Teach Yourself VISUAL CAFÉ™ 2

in 21 days

Teach Yourself
VISUAL CAFÉ™ 2
in 21 days

Mike Cohn

201 West 103rd Street
Indianapolis, Indiana 46290

President: Richard K. Swadley
Publisher and Director of Acquisitions: Jordan Gold
Director of Product Development: Dean Miller
Executive Editor: Christopher Denny
Managing Editor: Kitty Wilson Jarrett
Indexing Manager: Johnna L. VanHoose
Director of Marketing: Kelli S. Spencer
Product Marketing Manager: Wendy Gilbride
Marketing Coordinator: Linda Beckwith

Acquisitions Editor
Christopher Denny

Development Editor
Anthony Amico

Software Development Specialist
Brad Myers

Production Editor
Kate Shoup

Copy Editor
Kimberly K. Hannel

Indexer
Bruce Clingaman

Technical Reviewer
Greg Guntle

Editorial Coordinators
Mandie Rowell
Katie Wise

Technical Edit Coordinator
Lynette Quinn

Editorial Assistants
Carol Ackerman
Andi Richter
Rhonda Tinch-Mize
Karen Williams

Cover Designer
Tim Amrhein

Book Designer
Gary Adair

Copy Writer
David Reichwein

Production Team Supervisor
Brad Chinn

Production
Jeanne Clark
Polly Lavrick
Carl Pierce
Janet Seib
Andrew Stone

Dedication

To Savannah, my Little Princess, and Laura, my Princess Bride.

Overview

Contents

Acknowledgments

I would like to thank everyone at Sams.net. In particular, Chris Denny, Tony Amico, Kate Shoup, and Kim Hannel were invaluable throughout the process. Your professionalism, talent, and dedication are appreciated. Additional thanks also to technical editor Greg Guntle. Special thanks to Tim Lopez of Symantec for answering all of my questions.

I am grateful to Chris Hockett, Ken Kaplan, Steve Organ, and especially Andrew Meckler for the suggestions they made on early drafts. This book is immeasurably improved by the comments offered by these insightful readers.

I would like to thank John Barr and Mike Myers, both of Access Health, for grabbing hold of the Java vision and helping to make it a reality in Access Health's products. Thanks also to all of the programmers of Access Health, both in Sacramento and Boulder, who are beginning to demonstrate what Java can do.

I have benefited greatly in my career by working for a series of great bosses: Allan Siposs taught me to value quality over speed; Rob Brunner taught me the difference between programming as a hobby and programming as a career; Steven Adler offered me more variety and challenges every year than most people get in a lifetime; Jim Kearns taught me how to succeed by managing user expectations; Jim Steeb provided a constantly changing environment that needed tools like Java. Without each of these individuals, my career would have taken a different form. This book is strengthened by my association and friendship with each.

Thanks to everyone at Access Health (or soon to return to Access Health) who has encouraged my writing efforts: Shannon Folena, Kristy Hill, Jennifer Westerberg, and Lisa Williams. Thanks to Lisa Lord for showing me how to do it right the first time. Thanks to Pan for the collision. Thanks to Professor Bill Junk of the University of Idaho for teaching me the difference between programming and software engineering. Thanks to Matt Harris for showing me that the class of 2003 already has some great programmers. Thanks to my mom, dad, and sister for their encouragement and support in everything I do. Finally, thanks to Laura and Savannah for remembering who I am despite all the time this book took away from them.

About the Author

Mike Cohn is a Director of System Development at Access Health, Inc., the leading provider of personal health management services. Before that he was with Andersen Consulting and the Adler Consulting Group in New York. He holds a Masters degree in Computer Science from the University of Idaho and has been programming for sixteen years. Mike lives in Cameron Park, California, with his wife, Laura, and their daughter, Savannah. Mike was the lead author of *Database Developer's Guide with Borland C++ 5.0*, *Java Developer's Reference*, and *Web Programming with Visual J++*.

Tell Us What You Think!

As a reader, you are the most important critic and commentator of our books. We value your opinion and want to know what we're doing right, what we could do better, what areas you'd like to see us publish in, and any other words of wisdom you're willing to pass our way. You can help us make strong books that meet your needs and give you the computer guidance you require.

Do you have access to the World Wide Web? Then check out our site at http://www.mcp.com.

 NOTE

> If you have a technical question about this book, call the technical support line at 317-581-3833, or send e-mail to support@mcp.com.

As the team leader of the group that created this book, I welcome your comments. You can fax, e-mail, or write me directly to let me know what you did or didn't like about this book—as well as what we can do to make our books stronger. Here's the information:

Fax: 317-581-4669

E-mail: programming_mgr@sams.mcp.com

Mail: Christopher Denny
           Comments Department
           Sams Publishing
           201 W. 103rd Street
           Indianapolis, IN 46290

Introduction

By now there is little doubt that the Java language will profoundly affect both how you write programs and the programs you write. Java influences how you write programs because it achieves a new level of power combined with simplicity. Java influences the programs you write because *Java is an enabling technology*. With Java you can write programs you could not write without it. There are, of course, the simple things that Java allows, such as adding animation to Web pages. However, with Java so much more is possible. With Java you can write a single program that will run on Windows NT, Window 95, a Macintosh, or UNIX. With Java you can write a distributed program that can access resources on any machine on the Internet. In less than ten lines of Java code, you can write a program to display an image retrieved from a computer 5,000 miles away. And even better, your 10-line program can be run from almost any computer in use today or in the future.

When a powerful language like Java is combined with a powerful development environment, you have an unbeatable combination. In this book you will learn how Java and Visual Café work together to be this unbeatable combination. Although there are now many Java development environments available, Visual Café is the most fully capable of taking advantage of all of the features of Java. In this book, you will learn about the many unique features of Visual Café that enhance the power of Java.

Who Should Read This Book

You should read this book if you're already convinced that Java is part of your future. This book doesn't attempt to convince you that Java is the next great thing, the Holy Grail, or a silver bullet with which to slay a project's demons. You won't find a discussion in this book about how Java was named or how it started as a project for consumer electronics. Instead, what you will find in this book is a lot of useful information and a commitment to helping you become a proficient Java programmer in Visual Café by the end of the book.

Teach Yourself Visual Café 2 in 21 Days does not assume any specialized programming knowledge, although it does assume you have programmed in at least some language prior to reading this book. Perhaps that language is Visual Basic, C, C++, Smalltalk, Pascal, Delphi, or PowerBuilder.

This book takes the approach that the Java language itself is relatively simple and straight-forward to learn. On the other hand, it is the library of the classes that are used in a Java program that are time-consuming, but not difficult, to learn. Because of this, many of the chapters of *Teach Yourself Visual Café 2 in 21 Days* are dedicated to illustrating the most useful classes of Java and Visual Café. Many of these classes are demonstrated in one or more of the many sample programs included in the text. To help you solidify the knowledge you gain each day, each chapter concludes with a quiz and a series of exercises.

So if you already believe that Java is an important enough language to justify reading a book, have had at least some prior exposure to programming, want to master the Java class library, like to see examples of how things are done, and like a hands-on approach with quizzes and exercises, this book is for you.

How to Use This Book

This book has been divided into chapters that I believe can reasonably be covered in a day. But I realize that everyone is different and that you might be able to cover more than I had planned. If you feel you can do more, go for it! But don't become complacent. Try to work through the exercises, anyway. At the same time, there may chapters where you might be challenged. Do not lose heart. Just work at your own pace and endeavor to completely understand the subjects. Try to do the exercises and use them to reenforce the material.

You will find that the topics are presented in a progressive manner, designed to teach you things you don't know by building on those things you do know. It accomplishes this by making use of time-proven teaching methods. It first describes a concept, then demonstrates the concept in an easy-to-follow example. Finally, it discusses the results of the application of that concept.

Over the years, I have found that a *Teach Yourself* book should be friendly and easy to read. Much of the text will be formatted as you see here. I have also found that some important details should stand out and be separated from the normal text. So I have established some conventions, as you can see below:

- ☐ **Code/reserved words:** Terms, functions, variables, keywords, listings, and so on, that are taken from or are part of code, are set in a `monospaced type`.
- ☐ **Placeholders:** Placeholders are words that stand for what you will actually type. They appear appear in `monospaced italic`.
- ☐ **Commands:** When I am identifying commands from menus, I separate the different levels by using a vertical bar (|). For example, File | Open indicates that you pull down the File menu and select the Open command.

☐ **Code continuation:** When a line of code exceeds what I can show on a line in the book, I use a continuation character (➡). When you see this character, it means that the code continues on the next line. If you are typing, you should just ignore the character and continue typing. Do not use the return key to separate the code.

Some of the special visual elements I use in the book and their meanings are shown next:

Do	Don't

Do/Don't Boxes: These boxes are a way for me to give you a little insight into what I've learned through my experiences. They help you by providing guidance on what to do and what to avoid doing as you apply what you've learned.

WARNING

These boxes point out areas where care must be taken to prevent catastrophe. They should be avoided until you become more experienced.

NOTE

These provide essential background material or different ways of viewing the information to help you understand the concepts behind the implementations.

NEW TERM This icon indicates the presence of a definition for an important term that you will encounter as you progress through the book. The term appears in italics.

TIP

These boxes are the opposite of warning boxes. They tell you about techniques that are beneficial and that you might pursue.

ANALYSIS This icon tells you that I'm describing an example in detail. You might think of it as a kind of detour to a scenic overlook on your journey to learning this new technology.

Since I consider examples to be one of the most important elements of any book, I have taken great pains to make the examples stand out from the rest of the text and make them easy to follow. If code listings are used in the example, they are always numbered to help you keep track of your place. If you are entering the code in an editor, make sure you don't type the line number. Speaking of code, you can find all the listings as well as many other useful applications on the Macmillan Computer Publishing (MCP) Web site at (`www.mcp.com/info/1-57521/1-57521-303-6`).

Week 1

1
2
3
4
5
6
7

At A Glance

In this first week, you will establish a solid foundation. On Day 1, "A Java Language Refresher," you will learn everything you need to know about the Java language itself. This chapter outlines the core syntax and constructs of the Java language. You will learn how to declare Java variables and write Java methods. You will see how Java's minimal set of primitive types can be combined with its rich object model to fulfill the goals of object-oriented programming. You will also learn how to use exception handling to trap errors.

On Day 2, "Getting Started with Visual Café," you will begin to get familiar with Visual Café. You will be introduced to some of the items on the Visual Café desktop that you will use the most, including the Form Designer, the Component palette, the Project window, the Property List, and the Interaction wizard. You will also learn about the unique features of Visual Café's source-code editing windows and how they allow you to easily add methods to a class. You will learn how to create two sample applets and a sample application, and will see how Visual Café generates source code based on your actions in the development environment.

On Day 3, "Programming Applets and Handling Events," you learn the fundamentals of Java applet programming. You learn about the four methods that control the life span of an applet, as well as how to write code to respond to events generated by an applet's graphical user interface. You will also see how to embed an applet into a Web page and how to use applet parameters to control the behavior of a program.

On Day 4, "Java Strings," you will learn about the `String` and `StringBuffer` classes, two of the classes you will use most in your Java programming career. You will learn how to convert other object types into strings so they can be displayed. You will also learn how to perform a number of other operations on strings, including case conversion, searching for characters or substrings, and comparing strings. You will learn how the `StringBuffer` class offers an alternative to the `String` class and how it is more useful when working with text that is likely to change. Finally, you will learn how to use the many methods for appending or inserting into a `StringBuffer`.

On Day 5, "Using the Abstract Windowing Toolkit," you will learn about the Abstract Windowing Toolkit (AWT), which is the foundation of Java user interface programming. You will learn how to use the AWT to create buttons, text fields, text areas, labels, checkboxes, lists, choices, and scrollbars.

On Day 6, "Debugging, Customizing, and Managing Projects," you will learn about the Visual Café debugger and how it can save you time by allowing you to inspect variables, set conditional and nonconditional breakpoints, debug multiple threads, and step through your code line by line. You will learn how to customize Visual Café by creating and defining your own workspaces. You will also learn about many other tools that are included with Visual Café. You will learn about the Class browser, the Hierarchy editor, and Visual Café's project-management tools.

On Day 7, "The Form Designer, Layout Managers, and Panels," you will learn how to go beyond the AWT and learn about three topics that will help you enhance and fine-tune a program's user interface. First, you will learn about additional features of the Visual Café Form Designer. Next, you will learn how to use the layout managers to position components so that they remain properly placed regardless of the user's screen resolution. Finally, you will learn about the `Panel` class and its many subclasses.

Day 1

A Java Language Refresher

If you are an experienced programmer who is already comfortable with an object-oriented language but you don't know Java, or if you have already started learning Java but need a quick refresher, this chapter is for you because it outlines the core syntax and constructs of the Java language. You will learn how to declare Java variables and write Java methods. You will see how Java's minimal set of primitive types can be combined with its rich object model to fulfill the goals of object-oriented programming. You will also learn how to use exception handling to trap errors.

If you are already proficient with Java and are anxious to dive right into the specifics of Visual Café, you might want to skim this lesson before moving on to Day 2, "Getting Started with Visual Café."

The Structure of a Java File

This lesson presents the Java language by starting with its smallest pieces—reserved words, operators, and primitive types. Building on this foundation, you'll learn how to control the flow of a Java program and then how to create new Java classes. To augment this bottom-up approach, it is useful to start by taking a look at an example of a Java class in its entirety. This overview will help place the rest of this lesson in context. Listing 1.1 contains the complete definition of a Java class named MyClass.

Listing 1.1. A simple class definition.

```
1:      import java.applet.*;
2:      import java.awt.Graphics;
3:
4:      public class MyClass extends Applet
5:      {
6:          private String aString;
7:          private int xPosition;
8:
9:          public void init()
10:         {
11:             xPosition = 32;
12:             aString = "This is a string";
13:         }
14:
15:         public void paint(Graphics g)
16:         {
17:             g.drawString(aString, xPosition, 10);
18:         }
19:     }
```

ANALYSIS The statement `public class MyClass extends Applet` (line 4) creates a new class named MyClass. This class extends Applet, meaning that MyClass inherits the properties of the class named Applet and that MyClass extends Applet by adding functionality or modifying the functionality of Applet. If a class did not extend the functionality of the class on which it was based, there would be little reason for defining the new class.

NEW TERM A *class* is a way of combining the behavior and state of an entity. A class is a template for its runtime *instances* or *objects*. For example, for a class named Cake, an instance of that class may be my 1997 birthday cake or your wedding cake. Classes exist at design and compile time; objects exist when a program is executing.

Within the class, its member variables and methods are defined. In the case of `MyClass`, it includes a variable named `aString` of type `String`, and a variable named `xPosition` that is of type `int`. Each of these variables is defined as `private`, indicating that the variable cannot be accessed from outside the class.

 A *method* is a function or procedure that is part of a class.

 A *member* of a class is either a variable or a method declared within the class. In this way it is correct to speak of *member methods* and *member variables.*

Next within the class in Listing 1.1 is the definition of a method called `init()` (lines 9–13). This method is defined as `public` and `void`. The `public` keyword indicates that the method can be accessed outside the current class while `void` indicates that the method has no return value. The `init()` method sets the initial values of the `aString` and `xPosition` variables (lines 11 and 12).

Finally, the `paint` method, also declared as `public` and `void`, is presented (lines 15–18). Unlike `init()`, `paint` is passed a parameter. The parameter is named `g` and is of type `Graphics`. The code within `paint` invokes the `drawString` method of the `Graphics` class to draw the string stored in `aString` on the screen.

At the top of this sample class are two `import` statements (lines 1–2). In Java, classes are collected into packages. Classes and packages may then be reused in other programs by using the `import` statement.

 A *package* is a collection of classes that have been grouped into a logical unit for ease of reference and use.

The first `import` statement in Listing 1.1 is used to instruct Java to import all the classes stored in the package identified by the name `java.applet`. The `.*` at the end of the `import` statement indicates that all classes in this package are to be imported. Instead, a specific class name could have been listed. For example, line 2 of Listing 1.1 imports the `Graphics` class from the `java.awt` package.

Comments

Missing in the sample class you just saw were comments. I'd like to correct that right now so that code samples throughout the rest of this lesson can include comments. Java supports three types of comment delimiters—the traditional `/*` and `*/` of C, the `//` of C++, and a new variant that starts with `/**` and ends with `*/`.

The `/*` and `*/` delimiters are used to enclose text that is to be treated as a comment by the compiler. These delimiters are useful when you want to designate a lengthy piece of code as a comment, as shown in the following:

```
/* This is a comment that will span multiple
source code lines. */
```

The `//` comment delimiter is borrowed from C++ and is used to indicate that the rest of the line is to be treated as a comment by the Java compiler. This type of comment delimiter is particularly useful for adding comments adjacent to lines of code, as shown in the following:

```
Date today = new Date();        // create an object with today's date
System.out.println(today);      // display the date
```

Finally, the `/**` and `*/` delimiters are new to Java and are used to indicate that the enclosed text is to be treated as a comment by the compiler, but that the text is also part of the automatic class documentation that can be generated using the JavaDoc utility program that is provided by Sun with the Java Development Kit. These delimiters can be used to enclose multiple lines of text, identically to how `/*` and `*/` behave, as follows:

```
/** The NeuralNetwork class implements a back-propagation
network and ... */
```

The Java comment delimiters are summarized in Table 1.1.

Table 1.1. The Java comment delimiters.

Start	End	Purpose
`/*`	`*/`	The enclosed text is treated as a comment.
`//`	(none)	The rest of the line is treated as a comment.
`/**`	`*/`	The enclosed text is treated as a comment by the compiler but is used by JavaDoc to automatically generate documentation.

WARNING

You cannot nest comments in Java source code. Therefore, `/*` and `*/` appearing within a `//` comment are ignored, as is the pattern `//` appearing within `/*` or `/**` comments. Comments cannot be placed within quoted strings, and if comment delimiters occur within a quoted string, they will be considered part of the quoted string.

1

Java Keywords

The following is a list of Java keywords:

Java Keywords

abstract	float	public
boolean	for	return
break	if	short
byte	implements	static
case	import	super
catch	instanceof	switch
char	int	synchronized
class	interface	this
continue	long	throw
default	native	throws
do	new	transient
double	null	try
else	operator	void
extends	package	volatile
final	private	while
finally	protected	

Additionally, the Java specification reserves more keywords that will be used in the future but are not part of the current language specification. The following is a list of reserved Java keywords that are not currently used:

Reserved Java Keywords

byvalue	generic	outer
cast	goto	rest
const	inner	var
future	operator	

NOTE

You might have noticed that true and false are missing from the list of Java keywords. They are actually Boolean literals.

Primitive Types

A language's *primitive types* are the building blocks from which more complicated types, such as classes, are built. Java supports a set of eight primitive types; they are shown in Table 1.2.

Table 1.2. The Java primitive types.

Type	Description
byte	8-bit signed integer
short	16-bit signed integer
int	32-bit signed integer
long	64-bit signed integer
float	32-bit floating-point number
double	64-bit floating-point number
char	16-bit Unicode character
boolean	Can hold true or false

Because most of the machines that will run Java programs will do so in a 32-bit environment, the sizes of the primitive types have been defined with 32-bit optimization in mind. This means that some Java primitives might use more storage space than you are accustomed to if you come to Java from a 16-bit programming background.

In Java you declare a variable by giving its type followed by its name, as in the following examples:

```
int x;
float LifeRaft;
short people;
long TimeNoSee;
double amountDue, amountPaid;
```

In the preceding code, x is declared as an int (integer), LifeRaft is declared as a floating-point variable, people is declared as a short integer, TimeNoSee is declared as a long integer, and amountDue and amountPaid are declared as double-precision floating-point values.

NOTE

If you are a C++ programmer, you should notice from Table 1.2 that Java adds both the byte and boolean types. Some recent C++ compilers have added support for the new C++ boolean type, so you may already be using it in your code. Because Java provides unicode support, you should notice that its char type is 16 bits wide. This is also why the 8-bit byte type is included as a primitive type. In C++, you have

probably been emulating a byte type with something similar to the following:

```
type unsigned char byte;
```

There are a couple other extremely important differences between the Java and C++ primitive types. The Java primitives are each of a known and guaranteed size. This is critical to Java because of its goal of portability across hardware and operating systems. If an int is 16 bits on one platform and 32 bits on another platform, a program is asking for trouble if it expects to be run on both platforms. C++ guarantees certain relationships among its primitive types. For example, a C++ long is guaranteed to be at least as big as a C++ int. Java takes this further and prescribes an exact size for each primitive. You should take care to notice the sizes of the Java primitives. In particular, you should notice that a Java int is 32 bits and a Java long is 64 bits.

Also worth pointing out is that all Java primitive types are signed. This means that C++ declarations like the following are not allowed in Java:

```
unsigned long bigLong;      // not legal in Java
unsigned double salary;     // not legal in Java
```

Finally, the Java boolean primitive can be set to a value of true or false. In traditional C and C++ programming, true and false are defined by using the preprocessor to be equal to 1 and 0, respectively.

Integer Types

Java consists of four integer types: byte, short, int, and long, which are defined as 8-, 16-, 32-, and 64-bit signed values, as summarized in Table 1.3.

Table 1.3. The Java integer primitive types.

Type	Bit Size	Minimum Value	Maximum Value
byte	8	-256	255
short	16	-32,768	32,767
int	32	-2,147,483,648	2,147,483,647
long	64	-9,223,372,036,854,775,808	9,223,372,036,854,775,807

The operations that may be performed on integer primitives are shown in Table 1.4. A more detailed discussion of the Java operators is deferred until the section titled "Operators," later today.

Table 1.4. Operators that can be used on integer primitives.

Operator	Operation
=	Equality
!=	Inequality
>	Greater than
<	Less than
>=	Greater than or equal to
<=	Less than or equal to
+	Addition
-	Subtraction
*	Multiplication
/	Division
%	Modulus
++	Increment
--	Decrement
~	Bitwise logical negation
&	Bitwise AND
¦	Bitwise OR
^	Bitwise XOR
<<	Left shift
>>	Right shift
>>>	Right shift with zero fill

If either or both of the operands is of type `long`, the result of the operation will be a 64-bit `long`. If either operand is not a `long`, it will be cast to a `long` prior to the operation.

 To *cast* a variable is to convert it from one type (such as `float`) to another (such as `int`).

If neither operand is a `long`, the operation will be performed with the 32-bit precision of an `int`. Any `byte` or `short` operands will be cast to `int` prior to the operation.

> In Java, you cannot cast between an integer type and a Boolean type.

WARNING

1

Floating-Point Types

Support for floating-point numbers in Java is provided through two primitive types—`float` and `double`, which are 32- and 64-bit values, respectively. The operators available for use on these primitive types are shown in Table 1.5.

Table 1.5. Operators that can be used on floating-point primitives.

Operator	Operation
=	Equality
!=	Inequality
>	Greater than
<	Less than
>=	Greater than or equal to
<=	Less than or equal to
+	Addition
-	Subtraction
*	Multiplication
/	Division
%	Modulus
++	Increment
--	Decrement

Java floating-point numbers will behave as specified in IEEE Standard 754. Java variables of type `float` and `double` can be cast to other numeric types but cannot be cast to be of the `boolean` type.

If either or both of the operands is a floating-point type, the operation is considered to be a *floating-point operation*. If either of the operands is a `double`, each will be treated as a `double` with the necessary casts being performed. If neither operand is a `double`, each operand will be treated as a `float` and cast as necessary.

Floating-point numbers can take on any of the following values:

☐ Negative infinity

☐ Negative, finite values

☐ Negative zero

☐ Positive zero

☐ Positive, finite values

☐ Positive infinity

☐ NaN, or "Not a Number"

This last value, NaN, is used to indicate values that do not fit within the scale of negative infinity to positive infinity. For example, the following will produce a value of NaN:

```
0.0f / 0.0f
```

The inclusion of NaN as a floating-point value can cause some unusual effects when floating-point values are compared with the relational operators. Because NaN does not fit within the scale of negative infinity through positive infinity, comparing against it will always result in false. For example, both 5.3f > NaN and 5.3f < NaN are false. In fact, when NaN is compared to itself with ==, the result is false.

On the other hand, although negative and positive zero may sound like different values, comparing them with == will result in true.

Other Primitive Types

In addition to the integer and floating-point primitive types, Java includes two more primitive types—boolean and char. Variables of type boolean can hold either true or false, while variables of type char can hold a single unicode character.

WARNING

Remember, a Java boolean variable is not a 1 or 0 in disguise as it is C and C++. Because of this, you cannot cast between boolean and numeric types.

Default Values

One common source of programming errors is the use of an uninitialized variable. Frequently, this type of bug shows itself in a program that behaves erratically. Sometimes the program does what it's supposed to; other times it reformats your hard drive, overwrites your CMOS, declares war on a foreign country, or manifests some other undesirable side effect. It does this because an uninitialized variable may take on the value of whatever random garbage is in its memory location when the program runs. Java circumvents this problem, and possibly prevents World War III, by assigning a default value to any uninitialized variables. Default values are assigned based on the type of the variable, as shown in Table 1.6.

Table 1.6. The standard default values for Java primitive types.

Primitive	Default
byte	0
short	0
int	0
long	0L
float	0.0f
double	0.0d
char	null
boolean	false
all references	null

TIP

It's certainly convenient and beneficial that Java will take care of assigning default values to uninitialized variables, but it is not wise to rely on this. Good programming practice suggests that you should initialize every variable you declare, without relying on default values. Although it is very unlikely that the default values would change (for example, the Boolean default of `false` is unlikely to change to `true`), other side effects are possible.

In a C program, I once spent hours tracking down a bug that was caused by my reliance on the compiler defaulting a global integer to `0`. The compiler did its job correctly; unfortunately, another programmer saw my bad practice of using an uninitialized global and corrected it by initializing it for me—to `1`. When I was reassigned to the maintenance of the program, I had no idea the change had been made.

Casting Between Primitive Types

Sometimes you have a variable that is of one type but you want to use it as another. For example, one of the first programs I wrote was used to predict the final scores in baseball games based on a huge number of input statistics. It would come up with results such as the Chicago Cubs beating the San Diego Padres with scores like 3.2 to 2.7. Because it was clearly impossible in real life to score a partial run, the results needed to be converted from floating-point to integer values. This is known as *casting* a variable.

In Java, you can cast a variable of one type to another as follows:

```
float fRunsScored = 3.2f;
int iRunsScored = (int)fRunsScored;
```

In this case, the floating-point value 3.2 that is stored in fRunsScored will be cast into an integer and placed in iRunsScored. When cast into an integer, the non-whole portion of the fRunsScored will be truncated so that iRunsScored will equal 3.

This is an example of what is known as a *narrowing conversion*. A narrowing conversion may lose information about the overall magnitude or precision of a numeric value, as you saw in this case. You should always be careful when writing a narrowing conversion because of this potential for data loss.

The other type of conversion is called a *widening conversion*. A widening conversion might lose information about precision in the least significant bits of the value, but it will not lose information about the magnitude of the value. In general, widening conversions are much safer to use. Table 1.7 shows the widening conversions that are possible between Java primitive types.

Table 1.7. Available widening conversions among Java primitive types.

From	To
byte	short, int, long, float, or double
short	int, long, float, or double
char	int, long, float, or double
int	long, float, or double
long	float or double
float	double

NOTE

Related to casting is the concept of *automatic coercion*. Automatic coercion occurs when a compiler *coerces*, or casts, a variable of one type into another automatically. For example, consider the following C++ code:

```
long aLong = 65536L;
unsigned int justAnInt;
justAnInt = aLong;
printf("%d", justAnInt);
```

In this example, the 65536 stored in aLong is also placed into justAnInt. Because no explicit cast is performed, an automatic coercion from a long to an unsigned int is performed. Unfortunately, on a 16-bit platform, this will result in an error because the value in aLong is too large to fit in justAnInt. The automatic coercion will place 0 into justAnInt instead of the desired 65536.

Because Java does not perform automatic coercions, you may need to slightly alter your thinking about some of your C++ programming habits. For example, in C++ you could write the following loop:

```
int count=10;
while (count) {
    // use count to do something
    count--;
}
```

In C++, the while loop will execute as long as count is nonzero. However, a Java while loop must be formed according to the following syntax:

```
while (booleanExpression)
    statement
```

What this means is that statements like while(count) do not work in Java because there is no automatic coercion of an integer (such as count) to the boolean, which a Java while loop expects. You need to rewrite the C++ code fragment to work in Java as follows:

```
int count=10;
while (count > 0) {
    // use count to do something
    count--;
}
```

This creates a Boolean expression that is evaluated on each pass through the loop. You will need to make similar adjustments with the Java for and do...while loops, as well.

Do   Don't

DO remember that all Java primitives are assigned default values, but don't become dependent on Java to initialize variables for you. It is still good programming practice to explicitly assign a value to each variable you declare.

DO be careful when using narrowing conversions.

DO try to declare each variable to be of an appropriate type based on required precisions and any memory or storage requirements.

Literals

NEW TERM   A *literal* is an explicit value that is used by a program. For example, your program may include a literal value of 3.1415 that is used whenever the value of pi is necessary, or it may include 65 as the mandatory retirement age. These values, 3.1415 and 65, are both literals.

Integer Literals

Integer literals can be specified in decimal, hexadecimal, or octal notation. To specify a decimal value, simply use the number as normal. To indicate that a literal value is a long, you can append either L or l to the end of the number. Hexadecimal values are given in base 16 and include the digits 0–9 and the letters A–F. To specify a hexadecimal value, use 0x followed by the digits and letters that comprise the value. Similarly, an octal value is identified by a leading 0.

For examples of specifying integer literals, see Table 1.8.

Table 1.8. Examples of integer literals.

Integer	Long	Octal	Hexadecimal
0	0L	0	0x0
1	1L	01	0x1
10	10L	012	0xA
15	15L	017	0XF
16	16L	020	0x10
100	100L	0144	0x64

Floating-Point Literals

Similar to integer literals are Java's *floating-point literals*. Floating-point literals can be specified in either the familiar decimal notation (for example, 3.1415) or exponential notation (for example, 6.02e23). To indicate that a literal is to be treated as a single-precision float, append either f or F to it. To indicate that it is to be treated as a double-precision value, append either d or D.

Java includes predefined constants, POSITIVE_INFINITY, NEGATIVE_INFINITY, and NaN, to represent the infinity and Not-a-Number values.

The following are some valid floating-point literals:

```
43.3F
3.1415d
```

```
-12.123f
6.02e+23f
6.02e23d
6.02e-23f
6.02e23d
```

Boolean Literals

Java supports two Boolean literals—true and false. Unlike in some other languages, notably C and C++, true and false are not merely defined to be values such as 1 and 0.

Character Literals

A *character literal* is a single character or an escape sequence enclosed in single quotes; for example, 'b'. Escape sequences are used to indicate special characters or actions, such as line feed, form feed, and carriage return. The available escape sequences are shown in Table 1.9. The following are examples of character literals:

```
'b'
'\n'
'\u15e'
'\t'
```

Table 1.9. Escape sequences.

Sequence	Purpose
\b	Backspace
\t	Horizontal tab
\n	Line feed
\f	Form feed
\r	Carriage return
\"	Double quote
\'	Single quote
\\	Backslash
\uxxxx	Unicode character

String Literals

Although there is no string primitive type in Java, you can include string literals in your programs. Most applications and applets will make use of some form of string literal, probably at least for error messages. A *string literal* consists of zero or more characters

(including the escape sequences shown in Table 1.9) enclosed in double quotes. The
following are examples of string literals:

```
"A String"
"Column 1\tColumn 2"
"First Line\r\nSecond Line"
"First Page\fSecond Page"
" "
```

Because Java does not have a string primitive type, each use of a string literal causes an object
of the String class to be created behind the scenes. However, because of Java's automatic
memory management, your program doesn't need to do anything special to free or release
the memory used by the literal or string once you are finished with it.

Java does include a powerful String class. The String class will be fully explored on Day 4,
"Java Strings."

Arrays

In Java, you declare an array using enclosing square bracket symbols ([ ]).

For example, consider the following array declarations:

```
int intArray[];
float floatArray[];
double [] doubleArray;
char charArray[];
```

Notice that the brackets can be placed before or after the variable name. Placing the [ ] after
the variable name follows the conventions of C, and if you are coming to Java from C or C++,
you might want to continue that tradition. However, there is an advantage to placing the
brackets before the variable name. By placing the brackets in front of the variable name, you
can more easily declare multiple arrays. For example, consider the following declarations:

```
int [] firstArray, secondArray;
int thirdArray[], justAnInt;
```

On the first line both firstArray and secondArray are arrays. On the second line, thirdArray
is an array, but justAnInt is, as its name implies, a lone integer. The ability to declare singleton
variables and arrays in the same statement, as on the second line in the preceding example,
is the source of many problems in other programming languages. Java helps prevent this type
of problem by providing an easy, alternative syntax for declaring arrays.

Allocation

Once an array is declared, it must be allocated. You probably noticed that the sizes of the arrays have not been specified in the examples so far. This is because, in Java, all arrays must be allocated with new. Declaring the following array would have resulted in a compile-time error:

```
int intArray[10];    // this is an error
```

To allocate an array you use new, as shown in the following examples:

```
int intArray[] = new int[100];
float floatArray[];
floatArray = new float[100];
long [] longArray = new long[100];
double [][] doubleArray = new double[10][10];
```

Initialization

An alternative way of allocating a Java array is to specify a list of element initializers when the array is declared. This is done as follows:

```
int intArray[] = {1,2,3,4,5};
char [] charArray = {'a', 'b', 'c'};
String [] stringArray = {"A", "Four", "Element", "Array"};
```

In this case, intArray will be a five-element array holding the values 1 through 5. The three-element array charArray will hold the characters a, b, and c. Finally, stringArray will hold the strings shown.

Array Access

Items in a Java array are known as the *components* of the array. You can access a component at runtime by enclosing the component number you want to access with brackets, as shown in the following:

```
int intArray[] = {100, 200, 300, 400, 500};
int a = intArray[0];         // a will be equal to 100
int b = intArray[1];         // b will be equal to 200
int c = intArray[2];         // c will be equal to 300
int d = intArray[3];         // d will be equal to 400
int e = intArray[4];         // e will be equal to 500
```

Java arrays are numbered from 0 to 1 less than the number of components in the array. Attempting to access an array beyond the bounds of the array (for example, intArray[42] in the preceding example) will result in a runtime exception, ArrayIndexOutOfBoundsException.

Do	Don't

DON'T forget that Java arrays start with **0**.

DO remember that an array declaration does not allocate memory for the array.

DO consider the alternatives before using an array to store an unknown quantity of objects. The Vector class (described in Day 12, "The Java Utility Classes") is an excellent alternative in many cases.

Operators

A language's operators can be used to combine or alter a program's values. Java contains a very rich set of operators. Here is the complete list:

The Complete List of Java Operators

=	>	<	!	~
?	:	==	<=	>=
¦=	&&	¦¦	++	--
+	-	*	/	&
¦	^	%	<<	>>
>>>	+=	-=	*=	/=
&=	¦=	^=	%=	<<=
>>=	>>>=			

Operators on Integers

The bulk of the Java operators work on integer values. The *binary operators* (those that require two operands) are shown in Table 1.10. The *unary operators* (those that require a single operand) are shown in Table 1.11. Each table gives an example of the use of each operator.

Table 1.10. Binary operators on integers.

Operator	Operation	Example
=	Assignment	a = b
==	Equality	a == b
!=	Inequality	a != b
<	Less than	a < b
<=	Less than or equal to	a <= b
>=	Greater than or equal to	a >= b
>	Greater than	a > b

Operator	Operation	Example
+	Addition	a + b
-	Subtraction	a - b
*	Multiplication	a * b
/	Division	a / b
%	Modulus	a % b
<<	Left shift	a << b
>>	Right shift	a >> b
>>>	Right shift with zero fill	a >>> b
&	Bitwise AND	a & b
¦	Bitwise OR	a ¦ b
^	Bitwise XOR	a ^ b

Table 1.11. Unary operators on integers.

Operator	Operation	Example
-	Unary negation	-a
~	Bitwise logical negation	~a
++	Increment	a++ or ++a
--	Decrement	a-- or --a

In addition to the operators shown in Tables 1.10 and 1.11, Java also includes an assortment of assignment operators that are based on the other operators. These operators will operate on an operand and store the resulting value back in the same operand. For example, to increase the value of a variable x, you could do the following:

```
x += 3;
```

This is equal to the more verbose x = x + 3. Each of the specialized Java assignment operators performs its normal function on the operand and then stores the value in the operand. The following assignment operators are available:

Integer Assignment Operators

+=	-=	*=
/=	&=	¦=
^=	%=	<<=
>>=	>>>=	

NOTE

You might have noticed that operator overloading is not mentioned in this discussion of operators. Initially, operator overloading was an exciting feature of C++ that promised to allow programmers to treat all data types, whether primitive or not, equivalently. The reasoning went that if there was a logically intuitive action that should be performed by an operator, the language should support overloading the operator to perform that action. Unfortunately, reality intervened, and many uses of operator overloading in C++ have led to unnecessary bugs. Because of the potential for introducing bugs through operator overloading, the developers of Java wisely chose to leave it out.

Operators on Floating-Point Values

The Java operators on floating-point values are a subset of those available to Java integer types. The operators on floats and doubles are shown in Table 1.12, which also gives examples of their use.

Table 1.12. Operators on floating-point values.

Operator	Operation	Example
=	Assignment	a = b
==	Equality	a == b
!=	Inequality	a != b
<	Less than	a < b
<=	Less than or equal to	a <= b
>=	Greater than or equal to	a >= b
>	Greater than	a > b
+	Addition	a + b
-	Subtraction	a - b
*	Multiplication	a * b
/	Division	a / b
%	Modulus	a % b
-	Unary negation	-a
++	Increment	a++ or ++a
--	Decrement	a-- or -a

Operators on Boolean Values

The Java Boolean operators are summarized in Table 1.13. If you are coming to Java from a C or C++ background, you are probably already familiar with these. If you are not, the conditional operator will be a new experience.

Table 1.13. Operators on Boolean values.

Operator	Operation	Example
!	Negation	!a
&&	Conditional AND	a && b
¦¦	Conditional OR	a ¦¦ b
==	Equality	a == b
!=	Inequality	a != b
?:	Conditional	a ? expr1 : expr2

The conditional operator is Java's only *ternary* (three-operand) operator and has the following syntactic form:

```
booleanExpr ? expr1 : expr2
```

The value of `booleanExpr` is evaluated and, if it is `true`, the expression `expr1` is executed; if it is `false`, expression `expr2` is executed. This makes the conditional operator a convenient shorthand for the following:

```
if(booleanExpression)
    expr1
else
    expr2
```

NOTE

In Java, unlike in C++, Boolean operators operate only on Boolean expressions. For example, consider the following C++ fragment:

```
int x = 1;
int y = 7;
if (x && y) {
    // do something
}
```

This same code is illegal in Java. Because the `&&` operator expects two `boolean` operands and there is no automatic coercion from an integer, the Java compiler does not know how to interpret this statement. In Java, it needs to be rewritten as follows:

```
int x = 1;
int y = 7;
if (x != 0 && y != 0) {
    // do something
}
```

In this case, the two integer values have been converted into explicit tests. Because these tests are Boolean expressions, the code can now be compiled.

Controlling Your Program

The Java keywords for controlling program flow are nearly identical to C and C++. This is one of the most obvious ways in which Java shows its legacy as a derivative of these two languages. In this section, you will see how to use Java's control-flow commands to write methods.

Selection

The Java language provides two structures—if statements and switch statements—for selecting among alternatives. Although it would be possible to spend your entire Java programming career using only one of these at the expense of the other, each has its definite advantages.

The if Statement

A Java if statement is a test of any Boolean expression. If the Boolean expression evaluates to true, the statement following the if is executed. On the other hand, if the Boolean expression evaluates to false, the statement following the if is not executed. For example, consider the following code fragment:

```
import java.util.Date;
Date today = new Date();
if (today.getDay == 0) then
    System.out.println("It is Sunday.");
```

This code uses the java.util.Date package and creates a variable named today that will hold the current date. The getDay member method is then applied to today, and the result is compared to 0. A return value of 0 for getDay indicates that the day is Sunday, so if the Boolean expression today.getDay == 0 is true, a message is displayed. If today isn't Sunday, no action occurs.

1

> **NOTE**
>
> If you are coming to Java from a C or C++ background, you may have been tempted to rewrite the preceding example as follows:
>
> ```java
> import java.util.Date;
> Date today = new Date();
> if (!today.getDay) then
>     System.out.println("It is Sunday.");
> ```
>
> In C and C++, the expression `!today.getDay` would evaluate to 1 whenever `today.getDay` evaluated to `0` (indicating Sunday). In Java, the expression used within an `if` statement must evaluate to a Boolean. Therefore, this code doesn't work because `!today.getDay` will evaluate to `0` or `1`, depending on which day of the week it is. And, as you learned earlier today, integer values cannot be cast to Boolean values. This is, of course, an example where Java's nuances may take a little getting used to for C and C++ programmers. Once you're accustomed to the change, however, you will find your code more readable, reliable, and maintainable.

Of course, an `if` statement without an `else` is as incomplete as a Labrador retriever without a bandanna around his neck. Not wanting to be accused of cruelty to animals or programmers, the Java developers included an `else` statement that can be executed whenever an `if` statement evaluates to `false`. This can be seen in the following sample code:

```java
import java.util.Date;
Date today = new Date();
if (today.getDay == 0) then
    System.out.println("It is Sunday.");
else
    System.out.println("It is NOT Sunday.");
```

In this case, the same message as before will be displayed whenever it is Sunday, but a different message will be displayed whenever it is not Sunday. Both examples so far have only shown the execution of a single statement within the `if` or the `else` cases. By enclosing the statements within curly braces, you can execute as many lines of code as you like. You can see this in the following example, which makes some suggestions about how to spend each day of the week:

```java
import java.util.Date;
Date today = new Date();
if (today.getDay == 0) then {
    System.out.println("It is Sunday.");
    System.out.println("And a good day for golf.");
}
else {
    System.out.println("It is NOT Sunday.");
    System.out.println("But still a good day for golf.");
}
```

Because it's possible to execute whatever code you desire in the `else` portion of an `if...else` block, you may have already reasoned that it is possible to execute another `if` statement inside the `else` statement of the first `if` statement. This is commonly known as an *if...else if...else block*, an example of which follows:

```
import java.util.Date;
Date today = new Date();
if (today.getDay == 0) then
    System.out.println("It is Sunday.");
else if (today.getDay == 1) then
    System.out.println("It is Monday.");
else if (today.getDay == 2) then
    System.out.println("It is Tuesday.");
else if (today.getDay == 3) then
    System.out.println("It is Wednesday.");
else if (today.getDay == 4) then
    System.out.println("It is Thursday.");
else if (today.getDay == 5) then
    System.out.println("It is Friday.");
else
    System.out.println("It must be Saturday.");
```

The `switch` Statement

As you can see from the preceding code sample, a lengthy series of `if...else if...else` statements can get convoluted and hard to read as the number of cases increases. Fortunately, you can avoid this problem by using Java's `switch` statement. Like its C and C++ cousins, the Java `switch` statement is ideal for testing a single expression against a series of possible values and executing the code associated with the matching `case` statement, as shown in Listing 1.2.

Listing 1.2. Using the `switch` and `case` statements.

```
1:     import java.util.Date;
2:     ...
3:     Date today = new Date();
4:     switch (today.getDay) {
5:         case 0:    // Sunday
6:             System.out.println("It is Sunday.");
7:             break;
8:         case 1:    // Monday
9:             System.out.println("It is Monday.");
10:            break;
11:        case 2:    // Tuesday
12:            System.out.println("It is Tuesday.");
13:            break;
14:        case 3:    // Wednesday
15:            System.out.println("It is Wednesday.");
16:            break;
17:        case 4:    // Thursday
18:            System.out.println("It is Thursday.");
19:            break;
20:        case 5:    // Friday
```

1

```
21:              System.out.println("It is Friday.");
22:              System.out.println("Have a nice weekend!");
23:              break;
24:        default:   // Saturday
25:              System.out.println("It must be Saturday.");
26:     }
27:     System.out.println("All done!");
```

ANALYSIS You should have noticed that each day has its own case within the switch. The Saturday case (where today.getDay=6) is not explicitly given but is instead handled by the default case (lines 24–25). Any switch block may include an optional default case that will handle any values not caught by an explicit case.

Within each case, there can be multiple lines of code. The block of code that will execute for the Friday case (lines 20–23), for example, contains three lines. The first two lines will simply display informational messages, but the third is a break statement. The keyword break is used within a case statement to indicate that the flow of the program should move to the first line following the switch block. In this example, break appears as the last statement in each case except the default, and will cause program execution to move to the line that prints All done! (line 27). The break statement was left out of the default block because by that point in the code the switch block is ending, and there is no point in using an explicit command to exit the switch.

If, as Listing 1.2 seems to imply, you always need to include a break statement at the end of each block, why not just leave break out and have Java assume that after a block executes, control should move outside the switch block? The answer is that there are times when you do not want to break out of the switch statement after executing the code for a specific case value. For example, consider Listing 1.3, which could be used as a scheduling system for physicians.

Listing 1.3. A case **without a** break **falls through to the next** case.

```
1:     import java.util.Date;
2:     ...
3:     Date today = new Date();
4:     switch (today.getDay) {
5:         case 0:      // Sunday
6:         case 3:      // Wednesday
7:         case 6:      // Saturday
8:             System.out.println("It's Golf Day!");
9:             break;
10:        case 2:      // Tuesday
11:            System.out.println("Tennis at 8:00 am");
```

continues

Listing 1.3. continued

```
12:        case 1:      // Monday
13:        case 4:      // Thursday
14:        case 5:      // Friday
15:            System.out.println("Office Hours: 10:00 - 5:00");
16:            break;
17:    }
18:    System.out.println("All done!");
```

ANALYSIS Listing 1.3 illustrates a couple key concepts about `switch` statements. First, you'll notice that it is possible to have multiple `cases` execute the same block of code, as was done for Sunday, Wednesday, and Saturday (lines 5–7). For each of these days the program will display the message `It's Golf Day.`. If you collect the three `cases` together without any intervening `break` statements, each will execute the same code.

But consider what happens on Tuesday when the code in lines 10 and 11 executes. Certainly a reminder about the tennis match will be displayed, but this case doesn't end with a `break` statement. Because Tuesday's code doesn't end with a `break` statement, the program will continue executing the code in the following cases until a `break` is encountered. This means that Tuesday's code flows into the code used for Monday, Thursday, and Friday. This will result in the following messages being displayed every Tuesday:

```
Tennis at 8:00 am
Office Hours: 10:00 - 5:00
```

On Monday, Thursday, and Friday, only the latter message will display.

In addition to writing `switch` statements that use integer cases, you can use character values, as shown in the following example:

```
switch (aChar) {
    case 'a':
    case 'e':
    case 'i':
    case 'o':
    case 'u':
        System.out.println("It's a vowel!");
        break;
    default:
        System.out.println("It's a consonant!");
}
```

Iteration

Iteration is an important concept in any computer language. Without the ability to loop or iterate through a set of values, our ability to solve real-world problems would be severely limited. Java's iteration statements are nearly identical to those found in C and C++ and include `for` loops, `while` loops, and `do...while` loops.

The `for` **Statement**

The syntax of the Java `for` statement is very powerful and concise. The first line of a `for` loop enables you to specify a starting value for a loop counter, specify the test condition that will exit the loop, and indicate how the loop counter should be incremented after each pass through the loop. This is definitely a statement that offers a lot of bang for the buck. The syntax of a Java `for` statement is as follows:

```
for (initialization; testExpression; increment)
    statement
```

For example, a sample `for` loop may appear as follows:

```
int count;
for (count=0; count<100; count++)
    System.out.println("Count = " + count);
```

In this example, the initialization statement of the `for` loop sets `count` to `0`. The test expression, `count < 100`, indicates that the loop should continue as long as `count` is less than 100. Finally, the increment statement increments the value of `count` by 1. As long as the test expression is `true`, the statement following the `for` loop setup will be executed, as follows:

```
System.out.println("Count = " + count);
```

Of course, you probably need to do more than one thing inside the loop. This is as easy to do as using curly braces to indicate the scope of the `for` loop, as shown in the following:

```
int count;
for (count=0; count<100; count++) {
    YourMethod(count);
    System.out.println("Count = " + count);
}
```

One nice shortcut that can be taken with a Java `for` loop is to declare and initialize the variable used in the loop. For example, in the following code, the variable `count` is declared directly within the `for` loop:

```
for (int count=0; count<100; count++)
    System.out.println("Count = " + count);
```

It may look like an inconsequential difference whether you declare a variable before a `for` loop or within the loop. However, there are advantages to declaring the variable within the loop. First, it makes clear your intention to use the variable within the loop. If the variable is declared above the `for` loop, how will you remember (and how will future programmers know) that the variable was intended for use only *within* the loop? Second, a variable declared within the `for` loop will go out of scope at the end of the loop. This means you could not write the following code:

```
for (int count=0; count<100; count++)
    System.out.println("Count = " + count);
System.out.println("Loop exited with count = " + count);
```

The last line cannot find a variable named count because count goes out of scope when the for loop terminates. This means that, in addition to making the intended purpose of the variable more clear, it is also impossible to accidentally bypass that intent and use the variable outside the loop.

You can also leave out portions of the first line of a for loop. In the following example, the increment statement has been left out:

```
for (int count=0; count<100; ) {
    count += 2;
    System.out.println("Count = " + count);
}
```

Of course, leaving the increment statement out of the for loop declaration in this example doesn't achieve any useful purpose because count is incremented inside the loop.

It is possible to get even fancier with a Java for loop by including multiple statements or conditions. For example, consider the following code:

```
for (int up=0, down = 20; up < down; up++, down -= 2 ) {
    System.out.println("Up = " + up + "\tDown = " + down);
}
```

This loop starts the variable up at 0 and increments it by 1. It also starts the variable down at 20 and decrements it by 2 for each pass through the loop. The loop continues until up has been incremented enough that it is equal to or greater than the variable down.

The test expression portion of a Java for loop can be any Boolean expression. Because of this, it does not need to be a simple test (x < 10) as shown in the preceding examples. The test expression can be a method call, a method call combined with a value test, or anything that can be phrased as a Boolean expression. For example, suppose you want to write a method that will display a message indicating the first year since World War II that the Chicago Cubs appeared in the World Series. You could do this as shown in Listing 1.4.

Listing 1.4. A for loop can use any Boolean expression.

```
1:     public boolean DidCubsPlayInWorldSeries(int year) {
2:         boolean retval;
3:
4:         switch(year) {
5:             case 1907:    // these are years the Cubs won
6:             case 1908:
7:                 retval = true;
8:                 break;
9:             case 1906:    // these are years the Cubs lost
10:            case 1910:
11:            case 1918:
12:            case 1929:
13:            case 1932:
14:            case 1935:
```

```
15:              case 1938:
16:              case 1945:
17:                  retval = true;
18:                  break;
19:              default:
20:                  retval = false;
21:          }
22:          return retval;
23:      }
24:
25:      public void FindFirstAfterWWII() {
26:          for (int year=1946; DidCubsPlayInWorldSeries(year) ==
27:                  false; year++) {
28:              System.out.println("The Cubs didn't play in " + year);
29:          }
30:      }
```

ANALYSIS   The method DidCubsPlayInWorldSeries (lines 1–23) is passed an integer value indicating the year and returns a Boolean value that indicates whether the Cubs made it to the World Series in that year. This method is an example of the switch statement shown earlier today.

The method FindFirstAfterWWII (lines 25–30) uses a for loop to find a year in which the Cubs played in the World Series. The loop starts year with 1946 and increments year by 1 for each pass through the loop. The test expression for the loop will allow the loop to continue as long as the method DidCubsPlayInWorldSeries returns false. This is a useful example because it shows that a method can be called within the test expression of a for loop. Unfortunately, it is a bad example in that the Cubs haven't won the World Series since the goose step was popular in Berlin, and there is no sign of that changing in the near future. In other words, a loop that looks for a Cubs World Series appearance after 1945 is an infinite loop.

The while Statement

Related to the for loop is the while loop. The syntax for a while loop is as follows:

```
while (booleanExpression)
    statement
```

As you can tell from its simplicity, the Java while loop does not have the built-in support for initializing and incrementing variables that the Java for loop does. Because of this, you need to be careful to initialize loop counters prior to the loop and increment them within the body of the while loop. For example, the following code fragment will display a message five times:

```
int count = 0;
while (count < 5) {
    System.out.println("Count = " + count);
    count++;
}
```

The do...while **Statement**

The final looping construct in Java is the do...while loop. The syntax for a do...while loop is as follows:

```
do {
    statement
} while (booleanExpression);
```

This is similar to a while loop, except that a do...while loop is guaranteed to execute at least once. It is possible that a while loop might not execute at all, depending on the test expression used in the loop. For example, consider the following method:

```
public void ShowYears(int year) {
    while (year < 2000) {
        System.out.println("Year is " + year);
        year++;
    }
}
```

This method is passed a year value and then loops over the year, displaying a message as long as the year is less than 2000. If year starts at 1996, messages will be displayed for the years 1996, 1997, 1998, and 1999. But what happens if year starts at 2010? Because the initial test, year < 2000, will be false, the while loop will never be entered. Fortunately, a do...while loop can solve this problem. Because a do...while loop performs its expression testing after the body of the loop has executed for each pass, it will always be executed at least once. This is a valid distinction between the two types of loop, but it can also be a source of potential errors. Whenever you use a do...while loop, you should be careful to consider the first pass through the body of the loop.

Jumping

Of course, it is not always easy to write all your for, while, and do...while loops so that they are easy to read and still terminate on exactly the right pass through the loop. Java makes it easier to jump out of loops and to control other areas of program flow with its break and continue statements.

The break **Statement**

Earlier today, you saw how the break statement is used to exit a switch statement. In a similar manner, break can be used to exit a loop. (See Figure 1.1.)

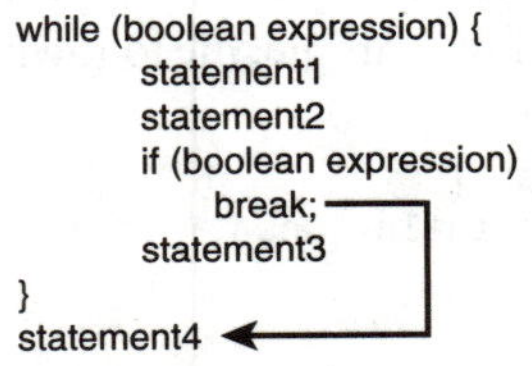

Figure 1.1.

The flow of control with a break *statement.*

```
while (boolean expression) {
    statement1
    statement2
    if (boolean expression)
        break;
    statement3
}
statement4
```

As Figure 1.1 illustrates, if the break statement is encountered, execution will continue with statement4. As an example of this, consider the following code:

```
int year = 1909;
while (DidCubsWinTheWorldSeries(year) == false) {
    System.out.println("Didn't win in " + year);
    if (year >= 3000) {
        System.out.println("Time to give up. Go White Sox!");
        break;
    }
}
System.out.println("Loop exited on year " + year);
```

This example shows a while loop that will continue to execute until it finds a year that the Chicago Cubs won the World Series. Because they haven't won since 1908 and the loop counter year starts with 1909, it has a lot of looping to do. For each year they didn't win, a message is displayed. Even die-hard Cubs fans will eventually give up and change allegiances to the Chicago White Sox. In this example, if the year is 3000 or later, a message is displayed and then a break is encountered. The break statement will cause program control to move to the first statement after the end of the while loop. In this case, that will be the following line:

```
System.out.println("Loop exited on year " + year);
```

The continue Statement

Just as a break statement can be used to move program control to immediately after the end of a loop, the continue statement can be used to force program control back to the top of a loop. (See Figure 1.2.)

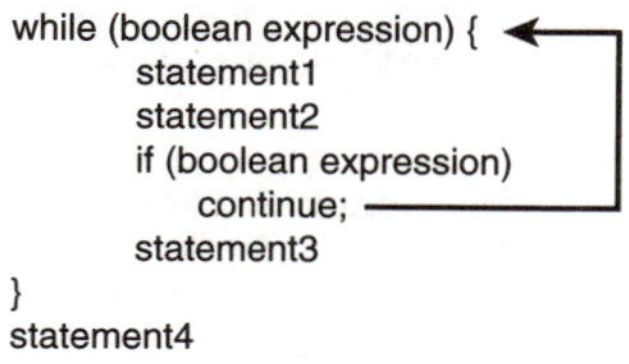

Figure 1.2.

The flow of control with a continue statement.

```
while (boolean expression) {
    statement1
    statement2
    if (boolean expression)
        continue;
    statement3
}
statement4
```

Suppose you want to write a method that will count and display the number of times the Cubs have won the World Series this century. One way to do this would be to first see whether the Cubs played in the World Series and then see whether they won. This could be done as follows:

```
int timesWon = 0;
for (int year=1900; year <= 2000; year++) {
    if (DidCubsPlayInWorldSeries(year) = false)
        continue;
```

```
    if (DidCubsWinWorldSeries(year)) {
        System.out.println("Cubbies won in " + year + "!");
        timesWon++;
    }
}
System.out.println("The Cubs won " + timesWon + " times.");
```

In this case, a for loop is used to iterate through the years from 1900 to 2000. The first line within the loop tests to see whether the Cubs played in the World Series. If they didn't, the continue statement is executed. This moves program control back to the for loop. At that point, year is incremented, and the expression year <= 2000 is retested. If year is less than or equal to 2000, the loop continues. If, however, DidCubsPlayInWorldSeries equals true, the continue statement is skipped and the next test is performed to see whether the Cubs won that year.

Using Labels

Java does not include a goto statement, but the fact that goto is a reserved word indicates that it may be added in a future version. Instead of goto, Java allows you to combine break and continue with a label. This has an effect similar to a goto in that it allows a program to reposition control. In order to understand the use of labels with break and continue, consider Listing 1.5.

Listing 1.5. Using labels to control the flow.

```
1:      public void paint(Graphics g) {
2:          int line=1;
3:
4:          outsideLoop:
5:          for(int out=0; out<3; out++) {
6:              g.drawString("out = " + out, 5, line * 20);
7:              line++;
8:
9:              for(int inner=0;inner < 5; inner++) {
10:                 double randNum = Math.random();
11:                 g.drawString(Double.toString(randNum), 15,
12:                         line * 20);
13:                 line++;
14:                 if (randNum < .10) {
15:                     g.drawString("break to outsideLoop",
16:                             25, line * 20);
17:                     line++;
18:                     break outsideLoop;
19:                 }
20:                 if (randNum < .60) {
21:                     g.drawString("continue to outsideLoop",
22:                             25, line * 20);
23:                     line++;
24:                     continue outsideLoop;
25:                 }
26:             }
27:         }
```

```
28:        g.drawString("all done", 50, line * 20);
29:    }
```

 ANALYSIS This example includes two loops. The first loops on the variable out (lines 5–27), and the second loops on the variable `inner` (lines 9–26). The outer loop has been labeled by the following line:

```
outsideLoop:
```

This statement will serve as a placeholder and as a name for the outer loop. A random number between 0 and 1 is generated for each iteration through the inner loop (line 10). This number is displayed on the screen (lines 11–12). If the random number is less than 0.10, the statement `break outsideLoop` is executed (line 18). A normal `break` statement in this position would break out of the inner loop. However, because this is a labeled `break` statement, it has the effect of breaking out of the loop identified by the name. In this case, program control passes to the line that displays `all done` (line 28) because that is the first line after `outsideLoop`.

On the other hand, if the random number is not less than 0.10, the number is compared to 0.60 (line 20). If it is less than that number, the statement `continue outsideLoop` is executed (line 24). A normal, unlabeled `continue` statement at this point would have the effect of transferring program control back to the top of the inner loop. Because this is a labeled `continue` statement, program control is transferred to the start of the named loop (line 5). A sample run of this method is shown in Figure 1.3.

Figure 1.3.

The results of executing the code in Listing 1.5.

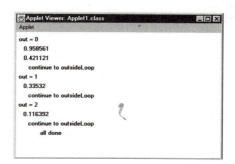

As you can see in Figure 1.3, the first pass through the outer loop resulted in two passes through the inner loop. When the value 0.421121 was generated, it caused the `continue outsideLoop` to execute because the number is less than 0.60. The next pass through the outer loop was similar, except that it did a `continue` of the outer loop after only one iteration through the inner loop. Finally, on the third pass through the outer loop, the program generated a value lower than 0.10, which caused the program to break to the outer loop. You can see that, at this point, the next line of code to be executed was line 28, and that it printed `all done`.

DO declare and initialize variables within a `for` loop if the variables are used only within the loop.

DON'T forget that a `do...while` loop will execute at least once.

DON'T fall into the habit of always using one particular type of loop. Each type of loop—`for`, `while`, and `do...while`—has its unique advantages. Take advantage of them.

Java Classes

Now that you've seen most of the low-level details of the Java language, it's time to turn your attention to Java classes and see how Java is able to live up to its claim of being an object-oriented language. A Java *class* is a compile-time concept that represents a runtime object. In other words, a class is a definition or template for an object that will exist within the program. For example, if you have a class called `Car`, you might have a particular instance of that class that is a 1966 Volkswagen Beetle. The instances (such as `1966 Volkswagen Beetle`) of a class (`Car`) are known as *objects*. To define a class in Java, you would do something similar to the following:

```
class Car {
    // member variables
    // member methods
}
```

NOTE

The design of Java's object model and its support for classes were certainly influenced by C++. But Java classes borrow less from C++ than do many other aspects of Java and its syntax. While classes are undeniably important in C++, they are mandatory and central to everything you do in Java. In Java, there are no free-standing variables or functions. Everything must be encapsulated within a class. Further, every class in Java can trace back through its inheritance hierarchy and find itself to be a descendant of the `Object` class.

1

Field Declarations

Car is now an empty class. In order to make it usable and useful, you need to add some fields to the class.

NEW TERM A *field* can be either a member variable or a member method.

To declare member variables, all you need to do is identify the variable by type and name in the class definition, as shown in the following:

```
class Car {
    // these are member variables
    String manufacturer;
    String model;
    int year;
    int passengers;
}
```

In this example, Car has been extended to include String variables for manufacturer and model, and integer variables for the year it was built and the number of passengers it can hold. From this class definition, it is then possible to create instances, or objects, at runtime, as shown in Figure 1.4.

Figure 1.4.

The Car *class and its objects.*

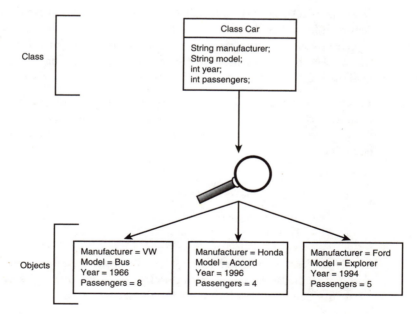

Field Access

One of the principal advantages of object-oriented programming is encapsulation.

 Encapsulation is the ability to define classes that hide their implementation details from other classes, exposing only their public interfaces to those other classes.

Support for encapsulation in Java comes from the three keywords `public`, `private`, and `protected`. When you are defining a class, these field-access modifiers are used to control who has access to each field in the class.

 A *field-access modifier*—`public`, `private`, or `protected`—determines who can access a field.

By declaring a field as `public`, you are indicating that it is entirely accessible to all other classes. Continuing with the `Car` example, to declare all the fields as `public`, do the following:

```
class Car {
    public String manufacturer;
    public String model;
    public int year;
    public int passengers;
}
```

Of course, declaring everything as `public` doesn't exactly achieve the goal of encapsulation because it lets other classes directly access variables in the `Car` class. Consider what would happen if you needed to create an instance of this class for a 1964-and-a-half Mustang. Because year only holds integer values, it would have to be changed to a float so that it could hold `1964.5`. If code in other classes directly accessed year, that code could conceivably break.

To restrict access to a field, use the keyword `private`. A class cannot access the private fields of another class. Suppose the `Car` class is intended for use in a used car sales application. In this case, you might want to define `Car` as follows in order to hide your cost for a car from potential buyers:

```
class Car {
    public String manufacturer;
    public String model;
    public int year;
    public int passengers;
    private float cost;
}
```

Finally, the keyword `protected` is used to indicate that fields are accessible within the current class and to all classes derived from the class, but not to other classes. The ability to derive a class from another class is discussed in the section "Class Inheritance," later today.

Setting Initial Values

One extremely nice aspect of Java class declarations is the capability to specify initial values for member variables in the variable declaration. For example, because most cars will hold four passengers, it may be reasonable to default the passengers member variable to 4, as shown in the following code:

```
class Car {
    public String manufacturer;
    public String model;
    public int year;
    public int passengers = 4;
    private float cost;
}
```

Static Members

In addition to private, protected, and public members, a Java class can also have static members.

NEW TERM A *static* member is one that belongs to the class itself, not to the instances of the class.

Regardless of how many instances of a class have been created by a program at runtime, there will exist exactly one instance of each static member. Declaring a static member is done by adding the keyword static to any of the other field-access modifiers, as shown in the following:

```
class Car {
    public String manufacturer;
    public String model;
    public int year;
    public int passengers = 4;
    private float cost;
    public static int tireQty = 4;
}
```

In this case, the variable tireQty has been added and is set to 4. Because every car will have four tires, tireQty was declared as static. Also, because I want tireQty to be accessible to other classes, it has been declared public.

It is also possible to declare member methods as static.

Member Methods

In addition to member variables, most classes will also have member methods. Because member methods, like member variables, are fields, access to them can be controlled with the public, protected, and private modifiers. A member method is declared according to the following syntax, in which elements enclosed in square brackets ([...]) are optional:

```
[methodModifiers] resultType methodName [throws exceptionList] {
    // method body
}
```

The methodModifiers are the familiar public, protected, and private keywords you've already seen, as well as some additional modifiers. The method modifiers are described in Table 1.14.

Table 1.14. Method modifiers.

Modifier	Purpose
public	Accessible outside the class in which it is declared.
protected	Accessible by the class in which it is declared and by subclasses of that class.
private	Accessible only by the class in which it is declared.
static	A method of the class rather than of a particular instance of the class.
abstract	A method that is not implemented.
final	Cannot be overriden in subclasses.
native	A platform-dependent implementation of the method in another language, typically C or assembly.
synchronized	Used to indicate a critical method that will lock the object to prevent execution of other methods while the synchronized method executes.

The resultType of a method declaration can be one of the primitive types (for example, int, float, char), another class, or void. A resultType of void indicates that no result is passed back to the caller of the method. After the method name is given, a list of exceptions throwable by the method is given. If no exceptions are thrown by the method, this list is not necessary. (Exception handling is discussed in the section titled "Exception Handling," later today.)

As an example of adding a method to the Car class, consider the following sample code:

```
class Car {
    public String manufacturer;
    public String model;
    public int year;
    public int passengers;
    public float CalculateSalePrice() {
        return cost * 1.5;
    }
    private float cost;
}
```

In this case, the Car class has had a public member method, CalculateSalePrice, added. The method returns a float, and the body of the method calculates this return value. To calculate the sale price of a car, the private member variable cost is multiplied by 1.5, reflecting a markup of 50% over the amount the car was purchased for.

Overloaded Methods

The ability to overload methods is one of the biggest advantages to working in an object-oriented language, and Java certainly doesn't disappoint.

 Overloading a method means to use the same method name for more than one method.

As an example of overloading, the Car class can include two `CalculateSalePrice` methods, as follows:

```
public float CalculateSalePrice() {
    return cost * 1.5;
}
public float CalculateSalePrice(double margin) {
    return cost * (1 + margin);
}
private float cost;
```

In this case, the first version of `CalculateSalePrice` is not passed any parameters and bases the sale price on the cost plus 50% (`cost * 1.5`). The second version is passed a margin by which the car should be marked up in determining the car's sale price.

At runtime, Java is able to distinguish between these methods by the parameters passed to each. Because of this, you can overload a method as many times as you want as long as the parameter lists of each version are unique. In other words, you could not do the following:

```
public float CalculateSalePrice() {
    return cost * 1.5;
}
public float CalculateSalePrice(double margin) {
    return cost * (1 + margin);
}
// this method declaration conflicts with the preceding method
public float CalculateSalePrice(double multiplier) {
    return cost * margin;
}
private float cost;
```

In this situation, the last two declarations are in conflict because each is passed a `double`. Different parameter names are insufficient to distinguish between two versions of the same overloaded function. They must differ by at least one parameter type.

Constructors

A special type of member method is known as a constructor.

NEW TERM A *constructor* is a method that is used to create new instances of that class.

You can identify a constructor because it will have the same name as the class. As with any other method, a constructor can be overloaded as long as the versions are distinguishable by the parameter types passed to each. Typically, a constructor will set the member variables of an object to values appropriate for that instance. As an example, consider the following variation on the Car class:

```
public class Car {
    String manufacturer;
    String model;
    int year;
    int passengers;
    float cost;
    // calculate the sale price of a car based on its cost
    public double CalculateSalePrice() {
        return cost * 1.5;
    }
    // a public constructor
    public Car(String madeBy, String name, int yr, int pass,
            float cst) {
        manufacturer = madeBy;
        model = name;
        year = yr;
        passengers = pass;
        cost = cst;
    }
    // create and return a string with the basic details about
    // this particular car
    public String GetStats() {
        return new String(year + " " + manufacturer + " " + model);
    }
}
```

A constructor, Car, has been added to this version of the Car class. The constructor is passed five parameters that will be used as initial values for the instance variables manufacturer, model, year, passengers, and cost. The code for the constructor simply sets the five instance variables. The Car class has also received a new public member, GetStats, that creates a string that contains the basic facts about the car. By using the constructor and the new GetStats method, you can now display some information about a car. For example, the following code will display 1967 VW Bug:

```
Car myCar = new Car("VW", "Bug", 1967, 4, 3000);
String str = myCar.GetStats();
System.out.println(str);
```

The new instance of the class Car was created with the following line:

```
Car myCar = new Car("VW", "Bug", 1967, 4, 3000);
```

The use of the Java keyword new instructs Java to create a new object of type Car by allocating memory for it and to invoke the constructor for Car whose signature matches the parameter list. In this case, Car has only one constructor, so it is invoked and will set the instance variables to the values of the parameters. Once the variable myCar goes out of scope at the end of the method in which it is declared, the automatic memory-management features of Java will detect that the memory that was allocated by new is no longer referenced, so it will be released.

TIP

> If a class does not specifically include a constructor, Java will provide a default constructor that takes no parameters. This constructor will allow you to create new instances of a class and will set all member variables to their Java system default values. However, it is a dangerous and unwise practice to rely on the existence of a Java default constructor. In general, you should always provide at least one constructor for each class you define.

The this Variable

All Java classes contain a hidden member variable named this. The this member can be used at runtime to reference the object itself. One excellent use of this is in constructors. It is very common to have a set of instance variables in a class that must be set to values that are passed to a constructor. When you are doing this, it would be nice to have code that is similar to the following:

```
year = year;
```

Ideally, the variable on the left could be the instance variable, and the variable on the right could be the parameter passed to the constructor. Unfortunately, I don't know of any languages that would be able to make this distinction. The typical solution most programmers have settled on is similar to the following:

```
public class Car {
    String manufacturer;
    String model;
    int year;
    int passengers;
    // a public constructor
    public Car(String madeBy, String name, int yr, int pass,
            float cst) {
        manufacturer = madeBy;
        model = name;
        year = yr;
        passengers = pass;
        cost = cst;
    }
}
```

Here, we've had to come up with two names for each concept: The best variable names (manufacturer, model, and so on) are used as the instance variables in the class declaration;

the less satisfactory names are passed as parameters so as to distinguish them from the instance variables. The assignment statements are then very readable by Java, but seem a little contrived to human readers. Java's this keyword provides a very effective solution to this problem in that the constructor can be written as follows:

```java
public class Car {
    String manufacturer;
    String model;
    int year;
    int passengers;
    float cost;
    // calculate the sale price of a car based on its cost
    public double CalculateSalePrice() {
        return cost * 1.5;
    }
    // a public constructor
    public Car(String manufacturer, String model, int year,
            int passengers, float cost) {
        this.manufacturer = manufacturer;
        this.model = model;
        this.year = year;
        this.passengers = passengers;
        this.cost = cost;
    }
}
```

In this case, the variables like this.year refer to the instance variables, whereas the unqualified variables like year refer to the constructor's parameters.

Of course, this is only one example of how you can use this. It is also frequently used as a parameter to other functions from within member methods.

Class Inheritance

In Java, every class you declare will be derived from another class. You can specify the class to derive from by using the extends keyword as follows:

```java
public class ClassicCar extends Car {
    // member methods and variables
}
```

As you probably noticed, extends was left out of all the prior examples in today's lesson. This is because if a class is not declared as being derived from a specific class, it is assumed to be derived from the Java base class, Object. This means that the following two class declarations are equivalent:

```java
public class Car {
    // member methods and variables
}
public class Car extends Object {
    // member methods and variables
}
```

Object is the class from which all other Java classes are ultimately derived, which provides a common set of functionality among all Java classes. Most notably, garbage collection is possible because all classes will ultimately trace their lineage back to Object, as shown in Figure 1.5.

Figure 1.5.

Everything is (eventually) derived from Object.

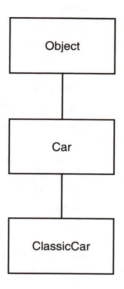

A derived class is commonly referred to as a *subclass*, while the class it is derived from is commonly referred to as a *superclass*. The term *immediate superclass* is used to describe the class from which a subclass is directly derived.

In Figure 1.5, for example, ClassicCar is a subclass of both Car and Object. Car and Object are both superclasses of ClassicCar, but only Car is the immediate superclass of ClassicCar.

Overriding Member Methods

When you create a subclass, you inherit all the functionality of its superclass, and then you can add to or change this functionality as desired. As an example of this, consider the altered declaration of a Car class in the following code:

```
public class Car {
    private int year;
    private float originalPrice;
    // calculate the sale price of a car based on its cost
    public double CalculateSalePrice() {
        double salePrice;
        if (year > 1994)
            salePrice = originalPrice * 0.75;
```

```
            else if (year > 1990)
                salePrice = originalPrice * 0.50;
            else
                salePrice = originalPrice * 0.25;
            return salePrice;
        }
        // a public constructor
        public Car(int year, float originalPrice) {
            this.year = year;
            this.originalPrice = originalPrice;
        }
    }
}
```

This version of the Car class holds information about the year and the original purchase price of the car. It has a member method, CalculateSalePrice, that determines the price for which to sell the car based on its age. Depending upon the age of the car, it can sell for 75%, 50%, or 25% of its original price.

Although very simplistic, this is a good start for most cars. However, it is completely inadequate for classic cars. This algorithm would indicate that a 1920 Model T would be worth only 25% of its original 1920 price. A slight improvement on this would be to assume that every ClassicCar is worth $10,000. To do this, ClassicCar is derived from Car, as follows:

```
public class ClassicCar extends Car {
    // calculate the sale price of a car based on its cost
    public double CalculateSalePrice() {
        return 10000;
    }
    // a public constructor
    public ClassicCar(int year, float originalPrice) {
        super(year, originalPrice);
    }
}
```

Because ClassicCar is derived from Car, it inherits all the functionality of Car, including its member variables year and originalPrice. The function CalculateSalePrice appears in both class declarations. This means that the occurrence of this function in ClassicCar overrides the occurrence of it in Car for object instances of ClassicCar. As an example of how this works, consider the following:

```
ClassicCar myClassic = new ClassicCar(1920, 1400);
double classicPrice = myClassic.CalculateSalePrice();
Car myCar = new Car(1990, 12000);
double price = myCar.CalculateSalePrice();
```

The variable myClassic is of type ClassicCar and is constructed using that class's constructor, which is passed an original price for the car of $1,400. The sale price of this car is calculated and stored in classicPrice. Because myClassic is a ClassicCar, the sale price will be $10,000. Next, myCar is constructed as a new object of type Car with an original cost of $12,000. Its sale price is determined and stored in price. Because myCar is a Car, its sale price will be based on the year it was made (1990) and will be 25% of $12,000, or $3,000.

The super **Variable**

In the preceding declaration for ClassicCar, you may have noticed that the constructor made use of a variable named super. Just as each object has a this variable that references itself, each object (other than those of type Object itself) has a super variable that represents the parent class. In this case, super(year, originalPrice) invokes the constructor of the superclass Car.

Class Modifiers

Classes that are created in Java can be modified by class modifiers. The Java class modifiers are public, final, and abstract. If no class modifier is used, the class may only be used within the package in which it is declared. A public class is a class that can be accessed from other packages. A class that is declared as final cannot be derived from, meaning it cannot have subclasses.

Abstract Classes

Sometimes you might want to declare a class but not know how to define all the methods that belong to that class. For example, you might want to declare a class called Mammal and include in it a member method called MarkTerritory. However, you don't know how to write MarkTerritory because it is different for each type of mammal. Of course, you plan to handle this by deriving subclasses of Mammal, such as Dog and Human. But what code do you put in the MarkTerritory function of Mammal itself?

In Java you can declare the MarkTerritory function of Mammal as an abstract method, which allows you to declare the method without writing any code for it in that class. However, you can write code for the method in the subclass. If a method is declared as abstract, the class must also be declared as abstract. For Mammal and its subclasses, this means they would appear as follows:

```
abstract class Mammal {
    abstract void MarkTerritory();
}
public class Human extends Mammal {
    public void MarkTerritory() {
        // mark territory by building a fence
    }
}
public class GangMember extends Mammal {
    public void MarkTerritory() {
        // mark territory with graffiti
    }
}
public class Dog extends Mammal {
    public void MarkTerritory() {
        // mark territory by doing what dogs do
    }
}
```

In the preceding declarations, the Mammal class contains no code for MarkTerritory. The Human class could contain code that would mark territory by building a fence around it, while the GangMember class could contain code that would mark territory by spray-painting graffiti. The Dog class would mark territory by raising the dog's leg and doing what dogs do to mark territory.

NOTE   A method that is private or static cannot also be declared as abstract. Because a private method cannot be overridden in a subclass, a private abstract method would not be usable. Similarly, because all static methods are implicitly final, static methods cannot be overridden.

Implementing Interfaces

Typically, an abstract class will have some methods that are declared as abstract and some that are not. If you find yourself declaring a class that is entirely abstract, you are probably declaring what is known in Java as an interface.

NEW TERM   An *interface* is an entirely abstract class.

You can derive subclasses from an interface in a manner completely analogous to deriving a subclass from another class. For example, suppose you are building an application that must display the hour of the day. Users will have two options for getting this information: They can get it from either a watch or a cuckoo clock. This could be implemented as follows:

```
interface Clock {
    public String GetTime(int hour);
}
class Cuckoo implements Clock  {
    public String GetTime(int hour) {
        StringBuffer str = new StringBuffer();
        for (int i=0; i < hour; i++)
            str.append("Cuckoo ");
        return str.toString();
    }
}
class Watch implements Clock  {
    public String GetTime(int hour) {
        return new String("It is " + hour + ":00");
    }
}
```

In this example, Clock is an interface that provides a single function, GetTime. What this means is that any class that is derived from (or, in other words, *implements*) the Clock interface must provide a GetTime function. Cuckoo is an example of a class that implements Clock, and you'll notice that instead of the class Cuckoo extends Clock syntax that would have been used if Clock were an abstract class, it is instead declared with class Cuckoo implements Clock.

Because Cuckoo implements the Clock interface, it provides a GetTime function. In this case, a string is created that will hold as many cuckoos as specified by the hour parameter. The class Watch also implements Clock and provides a GetTime function. Its version is a simple message stating the hour.

NOTE

> Although interfaces and abstract classes may at first appear the same, they are not. Remember, Java does not support multiple inheritance of classes, only of interfaces. Also, an interface cannot provide implementations of any of its methods and cannot include variable declarations.

Interfaces and superclasses are not mutually exclusive. A new class can be derived from a superclass and one or more interfaces. This could be done as follows for a class that implements two interfaces and has one superclass:

```
class MySubClass extends MySuperClass implements FirstInterface,
      SecondInterface {
    // class implementation
}
```

Because it is possible for one class to implement more than one interface, interfaces are a very convenient method for implementing a form of multiple inheritance.

Exception Handling

When something goes wrong inside a Java method, the method can *throw an exception*. Throwing an exception refers to generating an instance of a class that represents an error or warning and passing the object back to the calling code. Exception handling can streamline the code you must write to handle errors or unlikely conditions.

Trying and Catching

In Java, exception handling is performed through the use of try...catch blocks. The code within a try block is executed, and if an exception occurs, execution is transferred to a catch block (if one is provided) that handles the type of exception that occurred. The catch block is passed an object of the exception class as a parameter. For example, consider the following code:

```
public class MyClass extends Applet
{
    public void paint(Graphics g)
    {
```

```
        String [] stringArray = {"A", "Four", "Element", "Array"};
        try {
            for(int i=0;i<5;i++)
                g.drawString(stringArray[i], 10, 30+10*i);
        }
        catch (ArrayIndexOutOfBoundsException e) {
            g.drawString("oops: array too small", 10, 10);
        }
    }
}
```

In this example, a try block surrounds a for loop. The for loop will iterate one time too many through a four-element array. This will generate the exception ArrayIndexOutOfBoundsException, which is caught by a catch block. The catch block is passed an object, e, of type ArrayIndexOutOfBoundsException. In this example, the catch block does not need to use this object, but it could if necessary.

Sometimes a block of code can generate more than one possible exception. In these cases you can use multiple catch blocks, one for each of the possible exceptions, as shown in Listing 1.6.

Listing 1.6. Catching exceptions with try...catch.

```
1:      public class MyClass extends Applet
2:      {
3:
4:          public void paint(Graphics g)
5:          {
6:              String [] stringArray = {"A", "Four",
7:                                       "Element", "Array"};
8:
9:              try {
10:                 for(int i=0;i<4;i++)
11:                     g.drawString(stringArray[i],10,30+10*i);
12:
13:                 char ch = stringArray[0].charAt(43);
14:             }
15:             catch (ArrayIndexOutOfBoundsException e) {
16:                 g.drawString("oops: array too small",10,10);
17:             }
18:             catch (StringIndexOutOfBoundsException e) {
19:                 g.drawString("oops: string index error",10,10);
20:             }
21:         }
22:     }
```

ANALYSIS In this case, the program loops through the four items in the array (lines 10–11) and then uses charAt to get the character at position 43 in a one-character string (line 13). This generates the StringIndexOutOfBoundsException that is handled by the second catch block (lines 18–20).

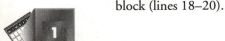

Using a `finally` Block

In addition to `try` and `catch` blocks, Java also allows you to specify a `finally` block that will execute regardless of any exceptions that may have occurred. For an example of a `finally` block, consider the following class:

```
public class MyClass extends Applet
{
    public void paint(Graphics g)
    {
        String [] stringArray = {"A", "Four", "Element", "Array"};
        try {
            for(int i=0;i<5;i++)
                g.drawString(stringArray[i], 10, 30+10*i);
        }
        catch (ArrayIndexOutOfBoundsException e) {
            g.drawString("oops: array too small", 10, 10);
        }
        finally {
            g.drawString("in the finally", 10, 100);
        }
    }
}
```

Here, an exception will be thrown when the loop attempts to access the fifth item in the four-item array. The exception is caught and handled by displaying a message on the screen; then the `finally` block is executed and another message is displayed.

Summary

This lesson covers a great deal of information. You were introduced to Java's primitive types and the operators that are available for these types. Next, you learned how to control the flow of a Java program through its selection statements (`if`, `switch`, and `case`), its iteration statements (`for`, `while`, and `do...while`), and jumping (`break` and `continue`). You learned how to put all this together and create new classes by deriving them from existing classes or interfaces. Finally, you learned how to effectively handle errors with exception handling.

Q&A

Q Why doesn't Java have a goto statement?

A The designers of Java were probably influenced by the years of arguments about the inherent evils of goto. It is long been argued that using goto results in less struc-tured programs that are therefore more difficult to maintain. If this is the thinking that led to leaving goto out of Java, it is surprising that its designers opted to include labeled jumps, because they are gotos in disguise.

Q I'm a C++ programmer who is contemplating using Java. In C++, I use templates extensively, but I notice that Java doesn't include templates. Will this cause problems?

A No, it shouldn't. Many of the problems that are addressed by C++ templates are not problems in Java because Java is a more complete object-oriented language. In Java, all objects can ultimately trace their ancestry to the `Object` class. Because of this, any Java class can be passed to a method that expects an `Object` parameter.

Q Why would I ever use an abstract class?

A Abstract classes represent a very useful way to combine behavior into a superclass and then add supplemental behavior in the subclasses. For example, suppose you are working on a universal inbox application that will allow users to retrieve both their e-mail and voice mail from a single program. One likely design for this would include an abstract `Message` class with the subclasses `VoiceMailMessage` and `EmailMessage`. The `Message` class would include methods that are common to each type of message (for example, `GetSenderName`, `GetDateSent`, and so on). The `Message` class would also include abstract methods (just the method signatures) for methods that exist for each message type but that are implemented differently. For example, `GetMessage` might start an audio playback for `VoiceMailMessage` but display text on the screen for `EmailMessage`. `GetLength` might return the number of seconds for `VoiceMailMessage` but the number of bytes for `EmailMessage`.

Workshop

The workshop includes quiz questions to help you gauge your understanding of the material in this chapter, and also includes exercises to provide hands-on experience with what you've learned in this chapter. You can find the answers to these questions and exercises in Appendix D, "Answers."

Quiz

1. What is a package?
2. Explain the difference between `public`, `private`, and `protected`.
3. What are Java's eight primitive types?
4. How many bytes are there in a Java `int`? How many in a `long`?
5. Give an example of a widening conversion.
6. What is the meaning of NaN?
7. What is the immediate superclass of `MyClass` in the following declaration?
   ```
   class MyClass {
   ...
   }
   ```

8. A class can use super to refer to its superclass; how does a class refer to itself?

9. How many immediate superclasses can a class have?

10. How many superclasses can a class have?

11. How many interfaces can a class implement?

12. What can you not do to a class that is declared as final?

13. What Java keywords are used to support exception handling?

Exercises

1. **Bug Hunt:** What is wrong with the following code?

```
for(int val=0; val<10; val++)
    ShowCurrentValue(val);
ShowFinalValue(val);
```

2. How can you correct the code in Exercise 1?

3. What will the following code display?

```
if (Float.NaN == Float.Nan)
    display("equal");
else
    display("not equal");
```

4. What is the difference between the following two lines of code?

```
int [] firstArray, secondArray;
int thirdArray[], justAnInt;
```

5. What will the following code display?

```
int x = 4;
display(x == 4 ? "Hi Mom" : "Hi Dad");
```

6. **Bug Hunt:** What's wrong with the following code? How can it be fixed?

```
int x = GetRandomValue();
if (!x)
    display("in the if");
else
    display("in the else");
```

Day 2

Getting Started with Visual Café

Today you will begin to get familiar with Visual Café. You will be introduced
to some of the items on the Visual Café desktop that you will use the most,
including the Form Designer, the Component palette, the Project window, the
Property List, and the Interaction wizard. You will also learn about the unique
features of Visual Café's source code editing windows and how they allow you
to easily add methods to a class. You will learn how to create two sample applets
and a sample application, and will see how Visual Café generates source code
based on your actions in the development environment.

The Visual Café Desktop

When you first start using Visual Café, the environment may seem overwhelm-
ing with all its windows popping up, coming and going. After a short time,
however, you will probably begin to feel at home and will come to understand
the purpose of each of the Visual Café windows and tools. Naturally, the Visual
Café desktop is highly configurable, but a very typical desktop is shown in Figure 2.1.

Figure 2.1.

*A typical view of the
Visual Café desktop.*

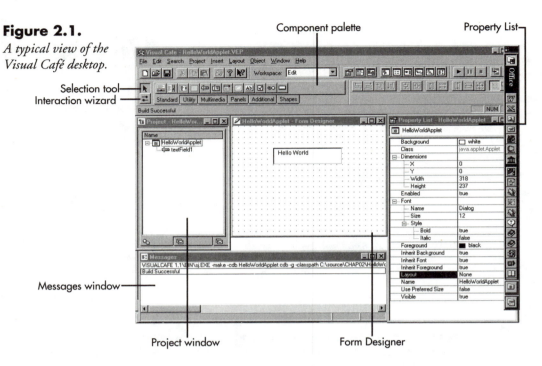

In Figure 2.1, you can see many of the most important or commonly used features of Visual
Café:

- [ ] The Form Designer
- [ ] The Component palette
- [ ] The Project window
- [ ] The Property List
- [ ] The Messages window
- [ ] The Selection tool
- [ ] The Interaction wizard

The Form Designer

The Form Designer is used whenever you want to visually lay out an applet, frame, or dialog
box. Both visual and nonvisual components can be placed on the Form Designer by dragging
them from the Component palette.

NEW TERM   Visual Café uses the term *form* to refer to an applet, a frame, a window, or a
dialog box.

A *visual component* is an element of the user interface, such as a button, text field, or checkbox. A *nonvisual component* is placed onto a form at design time as a visual component is, but does not appear in the user interface when the program is run.

In discussing Java programs, it has become standard to refer to Java programs that are embedded in another language as *applets* and to standalone programs as *applications*. For example, when using Java to augment a World Wide Web page, the Java code is embedded within HTML code. Therefore, this is referred to as an applet. On the other hand, a Java program that is not embedded within HTML or any other language and can stand on its own is referred to as an application.

There is a subtle implication within these definitions that applications are larger (and, therefore, presumably more complex) than applets. But this is not necessarily true. Applications and applets alike can range from simple, one-class programs to programs with hundreds of classes. The implication that an applet is somehow less than an application is unfortunately a connotation it is necessary to live with in an otherwise valid distinction.

NEW TERM Java programs that are embedded in another program, such as a browser, are *applets*. Java programs that are standalone programs not depending upon another program are referred to as *applications*.

Using the Form Designer you can use a positional layout manager that places each component at the precise X,Y coordinates you drag it to. Or, you can use the Java layout managers. (See Day 7, "The Form Designer, Layout Managers, and Panels," for a thorough discussion of the layout managers.)

The Component Palette

The Component palette is a toolbar that contains a series of tabs. Each tab contains various components that can be placed onto a form. For example, the Standard tab contains a component for each of the main classes in the Java Abstract Windowing Toolkit (AWT). The Standard tab of the Component palette in Figure 2.1 shows icons representing the following components:

 Horizontal scrollbar

 Vertical scrollbar

 List

 Canvas

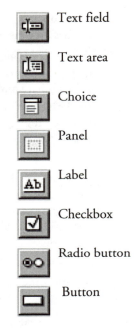

Text field

Text area

Choice

Panel

Label

Checkbox

Radio button

Button

To add a component to the Form Designer, you select the component by clicking the left mouse button with the mouse pointer over the desired component and then clicking the left mouse button again over the desired location in the Form Designer. This will add a component at its default size. To add a component of a specific size, you can hold down the left mouse button when placing the component and draw an outline of the desired size.

NOTE

Not every component on the Component palette represents a unique class. For example, the first component is a horizontal scrollbar, and the second is a vertical scrollbar. Each of these is based on the Scrollbar class, but each constructs the scrollbar in a different orientation.

Additionally, not every component supplied with Visual Café is shown on the Component palette. To see every available component, select Component from the Insert menu. On Day 6, "Debugging, Customizing, and Managing Projects," you learn how to customize the Component palette to show only those components you desire. Also, on Day 22, "Reusable Packages, Forms, and Projects," you will learn how to add your own components to the Component palette.

The Project Window

The Project window, shown along the left edge of the screen in Figure 2.1, is a tabbed window that contains three panes. The first pane (and the one shown in Figure 2.1) is the Objects pane. The Objects pane of the Project window shows you the classes and components that comprise a project. For example, the Project window of Figure 2.1 shows that there is a class named `HelloWorldApplet` that contains an object named `textField1`. If you look at the Form Designer in Figure 2.1, you should be able to identify this object.

The second pane of the Project window is the Packages pane. This pane lists the packages that are available to the current project. The Packages pane is shown in Figure 2.2. The final pane of the Project window is the Files pane. This pane shows the files that are included in the project.

Figure 2.2.

The Packages pane of the Project window.

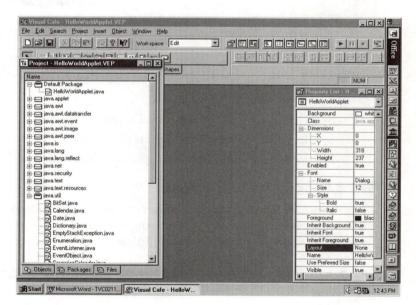

The Property List

The Property List, shown on the right side of the screen in Figure 2.1, allows you to interactively set the values for object properties. For example, the `Foreground` property shown in Figure 2.1 allows you to set the foreground color of the applet. In Figure 2.3, you can see the drop-down list of colors from which to choose.

Values that are set in the Property List result in code that is automatically generated by Visual Café. For example, selecting a foreground color in the Property List will result in a call to the `setForeground` method of the `Component` class.

Figure 2.3.

*Selecting the fore-
ground color of an
object in the Property
List.*

To set the properties of an object, you must first select the object. This can be done in the
following three ways:

☐ By selecting the object in the Form Designer

☐ By selecting the object in the Objects pane of the Project window

☐ By selecting the object from the list of objects at the top of the Property List

The Messages Window

The Visual Café Messages window displays various status, warning, and error messages to you
as you develop your Java programs. For example, Figure 2.4 shows the Messages window after
attempting to build an applet that included an error in the source code.

Figure 2.4.

*Viewing compile
errors in the Messages
window.*

 TIP   You can double-click the mouse on a line in the Messages window to
open a source code window on the offending line of code.

The Selection Tool and the Interaction Wizard

The Selection tool and Interaction wizard are activated by clicking the and buttons, respectively, near the top left of the screen in Figure 2.1. Of the Selection tool and the Interaction wizard, only one can be active at any time. The Selection tool is used to select components, enter component property values, edit source code, and perform most activities in the development environment. The Interaction wizard is used to define an interaction between two components.

Clicking the Interaction wizard button will change the cursor to an arrow accompanied by two small boxes that are connected by a line. This cursor is shown in Figure 2.5. Using this cursor, you can click on one component in the Form Designer and drag a connecting line to another component. When you release the cursor, the Interaction wizard will appear, as shown in Figure 2.6.

Figure 2.5.

The cursor that is used to draw interactions between components.

Figure 2.6.

The Interaction wizard allows you to draw interactions between components.

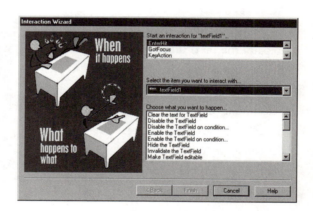

The Interaction wizard allows you to select an action that can occur to the first component. For example, if the first component is a button, the following actions are available:

☐ Clicked

☐ GotFocus

☐ LostFocus

You can also select the component that will interact with the first component. By default, this will be set to the component you dragged the mouse to in order to activate the Interaction wizard. Finally, you can select what you want to happen to the second component. Each component has its own list of actions that can be performed. For example, for a text field component you can set whether the text is editable. Because this action does not make sense for a button component, it is not available when the second component is a button. As an example of the rich variety of actions that can be taken on a component, consider the following list of available actions on a text field:

- ☐ Clear the text for `TextField`
- ☐ Disable the `TextField`
- ☐ Disable the `TextField` on condition
- ☐ Enable the `TextField`
- ☐ Enable the `TextField` on condition
- ☐ Hide the `TextField`
- ☐ Invalidate the `TextField`
- ☐ Make `TextField` editable
- ☐ Make `TextField` read only
- ☐ Move focus to the next component
- ☐ Repaint the `TextField`
- ☐ Request the focus
- ☐ Select all the text
- ☐ Select none of the text
- ☐ Set echo character in `TextField`
- ☐ Set editability on condition
- ☐ Set the background color
- ☐ Set the foreground color
- ☐ Set the text for `TextField`
- ☐ Set the `TextField`'s font
- ☐ Show the `TextField`
- ☐ Show the `TextField` on condition
- ☐ Toggle editability
- ☐ Toggle enabled
- ☐ Toggle show/hide

When you see how to create sample applets later today, you will learn more about using the Interaction wizard and how it allows you to "write" interactions without actually writing the code yourself. The Interaction wizard does this by adding code to your program for you. You can then maintain that code by editing it or by working with the Property List to set values that show up in the generated code.

TIP

> As you become proficient with Visual Café, you will undoubtedly want to create your own component classes. Visual Café allows you to customize the Interaction wizard so that it can create interactions for classes you add. To learn how to do this, see Day 22.

2

Do | **Don't**

DO experiment with the Interaction wizard to see what types of interactions it can simplify.

DON'T become overly reliant on the Interaction wizard to write all your interaction code for you. With experience, you will find that you can write many interactions more quickly using only the source code editing window.

A Sample Applet

One of the best ways to start learning a new tool is to see that tool in action. In this section, you will get a chance to create a couple programs with Visual Café and see how Visual Café can make your programming life easier. Ever since the Dead Sea scrolls were found to include a sample of a "Hello World" program in COBOL, it has been a programming tradition to begin using a new tool by writing a program that displays `Hello World`. With Visual Café, writing this can be accomplished without your having to write any code.

Saying "Hello World," Visual Café Style

By now you've seen enough of the Visual Café development environment that you're ready to get to it and write an actual applet. Go ahead and start Visual Café and close any projects that it opens. (You can do this by selecting the Project window and then choosing Close from the File menu.) Create a new project by selecting New Project from the File menu. You should see the New Project window, similar to what is shown in Figure 2.7.

Figure 2.7.
The New Project window.

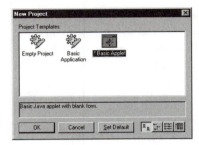

From the New Project window you can elect to create a basic applet, a basic application, or an empty project. Because our first goal is to write a Hello World applet, select Basic Applet and click the OK button. This will create a new project that will include a class that will probably be named `Applet1`. Remember, you can see the names of the classes in your project by looking at the Objects pane of the Project window. Because an applet can have a user interface, the Form Designer is also displayed and shows an empty applet window.

At this point you do have a full-fledged, runnable Java applet. Unfortunately, since neither you nor the Interaction wizard has written any code yet, the applet doesn't do much. However, you can run it to see it in action. To run the applet, select Execute from the Project menu. This will run the applet and should be similar to the less-than-exciting Figure 2.8.

Figure 2.8.
The initial applet doesn't do much, but it is easy to write.

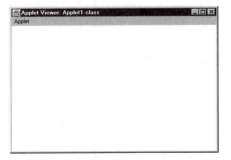

Because `Applet1` is a horrible name for an applet, go ahead and change it to `HelloWorldApplet`. To do this, select the applet by clicking on its name, either in the Objects pane of the Project window or in the Form Designer that is displaying the applet window. If the Property List is not visible, activate it by either pressing F4 or selecting Property List from the Window menu. To change the name of the applet, locate `Name` in the first column of the Property List. In the second column, next to `Name`, enter the new name of the applet: `HelloWorldApplet`.

Because the goal of this applet is to display a message to the user, the next step is to place a component on the applet to handle this task. A natural choice for doing this is the `TextField` component, located on the Standard tab of the Component palette. Select this component by clicking it. Then move the mouse cursor over the Form Designer and hold down the left mouse button while drawing a rectangle you think will be large enough to display Hello World. You don't have to worry too much about the precise size because you can change it later.

After you've dropped the TextField component onto the applet, it should remain selected. If so, at the top of the Property List you will see the name of the component: textField1. With textField1 selected in the Property List, change the value of the Text property to Hello World. After entering Hello World, move the focus off the Text property by clicking the text field in the Form Designer. When you do so, the Form Designer will automatically update with the text you entered in the Property List.

If everything has gone well up to this point, you are ready to greet the world. Run the applet by selecting Execute from the Project menu. Except for the difference in the size of the TextField you placed on your applet, our applets should look the same. Mine is shown in Figure 2.9.

Figure 2.9.
Running
HelloWorldApplet.

Examining the Source Code

It's not much; but, on the other hand, HelloWorldApplet was done without any real coding. To help understand what went on behind the scenes, take a look at Listing 2.1. The entire contents of this listing were generated by Visual Café based on what you did in the development environment.

NOTE   Because of the limited width of a printed page, the line numbers may differ between the source code generated by Visual Café on your system and the code shown here. The code itself will be the same, but due to line wrapping it might appear slightly different in the source listings in this book.

Listing 2.1. `HelloWorld.java` **as generated by Visual Café.**

```
1:   /*
2:        A basic extension of the java.applet.Applet class
3:    */
4:
5:   import java.awt.*;
6:   import java.applet.*;
7:
8:   public class HelloWorldApplet extends Applet {
9:
10:      public void init() {
11:          // Call parents init method.
12:          super.init();
13:      }
14:
15:      public void addNotify() {
16:          // Take out this line if you don't use
17:          // symantec.itools.net.RelativeURL
18:          symantec.itools.lang.Context.setDocumentBase(
19:              getDocumentBase());
20:
21:          // Call parents addNotify method.
22:          super.addNotify();
23:
24:          // This code is automatically generated by Visual Café
25:          // when you add components to the visual environment.
26:          // It instantiates and initializes the components. To
27:          // modify the code, only use code syntax that matches
28:          // what Visual Cafe can generate, or Visual Cafe may
29:          // be unable to back parse your Java file into its
30:          // visual environment.
31:          //{{INIT_CONTROLS
32:          setLayout(null);
33:          resize(426,266);
34:          textField1 = new java.awt.TextField();
35:          textField1.setText("Hello World");
36:          textField1.reshape(84,48,216,36);
37:          add(textField1);
38:          //}}
39:      }
40:
41:      //{{DECLARE_CONTROLS
42:      java.awt.TextField textField1;
43:      //}}
44:  }
```

 TIP

Because you haven't had to write any actual source code yet, I haven't shown you a Visual Café source code editing window. Because there are some unique, powerful features of this window, it isn't discussed until the section titled "Using a Source Code Window," later today.

However, in order to compare your source code to that shown in Listing 2.1, you might want to open a source code window. To do so, double-click the left mouse button over the Form Designer. This will open a source code window for the class shown in the Form Designer. Because this applet uses only one class, this will open the appropriate file. Alternatively, you can highlight the class name (HelloWorldApplet) in the Objects pane of the Project window, hold the right mouse button down to display a context menu, and then select Edit Source.

ANALYSIS Because HelloWorldApplet is an applet, lines 5 and 6 import the necessary packages. On line 8, the class HelloWorldApplet is declared. As you'll recall, this is the name you gave the applet class in the Property List. If you had not changed this property from Applet1, line 8 would have appeared as follows:

```
public class Applet1 extends Applet {
```

Inside the HelloWorldApplet class, you'll notice three main blocks of code:

- ☐ An init method (lines 10–13)
- ☐ An addNotify method (lines 15–39)
- ☐ A strange-looking section following a comment that says {{DECLARE_CONTROLS (lines 41–43)

Source Code Tags

Although lines 41 and 43 are both comments (because they begin with //), these lines are actually very important, and Visual Café generated them for a reason. Line 41 indicates the beginning of the section within this class that declares the controls that are used by the class. Line 43 indicates the end of the control declaration section. Visual Café marks these sections with tags so that it can continue to maintain these sections of code for you as you work within the development environment.

Line 42 declares a class member variable named textField1 that is of type java.awt.TextField (or, more commonly, just TextField). This is the TextField that you dragged from the Component Library onto the form. Line 42 is placed in the control declaration section (defined by the special comments on lines 41 and 43) to indicate that it is code that will be managed for you by Visual Café.

Because when you placed the text field on the applet you did not change its name in the Property List, it is declared in this section with the name textField1. To see how Visual Café manages this section of code for you, try this experiment: In the Property List, rename `textField1` to `helloMessage`. If you look at the source code, you will see that line 42 now declares a `TextField` named `helloMessage`.

Now try the opposite experiment. Open the Property List on `textField1`. Then edit the source code and change every occurrence of `textField1` to `myTextField`. In the Property List, you should see that the `Name` property is still `textField1`. Although it appears that Visual Café is a one-way tool that only recognizes changes made in the Property List, this is not the case. For a change in the source to show up in the Property List, Visual Café needs a chance to parse the source code. To give it this chance, select Parse All from the Project menu. Now you should see `myTextField` appear in the Property List.

You might have noticed that line 31 contains a comment similar to the `DECLARE_CONTROLS` tag on line 41. Line 31, however, uses the `INIT_CONTROLS` tag. This tag serves a similar purpose, but instead of declaring controls, the section that starts with the `INIT_CONTROLS` tag contains code that resizes the applet and creates the controls on the applet. The `INIT_CONTROLS` section continues through line 38 and its `//}}` comment delimiter.

In Listing 2.1, you can see that `textField1` is constructed using `new` (line 34). Next, `setText` is passed the string you entered in the Property List (line 35). The text field is then reshaped to make it the size you drew when you placed it on the applet (line 36). Finally, `textField1` is added to the applet (line 37).

Do	Don't

DO exercise caution when editing source code between tags.

DON'T hesitate to edit source code between tags, but be aware that you may need to reparse the project.

DO make sure you followed along and created `HelloWorldApplet` on your own.

Adding Interactions

The `HelloWorldApplet` is pretty boring, and one of the things that makes it so is that the user cannot interact with it. It just sits there and says hello. In this section, you will see how the Interaction wizard makes it easy to write a program that takes user input and modifies its behavior based on the user input. The `BilingualHelloApplet`, shown in Figure 2.10, knows how to say hello in English and French.

To create this applet, close any open projects and select New Project... from the File menu. As before, select Basic Applet from the New Project window. In the Property List, set the name of the applet to `BilingualHelloApplet`. Drag a `TextField` component from the

Component palette onto the Form Designer. In the Property List, set the text field's name to `helloMessage` and its text to `Hello`. Except for some name differences, these are the same steps you took to create `HelloWorldApplet`.

Figure 2.10.

Running `BilingualHello-Applet`.

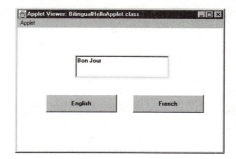

Complete the user interface for the applet by adding the buttons. First, drag a Button component from the Standard tab of the Component palette onto the Form Designer. As you place the button, make it of a size similar to the buttons shown in Figure 2.10. Name the button `englishButton` and set its label to `English`.

To create the second button, you can either repeat this process using `frenchButton` and `French` as the name and label, or you can copy the English button. To copy the button, press Ctrl+C or select Copy from the Edit menu. Paste the copied button by pressing Ctrl+V or selecting Paste from the Edit menu. The new button is added to the top left of the applet, and you can move it to the desired location. One advantage to copying the button instead of adding a second button from the Component palette is that it makes it very simple to ensure that both buttons are the same size.

Using the Interaction Wizard

With two buttons and a text field on the applet, you are now ready to add interactions between these components. When the English button is clicked, the applet needs to display `Hello` in the text field. Similarly, when the French button is clicked, the applet needs to display `Bon Jour` in the text field.

To add the interaction between the English button and the text field, select the Interaction wizard by clicking its button on the toolbar. (If you can't find it, refer to Figure 2.1.) With the Interaction wizard cursor, draw a line from the English button to the text field. This will cause the Interaction wizard to pop up, as shown in Figure 2.11.

TIP

Alternatively, you can start the Interaction wizard by selecting the component in the Form Designer, displaying its context menu by holding down the right mouse button, and selecting Add Interaction. It is frequently quicker to do this than to move the mouse to the Interaction Wizard button. However, the one disadvantage is that the destination component will not be automatically selected. You will need to choose it from a list.

Figure 2.11.

Starting to add an interaction between the English button and the text field.

In the Interaction wizard, you should confirm that `Clicked` is selected in the top list and `helloMessage` is selected in the middle list. These two selections indicate that when the English button is clicked, something is going to happen to `helloMessage`. What happens to `helloMessage` is determined by your selection in the bottom list. In that list, scroll down and select `Set the text for TextField`. Then click the Next button to move the second page of the wizard, which is shown in Figure 2.12.

Figure 2.12.

Completing the interaction between the English button and the text field.

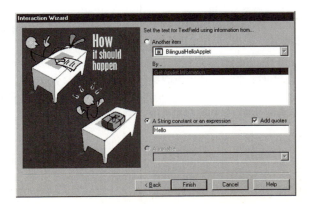

On the second page of the Interaction wizard, you can opt to set the text field based on another item, a string, or a variable. For this example, select a string constant or an expression. Then enter Hello in the field beneath that option. Make sure the Add quotes box is checked, and select the Finish button.

Using a Source Code Window

At this point, you could repeat this process and use the Interaction wizard to connect the French button to the text field and set the text to Bon Jour. However, there is another way to do this that is in some ways even easier than using the Interaction wizard. As an alternative to the Interaction wizard, open a source code window for the BilingualHelloApplet class. You can do this by selecting the class in the Project window, displaying the context menu, and then selecting Edit Source, or you can double-click the mouse on the applet in the Form Designer. Using either approach, the open source code window should appear similar to the one shown in Figure 2.13.

Figure 2.13.

Editing the source code to BilingualHello-Applet.

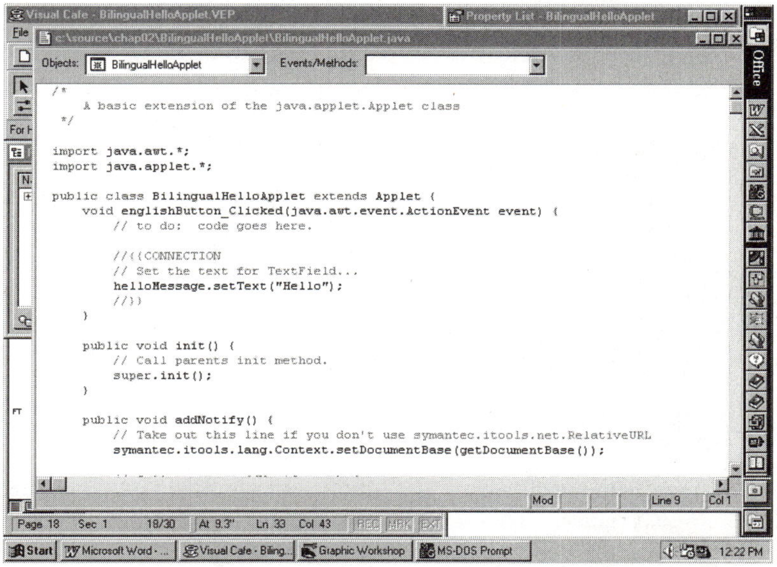

At the top of the source code window are two important drop-down lists. At the top left is the Objects list. To the right of that list is the Events/Methods list. You can use these lists to navigate to locations in the source code file or to create new event-handling methods in the class.

Because a click of the French button is still unhandled by the applet, you can use these lists to add an event handler for it. To do this, select frenchButton in the Objects list. Then select

Clicked from the Events/Methods list. Doing so will add code to the class to handle this event. First, a method named frenchButton_Clicked is added as follows:

```
void frenchButton_Clicked(java.awt.event.ActionEvent event) {
    // to do:  code goes here.
}
```

Because you didn't use the Interaction wizard, Visual Café doesn't know what you want to do in this event handler, so it just placed a "to do" comment in the method body. You can fill this in however you like. For this example, you can replace the comment with helloMessage.setText("Bon Jour"), and you are ready to run the applet.

> **NOTE**
>
> It is really a matter of personal preference whether you add event-handling methods through the Interaction wizard or by using the drop-down lists in the source code windows. I find that for simple interactions, such as setting the text of a text field, this is easier in the source window. However, more complicated or less frequently used interactions are more easily added with the Interaction wizard.

Navigating

Another way you can use the Objects and Events/Methods lists in a source code window is to navigate within that class file. If you are working with a lengthy file, it can sometimes be difficult to locate the method you are looking for. Visual Café streamlines this process significantly.

To position a source code window to a specific method, select the desired component in the Objects list and the desired event in the Events/Methods list. When you display the Events/Methods list, you will notice that some methods are listed in bold. These are methods that have been written already.

As an example of navigating a source code window, you should be able to scroll the window so that the frenchButton_Clicked method is not visible. Then select frenchButton in the Objects list and Clicked in the Events/Methods list. The window will be automatically scrolled so that frenchButton_Clicked is visible.

Examining the Source Code

The source code for BilingualHelloApplet is shown in Listing 2.2. You will probably be able to recognize sections of Listing 2.2 from the prior analysis of the HelloWorldApplet of Listing 2.1, but there are a couple new aspects to Listing 2.1.

Listing 2.2. `BilingualHelloApplet.java.`

```
1:    /*
2:         A basic extension of the java.applet.Applet class
3:    */
4:
5:    import java.awt.*;
6:    import java.applet.*;
7:
8:    public class BilingualHelloApplet extends Applet {
9:        void frenchButton_Clicked(java.awt.event.ActionEvent
10:               event) {
11:           helloMessage.setText("Bon Jour");
12:        }
13:
14:        void englishButton_Clicked(java.awt.event.ActionEvent
15:               event) {
16:           // to do:  code goes here.
17:           //{{CONNECTION
18:           // Set the text for TextField...
19:           helloMessage.setText("Hello");
20:           //}}
21:        }
22:
23:        public void init() {
24:            // Call parents init method.
25:            super.init();
26:        }
27:
28:        public void addNotify() {
29:            // Take out this line if you don't use
30:            //     symantec.itools.net.RelativeURL
31:            symantec.itools.lang.Context.setDocumentBase(
32:                getDocumentBase());
33:
34:            // Call parents addNotify method.
35:            super.addNotify();
36:
37:            // This code is automatically generated by Visual Café
38:            // when you add components to the visual environment.
39:            // It instantiates and initializes the components. To
40:            // modify the code, only use code syntax that matches
41:            // what Visual Cafe can generate, or Visual Cafe may
42:            // be unable to back parse your Java file into its
43:            // visual environment.
44:            //{{INIT_CONTROLS
45:            setLayout(null);
46:            resize(426,266);
47:            helloMessage = new java.awt.TextField();
48:            helloMessage.reshape(120,48,227,64);
49:            add(helloMessage);
50:            englishButton = new java.awt.Button("English");
51:            englishButton.reshape(60,156,120,36);
52:            add(englishButton);
```

continues

2

Listing 2.2. continued

```
53:        frenchButton = new java.awt.Button("French");
54:        frenchButton.reshape(264,156,120,36);
55:        add(frenchButton);
56:        //}}
57:
58:        //{{REGISTER_LISTENERS
59:        Action lAction = new Action();
60:        englishButton.addActionListener(lAction);
61:        frenchButton.addActionListener(lAction);
62:        //}}
63:    }
64:
65:    //{{DECLARE_CONTROLS
66:    java.awt.TextField helloMessage;
67:    java.awt.Button englishButton;
68:    java.awt.Button frenchButton;
69:    //}}
70:
71:    class Action implements java.awt.event.ActionListener {
72:        public void actionPerformed(java.awt.event.ActionEvent
73:            event) {
74:          Object object = event.getSource();
75:          if (object == englishButton)
76:            englishButton_Clicked(event);
77:          else if (object == frenchButton)
78:            frenchButton_Clicked(event);
79:        }
80:    }
81: }
```

ANALYSIS The method frenchButton_Clicked (lines 9–12) is the event-handling method that was created in the source code window. The method englishButton_Clicked (lines 14–21) was created as a result of using the Interaction wizard to tie a click of the English button to the contents of the text field. Within englishButton_Clicked, you can see that line 17 uses //{{CONNECTION to declare the start of a new section. This section ends a few lines later on line 20 with //}}. Between these symbols is the code that was generated by using the Interaction wizard. Notice that frenchButton_Clicked does not include a CONNECTION section because you wrote the code for that method yourself instead of using the Interaction wizard.

What I've neglected to mention so far is how the applet knows to invoke frenchButton_Clicked and englishButton_Clicked when these buttons are clicked. Event-handling in Java is supported through the use of *listeners*. When a class is interested in receiving event notifications, it registers listeners for those events. Event handling and listeners are discussed in detail in Day 3, "Programming Applets and Handling Events." For now, however, you should be able to see that listeners are registered between lines 58 and 62.

The addNotify method should appear very familiar except that code is now included to construct, size, and add the English button (lines 50–52) and the French button (53–55). Similarly, the DECLARE_CONTROLS section (lines 65–69) appears as it did in Listing 2.1, with the addition of the two buttons.

Do	Don't

DO experiment with the many selections available to you within the Interaction wizard.

DO get comfortable with using the Objects list and the Events/Methods list to navigate your source code. This can be a great time saver.

DON'T use the Interaction wizard to make random interactions and then delete the method bodies. It is far simpler to create an empty event handler with the lists in the source code window.

A Sample Application

So far, you've seen two sample applets that can be easily created with Visual Café. Fortunately, Visual Café can also be used to create applications. In the same way that you created an initial applet, you can create an initial application by selecting New Project... from the file menu. Then select Basic Application from the New Project dialog box.

TIP

Whenever it is displayed, the New Project dialog box will, by default, assume you want to create a basic applet. If you find yourself preferring to create empty projects or applications, you can establish one of these choices as the default new project. To do so, highlight the desired item and click the Set Default button in the New Project dialog box.

It is also possible to create your own project templates and add them to the New Project dialog. Doing so is described on Day 22.

Like the basic applet, the basic application can be compiled and run without modification. Doing so should look like the screen shown in Figure 2.14. Additionally, the basic application includes an About screen (shown in Figure 2.15), and it prompts for confirmation when the user attempts to close the program (see Figure 2.16).

Figure 2.14.

The main screen of the basic application includes a menu system.

Figure 2.15.

The basic application includes an about screen.

Figure 2.16.

When closing the basic application, the user is asked to confirm.

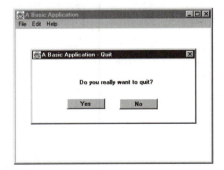

As you can see in Figure 2.14, the basic application includes a menu system. Just as Visual Café provides a Form Designer for visually creating forms, it also includes a Menu editor for visually designing menus. The Menu editor is described on Day 11, "Menus and Toolbars."

Because there are three forms in a basic application, there are three source files. You can confirm this by looking at the Objects pane of the Project window. Although it is not necessary to examine each of these source files, it is worth examining the source for the frame class that constitutes the main part of the application's user interface. This file, Frame1.java, is shown in Listing 2.3.

2

Listing 2.3. `Frame1.java` **from a basic application, as generated by Visual Café.**

```
1:   /*
2:        This simple extension of the java.awt.Frame class
3:        contains all the elements necessary to act as the
4:        main window of an application.
5:   */
6:
7:   import java.awt.*;
8:
9:   public class Frame1 extends Frame {
10:      void About_Action(java.awt.event.ActionEvent event) {
11:         //{{CONNECTION
12:         // Action from About Create and show as modal
13:         (new AboutDialog(this, true)).show();
14:         //}}
15:      }
16:
17:      void Exit_Action(java.awt.event.ActionEvent event) {
18:         //{{CONNECTION
19:         // Action from Exit Create and show as modal
20:         (new QuitDialog(this, true)).show();
21:         //}}
22:      }
23:
24:      void Open_Action(java.awt.event.ActionEvent event) {
25:         //{{CONNECTION
26:         // Action from Open... Show the OpenFileDialog
27:         openFileDialog1.show();
28:         //}}
29:      }
30:
31:      void Frame1_WindowClosing(java.awt.event.WindowEvent
32:         event) {
33:         hide();          // hide the Frame
34:         dispose();       // free the system resources
35:         System.exit(0); // close the application
36:      }
37:
38:      public Frame1() {
39:
40:      }
41:
42:      public Frame1(String title) {
43:         this();
44:         setTitle(title);
45:      }
46:
47:      public synchronized void show() {
```

continues

Listing 2.3. continued

```
48:         move(50, 50);
49:         super.show();
50:     }
51:
52:     static public void main(String args[]) {
53:         (new Frame1()).show();
54:     }
55:
56:   public void addNotify() {
57:         // Call parents addNotify method.
58:         super.addNotify();
59:
60:         // This code is automatically generated by Visual Café
61:         // when you add components to the visual environment.
62:         // It instantiates and initializes the components. To
63:         // modify the code, only use code syntax that matches
64:         // what Visual Cafe can generate, or Visual Cafe may
65:         // be unable to back parse your Java file into its
66:         // visual environment.
67:         //{{INIT_CONTROLS
68:         setLayout(null);
69:         resize(insets().left + insets().right + 405,
70:                 insets().top + insets().bottom + 305);
71:         openFileDialog1 = new java.awt.FileDialog(this, "Open",
72:                 FileDialog.LOAD);
73:         //$$ openFileDialog1.move(36,276);
74:         setTitle("A Basic Application");
75:         //}}
76:
77:         //{{INIT_MENUS
78:         mainMenuBar = new java.awt.MenuBar();
79:
80:         menu1 = new java.awt.Menu("File");
81:         menu1.add("New");
82:         Open = new java.awt.MenuItem("Open...");
83:         menu1.add(Open);
84:         menu1.add("Save");
85:         menu1.add("Save As...");
86:         menu1.addSeparator();
87:         Exit = new java.awt.MenuItem("Exit");
88:         menu1.add(Exit);
89:         mainMenuBar.add(menu1);
90:
91:         menu2 = new java.awt.Menu("Edit");
92:         menu2.add("Cut");
93:         menu2.add("Copy");
94:         menu2.add("Paste");
95:         mainMenuBar.add(menu2);
96:
97:         menu3 = new java.awt.Menu("Help");
98:         mainMenuBar.setHelpMenu(menu3);
99:         About = new java.awt.MenuItem("About");
```

```
100:        menu3.add(About);
101:        mainMenuBar.add(menu3);
102:        setMenuBar(mainMenuBar);
103:        //$$ mainMenuBar.move(4,277);
104:        //}}
105:
106:        //{{REGISTER_LISTENERS
107:        Window lWindow = new Window();
108:        addWindowListener(lWindow);
109:        Action lAction = new Action();
110:        Open.addActionListener(lAction);
111:        About.addActionListener(lAction);
112:        Exit.addActionListener(lAction);
113:        //}}
114:    }
115:
116:    //{{DECLARE_CONTROLS
117:    java.awt.FileDialog openFileDialog1;
118:    //}}
119:
120:    //{{DECLARE_MENUS
121:    java.awt.MenuBar mainMenuBar;
122:    java.awt.Menu menu1;
123:    java.awt.MenuItem Open;
124:    java.awt.MenuItem Exit;
125:    java.awt.Menu menu2;
126:    java.awt.Menu menu3;
127:    java.awt.MenuItem About;
128:    //}}
129:
130:    class Window extends java.awt.event.WindowAdapter {
131:        public void windowClosing(java.awt.event.WindowEvent
132:            event) {
133:          Object object = event.getSource();
134:          if (object == Frame1.this)
135:             Frame1_WindowClosing(event);
136:        }
137:    }
138:
139:    class Action implements java.awt.event.ActionListener {
140:        public void actionPerformed(java.awt.event.ActionEvent
141:            event) {
142:          Object object = event.getSource();
143:          if (object == Open)
144:             Open_Action(event);
145:          else if (object == About)
146:             About_Action(event);
147:          else if (object == Exit)
148:             Exit_Action(event);
149:        }
150:    }
151: }
```

ANALYSIS   What is important to notice in Listing 2.3 is that this file includes new section tags, similar to the DECLARE_CONTROLS, INIT_CONTROLS, and CONNECTION sections described earlier. The Frame1 class uses the DECLARE_MENUS tag to identify a menu declaration section (lines 120–128). These same menus are then created and menu items are added in the INIT_MENUS section between lines 77 and 104.

Do	Don't

DON'T worry if you don't understand all the code related to menus in Listing 2.3. Menus are the subject of Day 11.

DO read through Listing 2.3 to make sure you understand the code that Visual Café generated and why that code was generated.

Summary

Having completed this lesson, you now have a basic level of familiarity with the Visual Café desktop and many of the tools and windows you will use most frequently. You learned about and used the Form Designer, the Component palette, the Project window, the Property List, and the Interaction wizard. You also learned how to easily create event-handling methods in Visual Café's source code editing windows. To put this knowledge into practice, you wrote two simple applets and generated a basic application. Tomorrow you will learn about the Applet class and how it simplifies development of Java programs for use in Web pages.

Q&A

Q **How accurately does the Form Designer reflect what a form will actually look like when an applet is run?**

A Visual Café includes a built-in Java Virtual Machine that allows it to accurately execute Java code while you work in the development environment. Because of this, the Form Designer will display forms exactly as they will appear in the applet at runtime.

Q **I thought Visual Café came with many more components than are shown on the Component palette. Are some of my components missing?**

A No, they aren't missing. The Component palette displays what are expected to be the most frequently used components. You can see the entire collection of available components by selecting Component from the Insert menu. This will display a list of components, including those shown on the Component palette.

Q **If I can edit the generated code between tags such as INIT_CONTROLS, what is the purpose of these tags?**

A The tags tell the Visual Café parser where different sections begin and end. For example, if you add a new component to the Form Designer, Visual Café locates the DECLARE_CONTROLS section of the class and adds a declaration for the new component. If you've edited this section, Visual Café will still be able to find it, as long as you were careful and didn't edit the tags that delimit the section.

Workshop

The workshop includes quiz questions to help you gauge your understanding of the material in this chapter. The workshop also includes exercises to provide hands-on experience with what you've learned in this chapter. For the answers to the quiz questions, see Appendix D, "Answers."

Quiz

1. What are the two ways of invoking the Interaction wizard?
2. What are the advantages of each way of invoking the Interaction wizard?
3. Besides the Interaction wizard, how can Visual Café help you write an event-handling method?
4. What is the purpose of the Component palette?
5. What is the relationship between the Property List and the source code in a Visual Café project?
6. Summarize the steps you took to create HelloWorldApplet.
7. Name three of the source code tags added by Visual Café to indicate special sections of code.
8. Why should you never edit the source code placed between source code tags?

Exercises

1. Use the NervousText component (on the Multimedia tab of the Component palette) to write an applet called HelloNervousWorld. Have the applet say Hello World. Observe the behavior of the applet in the Form Designer and convince yourself that Visual Café does include a Java Virtual Machine in its development environment.

2. Write an applet with two buttons and a text field. Use the Interaction wizard to create the following interactions:

   ☐ When the first button is clicked, set the text field to Button 1 Was Pressed. Also have it toggle the second button between enabled and disabled.

   ☐ When the second button is clicked, set the text field to the label of the second button.

Day 3

Programming Applets and Handling Events

Today you will learn the fundamentals of Java applet programming. You will learn about the four methods that control the life span of an applet, as well as how to write code to respond to events generated by an applet's graphical user interface. You will also see how to embed an applet into a Web page and how to use applet parameters to control the behavior of a program.

The Applet Class

To create your own applets, you derive a class from Java's Applet class and then add the desired functionality. The Applet class contains methods for actions such as interacting with the browser environment, for retrieving images, for playing sound files, and for resizing the applet's host window. In this section you will learn about the most frequently used methods in this important class.

The Life and Death of an Applet

On a typical Java-enhanced Web page, Java applets start and stop frequently as the user switches among pages. As pages are loaded into the browser, viewed, and then left, applets are started and terminated in response to messages passed to the Applet class. The four most important methods in the life of an applet are init, start, stop, and destroy. They are described in Table 3.1.

Table 3.1. Important methods over the life of an applet.

Method	Purpose
init	Called when the applet is initially loaded
start	Called each time the user loads the host Web page
stop	Called each time the user leaves the host Web page
destroy	Called to release resources allocated by the applet

The init Method

When an applet is loaded by either a browser or a standalone interpreter such as the one provided with Visual Café, the init method is called. This allows the applet to execute any necessary startup code. Usually, an applet resizes itself and may also acquire and load resources such as images or sound at this point. The init method is called once each time the applet is loaded.

The destroy Method

The destroy method is called when the browser is closing an applet. Ideally, this method should be used to release any resources that have been allocated during the life of the applet; however, because Java performs garbage collection, it is not necessary to release resources.

TIP

Although you do not need to explicitly release resources, it is generally a good practice to do so. If you explicitly release a resource rather than waiting for Java's garbage detection to notice a resource has been released, your program will be able to reuse the resource sooner.

The start and stop Methods

The start method is similar to init except that start is called each time the Web page in which the applet is embedded is loaded. The most frequent use of the start method is to create a new thread. Similarly, the stop method is called whenever the browser moves off the Web page that hosts the applet.

The distinction between a method that gets called when an applet is loaded versus when its host page is loaded may seem minor, but understanding this distinction enables you to write more efficient applets. In Netscape Navigator 3 and Microsoft Internet Explorer 3, the init and start methods are called when a page containing a Java applet is loaded. If the user follows a link from the page, the applet's stop method is called. If the user backs up to the page, the applet's start method is called, but not its init method.

In Netscape Navigator, reloading a page that contains an applet will stop and then start the applet. Performing the equivalent function in Microsoft Internet Explorer, however, causes the stop, destroy, init, and start methods all to be invoked, in that order. This information is summarized in Table 3.2.

Table 3.2. Applet method calls under Navigator and Internet Explorer.

Action	Navigator	Internet Explorer
Page first loaded	init + start	init + start
Forward then backward	stop + start	stop + start
Reload/Refresh	stop + start	stop + destroy + init + start

An Example

The best way to understand how the init, start, stop, and destroy methods interact is to build an applet that demonstrates their use. Listing 3.1 shows a class that does exactly this. The LifeApplet class includes a private String member named history that is initially empty. As the various methods are called, text is added to this string to indicate the sequence in which the methods were called. Parentheses are placed around the start and stop messages to improve readability.

Listing 3.1. LifeApplet.java.

```
1:  import java.awt.*;
2:  import java.applet.*;
3:
4:  public class LifeApplet extends Applet {
5:
6:      public void init() {
7:          // Call parents init method.
8:          super.init();
9:
10:         history = history + "init ";
11:         resize(320, 240);
12:     }
13:
14:     public void addNotify() {
15:         // Call parents addNotify method.
```

continues

Listing 3.1. continued

```
16:          super.addNotify();
17:
18:          // This code is automatically generated by Visual Café
19:          // when you add components to the visual environment.
20:          // It instantiates and initializes the components. To
21:          // modify the code, only use code syntax that matches
22:          // what Visual Café can generate, or Visual Café may
23:          // be unable to back parse your Java file into its
24:          // visual environment.
25:          //{{INIT_CONTROLS
26:          setLayout(null);
27:          resize(426,266);
28:          //}}
29:      }
30:
31:    public void start() {
32:          history = history + "(start ";
33:    }
34:
35:    public void stop() {
36:          history = history + "stop) ";
37:    }
38:
39:    public void destroy() {
40:          history = history + "destroy ";
41:    }
42:
43:    public void paint(Graphics g) {
44:          g.drawString(history, 10, 10);
45:    }
46:
47:    private String history = "";
48:
49:    //{{DECLARE_CONTROLS
50:    //}}
51: }
```

NOTE

Even though the code in the destroy method of Listing 3.1 will execute, the results of adding this text will not be apparent. Because the history string is only displayed by the paint method and paint is not called after destroy, you will not be able to see the destroy message. You've got two options: either trust me or run LifeApplet in the debugger after setting a breakpoint in destroy. The Visual Café debugger is covered on Day 6, "Debugging, Customizing, and Managing Projects."

3

ANALYSIS   The result of a sample run of `LifeApplet` is shown in Figure 3.1. In this case, Netscape Navigator was used to run the applet. After the applet was loaded, the Reload button was clicked repeatedly. This had the effect of stopping and starting the applet each time, as you can see in Figure 3.1. Closing Navigator will stop the applet and then destroy it.

Figure 3.1.

Reloading an applet in Netscape Navigator.

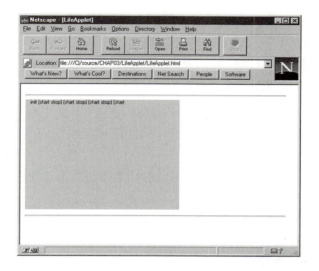

NOTE   To load a local applet from a file using Netscape Navigator, select Open File from the File menu. You can then navigate to the desired directory and file. Similarly, with Internet Explorer, select File | Open and then the Browse button.

Unlike Navigator, Microsoft Internet Explorer does not simply stop and start an applet when refreshing a page. Figure 3.2 shows Internet Explorer while running `LifeApplet` after the Refresh button was clicked repeatedly. As you can see, only `init` and `start` have been called. This is because Internet Explorer completely reloads an applet when refreshing it. This causes the `history` string to be reset each time the applet is reloaded.

Figure 3.2.

Reloading an applet in Internet Explorer.

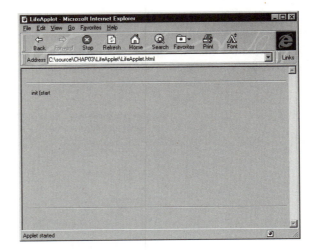

Adding an Applet to a Web Page

An applet is included in a Web page through the use of the `<applet>` HTML tag. This tag is embedded into an HTML form in the same manner as any other tag and is used to specify the name of the Java class to execute, the width and height to use for the applet, and other optional parameters. A simple example of adding an applet to a Web page is shown in Listing 3.2.

Listing 3.2. Applets are included on Web pages via the `<applet>` tag.

```
 1:     <html>
 2:     <head>
 3:     <title>A Java Applet</title>
 4:     </head>
 5:     <body>
 6:     <hr>
 7:     <applet
 8:         code="YourClassName.class"
 9:         width=320
10:         height=240>
11:     </applet>
12:     <hr>
13:     </body>
14:     </html>
```

ANALYSIS　In this case, the applet `YourClassName` is added to the page. The `<applet>` tag begins on line 7 and ends with the use of the `</applet>` tag on line 11. On line 8, the `code` attribute identifies the name of the applet to run. Lines 9 and 10 use the `width` and `height` attributes to set the dimensions of the applet.

There is no magic to HTML files. HTML stands for Hypertext Markup Language and is the language that is used to design Web pages. As shown in Listing 3.2, an HTML file is a plain-text file that can be created in any editor that can output text files. HTML tags are enclosed with angle brackets, and each tag may include one or more parameters. In Listing 3.2, `<applet>` is a tag, and `code`, `width`, and `height` are parameters of that tag. Many tags remain in effect until they are terminated with a similar tag that begins with a forward slash. For example, in Listing 3.2, the `<body>` tag on line 5 begins the body of the HTML document. The body continues until `</body>` is used on line 13.

In Listing 3.2, you saw how the `code`, `width`, and `height` attributes of the `<applet>` tag are used. In addition to these, the `<applet>` tag has other attributes that are sometimes useful:

- ☐ `codebase`
- ☐ `param`
- ☐ `hspace`
- ☐ `vspace`
- ☐ `align`

codebase **and** code

As you've seen, the `code` attribute indicates the location of the class file to run. This class file is assumed to be located in the same directory as the HTML file that includes it. If the class file is located in a different directory, you must use the `codebase` attribute to indicate the proper directory. For example, if you keep all your Java applets in a subdirectory beneath the directory with your HTML files, you could use the following:

```
<applet
    code="YourClassName.class"
    codebase="applets"
    width=320
    height=240>
</applet>
```

This locates the file `YourClassName.class` in the applet's subdirectory of the directory containing this HTML file. You can also specify a fully qualified path name, as follows:

```
<applet
    code="YourClassName.class"
    codebase="C:\java\classes"
    width=320
    height=240>
</applet>
```

This loads the class file `C:\java\classes\YourClassName.java`. An applet can determine the `codebase` from which it was loaded by calling the `getCodeBase` method in the `Applet` class.

hspace **and** vspace

The `hspace` and `vspace` attributes can be used to specify the amount of vertical and horizontal space that will surround the applet. For example, the following code places 50 pixels of space around the applet vertically and 150 horizontally:

```
<applet
    code="MyClass.class"
    vspace=50
    hspace=150
    width=222
    height=40>
</applet>
```

align

The `align` attribute can be used to control how the applet will be placed on the page. The valid values and their meanings are shown in Table 3.3. It can be used as follows:

```
<applet
    code=" MyClass.class"
    align=left
    width=222
    height=40>
</applet>
```

Table 3.3. Valid values for the `align` attribute.

Value	Meaning
absbottom	Align the bottom of the applet with the bottom of the lowest item in the current line
absmiddle	Align the vertical center of the applet with the center of the tallest item on the current line
baseline	Align the bottom of the applet with the baseline of the text
bottom	The same as `baseline`
left	Align the left of the applet with the left margin
middle	Align the vertical center of the applet with the baseline of the text
right	Align the right of the applet with the right margin
texttop	Align the top of the applet with the top of the text
top	Align the top of the applet with the top of the tallest item in the current line

param

In the traditional, non-Java programming world, it is common to write a program that uses command-line parameters to modify its behavior. For example, the grep program searches for string patterns in files. To search for java.awt in all files with a java extension, you would use the following command line:

```
grep java.awt *.java
```

Without command-line parameters, the grep program would be useless because it wouldn't know the pattern to look for or the files to search. Because Java applets are *not* run from a command line, an applet cannot be passed a parameter in this fashion. However, a Java applet is embedded in a host HTML file, and parameters to the applet can be embedded in the HTML file.

To embed a parameter in a host HTML document, use the <param name> tag with the <applet> tag. For each parameter you create with this tag, specify a name and a value. For example, Listing 3.3 is the host HTML file for the ParameterDemo applet. It describes three parameters: message, xPos, and yPos. The message parameter is displayed in the browser window by the applet and is set to Hello World. The xPos and yPos parameters indicate the coordinates at which the message will be displayed.

Listing 3.3. ParameterDemo.html.

```
1:    <html>
2:    <head>
3:    <title>ParameterDemo</title>
4:    </head>
5:    <body>
6:    <hr>
7:    <applet
8:        code=ParameterDemo.class
9:        width=320
10:       height=240 >
11:       <param name=message value="Hello World">
12:       <param name=xPos value=30>
13:       <param name=yPos value=40>
14:   </applet>
15:   <hr>
16:   </body>
17:   </html>
```

NOTE   To add an HTML file to a Visual Café project, select Files into Project from the Insert menu, navigate to the desired file, and click the Add button.

Reading Applet Parameters

An applet can read parameters from its host HTML file by using the getParameter method of the Applet class. The signature of getParameter is as follows:

```
public String getParameter(String name)
```

The getParameter method is passed the name of the parameter to read and returns the value of that parameter as a string. Although all parameters are read as string values, they can easily be converted to integers or any other more appropriate data type. This is illustrated in Listing 3.4, which shows the ParameterDemo applet. This applet reads the message, xPos, and yPos parameters that were embedded in the HTML file of Listing 3.3. An illustration of this applet being run is shown in Figure 3.3.

Listing 3.4. ParameterDemo.java.

```
1:    import java.awt.*;
2:    import java.applet.*;
3:
4:    public class ParameterDemo extends Applet {
5:
6:        public void init() {
7:            // Call parents init method.
8:            super.init();
9:
10:           String param;
11:
12:           param = getParameter("message");
13:           if (param != null)
14:               message = param;
15:
16:           param = getParameter("xPos");
17:           if (param != null)
18:               xPos = Integer.parseInt(param);
19:
20:           param = getParameter("yPos");
21:           if (param != null)
22:               yPos = Integer.parseInt(param);
23:       }
24:
25:       public void addNotify() {
26:           // Call parents addNotify method.
27:           super.addNotify();
28:
29:           // This code is automatically generated by Visual Café
30:           // when you add components to the visual environment.
31:           // It instantiates and initializes the components. To
32:           // modify the code, only use code syntax that matches
33:           // what Visual Café can generate, or Visual Café may
34:           // be unable to back parse your Java file into its
35:           // visual environment.
36:           //{{INIT_CONTROLS
```

3

```
37:        setLayout(null);
38:        resize(320,240);
39:        //}}
40:    }
41:
42:    public void paint(Graphics g) {
43:        g.drawString(message, xPos, yPos);
44:    }
45:
46:    private String message = "";
47:    private int xPos = 10;
48:    private int yPos = 10;
49:
50:    //{{DECLARE_CONTROLS
51:    //}}
52: }
```

Figure 3.3.

The ParameterDemo *applet displays a parameter from its host HTML file.*

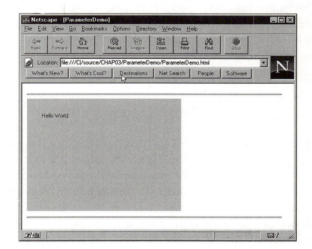

Using applet parameters is a very effective way to avoid hard-coding values into an applet. For example, if you want to write an applet that displays a customizable message, the text of the message can be passed to the applet as a parameter.

TIP

Not all browsers support Java. This is especially true for the millions of users who use browsers that were released before the Java revolution. You can help these poor souls by including text between the `<applet>` and `</applet>` tags. This text is displayed instead of the applet in browsers that do not support Java. For example, the following code will display `Buy a real browser, buddy!` to users without Java support.

```
<applet
    code=" MyClass.class"
    width=222
    height=40 >
Buy a real browser, buddy!
</applet>
```

Event Handling

One of the most frequently heard criticisms of the initial release of Java was of its approach to event handling. The 1.1 release of the Java Development Kit (JDK) addressed the criticism by introducing a new delegation model of event handling. The new event-handling approach is supported by the following three types of objects:

- ☐ Events
- ☐ Event sources
- ☐ Event listeners

An event source is an object such as a dialog, frame, button, or menu item. When something happens to an event source, it generates an event that is then sent to any event listeners who have requested to know about events for that object. I consider this to be similar to how I have told my personal information management software to remind me seven days before Valentine's Day, my wife's birthday, and our anniversary. I have *registered* with the program for those dates. It *listens* for those dates to occur and then sends me a message. By contrast, and as a way to understand the flaw with the older Java 1.0 event-handling mechanism, consider the usefulness of a personal information manager that automatically notifies you of every person in the world's birthday or anniversary.

Events

Events in Java are represented by instances of a descendant of the `EventObject` class. Whenever an event source needs to announce the occurrence of an event, it does so by creating an object and then sending that object to the registered listeners. Figure 3.4 shows the inheritance hierarchy that begins with `EventObject`.

The Java event classes can be split into two general classifications: low-level events and semantic events.

NEW TERM   A *low-level event* corresponds to low-level user interface or system events such as a mouse move, mouse click, or key press.

Figure 3.4.

The EventObject *inheritance hierarchy.*

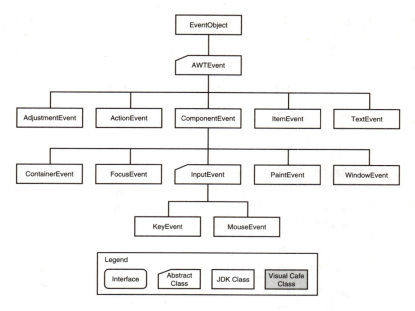

NEW TERM A *semantic event* is generated as a result of a higher level event such as a mouse click over a specific button or moving a scrollbar.

Table 3.4 shows the low-level events and the conditions that generate them. Table 3.5 shows the same information for the semantic events.

Table 3.4. Low-level events and the conditions that generate them.

Event	Generated
ComponentEvent	Generated when a component is hidden, moved, resized, or shown.
ContainerEvent	Generated when a component is added to or removed from a container.
FocusEvent	Generated when a component gains or loses focus.
InputEvent	This is an abstract class that is never directly generated.
KeyEvent	Generated whenever a key is pressed, released, or typed.
MouseEvent	Generated whenever the mouse button is pressed, released, or clicked, or when the mouse enters or exits the space occupied by a component.
PaintEvent	Generated when a component is painted or updated.
WindowEvent	Generated when a window is activated, closed, deactivated, deiconified, iconified, or opened.

Table 3.5. Semantic events and the conditions that generate them.

Event	Generated
ActionEvent	Generated whenever an action occurs.
AdjustmentEvent	Generated whenever a value is adjusted.
ItemEvent	Generated whenever the state of an item changes.
TextEvent	Generated whenever the text of an object changes.

Listening for Events

Now that you know what events are available, you need to know how to listen for them. This is done by writing a class that implements one of the listener interfaces that are included with Java. The following is a list of the available low-level listener interfaces:

- ComponentListener
- ContainerListener
- FocusListener
- KeyListener
- MouseListener
- MouseMotionListener
- WindowListener

In addition, the following semantic listeners are available:

- ActionListener
- AdjustmentListener
- ItemListener
- TextListener

You create a listener class in the same way you would implement any other Java interface. For example, Listing 3.5 declares a class named Action that implements the ActionListener interface.

Listing 3.5. The Action class implements the ActionListener interface.

```
1:    class Action implements ActionListener {
2:        public void actionPerformed(ActionEvent event) {
3:            Object object = event.getSource();
4:                if (object == myButton)
5:                    myButton_Clicked(event);
6:        }
7:    }
```

In this case, the getSource method is used to compare the object that generated the event to a button object. If the two are equal, the method myButton_Clicked is called.

NOTE

> Do not try to compile the class shown in Listing 3.5. Although this class uses the variable myButton, that variable is not declared within the scope of the class. This will prevent the class from compiling unless it is an inner class of a class that declares this variable. You will learn about inner classes later in this lesson in the section titled "Improving Things with Inner Classes."

When you implement an interface to create a listener class, you must be sure to provide a body for each method in the interface. Although the Action class of Listing 3.5 includes only one method, it is a complete implementation of the ActionListener interface because that interface includes only one method. Table 3.6 shows the methods that are required for each of the low-level listener interfaces. Table 3.7 does the same for the semantic listener interfaces.

Table 3.6. The methods provided by each low-level listener interface.

Interface	Methods
ComponentListener	void componentHidden(ComponentEvent)
	void componentMoved(ComponentEvent)
	void componentResized(ComponentEvent)
	void componentShown(ComponentEvent)
ContainerListener	void componentAdded(ContainerEvent)
	void componentRemoved(ContainerEvent)
FocusListener	void focusGained(FocusEvent)
	void focusLost(FocusEvent)
KeyListener	void keyPressed(KeyEvent)
	void keyReleased(KeyEvent)
	void keyTyped(KeyEvent)
MouseListener	void mouseClicked(MouseEvent)
	void mouseEntered(MouseEvent)
	void mouseExit(MouseEvent)
	void mousePressed(MouseEvent)
	void mouseReleased(MouseEvent)
MouseMotionListener	void mouseDragged(MouseEvent)
	void mouseMoved(MouseEvent)

continues

Table 3.6. continued

Interface	Methods
WindowListener	void windowActivated(WindowEvent)
	void windowClosed(WindowEvent)
	void windowClosing(WindowEvent)
	void windowDeactivated(WindowEvent)
	void windowDeiconified(WindowEvent)
	void windowIconified(WindowEvent)
	void windowOpened(WindowEvent)

Table 3.7. The methods provided by each semantic listener interface.

Interface	Methods
ActionListener	void ActionPerformed(ActionEvent)
AdjustmentListener	void adjustmentValueChanged(AdjustmentEvent)
ItemListener	void itemStateChanged(ItemEvent)
TextListener	void textValueChanged(TextEvent)

TIP

Do not be concerned that you need to provide method bodies for all methods in a listener interface. The section "Using Adapters" (later in this lesson) shows how you can get around this extra work by using adapter classes.

Registering a Listener

After you create a listener class, you must register it with the objects to which it will listen. This is done by calling one of the methods shown in Table 3.8. Each of these methods is passed an instance of the listener class. For example, to register the listener of Listing 3.5 to a button, the following code could be used:

```
Action lAction = new Action();
myButton.addActionListener(lAction);
```

The first line of this example simply creates an instance of the Action listener class. The next line uses addActionListener to assign the listener, lAction, to the button myButton.

3

Table 3.8. Methods that register a listener class.

Method	Provided in
addActionListener	Button, List, MenuItem, TextField
addAdjustmentListener	Adjustable, Scrollbar
addComponentListener	Component
addContainerListener	Container
addFocusListener	Component
addItemListener	Checkbox, CheckboxMenuItem, Choice, ItemSelectable, List
addKeyListener	Component
addMouseListener	Component
addMouseMotionListener	Component
addTextListener	TextComponent
addWindowListener	Window

Using Adapters

One problem with creating a listener class by implementing an interface, especially a low-level listener interface, is that you must provide a body for each method in the interface. This means that if you are implementing the MouseListener interface because you want to write a mouseEntered method, you must also provide bodies for four other methods. Even though the method bodies can be empty, you get the feeling that there must be a better way. Fortunately there is.

Instead of having a listener class implement a listener interface, you can base the listener class on one of Java's adapter classes. Each adapter class implements one of the listener interfaces and simply saves you the work of providing empty bodies for methods you are not interested in. The following adapter classes are available:

- ☐ ComponentAdapter
- ☐ ContainerAdapter
- ☐ FocusAdapter
- ☐ KeyAdapter
- ☐ MouseAdapter
- ☐ MouseMotionAdapter
- ☐ WindowAdapter

No adapter classes are provided for the semantic listener interfaces because those interfaces each only include one method. As an example of how an adapter class can simplify things, consider the code shown in Listing 3.6. This example declares two listener classes. Even though one extends MouseMotionAdapter and the other implements MouseMotionListener, they are equivalent.

Listing 3.6. Two equivalent listener classes: One implements an interface, the other extends a class.

```
1:    class MouseMotionListener extends MouseMotionAdapter {
2:        public void mouseDragged(MouseEvent e) {
3:            // do something here
4:        }
5:    }
6:
7:    class MouseMotionListener2 implements MouseMotionListener {
8:        public void mouseDragged(MouseEvent e) {
9:            // do something here
10:       }
11:       public void mouseMoved(java.awt.event.MouseEvent e) {
12:           // do something here
13:       }
14:   }
```

Event Sources

Just as certain classes can listen for events, other classes can generate events. Low-level events can be generated by the following components:

- [ ] Component
- [ ] Dialog
- [ ] Frame

Semantic events can be generated by the following components:

- [ ] Button
- [ ] Choice
- [ ] Checkbox
- [ ] CheckboxMenuItem
- [ ] List
- [ ] MenuItem
- [ ] Scrollbar
- [ ] TextField

3

An Example

As an example of how to write your own event-handling code, the ListenerDemo applet is included on the MCP Web site (www.mcp.com/info/1-57521/1-57521-303-6) and is shown in Listing 3.7. Running this applet will display the screen shown in Figure 3.5. When the button is clicked, it displays the message Hi Mom in the text field.

Listing 3.7. ListenerDemo.java.

```
1:    import java.awt.*;
2:    import java.applet.*;
3:    import java.awt.event.*;
4:
5:    public class ListenerDemo extends Applet
6:            implements ActionListener {
7:
8:        public void init() {
9:            // Call parents init method.
10:           super.init();
11:
12:           button.addActionListener(this);
13:       }
14:
15:       public void addNotify() {
16:           // Call parents addNotify method.
17:           super.addNotify();
18:
19:           // This code is automatically generated by Visual Café
20:           // when you add components to the visual environment.
21:           // It instantiates and initializes the components. To
22:           // modify the code, only use code syntax that matches
23:           // what Visual Café can generate, or Visual Café may
24:           // be unable to back parse your Java file into its
25:           // visual environment.
26:           //{{INIT_CONTROLS
27:           setLayout(null);
28:           resize(426,266);
29:           button = new java.awt.Button("button");
30:           button.reshape(36,12,108,43);
31:           add(button);
32:           textField = new java.awt.TextField();
33:           textField.reshape(36,96,144,31);
34:           add(textField);
35:           //}}
36:
37:           //{{REGISTER_LISTENERS
38:           //}}
39:       }
40:
41:       public void actionPerformed(ActionEvent event) {
42:           Object object = event.getSource();
43:           if (object == button)
44:               textField.setText("Hi Mom");
```

continues

Listing 3.7. continued

```
45:        }
46:
47:        //{{DECLARE_CONTROLS
48:        java.awt.Button button;
49:        java.awt.TextField textField;
50:        //}}
51:    }
```

Figure 3.5.

The ListenerDemo
sample applet after the
button has been
clicked.

ANALYSIS   Because ListenerDemo will be handling events, it includes the package java.awt.event (line 3). Although you must provide a listener class, there is nothing that prevents a listener class from doing double duty. In this case, ListenerDemo is declared as extending Applet (line 5) and implementing ActionListener (line 6). To implement this interface, it is necessary to include the actionPerformed method (lines 41–45). This method checks to see what object generated the event (line 42), and, if it was the button, it sets the text of the text field (line 44).

Because you want to listen for messages generated by the button, you must register the listener class that will listen for button events. This is done on line 12 by a call to addActionListener. Because the class containing this code is itself the listener, this is passed to addActionListener.

Improving Things with Inner Classes

One problem with the approach to event handling shown in Listing 3.7 is that the application logic and the event-handling logic become completely entangled. There is no separation between code that handles events and code that acts on those events. This was one of the criticisms of the Java 1.0 event-handling model. Fortunately, the 1.1 release of the Java Development Kit introduced another innovation that, when combined with the new delegation model of event handling, allows you to more appropriately separate application logic and user interface code. Java 1.1 accomplishes this through the addition of *inner classes*.

NEW TERM An *inner class* is a class that is defined within the scope of another class.

As an example of how to use an inner class to separate event-handling code from application logic, consider Listing 3.8. This listing shows the code to the InnerClassListenerDemo sample applet that is included on the MCP Web site. This applet is equivalent to the ListenerDemo applet of Listing 3.7 except that the new version uses an inner class.

Listing 3.8. InnerClassListenerDemo.java.

```
1:      import java.awt.*;
2:      import java.applet.*;
3:      import java.awt.event.*;
4:
5:      public class InnerClassListenerDemo extends Applet {
6:          public void init() {
7:              // Call parents init method.
8:              super.init();
9:
10:             Action lAction = new Action();
11:             button.addActionListener(lAction);
12:         }
13:
14:         public void addNotify() {
15:             // Call parents addNotify method.
16:             super.addNotify();
17:
18:             // This code is automatically generated by Visual Café
19:             // when you add components to the visual environment.
20:             // It instantiates and initializes the components. To
21:             // modify the code, only use code syntax that matches
22:             // what Visual Café can generate, or Visual Café may
23:             // be unable to back parse your Java file into its
24:             // visual environment.
25:             //{{INIT_CONTROLS
26:             setLayout(null);
27:             resize(426,266);
28:             button = new java.awt.Button("button");
29:             button.reshape(36,12,108,43);
30:             add(button);
31:             textField = new java.awt.TextField();
32:             textField.reshape(36,96,144,31);
33:             add(textField);
34:             //}}
35:
36:             //{{REGISTER_LISTENERS
37:             //}}
38:         }
39:
40:         void button_Action(ActionEvent e) {
41:             textField.setText("Hi Mom");
```

continues

Listing 3.8. continued

```
42:       }
43:
44:       //{{DECLARE_CONTROLS
45:       java.awt.Button button;
46:       java.awt.TextField textField;
47:       //}}
48:
49:       class Action implements ActionListener {
50:          public void actionPerformed(ActionEvent event) {
51:             Object object = event.getSource();
52:             if (object == button)
53:                button_Action(event);
54:          }
55:       }
56: }
```

ANALYSIS   The first difference you should notice is that the `Applet` class no longer implements the `ActionListener` interface. That duty is now performed by the `Action` class (lines 49–55). If you look carefully at this listing, you will see that although `Action` is a class, it has been defined within the body of the `InnerClassListenerDemo` class. Because `Action` implements the `ActionListener` interface, it supplies the `actionPerformed` method that was part of the `ListenerDemo` class in Listing 3.7. Instead of directly setting the text of the text field, `actionPerformed` now calls the `button_Action` method (lines 40–42), which is defined within `InnerClassListenerDemo`, not `Action`.

You must still register the listener class with the button. First, an instance of the `Action` class is created (line 10). That instance is then registered as a listener to the button (line 11).

NOTE As easy as event handling is with listeners, Visual Café makes it even easier. When you use the Interaction wizard or when you create an event handler by using the Events/Methods list in a source code editing window, it will automatically generate all the necessary code for you. As necessary for any event, Visual Café will generate an inner class, register the inner class as a listener, and create an empty method that is called by the inner class.

3

Summary

Today's lesson covers a lot of ground. You learned how an applet's `init`, `start`, `stop`, and `destroy` methods are executed over the life of an applet. This lesson also demonstrates how to embed an applet in a Web page and how to customize the behavior of an applet by using applet parameters embedded in the host HTML file. Because understanding event handling is critical to Java programming, this lesson covers Java's new delegation model of event handling. You learned about event sources, events, event listeners, and adapters. Finally, you learned about inner classes and how they can improve the separation of event-handling and application logic.

Q&A

Q How can I distinguish between clicks of the right mouse button and the left mouse button?

A You can't. The Abstract Windowing Toolkit (AWT) that provides Java's event handling does not distinguish between mouse buttons. This was a tradeoff that was made for the sake of portability. Macintosh systems use a mouse with a single button, so to ensure applet portability, the AWT supports only a single mouse button.

Q Why do Netscape Navigator and Internet Explorer differ in what methods they call when their Refresh or Reload buttons are clicked? Do I need to do anything special to code around this difference?

A It's unfortunate that there isn't a standard covering what a browser should do when reloading or refreshing a page that includes a Java applet. Internet Explorer is more conservative in that it calls `destroy` and `init` in addition to `stop` and `start`. For the most part, there is no special coding you need to do to account for this difference in strategy. However, because Navigator and Internet Explorer differ in this and many other ways, you should test your applets in both browsers.

Workshop

The workshop includes quiz questions to help you gauge your understanding of the material in this chapter. The workshop also includes exercises to provide hands-on experience with what you've learned in this chapter. Answers to the quiz questions can be found in Appendix D, "Answers."

3

Quiz

1. What is the difference between the `init` and `start` methods?

2. What is the difference between the `stop` and `destroy` methods?

3. In what order will the four methods `init`, `destroy`, `start`, and `stop` be called?

4. What is the difference between a low-level event and a semantic event?

5. What are the adapter classes used for?

6. What is the difference between the `code` and `codebase` attributes of the `<applet>` HTML tag?

7. What is the advantage of using inner classes?

Exercises

1. Write an applet that reads in up to ten applet parameters (`KEY_A` through `KEY_J`) that correspond to the capital letters A through J. Write an event handler that displays a string associated with the parameter for each key press of A through J.

2. Write an applet that displays a message every time a key is pressed or released.

3. Write an applet that displays an X onscreen wherever the mouse is pressed.

Day 4

Java Strings

Today you will learn about the `String` and `StringBuffer` classes, two of the classes you will use most in your Java programming career. You will learn how to convert other object types into strings so they can be displayed. You will also learn how to perform a number of other operations on strings, including case conversion, searching for characters or substrings, and comparing strings. You will learn how the `StringBuffer` class offers an alternative to the `String` class and how it is more useful when working with text that is likely to change. Finally, you will learn how to use the many methods for appending or inserting into a `StringBuffer`.

The `String` Class

The Java `String` class, a part of the `java.lang` package, is used to represent strings of characters. Unlike C and C++, Java does not use an array of characters to represent a string. The `String` class is used to represent a string that is fairly static, changing infrequently if at all. This section describes how to use this class and includes examples of many of the nearly 50 methods and constructors that are part of this important class.

Constructing New Strings

There are seven String constructors, as shown in Table 4.1.

Table 4.1. Constructors for the String class.

Constructor	Purpose
String()	Creates an empty string.
String(String)	Creates a string from the specified string.
String(char[])	Creates a string from an array of characters.
String(char[], int, int)	Creates a string from the specified subset of characters in an array.
String(byte[], int)	Creates a string from the specified byte array and unicode upper byte.
String(byte[],int,int,int)	Creates a string from the specified subset of bytes and unicode upper byte.
String(StringBuffer)	Creates a string.

For an example of using these constructors, consider the following code:

```
String str1 = new String();
String str2 = new String("A New String");
char charArray[] = {'A', 'r', 'r', 'a', 'y' };
String str3 = new String(charArray);
String str4 = new String(charArray, 2, 3);
StringBuffer buf = new StringBuffer("buffer");
String str5 = new String(buf);
```

In the first example, str1 is created as an empty string. The second string, str2, holds the text A New String. The next two examples, str3 and str4, are constructed from a character array. In the case of str3, the entire array is placed in the string. For str4, three characters starting in array position 2 are copied into the string. Because Java arrays are zero based, this results in str4 containing ray. In the final example, the string str5 is constructed from a StringBuffer, buf. The StringBuffer class has much in common with String and is described in detail in the section "The StringBuffer Class," later in this lesson.

In addition to these constructors, there are other ways to get a String object. Many Java classes include a toString method that can be used to generate a string representation of the object. For example, consider the following:

```
Long myLong = new Long(43);
String longStr = myLong.toString();
g.drawString(longStr + myLong.toString(), 10, 20);
```

In this case, a `Long` object is created and set to hold the value 43. Note that this is an object of type `Long`, not a primitive of type `long`. Because `myLong` is an instance of a class, the `toString` method is used to place a string directly into `longStr`. The call to `drawString` illustrates that the converted string in `longStr` can be used as a regular string, as can an inline use of `myLong.toString`.

Finally, Java supports the use of automatic strings, as follows:

```
g.drawString("This is an automatic string.", 10, 20);
```

In this case, the `drawString` method expects to be passed a string as its first parameter. To satisfy this expectation, a new `String` object is constructed using the quoted text. This happens behind the scenes automatically, and requires no special attention on your part.

Basic String Methods

The basic methods for manipulating and examining a string are shown in Table 4.2. The Java `String` class is meant to be used to hold text that does not change, so this table does not include a lot of methods for adding and inserting text. It does, however, include a simple `concat` method for adding one string to the end of another and a `replace` method for swapping one character for another.

Table 4.2. Basic string methods.

Method	Purpose
`concat(String)`	Concatenates one string onto another.
`length()`	Returns the length of the string.
`replace(char, char)`	Replaces all occurrences of one character with a different character.
`toLowerCase()`	Converts the entire string to lowercase.
`toUpperCase()`	Converts the entire string to uppercase.
`trim()`	Trims both leading and trailing whitespace from the string.

The `concat` method appends the specified string onto the current string and returns the result as a new string. This can be seen in the following, in which `str3` will contain `Hello World`:

```
String str1 = new String("Hello ");
String str2 = new String("World");
String str3 = str1.concat(str2);
```

The `replace` method can be used to change all occurrences of one character to a different character. The following example changes `Hi Mom` to `Hi Mum`, allowing the program to be run in England:

```
String str = new String("Hi Mom ");
String newStr = str.replace('o', 'u');
```

Like `concat`, `trim` works by returning a new string. In this case, all leading and trailing whitespace characters are first removed from the returned string. The following example will remove the tabs, carriage return, newline, and space characters at both ends of the string:

```
String str = new String("\t\t In The Middle \r\n");
String newStr = str.trim();
```

The `length` method simply returns the number of characters in the string. In the following example, `len` will be set to `12`:

```
String str = new String("Length of 12");
int len = str.length();
```

The `toUpperCase` and `toLowerCase` methods can be used to change the case of an entire string. Each works by returning a new string. In the following example, an uppercase version and a lowercase version of the same string are created:

```
String str = new String("This is MiXeD caSE");
String upper = str.toUpperCase();
String lower = str.toLowerCase();
```

Converting Variables to Strings

Because most of the display methods of Java's user interface classes use strings, it is important to be able to convert variables of other types into strings. Naturally, Java includes methods for doing this. The `String` class includes a set of static `valueOf` methods that can be used to create strings from other Java objects and primitive types. The `valueOf` methods are shown in Table 4.3.

Table 4.3. Useful static methods for converting strings.

Method	Purpose
`valueOf(char)`	Returns a string containing the one specified character.
`valueOf(char[])`	Returns a string with the same text as the specified character array.
`valueOf(char[], int, int)`	Returns a string with the same text as a subset of the specified character array.
`valueOf(boolean)`	Returns a string containing either `true` or `false`.
`valueOf(int)`	Returns a string containing the value of the `int`.

4

Method	Purpose
valueOf(long)	Returns a string containing the value of the long.
valueOf(float)	Returns a string containing the value of the float.
valueOf(double)	Returns a string containing the value of the double.

Each of these methods is passed the variable to convert and returns a String representation of that variable. Because these methods are static, they are invoked using the name of the class rather than the name of an instance of the class. For example, consider the following uses of valueOf to create strings from numeric values:

```
String intStr = String.valueOf(100);
String floatStr = String.valueOf(98.6F);
String doubleStr = String.valueOf(3.1416D);
```

Each of these lines will result in the creation of a string containing the number specified. Consider also the following examples of non-numeric conversions:

```
String boolStr = String.valueOf(true);
String charStr = String.valueOf('Y');
char charArray[] = {'A', 'r', 'r', 'a', 'y' };
String arrayStr1 = String.valueOf(charArray);
String arrayStr2 = String.valueOf(charArray, 2, 3);
```

In the first case, boolStr will be set to true. The variable charStr will be a string with a length of 1. The e⌷⌷⌷⌷⌷⌷⌷⌷⌷⌷⌷⌷⌷⌷⌷⌷ in arrayStr1, but only ray will be stored in arrayStr⌷⌷⌷

 TIP

Margaret Lim KL

Conver⌷⌷⌷

Of cours⌷
one of Ja⌷
into an i⌷
shown i⌷

```
String intString = "34";
String longString = "987654321";
int i = Integer.parseInt(intString);
long l = Long.parseLong(longString);
```

There is no one-step conversion possible from a String to either a float or a double. To make these conversions, you must first convert the string to Float or Double and then to float or double. This two-step process is achieved as follows:

```
String floatString = "3.14f";
String doubleString = "987654321.123";
Float myFloat = Float.valueOf(floatString);
float f = myFloat.floatValue();
Double myDouble = Double.valueOf(doubleString);
double d = myDouble.doubleValue();
```

The static member methods Float.valueOf and Double.valueOf are used to create Float and Double objects. Then the instance methods floatValue and doubleValue are used to convert the objects to their equivalent primitives.

WARNING

Each of these conversion methods can throw NumberFormatException, so you should catch this exception. This can be done as follows:

```
String badIntStr = "Hello";
int badInt = 100;
try {
    badInt = Integer.parseInt(badIntStr);
}
catch (NumberFormatException e) {
    badInt = 0;
}
g.drawString("badInt = " + String.valueOf(badInt), 10, 30;
```

In this case, an attempt is made to convert a string containing Hello to an int. The converted value of the string will be stored in badInt, which is initialized to 100, so you can verify that the exception is caught. When the exception NumberFormatException is raised, it is caught, and badInt is set to 0. After the conversion, the string is drawn on the screen so you can see that the exception was caught and badInt is set to 0.

Using Only Part of a String

Of course, sometimes the entire string is too much; you need just a portion of the string. Fortunately, the Java String class provides methods for accessing or creating a substring from a longer string. Each of the methods listed in Table 4.4 can be used to retrieve a portion of a string.

Table 4.4. Methods for using a substring.

Method	Purpose
charAt(int)	Returns the character at the specified location.
getBytes(int, int, byte[], int)	Copies the specified number of characters from the specified location into the byte array.
getChars(int, int, char[], int)	Copies the specified number of characters from the specified location into the char array.
substring(int)	Returns a substring beginning from the specified offset of the current string.
substring(int, int)	Returns a substring between the specified offsets of the current string.

The charAt method retrieves the single character at the index given. For example, the following will place the character a in ch:

```
String str = new String("This is a String");
char ch = str.charAt(8);
```

The getBytes and getChars methods are similar. The former moves a substring into an array of bytes; the latter moves a substring into an array of characters. For example, consider the following:

```
public void paint(Graphics g)
{
    String str = new String("Wish You Were Here");
    char charArray[] = new char[25];
    str.getChars(5, 13, charArray, 0);
    g.drawChars(charArray, 0, 8, 10, 10);
}
```

This code will extract You Were from str and move it into the charArray variable. It is then displayed using g.drawChars.

The two substring methods can be used to create new strings that are extracted from the current string. To create a substring from an offset to the end of the string, use the first version of substring, as follows:

```
String str = new String("This is a String");
String substr = str.substring(10);
```

In this case, substr will hold String. To create a substring from the middle of a string, you can specify an ending offset as an additional parameter to substring. The following code will place You Were into substr:

```
String str = new String("Wish You Were Here");
String substr = str.substring(5, 13);
```

The character given by the beginning index will be included in the new string, but the character given by the ending index will not be.

Comparing Strings

As you can see in Table 4.5, Java provides a number of methods for comparing one string to another. The compareTo method returns the difference between two strings by examining the first two characters that differ in the strings. The difference between the characters is returned. For example, the character a differs from c by two characters, so 2 will be returned if these are the first two characters that differ. Depending on which string contains the higher valued character, the return value could be positive or negative. For example, in the following, result1 will equal -2, but result2 will equal 2:

```
String str1 = new String("abc");
String str2 = new String("abe");
// compare str2 against str1
int result1 = str1.compareTo(str2);
// perform the same comparison but in the
// opposite direction (str1 against str2)
int result2 = str2.compareTo(str1);
```

Table 4.5. Methods for comparing strings.

Method	Purpose
compareTo(String)	Compares two strings. Returns 0 if they are equal, a negative value if the specified string is greater than the String, or a positive value otherwise.
endsWith	Returns true if the string ends with the specified string.
equalIgnoreCase	Returns true if, ignoring differences in capitalization, the string matches the specified string.
equals(Object)	Returns true if the string matches the Object.
equalTo(String)	Returns true if the string matches the specified string.

4

Method	Purpose
regionMatches(int,String,int,int)	Returns true if the specified region of the string matches the specified region of a different string.
regionMatches(boolean,int,String,int,int)	Returns true if the specified region of the string matches the specified region of a different string, optionally considering the case of the strings.
startsWith(String)	Returns true if the string starts with the specified string.
startsWith(String, int)	Returns true if the string starts with the specified string at the specified offset.

The `equals` and `equalTo` methods perform similar comparisons; however, they each return a Boolean value rather than a measure of how the strings differ. These can be used to compare one string against another string or against a string literal, as shown in the following:

```
public void paint(Graphics g)
{
    String str1 = new String("abc");
    // create str2 to have the same contents as str1
    String str2 = new String(str1);
    // compare str1 to the string made from it
    if (str1.equals(str2))
        g.drawString("str1 and str2 are equal", 10, 10);
    // compare str1 against a literal
    if (str1.equals("abc"))
        g.drawString("str1 equals abc", 10, 30);
}
```

In this case, `str1` is equal to both `str2` and the literal `abc`. To perform a case-insensitive comparison, use the `equalIgnoreCase` method, as follows:

```
String str1 = new String("abc");
boolean result = str1.equalsIgnoreCase("ABC");
```

The `endsWith` method (`String`) can be used to determine whether a string ends with a given string. Usually more useful are the two `startsWith` methods, which can be used to determine whether the string starts with a given string or whether that string appears at a specific location within the string. The `endsWith` and `startsWith` methods can be used as shown in the following:

```
// create two Strings
String str1 = new String("My favorite language is Java");
String str2 = new String("I like the Java language");
```

```
// see if str1 ends with "Java"
boolean result1 = str1.endsWith("Java");          // true
// see if str1 starts with "My"
boolean result2 = str1.startsWith("My");          // true
// see if starting in offset 11 str2 starts with "Java"
boolean result3 = str2.startsWith("Java", 11);    // true
```

The two regionMatches methods can be used to see whether a region in one string matches a region in a different string. The second regionMatches method allows for case-insensitive comparisons of this nature. As an example of using regionMatches, consider the following:

```
// create two longer Strings
String str1 = new String("My favorite language is Java");
String str2 = new String("I like the Java language");
// compare regions
// Start at offset 24 in str1 and compare against offset 11
// in str2 for 4 characters
boolean result = str1.regionMatches(24, str2, 11, 4);    // true
```

In this case, the strings are compared for a length of four characters starting with index 24 in str1 and index 11 in str2. Because each of these substrings is Java, result is set to true.

Searching Strings

In addition to comparing one string against another, you can also search a string for the occurrence of a character or another string. Unfortunately, you can only do a normal exact-character search; no regular expression or wildcard searching is possible. The methods that can be used to search a string are shown in Table 4.6.

Table 4.6. Methods for searching a string.

Method	Purpose
indexOf(int)	Searches for the first occurrence of the specified character.
indexOf(int, int)	Searches for the first occurrence of the specified character following the given offset.
indexOf(String)	Searches for the first occurrence of the specified string.
indexOf(String, int)	Searches for the first occurrence of the specified string following the given offset.
lastIndexOf(int)	Searches backward for the last occurrence of the specified character.
lastIndexOf(int, int)	Searches backward for the last occurrence of the specified character preceding the given offset.

Method	Purpose
lastIndexOf(String)	Searches backward for the last occurrence of the specified string.
lastIndexOf(String, int)	Searches backward for the last occurrence of the specified string preceding the given offset.

As you can see from Table 4.6, the search methods have various signatures but are named either indexOf or lastIndexOf. The indexOf methods search forward from the start of a string to its end; the lastIndexOf methods search in the opposite direction.

To search for a character from the beginning of the string, use the indexOf(int) method. The following code illustrates searching for the character Y:

```
String str = new String("Wish You Were Here");
int index = str.indexOf('Y');
```

In this case, a Y is found in index 5, so this value is placed in index. This works well for finding the first occurrence of a letter, but what if you need to find subsequent occurrences of the same letter? This can be done by using the indexOf(int, int) method. The additional parameter indicates the offset from which to start the search. By setting this value each time a matching character is found, a loop can be written to easily find all occurrences of a letter. For example, consider the following code fragment:

```
String str = new String("Wish You Were Here");
int fromIndex = 0;
while(fromIndex != -1)
{
    fromIndex = str.indexOf('W', fromIndex);
    if (fromIndex != -1)
    {
        // character was matched, use as desired
        fromIndex++;
    }
}
```

This example starts with str containing Wish You Were Here and uses a loop to find all W characters. The variable fromIndex is initially set to 0. This causes the str.indexOf method call to start at the beginning of the string on the first pass through the loop. If fromIndex is not -1, this indicates that the character was found. The value is appended to a results string and fromIndex is incremented to move past the matching character. In this case, a W is found at indexes 0 and 9.

Searching for a string is just as simple as searching for a character. The following example will search for the string er:

```
public void paint(Graphics g)
{
```

4

```
    String str = new String("Wish You Were Here");
    int count = 0;
    int fromIndex = 0;
    while(fromIndex != -1)
    {
        fromIndex = str.indexOf("er", fromIndex);
        if (fromIndex != -1)
        {
            count++;
            fromIndex++;
        }
    }
    g.drawString(String.valueOf(count), 10, 10);
}
```

This string will be found twice, once in Were and once in Here.

Do	**Don't**

DON'T forget that strings are objects of the String class, not arrays of characters as in other languages.

DO avoid using String for strings that change. In those cases, use the StringBuffer class instead.

DO remember that a String can be constructed in many ways other than with an explicit constructor. For example, the trim, toLowerCase, toUpperCase, and substring methods all create new strings and return them.

The StringBuffer Class

The primary limitation of the String class is that once the string is created, you cannot change it. If you need to store text that might need to be changed, you should use the StringBuffer class. The StringBuffer class includes methods for inserting and appending text. Additionally, a StringBuffer object may easily be converted into a String object when necessary.

To create a new StringBuffer, you can use any of the three constructors shown in Table 4.7. Examples of using these constructors are as follows:

```
StringBuffer buf1 = new StringBuffer(25);
StringBuffer buf2 = new StringBuffer();
StringBuffer buf3 = new StringBuffer("This is a StringBuffer");
```

In the first case, buf1 will be an empty StringBuffer with an initial length of 25. Similarly, buf2 will be an empty StringBuffer, but buf3 will contain This is a StringBuffer.

Table 4.7. The `StringBuffer` **constructors.**

Constructor	Purpose
`StringBuffer()`	Creates an empty `StringBuffer`.
`StringBuffer(int)`	Creates an empty `StringBuffer` with the specified length.
`StringBuffer(String)`	Creates a `StringBuffer` based on the specified string.

Useful `StringBuffer` Methods

In addition to the methods for inserting and appending text, the `StringBuffer` class contains other methods with which you will need to be familiar. (See Table 4.8.) The `capacity` method can be used to determine the storage capacity of the string buffer. Because each string buffer can grow as text is appended or inserted, the capacity of the string buffer can exceed the length of the text currently stored in it. While `capacity` returns the amount of text that could be stored in the currently allocated space of the string buffer, `length` returns how much of that space is already used. For example, consider the following:

```
StringBuffer buf = new StringBuffer(25);
buf.append("13 Characters");
int len = buf.length();
int cap = buf.capacity();
```

In this case, the constructor specifies a capacity of 25 for `buf`, but only 13 characters are placed in it with the `append` method. Because of this, the `length` of `buf` is 13 while its `capacity` is 25. These values will be stored in `len` and `cap`, respectively.

Table 4.8. Useful methods of the `StringBuffer` **class.**

Method	Purpose
`capacity()`	Returns the current capacity of the `StringBuffer`.
`charAt(int)`	Returns the character located at the specified index.
`ensureCapacity(int)`	Ensures the capacity of the `StringBuffer` is at least the specified amount.
`getChars(int,int,char[],int)`	Copies the specified characters from the `StringBuffer` into the specified array.
`length()`	Returns the length of the `StringBuffer`.
`setCharAt(int, char)`	Sets the value at the specified index to the specified character.

continues

Table 4.8. continued

Method	Purpose
setLength(int)	Sets the length of the StringBuffer to the specified value.
toString	Returns a string representing the text in the StringBuffer.

The ensureCapacity method can be used to increase the capacity of the string buffer, and the setLength method can be used to set the length of the buffer. If setLength is used to reduce the length, the characters at the end of the buffer are lost. If, instead, setLength is used to increase the length of a string buffer, null characters are used to fill the additional space at the end. This is shown in the following code:

```
StringBuffer buf = new StringBuffer("0123456789");
buf.setLength(5);
// buf now contains "01234"
buf.setLength(10);
// buf now contains "01234" followed by five null characters
```

The toString method will be one of the StringBuffer methods you will use most frequently. This method creates a string representation of the text in the string buffer. This is useful because so many of the Java library methods expect a string as a parameter. For example, the following code illustrates how to display the contents of a string buffer in an applet's paint method:

```
public void paint(Graphics g)
{
    StringBuffer buf = new StringBuffer("Hello, World");
    g.drawString(buf.toString(), 10, 10);
}
```

The charAt and setCharAt methods can be used to retrieve the character at a specific index and to set the character at a specific index, respectively. This is shown in the following:

```
StringBuffer buf = new StringBuffer("Hello");
char ch = buf.charAt(1);
buf.setCharAt(1, 'a');
```

Because StringBuffers are zero based, ch will contain e. The setCharAt method replaces this e, changing the StringBuffer to say Hallo. The getChars method can be used to retrieve characters from a StringBuffer and place them into a character array. The getChars method has the following signature:

```
public synchronized void getChars(int srcBegin, int srcEnd,
    char dst[], int dstBegin) ;
```

The srcEnd parameter indicates the first character after the desired end of the text. It will not be placed in the destination array, so you should be careful to specify the proper value. In the following example, getChars is used to place the characters of String into the array:

```
StringBuffer buf = new StringBuffer("A String Buffer");
char array[] = new char[10];
buf.getChars(2,8, array, 0);
```

WARNING

The getChars method will throw a StringIndexOutOfBoundsException if any of the parameters represents an invalid index.

Appending

Because the main distinction between the String and StringBuffer classes is the capability of a StringBuffer instance to increase in size, methods are provided for appending to a StringBuffer. Each of the following methods can be used to append to a StringBuffer:

- [ ] append(Object)
- [ ] append(String)
- [ ] append(char)
- [ ] append(char[])
- [ ] append(char[], int, int)
- [ ] append(boolean)
- [ ] append(int)
- [ ] append(long)
- [ ] append(float)
- [ ] append(double)

Use of these methods is demonstrated by the following:

```
StringBuffer buf = new StringBuffer("Hello");
buf.append(", World");
StringBuffer buf2 = new StringBuffer("Revolution #");
buf2.append(9);
StringBuffer buf3 = new StringBuffer("My daughter is ");
float ageSavannah = 18F/12F;
buf3.append(ageSavannah);
buf3.append(" years old");
```

In the first case, buf is set to contain Hello, and then append(String) is used to create Hello, World. The second case illustrates the use of append(int) to create the text Revolution #9. Finally, buf3 illustrates the use of append(float) combined with append(String).

Inserting

Of course, sometimes the text you want to add to a string buffer needs to go somewhere other than at the end. In these cases, append is of no use, and you need to use one of the provided insert methods. A variety of insert methods is provided:

- [ ] insert(int, Object)
- [ ] insert(int, String)
- [ ] insert(int, char[])
- [ ] insert(int, boolean)
- [ ] insert(int, char)
- [ ] insert(int, int)
- [ ] insert(int, long)
- [ ] insert(int, float)
- [ ] insert(int, double)

Each of these methods is passed the index at which to insert the text and then an object to be inserted. For example, the following code inserts the all-important half-month into a child's age:

```
StringBuffer buf = new StringBuffer("My daughter is 18 months old");
buf.insert(17, "-and-a-half");
```

An Example

To help solidify what you've learned about the String and StringBuffer classes, this section presents an example. This example, TabApplet, which is included on the MCP Web site (www.mcp.com/info/1-57521/1-57521-303-6), illustrates how to convert between spaces and tabs in a string. The detab method removes tabs from a string, replacing each tab with an appropriate number of space characters. The entab method does exactly the opposite: Where possible, space characters are removed from a string and replaced with a tab character.

Removing Tabs

It would be very simple to write a detab method that replaces each tab character with either four or eight spaces. However, this isn't what we want. Whenever a tab character is removed, we want to replace it with enough space characters to fill a string through the next tab stop. For the purposes of this example, tab stops are assumed to occur every eight characters. So, for example, if a string containing ABC\tD is processed by detab, it should be changed into ABC followed by five spaces and then the D. A detab method that does exactly that is shown in Listing 4.1.

Listing 4.1. The `detab` method removes tabs from a string.

```
 1:    private String detab(String in)
 2:    {
 3:        // save the length of the original string
 4:        int length = in.length();
 5:
 6:        // allocate a StringBuffer, guessing that its length will
 7:        // be the same as the original string
 8:        StringBuffer outBuffer = new StringBuffer(length);
 9:
10:        int outputColumn = 0;
11:
12:        // for each character in the string
13:        for(int pos = 0; pos < length; pos++) {
14:            char ch = in.charAt(pos);
15:
16:            // if the character is a tab...
17:            if (ch == '\t') {
18:                // loop adding spaces until the next tab stop
19:                do {
20:                    outBuffer.append(' ');
21:                    outputColumn++;
22:                } while ( (outputColumn % 8) != 0);
23:            }
24:            // if the character isn't a tab, just add it
25:            else {
26:                outBuffer.append(ch);
27:                outputColumn++;
28:            }
29:        }
30:        // return the buffer after conversion to a string
31:        return outBuffer.toString();
32:    }
```

ANALYSIS The `detab` method works by allocating a `StringBuffer` that is the same length as the original string (line 8). Instead, you could have allocated a zero-length buffer. However, because each tab will be converted to one or more spaces, you know the detabbed string will be at least as long as the input string. The variable `outputColumn`, declared on line 10, is used to keep track of the current position in the string being created.

The loop in lines 13–29 looks at each character. If the character is not a tab, it is simply added to the string buffer (line 26), and `outputColumn` is incremented (line 27). However, if the character is a tab character, an inner loop (lines 19–22) adds spaces until reaching the next tab stop.

The `while` statement on line 22 may look a little tricky. What we're doing here is comparing the remainder of `outputColumn` divided by 8. When the remainder is 0, `outputColumn` is on a tab stop and the loop breaks.

Because detab is passed a String parameter, it should return a String, not a StringBuffer. In line 31, toString is used to convert outBuffer from a StringBuffer to a String.

Adding Tabs

The entab method, shown in Listing 4.2, is similar to detab but is a little more complicated.

Listing 4.2. The entab method adds tabs to a string.

```
1:    private String entab(String in)
2:    {
3:        // save the length of the original string
4:        int length = in.length();
5:
6:        // allocate a StringBuffer, guessing that its length
7:        // will be the same as the original string
8:        StringBuffer outBuffer = new StringBuffer(length);
9:
10:       // outputColumn represents the current column of the
11:       // string as it will be displayed on screen
12:       int outputColumn = 0;
13:
14:       // for each character in the string...
15:       for(int pos = 0; pos < length; pos++) {
16:           // store the current column
17:           int tempColumn = outputColumn;
18:
19:           char ch = in.charAt(pos);    // get the next char
20:
21:           // while not at the end and while the character
22:           // is a space
23:           while (pos < length-1 && ch == ' ') {
24:               // increment the temporary column counter and
25:               // check to see if its at a tab position
26:               tempColumn++;
27:               if ((tempColumn % 8) == 0) {
28:                   // if so, output a tab and store the column
29:                   outBuffer.append('\t');
30:                   outputColumn = tempColumn;
31:               }
32:               // move forward through the string
33:               pos++;
34:               ch = in.charAt(pos);
35:           };
36:
37:           // ASSERT: at this point ch will not be a space
38:
39:           // output extra spaces (after the tab stop)
40:           for(; outputColumn < tempColumn; outputColumn++)
41:               outBuffer.append(' ');
42:           outBuffer.append(ch);
43:           outputColumn++;
44:       }
45:       return outBuffer.toString();
46:    }
```

ANALYSIS Like detab, entab begins by allocating a StringBuffer that is the same length as the original string. Because entab converts multiple spaces into a tab, the resulting string will most likely be shorter than the input string. However, the length of the input string still represents a reasonable guess of the resulting string's length.

The variable outputColumn (declared on line 12) serves the same purpose in entab that it did in detab. The outer loop of detab (lines 15–44) iterates through each character in the original string. The current character is read on line 19. Then, if the character is a space and not near the end of the input string, a loop (lines 23–35) is used to read the successive spaces from the string. A temporary column counter is incremented and then tested to see whether it represents a tab stop. If it does, a tab character is added to the output buffer (line 29). If it does not, the loop moves forward through the string and retrieves the next character (lines 33–34).

After looping through any spaces, the entab method is guaranteed to be on a nonspace character. This is shown by the ASSERT comment (line 37). Because it was possible to have found spaces that did not lead to a tab stop, these spaces are appended to outBuffer in lines 40–41. Finally, the current character is appended and outputColumn incremented (42–43).

Testing entab and detab

The entab and detab methods are included in TabApplet on the MCP Web site. The test method of this applet is shown in Listing 4.3. This method creates a TextArea called results to which various strings are appended. First, a row of numbers is appended to ensure that subsequent strings are lined up in the appropriate columns. Next, the strings are displayed without modification. Then, a detabbed instance of each string is created, and these strings are displayed. Finally, entab is used to restore the tabs in the detabbed strings. The results of executing TabApplet are shown in Figure 4.1.

Listing 4.3. Testing the entab and detab methods.

```
1:    private void test() {
2:        // output some column headings
3:        results.setText("123456789012345678901234567890\r\n");
4:
5:        // create two test strings
6:        String string1 = new String("ab\tc\td\r\n");
7:        String string2 = new String("\tx\tyz\r\n");
8:
9:        // display the strings without modification
10:       results.appendText("Untouched strings:\r\n");
11:       results.appendText(string1);
12:       results.appendText(string2);
13:
14:       // remove the tabs and display the new strings
15:       String detabbedString1 = detab(string1);
```

continues

Listing 4.3. continued

```
16:          String detabbedString2 = detab(string2);
17:          results.appendText("\r\nDetabbed strings:\r\n");
18:          results.appendText(detabbedString1);
19:          results.appendText(detabbedString2);
20:
21:          // restore the tabs and display the returned strings
22:          results.appendText("\r\nEntabbed strings:\r\n");
23:          results.appendText(entab(detabbedString1));
24:          results.appendText(entab(detabbedString2));
25:      }
```

Figure 4.1.

Testing the entab *and* detab *methods.*

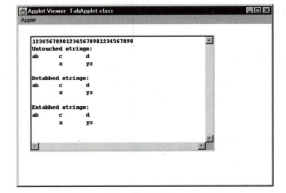

Summary

Today you learned about the String and StringBuffer classes, two of the most commonly used classes in Java programming. You learned that the String class is intended to hold nonchanging text. You saw many examples of using the member methods of the String class, including changing the case of a string, trimming whitespace, and accessing substrings. You learned how to convert variables of other types into strings and how to search and compare strings. Finally, you saw how the StringBuffer class is a more useful class for dynamic strings because text can be inserted and appended.

Q&A

Q You say that the String class is for strings that don't change. If this is true, why can I write code like the following?

```
String myString = new String ("Hello");
myString = myString + " World";
```

A This works because you are really creating two strings. On the first line, you have constructed an object named myString and set it to contain Hello. In the second

line, you have created a new String that contains the contents of the old String plus some new text. You have also told myString to reference the new String rather than the first String. The first String (containing just Hello) still exists, but because no variables reference it, it will be collected by the garbage collector.

Q I need to write a parser. It seems like a lot of work with the methods described in this lesson. Isn't there an easier way?

A Yes, there is. The StringTokenizer class provides a very powerful mechanism for parsing strings. This class is fully described on Day 12, "The Java Utility Classes."

Workshop

The workshop includes quiz questions to help you gauge your understanding of the material in this chapter. The workshop also includes exercises to provide hands-on experience with what you've learned in this chapter. To see the answers, look in Appendix D, "Answers."

Quiz

1. How would you select three characters, starting with the 10th character in a string?
2. What is the difference between the equalTo and compareTo methods in the String class?
3. How can you compare an object of an unknown type to a String without using toString on the unknown object?
4. What is the difference between indexOf and lastIndexOf in the String class?
5. When would you use a StringBuffer object instead of a String?
6. What is the difference between the length and the capacity of a string buffer?
7. To the StringBuffer class, what is the difference between inserting and appending?

Exercises

1. Modify the entab and detab methods so that they work with a vector of tab stops instead of fixed tab-stop positions.
2. Write an applet that allows the user to enter a string and two integer values. Whenever the user clicks a button named Upper, convert the characters between the two integer values to uppercase. Do the opposite when he clicks a Lower button.
3. Write a method that is passed an array of strings and that searches the array for lines beginning with The. Display each of the strings in a text area.
4. Write an applet that allows the user to interactively enter a short string and then append or insert that string into another string.
5. Write a method that reverses the contents of a String. When passed Hello, it should return olleH.

Day 5

Using the Abstract Windowing Toolkit

Back in the days before the graphical browser, the World Wide Web was dominated by boring, text-only pages, and the only people using the Web were researchers, programmers, and some college students. The graphical browser changed all that by presenting more visually appealing pages. Suddenly, everyone is surfing the Web. Clearly, the change to an appealing, graphical user interface has much to do with the growth in popularity of the Web. Today you will learn about the Abstract Windowing Toolkit (AWT) that is the foundation of Java user-interface programming.

Elements of an Applet's Interface

The Abstract Windowing Toolkit (AWT) includes classes that represent the following elements:

- Buttons
- Text fields
- Text areas
- Labels
- Checkboxes
- Lists
- Choices
- Scrollbars

These visual elements can be combined in any manner to create the user interface your applet needs. For example, Figure 5.1 shows a Web-based applet that enables golfers to enter their scores and submit them to a remote server. Of course, user-interface programming does not end with the classes included in the AWT. You can create your own subclasses of these classes, or you can use classes created by others. In addition to the user-interface classes of the AWT, Visual Café provides many other user-interface classes as part of its Object Library. These classes are described in Chapter 8, "Using the Object Library," and Chapter 9, "More Object Library Components."

Figure 5.1.

The golf scorekeeper applet illustrates most AWT user-interface components.

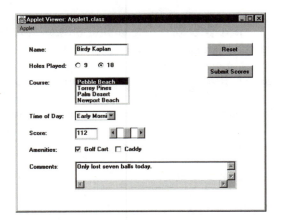

This figure shows all the common elements of an AWT user interface. The golfer's name is collected in a text field. The number of holes played (9 or 18) is a Checkbox group. A List component is used for the course, and a Choice component is used for the time of day. The score can be entered directly into a text field or can be increased or decreased by using the adjacent scrollbar. The amenities (Golf Cart and Caddy) are checkboxes. The comment area is a multiline text area. The use of each of these user-interface elements is explained in detail in the following sections.

Everything Is a Component

You were introduced to the Component class in Chapter 3, "Programming Applets and Handling Events," because of its importance in passing events from one subclass of Component to another. As you can see in Figure 5.2, Component serves as the base class for most of the AWT's user-interface classes.

Figure 5.2.

Some of the descendants of Component.

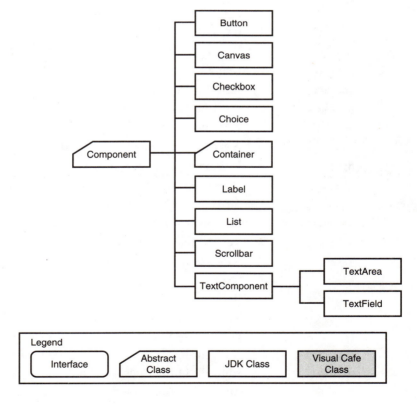

As the base class for Java's user-interface classes, Component does much more than provide a common set of event handlers for each user-interface object. Component is a very large class that makes over 70 methods available to its subclasses. The most important or frequently used methods of this class are shown in Table 5.1.

Table 5.1. Some useful public members of Component.

Method	Purpose
action	An event-handling method called when action events occur.
disable	Disables the component.
enable	Enables the component.
getBackground	Returns the background color of the component.
getFont	Returns the font in use on the component.
getFontMetrics	Returns the font metrics (character height, width, and so on) of the component's font.
getForeground	Returns the foreground color of the component.
getGraphics	Gets a reference to the graphics object for the component.
getParent	Gets the component's parent.
gotFocus	An event-handling method called when the component receives the focus.
handleEvent	A generic event-handling method.
hide	Makes the component invisible.
inside	Determines whether a position given by X,Y coordinates is inside the component.
isEnabled	Returns true if the component is enabled.
isVisible	Returns true if the component is visible.
lostFocus	An event-handling method called when the component loses the focus.
minimumSize	Returns the minimum size required by the component.
mouseDown	An event-handling method called when the mouse button is pressed down.
mouseDrag	An event-handling method called when the mouse is moved while the button is held down.
mouseEnter	An event-handling method called when the mouse enters the component.

Method	Purpose
mouseExit	An event-handling method called when the mouse exits the component.
mouseMove	An event-handling method called when the mouse is moved without holding down the button.
mouseUp	An event-handling method called when the mouse button is released.
move	Relocates the component.
nextFocus	Gives focus to the next component.
paint	Paints the component.
preferredSize	Returns the preferred dimensions of the component.
repaint	Causes the component to be repainted.
resize	Changes the dimensions of the component.
setBackground	Sets the background color of the component.
setFont	Sets the font that will be used by the component.
setForeground	Sets the foreground color of the component.
show	Makes the component visible.

Toolkits and Peers

One of the advantages of the AWT and its approach to platform independence is that user-interface components are displayed in a manner consistent with platform-specific programs. In other words, a scrollbar in a Java applet under Motif will look like any other scrollbar in Motif, even if the other program was developed in a language like C++. Java supports platform independence through its concepts of *toolkits* and *peers*.

NEW TERM   The Java idea of a *toolkit* is a way of encapsulating platform-specific aspects of a user interface. Java supports this by providing a subclass of the abstract class `java.awt.Toolkit` for each platform. Most applets do not need to use the `Toolkit` class directly; however, it does work behind the scenes to help create peers.

NEW TERM   A *peer* is a platform-specific representation of an AWT user-interface component. For example, `Checkbox` is an AWT class that is supported by a peer in the platform in which the program is executing. In Microsoft Windows, this means that the AWT `Checkbox` can be associated with a checkbox in the underlying Windows operating system.

5

By using toolkits and peer classes, the AWT is able to maintain a platform-specific look while remaining platform independent. Peers are created by many of the AWT classes through the `addNotify` method. You do not need to call `addNotify` yourself; whenever the AWT needs to create a peer, it will do so itself.

Buttons

Buttons are one of the simplest Java user-interface classes and are therefore a good starting point. To create a button, you can use either of the constructors shown in Table 5.2. Of course, you'll find the constructor that takes a label as a parameter much more useful than the one that does not, unless you want users to have to guess what a button does.

Table 5.2. Button constructors.

Constructor	Purpose
`Button()`	Creates a button without a label.
`Button(String label)`	Creates a button with the specified label.

As an example of how to construct and use a button, consider `SimpleButtonApplet`, shown in Listing 5.1. This is a no-frills example of placing a button on an applet and then displaying a message when the button is clicked.

Listing 5.1. `SimpleButtonApplet.java.`

```
 1:   import java.awt.*;
 2:   import java.applet.*;
 3:
 4:   public class SimpleButtonApplet extends Applet {
 5:       void button1_Clicked(java.awt.event.ActionEvent event) {
 6:           getGraphics().drawString("You pushed it!", 20, 20);
 7:       }
 8:
 9:       public void init() {
10:           // Call parents init method.
11:           super.init();
12:       }
13:
14:       public void addNotify() {
15:           // Call parents addNotify method.
16:           super.addNotify();
17:
18:           // This code is automatically generated by Visual Café
19:           // when you add components to the visual environment.
20:           // It instantiates and initializes the components. To
21:           // modify the code, only use code syntax that matches
```

```
22:        // what Visual Café can generate, or Visual Café may
23:        // be unable to back parse your Java file into its
24:        // visual environment.
25:        //{{INIT_CONTROLS
26:        setLayout(null);
27:        resize(426,266);
28:        button1 = new java.awt.Button("Push Me");
29:        button1.reshape(84,60,252,48);
30:        add(button1);
31:        //}}
32:
33:        //{{REGISTER_LISTENERS
34:        Action lAction = new Action();
35:        button1.addActionListener(lAction);
36:        //}}
37:    }
38:
39:    //{{DECLARE_CONTROLS
40:    java.awt.Button button1;
41:    //}}
42:
43:    class Action implements java.awt.event.ActionListener {
44:        public void actionPerformed(java.awt.event.ActionEvent event) {
45:            Object object = event.getSource();
46:            if (object == button1)
47:                button1_Clicked(event);
48:        }
49:    }
50: }
```

SimpleButtonApplet was created through the following steps:

1. A new applet was started and named SimpleButtonApplet.

2. A Button component was dragged from the Standard tab of the Component palette to the Form Designer.

3. In the Property List, the Label of the button is set to Push Me.

4. A source code window was opened, and a handler for the button's clicked event was added.

5. The body of the button1_Clicked method was written, as shown on line 6 of Listing 5.1.

ANALYSIS As you can see from Listing 5.1, Visual Café has taken care of creating the button and adding it to the applet (lines 28–30). Because add is defined in java.awt.Container and Applet is a subclass of Container, the button is added to the applet and will be displayed when the applet is run. Visual Café also created a listener class (43–49) that watches for the button click and calls your button1_Clicked method (5–7). The results of running this applet are shown in Figure 5.3.

Figure 5.3.

SimpleButtonApplet
*after the button has
been clicked.*

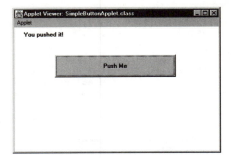

Public `Button` Methods

In addition to its constructors and to the methods available to it as a subclass of `Component`, the `Button` class provides the public member methods shown in Table 5.3.

Table 5.3. Public member methods of the `Button` class.

Method	Purpose
`addNotify()`	Creates a peer for the component.
`getLabel()`	Returns the button's current label.
`paramString()`	Returns the button's parameter string.
`setLabel(String)`	Sets the button's label to the specified string.

The `TwoButtons` applet is a more involved example of how to use the `Button` class and is shown in Listing 5.2. In this example, two buttons are created. As the buttons are clicked, the buttons become enabled or disabled, and their labels change.

Listing 5.2. `TwoButtons.java`.

```
1:    import java.awt.*;
2:    import java.applet.*;
3:
4:    public class TwoButtons extends Applet {
5:        int button1Count = 0;
6:
7:        void button1_Clicked(java.awt.event.ActionEvent event) {
8:            button1Count++;
9:
10:           switch(button1Count) {
11:               case 1:
12:                   button2.setLabel("Almost...");
13:                   break;
```

```
14:                case 2:
15:                    button2.setLabel("Now Push Me");
16:                    button2.enable();
17:                    button1.disable();
18:                    break;
19:            }
20:        }
21:
22:    void button2_Clicked(java.awt.event.ActionEvent event) {
23:        getGraphics().drawString("Thank you", 20, 60);
24:        button2.disable();
25:    }
26:
27:    public void init() {
28:        // Call parents init method.
29:        super.init();
30:    }
31:
32:    public void addNotify() {
33:        // Call parents addNotify method.
34:        super.addNotify();
35:
36:        // This code is automatically generated by Visual Café
37:        // when you add components to the visual environment.
38:        // It instantiates and initializes the components. To
39:        // modify the code, only use code syntax that matches
40:        // what Visual Café can generate, or Visual Café may
41:        // be unable to back parse your Java file into its
42:        // visual environment.
43:        //{{INIT_CONTROLS
44:        setLayout(null);
45:        resize(426,266);
46:        button2 = new java.awt.Button("I'm Disabled");
47:        button2.reshape(228,108,132,39);
48:        add(button2);
49:        button2.disable();
50:        button1 = new java.awt.Button("Push Me");
51:        button1.reshape(60,108,132,39);
52:        add(button1);
53:        //}}
54:
55:        //{{REGISTER_LISTENERS
56:        Action lAction = new Action();
57:        button2.addActionListener(lAction);
58:        button1.addActionListener(lAction);
59:        //}}
60:    }
61:
62:    //{{DECLARE_CONTROLS
63:    java.awt.Button button2;
64:    java.awt.Button button1;
65:    //}}
66:
```

5

continues

Listing 5.2. continued

```
67:     class Action implements java.awt.event.ActionListener {
68:         public void actionPerformed(java.awt.event.ActionEvent
69:             event) {
70:           Object object = event.getSource();
71:           if (object == button2)
72:               button2_Clicked(event);
73:           else if (object == button1)
74:               button1_Clicked(event);
75:         }
76:     }
77: }
```

ANALYSIS This applet was created by placing two buttons on the applet. The first button, button1, was given a label of Push Me. The second button, button2, was given a label of I'm Disabled, and its Enabled property was set to false in the Property List. This creates an applet that initially appears as shown in Figure 5.4.

Figure 5.4.

The TwoButtons *applet before either button is pushed.*

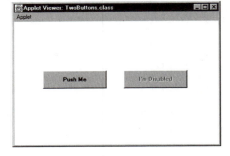

On line 5 of Listing 5.2, the button1Count variable is declared and set to 0. This variable is used by the button1_Clicked method (lines 7–20) to keep track of the number of clicks on button1. After the first click of button1, the label of button2 is changed to Almost..., as shown in Figure 5.5. On the second click, button2 is changed to read Now Push Me and is enabled. The first button is disabled to prevent further clicks. This is shown in Figure 5.6.

After the second button has been enabled, it can be clicked. Clicking it displays a message on the applet window (line 23) and then disables the button (line 24), as shown in Figure 5.7.

5

Figure 5.5.
The first button click changes the label of the second button.

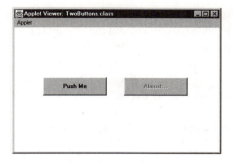

Figure 5.6.
After another click, the second button becomes enabled.

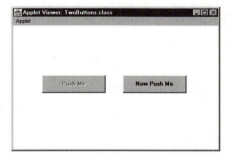

Figure 5.7.
After the second button is clicked, a message is displayed, and both buttons are disabled.

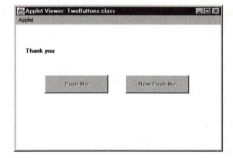

Text Fields and Areas

A text field is a one-line area for data entry. A text area is a multiline text field that includes scrollbars. There are various ways of constructing a text field or text area, as shown in the following examples:

```
TextField tf1 = new TextField(25);
TextField tf2 = new TextField("This is a TextField");
TextArea ta1 = new TextArea(10, 50);
TextArea ta2 = new TextArea("This is a 10 x 50 TextArea", 10, 50);
```

In this example, tf1 is constructed as a 25-column, one-row text field; tf2 is constructed as a text field wide enough to hold the string This is a TextField. Both text areas, ta1 and ta2, will be 10 rows by 50 columns, but ta2 will contain the initial text shown. There are additional constructors for the TextField and TextArea classes beyond those demonstrated in these examples. Tables 5.4 and 5.5 show the constructors available for the TextField and TextArea classes, respectively.

Table 5.4. Constructors for the TextField class.

Constructor	Purpose
TextField()	Creates a new, empty text field.
TextField(int)	Creates a new text field with the specified number of columns.
TextField(String)	Creates a new text field containing the specified string.
TextField(String, int)	Creates a new text field with the specified number of columns and containing the specified string.

Table 5.5. Constructors for the TextArea class.

Constructor	Purpose
TextArea()	Creates a new, empty text area.
TextArea(int, int)	Creates a new text area with the specified number of rows and columns.
TextArea(String)	Creates a new text area containing the specified string.
TextArea(String,int,int)	Creates a new text area with the specified number of rows and columns and containing the specified string.

Both TextField and TextArea are subclasses of the TextComponent class. This common base class provides the public methods listed in Table 5.6.

5

Table 5.6. Public members of `TextComponent`.

Method	Purpose
`getSelectedText()`	Returns the currently selected text.
`getSelectionEnd()`	Returns the ending column number of the selected text.
`getSelectionStart()`	Returns the starting column number of the selected text.
`getText()`	Returns the text in the `TextComponent`.
`isEditable()`	Returns `true` if the text component is editable.
`paramString()`	Returns a parameter string for the text component.
`removeNotify()`	Removes a text component's peer.
`select(int, int)`	Selects the text between the specified columns.
`selectAll()`	Selects all the text.
`setEditable(boolean)`	Indicates whether the text component is editable by the user.
`setText(String)`	Sets the text component to contain the specified string.

Beyond the methods shared through the `TextComponent` class, `TextField` and `TextArea` each implements its own additional member methods. They are listed in Tables 5.7 and 5.8.

Table 5.7. Public members of `TextField`.

Method	Purpose
`addNotify()`	Creates a peer for the component.
`echoCharIsSet()`	Returns `true` if an echo character has been set.
`getColumns()`	Returns the number of columns for the text field.
`getEchoChar()`	Returns the echo character that will be used.
`minimumSize(int)`	Returns the minimum dimensions for a text field with the specified number of columns.
`minimumSize()`	Returns the minimum dimensions for the text field.
`paramString()`	Returns a parameter string for the text field.
`preferredSize(int)`	Returns the preferred dimensions for a text field with the specified number of columns.
`preferredSize()`	Returns the preferred dimensions for the text field.
`setEchoCharacter(char)`	Sets the echo character to the specified character.

5

Table 5.8. Public members of TextArea.

Method	Purpose
addNotify()	Creates a peer for the component.
appendText(String)	Appends the specified string to the text area.
getColumns()	Returns the number of columns for the text area.
getRows()	Returns the number of rows for the text area.
insertText(String, int)	Inserts the specified string at the specified column.
minimumSize(int, int)	Returns the minimum dimensions for a text area with the specified number of rows and columns.
minimumSize()	Returns the minimum dimensions for the text area.
paramString()	Returns a parameter string for the text area.
preferredSize(int, int)	Returns the preferred dimensions for a text area with the specified number of rows and columns.
preferredSize()	Returns the preferred dimensions for the text area.
replaceText(String, int, int)	Uses the specified string to replace the text between the specified columns.

A TextField **and** TextArea **Example**

Figure 5.8 shows TextComponentApplet, which is a demonstration of using TextField and TextArea components. In this case, the user can enter text into either of two text fields and then click a button to append or insert the text into a text area. If the text is being inserted, the user can enter the column number at which the text will be inserted.

The code for TextComponentApplet is shown in Listing 5.3.

Listing 5.3. TextComponentApplet.java.

```
1:    import java.awt.*;
2:    import java.applet.*;
3:
4:    public class TextComponentApplet extends Applet {
5:        void insertButton_Clicked(java.awt.event.ActionEvent event) {
6:            int column = Integer.parseInt(insertColumn.getText());
7:            textArea1.insertText(insertText.getText(), column);
8:        }
9:
10:       void appendButton_Clicked(java.awt.event.ActionEvent event) {
11:           textArea1.appendText(appendText.getText());
12:           textArea1.appendText("\r\n");
```

5

```
13:     }
14:
15:     public void init() {
16:         // Call parents init method.
17:         super.init();
18:     }
19:
20:     public void addNotify() {
21:         // Call parents addNotify method.
22:         super.addNotify();
23:         // This code is automatically generated by Visual Café
24:         // when you add components to the visual environment.
25:         // It instantiates and initializes the components. To
26:         // modify the code, only use code syntax that matches
27:         // what Visual Café can generate, or Visual Café may
28:         // be unable to back parse your Java file into its
29:         // visual environment.
30:         //{{INIT_CONTROLS
31:         setLayout(null);
32:         resize(454,481);
33:         textArea1 = new java.awt.TextArea();
34:         textArea1.reshape(36,168,387,152);
35:         add(textArea1);
36:         appendButton = new java.awt.Button("Append");
37:         appendButton.reshape(336,36,84,31);
38:         add(appendButton);
39:         insertText = new java.awt.TextField();
40:         insertText.reshape(36,84,180,24);
41:         add(insertText);
42:         insertButton = new java.awt.Button("Insert");
43:         insertButton.reshape(336,84,84,31);
44:         add(insertButton);
45:         appendText = new java.awt.TextField();
46:         appendText.reshape(36,36,180,24);
47:         add(appendText);
48:         insertColumn = new java.awt.TextField();
49:         insertColumn.reshape(252,84,48,24);
50:         add(insertColumn);
51:         //}}
52:
53:         //{{REGISTER_LISTENERS
54:         Action lAction = new Action();
55:         insertButton.addActionListener(lAction);
56:         appendButton.addActionListener(lAction);
57:         //}}
58:     }
59:
60:     //{{DECLARE_CONTROLS
61:     java.awt.TextArea textArea1;
62:     java.awt.Button appendButton;
63:     java.awt.TextField insertText;
64:     java.awt.Button insertButton;
65:     java.awt.TextField appendText;
66:     java.awt.TextField insertColumn;
67:     //}}
```

5

continues

Listing 5.3. continued

```
68:
69:        class Action implements java.awt.event.ActionListener {
70:            public void actionPerformed(java.awt.event.ActionEvent
71:                    event) {
72:                Object object = event.getSource();
73:                if (object == insertButton)
74:                    insertButton_Clicked(event);
75:                else if (object == appendButton)
76:                    appendButton_Clicked(event);
77:            }
78:        }
79:    }
```

Figure 5.8.

Executing
TextComponentApplet.

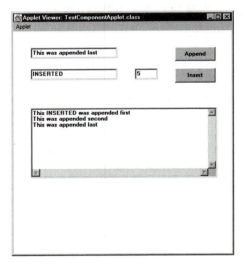

To create TextComponentApplet, take the following steps:

1. Create a new applet named TextComponentApplet.

2. Drag the TextField, TextArea, and Button components onto the Form Designer to match the user interface shown in Figure 5.8. Name the text fields appendText, insertText, and insertColumn. Name the buttons appendButton and insertButton.

3. Open a source code window and add an event handler for a click of appendButton. Write the body of the appendButton_Clicked method (lines 11–12).

4. Add an event handler for a click of insertButton. Write the body of the insertButton_Clicked method (lines 6–7).

Do	Don't

DO remember that you can make a text area or text field read-only by setting the `Editable` property to `false` or by using the `setEditable` method directly.

DON'T forget that you can use all the methods of the `TextComponent` class when working with `TextArea` and `TextField` objects.

DON'T expect a text area to be a word processor. The `TextArea` class provides the basic set of features required for editing multiple lines of text. Beyond that, you will need to write your own subclass or purchase one.

Labels

Of course, if you put a text field or text area on the screen, you should probably tell your user what you expect him to enter. You may have noticed that there is no capability to associate a prompt directly with a text field or text area. Instead, with the AWT, you use a different user-interface class to create prompts: `Label`. The `Label` class contains three constructors, as shown in Table 5.9.

Table 5.9. Constructors for the `Label` class.

Constructor	Purpose
`Label()`	Creates a label without a name.
`Label(String)`	Creates a new label with the specified string.
`Label(String, int)`	Creates a new label using the specified string and alignment value.

The alignment values specify how the text on the label should appear. Your choices are `Label.LEFT`, `Label.RIGHT`, and `Label.CENTER`. The following two lines will create two new labels:

```
add(new Label("Social Security Number:", Label.RIGHT);
add(new Label("First Name:");
```

In addition to its constructors, the `Label` class provides the public methods shown in Table 5.10. Among other things, these methods enable you to change a label's text and alignment while the applet is running.

Table 5.10. Public methods of the `Label` class.

Method	Purpose
addNotify()	Creates a peer for the component.
getAlignment()	Returns the alignment value for the label.
getText()	Returns the text on the label.
paramString()	Returns a parameter string for the label.
setAlignment(int)	Sets the alignment value for the label.
setText(String)	Sets the text of the label to the specified string.

An Example

`LabelDemo` is an example that could be the front end of a database program that lets users search for people in the database by social security number or name. When first loaded, the applet is ready to search by social security number, as shown in Figure 5.9.

Figure 5.9.

Searching `LabelDemo` *by social security number.*

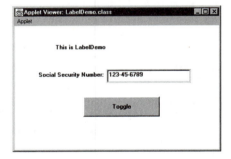

However, if the user doesn't know the social security number of the person he is searching for, he can select the Toggle button. This will change the search to a name search, as shown in Figure 5.10. The code for this applet is shown in Listing 5.4.

Figure 5.10.

In `LabelDemo`, *clicking the Toggle button enables you to search by name.*

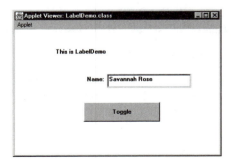

Listing 5.4. `LabelDemo.java`.

```
1:   import java.awt.*;
2:   import java.applet.*;
3:
4:   public class LabelDemo extends Applet {
5:       void toggleButton_Clicked(java.awt.event.ActionEvent
6:           event) {
7:           if(promptLabel.getText().equals("Name:"))
8:               promptLabel.setText("Social Security Number:");
9:           else
10:              promptLabel.setText("Name:");
11:      }
12:
13:      public void init() {
14:          // Call parents init method.
15:          super.init();
16:      }
17:
18:      public void addNotify() {
19:          // Call parents addNotify method.
20:          super.addNotify();
21:
22:          // This code is automatically generated by Visual Café
23:          // when you add components to the visual environment.
24:          // It instantiates and initializes the components. To
25:          // modify the code, only use code syntax that matches
26:          // what Visual Café can generate, or Visual Café may
27:          // be unable to back parse your Java file into its
28:          // visual environment.
29:          //{{INIT_CONTROLS
30:          setLayout(null);
31:          resize(426,266);
32:          label1 = new java.awt.Label("This is LabelDemo");
33:          label1.reshape(72,24,286,48);
34:          add(label1);
35:          promptLabel = new java.awt.Label(
36:              "Social Security Number:",Label.RIGHT);
37:          promptLabel.reshape(36,96,151,21);
38:          add(promptLabel);
39:          textField1 = new java.awt.TextField();
40:          textField1.reshape(192,96,175,29);
41:          add(textField1);
42:          toggleButton = new java.awt.Button("Toggle");
43:          toggleButton.reshape(144,156,158,41);
44:          add(toggleButton);
45:          //}}
46:
47:          //{{REGISTER_LISTENERS
48:          Action lAction = new Action();
49:          toggleButton.addActionListener(lAction);
50:          //}}
51:      }
52:
```

continues

5

Listing 5.4. continued

```
53:      //{{DECLARE_CONTROLS
54:      java.awt.Label label1;
55:      java.awt.Label promptLabel;
56:      java.awt.TextField textField1;
57:      java.awt.Button toggleButton;
58:      //}}
59:
60:      class Action implements java.awt.event.ActionListener {
61:          public void actionPerformed(java.awt.event.ActionEvent
62:              event) {
63:            Object object = event.getSource();
64:            if (object == toggleButton)
65:                toggleButton_Clicked(event);
66:        }
67:      }
68:  }
```

ANALYSIS Although most of the code in Listing 5.4 is typical of the code Visual Café generates, a couple key points are worth noticing. When promptLabel is constructed (lines 35–36), the parameter Label.RIGHT is specified. This right-justifies the label, as you can see in Figures 5.9 and 5.10. The toggleButton_Clicked method (lines 5–11) illustrates the use of setText and getText to manipulate the text of the labels.

TIP

> When working with labels, it is usually a good idea to use the Property List to set the Use Preferred Size property to true. This will automatically size the label to hold the label's text. Once Visual Café has resized the label, it will immediately reset the Use Preferred Size property to false.

Checkboxes and Checkbox Groups

Java checkboxes come in two varieties: grouped and ungrouped. Instances of the Java Checkbox classes are grouped using the CheckboxGroup class. If a checkbox group contains more than one checkbox, only one of the checkboxes in the group can be set at any given time. In other programming environments, you might be used to referring to grouped checkboxes as radio buttons. You can see an example of a checkbox group in Figure 5.11. The Male and Female buttons are grouped together and are therefore mutually exclusive.

Ungrouped checkboxes, on the other hand, can be checked or unchecked without regard to other checkboxes. In Figure 5.11, each of the sports is associated with an ungrouped checkbox because a user might need to mark more than one box.

Figure 5.11.

Grouped and ungrouped checkboxes in action.

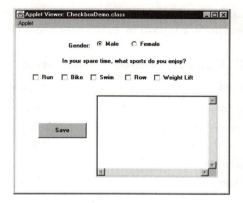

Visual Café simplifies the distinction between grouped and ungrouped checkboxes by including separate buttons on the Component palette for radio buttons and checkboxes. Selecting either item on the Component palette creates a new Checkbox object. However, when a radio button is dragged from the Component palette, it is automatically assigned to a checkbox group. All subsequent radio buttons are placed in this same group by default. This can be easily changed by entering a new value in the Property List for the desired radio buttons.

There are three constructors for the Checkbox class, as shown in Table 5.11. Only one of the constructors assigns the new Checkbox object to a checkbox group. The CheckboxGroup class has a single constructor that requires no parameters. The easiest way to assign a checkbox to a checkbox group is with the appropriate constructor. In the following code, a two-item group is created and then three ungrouped items are created:

```
CheckboxGroup genderGroup = new CheckboxGroup();
add(new Checkbox("Male",   genderGroup, false));
add(new Checkbox("Female", genderGroup, true));
add(new Checkbox("Option 1"));
add(new Checkbox("Option 2"));
add(new Checkbox("Option 3"));
```

Table 5.11. Constructors for the Checkbox class.

Constructor	Purpose
Checkbox()	Creates a checkbox without a label.
Checkbox(String)	Creates a checkbox using the specified string.
Checkbox(String, CheckboxGroup, boolean)	Creates a checkbox in the specified group, using the specified string and set to the specified default value.

In addition to their constructors, the Checkbox and CheckboxGroup classes offer additional public methods, as shown in Tables 5.12 and 5.13.

Table 5.12. Public methods of the Checkbox class.

Method	Purpose
addNotify()	Creates a peer for the component.
getCheckboxGroup()	Returns the checkbox group to which the checkbox belongs.
getLabel()	Returns the text on the checkbox.
getState()	Returns true if the checkbox is selected.
paramString()	Returns a parameter string for the checkbox.
setCheckboxGroup(CheckboxGroup)	Assigns the checkbox to the specified checkbox group.
setLabel(String)	Sets the text on the checkbox.
setState(boolean)	Checks or unchecks the checkbox.

Table 5.13. Public methods of the CheckboxGroup class.

Method	Purpose
getCurrent()	Returns the currently selected checkbox.
setCurrent(Checkbox)	Makes the specified checkbox the current selection for the group.
toString()	Returns a string showing the current values of the checkbox group. Useful for debugging.

An Example

For an example of using the Checkbox and CheckboxGroup classes, consider Figure 5.12, which shows the CheckboxDemo applet in action. The source code for this applet is shown in Listing 5.5.

5

Figure 5.12.

The results of the CheckboxDemo *applet.*

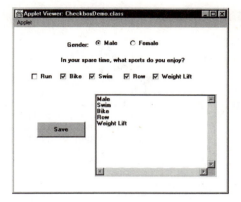

Listing 5.5. `CheckboxDemo.java.`

```
 1:  import java.awt.*;
 2:  import java.applet.*;
 3:
 4:  public class CheckboxDemo extends Applet {
 5:      void saveButton_Clicked(java.awt.event.ActionEvent
 6:          event) {
 7:          // clear the results area
 8:          results.setText("");
 9:
10:          // display the gender
11:          Checkbox current = genderGroup.getCurrent();
12:          results.appendText(current.getLabel() + "\r\n");
13:
14:          // check each of the sports
15:          if (swimCheckbox.getState() == true)
16:              results.appendText("Swim\r\n");
17:          if (bikeCheckbox.getState() == true)
18:              results.appendText("Bike\r\n");
19:          if (runCheckbox.getState() == true)
20:              results.appendText("Run\r\n");
21:          if (rowCheckbox.getState() == true)
22:              results.appendText("Row\r\n");
23:          if (weightCheckbox.getState() == true)
24:              results.appendText("Weight Lift\r\n");
25:      }
26:
27:      public void init() {
28:          // Call parents init method.
29:          super.init();
30:      }
31:
```

5

continues

Listing 5.5. continued

```
32:     public void addNotify() {
33:         // Call parents addNotify method.
34:          super.addNotify();
35:
36:         // This code is automatically generated by Visual Café
37:         // when you add components to the visual environment.
38:         // It instantiates and initializes the components. To
39:         // modify the code, only use code syntax that matches
40:         // what Visual Café can generate, or Visual Café may
41:         // be unable to back parse your Java file into its
42:         // visual environment.
43:         //{{INIT_CONTROLS
44:         setLayout(null);
45:         resize(442,354);
46:         label1 = new java.awt.Label("Gender:",Label.RIGHT);
47:         label1.reshape(72,24,84,28);
48:         add(label1);
49:         genderGroup = new CheckboxGroup();
50:         maleButton = new java.awt.Checkbox("Male",genderGroup,
51:             true);
52:         maleButton.reshape(168,24,58,21);
53:         add(maleButton);
54:         femaleButton = new java.awt.Checkbox("Female",
55:             genderGroup, false);
56:         femaleButton.reshape(240,24,71,21);
57:         add(femaleButton);
58:         label2 = new java.awt.Label(
59:            "In your spare time, what sports do you enjoy?");
60:         label2.reshape(84,60,272,21);
61:         add(label2);
62:         runCheckbox = new java.awt.Checkbox("Run");
63:         runCheckbox.reshape(36,96,54,21);
64:         add(runCheckbox);
65:         bikeCheckbox = new java.awt.Checkbox("Bike");
66:         bikeCheckbox.reshape(96,96,56,21);
67:         add(bikeCheckbox);
68:         swimCheckbox = new java.awt.Checkbox("Swim");
69:         swimCheckbox.reshape(156,96,60,21);
70:         add(swimCheckbox);
71:         rowCheckbox = new java.awt.Checkbox("Row");
72:         rowCheckbox.reshape(228,96,56,21);
73:         add(rowCheckbox);
74:         weightCheckbox = new java.awt.Checkbox("Weight Lift");
75:         weightCheckbox.reshape(288,96,93,21);
76:         add(weightCheckbox);
77:         saveButton = new java.awt.Button("Save");
78:         saveButton.reshape(48,204,100,33);
79:         add(saveButton);
80:         results = new java.awt.TextArea();
81:         results.reshape(180,144,246,198);
82:         add(results);
```

5

```
83:        //}}
84:
85:        //{{REGISTER_LISTENERS
86:        Action lAction = new Action();
87:        saveButton.addActionListener(lAction);
88:        //}}
89:    }
90:
91:    //{{DECLARE_CONTROLS
92:    java.awt.Label label1;
93:    java.awt.Checkbox maleButton;
94:    CheckboxGroup genderGroup;
95:    java.awt.Checkbox femaleButton;
96:    java.awt.Label label2;
97:    java.awt.Checkbox runCheckbox;
98:    java.awt.Checkbox bikeCheckbox;
99:    java.awt.Checkbox swimCheckbox;
100:    java.awt.Checkbox rowCheckbox;
101:    java.awt.Checkbox weightCheckbox;
102:    java.awt.Button saveButton;
103:    java.awt.TextArea results;
104:    //}}
105:
106:    class Action implements java.awt.event.ActionListener {
107:        public void actionPerformed(java.awt.event.ActionEvent
108:            event) {
109:          Object object = event.getSource();
110:          if (object == saveButton)
111:              saveButton_Clicked(event);
112:        }
113:    }
114: }
```

The `CheckboxDemo` applet can be created with the following steps:

1. Create a new applet named `CheckboxDemo`.

2. Drag a label component onto the Form Designer and set its `Text` property to `Gender`.

3. Add to the applet two `RadioButton` components from the Standard tab of the Component palette. Set their labels to `Male` and `Female` and their names to `maleButton` and `femaleButton`. Set the `Group` property for each to `genderGroup`. For `maleButton`, set the `State` property to `true`. (This selects male by default when the applet is started.)

4. Place a label on the applet prompting the user to select the sports he enjoys.

5. Add five `Checkbox` components, giving them the names `runCheckbox`, `bikeCheckbox`, `swimCheckbox`, `rowCheckbox`, and `weightCheckbox`. Assign each component an appropriate value for its `Label` property.

6. Add a Save button named `saveButton` and a text area named `results`.

7. Add a `click` event handler for `saveButton` and complete the `saveButton_Clicked` method as shown in Listing 5.5 (lines 5–25).

In `saveButton_Clicked` (lines 5–25), you can see how the currently selected gender radio button is identified (line 11) and its label is added to the `results` text area (line 12). For each of the checkboxes, `getState` is used to determine whether the checkbox is checked (lines 15–24).

A couple additional points are worth noticing about the code generated by Visual Café. The Male and Female radio buttons are constructed in lines 50–57. As you can see from these lines, even though you dragged a radio button component from the Component palette, what Visual Café constructs are two `Checkbox` objects. The only difference between these radio button checkboxes and normal checkboxes (such as used for the sports) is that the gender checkboxes are each assigned to the `genderGroup` checkbox group (lines 50–51 and 54–55).

Do	Don't

DON'T forget that checkboxes and radio buttons are really the same class (`java.awt.Checkbox`) at the AWT level.

DO remember to set the `Group` property whenever you want to create two or more radio button groups on the same form.

Lists and Choices

Checkboxes are not the only way to present options to your users. You can also use Java's `Choice` and `List` classes. In Java, a choice is a drop-down list from which the user may make a single selection. A list is a variable-sized region from which the user may select one or more items. Figure 5.13 shows a screen that makes use of a choice to gather a person's gender and a list of sports, similar to what was done with radio buttons and checkboxes in `CheckboxDemo`.

Figure 5.13.

A gender choice and a sports list.

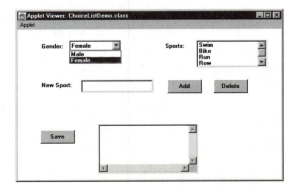

When you want to place a list or a choice onto an applet (or other Java container), you must take the following three steps:

1. Construct the new `List` or `Choice` object.
2. Add items to the `List` or `Choice` object.
3. Place the `List` or `Choice` object onto the applet.

TIP

When you place a list or choice onto a form in the Form Designer, Visual Café takes care of these steps for you.

The following code illustrates these steps in creating a new choice:

```
// create a Choice object
Choice genderChoice = new Choice();
// add items to the Choice
genderChoice.addItem("Male");
genderChoice.addItem("Female");
// then add the Choice to the applet
add(genderChoice);
```

The `Choice` class has only a single, no-parameter constructor. An object of the `List` class, however, can be created using either of the two constructors shown in Table 5.14. Usually you will use the second constructor in order to specify the number of visible rows and whether the user can select multiple items in the list.

Table 5.14. Constructors for the `List` class.

Constructor	Purpose
`List()`	Creates a new, empty list without any visible lines.
`List(int, boolean)`	Creates a new list with the specified number of visible lines. The `boolean` parameter specifies whether to allow multiple selections.

For an example of creating a new list and adding five items to it, consider the following:

```
// create a List object
List sportList = new List(5, true);

// add items to the List
sportList.addItem("Swim");
sportList.addItem("Bike");
sportList.addItem("Run");
sportList.addItem("Row");
sportList.addItem("Weight Lift");

// then add the List to the applet
add(sportList);
```

TIP

> You can add items to a list or choice by using the Property List to set
> the Items property. This property holds an array of strings that will be
> added to the object in the init method generated by Visual Café.

List and Choice **Public Methods**

Because of the many ways in which a user can interact with a list or a choice, these Java classes
include many public member methods. The public methods of List are shown in Table 5.15;
the public methods of Choice are shown in Table 5.16.

Table 5.15. Public methods of the List class.

Method	Purpose
addItem(String)	Adds the specified string to the bottom of the list.
addItem(String, int)	Adds the specified string at the specified index in the list.
addNotify()	Creates a peer for the component.
allowsMultipleSelection()	Returns true if the user can select multiple list items.
clear()	Removes all items from the list.
countItems()	Returns the quantity of items in the list.
delItem(int)	Deletes the item at the specified index.
delItems(int, int)	Deletes the specified range of items.
deselect(int)	Deselects the item at the specified index.
getItem(int)	Returns the item string at the specified index.
getRows()	Returns the number of visible rows.
getSelectedIndex()	Returns the index number of the selected item.
getSelectedIndexes()	Returns the index numbers of the selected items.
getSelectedItem()	Returns the item string of the selected item.
getSelectedItems()	Returns the item string of the selected items.
getVisibleIndex()	Returns the index of the last item passed to makeVisible.
isSelected(int)	Returns true if the specified item is selected.
makeVisible(int)	Makes the specified item visible in the list.

Method	Purpose
minimumSize(int)	Returns the minimum dimensions for a list with the specified number of rows.
minimumSize()	Returns the minimum dimensions for the list.
paramString()	Returns a parameter string for the list.
preferredSize(int)	Returns the preferred dimensions for a list with the specified number of rows.
preferredSize()	Returns the preferred dimensions for the list.
removeNotify()	Remove the list's peer.
replaceItem(String, int)	Replaces the item at the specified index with the specified string.
select(int)	Selects the specified item.
setMultipleSelection(boolean)	Enables or disables the selection of multiple items in the list.

Table 5.16. Public methods of the Choice class.

Method	Purpose
addItem(String)	Adds the specified string to the bottom of the choice.
addNotify()	Creates a peer for the component.
countItems()	Returns the quantity of items in the choice.
getItem(int)	Returns the item string at the specified index.
getSelectedIndex()	Returns the index number of the selected item.
getSelectedItem()	Returns the item string of the selected item.
paramString()	Returns a parameter string for the choice.
select(int)	Selects the specified item.
select(String)	Selects the specified string in the choice.

5

An Example

To illustrate the use of the List and Choice classes and some of their public member methods, consider the applet ChoiceListDemo, shown in Listing 5.6. This example creates the applet window shown in Figure 5.13.

Listing 5.6. `ChoiceListDemo.java.`

```
1:    import java.awt.*;
2:    import java.applet.*;
3:
4:    public class ChoiceListDemo extends Applet {
5:        void saveButton_Clicked(java.awt.event.ActionEvent event){
6:            // clear the results area
7:            results.setText("");
8:
9:            // display the gender
10:           String gender = genderChoice.getSelectedItem();
11:           results.appendText(gender + "\r\n");
12:
13:           for(int i=0;i<sportList.countItems();i++) {
14:               if(sportList.isSelected(i))
15:                   results.appendText(sportList.getItem(i)+"\r\n");
16:           }
17:       }
18:
19:       void deleteButton_Clicked(java.awt.event.ActionEvent
20:               event) {
21:           for(int i=sportList.countItems()-1; i>=0; i--) {
22:               if(sportList.isSelected(i))
23:                   sportList.delItem(i);
24:           }
25:       }
26:
27:       void addButton_Clicked(java.awt.event.ActionEvent event) {
28:           String sport = newSport.getText();
29:           if(sport.length() > 0) {
30:               sportList.addItem(sport);
31:               newSport.setText("");
32:           }
33:       }
34:
35:       public void init() {
36:           // Call parents init method.
37:           super.init();
38:       }
39:
40:       public void addNotify() {
41:           // Call parents addNotify method.
42:           super.addNotify();
43:
44:           // This code is automatically generated by Visual Café
45:           // when you add components to the visual environment.
46:           // It instantiates and initializes the components. To
47:           // modify the code, only use code syntax that matches
48:           // what Visual Café can generate, or Visual Café may
49:           // be unable to back parse your Java file into its
50:           // visual environment.
51:           //{{INIT_CONTROLS
52:           setLayout(null);
53:           resize(549,322);
54:           sportList = new java.awt.List(0,true);
```

5

```
55:            sportList.addItem("Swim");
56:            sportList.addItem("Bike");
57:            sportList.addItem("Run");
58:            sportList.addItem("Row");
59:            sportList.addItem("Weight Lift");
60:            add(sportList);
61:            sportList.reshape(372,24,147,58);
62:            genderChoice = new java.awt.Choice();
63:            genderChoice.addItem("Male");
64:            genderChoice.addItem("Female");
65:            try {
66:               genderChoice.select(1);
67:            } catch (IllegalArgumentException e) {
68:            }
69:            add(genderChoice);
70:            genderChoice.reshape(108,24,108,21);
71:            label1 = new java.awt.Label("Gender:",Label.RIGHT);
72:            label1.reshape(24,24,72,24);
73:            add(label1);
74:            label2 = new java.awt.Label("Sports:",Label.RIGHT);
75:            label2.reshape(276,24,72,24);
76:            add(label2);
77:            label3 = new java.awt.Label("New Sport:",Label.RIGHT);
78:            label3.reshape(36,108,78,21);
79:            add(label3);
80:            newSport = new java.awt.TextField();
81:            newSport.reshape(132,108,150,27);
82:            add(newSport);
83:            addButton = new java.awt.Button("Add");
84:            addButton.reshape(312,108,71,29);
85:            add(addButton);
86:            deleteButton = new java.awt.Button("Delete");
87:            deleteButton.reshape(408,108,71,29);
88:            add(deleteButton);
89:            saveButton = new java.awt.Button("Save");
90:            saveButton.reshape(48,216,71,29);
91:            add(saveButton);
92:            results = new java.awt.TextArea();
93:            results.reshape(168,204,207,106);
94:            add(results);
95:            //}}
96:
97:            //{{REGISTER_LISTENERS
98:            Action lAction = new Action();
99:            saveButton.addActionListener(lAction);
100:           deleteButton.addActionListener(lAction);
101:           addButton.addActionListener(lAction);
102:           //}}
103:        }
104:
105:     //{{DECLARE_CONTROLS
106:     java.awt.List sportList;
107:     java.awt.Choice genderChoice;
108:     java.awt.Label label1;
109:     java.awt.Label label2;
```

continues

Listing 5.6. continued

```
110:      java.awt.Label label3;
111:      java.awt.TextField newSport;
112:      java.awt.Button addButton;
113:      java.awt.Button deleteButton;
114:      java.awt.Button saveButton;
115:      java.awt.TextArea results;
116:      //}}
117:
118:      class Action implements java.awt.event.ActionListener {
119:          public void actionPerformed(java.awt.event.ActionEvent
120:                  event) {
121:              Object object = event.getSource();
122:              if (object == saveButton)
123:                  saveButton_Clicked(event);
124:              else if (object == deleteButton)
125:                  deleteButton_Clicked(event);
126:              else if (object == addButton)
127:                  addButton_Clicked(event);
128:          }
129:      }
130: }
```

ANALYSIS   In the addNotify method, when the List object sportList is created (lines 54–59), you can see that Visual Café has generated code using addItem to fill the list. The items added in these lines are the result of setting the Items property for the list in the Property List. Similarly, the genderChoice Choice object is constructed, and addItem is used to fill the list with values (lines 62–64). You should also notice that the constructor for sportList (line 54) was passed true as the second parameter. This will allow multiple selections to be made in the list and is the result of setting the list's Multiple Selection property to true.

If the Save button is clicked, the saveButton_Clicked method is called. This method clears the results text area and then uses genderChoice.getSelectedItem to create a string indicating whether Male or Female was selected (line 10). This string is written to the results text area (line 11). Next, the code loops through the items in sportList (lines 13–16). For each selected item that is found, the getItem method is used to retrieve the text of the selected item. This text is also added to results.

If the Add button is clicked, the text in the newSport text field is retrieved (line 28). If this text field is not empty, sportList.addItem is used to add the new sport to the bottom of the list (line 30).

Finally, if the Delete button is clicked, the code loops through sportList using delItem to delete any selected items (lines 21–24). Note that the loop counts down from sportList.countItems()-1 to 0. To have counted up would have possibly caused invalid numbers to be passed to delItem. The result of ChoiceListDemo after having added and deleted a few items is shown in Figure 5.14.

Figure 5.14.

The ChoiceListDemo *applet after adding and deleting some sports.*

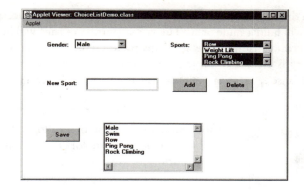

Scrollbars

Scrollbars can be used to satisfy a number of user-interface goals. They are used on windows and List components to indicate that there is more to the object than meets the eye. They can also be used to allow a user to select a value from a range of values. For example, if you were designing a user interface that represented a home thermostat, a scrollbar would be an excellent choice. In Java, scrollbars can be created by using the Scrollbar class. The constructors for this class are shown in Table 5.17.

Table 5.17. Constructors for the Scrollbar class.

Constructor	Purpose
Scrollbar()	Creates a vertical scrollbar.
Scrollbar(int)	Creates a scrollbar in the specified orientation.
Scrollbar(int,int,int,int,int)	Creates a scrollbar with the specified orientation, initial value, visible area, and minimum and maximum values.

As you can see from Table 5.17, it is possible to construct a scrollbar in more than one screen orientation. The values Scrollbar.HORIZONTAL and Scrollbar.VERTICAL are defined in java.awt.Scrollbar. By default, a scrollbar will be positioned vertically. To create scrollbars using these constructors, consider the following examples:

```
Scrollbar bar1 = new Scrollbar(Scrollbar.HORIZONTAL, 50, 10, 0, 100);

Scrollbar bar2 = new Scrollbar();

Scrollbar bar3 = new Scrollbar(Scrollbar.VERTICAL);
```

5

In this case, bar1 is created as a horizontal bar that can accept values from 0 to 100. Initially, it will hold a value of 50. The visible portion of bar1 will be 10. In the second example, bar2 is created using the default constructor, which means it will be oriented vertically. Finally, bar3 is created using the constructor that requires only a parameter for the orientation. Because Scrollbar.VERTICAL is passed, a vertical scrollbar will be created.

 TIP

> To streamline the creation of scrollbars, Visual Café includes a button on the Component palette for creating a horizontal scrollbar and a separate button for creating a vertical scrollbar. In both cases, a Scrollbar object is created; however, the Orientation property is set to the proper value.

The Scrollbar class offers a number of public methods. They are shown in Table 5.18.

Table 5.18. Public methods of the Scrollbar class.

Method	Purpose
addNotify()	Creates a peer for the component.
getLineIncrement()	Returns the amount by which the scrollbar will change when moving one line.
getMaximum()	Returns the maximum value for the scrollbar.
getMinimum()	Returns the minimum value for the scrollbar.
getOrientation()	Returns the orientation of the scrollbar.
getPageIncrement()	Returns the amount by which the scrollbar will change value when moving by a page.
getValue()	Returns the current value of the scrollbar.
getVisible()	Returns a value indicating how much of the scrollbar is visible.
paramString()	Returns a parameter string for the choice.
setLineIncrement()	Sets the amount by which to change the current value when moving one line.
setPageIncrement()	Sets the amount by which to change the current value when moving one page.
setValue()	Sets the current value of the scrollbar.
setValues(int,int,int,int)	Sets the current value, visible amount, and minimum and maximum values of the scrollbar.

An Example

As an example of using the `Scrollbar` class in the user interface of an applet, consider `ScrollbarDemo`, shown in Listing 5.7. In this example, the user is asked to enter his score for a round of golf using a horizontal scrollbar. The scrollbar is associated with a read-only text field that displays the value of the scrollbar. This is shown in Figure 5.15.

Listing 5.7. `ScrollbarDemo.java.`

```
1:  import java.awt.*;
2:  import java.applet.*;
3:
4:  public class ScrollbarDemo extends Applet {
5:      void scoreBar_AdjustmentValueChanged(
6:              java.awt.event.AdjustmentEvent event) {
7:          int value = scoreBar.getValue();
8:          String str = String.valueOf(value);
9:
10:         score.setText(str);
11:     }
12:
13:     public void init() {
14:         // Call parents init method.
15:         super.init();
16:
17:         // put the value in the scrollbar into the text field
18:         score.setText(String.valueOf(scoreBar.getValue()));
19:     }
20:
21:     public void addNotify() {
22:         // Call parents addNotify method.
23:         super.addNotify();
24:
25:         // This code is automatically generated by Visual Café
26:         // when you add components to the visual environment.
27:         // It instantiates and initializes the components. To
28:         // modify the code, only use code syntax that matches
29:         // what Visual Café can generate, or Visual Café may
30:         // be unable to back parse your Java file into its
31:         // visual environment.
32:         //{{INIT_CONTROLS
33:         setLayout(null);
34:         resize(426,266);
35:         label1 = new java.awt.Label("Score:",Label.RIGHT);
36:         label1.reshape(36,36,60,21);
37:         add(label1);
38:         score = new java.awt.TextField();
39:         score.setEditable(false);
40:         score.reshape(108,36,48,23);
41:         add(score);
42:         scoreBar=new java.awt.Scrollbar(Scrollbar.HORIZONTAL,
43:                 72,10,50,120);
```

continues

Listing 5.7. continued

```
44:        scoreBar.reshape(180,36,137,26);
45:        add(scoreBar);
46:        //}}
47:
48:        //{{REGISTER_LISTENERS
49:        Adjustment lAdjustment = new Adjustment();
50:        scoreBar.addAdjustmentListener(lAdjustment);
51:        //}}
52:    }
53:
54:    //{{DECLARE_CONTROLS
55:    java.awt.Label label1;
56:    java.awt.TextField score;
57:    java.awt.Scrollbar scoreBar;
58:    //}}
59:
60:    class Adjustment implements
61:            java.awt.event.AdjustmentListener {
62:        public void adjustmentValueChanged(
63:                java.awt.event.AdjustmentEvent event) {
64:            Object object = event.getSource();
65:            if (object == scoreBar)
66:                scoreBar_AdjustmentValueChanged(event);
67:        }
68:    }
69: }
```

Figure 5.15.

Entering a golf score of 79 in the ScrollbarDemo *applet.*

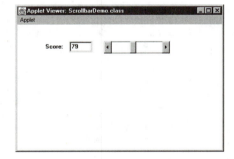

ANALYSIS In ScrollbarDemo, the member variable scoreBar is used to represent the scrollbar. Its constructor (lines 42–43) specifies horizontal alignment, an initial value of 72, a visible region of 10, a minimum value of 50, and a maximum value of 120. The scrollbar is oriented horizontally because the horizontal scrollbar icon was selected on the Component palette. The initial value, visible region, minimum value, and maximum value were all established by setting properties in the Property List.

5

The text field score is created on line 38 and made read-only on line 39. It is made read-only to prevent the user from entering a score other than by using the scrollbar. At the end of the init method, the text field is set to display the current value of the scrollbar (line 18).

The event handling in this example is a little different from other examples in this chapter. Because scrollbars generate different events than do the other AWT components, the listener class (lines 60–68) implements the AdjustListener interface.

Summary

This chapter covers a lot of territory. Along the way you learned that the Component class is the base class for many of the Java user-interface classes. You learned about the Button, TextField, TextArea, Label, Checkbox, List, Choice, and Scrollbar classes and how you can use them to create an applet's user interface.

Q&A

Q If a text field can only have one row, why does the Form Designer let me draw it tall enough to hold multiple rows?

A Because the Form Designer has no way of knowing what font sizes will be used (this isn't known until the program is running on the user's machine), it allows you to draw a text field of whatever size you want.

Q I've heard a lot of people complain that the AWT is insufficient for writing user interfaces. Is this true?

A While the AWT is definitely less powerful than similar native frameworks such as the Microsoft Foundation Classes for Windows, it is sufficient for many programs. You probably noticed that the AWT is missing many of the user-interface components found in today's state-of-the-art programs. For example, there is no direct way to create tabbed dialog boxes or image lists with the AWT. However, components that provide these features are included in Visual Café's Object Library and are available from other third-party vendors. Also, remember that using the AWT is not an all-or-nothing proposition. You can freely mix AWT components with components from Java tool vendors.

Workshop

The workshop includes quiz questions to help you gauge your understanding of the material in this chapter. The workshop also includes exercises to provide hands-on experience with what you've learned in this chapter. You can find the answers in Appendix D, "Answers."

Quiz

1. Explain the concepts of *toolkit* and *peer*.

2. What is the difference between a text field and a text area?

3. What is the `TextComponent` class used for?

4. How would you create a `Label` that is right-aligned?

5. What is another name for a grouped checkbox?

6. What extra steps must be taken to create a radio button instead of a checkbox?

7. How many items can be simultaneously selected in a `Choice` object?

8. How many items can be simultaneously selected in a `List` object?

9. What purpose does the page-increment value serve in the `Scrollbar` class?

Exercises

1. Write an applet that includes a list, a checkbox, a button, and a text area. Use the checkbox to toggle whether the list allows multiple selections. When the button is clicked, write a message to the text area indicating whether the list currently allows multiple selections and then list all selections.

2. Write a user interface that includes a group of radio buttons labeled `English`, `Spanish`, and `French`. Have a button on the applet that says `Exit` when English is selected, `Adios` when Spanish is selected, and `Adieu` when French is selected.

3. Write an applet that uses a scrollbar to grade college students. When the value in the scrollbar is below 50, have a text field say `F`; when it's between 51–70, have it say `D`; when it's between 71–80, have it say `C`; when it's between 81–90, have it say `B`; and when it's above 90, have it say `A`.

Day 6

Debugging, Customizing, and Managing Projects

In this chapter, you will learn about the Visual Café debugger and how it can save you time by allowing you to inspect variables, set conditional and nonconditional breakpoints, debug multiple threads, and step through your code line by line. You will learn how to customize Visual Café by creating and defining your own workspaces. You will also learn about many other tools that are included with Visual Café. You will learn about the Class browser, the Hierarchy editor, and Visual Café's project-management tools.

The Debugger

Writing a program is very simple. Writing a bug-free program is very difficult. To assist in writing bug-free programs, Visual Café includes a state-of-the-art debugger. Among other things, the Visual Café debugger allows you to perform the following tasks:

☐ Inspect the values of program variables

☐ Set conditional and nonconditional breakpoints to stop execution of the program

☐ Set watches on variables to easily monitor changes in value

☐ View the call stack

☐ Debug multiple threads

An example of the debugger in action is shown in Figure 6.1. In this figure, you can see the Variables, Calls, Breakpoints, Watch, and Threads windows. The use of each of these windows is described in the following sections.

Figure 6.1.

Viewing the Visual Café debugger.

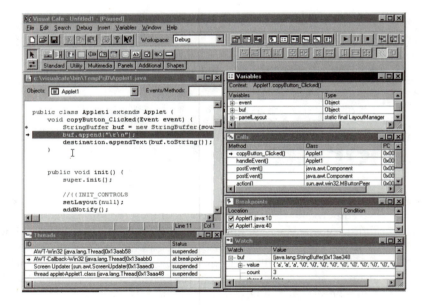

Setting Breakpoints

Breakpoints can be set on individual lines of code and act as instructions to the debugger to stop execution at the breakpoint. Breakpoints are useful because they allow the debugger to run the program at near full speed until it gets close to the code in which you suspect a bug might be present.

NEW TERM A *breakpoint* is a line of code that will stop the execution of the debugger.

Before you set a breakpoint, position the cursor into the desired source code line. You then have three options for setting the actual breakpoint:

☐ Click the right mouse button to display a context menu and then select Set Breakpoint.

☐ Select Set Breakpoint from the Source menu.

☐ Press the F9 button.

TIP

> If you try to set a breakpoint on a line and Visual Café appears to be ignoring you, it is because you are trying to set a breakpoint on a nonexecutable line.

The Edit window will indicate that a breakpoint has been set by putting a small red diamond in the left margin, as shown in Figure 6.2. Additionally, a new row will be added to the Breakpoints window that shows the name of the class and the line number on which the breakpoint was set.

Figure 6.2.

A small red diamond in the left margin indicates the presence of a breakpoint.

```
c:\source\chap06\DebugApplet\DebugApplet.java                          _ □ X

Objects: [  DebugApplet          ▼]   Events/Methods: [                    ▼]

public class DebugApplet extends Applet {
    int lineNumber = 0;

    void copyButton_Clicked(Event event) {
        lineNumber++;
        StringBuffer buf = new StringBuffer(source.getText());
        buf.append("\r\n");
        destination.appendText(String.valueOf(lineNumber) + " ");
        destination.appendText(buf.toString());
    }


    public void init() {
        super.init();
                                                          Line 18    Col 1
```

6

To remove a breakpoint, simply repeat the process by which you added it. A breakpoint can be removed in the following ways:

☐ Click the right mouse button to display a context menu and then select Clear Breakpoint.

☐ Select Clear Breakpoint from the Source menu.

☐ Press the F9 button.

Conditional Breakpoints

A breakpoint is great—every time the program encounters that line of code, it will stop. Sometimes, however, your bugs don't cooperate, and you have one that occurs only after a method has executed 100 times or when a variable is equal to some specific value. It would be terribly inconvenient to hit a breakpoint 99 times before getting to the case you really want to examine. Fortunately, the Visual Café debugger supports conditional breakpoints.

 A *conditional breakpoint* is a line of code that will stop the execution of the debugger if a specified condition is true.

To set a conditional breakpoint, position the cursor on the desired line of code and select Set Conditional Breakpoint from the Source menu. You will be presented with the Conditional Breakpoint dialog, which is shown in Figure 6.3.

Figure 6.3.

Conditional breakpoints stop execution when an expression is true.

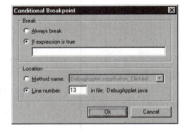

In the Conditional Breakpoint dialog box, you can specify an expression that will be evaluated whenever the breakpoint is hit. If the expression evaluates to true, the debugger will stop execution at the breakpoint. Otherwise, it will skip over the breakpoint, and execution will continue. As an example, suppose you are debugging the code in Listing 6.1.

Listing 6.1. A method to be debugged.

```
1:    int lineNumber = 0;
2:
3:    void copyButton_Clicked(java.awt.event.ActionEvent event) {
4:        lineNumber++;
5:        StringBuffer buf = new StringBuffer(source.getText());
6:        buf.append("\r\n");
7:        destination.appendText(String.valueOf(lineNumber) + " ");
8:        destination.appendText(buf.toString());
9:    }
```

You suspect there is a bug in the `copyButton_Clicked` method, but it only happens after the method is called 20 times. You could track the bug down by setting a breakpoint and then telling the debugger to continue running each of the 20 times the breakpoint in encountered. Or you could set a conditional breakpoint with an expression that will only evaluate to `true` after 20 calls to the method. To do the latter, place the cursor on line 4 of Listing 6.1, display the Conditional Breakpoint dialog box by selecting Set Conditional Breakpoint from the Source menu, and enter `lineNumber > 19` as the expression to evaluate. This is shown in Figure 6.4.

Figure 6.4.

A conditional breakpoint that will stop execution after 19 calls to this method.

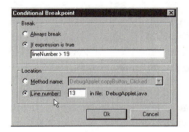

The next time you run the program, this expression will be `false`, and the debugger will skip over the breakpoint the first 19 times it is encountered. On subsequent encounters, however, the expression will be `true`, and the debugger will stop execution.

Disabling Breakpoints

Sometimes you want to temporarily disable a breakpoint without clearing it. To temporarily disable a breakpoint, activate the Breakpoints window, select the breakpoint you want to disable, and select Disable from the context menu. Enabled breakpoints appear in the Breakpoints window with a small checkmark in the left column. When a breakpoint is disabled, the checkmark is removed. This is shown in Figure 6.5.

Figure 6.5.

Enabled breakpoints have a checkmark to their left in the Breakpoints window; disabled breakpoints do not.

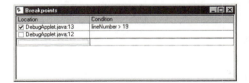

Similarly, disabled breakpoints are shown in the Edit window with an outline of a diamond (instead of a solid diamond) in the leftmost column.

TIP

> The Context menu for the Breakpoints window also includes selections that will disable all breakpoints, enable the selected breakpoint, and enable all breakpoints. You can also enable or disable a breakpoint by clicking the outline square in the Breakpoints window where the checkmark appears. This toggles a breakpoint between enabled and disabled.

Controlling Program Execution

To start debugging a Visual Café project, load the project into memory and then select Run in Debugger from the Project menu. (Alternatively, you can press the F5 key.) This starts the Visual Café debugger, and your program will begin to execute. When executing, a program will continue to run until it encounters a breakpoint or you tell it to stop.

After an executing program has stopped, you have the option of stepping through it a line at a time. The easiest way to control a stopped program is with the Debug toolbar. This toolbar, shown in Figure 6.6, contains buttons that perform the following actions:

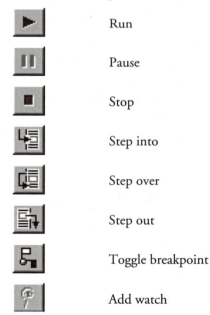

Run

Pause

Stop

Step into

Step over

Step out

Toggle breakpoint

Add watch

The Run button instructs Visual Café to begin executing the program again until it encounters the next breakpoint. The Pause button temporarily suspends execution of the program; Stop terminates the current debugging session. The Step Into, Over, and Out buttons advance the debugger through the source code, but by different amounts. The Toggle Breakpoint button is another way of setting an unconditional breakpoint on a line. The Add Watch button allows you to establish a watch on a variable. The usefulness of watching variables is described in the section "Examining Variables," later in this chapter.

Figure 6.6.
The Debug toolbar.

Stepping In, Over, and Out

When you are debugging a method, there may be times when you are on a line of code that calls another method and you're not sure whether the bug you're after is in the method you're currently in or in the method that is about to be called. If you suspect the bug might be in the method about to be called, you can *step into* that method. If it is unlikely that the bug is in that method, you can *step over* that method call.

For example, suppose you have written the applet shown in Figure 6.7. This applet allows a user to enter text in the text field, click the Copy button, and have the text moved to the text area at the bottom. Each piece of text should be sequentially numbered and appear on its own line. Unfortunately, there's a bug in the applet, the result of which is shown in Figure 6.8.

Figure 6.7.
The Copy button copies text from the top field to the bottom and numbers each line.

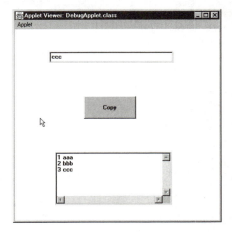

Figure 6.8.

Text should be appearing on separate lines.

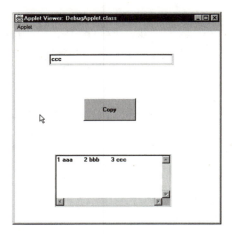

The complete code for this buggy applet is shown in Listing 6.2. You suspect there might be a bug in copyButton_Clicked, so you set a breakpoint on line 10 and start the program. The debugger will stop execution of the program when it hits line 10. At this point, you can step over line 10. Line 14 calls the StringBuffer constructor and the getText method of a TextField. Because these methods are part of standard Java, the best guess is that they work fine, so you step over line 14.

Listing 6.2. Code can be stepped into, over, or out of.

```
1:      import java.awt.*;
2:      import java.applet.*;
3:
4:      public class DebugApplet extends Applet {
5:          int lineNumber = 0;
6:
7:          void AddNewLine(StringBuffer buf) {
8:              buf.append("\t");
9:          }
10:
11:         void copyButton_Clicked(java.awt.event.ActionEvent
12:                 event) {
13:             lineNumber++;
14:             StringBuffer buf = new StringBuffer(source.getText());
15:             AddNewLine(buf);
16:             dest.appendText(String.valueOf(lineNumber) + " ");
17:             dest.appendText(buf.toString());
18:         }
19:
20:         public void init() {
21:             // Call parents init method.
22:             super.init();
23:         }
24:
25:         public void addNotify() {
```

```
26:        // Call parents addNotify method.
27:        super.addNotify();
28:
29:        // This code is automatically generated by Visual Café
30:        // when you add components to the visual environment.
31:        // It instantiates and initializes the components. To
32:        // modify the code, only use code syntax that matches
33:        // what Visual Cafe can generate, or Visual Cafe may
34:        // be unable to back parse your Java file into its
35:        // visual environment.
36:        //{{INIT_CONTROLS
37:        setLayout(null);
38:        resize(426,409);
39:        copyButton = new java.awt.Button("Copy");
40:        copyButton.reshape(144,144,108,48);
41:        add(copyButton);
42:        dest = new java.awt.TextArea();
43:        dest.reshape(84,264,242,113);
44:        add(dest);
45:        source = new java.awt.TextField();
46:        source.reshape(72,48,258,24);
47:        add(source);
48:        //}}
49:
50:        //{{REGISTER_LISTENERS
51:        Action lAction = new Action();
52:        copyButton.addActionListener(lAction);
53:        //}}
54:    }
55:
56:    //{{DECLARE_CONTROLS
57:    java.awt.Button copyButton;
58:    java.awt.TextArea dest;
59:    java.awt.TextField source;
60:    //}}
61:
62:    class Action implements java.awt.event.ActionListener {
63:        public void actionPerformed(java.awt.event.ActionEvent
64:            event) {
65:            Object object = event.getSource();
66:            if (object == copyButton)
67:                copyButton_Clicked(event);
68:        }
69:    }
70: }
```

ANALYSIS Line 15 calls the AddNewLine method (lines 7–9) that you wrote. This method is supposed to add \r\n to each line. Because this method is a likely candidate for the bug you're pursuing, you click the Step Into button on line 15. This causes the debugger to move to line 7, and you find the bug. (AddNewLine is appending a tab character, \t, instead of a carriage return and new line, \r\n.)

The Step Out command is useful when you are debugging a method you no longer want to debug. Suppose you've corrected the AddNewLine method to appear as follows:

```
void AddNewLine(StringBuffer buf)
{
    buf.append("\r");
    buf.append("\n");
}
```

Further, suppose that while debugging, you've stepped into AddNewLine and are on the line buf.append("\r"). After you notice that AddNewLine is adding both \r and \n, there is no point in stepping through the method. You can click the Step Out button, which tells the debugger to finish executing the code in the current method but stop execution on the next line in the method that called this one. In this example, stepping out of AddNewLine advances the debugger to line 16 of Listing 6.2.

Examining Variables

There are two ways you can look at variables in the Visual Café debugger. The first is through the Variables window. This window automatically includes information about every variable used in the method currently being debugged. An example of the Variables window debugging the AddNewLine method is shown in Figure 6.9.

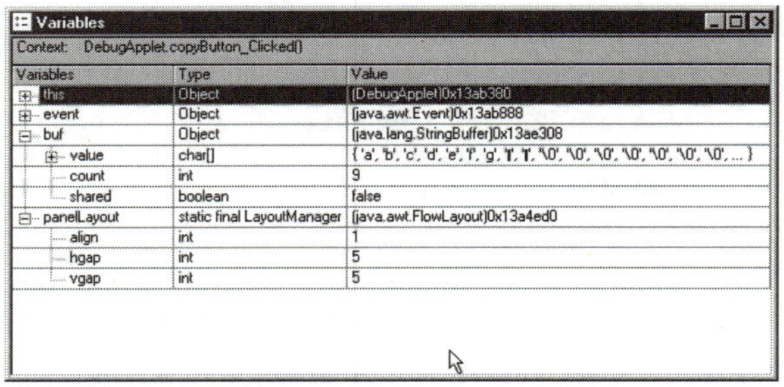

Figure 6.9.

The Variables window shows detailed information about each variable in a method.

Although the Variables window gives a nice overview of all the variables in a method, the more concise Watch window is frequently more useful. To add a variable to the Watch window, position the cursor over the variable name in a source code window, click the right mouse button to display the context menu, and select Add Watch. A sample Watch window is shown in Figure 6.10.

TIP

In addition to the Watch and Variables windows, Visual Café provides a third alternative for inspecting the value of a variable. If you position the mouse pointer over a variable name in an Edit window, a small window will appear adjacent to the mouse pointer. The value of the variable will be temporarily displayed in this window.

Figure 6.10.

The Watch window shows a more concise view of specific variables.

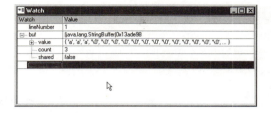

 TIP

In either the Variables window or the Watch window, you can edit the value of a variable. To do so, click on the line containing the variable you want to edit, press the Tab key to move to the value column, and then enter the desired value. There are many times when changing the value of a variable in the debugger can be useful. For example, if you suspect you have accidentally set a variable to the wrong value, you can change it in the debugger and then continue running the program.

Examining the Call Stack

Sometimes, the most important thing to know is the order in which methods were called. For example, if you have a method named ReadStringFromFile, it is probably a low-level method that is called from more than one place in your program. When debugging this method, it might be useful to know which method called it. This information can be found by examining the Calls window.

The Calls window shows the names of the most recently called methods. The currently executing method is shown at the top of the list. Figure 6.11 shows the Calls window as it would appear if you were debugging the AddNewLine method of Listing 6.2. As you can see, AddNewLine is at the top of the stack. Just below it is copyButton_Clicked, indicating that copyButton_Clicked called AddNewLine. As the program completes the execution of a method, that method is removed from the call stack; so when AddNewLine completes, copyButton_Clicked will be at the top of the Calls window.

6

Figure 6.11.

Viewing the call stack.

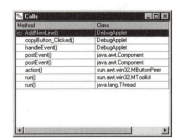

Debugging Threads

Because a Java program can contain multiple threads of execution, it is important that you be able to debug the various threads of your program. This is accomplished in the Visual Café debugger through the Threads window (see Figure 6.12).

Figure 6.12.

Viewing a program's threads.

In the Threads window, the thread you are currently debugging is indicated with an arrow to its left. In Figure 6-O¢, this arrow is adjacent to the `AWT-Callback-Win32` thread. As you can see in Figure 6.12, you are shown the status of each thread. You can suspend or resume threads by using the Threads window's context menu.

For details on using threads, see Chapter 14, "Multithreading."

Do	**Don't**

DO use conditional breakpoints to speed up the debugging process.

DO set watches instead of relying on the Variables window for variables you are particularly interested in.

DON'T rely on the debugger instead of your brain. You should never use the debugger instead of taking a few moments to thoroughly think through your code before executing it.

Customizing Visual Café

There is no way for a single development tool to be the right tool for every programmer. Symantec knew this when it designed Visual Café; therefore, Visual Café was built with customization options that allow you to turn it into just the tool you want. In this section, you will learn about some of the features and tools that let you customize Visual Café.

Understanding Workspaces

If you have been following the debugger examples in this chapter, you might have noticed that as soon as you started the debugger, Visual Café closed many of your open windows and opened a new set of windows for you. This is because Visual Café includes a Debug workspace that is loaded whenever you start debugging.

A *workspace* is a collection of windows, window locations, window sizes, and other environment options that can be saved, edited, and restored.

By default, your Visual Café installation should include two workspaces: Edit and Debug.

Creating a Workspace

To create a new workspace, select New from the Window | Workspaces menu. You will be presented with the New Workspace dialog box, as shown in Figure 6.13. Enter a descriptive name and click OK. You have just created a new workspace based on your currently open windows.

Figure 6.13.

Creating a new workspace.

 TIP

> The Window | Workspaces menu also includes options to delete or rename workspaces.

Selecting a Workspace

To select a different workspace, you have two options:

☐ Select Workspaces from the Window menu. This will display a submenu with each of the workspaces. Select the desired workspace, and it will be loaded.

☐ Select the desired workspace from the Workspaces listbox on the toolbar.

As an experiment, try selecting the Debug workspace. You should see some of the familiar debug windows appear. Next, select the workspace you created. This will restore that workspace; the windows of that workspace will be restored and repositioned.

 NOTE

> Workspaces are independent of Visual Café projects. If you create a new workspace, it will be immediately available to any project you load.

Customizing Your Environment

Visual Café allows a tremendous amount of customization through the Environment Options item in the File menu. The purposes of the seven tabs in the Environment Options dialog are listed in Table 6.1.

Table 6.1. The tabs of the Environment Options dialog.

Tab	Purpose
General	Configure what Visual Café should do at startup (load the last project or create a new project), indicate whether the Debug workspace should be loaded when debugging, specify source code directories and help filenames.
Format	Indicate how source should be formatted, including tab spacing, automatic indentation, and keyword highlighting.
Keyboard	Assign commands to keyboard shortcuts.
Display	Configure fonts and colors for each of Visual Café's windows.
Backup	Configure automatic backup and save options, establish how many levels of actions can be undone.
Editing	Configure the appearance and behavior of source code windows, the Class Browser, and the Hierarchy editor. (The Class Browser and Hierarchy editor are described later in this chapter.)
Component Palette	Allows you to customize which components are displayed on the Component palette.

Configuring the Component Palette

The Component Palette tab of the Environment Options dialog, shown in Figure 6.14, allows you to specify which components appear on the Component palette. In this dialog, you can assign components to existing tabs of the Component palette, or you can create your own Component Palette tabs and add components to them.

Figure 6.14.

The Component Palette tab is used to specify which components are available on the Component palette.

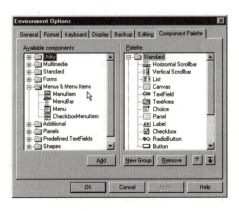

To add a new tab, select the New Group button. A new group will be added and the cursor positioned so that you are ready to type a name for the group. To add components to a group, either highlight the component in the left list and click the Add button, or drag the component from the left list to the right. Components can be removed from a group by selecting the component and clicking the Remove button. The component remains available to be placed in another group.

TIP

> You can also add your own components to the Component palette. Chapter 22, "Reusable Packages, Forms, and Projects," addresses this topic.

Dockable Toolbars

Each of the Visual Café toolbars is a docking toolbar.

 NEW TERM A *docking toolbar* is a toolbar that can be positioned beneath the program's menu bar in its *docked* position or that can be moved around the desktop as a free-floating window.

If you don't like the location of one of the toolbars, you can drag it from its current position and create a free-floating toolbar. You can also control which toolbars are visible by right-clicking the toolbars and selecting the desired toolbars.

Managing Visual Café Projects

Visual Café allows you to set a variety of project options by selecting Options from the Project menu. This displays the Project Options dialog, shown in Figure 6.15, which contains four tabs of project information. The Project tab allows you to indicate whether you are building an applet or application, any program arguments, and the name of the host HTML file. The Compiler tab allows you to configure which warning messages will be displayed and which compiler and optimizations to use. On the Directories tab, you can specify the directories to use for classes, output, and source code. On the Debugger tab, you can set options for remote and exception debugging.

6

WARNING

> Even though you can turn off the display of compiler warnings, this does not mean that the cause of the warning no longer exists. In general, it is wise to write code that will compile cleanly without warnings.

Figure 6.15.

The Project Options dialog includes four tabs of information.

Adding Files

To add an existing file to a project, you can select Files into Project from the Insert menu. This displays the Project Files dialog, shown in Figure 6.16. From this dialog you can navigate your directory structure and add one or more files to your project.

Figure 6.16.

The Project Files dialog allows you to add files to a project.

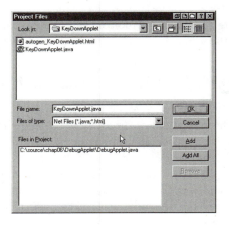

Another way to add to a project is to create your own components, add them to the Component palette, and then add the component to a project. This topic is covered in Chapter 18.

Creating New Classes

If you need to create a new class and add it to a project, you can do so by selecting Class... from the Insert menu. This displays the Insert Class dialog, shown in Figure 6.17.

Figure 6.17.

The Insert Class dialog allows you to create a new class by selecting its superclass and interfaces.

In the Insert Class dialog, you can enter the name of your new class and a file in which to store the class. You can also select the classes and interfaces on which the new class will be based. Classes are shown in a normal typeface, and interfaces are shown in italics. To select a superclass or interface, select its name in the Base Class field of the Insert Class dialog. You can select multiple items by holding down the Ctrl key while clicking the item. Of course, you cannot do this to create a subclass of two superclasses, but you can select a superclass and one or more interfaces.

Working with Source Code

When you get right down to it, programming means writing source code. So any tool that is going to earn a permanent place on your system needs to have a strong set of source code editing tools. Fortunately, Visual Café delivers in this regard.

The Class Browser

The Class browser is a powerful tool that enables you to quickly navigate a program's source code without being concerned with files and file locations. The Class browser, an example of which is shown in Figure 6.18, includes three panes: Classes, Members, and Code. The Classes pane lists all the packages and classes. When you highlight a class in the Classes pane, its members are displayed in the Members pane. When you select an item in the Members pane, the associated source code is shown in the Code pane.

In Figure 6.18, you can see that the class DebugApplet has been selected in the Classes pane, and the method copyButton_Clicked is selected in the Members pane. Therefore, the code for copyButton_Clicked is shown in the Code pane.

The Hierarchy Editor

The Visual Café Hierarchy editor can be used to change the relationships among classes in a program. For example, suppose you have added a class called MyClass to an applet. In this case, the Hierarchy editor will appear as shown in Figure 6.19.

Figure 6.18.

The Class browser includes three panes: Classes, Members, and Code.

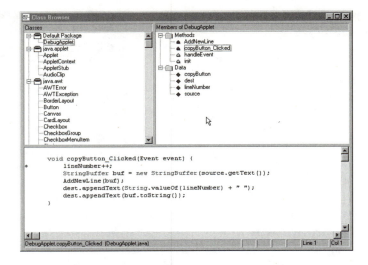

Figure 6.19.

The Hierarchy editor with MyClass *added.*

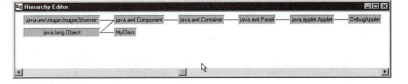

If you want to create another class, MySecondClass, you can do so right in the Hierarchy editor instead of using the Insert Class dialog. To do this, click the desired superclass and drag a line into an empty area of the Hierarchy editor screen. This displays a dialog identical to the Insert Class dialog that will allow you to give the new class a name and file location. Adding the class MySecondClass as a subclass of Object will result in the Hierarchy editor appearing as shown in Figure 6.20.

Figure 6.20.

Creating MySecondClass *as a subclass of* Object.

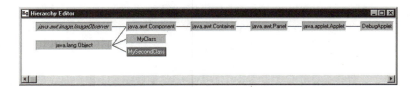

What if you want MyClass to be the superclass of MySecondClass instead of Object? To do this, click the line between the two classes and drag the end attached to Object to MyClass. The change will be made and the Hierarchy editor updated to reflect the change, as shown in Figure 6.21.

Figure 6.21.

MySecondClass `has` *been made a subclass of* `MyClass` *by dragging the inheritance line away from* `Object`.

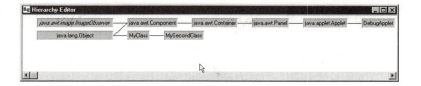

Summary

In this chapter, you have learned about the Visual Café debugger. You have learned how to set breakpoints, including conditional breakpoints that only stop program execution when they've met conditions you establish. You have learned how to inspect variables, debug multiple threads, examine the call stack, and step through a program in the debugger. You have also learned how to create and manage workspaces. The Class browser and Hierarchy editor are also described here, and you have learned how to use these tools to help examine existing classes and create new classes.

Q&A

Q While debugging an applet, I discovered the problem. I fixed the code and continued debugging. Nonetheless, the bug still happens even though the source code has been fixed.

A Before your changes can take effect, you must rebuild your project. The debugger executes a program based on the class files that were created when the program was last built. Class files are not automatically rebuilt when you edit the source files. To see the effect of your changes, stop the debugger, rebuild your project, and then restart the debugger.

Q I've noticed that the Hierarchy editor lets me change the superclass of the classes that come with Java. Isn't this dangerous?

A No more dangerous than driving a Volkswagon Beetle up a steep hill. Even though the Hierarchy esditor allows it, you should never change the superclass of a class you didn't create. This is especially true of the classes provided as part of the Java Development Kit. To help prevent accidental changes, make sure Confirm Inheritance Change is selected on the Editing tab of the Environment Options dialog box.

Workshop

The workshop includes quiz questions to help you gauge your understanding of the material in this chapter, and you can find the answers in Appendix D, "Answers." The workshop also includes exercises to provide hands-on experience with what you've learned in this chapter.

Quiz

1. What are the three ways you can examine the value of a variable in the debugger?
2. Why would you ever view the Calls window?
3. What is a conditional breakpoint?
4. When would you want to step out of a method?
5. Why does Visual Café load the Debug workspace when the debugger is started?
6. Why doesn't Visual Café allow you to configure the Component palette?
7. In what way can the appearance of Visual Café's toolbars be changed?
8. Name two ways to create a new class.

Exercises

1. Load and debug the `DebugApplet` provided on the MCP Web site (www.mcp.com/info/1-57521/1-57521-303-6). Set breakpoints in the `handleEvent` and `copyButton_Clicked` methods. When the first breakpoint is hit, tell the applet to continue running to the second breakpoint. When the `copyButton_Clicked` breakpoint is hit, step into the `AddNewLine` method. Step out of the `AddNewLine` method.

2. With the `DebugApplet` loaded and the breakpoints set, disable the `handleEvent` breakpoints. Predict how the program will behave and re-execute the program. Did it behave as you predicted?

3. With `DebugApplet` still loaded, disable all breakpoints (one should already be disabled). Then enable all breakpoints.

4. Use the Hierarchy editor to create a new class based on the `Button` class.

Day 7

The Form Designer, Layout Managers, and Panels

Earlier this week you learned about the Abstract Windowing Toolkit (AWT) and the user-interface components it includes. You also learned a little about the Visual Café Form Designer and how to use it to easily create your program's user interface. Today you will learn about three topics that will help you enhance and fine-tune a program's user interface. First, you will learn about additional features of the Visual Café Form Designer. Next, you will learn how to use the layout managers to position components so that they remain properly placed regardless of the user's screen resolution. Finally, you will learn about the `Panel` class and its many subclasses.

The Form Designer

You've already encountered Visual Café's Form Designer. In many of the examples in the past six days, you used it to visually place components onto an applet. But you've barely scratched the surface of what you can do with the Form

Designer. So far all you've done is place components onto a form without a great deal of concern for exactly where they are placed or where they appear at runtime. In this section, you will learn how to take advantage of the more advanced features of the Form Designer for laying out controls.

Placing Components

After you've placed a component on a form, you must make sure it is properly aligned, positioned, and sized relative to other components on the form. The easiest way to do this is with the Layout toolbar. The Layout toolbar contains buttons that perform the following functions:

 Align left edges

 Align right edges

 Align top edges

 Align bottom edges

 Center vertically

 Center horizontally

 Space evenly (vertically)

 Space evenly (horizontally)

 Same size vertically

 Same size horizontally

 Same size vertically and horizontally

 View grid

 View invisible

The Layout toolbar is shown in Figure 7.1.

Figure 7.1.
The Layout toolbar.

Aligning Components

To align a component with another component on the form, you must first select the components in the Form Designer. To select more than one component, hold down the Ctrl key while clicking the mouse button when the mouse is over the desired components. When two or more components have been selected, you can select one of the alignment buttons (left, right, top, or bottom) from the Layout toolbar or choose Layout | Align from the menu bar and then choose an alignment. Figure 7.2 shows three differently sized buttons that have been left aligned.

Figure 7.2.
Three differently sized buttons that have been left aligned.

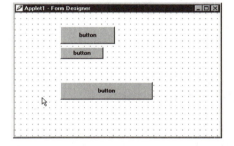

Centering Components

To center a component or group of components, select the components and then click the Center Vertically or the Center Horizontally button on the Layout toolbar. Alternatively, you can choose Layout | Center from the menu bar and make your selection there. Either of these actions will center the components on the form. If multiple components are selected, the spacing between the components will be maintained, and the components as a group will be centered on the form.

To see how multiple components are centered, consider Figure 7.3, which shows three components before they are centered vertically. From this figure you should be able to see that Button1 and Button2 are separated by less vertical space than are Button2 and Button3.

Figure 7.4 shows the result of vertically centering these three components. As you can see, the spacing between the buttons has not changed, and Button2 is closer to Button1 than it is to Button3. That the components are vertically centered can be seen by the fact that there is the same amount of space above Buttton1 as there is below Button3.

7

Figure 7.3.

*Non-centered
components with
different amounts of
space between them.*

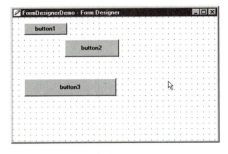

Figure 7.4.

*Vertically centered
components with
uneven spacing
between them.*

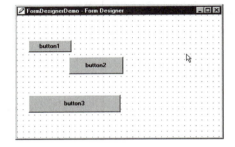

Spacing Components

But what if this isn't what you wanted? What if you wanted consistent spacing between components? To achieve consistent spacing between components, you use the Layout toolbar's Space Evenly (Vertically) and Space Evenly (Horizontally) buttons (or, of course, by making equivalent selections from the menu bar after choosing Layout | Space Evenly). When components are spaced evenly, they are positioned within the space occupied by the set of selected components so that there is a consistent amount of space between all the components.

As an example of vertically spacing components, suppose you are working again with the components of Figure 7.3. Choosing to space these components vertically will change the form to appear as shown in Figure 7.5. Here, you can see that the only component to have moved is Button2. Button1 and Button3 remained in the same places, but Button2 moved lower to equalize the vertical spacing among the components.

Figure 7.5.

*When three compo-
nents are spaced
vertically, only the
middle component
moves.*

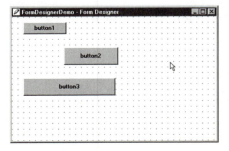

NOTE

To evenly space components, you must first select at least three components. Because the Form Designer spaces components by placing the same amount of space between each component, it doesn't make sense to perform this operation on only two components. Because there is only one space between two components, there is nothing to compare this space to. In other words, if you select only two components, they are already evenly spaced.

Sizing Components

When dragging components from the Component palette to the Form Designer, it is difficult to make each of your components the proper size. To help solve this problem after the components are on the form, you can use the Layout toolbar's Same Size Vertically, Same Size Horizontally, and Same Size Vertically and Horizontally buttons. When two or more components are selected, these buttons will change the indicated dimension of the components so that all are the same height, width, or both. For example, Figure 7.6 shows what happens when the components in Figure 7.5 are made the same size in both dimensions.

Figure 7.6.

Components can be made the same size vertically and horizontally.

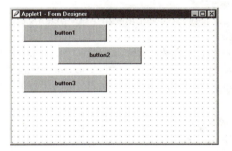

The Layout Grid

In working with the Form Designer, you might have noticed that it includes rows and columns of dots. These dots are known as the *layout grid* and are there to assist you in placing controls. By default, components will snap to these dots: If the top left of a component is placed near, but not on, one of these dots, the Form Designer will automatically move the component so that it is aligned on a dot. This is a benefit when trying to position components in an aligned, orderly manner.

On the other hand, having your components snap to a grid gets in the way of precisely controlling their placement. Sometimes you want the component to stay precisely where you place it. Fortunately, this is configurable with the Grid Options dialog, shown in Figure 7.7. You can access this dialog by selecting Grid Options from the Layout menu.

7

Figure 7.7.

*Configuration options
for the Form
Designer's layout grid.*

The Grid Options dialog allows you to hide the grid, choose whether components will snap to the grid, and set the spacing of the dots on the grid.

Working with Invisible Components

Some Visual Café components are invisible when the program is run. For example, the Timer control (located on the Utility tab of the Component palette) has no visual runtime representation. If you are designing a form that uses many invisible components, it might be difficult to visualize what the form will look like when the program is run. To solve this problem, you can hide invisible components by selecting Invisibles from the Layout menu. This will toggle the display of invisible components.

Using Layout Managers

So far, you've been designing forms by placing controls at specific coordinates. For example, you might have created a button 70 pixels wide and 20 pixels tall that was to be placed 400 pixels in from the left corner and 200 pixels down from the top. This may look great in the Form Designer or in the browser you run on your machine, but unfortunately, it might not look so great to someone running with a different screen resolution. To get around this, Java includes layout managers.

 A *layout manager* is a class that controls the placement of components on Java container classes.

Visual Café and the Java Software Development Kit (SDK) support five layout managers and you can write your own:

- ☐ FlowLayout
- ☐ BorderLayout
- ☐ CardLayout
- ☐ GridLayout
- ☐ GridBagLayout

A layout manager can be used by each of the Java classes that can hold user-interface components: Applet, Panel, Frame, and Dialog. (You will learn about frames and dialogs on Day 10, "Windows, Frames, and Dialogs.") Each of these classes has a default layout manager associated with it, as shown in Table 7.1. However, any layout manager can be used with any of these classes.

Table 7.1. The default layout managers for the classes.

Class	Default layout manager
Applet	FlowLayout
Dialog	BorderLayout
Frame	BorderLayout
Panel	FlowLayout

NOTE

You can set a form's layout manager by modifying the Layout property in the Property List. The Applet, Panel, Frame, and Dialog classes each have a default layout manager assigned by the Java Development Kit. However, Visual Café overrides these defaults and assumes that you do not want to use a layout manager but instead want to position components at specific coordinates. To achieve this, the Layout property is set to None. This generates code similar to the following for the form:

```
setLayout(null);
```

FlowLayout

The FlowLayout control is the default layout manager for the Applet and Panel classes. What FlowLayout does is continue placing components on the same line until no more will fit. If a component won't fit on the current line, FlowLayout moves to the next line and places the component there. Components are placed on the screen in the order they are added to the applet.

To see how this works, create a new applet and set the applet's Layout property to FlowLayout. Then drag a button component onto the applet in the Form Designer. When you place the button, draw it as a very large button near the bottom of the form. When you stop drawing the button, it will be resized and centered at the top of the form. This is shown in Figure 7.8.

To understand how the FlowLayout layout manager works, continue adding button components to the form until the top row of the form is nearly filled with buttons. (You might want to shrink the width of the form to reduce the number of buttons you need to add.) Then attempt to add one more button to the end of the row of buttons. The new button will be automatically placed in the center of a new row of buttons. (See Figure 7.9.) From this exercise, you can see how the components have flowed from one line to the next. As long as a new component could fit on the current line, it was positioned there. If, however, the component was wider than the remaining space on the line, it was centered on a new line.

7

Figure 7.8.

The button is centered on the top of the form.

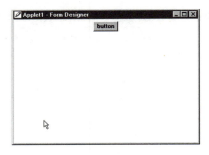

Figure 7.9.

With FlowLayout, *components are placed in the order they are added to the form.*

Sometimes you can achieve desirable results this way, but you might have to work at it a bit. For example, consider Figure 7.10. I wanted to create a form that was this width; however, with FlowLayout enabled, the components look horrible. The checkboxes span two lines and are on the same line with their prompt. The radio buttons span one line, but the associated prompt is hard to locate. I was able to fix this by changing the dimensions of my form, as shown in Figure 7.11.

Figure 7.10.

An absolutely horrible-looking form that uses FlowLayout.

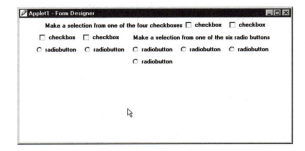

Unfortunately, you have no guarantee about the size your forms will appear in a user's browser. In some cases the appearance of a form may improve (as between Figures 7.10 and 7.11). In other cases the appearance might get worse (you could have planned for your users to see Figure 7.11, but instead they actually see Figure 7.10).

Figure 7.11.

The appearance of a form using FlowLayout *can change dramatically if the form is resized.*

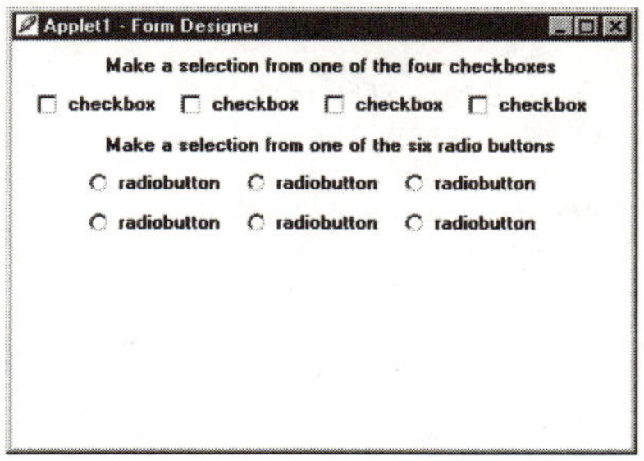

BorderLayout

The BorderLayout class is very useful when you have a relatively small number of components to place and you want to have more control over how they are placed than is available with FlowLayout. BorderLayout can control up to five components. Each component is placed in one of the following areas:

- ☐ North
- ☐ South
- ☐ East
- ☐ West
- ☐ Center

When you add a component using a BorderLayout, you specify the location in which to place the component. In the Property List, you do this by setting the Placement property of the component being positioned. If you don't see a Placement property on the component you are positioning, it is because the form is not using BorderLayout. The Placement property appears only for components that are placed on a form using BorderLayout.

As you would expect, the north is the top of a container, the south is the bottom, the east is the right, and the west is the left. The center is everything else. Usually this means that a component placed in the center will be larger than other components. For example, Figure 7.12 illustrates an applet that created five buttons, one in each position. Notice how the center button grew to fill the available space, in much the same manner as my waist grows to fill the last available hole in my belt.

Of course, Visual Café generates the code for placing components with a BorderLayout, but it helps to be familiar with what it will generate. To use a BorderLayout, you use the setLayout method and then place the components on the container with add. The add method is first passed a string indicating where the component should be placed and is then passed the component. The applet shown in Figure 7.12 was created with the following code:

7

```
setLayout(new BorderLayout());

add("North", new Button("North"));
add("South", new Button("South"));
add("East", new Button("East"));
add("West", new Button("West"));
add("Center", new Button("Center"));
```

Figure 7.12.

The center of a
BorderLayout *grows*
to fill the remaining
space.

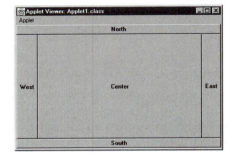

CardLayout

The CardLayout class is useful for presenting a user interface in which components can come and go. For example, you could use CardLayout to create an interface that included property pages or tabbed dialogs. Each page would be a separate card in this layout manager's lexicon. Using the methods of CardLayout, you can allow a user the freedom to switch between cards. For example, consider the code in Listing 7.1.

Listing 7.1. CardLayoutDemo.java.

```
1:    import java.awt.*;
2:    import java.applet.*;
3:
4:    public class CardLayoutDemo extends Applet {
5:        void button1_Clicked(java.awt.event.ActionEvent event) {
6:            CardLayout layout = (CardLayout)getLayout();
7:            layout.next(this);
8:        }
9:
10:       void button2_Clicked(java.awt.event.ActionEvent event) {
11:           CardLayout layout = (CardLayout)getLayout();
12:           layout.last(this);
13:       }
14:
15:       void button3_Clicked(java.awt.event.ActionEvent event) {
16:           CardLayout layout = (CardLayout)getLayout();
17:           layout.first(this);
18:       }
19:
20:       public void init() {
21:           // Call parents init method.
22:           super.init();
```

```
23:        }
24:
25:        public void addNotify() {
26:            // Call parents addNotify method.
27:            super.addNotify();
28:
29:            //{{INIT_CONTROLS
30:            setLayout(new CardLayout(0,0));
31:            resize(286,214);
32:            button1 = new java.awt.Button(
33:                "This is page 1, Click to go to Page 2");
34:            button1.reshape(0,0,286,195);
35:            add("CardName", button1);
36:            button2 = new java.awt.Button(
37:                "This is page 2, Click to go to Page 3");
38:            button2.reshape(0,0,286,195);
39:            add("CardName", button2);
40:            button3 = new java.awt.Button(
41:                "This is page 3, Click to go to Page 1");
42:            button3.reshape(0,0,286,195);
43:            add("CardName", button3);
44:            //}}
45:
46:            //{{REGISTER_LISTENERS
47:            Action lAction = new Action();
48:            button3.addActionListener(lAction);
49:            button2.addActionListener(lAction);
50:            button1.addActionListener(lAction);
51:            //}}
52:        }
53:
54:        //{{DECLARE_CONTROLS
55:        java.awt.Button button1;
56:        java.awt.Button button2;
57:        java.awt.Button button3;
58:        //}}
59:
60:        class Action implements java.awt.event.ActionListener {
61:            public void actionPerformed(java.awt.event.ActionEvent
62:                    event) {
63:                Object object = event.getSource();
64:                if (object == button3)
65:                    button3_Clicked(event);
66:                else if (object == button2)
67:                    button2_Clicked(event);
68:                else if (object == button1)
69:                    button1_Clicked(event);
70:            }
71:        }
72:    }
```

7

ANALYSIS   In this example, the goal is to create an applet that displays a page with a button on it. Clicking the button will move the user to another page with another button. When the user reaches the final page, he or she can click a button that will return him or her to the first page, where it all starts again. Hopefully the user will figure out that the cycle is repeating itself and, unlike Sisyphus, will stop before repeating the process too many times. An example of the first page of the applet is shown in Figure 7.13.

Figure 7.13.

An example of the first page of a CardLayout.

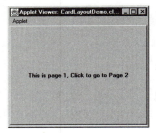

After setting the Layout property of a container to CardLayout, you can drag components onto the container. The first component will be placed on the first card of the layout, the second component will be placed on the second card, and so on. The CardLayoutDemo applet was created by setting the Layout property and then dragging three button components onto the form in the Form Designer.

The button1_Clicked, button2_Clicked, and button3_Clicked methods are called in response to clicks of the buttons on the applet. Each of these methods uses the getLayout method of the Container class to get a reference to the layout manager in use on the applet. Because this is a CardLayout object, the returned value is cast to CardLayout (lines 6, 11, and 16). The methods next, last, and first are then used to select different cards. (There is an analogous method, previous, that was not used in this example.)

NOTE

> One potentially disconcerting fact about CardLayout is that each card, or page, can contain only one component. This is why only a single button was placed on each card in CardLayoutDemo. However, this limitation is not a real concern because Java includes a Panel class. You can place multiple components on a panel and then place a single panel on a card. The Panel class is described in the section titled "The Panel Class," later in this chapter.

GridLayout

The GridLayout class is useful when you have a set of controls you want to place that are all the same size. For example, Figure 7.14 shows the GridLayoutDemo applet, which creates a grid that is three rows by three columns. Each of the grid's components—eight buttons and a text field—is made the same size by GridLayout.

In the Property List, you can set values for the vertical gap and horizontal gap to use when placing components on the grid. These values are expressed in pixels and are set to 0 by default. You can see the impact of these properties in Figure 7.15, which shows the same grid as Figure 7.14 but with gaps of 10 instead of 0.

Figure 7.14.

Using a 3×3 GridLayout.

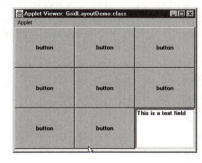

Figure 7.15.

Vertical and horizontal gaps can be set in the Property List.

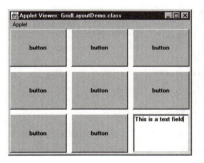

At the start of the section on layout managers, I made the claim that using layout managers was a better strategy than placing components at fixed locations on forms. The GridLayoutDemo is a good illustration of why. Suppose a user of this applet is running in a different resolution or has resized his browser. If components are coded to appear at fixed locations, this user might not see some components. With a layout manager, however, the components will shrink and expand. (See Figure 7.16.) This figure shows the GridLayoutDemo after it has been made shorter and wider. As you can see, the buttons and text field have resized themselves, and the applet remains usable.

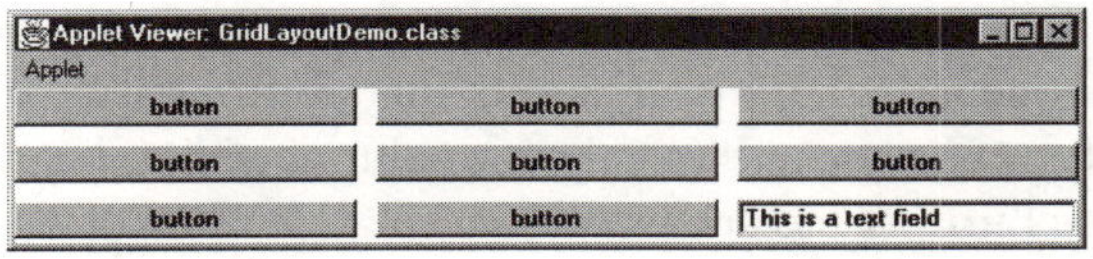

Figure 7.16.

When using a layout manager, components will be resized to fit the available space.

7

GridBagLayout

The final layout manager, GridBagLayout, is the most involved to use but also gives you the most flexibility in placing your components. When using this layout manager, each of the components on the form has additional properties added to its Property List. These additional properties appear under the heading Grid Bag Constraints in the Property List and correspond to the Java class GridBagConstraints. The properties that can be set under Grid Bag Constraints for each component are the following:

- ☐ Grid X
- ☐ Grid Y
- ☐ Grid Width
- ☐ Grid Height
- ☐ Weight X
- ☐ Weight Y
- ☐ Anchor
- ☐ Fill
- ☐ Insets
- ☐ Internal Pad X
- ☐ Internal Pad Y

The Fill Property

Each of the Grid Bag Constraints properties influences how the components using a GridBagLayout appear. The Fill property specifies how a component stretches to fill its cell in the grid. It can be set to Horizontal, Vertical, Both, or None. By default, Fill is set to None, and the component will remain its default size. For most of the examples in this section, Fill will be set to Both because this helps visualize the area occupied by a cell in the grid.

The Grid Width and Grid Height Properties

The Grid Width and Grid Height properties determine the width and height of the cell in the grid. Each of these properties can hold a value between 0 and 32,767. Entering 0 indicates that the cell is the last cell in that row or column. For example, consider the form in Figure 7.17.

All the buttons in Figure 7.17 have Fill set to Both. Button1 and Button2 have Grid Width and Grid Height set to 1. Button3 has Grid Width set to 0 to indicate that it is the last component on the line. Because of that, Button4 starts its own line; and because Button4 has Grid Width set to 1, it is only one column wide. This is changed, however, in Figure 7.18, where Button4 has Grid Width set to 2.

Figure 7.17.

The grid width of Button3 is 0, *indicating that it is the last component on the line.*

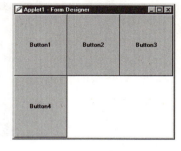

Figure 7.18.

The grid width of Button4 is 2, *so Button4 is two columns wide.*

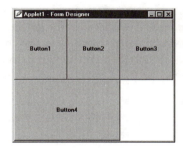

If the grid width of Button4 is set to 0, it indicates that Button4 is the last (and only) component on the row. This results in a form like the one shown in Figure 7.19.

Figure 7.19.

With a grid width of 0, *Button4 is made the last component on the row, and it expands to fill the entire row.*

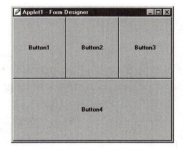

The `Insets` Property

By using the `Insets` property, you can specify an amount by which a component will be moved in from its cell borders. Separate values can be given for `Top`, `Bottom`, `Left`, and `Right` insets. For an example of how `Insets` can alter the appearance of a form, consider Figure 7.20. In this figure, Button1 has `Fill` set to `Both`, but it is inset 40 pixels on its right edge and 10 pixels on all other edges.

7

Figure 7.20.
By using the Insets
*property, you can
move a component
away from its cell
borders.*

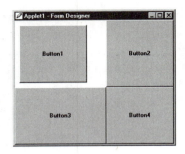

The Anchor **Property**

When a component is smaller than the grid cell into which it is placed, you can use the Fill property to instruct Visual Café how to stretch the component. You can also use the Anchor property to position the component within its cell. The Anchor property can be set to any of the following values:

- ☐ CENTER
- ☐ EAST
- ☐ NORTH
- ☐ NORTHEAST
- ☐ NORTHWEST
- ☐ SOUTH
- ☐ SOUTHEAST
- ☐ SOUTHWEST
- ☐ WEST

As an example of how the Anchor property can be used, Figure 7.21 shows a button that has been anchored to the southeast corner of its grid cell.

Figure 7.21.
*Button4 is placed in
the southeast corner of
its cell by using the
Anchor property.*

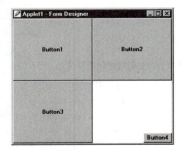

The Internal Padding Properties

The `Internal Pad X` and `Internal Pad Y` properties can be used to set the minimum size of a component. By default, each of these properties is `0`. If set to a value other than `0`, the minimum size of a component will be increased by twice the internal padding value. (Twice, because the padding is added to both sides of the component.)

The `Weight X` and `Weight Y` Properties

These properties are used to tell the `GridBagLayout` layout manager how to distribute space between the cells in a grid. For example, Figure 7.22 shows three buttons. All the buttons have `Weight X` and `Weight Y` set to `0`, so even though each of the buttons has `Fill` set to `Both`, they have clustered together in the middle of the form.

Figure 7.22.

With `Weight X` *and* `Weight Y` *set to* `0` *for all components, they cluster together in the middle of the form.*

It is important that at least one component in each row has a `Weight X` of `1`, and at least one component in each column has a `Weight Y` of `1` to avoid this clustering. This instructs the layout manager that these components are more heavily weighted and should be allocated additional space. Figure 7.23 illustrates this; in the figure, both the `Weight X` and the `Weight Y` of Button1 are `1`.

Figure 7.23.

Button 1 has `Weight X` *and* `Weight Y` *set to* `1`, *so it receives additional space.*

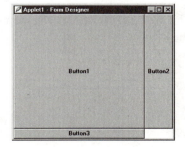

The `Grid X` and `Grid Y` Properties

You use the `Grid X` and `Grid Y` properties to specify the cell to the upper left of the component. The first cell in a grid has `Grid X` and `Grid Y` equal to `0`. The default value, `-1`, for these properties will position the component to the right or below the last component added. Normally, it is best to leave these properties at their defaults.

Do	Don't

DON'T forget that your users may be running a variety of operating systems and browsers, and that they probably are using every known screen resolution.

DO design your programs to be resolution independent so they will look good regardless of how they are being run.

Containers

You have probably noticed that a fundamental problem with many of these layout managers is that they can put only a limited number of components on the screen. For example, think about the BorderLayout layout manager. It enables you to place a component in the north, south, east, west, or center. If there are only five locations you can put a component, where do you put a sixth?

Similarly, there are many occasions when it would be convenient to treat more than one component (for example, a label and a text field) as a group. For example, instead of placing each component onto the user interface one at a time, it would be nice to be able to create a group of components and then place the group on the user interface.

Fortunately, Java provides a solution to these problems in the form of its Container classes. A Container class can be used to hold components. And because Container is a subclass of Component, you can place a Container on the user interface just like you'd place a Checkbox, TextField, or any other Component.

As shown in Figure 7.24, Container serves as a superclass for a number of other classes, one of which is the familiar Applet class.

Figure 7.24.

The Java Container *classes.*

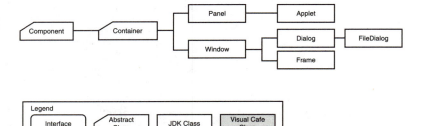

The `Panel` **Class**

The `Panel` class is the simplest of the Java container classes. When an applet creates a panel, no new window is created, and the panel is unseen by the user. However, by using panels you can exert more explicit control over the placement of components in an applet's user interface. To create a new panel, drag a `Panel` component from the Component palette onto the Form Designer. Visual Café will create code in the form's `init` method that calls the `Panel` constructor, as follows:

```
panel1 = new java.awt.Panel();
```

After a panel is created, you can add components to it exactly as if it were an applet or any other form. Each panel uses its own layout manager that is independent of the layout manager of the form on which the panel is placed. By default, `Panel` uses the `FlowLayout` layout manager, but Visual Café overrides this in the Property List to use no layout manager. Because a panel can have a different layout manager than its parent, `Container`, you can create user interfaces that are as complex and precise as you want.

A Panel Example

As an example of how you can use panels, the `PanelDemo` applet is shown in Figure 7.25. This applet illustrates a couple important concepts related to the use of panels, including the use of different layout managers. This interface was created by using `GridLayout` on the applet to create a grid that is two rows by two columns.

Figure 7.25.

Running `PanelDemo`
*creates three panels
and a panelless area
with a large button.*

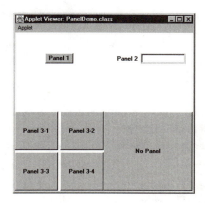

ANALYSIS   The top-left cell of the grid contains a panel that uses the `FlowLayout` layout manager and contains a single button labeled `Panel 1`. The top-right cell also contains a panel that uses `FlowLayout`. This panel, however, contains two components: a label and a text field. The bottom-left cell contains a panel that uses the `GridLayout` to make a 2×2 grid. Four buttons are placed on this panel.

7

Finally, in the bottom-right cell of the applet's grid, a button is placed directly onto the applet. Because the applet is using a GridLayout layout manager, the size of the button is increased so that it fills the entire grid cell, as you saw in Figure 7.25.

You should take a moment to think about the different layout managers that are in use in this example. The applet itself is being laid out under the control of GridLayout. The first two cells in this grid are using FlowLayout. The third cell is again using GridLayout. This means the third cell is placed on the applet as part of a grid and that it will lay out its components as part of a grid within the grid. Finally, the fourth cell of the applet's GridLayout does not use a panel at all, and its button is placed directly on the applet.

Placing a Panel on a Panel

What if, instead of the screen shown in Figure 7.25, you wanted to create the screen shown in Figure 7.26? The only change here is in the top-right cell. Here, a label is displayed in the top of the panel, and a second label is displayed at the bottom of the panel. How can you create this look?

Figure 7.26.

PanelOnPanelDemo *illustrates the placement of a panel on a panel.*

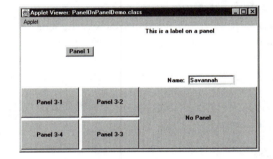

It's actually fairly simple. The answer lies in the ability to put a panel on another panel. The PanelOnPanelDemo applet creates a new GridLayout instance and creates the first cell in the same way as was done in PanelDemo. The second panel is created and told to use BorderLayout. A label, This is a label on a panel, is created and placed in the north of the panel.

Here is where things get interesting. Another panel is created and placed at the south of the second panel. This subpanel is then told to use the FlowLayout layout manager. Finally, a label and text field are placed on the subpanel to create the desired look.

Visual Café's Panel Classes

Because the Panel class provided with the Java Development Kit is relatively boring and limited in its display options, Visual Café includes its own set of additional panels:

    ☐ BorderPanel

☐ RadioButtonGroupPanel

☐ KeyPressManagerPanel

☐ ScrollingPanel

☐ SplitterPanel

☐ TabPanel

Many of these classes are intended to work in conjunction with the Panel class. Each of these classes is discussed in detail in the following sections.

The BorderPanel Class

The BorderPanel class is an extension of the Panel class and draws a border around the panel. This is very useful when the panel is used to group similar components. With the BorderPanel class, you can also specify a label that will be placed on the top line of the border and will be centered, left aligned, or right aligned. You can also specify the type of line to be drawn as the border. Finally, you can specify the padding that will be placed around the inside and outside of the panel.

To control these options, the BorderPanel adds a number of properties to the Property List. (See Table 7.2.)

Table 7.2. Additional properties of BorderPanel.

Property	Purpose
Border Color	Specifies the color of the border.
Inset Padding Bottom	Specifies space at the bottom of the panel that will not hold components.
Inset Padding Sides	Specifies space at the sides of the panel that will not hold components.
Inset Padding Top	Specifies space at the top of the panel that will not hold components.
Label	Specifies a label for the panel.
Label Alignment	Specifies the alignment of the label: ALIGN_CENTERED, ALIGN_LEFT, ALIGN_RIGHT.
Label Color	Specifies the color of the label.
Padding Bottom	Specifies the amount of empty space beneath the panel.
Padding Left	Specifies the amount of empty space to the left of the panel.

continues

7

Table 7.2. continued

Property	Purpose
Padding Right	Specifies the amount of empty space to the right of the panel.
Padding Top	Specifies the amount of empty space above the panel.
Style	Specifies the type of border: BEVEL_NONE, BEVEL_LINE, BEVEL_LOWERED, BEVEL_RAISED.

To understand how these properties work together, consider Figure 7.27. The BorderPanelDemo applet of Figure 7.27 uses GridLayout to create a grid that is two rows by two columns. Each cell of this grid contains a border panel. Three of the border panels contain a button that helps illustrates the size of the border panel.

Figure 7.27.

The BorderPanel- Demo *applet illustrates various* BorderPanel *options.*

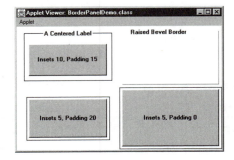

The border panel in the top-left cell uses a centered label, and each of the three insets (top, sides, and bottom) has been set to 10. Each of the padding values has been set to 15. Contrast this with the border panel in the bottom-left cell, which has its insets set to 5 and its padding set to 20. You should be able to see that the bottom button is much closer to the border of the panel. This is the result of the smaller Insets value on the bottom panel.

You can also see that the top-left border panel is surrounded by less whitespace than is the bottom-left border panel. This is the influence of the padding values. Because the bottom panel has more padding, the border panel takes up less of the cell. As an extreme, compare these border panels to the border panel in the bottom-right cell. It appears much larger because it has no padding, so the border panel occupies the entire cell.

Each of these three border panels has used BEVEL_LINE for its Style property. This resulted in a solid line being drawn completely around the panel. The border panel in the top-right cell uses a Style of BEVEL_RAISED. This causes the border to be drawn at the bottom and to the right of the panel, giving the panel a raised look.

Naturally, the properties you can set in the Form Designer while designing a form are also available at runtime. The BorderPanel class includes many new methods that correspond to the properties of Table 7.2. Some of the most useful of these are shown in Table 7.3.

Table 7.3. Some useful methods of BorderPanel.

Method	Purpose
countComponents()	Returns the number of components on the panel.
getAlignStyle()	Returns the alignment style for the border label.
getBevelStyle()	Returns the current border style.
getLabel()	Returns the current border label.
getLabelColor()	Returns the current border label color.
getPaddingBottom	Returns the amount of bottom padding.
getPaddingLeft	Returns the amount of left padding.
getPaddingRight	Returns the amount of right padding.
getPaddingTop()	Returns the amount of top padding.
setAlignStyle(int)	Sets the alignment style for the border label.
setBevelStyle(int)	Sets the type of bevel that borders the panel.

The RadioButtonGroupPanel Class

As you learned on Day 5, "Using the Abstract Windowing Toolkit," when you place checkboxes onto a form you can group them so they behave like radio buttons. As an alternative to specifying a group when creating a radio button, you can use Visual Café's RadioButtonGroupPanel. This panel provides a more visual approach to placing radio buttons on a form.

To use the RadioButtonGroupPanel class, drag the component from the Panels tab of the Component library and place it on your form. Then drag as many radio buttons as desired from the Standard tab of the Component library and place them on the panel you just added.

When the program is run, the RadioButtonGroupPanel class will take care of setting the Group property of all radio buttons placed on it. If you need a form that has multiple radio button groups, simply place two RadioButtonGroupPanel objects onto the form.

7

The `KeyPressManagerPanel` **Class**

The `KeyPressManagerPanel` class works to augment the AWT with improved keyboard handling. `KeyPressManagerPanel` allows users to use the Tab key and Shift+Tab keystroke to move between components. You can also use `KeyPressManagerPanel` to assign a default button that will be clicked whenever the user presses Enter, and a Cancel button that will be clicked whenever the user presses Esc. Additionally, you can assign events to the function keys so that whenever a function key is pressed, an event is generated.

To create a `KeyPressManagerPanel` on your form, drag one from the Component palette to the Form Designer. A `KeyPressManagerPanel` is particularly useful when used in combination with the panel types, such as `BorderPanel`, `SplitterPanel`, or `TabPanel`. This allows you to gain the benefits of multiple panel types.

The most common use of `KeyPressManagerPanel` is to allow users to tab through a form's components. This can be accomplished without having to write a line of code. (Almost makes you feel guilty collecting a paycheck, doesn't it?) The order in which components will be tabbed through is the same order in which they were placed on the form.

However, to take advantage of other `KeyPressManagerPanel` features, you do need to write some code. For example, if a form contains a button that you want to have clicked whenever the user presses Esc or Enter, you use the `setCancelButton` or `setDefaultButton` methods. The signatures for these methods are

```
void setCancelButton(Button button)
```

```
void setDefaultButton(Button button)
```

When Esc is pressed, the button that was passed to `setCancelButton` will be clicked. Similarly, the button passed to `setDefaultButton` is clicked when the user presses Enter. Just as default and Cancel buttons can be assigned, they can also be removed. To do this, use the following methods:

```
void removeCancelButton()
```

```
void removeDefaultButton()
```

An Example

The `KeyPressManagerDemo` applet is a complete example of the use of `KeyPressManagerPanel`. Figure 7.28 shows what this applet looks like when run, and Listing 7.2 shows the complete source code.

Figure 7.28.

The KeyPress-
ManagerDemo *applet
in action.*

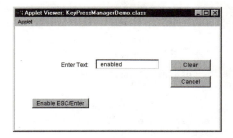

Listing 7.2. `KeyPressManagerDemo.java.`

```
 1:  import java.awt.*;
 2:  import java.applet.*;
 3:
 4:  public class KeyPressManagerDemo extends Applet {
 5:      void enableKeysBtn_Clicked(java.awt.event.ActionEvent
 6:          event) {
 7:        if(enableKeysBtn.getLabel().equals(enableKeysMsg))
 8:          disableDefaultButtons();
 9:        else
10:          enableDefaultButtons();
11:      }
12:
13:      void enableDefaultButtons() {
14:        keyMgr.setDefaultButton(clearButton);
15:        keyMgr.setCancelButton(cancelButton);
16:        enableKeysBtn.setLabel(enableKeysMsg);
17:        results.setText("enabled");
18:      }
19:
20:      void disableDefaultButtons() {
21:        keyMgr.removeDefaultButton();
22:        keyMgr.removeCancelButton();
23:        enableKeysBtn.setLabel(disableKeysMsg);
24:        results.setText("disabled");
25:      }
26:
27:      void cancelButton_Clicked(java.awt.event.ActionEvent
28:          event) {
29:        results.setText("cancelled");
30:      }
31:
32:      void clearButton_Clicked(java.awt.event.ActionEvent
33:          event) {
34:        results.setText("cleared");
35:      }
36:
37:      public void init() {
```

continues

7

Listing 7.2. continued

```
38:        // Call parents init method.
39:        super.init();
40:
41:        enableDefaultButtons();
42:    }
43:
44:    public void addNotify() {
45:        // Call parents addNotify method.
46:        super.addNotify();
47:
48:        // This code is automatically generated by Visual Café
49:        // when you add components to the visual environment.
50:        // It instantiates and initializes the components. To
51:        // modify the code, only use code syntax that matches
52:        // what Visual Cafe can generate, or Visual Cafe may
53:        // be unable to back parse your Java file into its
54:        // visual environment.
55:        //{{INIT_CONTROLS
56:        setLayout(new BorderLayout(0,0));
57:        resize(426,220);
58:        keyMgr = new symantec.itools.awt.KeyPressManagerPanel();
59:        keyMgr.setLayout(null);
60:        keyMgr.reshape(0,0,426,220);
61:        add("Center", keyMgr);
62:        enableKeysBtn = new java.awt.Button("Disable ESC/Enter");
63:        enableKeysBtn.reshape(36,156,118,21);
64:        keyMgr.add(enableKeysBtn);
65:        cancelButton = new java.awt.Button("Cancel");
66:        cancelButton.reshape(324,108,83,24);
67:        keyMgr.add(cancelButton);
68:        clearButton = new java.awt.Button("Clear");
69:        clearButton.reshape(324,72,83,24);
70:        keyMgr.add(clearButton);
71:        results = new java.awt.TextField();
72:        results.reshape(168,72,132,21);
73:        keyMgr.add(results);
74:        label1 = new java.awt.Label("Enter Text:");
75:        label1.reshape(96,72,71,23);
76:        keyMgr.add(label1);
77:        //}}
78:
79:        //{{REGISTER_LISTENERS
80:        Action lAction = new Action();
81:        enableKeysBtn.addActionListener(lAction);
82:        cancelButton.addActionListener(lAction);
83:        clearButton.addActionListener(lAction);
84:        //}}
85:    }
86:
87:    String enableKeysMsg  = "Enable ESC/Enter";
88:    String disableKeysMsg = "Disable ESC/Enter";
89:
```

```
90:        static int CUSTOM_EVENT     = 2000;
91:        static int CUSTOM_EVENT_1   = 1 + CUSTOM_EVENT;
92:        static int CUSTOM_EVENT_2   = 2 + CUSTOM_EVENT;
93:
94:        //{{DECLARE_CONTROLS
95:        symantec.itools.awt.KeyPressManagerPanel keyMgr;
96:        java.awt.Button enableKeysBtn;
97:        java.awt.Button cancelButton;
98:        java.awt.Button clearButton;
99:        java.awt.TextField results;
100:       java.awt.Label label1;
101:       //}}
102:
103:       class Action implements java.awt.event.ActionListener {
104:          public void actionPerformed(java.awt.event.ActionEvent
105:              event) {
106:             Object object = event.getSource();
107:             if (object == enableKeysBtn)
108:                enableKeysBtn_Clicked(event);
109:             else if (object == cancelButton)
110:                cancelButton_Clicked(event);
111:             else if (object == clearButton)
112:                clearButton_Clicked(event);
113:          }
114:       }
115: }
```

ANALYSIS   The button labeled Enable ESC/Enter in Figure 7.28 is used to toggle whether default and Cancel buttons are assigned. The method enableKeysBtn_Clicked (lines 5–11) determines the current state of these buttons and then calls either disableDefaultButtons (lines 20–25) or enableDefaultButtons (lines 13–18).

Whenever the Cancel button is clicked (or if Esc is pressed while assigned to the Cancel button), cancelled is displayed in the form's text field. If Clear is clicked (or if Enter is pressed while assigned as the default button), cleared is displayed in the text field. These functions are performed by the event-handling methods cancelButton_Clicked (lines 27–30) and clearButton_Clicked (lines 32–35).

The ScrollingPanel **Class**

The ScrollingPanel class provides an easy mechanism for allowing a user to scroll through a panel that would otherwise be too large to be displayed. To create a scrolling panel, take the following steps:

1. Drag a ScrollingPanel object from the Component palette to the Form Designer.
2. Drag another panel object onto the scrolling panel.
3. Set the dimensions of the second panel so that it is larger than the scrolling panel.
4. Place additional components on the second panel.

7

> **TIP**   If you want to place an existing panel into a `ScrollingPanel`, you can
> do so in the Form Designer. Select the panel and drag it over the
> scrolling panel. When the icon that appears next to the mouse pointer
> is over the scrolling panel, release the mouse button, and the panel will
> now be a component on the scrolling panel.

A sample applet, `ScrollingPanelDemo`, created from these steps, is included on the MCP Web
site (`www.mcp.com/info/1-57521/1-57521-303-6`). This applet needs to display a rather large
area, as shown in Figure 7.29. Unfortunately, the Web page for which this applet is intended
does not have this much room. The solution is to use a scrolling panel, as shown in Figure 7.30.

Figure 7.29.

The `Scrolling-`
`PanelDemo` *needs*
more display space
than is available to it.

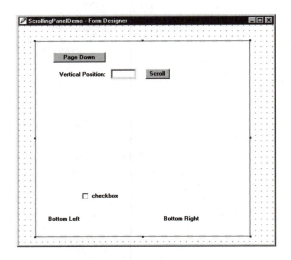

Figure 7.30.

`ScrollingPanel`
presents the user with
a view into a panel
that is larger than the
scrolling panel.

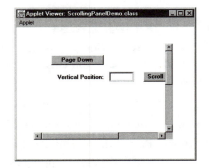

The behavior and appearance of a scrolling panel can be customized by setting the many properties available in the Property List. The most important of the new properties available to a scrolling panel are shown in Table 7.4.

Table 7.4. Useful new properties of `ScrollingPanel`.

Property	Purpose
Auto Tab	Indicates whether the Tab key can be used to move between components on the panel.
Scroll Increment	Sets the increment by which the panel will scroll each time a scrollbar arrow is clicked.
Show Horizontal Scrollbar	Indicates whether horizontal scrollbars are visible when necessary.
Show Vertical Scrollbar	Indicates whether vertical scrollbars are visible when necessary.

Because `ScrollingPanel` is a subclass of `KeyPressManagerPanel`, setting the `Auto Tab` property allows a scrolling panel to process Tab keys in the same way as a `KeyPressManagerPanel`. Visual Café sets the `Scroll Increment` property to a default of 1. This causes the panel to scroll by one pixel each time a scrollbar arrow (up, down, left, or right) is clicked. For many programs, this is too small and a larger value provides smoother scrolling. Of course, this is highly dependent on the contents of the panel being scrolled.

TIP

Because the panel that is placed in the scrolling panel is usually very large, it is sometimes difficult to place components on this panel. One way to simplify this is to make the scrolling panel as large as possible while placing components. Ideally, you can make the scrolling panel the same size as the panel being placed on it. Once you've finished placing components, you can shrink the scrolling panel back to the desired size.

In addition to its design-time properties, the `ScrollingPanel` class has many useful methods, the most useful of which are summarized in Table 7.5.

7

Table 7.5. Some useful methods of `ScrollingPanel`.

Method	Purpose
`getScrollLineIncrement()`	Returns the pixel amount that will be scrolled each time a scrollbar arrow is clicked.
`getShowHorizontalScroll()`	Returns `true` if the horizontal scrollbar is enabled.
`getShowVerticalScroll()`	Returns `true` if the vertical scrollbar is enabled.
`scrollDown()`	Scrolls down one pixel.
`scrollHorizontalAbsolute(int)`	Scrolls to an absolute horizontal position.
`scrollLeft()`	Scrolls left one pixel.
`scrollPageDown()`	Scrolls down one page.
`scrollPageLeft()`	Scrolls left one page.
`scrollPageRight()`	Scrolls right one page.
`scrollPageUp()`	Scrolls up one page.
`scrollRight()`	Scrolls right one pixel.
`scrollUp()`	Scrolls up one pixel.
`scrollVerticalAbsolute(int)`	Scrolls to an absolute vertical position.
`setScrollLineIncrement(int)`	Sets the pixel amount to scroll each time a scrollbar arrow is clicked.

To see how a couple of these methods are used, consider the following event handlers from the `ScrollingPanelDemo` applet:

```
void verticalPosButton_Clicked(java.awt.event.ActionEvent event) {
    int vPos = Integer.parseInt(verticalPos.getText());
    scroller.scrollVerticalAbsolute(vPos);
}

void pgDnButton_Clicked(Event event) {
    scroller.scrollPageDown();
}
```

The first method, `verticalPosButton_Clicked`, is called in response to a click of the Scroll button of Figure 7.29. When this button is clicked, the scrolling panel is positioned to the absolute vertical location entered by the user in a text field. This is performed with the `scrollVerticalAbsolute` method and passed a parameter that is an integer value converted from the contents of the text field, `verticalPos`.

Figure 7.30 also shows a Page Down button. Clicking this button has the same effect as clicking in the vertical scrollbar beneath the thumbprint. This is done in the `pgDnButton_Clicked` method by calling the `scrollPageDown` method for the scrolling panel.

TIP The example in this chapter shows a `Panel` being placed into a `ScrollingPanel`. Any `Panel` object can be placed into a `ScrollingPanel`.

The `SplitterPanel` Class

The `SplitterPanel` class allows you to create a panel that is composed of resizable subpanels. This is extremely useful whenever you are designing a form and cannot know how much space should be allocated to each area of the screen. For example, the Visual Café Form Designer is split vertically: The left side displays the name of each property, and the right side displays the value for each property. Depending on the property you're working with, you might want to move the vertical split so that more space is allocated on the side you are interested in.

The Visual Café `SplitterPanel` class allows you to create vertical splits or horizontal splits. In fact, once an area has been split one way, you can split it again in either direction. This allows you complete freedom in how you allocate space for your user interface.

For an example of what can be done with splitter panels, consider Figure 7.31. This figure contains six distinct areas that can be reallocated with splitter panels:

☐ The top-left area (containing five buttons, each labeled `button`)

☐ The top-left button, labeled `One`

☐ The button labeled `Two`

☐ The button labeled `Three`

☐ The bottom-left area containing the buttons labeled with colors and widths

☐ The bottom-right button

Figure 7.31.
Running the
`SplitterPanelDemo`
applet.

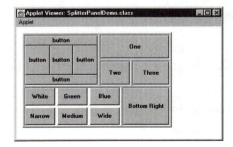

Creating a `SplitterPanel`

To create a splitter panel, you must take the following steps:

1. Drag a `SplitterPanel` object from the Component palette to the Form Designer.

2. Build the splitter panel's subpanels by dragging other panels onto the form, but do not place them on the splitter panel.

3. Place additional components on the subpanels in the Form Designer.

4. Write code to split the splitter panel in the desired ways and to move the subpanels onto the splitter panel.

The central differences between creating splitter panels and other types of panels are that for splitter panels, you must write some code, and that you lay out subpanels separately and then move them onto the splitter panel at runtime. To better understand this, look at Figure 7.32. This figure is the design-time equivalent of Figure 7.31 and shows what the SplitterPanelDemo applet, which can be found on the MCP Web site, looks like in the Form Designer.

Figure 7.32.

The subpanels of SplitterPanelDemo *are designed to the side of the splitter panel.*

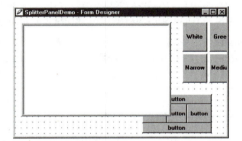

As you can see, the top- and bottom-left panels of SplitterPanelDemo have been placed off to the side of the SplitterPanel itself. This design allows you to take advantage of the visual layout capabilities of the Form Designer when using a splitter panel.

Because working with a splitter panel requires that you write more code than with most other panel types, the SplitterPanel class includes many methods. These methods can be used to select individual subpanels, to create new subpanels, and to set parameters such as gap and border sizes and colors. A summary of the methods you will use most frequently is shown in Table 7.6.

Table 7.6. Some useful methods of SplitterPanel.

Method	Purpose
getBottomLeftPanel()	Returns the bottom-left panel.
getBottomPanel()	Returns the bottom panel.
getBottomRightPanel()	Returns the bottom-right panel.
getLeftPanel()	Returns the left panel.
getRightPanel()	Returns the right panel.

Method	Purpose
getSplitType()	Returns the type of split (SPLIT_HOR or SPLIT_VER).
getSub2Panel(int,int,int,int)	Returns the specified pane within a doubly split panel.
getSubPanel(int)	Returns the subpanel based on the specified panel number (starting with 1).
getTopLeftPanel()	Returns the top-left panel.
getTopRightPanel()	Returns the top-right panel.
setBdrSizes(int)	Sets the inside and outside borders to the specified sizes.
setBdrSizes(int, int)	Sets the inside and outside borders to the specified sizes.
setGapColor(Color)	Sets the color to be used to fill internal and external gaps.
setGapSizes(int)	Sets all gap sizes to the specified value.
setGapSizes(int, int)	Sets all gaps to the width and height specified.
setGapSizes(int, int, int, int	Sets internal and external gap width and height to the values specified.
split(int)	Splits a panel vertically (SPLIT_VER) or horizontally (SPLIT_HOR).

To see how many of these methods are used, consider Listing 7.3. This listing shows the formatSplitter method of the SplitterPanelDemo. When run, this method converts the layout of Figure 7.32 into the runtime display of Figure 7.31.

Listing 7.3. The formatSplitter method of the SplitterPanelDemo applet.

```
1:    private void formatSplitter() {
2:      splitter.split(splitter.SPLIT_HOR);
3:      splitter.getTopPanel().split(splitter.SPLIT_VER);
4:      splitter.getBottomPanel().split(splitter.SPLIT_VER);
5:
6:      // TOP LEFT
7:      splitter.getTopLeftPanel().add(panel1);
8:      remove(panel1);
9:
10:     // TOP RIGHT
11:     splitter.getTopRightPanel().split(splitter.SPLIT_HOR);
```

continues

7

Listing 7.3. continued

```
12:     splitter.getTopRightPanel().getSubPanel(1).add(
13:         new Button("One"));
14:     splitter.getTopRightPanel().getSubPanel(2).split(
15:         splitter.SPLIT_VER);
16:
17:     splitter.getTopRightPanel().getSub2Panel(
18:         2, splitter.SPLIT_HOR, 1, splitter.SPLIT_VER).add(
19:         new Button("Two"));
20:
21:     splitter.getTopRightPanel().getSubPanel(2).getSubPanel(2).
        ➥add(new Button("Three"));
22:
23:     // BOTTOM LEFT
24:     splitter.getBottomLeftPanel().add(panel2);
25:     remove(panel2);
26:
27:     // BOTTOM RIGHT
28:     splitter.getBottomRightPanel().add(new
29:     Button("Bottom Right"));
30: }
```

ANALYSIS The first thing formatSplitter does is use split to create a horizontal split. In Figure 7.31, this can be seen as the line separating the bottom buttons (the color and width buttons plus the Bottom Right button) from those above them. In line 3, getTopPanel is used to select the upper panel, and split is then used to split this panel vertically. Using getBottomPanel, this process is then repeated in line 4 for the lower panel. At this point the splitter has been split into four areas, none of which has had any components added to it.

The variable panel1 represents the block of buttons that need to be placed on the top left of the splitter. This panel is added to the splitter in line 7. To prevent this panel from appearing on the splitter and on the applet window, line 8 removes it from the applet.

The top-right area of the splitter panel is created between lines 11 and 21. Line 11 selects the top-right panel and then splits it horizontally. Lines 12 and 13 place a button in the top half of this split. To accomplish this, getTopRightPanel is used to select the top-right quadrant of the splitter. Because this was just split horizontally, getSubPanel(1) is used to select the first subpanel (the top one). The button is then added to this panel.

Lines 14–15 use getSubPanel(2) to select the second panel in the top right. This is the bottom half of the horizontally split panel. This panel is then split vertically to make room for the buttons labeled Two and Three.

Lines 17–19 take care of making the Two button. First, the top-right panel is selected. Then getSub2Panel is used to select the desired panel. The signature for getSub2Panel is as follows:

```
SplitterPanel getSub2Panel(int n1, int splitType1,
        int n2, int splitType2)
```

The first two parameters to `getSub2Panel` are used together to select a panel. The `n1` parameter is a panel number (beginning with 1), and the `splitType1` parameter is `SPLIT_HOR` or `SPLIT_VER`, depending on the split type. So, to select the bottom of a horizontally split panel, `n1` is 2 and `splitType1` is `SPLIT_HOR`. The third and fourth parameters specify similar information about the subpanel selected by the first two parameters. This means that lines 17–19 select the left side of a vertical split within the bottom of a horizontally split panel. You should be able to look back at Figure 7.31 and convince yourself that this is where the Two button is located. Finally, line 21 creates the Three button by using successive calls to `getSubPanel`.

NOTE

> The `formatSplitter` method was written with the goal of demonstrating the use of as many `SplitterPanel` methods as possible. Because of this, it might seem to inconsistently use the various subpanel-selection methods. For example, on line 12 of Listing 7.3 you could have used `getTopPanel` instead of `getSubPanel(1)`.

The `TabPanel` **Class**

Tabbed dialogs have become so common that almost every significant program includes at least one. Fortunately, Visual Café includes the `TabPanel` class. This class makes creating tabbed dialogs a breeze. To create a tab panel, you take the following steps:

1. Drag a `TabPanel` object from the Component palette to the Form Designer.
2. Set the `Tab Labels` property to contain an entry for each tab of the panel.
3. For each tab you want to create, drag a panel from the Component palette and place it on the tab panel. As panels are placed on the tab panel, additional tabs will appear on the `TabPanel` object.
4. To work with a panel on an individual tab of the tab panel, select the tab by clicking on it. Place components as usual onto the selected tab. Repeat this process for each tab on the tab panel.

TIP

> By default, tab panels are displayed in white. If the form on which you are placing the tab panel is also white, it makes it difficult to see the individual tabs. To make it easier to see the tabs in the Form Designer you may want to set the `Background` property of the tab panel. If you want the tab panel to be white when run, you can reset the `Background` property when you've finished designing the form.

Because `TabPanel` is a subclass of `BaseTabbedPanel`, `TabPanel` objects can use methods from either class. Table 7.7 describes the most useful methods of these two classes.

Table 7.7. Some useful methods available to `TabPanel` objects.

Method	Purpose
`countTabs()`	Returns the number of tabs on the panel.
`enableTabPanel(boolean, int)`	Enables or disables the specified tab number.
`getCurrentNdx()`	Returns the zero-based tab number of the current tab.
`getLabel(int)`	Returns a string that is the label of the current tab.
`getPanelLabels()`	Returns an array of strings containing the label of each tab.
`getTabsPosition()`	Returns TOP or BOTTOM to indicate where the tabs are located.
`setCurrentPanelNdx(int)`	Sets the current tab to the specified tab number.
`setTabsOnBottom(boolean)`	Specifies whether tabs are to be placed on the top or the bottom of the panel.
`setTab(String, tabNum)`	Sets the label of the specified tab number.
`tabIsEnabled(int)`	Returns true if the tab is enabled or false if not.

WARNING

Remember, the individual tabs within a tab panel are numbered starting with 0.

Figure 7.33 shows the first tab of a sample applet created with the `TabPanel` component. As you can see, the applet includes four tabs across the top of the tab panel. The first tab includes two buttons that can be used to move the tabs between the top and bottom of the panel. Figure 7.34 shows the result of moving the tabs to the bottom of the tab panel.

The event-handling methods associated with these buttons are as follows:

```
void bottomButton_Clicked(java.awt.event.ActionEvent event) {
    tabPanel1.setTabsOnBottom(true);
    bottomButton.disable();
    topButton.enable();
}
```

```
void topButton_Clicked(java.awt.event.ActionEvent  event) {
    tabPanel1.setTabsOnBottom(false);
    topButton.disable();
    bottomButton.enable();
}
```

Figure 7.33.

Tabs can be placed on the top of the panel...

Figure 7.34.

...or you can place the tabs on the bottom of the panel.

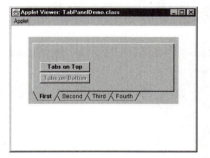

You can see that in both cases, setTabsOnBottom was used. When passed true, the tabs are moved to the bottom; when passed false, the tabs are moved to the top.

The second tab of this sample applet, shown in Figure 7.35, contains a single button that can be used to toggle the availability of the third panel. This is done with the following method:

```
void enableButton_Clicked(java.awt.event.ActionEvent event) {
    if (tabPanel1.tabIsEnabled(2))
        tabPanel1.enableTabPanel(false, 2);
    else
        tabPanel1.enableTab(true, 2);
}
```

In this case, tabIsEnabled is used to determine whether the third tab is enabled. (Remember, tab numbers are zero-based.) Then enableTabPanel is passed either true or false to toggle the state of the tab. If you look closely at Figure 7.35, you will notice that the label of the Third tab is grayed out, indicating that the tab is unavailable.

7

Figure 7.35.

The Third tab is disabled.

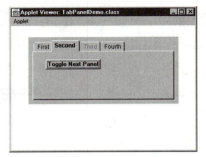

When the Third tab is selected, it looks like Figure 7.36. This tab illustrates the ability to dynamically change a tab's label. The user can enter text in a text field and then click the Set Label button to use the new label. This is done with the setLabel method, as follows:

```
void setLabelButton_Clicked(java.awt.event.ActionEvent event) {
    tabPanel1.setLabel(newLabel.getText(), 2);
}
```

Figure 7.36.

A tab's label can be changed at runtime.

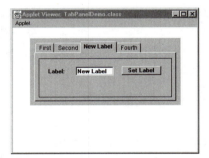

All of the tabs you've seen so far were created by dragging a Panel component onto the tab panel. You are not limited to dragging only plain Panel components onto a tab panel, however. Instead, you can use any of the subclasses of Panel, including another TabPanel. The Fourth tab of TabPanelDemo, shown in Figure 7.37, illustrates this.

TIP

By default, a tab panel will start by displaying its last tab. Usually this is the opposite of what you want. To start with a different tab, set the Active Tab property or use the setCurrentPanelNdx method. For example, the following will select the first tab on a tab panel:

```
tabPanel1.setCurrentPanelNdx(0);
```

Figure 7.37.

A tab can even contain another tab panel.

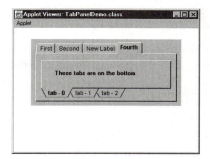

Do	Don't

DO place one type of panel onto another type of panel to take advantage of both panel types. For example, a KeyPressManagerPanel placed on a TabPanel allows users to tab through the components on a tab.

DO keep in mind that the tabs of a TabPanel are numbered starting with 0, but the panels of a SplitterPanel are numbered starting with 1.

DON'T overuse tabbed panels. Generally it is best to avoid more than one level of nested tab panels.

DO use scrolling panels to make the most of a program's screen space. Keep in mind that you don't know the resolution of your users' monitors.

Summary

Today you learned how to fine-tune and optimize a program's user interface. You learned all the details about the Form Designer and how it can help you properly position and size components. You also learned about Java's five layout managers and how you can use them to create user interfaces that appear correctly regardless of the user's screen resolution. You learned how FlowLayout continues placing as many components as possible on each line of the form. You saw how to use BorderLayout to position components in the north, south, east, west, and center of a form. You now know how CardLayout can be used to create changeable displays. You learned how to use GridLayout when creating forms that are organized into rows and columns, and you learned about GridBagLayout and the flexibility it provides.

Then, you turned your attention to the Panel class and learned how it can be used to create even more precise user interfaces. Finally, you learned about the subclasses of Panel that were provided with Visual Café: BorderPanel, RadioButtonGroupPanel, KeyPressManagerPanel, ScrollingPanel, SplitterPanel, and TabPanel.

7

Q&A

Q **I'm writing an intranet application. All my users are using the same size of monitor and the same browser. Should I still use layout managers?**

A Yes. Using a layout manager allows you to create forms that will appear correctly regardless of what your users do or use. Even if you are assured that all users are running in identical environments, you have no assurance that some users won't resize some of an applet's windows.

Q **I'm trying to create a scrolling panel, but when I run my applet I don't see any scrollbars. What happened?**

A After you placed a `ScrollingPanel` object on the form, you probably added a panel to the form and then placed your components on this panel. Somehow, the panel was inadvertently moved off of the `ScrollingPanel` object in the Form Designer. To check this, look at the drop-down list at the top of the Property List and see if your panel is indented beneath the `ScrollingPanel` object. If it is not, go to the Form Designer and drag the panel onto the `ScrollingPanel` object.

Q **I am trying to create a tabbed panel. I've placed a `TabPanel` on the form, but when I drop a button on the first tab the button is resized to the entire size of the `TabPanel`. What's wrong?**

A When you drop a component directly onto a `TabPanel`, the Form Designer thinks you want to make a new tab. You should, instead, drop a `Panel` onto the `TabPanel` and then drop the button onto the panel.

Q **When I drop panels onto a `TabPanel` my tabs are named `tab-0`, `tab-1`, and so on. What's wrong?**

A These are the default labels used by Visual Café whenever you don't provide a label. The easiest way to supply your own labels is by entering them into the `Tab Labels` property in the Property List. Alternatively, you could use the `setPanelLabels` method and pass it an array of strings.

Workshop

The workshop includes quiz questions to help you gauge your understanding of the material in this chapter. The workshop also includes exercises to provide hands-on experience with what you've learned in this chapter. For the answers to the quiz questions, see Appendix D, "Answers."

Quiz

1. Is `Component` a subclass or superclass of `Container`?

2. What are the five layout managers?

3. How does the `FlowLayout` manager determine where to position its components?

4. In what areas can components on a `BorderLayout` be placed?

5. What happens if all components on a form using `GridBagLayout` have `Weight X` and `Weight Y` values of `0`?

6. What are the four values that can be used for the `Fill` property of a `GridBagLayout`, and what does each do?

7. Why should the subpanels of a `SplitterPanel` be designed to the side of the `SplitterPanel` in the Form Designer?

Exercises

1. Use `CardLayout` to create an applet that includes three cards. Above the cards, have buttons that move between the cards: First, Previous, Next, and Last. The user should be able to use the Tab key and Shift+Tab keystroke to move between these buttons. On the first card, include a label that says `This is the first card`. On the middle card, use a layout manager to pleasingly place a prompt and a text field. On the third card, display the text that was entered on the second card.

2. Write a program that allows two human players to play Tic Tac Toe.

3. Enhance the Tic Tac Toe program so that the cells are all resizable.

4. Modify line 21 of Listing 7.3 so that it uses `getSub2Panel`.

5. Write an applet that uses a `ScrollingPanel` to allow the user to scroll through a very tall `TabPanel`.

7

In Review

Week 1 provided you with a solid foundation upon which to build in the coming weeks. On Day 1, "A Java Language Refresher," you were introduced to Java's primitive types and the operators that are available for these types. Next, you learned how to control the flow of a Java program through its selection statements (`if`, `switch`, and `case`), its iteration statements (`for`, `while`, and `do...while`), and jumping (`break` and `continue`). You learned how to put all this together and create new classes by deriving them from existing classes or interfaces. Finally, you learned how to effectively handle errors with exception handling.

On Day 2, "Getting Started with Visual Café," you gained a solid level of familiarity with the Visual Café desktop and many of the tools and windows you will use most frequently. You learned about and used the Form Designer, the Component palette, the Project window, the

Property List, and the Interaction wizard. You also learned how to easily create event-handling methods in Visual Café's source-code editing windows. To put this knowledge into practice, you wrote two simple applets and generated a basic application.

On Day 3, "Programming Applets and Handling Events," you learned how an applet's `init`, `start`, `stop`, and `destroy` methods are executed over the life of an applet. Because understanding event handling is critical to applet development, this chapter presents numerous examples of how to handle events. Finally, this chapter demonstrats how to embed an applet in a Web page and how to customize the behavior of an applet by using applet parameters embedded in the host HTML file.

On Day 4, "Java Strings," you learned about the `String` and `StringBuffer` classes, two of the most commonly used classes in Java programming. You learned that the `String` class is intended to hold nonchanging text. You saw many examples of using the member methods of the `String` class, including changing the case of a string, trimming whitespace, and accessing substrings. You learned how to convert variables of other types into strings and how to search and compare strings. Finally, you saw how the `StringBuffer` class is a more useful class for dynamic strings because text can be inserted and appended.

On Day 5, "Using the Abstract Windowing Toolkit," you learned that the `Component` class is the base class for many of the Java user-interface classes. You learned about the `Button`, `TextField`, `TextArea`, `Label`, `Checkbox`, `List`, `Choice`, and `Scrollbar` classes and how you can use them to create an applet's user interface.

On Day 6, "Debugging, Customizing, and Managing Projects," you learned about the Visual Café debugger. You learned how to set breakpoints, including conditional breakpoints that stop program execution only when they've met conditions you establish. You learned how to inspect variables, debug multiple threads, examine the call stack, and step through a program in the debugger. You also learned how to create and manage workspaces. The Class browser and Hierarchy editor were also described, and you learned how to use these tools to examine existing classes and create new classes.

On Day 7, "The Form Designer, Layout Managers, and Panels," you learned how to fine-tune and optimize a program's user interface. You learned all the details about the Form Designer and how it can help you properly position and size components. You also learned about Java's five layout managers and how you can use them to create user interfaces that appear correctly regardless of the user's screen resolution. You learned how `FlowLayout` continues placing as many components as possible on each line of the form. You saw how to use `BorderLayout` to position components in the north, south, east, west, and center of a form. You now know how `CardLayout` can be used to create changeable displays. You learned how to use GridLayout when creating forms that are organized into rows and columns, and you learned about GridBagLayout and the flexibility it provides. Then, you turned your attention to the Panel class and learned how it can be used to create even more precise user interfaces. Finally, you learned about the subclasses of Panel that were provided with Visual Café: BorderPanel, RadioButtonGroupPanel, KeyPressManagerPanel, ScrollingPanel, SplitterPanel, and TabPanel.

At A Glance

During this week you will learn about the components in Visual Café's Object Library. You will also learn how to create more advanced user interfaces by creating your own windows, menus, and toolbars. You will improve your Java knowledge by learning about streams, multithreading, and Java's utility classes.

Day 8, "Using the Object Library," is the first of two chapters dedicated entirely to the Visual Café Object Library. In this chapter you will learn about the `WrappingLabel`, `Label3d`, `TreeView`, slider, `InvisibleButton`, HTML link, `StatusBar`, `ProgressBar`, `Timer`, `Calendar`, `ComboBox`, and formatted text field components. This chapter covers a lot of ground; by the end of it you will be able to use these powerful new components in your own Java programs.

8

9

10

11

12

13

14

On Day 9, "More Object Library Components," you'll continue your exploration of the Visual Café Object Library. On this day you will learn about the `MultiList`, `LabelButton`, `ImageListBox`, `NumericSpinner`, `ListSpinner`, `DaySpinner`, `MonthSpinner`, `DirectionButton`, and `StateCheckBox` components.

On Day 10, "Windows, Frames, and Dialogs," you'll learn how to create standalone windows, frames, and dialogs. By placing AWT and Object Library components on standalone windows, you can create more powerful user interfaces.

On Day 11, "Menus and Toolbars," you will learn how to create menus and toolbars. Visual Café includes a Menu editor that greatly simplifies menu creation. You will learn how to use the Menu editor to create menu bars, menus, menu items, separators, submenus, and checkbox menu items. Toolbars are often used instead of or in addition to menus, and Visual Café's Object library includes classes that aid in creating toolbars. In this chapter, you will learn how easy it is to create a fully functional toolbar without writing a single line of code.

On Day 12, "The Java Utility Classes," you'll learn about the `java.util` package. This package provides some very useful Java classes on which you will come to rely. This chapter introduces the following classes and interfaces: `BitSet`, `Date`, `Enumeration`, `Hashtable`, `Properties`, `Observable`, `Random`, `Vector`, `Stack`, and `StringTokenizer`.

On Day 13, "Using Streams for Input and Output," you will learn how to move data into and out of your Visual Café programs through the use of streams. Along the way, you will learn about Java's byte streams, character, and object streams. You will see how you can use streams to write to and read from files and strings. You will see how to improve the performance of streams by buffering them, and you will see some special-purpose streams that add features such as line numbering and the capability to push data back into a stream.

On Day 14, "Multithreading," you will learn how to work with Java threads. By using threads, you can write programs that give the appearance of doing more than one task at a time. For example, a multithreaded program may be downloading graphics in one thread, connecting to a database in another, and interacting with the user in a third.

Day 8

Using the Object Library

This is the first of two lessons dedicated entirely to the Visual Café Object Library. In this lesson you will learn about the WrappingLabel, Label3D, TreeView, slider, InvisibleButton, HTML link, StatusBar, ProgressBar, Timer, Calendar, ComboBox, and formatted text field components. This lesson covers a lot of ground in describing each of these components, but by the end of it you will be able to use these powerful new components in your own Java programs.

The Label Components

In addition to the Label component provided by the AWT (Abstract Windowing Toolkit), Visual Café provides two additional label components: WrappingLabel and Label3D.

WrappingLabel

The `WrappingLabel` component is useful when you need to place a lengthy label. While an AWT label is limited to one line, a wrapping label can take up multiple lines, and text will wrap from one line to the next as necessary, as shown in Figure 8.1. Additionally, you can specify whether a wrapping label will be left, right, or center aligned. By default, wrapping labels are left aligned.

Figure 8.1.

`WrappingLabel` *extends* `Canvas` *and implements* `AlignStyle`.

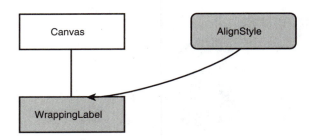

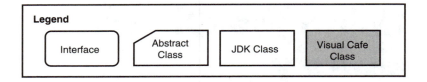

You can create a new wrapping label by dragging the component onto the Form Designer or by using one of the two constructors shown in the following code fragment:

```
WrappingLabel label1 = new WrappingLabel("Hello");
WrappingLabel label2 = new WrappingLabel("Goodbye",
        WrappingLabel.ALIGN_RIGHT);
```

In this case, the first label will be left aligned (the default) while the second label is explicitly right aligned. To left- or center-align a wrapping label, you can use the constants `WrappingLabel.ALIGN_LEFT` and `WrappingLabel.ALIGN_CENTERED`.

NOTE   Visual Café does not automatically add an import statement for any packages you add from the Component palette. If you do not work with a component in code, but instead use only the Form Designer and the Property List, this works. However, if you manipulate the component with code, you should include the following import statement:
`import symantec.itools.awt.*;`

8

If you do not know which alignment style is appropriate when the label is constructed, you can alter it with the `setAlignStyle` method. For example, the following code creates a left-aligned label and then changes it to be right aligned:

```
WrappingLabel label = new WrappingLabel("Hello");
label.setAlignStyle(WrappingLabel.ALIGN_RIGHT);
```

Additionally, the `getAlignStyle` method can be used to retrieve a wrapping label's current alignment. The text of the label can be retrieved or set using `getText` and `setText`. The constructors and useful methods of `WrappingLabel` are summarized in Table 8.1.

Table 8.1. Constructors and useful methods of `WrappingLabel`.

Method	Purpose
WrappingLabel()	Creates a new label without any text. Only useful if `setText` is used subsequently.
WrappingLabel(String)	Creates a new label with the specified text.
WrappingLabel(String, int)	Creates a new label with the specified text and alignment style.
getAlignStyle()	Returns the current alignment style of the wrapping label.
getText()	Returns the text of the label.
setAlignStyle(int)	Sets the alignment style of the wrapping label to the specified type.
setText(String)	Sets the text of the label.

An Example

As an example of how to manipulate a wrapping label, the sample applet `LabelDemo` is shown in Listing 8.1 and Figure 8.2. This applet is included on the MCP Web site (www.mcp.com/info/1-57521/1-57521-303-6).

Listing 8.1. `LabelDemo.java`.

```
1:    import java.awt.*;
2:    import java.applet.*;
3:
4:    public class LabelDemo extends Applet {
5:       String labelText = "This WrappingLabel is currently ";
6:
7:       void nextButton_Clicked(java.awt.event.ActionEvent event){
8:          int align = wrapLabel.ALIGN_LEFT;
9:
```

continues

Listing 8.1. continued

```
10:            try {
11:                switch(wrapLabel.getAlignStyle()) {
12:                    case wrapLabel.ALIGN_LEFT:
13:                      align = wrapLabel.ALIGN_CENTERED;
14:                      wrapLabel.setText(labelText+"center aligned.");
15:                      break;
16:                    case wrapLabel.ALIGN_CENTERED:
17:                       align = wrapLabel.ALIGN_RIGHT;
18:                       wrapLabel.setText(labelText+"right aligned.");
19:                       break;
20:                    case wrapLabel.ALIGN_RIGHT:
21:                       align = wrapLabel.ALIGN_LEFT;
22:                       wrapLabel.setText(labelText+"left aligned.");
23:                       break;
24:                }
25:                wrapLabel.setAlignStyle(align);
26:                wrapLabel.repaint();
27:            }
28:            catch (java.beans.PropertyVetoException e) {
29:            }
30:        }
31:
32:        public void init() {
33:            // Call parents init method.
34:            super.init();
35:        }
36:
37:        public void addNotify() {
38:            // Call parents addNotify method.
39:            super.addNotify();
40:
41:            //{{INIT_CONTROLS
42:            setLayout(null);
43:            resize(426,149);
44:            wrapLabel = new symantec.itools.awt.WrappingLabel();
45:            wrapLabel.reshape(36,60,168,36);
46:            add(wrapLabel);
47:            try {
48:                wrapLabel.setText(
49:                    "This wrapping label is currently left aligned");
50:            }
51:            catch (java.beans.PropertyVetoException veto) { }
52:            nextButton = new java.awt.Button("Next");
53:            nextButton.reshape(228,60,96,24);
54:            add(nextButton);
55:            //}}
56:
57:            //{{REGISTER_LISTENERS
58:            Action lAction = new Action();
59:            nextButton.addActionListener(lAction);
60:            //}}
61:        }
62:
```

```
63:    //{{DECLARE_CONTROLS
64:    symantec.itools.awt.WrappingLabel wrapLabel;
65:    java.awt.Button nextButton;
66:    //}}
67:
68:    class Action implements java.awt.event.ActionListener {
69:       public void actionPerformed(java.awt.event.ActionEvent
70:             event) {
71:          Object object = event.getSource();
72:          if (object == nextButton)
73:             nextButton_Clicked(event);
74:       }
75:    }
76: }
```

Figure 8.2.

The LabelDemo *with a left-aligned label.*

ANALYSIS In this case, the wrapping label, wrapLabel, was dragged onto the Form Designer. Therefore, code to create it was generated by Visual Café (lines 44–51). The nextButton_Clicked method (7–30) is executed whenever the user clicks the Next button. Clicking this button causes the alignment of the label's text to change from left to centered to right, and back again. Figure 8.3 shows the LabelDemo applet after the Next button was clicked twice, causing the label to become right aligned.

Figure 8.3.

After the user clicks Next twice, the label is right aligned.

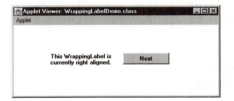

 NOTE Unfortunately, WrappingLabel does not translate newline (\n) or carriage-return (\r) sequences into new lines, so you cannot specify where new lines occur.

Label3D

The second type of label provided by Visual Café is the Label3D class. As shown in Figure 8.4, Label3D extends Canvas and implements the AlignStyle and BevelStyle interfaces. This class allows you to create labels with a 3D, beveled appearance. In addition to the usual customizations available for any component, you can also customize the following attributes of a Label3D object:

- ☐ The type of bevel that appears around the label
- ☐ The color of the border
- ☐ The amount by which the border is indented
- ☐ Whether the text should be left, right, or center aligned
- ☐ The color of the text

Figure 8.4.

Label3D *extends* Canvas *and implements* AlignStyle *and* BevelStyle.

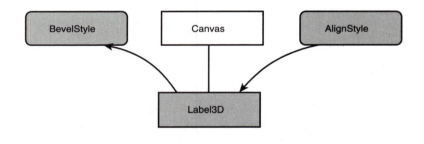

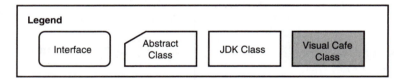

You can create a Label3D by dragging it from the Component palette to the Form Designer; the following constructors are available:

```
Label3D()

Label3D(String text, int alignStyle, int bevelStyle)

Label3D(String text, int alignStyle, int bevelStyle,
        Color textColor)

Label3D(String text, int alignStyle, int bevelStyle,
        Color textColor, int borderIndent)

Label3D(String text, int alignStyle, int bevelStyle,
        int borderIndent)
```

You can left-, right-, or center-align the label by using `Label3D.ALIGN_LEFT`, `Label3D.ALIGN_RIGHT`, or `Label3D.ALIGN_CENTERED`. Additionally, you can change the alignment of a label after it has been constructed by using `setAlignStyle` and passing it one of these constants. There is also a `getAlignStyle` method that will return the current alignment style.

The valid values for specifying the bevel style of a `Label3D` object are `Label3D.BEVEL_NONE`, `Label3D.BEVEL_LOWERED`, `Label3D.BEVEL_RAISED`, and `Label3D.BEVEL_LINE`. These values can be passed to all but one of the constructors or to `setBevelStyle`. Additionally, `getBevelStyle` will return the current bevel style.

These methods and other useful members of `Label3D` are summarized in Table 8.2.

Table 8.2. Useful methods of `Label3D`.

Method	Purpose
`getAlignStyle()`	Returns the current alignment style of the label.
`getBevelStyle()`	Returns the current bevel style of the label.
`getBorderIndent()`	Returns the current amount of the border indent.
`getText()`	Returns the text of the label.
`getTextColor()`	Returns the color used for the text.
`setAlignStyle(int)`	Sets the alignment style of the label to the specified type.
`setBevelStyle(int)`	Sets the bevel style of the label to the specified type.
`setBorderedColor(Color)`	Sets the color to use for the borders.
`setBorderIndent(int)`	Sets the amount by which to indent the border.
`setText(String)`	Sets the text of the label.
`setTextColor(Color)`	Sets the color to use for the text.

An Example

The applet `Label3DDemo`, included on the MCP Web site, is an example of using the `Label3D` component. This applet allows you to visually experiment with the alignment and bevel options for a label, as can be seen in Figure 8.5.

When the Apply button is clicked, the label is repainted using the alignment and bevel values selected by the user. Figure 8.6 shows the applet after the user selected the Right and Lowered options and clicked Apply.

The code that is executed when the Apply button is clicked is shown in Listing 8.2.

Figure 8.5.

In `Label3DDemo`, *the label is initially center aligned with a raised bevel.*

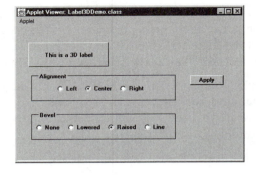

Figure 8.6.

A `Label3D` *that is right aligned and has a lowered bevel.*

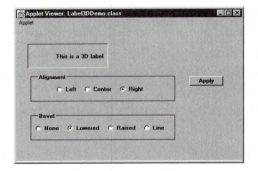

Listing 8.2. The `applyButton_Clicked` method of `Label3DDemo`.

```
1:  void applyButton_Clicked(java.awt.event.ActionEvent event) {
2:      int alignStyle = Label3D.ALIGN_LEFT;
3:      int bevelStyle = Label3D.BEVEL_RAISED;
4:
5:      // change the alignment
6:      Checkbox selectedAlignment = alignGroup.getCurrent();
7:      if (selectedAlignment == alignCenter)
8:          alignStyle = Label3D.ALIGN_CENTERED;
9:      else if (selectedAlignment == alignLeft)
10:         alignStyle = Label3D.ALIGN_LEFT;
11:     else if (selectedAlignment == alignRight)
12:         alignStyle = Label3D.ALIGN_RIGHT;
13:
14:     // apply the selected alignment style
15:     try {
16:         label.setAlignStyle(alignStyle);
17:     }
18:     catch (java.beans.PropertyVetoException e) {
19:     }
20:
21:     // change the bevel style
22:     Checkbox selectedBevel = bevelGroup.getCurrent();
23:     if (selectedBevel == bevelNone)
24:         bevelStyle = Label3D.BEVEL_NONE;
```

```
25:    else if (selectedBevel == bevelLowered)
26:        bevelStyle = Label3D.BEVEL_LOWERED;
27:    else if (selectedBevel == bevelRaised)
28:        bevelStyle = Label3D.BEVEL_RAISED;
29:    else if (selectedBevel == bevelLine)
30:        bevelStyle = Label3D.BEVEL_LINE;
31:
32:    // apply the selected bevel style
33:    try {
34:        label.setBevelStyle(bevelStyle);
35:    }
36:    catch (java.beans.PropertyVetoException e) {
37:    }
38:
39:    // repaint the label
40:    label.repaint();
41: }
```

Do	Don't

DO be consistent in your use of labels. Avoid using many different label classes (WrappingLabel, Label3D, and Label) on the same form or within the same program. Similarly, select one bevel type (such as BEVEL_RAISED) and stick with it as much as possible. Using more than one bevel style creates a confusing user interface.

DON'T overuse the WrappingLabel component. Because most labels occur on only a single line, users will not expect to see a label that wraps across more than one line.

TreeView

The TreeView component displays a hierarchical list of items. While working with Visual Café, you have encountered tree components on a variety of dialogs. For example, consider the Insert Object dialog, shown in Figure 8.7 (access it onscreen by selecting Component from the Insert menu). The Visual Café TreeView component is a subclass of Panel, as can be seen in Figure 8.8.

NEW TERM The items in a TreeView are known as *nodes*. Each node can be *expanded* (meaning its child nodes are viewable) or *collapsed* (meaning its child nodes are not viewable).

NEW TERM A *visible* node is one that can be seen on the screen at the present time. A *viewable* node is one whose parent has been expanded so that the node will be visible if the user scrolls appropriately within the TreeView. A node can be viewable but not visible. A node cannot be visible but not viewable.

Figure 8.7.

Visual Café uses tree
*components on its
dialogs, including the
Insert Object dialog.*

Figure 8.8.

TreeView *extends*
Panel.

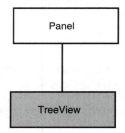

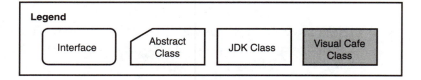

Adding Nodes to a TreeView

The easiest way to create the nodes of a tree is to use the Property List. To do this, drag a
TreeView component onto the Form Designer and select the Items property in the Property
List. Create nodes by entering each node's text in the Property List. To create a new node,
press Ctrl+Enter. To make a node a child of the preceding node, add a space to the front of
the node text. Use an additional space character to indicate each level of indentation in the
tree. So if an item is to be the child of a node that starts with one space, the child must start
with two spaces.

Setting the Tree Structure

Another way to add nodes to a TreeView is with the method setTreeStructure. This method
is passed an array of strings with the spaces at the front of each string used to indicate the item's
level of indentation in the tree. For example, the following code will create the tree shown
in Figure 8.9:

```
void loadTreeStructure() {
    String[] strArray = new String[15];
    strArray[0]  = new java.lang.String("Menu");
    strArray[1]  = new java.lang.String(" Salads");
    strArray[2]  = new java.lang.String("  Caesar");
    strArray[3]  = new java.lang.String("  Green");
    strArray[4]  = new java.lang.String("  Fruit");
    strArray[5]  = new java.lang.String(" Sandwiches");
    strArray[6]  = new java.lang.String("  Hamburger");
    strArray[7]  = new java.lang.String("  Chili Burger");
    strArray[8]  = new java.lang.String("  Chicken Sandwich");
    strArray[9]  = new java.lang.String("  Tuna Melt");
    strArray[10] = new java.lang.String(" Side Dishes");
    strArray[11] = new java.lang.String("  Fries");
    strArray[12] = new java.lang.String("   Small");
    strArray[13] = new java.lang.String("   Large");
    strArray[14] = new java.lang.String("  Baked Potato");
    tree.setTreeStructure(strArray);
}
```

Figure 8.9.

*A tree that was
loaded using*
setTreeStructure.

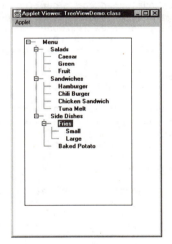

Appending and Inserting Nodes

The final way you can create the nodes of a tree is to use the append and insert methods, whose signatures are as follows:

```
void append(TreeNode newNode)
```

```
void insert(TreeNode newNode, TreeNode relativeNode, int position)
```

Both methods rely on the TreeNode class. TreeNode is used to represent the individual nodes in a TreeView. The easiest way to create a TreeNode is with its constructor that is passed only a string, as can be seen in the following examples:

```
TreeNode tn1 = new TreeNode("Tuna Melt");

TreeNode tn1 = new TreeNode("Baked Potato");
```

The append method will create a new root-level node, while insert is used to add new nodes relative to existing nodes. With insert you can place a new node before an existing node, after an existing node, or as a child of an existing node. Listing 8.3 illustrates the use of append and insert. This listing will create the exact tree that was shown in Figure 8.9.

Listing 8.3. Using append and insert to create the same tree.

```
 1:    void insertNodes() {
 2:        // add the root node "Menu"
 3:        TreeNode menuNode = new TreeNode("Menu");
 4:        tree.append(menuNode);
 5:
 6:        // add the "Salad" node and its children
 7:        TreeNode saladNode = new TreeNode("Salads");
 8:        tree.insert(saladNode, menuNode, TreeView.CHILD);
 9:        tree.insert(new TreeNode("Caesar"), saladNode,
10:              TreeView.CHILD);
11:        tree.insert(new TreeNode("Green"), saladNode,
12:              TreeView.CHILD);
13:        tree.insert(new TreeNode("Fruit"), saladNode,
14:              TreeView.CHILD);
15:
16:        // add the "Sandwiches" node and its children
17:        TreeNode sandwichNode = new TreeNode("Sandwiches");
18:        tree.insert(sandwichNode, menuNode, TreeView.CHILD);
19:        tree.insert(new TreeNode("Hamburger"), sandwichNode,
20:              TreeView.CHILD);
21:        tree.insert(new TreeNode("Chili Burger"),
22:              sandwichNode, TreeView.CHILD);
23:        tree.insert(new TreeNode("Chicken Sandwich"),
24:              sandwichNode, TreeView.CHILD);
25:        tree.insert(new TreeNode("Tuna Melt"),
26:              sandwichNode, TreeView.CHILD);
27:
28:        // add the "Side Dishes" node
29:        TreeNode sidesNode = new TreeNode("Side Dishes");
30:        tree.insert(sidesNode, menuNode, TreeView.CHILD);
31:
32:        // add the "Fries" node and its children
33:        TreeNode friesNode = new TreeNode("Fries");
34:        tree.insert(friesNode, sidesNode, TreeView.CHILD);
35:        tree.insert(new TreeNode("Small"), friesNode, TreeView.CHILD);
36:        tree.insert(new TreeNode("Large"), friesNode, TreeView.CHILD);
37:
38:        // add the "Potato" node to "Side Dishes"
39:        tree.insert(new TreeNode("Baked Potato"), sidesNode,
40:              TreeView.CHILD);
41:    }
```

ANALYSIS   On lines 3 and 4 the root node, menuNode, is constructed and added to the tree with append. The salad menu is created between lines 7 and 14. First the salad node itself is created (line 7) and a reference to it is saved in saladNode. Next, saladNode is added to the tree with insert (8). Because Salad needs to appear as a child of Menu, TreeView.CHILD is specified as the final parameter to insert. Finally, the children of saladNode are inserted. References to the child nodes are not stored because those nodes are not manipulated or passed to other methods.

The sandwiches part of the tree is created in an identical manner. However, the side-dishes part of the tree is more complicated because it includes a node with its own children. (Fries includes child nodes of Small and Large.) This part of the tree is made by first adding the sidesNode (lines 29–30). Next, friesNode is constructed and a reference to it is saved (line 33). The children of the friesNode are then inserted (lines 35–36). Finally, Baked Potato is inserted as a child of sidesNode (lines 39–40). This makes it at the same level as, or a sibling of, friesNode.

Multiple Root Nodes

It is also possible to create multiple root nodes, as can be seen in Listing 8.4. In this example, append is used to add Salad and Sandwich as root-level nodes (lines 4 and 11). Side Dishes could also have been added with append, but it was added with insert instead (line 24). However, Side Dishes appears as a root-level node because TreeView.NEXT causes it to be added as the next sibling of sandwichNode. If line 24 had used TreeView.PREVIOUS instead, the Side Dishes would have appeared before Sandwiches in the tree. The tree created by Listing 8.4 is shown in Figure 8.10.

Listing 8.4. Multiple root nodes can also be created.

```
1:      void insertMultipleRootNodes() {
2:          // add the "Salad" node and its children
3:          TreeNode saladNode = new TreeNode("Salads");
4:          tree.append(saladNode);
5:          tree.insert(new TreeNode("Caesar"), saladNode, TreeView.CHILD);
6:          tree.insert(new TreeNode("Green"), saladNode, TreeView.CHILD);
7:          tree.insert(new TreeNode("Fruit"), saladNode, TreeView.CHILD);
8:
9:          // add the "Sandwiches" node and its children
10:         TreeNode sandwichNode = new TreeNode("Sandwiches");
11:         tree.append(sandwichNode);
12:
13:         tree.insert(new TreeNode("Hamburger"), sandwichNode,
14:               TreeView.CHILD);
15:         tree.insert(new TreeNode("Chili Burger"), sandwichNode,
16:               TreeView.CHILD);
17:         tree.insert(new TreeNode("Chicken Sandwich"),
18:               sandwichNode, TreeView.CHILD);
```

continues

Listing 8.4. continued

```
19:         tree.insert(new TreeNode("Tuna Melt"), sandwichNode,
20:             TreeView.CHILD);
21:
22:         // add the "Side Dishes" node
23:         TreeNode sidesNode = new TreeNode("Side Dishes");
24:         tree.insert(sidesNode, sandwichNode, TreeView.NEXT);
25:
26:         // add the "Fries" node and its children
27:         TreeNode friesNode = new TreeNode("Fries");
28:         tree.insert(friesNode, sidesNode, TreeView.CHILD);
29:         tree.insert(new TreeNode("Small"), friesNode,
30:             TreeView.CHILD);
31:         tree.insert(new TreeNode("Large"), friesNode,
32:             TreeView.CHILD);
33:
34:         // add the "Potato" node to "Side Dishes"
35:         tree.insert(new TreeNode("Baked Potato"), sidesNode,
36:             TreeView.CHILD);
37:    }
```

 NOTE

> A sample applet, TreeViewAddDemo, is included on the MCP Web site and can be used to test the behavior of each of the examples given here on how to add nodes to a tree.

Figure 8.10.

A tree with multiple root nodes.

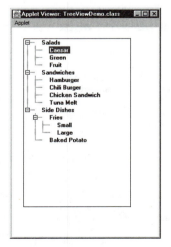

8

Expanding and Collapsing Nodes

If you attempted to run the preceding examples that illustrated how to write code to construct a tree, you probably noticed that when the tree was initially displayed, all of its nodes were collapsed. To expand a node, you must call its expand method. Similarly, collapse can be used to collapse a node, hiding its children. As an example, consider the following:

```
TreeNode saladNode = new TreeNode("Salads");
tree.append(saladNode);
tree.insert(new TreeNode("Caesar"), saladNode, TreeView.CHILD);
tree.insert(new TreeNode("Green"), saladNode, TreeView.CHILD);
tree.insert(new TreeNode("Fruit"), saladNode, TreeView.CHILD);
saladNode.expand();
```

In this case, a new node, saladNode, is created and added to the tree. Three children are added and then expand is used to make the children viewable. (Remember, *viewable* is not the same as *visible*.)

If expand makes a node viewable and that node has children of its own, the children are not expanded. In other words, expanding a node will make its children viewable, but not its grandchildren. In order to fully expand the Side Dishes node of Listing 8.4, both sidesNode and friesNode would need to be expanded, as follows:

```
sidesNode.expand();
friesNode.expand();
```

Adding Images

One of the nice features of TreeView is its capability to add small images next to the nodes. The tree shown in Figure 8.11 illustrates this by displaying a blue ball next to a collapsed node and a green ball next to an expanded node.

Figure 8.11.

You can specify different images to use when a node is collapsed or expanded.

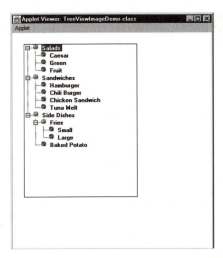

The images to use are specified when the `TreeNode` is created. In prior examples, a simple `TreeNode` constructor was used that was passed only a string. There is an additional constructor whose signature is

```
TreeNode(String str, Image collapsed, Image expanded)
```

Therefore, you can create a node that will display images as follows:

```
Image collapsedImg = getImage(getDocumentBase(), "blue.gif");
Image expandedImg = getImage(getDocumentBase(), "green.gif");
TreeNode newNode = TreeNode("Hi", collapsedImg, ExpandedImg);
```

NOTE   The `Image` class and the `getImage` method are described on Day 16, "Working with Graphics."

After a `TreeNode` has been created with this new constructor, the node can be added to the tree with `append` or `insert` just like any other node. Listing 8.5 illustrates how to create the tree shown in Figure 8.11 with a portion of code from the `TreeViewImageDemo` sample applet that is included on the MCP Web site.

Listing 8.5. A portion of `TreeViewImageDemo.java`.

```
1:   TreeNode makeNode(String str) {
2:       return new TreeNode(str, collapsedImg, expandedImg);
3:   }
4:
5:   private void FillTree() {
6:       MediaTracker tracker = new MediaTracker(this);
7:       collapsedImg = getImage(getDocumentBase(), "blue.gif");
8:       tracker.addImage(collapsedImg, 0);
9:       expandedImg = getImage(getDocumentBase(), "green.gif");
10:      tracker.addImage(expandedImg, 1);
11:
12:      int status;
13:      for(;;) {
14:          status = tracker.statusAll(true);
15:          if (status == MediaTracker.COMPLETE)
16:              break;
17:      }
18:
19:      // add the "Salad" node and its children
20:      TreeNode saladNode = makeNode("Salads");
21:      tree.append(saladNode);
22:      tree.insert(makeNode("Caesar"),saladNode,TreeView.CHILD);
23:      tree.insert(makeNode("Green"),saladNode,TreeView.CHILD);
24:      tree.insert(makeNode("Fruit"),saladNode,TreeView.CHILD);
25:
```

```
26:        // add the "Sandwiches" node and its children
27:        TreeNode sandwichNode = makeNode("Sandwiches");
28:        tree.insert(sandwichNode, saladNode, TreeView.NEXT);
29:        tree.insert(makeNode("Hamburger"), sandwichNode,
30:             TreeView.CHILD);
31:        tree.insert(makeNode("Chili Burger"), sandwichNode,
32:             TreeView.CHILD);
33:        tree.insert(makeNode("Chicken Sandwich"),
34:             sandwichNode, TreeView.CHILD);
35:        tree.insert(makeNode("Tuna Melt"), sandwichNode,
36:             TreeView.CHILD);
37:
38:        // add the "Side Dishes" node
39:        TreeNode sidesNode = makeNode("Side Dishes");
40:        tree.insert(sidesNode, sandwichNode, TreeView.NEXT);
41:
42:        // add the "Fries" node and its children
43:        TreeNode friesNode = makeNode("Fries");
44:        tree.insert(friesNode, sidesNode, TreeView.CHILD);
45:        tree.insert(makeNode("Small"), friesNode,
46:             TreeView.CHILD);
47:        tree.insert(makeNode("Large"),friesNode,TreeView.CHILD);
48:
49:        // add the "Potato" node to "Side Dishes"
50:        tree.insert(makeNode("Baked Potato"), sidesNode,
51:             TreeView.CHILD);
52:
53:        // expand all of the nodes
54:        saladNode.expand();
55:        sandwichNode.expand();
56:        sidesNode.expand();
57:        friesNode.expand();
58:   }
```

 In Listing 8.5, the makeNode method (lines 1–3) is provided as a convenience method to simplify the FillTree method. The TreeNode that is returned from makeNode always uses the images that are created at the top of FillTree (lines 7 and 9).

When the images are created with getImage, they are added to a MediaTracker object. This is done because getImage does not actually load the image. By using a MediaTracker object, you can ensure that the images are loaded before the tree is displayed, as is done in the loop between lines 13 and 17.

 NOTE

The MediaTracker class is discussed on Day 17, "Multimedia Programming." It is not necessary to understand MediaTracker at this point.

Searching for Nodes

`TreeView` includes two methods you can use to search for a specific node. Both are named `exists`, but they are overloaded to take different parameters as follows:

```
boolean exists(String str)

boolean exists(TreeNode node)
```

These methods return `true` if a matching string or node is found. This can be seen in the following code taken from the `TreeViewFindDeleteDemo` applet that is included on the MCP Web site

```
void findButton_Clicked(java.awt.event.ActionEvent event) {
    if(tree.exists(nodeTextField.getText()) == true)
        resultField.setText("Found");
    else
        resultField.setText("Not Found");
}
```

This example passes the contents of a text field to `exists`. If a matching node is found, a different text field will be set to `Found`; if not, the text field will be set to `Not Found`. This can be seen in Figure 8.12, which shows the result of searching for `Tuna Melt`.

Figure 8.12.

The `TreeView-`
`FindDeleteDemo`
*applet can be used to
search for or delete
nodes.*

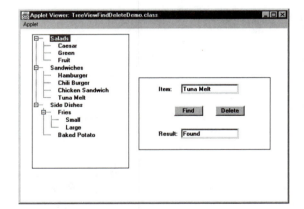

Deleting Nodes

Nodes can also be deleted. This is done using either of the `remove` methods:

```
TreeNode remove(String str)

TreeNode remove(TreeNode node)
```

If `remove` does not find the node to delete, it returns `null`. If the node is found and deleted, `remove` returns a reference to the node. In most cases you can simply ignore the returned

TreeNode; however, the returned node can sometimes be used, as shown in the following code fragment:

```
void deleteButton_Clicked(java.awt.event.ActionEvent event) {
    TreeNode tn = tree.remove(nodeTextField.getText());
    if (tn != null) {
        resultField.setText("Deleted: " + tn.getText());
        tree.redraw();
    }
    else
        resultField.setText("Not Found");
}
```

A TreeView object does not automatically repaint itself after a node has been removed. Therefore, the call to redraw was included in the preceding fragment so that the tree is redrawn to reflect the deleted node. You cannot call repaint because repaint is not aware of any changes to the tree (such as deleted nodes).

When a node is removed, its children are also removed. You can verify this by running TreeViewFindDeleteDemo and deleting one of the nodes that has children.

The Slider Components

Visual Café includes components for creating horizontal and vertical sliders. Some examples of how these components can be customized are shown in Figure 8.13.

Figure 8.13.

Various HorizontalSlider *and* VerticalSlider *objects.*

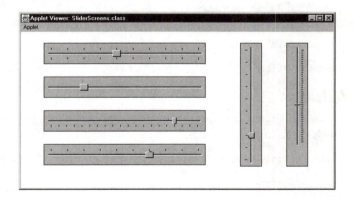

Figure 8.13 was created using the HorizontalSlider and VerticalSlider components. These are both subclasses of the abstract class Slider, as shown in Figure 8.14.

Figure 8.14.
Slider *extends*
Canvas;
HorizontalSlider
and
VerticalSlider
extend Slider.

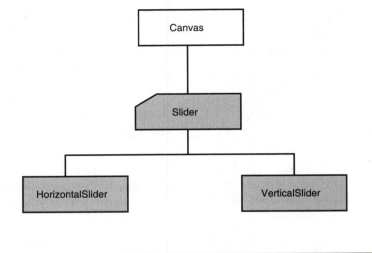

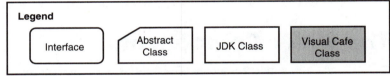

To create a new slider, either drag one from the Component palette or use one of the
following constructors:

```
HorizontalSlider()
```

```
VerticalSlider()
```

Values

Each slider has a minimum, maximum, and current value. The values can be manipulated
with the following methods:

```
void setMinimumValue(int value)
```

```
int getMinimumValue()
```

```
void setMaximumValue(int value)
```

```
int getMaximumValue()
```

```
void setValue(int value)
```

```
int getValue()
```

The following illustrates how to use these methods to create a new slider with a minimum value of 25, a maximum value of 75, and a current value of 50:

```
HorizontalSlider slider = new HorizontalSlider();
slider.setMinimumValue(25);
slider.setMaximumValue(75);
slider.setValue(50);
```

Customizing the Tick Marks

You can customize where the tick marks appear on a slider. If you refer to Figure 8.13, you will notice that each of the four horizontal sliders has its tick marks in a different location. The topmost horizontal slider has tick marks above and below the gauge. The next slider has no tick marks, while the third and fourth sliders show the tick marks below and above. Similarly, the first vertical slider shows the tick marks on the left and the second vertical slider has its tick marks on the right.

A slider's tick marks are set with a call to setTickStyle. A slider's tick-mark style can be retrieved with a call to getTickStyle. This can be seen in the following code fragment:

```
slider.setTickStyle(Slider.TICK_BOTH);
int style = slider.getTickStyle();
```

For a horizontal slider, the following tick-mark styles are available:

- ☐ TICK_BOTH
- ☐ TICK_BOTTOM
- ☐ TICK_TOP
- ☐ TICK_NONE

For a vertical slider, the following tick-mark styles are available:

- ☐ TICK_BOTH
- ☐ TICK_LEFT
- ☐ TICK_RIGHT
- ☐ TICK_NONE

In addition to the style of tick marks, you can also set the tick-mark frequency. The tick-mark frequency determines how many tick marks appear on the slider. For example, if a slider has a minimum value of 1, a maximum value of 10, and a tick frequency of 1, there will be 10 tick marks. If the same slider instead had a tick frequency of 2, there would be five tick marks. Use setTickFreq and getTickFreq to work with a slider's tick frequency. The following example will double a slider's current tick-mark frequency:

```
int current = slider.getTickFreq();
slider.setTickFreq(current * 2);
slider.repaint();
```

An Example

The SliderDemo applet, which is included on the MCP Web site, illustrates how the various methods can be used to customize the appearance and behavior of a slider. As you can see in Figure 8.15, this applet allows you to enter values for the slider's current value, minimum value, maximum value, and tick frequency. You can also indicate where tick marks should appear. When the Apply button is clicked, the indicated changes will be made and the slider updated. The relevant source from the SliderDemo applet is shown in Listing 8.6.

Figure 8.15.

The SliderDemo
*applet illustrates how
to customize a
horizontal slider.*

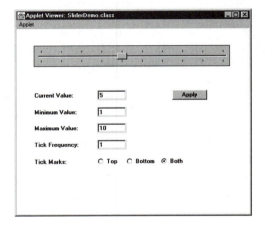

Listing 8.6. A portion of SliderDemo.java.

```
1:   void slider_MouseMove(java.awt.event.MouseEvent event) {
2:       currentValue.setText(String.valueOf(slider.getValue()));
3:   }
4:
5:   void applyButton_Clicked(java.awt.event.ActionEvent event) {
6:       try {
7:           slider.setMinValue(Integer.parseInt(
8:                   minValue.getText()));
9:           slider.setMaxValue(Integer.parseInt(
10:                  maxValue.getText()));
11:
12:          slider.setTickFreq(Integer.parseInt(
13:                  tickFrequency.getText()));
14:
15:          if(tickGroup.getCurrent() == topTicks)
16:              slider.setTickStyle(Slider.TICK_TOP);
17:          else if(tickGroup.getCurrent() == bottomTicks)
18:              slider.setTickStyle(Slider.TICK_BOTTOM);
19:          if(tickGroup.getCurrent() == bothTicks)
20:              slider.setTickStyle(Slider.TICK_BOTH);
21:
22:          slider.setValue(Integer.parseInt(
23:                  currentValue.getText()));
```

```
24:         slider.repaint();
25:     }
26:     catch (java.beans.PropertyVetoException e) {
27:     }
28: }
```

InvisibleButton

The InvisibleButton class allows an applet to define buttons that are not visible to users. However, if the user clicks an invisible button, the button can respond to events like any other button. As shown in Figure 8.16, InvisibleButton extends Canvas.

Figure 8.16.

InvisibleButton
extends Canvas.

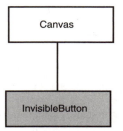

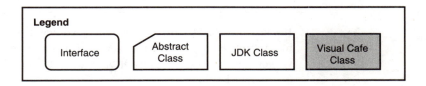

You can create and use an invisible button in exactly the same manner as you would any other button component.

The HTML Link Components

Visual Café includes three classes that can be used to load a new HTML page:

- ☐ LabelHTMLLink
- ☐ ImageHTMLLink
- ☐ InvisibleHTMLLink

Each of these components can be placed on a form and then used to generate a call to the AppletContext object's showDocument method. This method loads a different HTML page. The inheritance hierarchy of these classes is shown in Figure 8.17.

Figure 8.17.

*The inheritance
hierarchy of the
HTML link classes.*

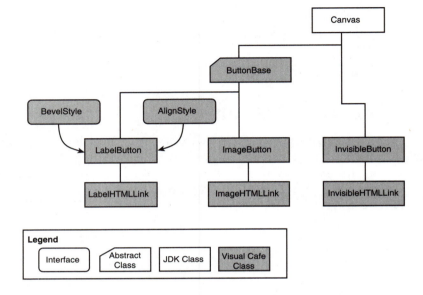

Each HTML link component creates an onscreen area that will load a new HTML page when clicked. Listing 8.7 shows the code from the HTMLDemo sample applet, which illustrates how to use these classes and is included on the MCP Web site.

TIP

Because the HTML link components load new HTML pages, you need to test applets that use them in a Web browser rather than in the applet viewer. To run HTMLDemo, load HTMLDemo.html from Netscape Navigator or Internet Explorer.

Listing 8.7. HTMLDemo.java.

```
1:   import java.awt.*;
2:   import java.applet.*;
3:   import symantec.itools.awt.*;
4:   import java.net.*;
5:
6:   public class HTMLDemo extends Applet {
7:
8:       public void init() {
9:           // Call parents init method.
10:          super.init();
11:          AddLabelLink();
12:      }
13:
14:      void AddLabelLink() {
```

```
15:        labelLink = new LabelHTMLLink();
16:
17:        labelLink.setBackground(Color.red);
18:
19:        try {
20:           URL url=new URL(getDocumentBase(),"FromLabel.html");
21:           try {
22:              labelLink.setURL(url);
23:           }
24:           catch (java.beans.PropertyVetoException e) {
25:            }
26:        }
27:        catch(MalformedURLException e) {}
28:
29:        add(labelLink);
30:     }
31:
32:     public void addNotify() {
33:        // Call parents addNotify method.
34:        super.addNotify();
35:
36:        //{{INIT_CONTROLS
37:        setLayout(new FlowLayout(FlowLayout.CENTER,5,5));
38:        resize(426,266);
39:        //}}
40:     }
41:
42:     LabelHTMLLink labelLink;
43:
44:     //{{DECLARE_CONTROLS
45:     //}}
46:  }
```

ANALYSIS The method AddLabelLink (lines 14–30) constructs a new LabelHTMLLink named labelLink. A new URL is then created and assigned to labelLink using setURL on line 22. If the user clicks this label, the browser will load FromLabel.html (the URL passed to setURL).

NOTE

> When the user clicks any HTML link component and loads a new HTML document, this will stop execution of the current applet. However, any applet embedded in the new HTML document will be loaded.

StatusBar

The StatusBar component is frequently placed on the bottom of a form and can be used to display any information the user might need. As shown in Figure 8.18, StatusBar is a subclass of BorderPanel, which itself is a subclass of Panel.

Figure 8.18.
`StatusBar` *descends*
from `Panel`.

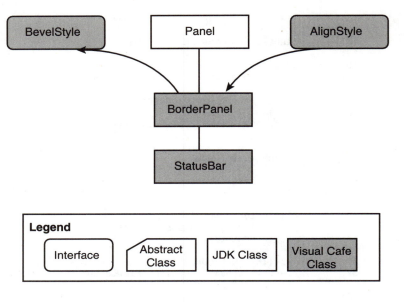

To create a new status bar, you can either drag one from the Component palette or use the following constructor:

`StatusBar()`

The text displayed by a status bar can be set or retrieved using one of the following methods:

`void setStatusText(String);`

`String getStatusText();`

The color in which the text is displayed can be set or retrieved using one of the following methods:

`void setStatusTextColor(Color);`

`Color getStatusTextColor();`

Figure 8.19 shows the sample applet `StatusBarDemo`, which is included on the MCP Web site. As is usually the case, this example shows a status bar placed across the bottom of a form.

TIP   The easiest way to place a status bar at the bottom of a panel and ensure that it remains there, even if the user resizes the form, is to use the `BorderLayout` layout manager. You learned about this class on

Day 7, "The Form Designer, Layout Managers, and Panels." To place a status bar on the bottom of a form, use the `BorderLayout` on the form and then add the status bar to the form and set its `Placement` property to `South`.

Figure 8.19.

Status bars are frequently placed at the bottom of a form.

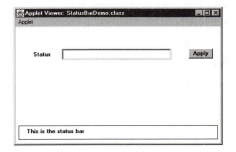

ProgressBar

The `ProgressBar` component can be used to keep the user apprised of the progress of lengthy operations. You've undoubtedly seen progress bars used in setup programs to show how much of the program has been installed. As shown in Figure 8.20, `ProgressBar` is a subclass of `Canvas`.

Figure 8.20.

`ProgressBar` *extends* `Canvas` *and implements* `AlignStyle` *and* `BevelStyle`.

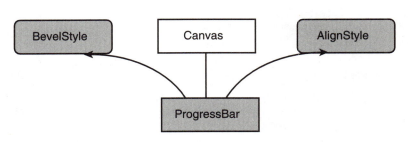

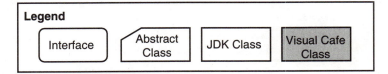

To construct a new progress bar, you can either drag one from the Component palette or use either of the following constructors:

```
ProgressBar()
```

```
ProgressBar(int alignStyle, int bevelStyle, int borderIndent)
```

A progress bar may optionally display a text message stating what percentage has been completed. The placement of this text message is controlled by the *alignStyle* parameter, which can be any of the following values:

- ☐ ProgressBar.ALIGN_LEFT
- ☐ ProgressBar.ALIGN_CENTERED
- ☐ ProgressBar.ALIGN_RIGHT

The *bevelStyle* parameter specifies what type of border will be drawn around the bar. Any of the following values can be used for *bevelStyle*:

- ☐ ProgressBar.BEVEL_LOWERED
- ☐ ProgressBar.BEVEL_RAISED
- ☐ ProgressBar.BEVEL_LINE
- ☐ ProgressBar.BEVEL_NONE

Finally, the *borderIndent* parameter indicates how far in from its border the progress bar will be drawn. This parameter can be set to any of the following values:

- ☐ ProgressBar.INDENT_ZERO
- ☐ ProgressBar.INDENT_ONE
- ☐ ProgressBar.INDENT_TWO

Controlling a Progress Bar's Appearance

There are two types of bars that can be displayed with the Visual Café ProgressBar component: a solid bar and a bar composed of individual boxes. If you opt to use boxes, you can set the width of the boxes as well as the gap between them. Figure 8.21 illustrates the difference between a solid progress bar and one filled with boxes.

Figure 8.21.

A progress bar can be solid or filled with boxes.

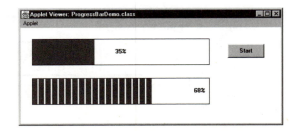

You can use the following methods to control if and how a progress bar is drawn with individual boxes:

```
void setDrawBoxes(boolean boxes)
```

```
boolean getDrawBoxes()
```

```
void setBoxWidth(int width)
```

```
int getBoxWidth()
```

```
void setGapWidth(int width)
```

```
int getGapWidth()
```

For example, the following code will configure a progress bar to use boxes that are 11 pixels wide with a three-pixel gap between each box:

```
progBar.setDrawBoxes(true);
progBar.setBoxWidth(11);
progBar.setGapWidth(3);
```

Updating Progress

To update the progress of a bar, you can use either of the following methods:

```
void setValue(int progress)
```

```
void updateProgress(int progress)
```

These methods will behave exactly the same. It is not unusual to see a loop similar to the following when a progress bar is in use:

```
for (int progress = 1; progress <= 100; progress++) {
    // do 1% of activity here
    progBar1.updateProgress(progress);
}
```

A loop like this can be found in the ProgressBarDemo sample applet that is included on the MCP Web site.

To find out how much progress has been made, use getValue, the signature of which is as follows:

```
int getValue()
```

The display of the text on the progress bar can be temporarily suspended. This is controlled by a flag whose value can be set or retrieved using one of the following methods:

```
void setShowProgress(boolean showProgress)
```

```
boolean getShowProgress()
```

Additional Methods

There are additional methods that can be used to set or retrieve the values that control such aspects of a progress bar as its alignment, bevel style, border color, border indent, bar color, and text color. These methods are summarized in Table 8.3.

Table 8.3. Additional `ProgressBar` methods for controlling the appearance of a progress bar.

Method	Purpose
getAlignStyle()	Returns the current alignment style of the bar.
getBevelStyle()	Returns the current bevel style of the bar.
getBorderedColor()	Returns the color used for the border of the progress bar.
getBorderIndent()	Returns the current amount of the border indent.
getProgressBarColor()	Returns the color used to paint the progress bar.
getProgressBarTextColor()	Returns the color used to paint the text on the progress bar.
setAlignStyle(int)	Sets the alignment style of the bar to the specified type.
setBevelStyle(int)	Sets the bevel style of the bar to the specified type.
setBorderedColor(Color)	Sets the color to use for the borders.
setBorderIndent(int)	Sets the amount by which to indent the border.
setProgressBarColor(Color)	Sets the color to use for the progress bar.
setProgressBarTextColor(Color)	Sets the color to use for the text on the progress bar.

Do   **Don't**

DON'T assume you need to display a progress bar so the user has something to watch during a long operation. In many cases, a separate thread can be started to perform the lengthy operation while the user is allowed to continue working. For more on threads, see Day 14, "Multithreading."

8

Timer

It is not unusual for a program to need to perform operations or tests at set intervals. For example, if you are writing a clock program or class, you need to update the minute value every sixty seconds. Similarly, if a program is performing a lengthy operation, you might want to display a message to the user every five seconds informing of the program's progress. This can be done very simply by combining a Timer object with a ProgressBar object.

As you can see in Figure 8.22, Timer extends Object and implements the Runnable interface. The Runnable interface is closely related to the Java concepts of *threads*. You can use a timer without understanding threads, but you will learn about threading on Day 14.

Figure 8.22.

Timer *extends* Object *and implements* Runnable.

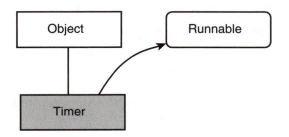

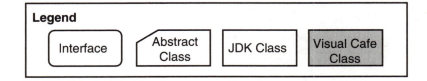

To create a new timer, either drag one from the Component palette to the Form Designer or use one of the following constructors:

```
Timer(Component target)

Timer(Component target, int delay)

Timer(Component target, int delay, boolean repeat)

Timer(Component target, int delay, boolean repeat, int eventType)
```

The *delay* parameter is the number of milliseconds that the timer should wait before generating each event. (Remember, a second is 1,000 milliseconds.) The *repeat* parameter indicates whether the timer should continue generating events. If not specified, a delay of

1,000 milliseconds (one second) is assumed. If *repeat* is false, the timer will generate a single event and then stop running. If *repeat* is true, the timer will continue generating events until it is told to stop. If *repeat* is not specified, it is assumed to be false.

The *eventType* parameter is the type of event you want the timer to generate. If not specified, the timer will generate ACTION_EVENT events. The *target* parameter is the component that will be sent the events the timer generates. In most cases, this is passed as the target. Consider the following examples of how to create a new Timer:

```
Timer t1 = new Timer(this);

Timer t2 = new Timer(this, 500);

Timer t3 = new Timer(this, 2000, true);

Timer t4 = new Timer(myButton, 1000, true, Event.MOUSE_DOWN);
```

The first three examples each send their events to the component in which this code is executed. The last example send its events to myButton. The first and fourth examples generate an event after 1,000 milliseconds, but t1 stops after generating its first event while t4 continues generating new events. The second timer, t2, generates a single event after half a second. The third timer, t3, repeatedly generates ACTION_EVENT events every two seconds.

Starting and Stopping

You can start or stop a timer by using the following methods:

```
public void start()

public void start(int delay)

public void start(boolean repeat)

public void start(int delay, boolean repeat)

public void stop()
```

Naturally, the *delay* and *repeat* parameters have the same meanings here as when passed to a constructor. However, they are provided as parameters to the start methods to give you additional flexibility when restarting a thread. If you stop a thread using stop, you can restart it using any of the provided start methods.

Additional Methods

There are additional methods that can be used to set or retrieve the values that control such aspects of a timer as its delay, event type, repeat status, and target. These methods are summarized in Table 8.4.

Table 8.4. Additional useful `Timer` methods.

Method	Purpose
`int getDelay()`	Returns the delay in milliseconds.
`int getEventType()`	Returns the event type generated by the timer.
`boolean getRepeat()`	Returns `true` if the timer repeats or `false` otherwise.
`Component getTarget()`	Returns the component to which events will be sent.
`void setDelay(int)`	Sets the delay in milliseconds.
`void setEventType(int)`	Sets the event type that will be generated by the timer.
`void setRepeat(boolean)`	Sets whether or not the timer will repeat.
`void getTarget(Component)`	Sets the component to which events will be sent.

NOTE

The demonstration applet `TimerDemo` is provided on the MCP Web site and illustrates using a timer object to control the updating of a progress bar.

Calendar

As shown in Figure 8.23, Visual Café provides a `Calendar` component. The calendar can be used to select a month from a drop-down list, the year with a numeric spinner, and the day by selecting it from a typical wall calendar display.

Figure 8.23.

The Visual Café `Calendar` *component.*

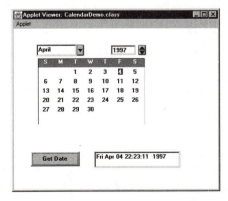

Calendar is a subclass of Panel, as can be seen in Figure 8.24. To create a new calendar, either drag one from the Component palette or use one of these constructors:

```
Calendar()
```

```
Calendar(Date date)
```

Figure 8.24.
Calendar *extends*
Panel.

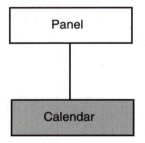

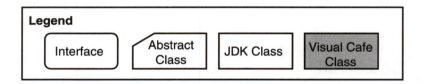

The first constructor will set the calendar to today's date. The second constructor will set the calendar on the date specified. For example, the following code will create a calendar that will display August 25, 1962:

```
Date myBirthday = new Date(62, 7, 25);
Calendar c = new Calendar(myBirthday);
```

WARNING

The 1.1 release of Visual Café includes bugs in the Calendar component that prevent the Calendar(Date) constructor and the setDate(String) methods from working. Hopefully, by the time you read this these methods will function as expected.

To retrieve the date a user has selected in a calendar, you use the getDate method. This method returns the selected date as a string in the following format:

```
Day Month Date Hours:Minutes:Seconds Year
```

8

An example can be seen in Figure 8.23, which is taken from the `CalendarDemo` applet that is included on the MCP Web site.

You can set the date of a calendar component with a call to `setDate(String newDate)`.

Finally, you can retrieve or set the selection color used by a calendar with the following two methods:

```
Color getSelectedColor()
```

```
void setSelectedColor(Color)
```

ComboBox

The Visual Café `ComboBox` class is a very powerful component that combines some of the best features of other components into a single component. As shown in Figure 8.25, `ComboBox` combines a text field with a drop-down list. Users can either make an entry in the text field or select an item from the list. As the programmer, you have a great deal of control over how a combo box behaves and interacts with the user. As can be seen in Figure 8.26, `ComboBox` extends `Panel`.

Figure 8.25.

`ComboBox` *combines a text field and a drop-down list into a single component.*

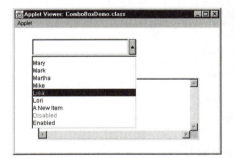

You can create a new `ComboBox` object by dragging it from the Component palette or by using either of the following constructors:

```
ComboBox()
```

```
ComboBox(boolean editable, boolean searchable)
```

The `boolean` parameters of the second constructor are two of the most significant ways in which you can customize the behavior of a combo box. If *editable* is `false`, the user cannot make an entry into the text field. If *searchable* is `true`, then as each character is typed, the combo box verifies that the user has thus far typed the beginning of a valid item in the combo box. The interactions of these two parameters are summarized in Table 8.5.

Figure 8.26.
ComboBox *extends*
Panel.

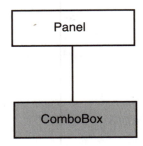

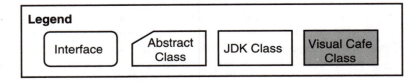

Table 8.5. Interaction of the *editable* **and** *searchable* **aspects of** ComboBox.

editable	searchable	Behavior
false	false	User can only select from the list.
false	true	User can select from the list or enter the text of an item in the list.
true	false	User can select from the list or enter any random text.
true	true	User can select from the list or enter any random text.

Adding Items

You can add an item or set the entire list of items used by a combo box with the following methods:

```
void setListItems(String[] values)

void addItem(String itemText)

void addItem(String itemText, boolean enabled)
```

The setListItems method removes any items currently in the list and replaces them with the strings contained in the specified array. For example, the following code will place six names into the combo box:

```
void LoadItems() {
    String[] names = new java.lang.String[6];
    names[0] = new String("Mary");
    names[1] = new String("Mark");
    names[2] = new String("Martha");
    names[3] = new String("Mike");
    names[4] = new String("Lisa");
    names[5] = new String("Lori");
    comboBox1.setListItems(names);
}
```

The addItem methods can be used to add simple string items. By default, items will be enabled when they are added but the *enabled* parameter can optionally be used to add disabled items. A disabled item appears in the combo box but is grayed out and cannot be selected. The following code adds three simple text-only items to a combo box:

```
comboBox.addItem("A New Item");
comboBox.addItem("Disabled", false);
comboBox.addItem("Enabled", true);
```

Items with Images

An item in a combo box can optionally display a small image adjacent to the text, as shown in Figure 8.27. To add an item with an image, use either of the following addItem methods:

```
void addItem(Image image, String itemText)
```

```
void addItem(Image image, String itemText, boolean enabled)
```

Figure 8.27.

Items in a combo box can display images to the left of their text.

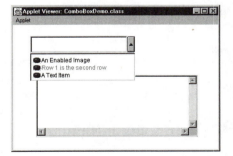

As an example of how to use these methods, consider Listing 8.8, which will create the combo box shown in Figure 8.27:

Listing 8.8. Adding items with images.

```
 1:    Image img;
 2:
 3:    void LoadItems() {
 4:        LoadImage();
 5:        try {
 6:            comboBox.addItem(img, "An Enabled Image");
 7:            comboBox.addItem(img, "A Disabled Image", false);
 8:            comboBox.addItem("A Text Item");
 9:        }
10:        catch (java.beans.PropertyVetoException e) {
11:        }
12:    }
13:
14:    void LoadImage() {
15:        MediaTracker tracker = new MediaTracker(this);
16:        img = getImage(getDocumentBase(), "blue.gif");
17:        tracker.addImage(img, 0);
18:
19:        int status;
20:        for(;;) {
21:            status = tracker.statusAll(true);
22:            if (status == MediaTracker.COMPLETE)
23:                break;
24:        }
25:    }
```

 ANALYSIS   The `LoadItems` method (lines 3–12) calls the `LoadImage` method (14–25), which loads the image that will be used. The image is loaded under the control of a `MediaTracker` object. This is done because `getImage` (line 16) does not actually load the image. By using a `MediaTracker` object, you can ensure that the image is loaded before the combo box is displayed.

> **NOTE**   Do not worry if you do not yet know how the `Image` and `MediaTracker` classes work. Each of these subjects is given in-depth coverage on subsequent days. The `Image` class and the `getImage` method are described on Day 16. The `MediaTracker` class is discussed on Day 17.

Changing Items

You can change the text or image associated with an item with the following methods:

```
void changeImage(int row, Image image)
```

```
void changeText(int row, String newText)
```

Rows in a combo box are numbered beginning with zero. The `changeImage` method can be used to change an image or to add an image to an item that previously had none.

```
comboBox.changeText(1,"Row 1 is the second row");
comboBox.changeImage(2, img);
```

Selecting Items

You can select or deselect items in the list portion of a combo box with the following methods:

```
void select(int rowNum)

void select(String text)

void deselect(int rowNum)

boolean isSelected(int rowNum)
```

The two `select` methods can be used to select a row in the list and then copy the text of the selection into the text field portion of the combo box. However, when `deselect` is used to deselect an item in the list, it does not remove the selected text from the text field.

Deleting Items

You can remove items from the list portion of a combo box with the following four methods:

```
void clear()

void delSelectedItem()

void delItem(int rowNum)

void delItems(int startRow, int endRow)
```

To remove all items from the list, use `clear`. A selected row can be removed with `delSelectedItem`. A single item can be removed with `delItem`. With `delItems`, all items on or between the *startRow* and *endRow* will be removed. Naturally, *endRow* must be greater than or equal to *startRow*. When these two parameters are equal, a single row is removed; it is equivalent to using `delItem`. For example, either of the following statements will delete row three from the list:

```
delItems(3, 3);

delItem(3);
```

Controlling Behavior and Appearance

A combo box can optionally display vertical or horizontal scrollbars on the list. You can set or get a combo box's scrollbar display status with the following methods:

```
void setShowHorizontalScroll(boolean showFlag)

boolean getShowHorizontalScroll()
```

```
void setShowVerticalScroll(boolean showFlag)
```

```
boolean getShowVerticalScroll()
```

You can control whether a combo box is editable, searchable, and/or case-sensitive using the following methods:

```
void setEditable(boolean editable)
```

```
boolean getEditable()
```

```
void setSearchable(boolean searchable)
```

```
boolean getSearchable()
```

```
void setCaseSensitive(boolean caseSensitive)
```

```
boolean getCaseSensitive()
```

Table 8.5 shows how the editable and searchable attributes of a combo box influence its behavior. If a combo box is case sensitive in addition to being searchable, the user must enter the text of a list item exactly as it appears in the list.

Finally, you can control whether individual items are enabled (selectable) or disabled with the following:

```
void disable(int rowNum)
```

```
void enable(int rowNum)
```

```
void enable(int rowNum, boolean enabled)
```

Retrieving Items

You can use the following methods to retrieve information from the combo box:

```
int countItems()
```

```
String getItem(int rowNum)
```

```
String[] getListItems()
```

```
int getSelectedIndex()
```

```
String getSelectedItem()
```

```
String getText()
```

To find out how many rows are in the list, use countItems. To retrieve the text from a particular row in the list, use getItem. To retrieve all the items in a list, use getListItem. For example, the following code will display the text of each list item in a text area:

```
String[] str = comboBox.getListItems();
```

8

```
for(int i= 0; i < str.length; i++)
    textArea1.appendText(str[i] + "\r\n");
```

The `getSelectedIndex` method can be used to find out what row number the user has selected in the combo box, while `getSelectedItem` will return the text of the selected item. To retrieve the text entered in the combo box's text field, use `getText`.

TIP If the combo box is editable, it is usually best to find out what the user entered by using `getText`. If the combo box is not editable, it is usually best to use `getSelectedItem` or `getSelectedIndex` to find out what selection was made in the list.

Fonts

A combo box can use separate fonts for its text field and list components. You can set or retrieve a combo box's font with the following methods:

```
Font getComboBoxFont()

void setComboBoxFont(Font newFont)

Font getFont()

void setFont(Font newFont)

Font getDropDownFont()

void setDropDownFont(Font newFont)

Font getEditFieldFont()

void setEditFieldFont(Font newFont)
```

The methods `getDropDownFont`, `setDropDownFont`, `getEditFieldFont`, and `setEditFieldFont` work with only one of the two fonts. The `setFont` and `setComboBoxFont` methods set both fonts to the specified *newFont*. The `getFont` and `getComboBoxFont` methods both return the same value as `getEditFieldFont`, under the assumption that both fonts have been set to the same value.

Formatted Text Fields

Most programs require user input, and many require users to enter some of this input in a specific format. For example, you would like users to enter United States long-distance telephone numbers in a format like `(123)456-7890`. But if you just put a `TextField` component on the screen, how is the user to know you want him to enter (123)456-7890 instead of 123 456 7890 or some other format? Equally important, how can you ensure that users follow the desired format?

 Visual Café provides the solution in the form of its formatted text fields. A formatted text field works by defining a *mask* for the field. A *mask* indicates the acceptable set of characters for each position within a formatted text field.

For example, when specifying a field's mask, the character 9 is used to indicate a field that can only contain a digit. So a field with the mask 999 would be able to hold any three-digit number, but would not accept user input such as ABC. The valid mask characters are shown in Table 8.6.

Table 8.6. Valid mask characters.

Mask	Allowable Characters
9	Any digit (0 through 9).
+	A plus (+) or minus (–) sign.
-	Any digit (0 through 9), a plus (+) or minus (–) sign.
A	Any uppercase alphabetic character (A through Z).
a	Any lowercase alphabetic character (a through z).
U	Any alphabetic character (A through Z, a through z). The character is converted to uppercase for use.
L	Any alphabetic character (A through Z, a through z). The character is converted to lowercase for use.
X	Any uppercase alphabetic character (A through Z) or digit (0 through 9).
x	Any lowercase alphabetic character (a through z) or digit (0 through 9).
N	Any alphabetic character (A through Z, a through z) or digit (0 through 9). The character is converted to uppercase for use.
n	Any alphabetic character (A through Z, a through z) or digit (0 through 9). The character is converted to lowercase for use.
*	Any character.
/	Causes the next character in the mask to be interpreted literally.

Formatted fields are supported in Visual Café through the FormattedTextField class. As can be seen in Figure 8.28, FormattedTextField is a subclass of the AWT TextField class.

8

Figure 8.28.
FormattedTextField
extends TextField.

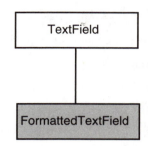

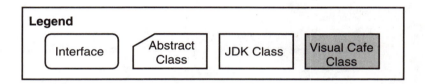

To create a new `FormattedTextField` object, either drag one onto a form from the Component palette or use one of the following constructors:

```
FormattedTextField()
```

```
FormattedTextField(int length)
```

```
FormattedTextField(String contents)
```

```
FormattedTextField(String contents, int length)
```

If the `length` is not specified, a length of 255 will be assumed. If no initial `contents` are specified, the field will initially be empty. The mask that is used by a formatted field is not passed to the constructor. It is passed as a parameter to `setMask`, as shown in the following:

```
FormattedTextField fld = new FormattedTextField(8);
fld.setMask("999/-9999");
```

In this case, a mask is created that is suitable for entering local phone numbers. You should notice that the escape character (/) was used to indicate that the - should be treated literally rather than as a part of the mask. In addition to `setMask`, `getMask` will return a `String` containing a field's current mask.

To set or get the font that is in use by a formatted text field, use the following methods:

```
void setEditFont(Font newFont)
Font getEditFont()
```

Predefined Text Fields

Visual Café includes the following predefined formatted text fields:

- ☐ `USLongDistPhoneNumber`
- ☐ `IntlLongDistPhoneNumber`
- ☐ `LocalPhoneNumber`
- ☐ `SocialSecurityNumber`
- ☐ `SocialInsuranceNumber`
- ☐ `ZipCode`
- ☐ `LongZipCode`
- ☐ `PostalCode`

Figure 8.29 shows the `FormattedTextFieldDemo` sample applet, which demonstrates the use of each of these classes. This sample applet is included on the MCP Web site.

Figure 8.29.

The `FormattedText-FieldDemo` *applet illustrates the mask for each field.*

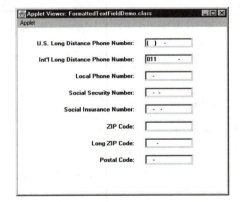

TIP

By default, Visual Café does not place the predefined formatted text fields on the Component palette. To add one to a form, select Component from the Insert menu and scroll down until you find the desired component.

Summary

Today you learned about some of the components in the Visual Café Object Library. You learned how to improve your Java programs with the `WrappingLabel`, `Label3D`, `TreeView`, slider, `InvisibleButton`, HTML link, `StatusBar`, `ProgressBar`, `Timer`, `Calendar`, `ComboBox`, and formatted text field components. However, you are not yet finished with the Object Library. In the next chapter you will encounter more Object Library components, including those for creating multicolumn lists, image lists, and spin buttons.

Q&A

Q **I would like to use a status bar to display both the current date and help messages. Is there a way to use a status bar to display two pieces of information?**

A You can certainly concatenate the two pieces of information into a single string and then display that string in the status bar. However, there is no reason why you cannot create two status bars and place each on the form. Usually, this is a better approach.

Q **I am using the `USLongDistPhoneNumber` formatted text field component to gather a phone number from the user. When I use `getText` to retrieve whatever the user entered, the string I get also contains the parentheses from the mask. How do I get just the phone number the user entered?**

A The formatted text field includes literal mask characters in the strings it returns. The only way to get rid of these characters is to write a method to strip them yourself.

Q **I am trying to use images in a `ComboBox` component but cannot find a way to increase the amount of space the `ComboBox` uses to draw the image. Is there a way to do this?**

A No, unfortunately, there is not. `ComboBox` uses an instance of `ImageListBox` to manage the drop-down list, and this class assumes a constant 19-pixel width for the image. The `ImageListBox` class will be discussed in more detail in the next lesson.

Workshop

The workshop includes quiz questions to help you gauge your understanding of the material in this chapter. The workshop also includes exercises to provide hands-on experience with what you've learned in this chapter. Answers to the quiz questions can be found in Appendix D, "Answers."

Quiz

1. What are the alignment styles that can be used with `WrappingLabel`?
2. What are the bevel styles that can be used with `Label3D`?
3. Define the following terms relative to their use with `TreeView` objects: node, visible node, and viewable node.

4. What is the purpose of the `setTreeStructure` method in the `TreeView` class?

5. How many root nodes can a `TreeView` object have?

6. What is the purpose of the HTML link components?

7. What two components are combined to create `ComboBox`?

8. How many milliseconds are there in a second?

9. What is the difference between the `9`, `+`, and `-` characters when used as part of the mask for a formatted text field?

Exercises

1. Write a program that updates a progress bar while counting from 1 to a value that can be set by the user with a slider component.

2. Use a timer to display the current time in a status bar.

3. Use the `TreeView` component that displays a node for each number from 1 to 50. If the number of the node is divisible by 5, add a subnode that says that the node is divisible by 5. If any node that is divisible by 5 is also divisible by 10, add a subnode of the prior subnode stating that the line is divisible by 10. This will create a tree whose top will look like the following:

```
1
2
3
4
5
     Divisible by 5
6
7
8
9
10
    Divisible by 5
    Divisible by 10
11
12
```

4. Write a program that allows a user to select a formatted text field mask from an editable combo box. Based on the selection in the combo box, change the mask of a formatted text field on the same form.

8

Day 9

More Object Library Components

Today you'll continue the exploration of the Visual Café Object Library that you began yesterday. Today you will learn about the `MultiList`, `LabelButton`, `ImageListBox`, `ListSpinner`, `DaySpinner`, `MonthSpinner`, `NumericSpinner`, `DirectionButton`, and `StateCheckBox` components.

MultiList

You can use the `MultiList` component to create multiple column lists or grids. A multilist includes a heading row and individual data rows. To create a new multilist, you can use any of the constructors shown in Table 9.1. As shown in Figure 9.1, `MultiList` extends `Panel`.

Table 9.1. Constructors for `MultiList`**.**

Method	Purpose
`MultiList()`	Creates a multilist without any columns.
`MultiList(int)`	Creates a multilist with the specified number of columns.
`MultiList(int, boolean)`	Creates a multilist with the specified number of columns that optionally allows multiple rows to be selected.
`MultiList(int, boolean, Color)`	Creates a multilist with the specified number of columns that optionally allows multiple rows to be selected and uses the specified background color.

Figure 9.1.
`MultiList` *extends*
`Panel`.

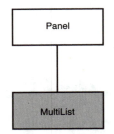

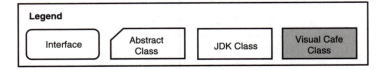

Adding Column Headings

Each column in a multilist includes a heading that identifies the contents of the column. To add headings to a multilist , you can use the `Column Headings` property in the Property List or you can add them yourself in code. The easiest way to add column headings with code is to use the `setHeadings` method, whose signature is

```
void setHeadings(String headings[])
```

Because `setHeadings` is passed an array of `String` objects, you need to create and fill this array before passing it as a parameter. The following example creates three column headings suitable for displaying information about programmers:

```
CreateHeadings() {
    String[] headings = new String[3];
    headings[0] = new String("Name");
    headings[1] = new String("Language");
    headings[2] = new String("Salary");
    try {
        MultiList.setHeadings(headings);
    }
    catch (java.beans.PropertyVetoException e) {
    }
}
```

WARNING

You must include headings in a multilist.

If you only want to set or change a single column heading, you can use `setHeading`. The signature for `setHeading` is

```
void setHeading(String heading, int column, int width)
```

The width is specified in pixels. Therefore, to change the heading of the first column you could do the following:

```
myList.setHeading("New Heading", 1, 30);
```

WARNING

For some reason, the *column* parameter of `setHeading` is one-based, while other multilist methods are zero-based. So to change the heading of the first column, specify column 1. However, later you will see other methods that consider this same column to be column 0.

TIP

A convenient way to change a column's heading but leave its width unchanged is to use the method `getColumnSize`. This method is passed a column number and returns the column's width in pixels. A call to `getColumnSize` can be conveniently used to provide the *width* parameter to `setHeading` as follows:

```
myList.setHeading("New Heading", 1, myList.getColumnSize(1));
```

If you want to retrieve one or all column headings, you can do so with getHeading or
getHeadings:

```
String getHeading(int column)
```

```
String[] getHeadings()
```

Use getHeading to retrieve the heading for a single specific column, and getHeadings to
retrieve a String array of all column headings.

Colors and Fonts

You can view or manipulate heading colors with the following methods:

```
Color getHeadingBg()
```

```
Color getHeadingFg()
```

```
void setHeadingBg(Color color)
```

```
void setHeadingColors(Color foreground, Color background)
```

```
void setHeadingFg(Color color)
```

You can view or change the font that will be used for headings with getHeadingFont and
setHeadingFont. The signatures of these methods are

```
Font getHeadingFont()
```

```
void setHeadingFont(Font newFont)
```

NOTE

> For some reason, the MultiList component does not provide a way to
> change the color it uses to indicate a selected row.

Adding Data Rows

Without data rows, a multilist is of very limited use, so it's time to see some examples of how
to add data. If you need to add more than one row, the easiest way is to create an array of
strings. Each element in the array represents a row in the multilist. Within each string,
separate each column with a semicolon (;) character. Then use setListItems and pass it the
array. Because setListItems can throw java.beans.PropertyVetoException, you must catch
this exception. Consider the following example:

```
void LoadData() {
    String[] data = new String[3];
    data[0] = new String("Herb;Visual Basic;33000");
    data[1] = new String("Mary;C++;44000");
    data[2] = new String("Bjarne;Java;80000");
```

```
try {
    multiList.setListItems(data);
}
catch (java.beans.PropertyVetoException e) {
}
}
```

When combined with the CreateHeadings method discussed in the section "Adding Column Headings," LoadData will create the multilist shown in Figure 9.2. These methods are from the SimpleMultiListDemo applet which can be found on the MCP Web site (www.mcp.com/info/1-57521/1-57521-303-6).

Figure 9.2.

The SimpleMulti-ListDemo *applet shows how to create headings and data rows.*

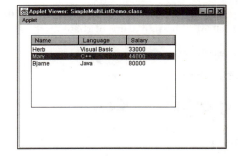

Column Alignment

You can set a column's alignment with the following method:

setColumnAlignment(int *column*, int *alignMode*)

The *alignMode* parameter can be set to any of the following values:

MultiList.LEFT

MultiList.RIGHT

MultiList.CENTER

By default, columns will be left aligned. As an example of using setColumnAlignment, the following method creates three column headings and then right-aligns the last column:

```
CreateHeadings() {
    String[] headings = new String[3];
    headings[0] = new String("Name");
    headings[1] = new String("Language");
    headings[2] = new String("Salary");
    try {
        multiList.setHeadings(headings);
        multiList.setColumnAlignment(2, multiList.RIGHT);
    }
    catch (java.beans.PropertyVetoException e) {
    }
}
```

Colors and Fonts

You can view or manipulate heading cell colors with the following methods:

```
Color getCellBg()
```

```
Color getCellFg()
```

```
void setCellBg(Color color)
```

```
void setCellColors(Color foreground, Color background)
```

```
void setCellFg(Color color)
```

You can view or change the font that will be used for cells with `getHeadingFont` and `setHeadingFont`. The signatures of these methods are

```
Font getCellFont()
```

```
void setCellFont(Font newFont)
```

Altering a Single Cell

To change the text in a single cell you can use the `addTextCell` method, whose signature is the following:

```
addTextCell(int row, int cell, String newText)
```

The row and column are both zero-based. If the row passed to `addTextCell` does not currently exist in the multilist, a new row will be created and added to the bottom. The column passed to `addTextCell` must exist. The `AddTextCellDemo` sample applet illustrates how to use `addTextCell` to write a simple applet that allows the user to enter new rows into a multilist. The relevant portions of this applet are shown in Listing 9.1. The entire applet can be found on the MCP Web site.

Listing 9.1. Portions of `AddTextCellDemo.java`.

```
1:   import java.awt.*;
2:   import java.applet.*;
3:
4:   public class AddTextCellDemo extends Applet {
5:       void addButton_Clicked(java.awt.event.ActionEvent event) {
6:           int row = multiList.getNumberOfRows();
7:
8:           multiList.addTextCell(row, 0, name.getText());
9:           multiList.addTextCell(row, 1, language.getText());
10:          multiList.addTextCell(row, 2, salary.getText());
11:      }
12:
13:      public void init() {
```

```
14:          // Call parents init method.
15:          super.init();
16:
17:          CreateHeadings();
18:          LoadData();
19:          multiList.redraw();
20:      }
21:
22:      public void addNotify() {
23:          // Call parents addNotify method.
24:          super.addNotify();
25:
26:          //{{INIT_CONTROLS
27:          setLayout(null);
28:          resize(426,354);
29:          multiList = new symantec.itools.awt.MultiList();
30:          multiList.reshape(12,24,286,153);
31:          add(multiList);
32:          label1 = new java.awt.Label("Name:");
33:          label1.reshape(24,204,51,21);
34:          add(label1);
35:          name = new java.awt.TextField();
36:          name.reshape(108,204,120,21);
37:          add(name);
38:          label2 = new java.awt.Label("Language:");
39:          label2.reshape(24,240,75,21);
40:          add(label2);
41:          language = new java.awt.TextField();
42:          language.reshape(108,240,120,21);
43:          add(language);
44:          label3 = new java.awt.Label("Salary:");
45:          label3.reshape(24,276,51,21);
46:          add(label3);
47:          salary = new java.awt.TextField();
48:          salary.reshape(108,276,120,21);
49:          add(salary);
50:          addButton = new java.awt.Button("Add");
51:          addButton.reshape(288,204,73,21);
52:          add(addButton);
53:          //}}
54:
55:          //{{REGISTER_LISTENERS
56:          Action lAction = new Action();
57:          addButton.addActionListener(lAction);
58:          //}}
59:      }
60:
61:      void CreateHeadings() {
62:          String[] headings = new String[3];
63:          headings[0] = new String("Name");
64:          headings[1] = new String("Language");
65:          headings[2] = new String("Salary");
66:          try {
67:              multiList.setHeadings(headings);
68:              multiList.setColumnAlignment(2, multiList.RIGHT);
```

continues

Listing 9.1. continued

```
69:             }
70:             catch (java.beans.PropertyVetoException e) {
71:             }
72:         }
73:
74:         void LoadData() {
75:             String[] data = new String[3];
76:             data[0] = new String("Herb;Visual Basic;33000");
77:             data[1] = new String("Mary;C++;44000");
78:             data[2] = new String("Bjarne;Java;80000");
79:             try {
80:                 multiList.setListItems(data);
81:             }
82:             catch (java.beans.PropertyVetoException e) {
83:             }
84:         }
85:
86:         //{{DECLARE_CONTROLS
87:         symantec.itools.awt.MultiList multiList;
88:         java.awt.Label label1;
89:         java.awt.TextField name;
90:         java.awt.Label label2;
91:         java.awt.TextField language;
92:         java.awt.Label label3;
93:         java.awt.TextField salary;
94:         java.awt.Button addButton;
95:         //}}
96:
97:         class Action implements java.awt.event.ActionListener {
98:             public void actionPerformed(java.awt.event.ActionEvent
99:                 event) {
100:                Object object = event.getSource();
101:                if (object == addButton)
102:                    addButton_Clicked(event);
103:            }
104:        }
105: }
```

ANALYSIS   The method `addButton_Clicked` (lines 5–11) determines the number of rows currently in the list and then passes that as the first parameter to `addTextCell`. The three successive calls to `addTextCell` are used to add the text for each of the columns in the multilist. The text is taken from the three text fields that appear on the screen. These can be seen in Figures 9.3 and 9.4.

TIP   In addition to `addTextCell`, you can also use `addCell` and `addImageCell`; however, these methods are normally used only when a cell displays an image. These methods will be discussed in the next section.

Figure 9.3.

The AddTextCellDemo *applet before any rows are added.*

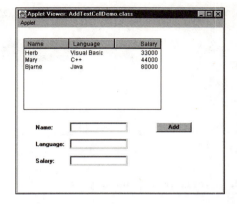

Figure 9.4.

The AddTextCellDemo *applet after two new rows are added.*

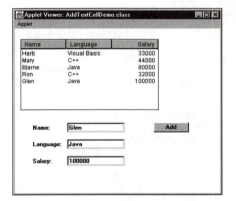

Using Images in Cells

In addition to text, a cell might also contain an image, as shown in Figure 9.5. To create a cell that contains an image, you can use either of the following methods:

```
void addCell(int row, int column, String text, Image img)

void addImageCell(int row, int column, Image img)
```

The `addCell` method can be used to create cells that contain both text and an image. To create a cell containing only an image, use `addImageCell`.

The code in Listing 9.2 can be used to create the applet shown in Figure 9.5. This code is from the `MultiListImageDemo` applet that appears on the MCP Web site.

Figure 9.5.

*In addition to
displaying text, cells
can also display
images.*

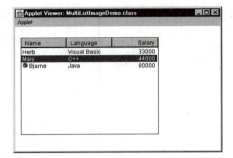

Listing 9.2. `MultiListImageDemo.java.`

```
 1:   import java.awt.*;
 2:   import java.applet.*;
 3:
 4:   public class MultiListImageDemo extends Applet {
 5:
 6:       public void init() {
 7:           // Call parents init method.
 8:           super.init();
 9:
10:           LoadImage();
11:           CreateHeadings();
12:           LoadData();
13:           multiList.redraw();
14:       }
15:
16:       public void addNotify() {
17:           // Call parents addNotify method.
18:           super.addNotify();
19:           //{{INIT_CONTROLS
20:           setLayout(null);
21:           resize(426,266);
22:           multiList = new symantec.itools.awt.MultiList();
23:           multiList.reshape(12,24,286,209);
24:           add(multiList);
25:           //}}
26:       }
27:
28:       void LoadImage() {
29:           MediaTracker tracker = new MediaTracker(this);
30:           img = getImage(getDocumentBase(), "blue.gif");
31:           tracker.addImage(img, 0);
32:
33:           int status;
34:           for(;;) {
35:               status = tracker.statusAll(true);
36:               if (status == MediaTracker.COMPLETE)
37:                   break;
38:           }
39:       }
```

```
40:
41:     void CreateHeadings() {
42:        String[] headings = new String[3];
43:         headings[0] = new String("Name");
44:         headings[1] = new String("Language");
45:         headings[2] = new String("Salary");
46:
47:         try {
48:            multiList.setHeadings(headings);
49:             multiList.setColumnAlignment(2, multiList.RIGHT);
50:         }
51:         catch (java.beans.PropertyVetoException e) {
52:         }
53:     }
54:
55:     void LoadData() {
56:         String[] data = new String[2];
57:         data[0] = new String("Herb;Visual Basic;33000");
58:         data[1] = new String("Mary;C++;44000");
59:
60:         try {
61:            multiList.setListItems(data);
62:         }
63:         catch (java.beans.PropertyVetoException e) {
64:         }
65:
66:         multiList.addCell(3, 0, "Bjarne", img);
67:         multiList.addTextCell(3, 1, "Java");
68:         multiList.addTextCell(3, 2, "80000");
69:     }
70:
71:     Image img;
72:
73:     //{{DECLARE_CONTROLS
74:     symantec.itools.awt.MultiList multiList;
75:     //}}
76: }
```

![ANALYSIS] The work of preparing the multilist for display is handled at the end of init between lines 10 and 13. First, the image is loaded by the call to LoadImage. Next, the headings are created by the call to CreateHeadings. Then, data is loaded into the cells by the call to LoadData. Finally, the multilist is redisplayed by calling redraw.

The LoadImage method (lines 28–39) loads the image blue.gif from the directory from which the applet was loaded. The image is loaded under the control of a MediaTracker object. This is done because getImage does not actually load the image. By using a MediaTracker object, you can ensure that the image is loaded before the multilist is displayed.

NOTE

Do not worry if you do not yet know how the `Image` and `MediaTracker` classes work. Each of these subjects is given in-depth coverage on subsequent days. The `Image` class and the `getImage` method are described on Day 16, "Working with Graphics." The `MediaTracker` class is discussed on Day 17, "Multimedia Programming."

The `LoadData` method (lines 55–69) is similar to the same-named method in the `AddTextCellDemo` of Listing 9.1. However, after the first two rows are added with `setListItems` (line 61), an additional row is added (lines 66–68). The first column is added with `addCell` and will include the text `Bjarne` and the image that was loaded in `LoadImage`. The remaining columns are text-only and are created with `addTextCell`.

Retrieving Cell Contents

You can retrieve the contents of a cell using `getCellText`. The signature for this method is as follows:

```
String getCellText(int row, int column)
```

To retrieve the contents of a specific row, use `getSelectedRow`. This method returns the currently selected row. The code in Listing 9.3 illustrates how to use `getSelectedRow` and `getCellText` to display the contents of each column of the selected row in a text area:

Listing 9.3. Displaying the columns of the selected row.

```
 1:    void getSelectedButton_Clicked(java.awt.event.ActionEvent
 2:        event) {
 3:      int row = multiList.getSelectedRow();
 4:
 5:      contents.setText("");
 6:      for(int i=0; i<multiList.getColumns(); i++) {
 7:          String str = multiList.getCellText(row, i);
 8:          contents.appendText(str + "\r\n");
 9:      }
10:    }
```

To retrieve all of the rows of a multilist, you can use `getListItems`. This method returns an array of strings as shown by its signature:

```
String[] getListItems()
```

Retrieving Multiple Selections

Don't forget that two of the MultiList constructors allow you to create lists that enable a user to simultaneously select more than one row. For example, the following will create a three-column, multiple-selection multilist:

```
multiList = new MultiList(3, true);
```

The method getSelectedRows can be used to return an integer array in which each item in the array is the row number of a selected row in the multilist. The signature of getSelectedRows is

```
int[] getSelectedRows()
```

The following example is similar to Listing 9.3 except that it supports multiple selections:

```
void getSelectedButton_Clicked(java.awt.event.ActionEvent event) {
    int rows[] = multiList.getSelectedRows();

    int lastCol = multiList.getColumns() - 1;
      contents.setText("");

      for(int i=0; i < rows.length; i++) {
        for(int col=0; col <= lastCol; col++) {
            String str = multiList.getCellText(rows[i], col);
            contents.appendText(str);
            if(col == lastCol)
                contents.appendText("\r\n");
            else
                contents.appendText(", ");
        }
      }
}
```

The result of executing this code is shown in Figure 9.6.

Figure 9.6.

The result of selecting multiple items in a multilist.

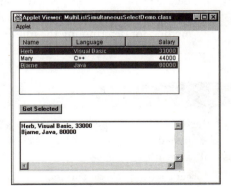

TIP

The current version of Visual Café does not support the creation of multiple select `MultiList` objects in the Form Designer. To create one yourself use one of the `MultiList` constructors as shown in the following example:

```
multiList = new MultiList(3, true);
```

This will create a three-column `MultiList` object that allows multiple selections.

Other Methods

Table 9.2 shows other `MultiList` methods that you might find useful.

Table 9.2. Additional `MultiList` member methods.

Method	Purpose
`clear()`	Deletes all rows of the list.
`getColumns()`	Returns the number of columns in the list. Equivalent to `getNumberOfCols`.
`getNumberOfCols()`	Returns the number of columns in the list. Equivalent to `getColumns`.
`setSelectedRow(int)`	Selects the specified row.

WARNING

Before using a multilist, you should be aware of two deficiencies. First, there is no method for removing a single row. Second, there is no method for determining the number of rows in the list.

Do   **Don't**

DO use the `MultiList` component whenever a list contains columns of items that need to be aligned. Using the AWT `List` class and attempting to align items with spaces will not work.

DON'T forget that the *column* parameter of `setHeading` is one-based, while other `MultiList` methods are zero-based.

9

LabelButton

The LabelButton component is very similar to the Abstract Windowing Toolkit's Button component. However, as shown in Figure 9.7, LabelButton extends ButtonBase, which extends Canvas rather than Button. LabelButton offers two significant enhancements over Button. First, a label button can be instructed to continuously generate events while it is depressed. Second, the border style around a label button can be set to create a three-dimensional appearance.

Figure 9.7.

LabelButton *extends*
ButtonBase *and*
implements
BevelStyle *and*
AlignStyle.

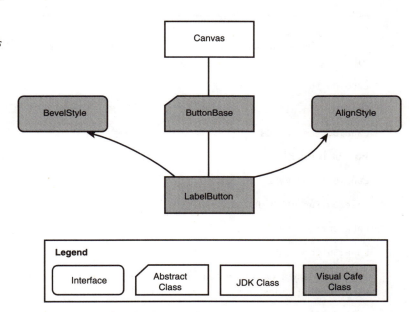

In addition to dragging LabelButton from the Component palette to the Form Designer, you can also create a label button with any of the constructors shown in Table 9.3.

Table 9.3. LabelButton **constructors.**

Method	Purpose
LabelButton()	Creates a new label button.
LabelButton(String, int, int)	Creates a new label button with the specified text, alignment style, and border bevel style.

continues

Table 9.3. continued

Method	Purpose
LabelButton(String, int, int, Color)	Creates a new label button with the specified text, alignment style, border bevel style, and text color.
LabelButton(String, int, int, int)	Creates a new label button with the specified text, alignment style, border bevel style, and border indent.

For the alignment parameters of the LabelButton constructors, you can pass any of the following values:

LabelButton.LEFT

LabelButton.RIGHT

LabelButton.CENTER

For the border bevel style parameters, you can pass any of the following values:

LabelButton.BEVEL_LOWERED

LabelButton.BEVEL_RAISED

LabelButton.BEVEL_LINE

LabelButton.NONE

For example, you can create a button labeled Hello that is left aligned with a raised bevel with the following code:

```
LabelButton button = new LabelButton("Hello",
        LabelButton.LEFT, LabelButton.BEVEL_RAISED);
```

Table 9.4 lists some additional LabelButton methods you will find useful. You have encountered all of this before, except for setNotifyDelay and setNotifyWhilePressed. These two methods work together to allow a label button to generate multiple events for a single button click. This is useful if a program needs to know how long a user holds down a button. For example, if you were implementing your own scrollbars, you might want to continue generating events as long as the user holds the mouse button down over a particular button.

Table 9.4. Useful methods of LabelButton.

Method	Purpose
getAlignStyle()	Returns the button's alignment style.
getBevelStyle()	Returns the button's bevel style.

Method	Purpose
getBorderIndent()	Returns the button's border indent amount.
getText()	Returns the button's label text.
getTextColor()	Returns the button's text color.
setAlignStyle(int)	Sets the button's alignment style.
setBevelStyle(int)	Sets the button's bevel style.
setBorderedColor(Color)	Sets the button's border color.
setBorderIndent(int)	Sets the border indent amount.
setNotifyDelay(int)	Sets the delay before each additional event is generated.
setNotifyWhilePressed(boolean)	Sets whether multiple events can be generated while the button is pressed.
setText(String)	Sets the button's label text.
setTextColor(Color)	Sets the button's text color.

To enable continuous notification, use setNotifyWhilePressed, passing it true. Use setNotifyDelay to specify how long in milliseconds to wait between generating successive events. For example, if you want a button to generate an event every second, you would do the following:

```
button.setNotifyWhilePressed(true);
button.setNotifyDelay(1000);
```

Rather than click events, a LabelButton generates action events. This can be seen in Listing 9.4. This listing contains the source to the LabelButtonDemo applet, which is shown running in Figure 9.8. This applet can be found on the MCP Web site.

Listing 9.4. LabelButtonDemo.java.

```
1:    import java.awt.*;
2:    import java.applet.*;
3:
4:    public class LabelButtonDemo extends Applet {
5:        void button_Action(java.awt.event.ActionEvent event) {
6:            status.appendText("Do Something...\r\n");
7:        }
8:
9:        public void init() {
10:           // Call parents init method.
11:           super.init();
12:       }
13:
14:       public void addNotify() {
```

continues

Listing 9.4. continued

```
15:           // Call parents addNotify method.
16:           super.addNotify();
17:
18:           //{{INIT_CONTROLS
19:           setLayout(null);
20:           resize(426,266);
21:           button = new symantec.itools.awt.LabelButton();
22:           button.reshape(12,24,144,36);
23:           button.setBackground(new Color(12632256));
24:           add(button);
25:           try {
26:               button.setNotifyWhilePressed(true);
27:           }
28:           catch (java.beans.PropertyVetoException veto) { }
29:           try {
30:               button.setNotifyDelay(500);
31:           }
32:           catch (java.beans.PropertyVetoException veto) { }
33:           try {
34:               button.setText("Press And Hold");
35:           }
36:           catch (java.beans.PropertyVetoException veto) { }
37:           try {
38:               button.setBorderIndent(
39:                       symantec.itools.awt.LabelButton.INDENT_ONE);
40:           }
41:           catch (java.beans.PropertyVetoException veto) { }
42:           status = new java.awt.TextArea();
43:           status.reshape(12,84,298,154);
44:           add(status);
45:           //}}
46:
47:           //{{REGISTER_LISTENERS
48:           Action lAction = new Action();
49:           button.addActionListener(lAction);
50:           //}}
51:       }
52:
53:       //{{DECLARE_CONTROLS
54:       symantec.itools.awt.LabelButton button;
55:       java.awt.TextArea status;
56:       //}}
57:
58:       class Action implements java.awt.event.ActionListener {
59:           public void actionPerformed(java.awt.event.ActionEvent
60:                   event) {
61:               Object object = event.getSource();
62:               if (object == button)
63:                   button_Action(event);
64:           }
65:       }
66:   }
```

9

Figure 9.8.

A LabelButton *can continue to generate events as long as the button is held down.*

ImageListBox

The ImageListBox component can be used to display lists that contain images and text. An example is shown in Figure 9.9. As shown in Figure 9.10, ImageListBox extends Panel.

Figure 9.9.

The ImageListBox *component can be used to display images and text in the same list.*

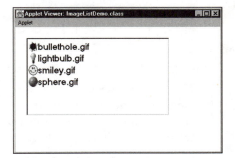

To create an image listbox, you can drag one from the Component palette to the Form Designer or use one of the following constructors:

```
ImageListBox()

ImageListBox(String label)

ImageListBox(String label, boolean multiSelect)

ImageListBox(String label, int rows, boolean multiSelect)

ImageListBox(Component parent, String label)

ImageListBox(Component parent, String label, int rows,
        boolean multiSelect)
```

The *rows* parameter to these constructors can be used to specify the number of visible rows in the list. The *label* parameter is not used. The *multiSelect* parameter indicates whether the multiple items can be simultaneously selected.

Figure 9.10.
`ImageListBox`
extends `Panel`.

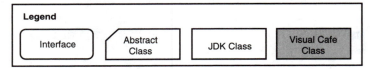

 NOTE

The `ImageListBox` class, as it currently ships with Visual Café, is of somewhat limited usefulness because you cannot set the width of the image. All images will be set to a width of 19 pixels. Hopefully a future enhancement will support larger images.

Adding Items

If you are adding items that include only text and not images, you can use `setListItems`. This method is passed a `String` array as its only parameter, as can be seen in the following example:

```
void SetItems() {
    String text[] = {  "This is line 1",
                       "This is line 2",
                       "This is line 3",
    };

    try {
        imgList.setListItems(text);
    }
    catch (java.beans.PropertyVetoException e) {
    }
}
```

If you want to add text rows one at a time, you can use either of the following methods:

```
addItem(String str)
```

```
addItem(String str, boolean enabled)
```

The second `addItem` method can be used to add an item and disable it at the same time. Disabled items appear grayed out to the user and cannot be selected.

Adding Items with Images

It is much more likely that you want to include images on at least some of the lines you use. To include images, you need to use one of the following `addItem` methods:

```
addItem(Image image, String str)
```

```
addItem(Image image, String str, boolean enabled)
```

```
addItem(Image image, String str, boolean enabled,
        Color textColor)
```

As an example of how to use `addItem`, consider the `LoadImages` method shown in Listing 9.5. This method is taken from the `ImageListDemo` applet on the MCP Web site.

Listing 9.5. Adding rows that include text and images.

```
 1:    void LoadImages() {
 2:        String fileNames[] = {  "bullethole.gif",
 3:                                "lightbulb.gif",
 4:                                "smiley.gif",
 5:                                "sphere.gif"
 6:        };
 7:
 8:        MediaTracker tracker = new MediaTracker(this);
 9:        Image images[] = new Image[fileNames.length];
10:
11:        for(int i=0; i< fileNames.length; i++) {
12:            images[i]=getImage(getDocumentBase(), fileNames[i]);
13:            tracker.addImage(images[i], i);
14:        }
15:
16:        int status;
17:        for(;;) {
18:            status = tracker.statusAll(true);
19:            if (status == MediaTracker.COMPLETE)
20:                break;
21:        }
22:
23:        try {
24:            for(int i=0; i< fileNames.length; i++)
25:                imgList.addItem(images[i], fileNames[i]);
26:        }
27:        catch (java.beans.PropertyVetoException e) {
28:        }
29:    }
```

ANALYSIS   Parts of Listing 9.5 might not be totally clear yet because you haven't yet reached the lessons about images and the `MediaTracker` class. These topics will be covered on Days 16 and 17. For now, it is sufficient to understand that new images are created by the call to `getImage` on line 12 and that the loop between lines 17 and 21 uses a `MediaTracker` object to ensure that the images are loaded before the list is displayed. The loop on lines 24 and 25 uses `addItem` to add each of the images to the list. Because `addItem` can throw `java.beans.PropertyVetoException`, this exception is caught on line 27.

TIP   The height of each line is dependent on the font used for the text. To create a square region for the image, set the font to 19 points.

Selecting Items

Depending on what constructor was used to create an image listbox, it can allow more than one row to be selected at a time. Additionally, a list can enable or disable multiple selection by using `setMultipleSelections`. The signature for this method is

```
void setMultipleSelections(boolean multiSelect)
```

Similarly, you can determine whether a list currently supports multiple selections by using `allowsMultipleSelections`. This method takes no parameters. As an example of using these two methods, consider the following, which can be used to toggle whether a list allows multiple selection:

```
bool newMode = !imgList.allowsMultipleSelections();
myList.allowsMultipleSelections(newMode);
```

The following methods can be used to select or deselect either one row or all of the rows in the list:

```
void select(int row)
```

```
void deselect(int row)
```

```
void selectAll()
```

```
void deselectAll()
```

To determine whether all rows in the list are selected, you can use `allSelected`. This method returns `true` if all rows have been selected.

Finally, you can use select(String *searchString*) to select the first string in the list that matches *searchString*. For example, the following SetItems method loads the list and then selects the second row in the list:

```
void SetItems() {
    String text[] = {  "This is line 1",
                       "This is line 2",
                       "This is line 2a",
    };

    try {
        imgList.setListItems(text);
    }
    catch (java.beans.PropertyVetoException e) {
    }

    // select the second row
    imgList.select("This is line 2");
}
```

Deleting and Disabling Items

Items can be deleted from an image listbox by using any of the following methods:

```
void delItem(int index)
```

```
void delSelectedItems()
```

```
void delItems(int startRow, int endRow)
```

The first of these methods deletes a single row. The second method deletes all currently selected rows. The final method deletes all rows between the starting and ending rows, including these rows. For example, consider the following method:

```
void SetItems() {
    String text[] = {  "This is line 0",
                       "This is line 1",
                       "This is line 2",
                       "This is line 3",
                       "This is line 4"
    };

    try {
        imgList.setListItems(text);
        imgList.delItems(2,3);
    }
    catch (java.beans.PropertyVetoException e) {
    }
}
```

When displayed, this list will not contain the third and fourth lines of text. (Passing 2 and 3 removes the third and fourth lines because the numbering is zero-based.) This can be seen in Figure 9.11.

Figure 9.11.

A range of items can be deleted with delItems(int *startRow,* int *endRow*).

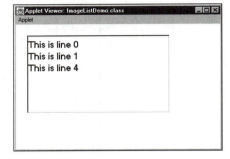

Disabled rows appear grayed out and cannot be selected by the user. You can disable or enable a row with the following methods:

```
void disable(int index)
```

```
void enable(int index)
```

```
void enable(int index, boolean isEnabled)
```

Finally, you can determine whether a row is currently enabled by using the following method:

```
boolean isEnabled(int row)
```

Retrieving Items

You can retrieve the image or text of a particular row with the following methods:

```
Image getImage(int row)
```

```
String getItem(int row)
```

Retrieving Selected Items

You can retrieve the text of the currently selected item with getSelectedItem. If the list supports multiple selections, you should use getSelectedItems, which returns an array. The signatures of these methods are as follows:

```
String getSelectedItem()
```

```
String[] getSelectedItems()
```

As an example of how to retrieve selected items, consider Listing 9.6. This method is taken from the ImageListRetrievalDemo applet on the MCP Web site. This method displays the text of each selected ImageListBox item in a text area, as can be seen in Figure 9.12.

Listing 9.6. Retrieving all selected items.

```
1:      void getSelItemsButton_Clicked(java.awt.event.ActionEvent
2:            event) {
3:         String items[] = imgList.getSelectedItems();
4:
5:         // blank the results text area
6:         results.setText("Items:\r\n");
7:
8:         // display each selected item
9:         for(int i = 0; i < items.length; i++)
10:            results.appendText(items[i] + "\r\n");
11:     }
```

Figure 9.12.

Selected items can be retrieved with getSelectedItems.

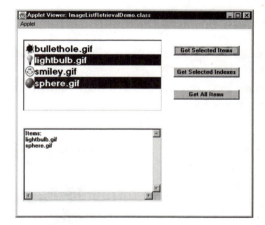

Sometimes you would prefer to work with the row numbers, or indexes, of the selected items. This can be done with the following methods:

```
int getSelectedIndex()
```

```
int[] getSelectedIndexes()
```

As an example of using getSelectedIndexes and getItem, consider Listing 9.7 from the ImageListRetrievalDemo sample applet.

Listing 9.7. Retrieving all selected indexes.

```
1:      void getSelIndexesBtn_Clicked(java.awt.event.ActionEvent
2:            event) {
3:         int items[] = imgList.getSelectedIndexes();
4:
5:         if (items.length > 0) {
```

continues

Listing 9.7. continued

```
6:          // blank the results text area
7:          results.setText("Indexes:\r\n");
8:
9:          // display each selected index number
10:         for(int i = 0; i < items.length; i++) {
11:             // display the index (row) number
12:             results.appendText(String.valueOf(items[i]) + "=");
13:
14:             // get the text for that row number
15:             results.appendText(" " + imgList.getItem(i) +
16:                     "\r\n");
17:         }
18:
19:     }
20:     else
21:         results.setText("Nothing selected!");
22: }
```

In this case, an array of integers is created by getSelectedIndexes. A loop iterates through this array to display each row number and the text of that row is retrieved by a call to getItem. This can be seen in Figure 9.13.

Figure 9.13.

Retrieve indexes of selected items with getSelectedIndexes.

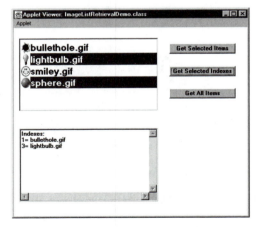

If you want to test to see whether a row is currently selected, you can use the isSelected method rather than retrieve the row's text. The signature of isSelected is as follows:

```
boolean isSelected(int row)
```

Retrieving All Items

If you want to retrieve the text for all items in an image listbox instead of just the selected items, you can do so with the following method:

```
String[] getListItems()
```

An example of using `getListItems` is taken from `ImageListRetrievalDemo` and shown in Listing 9.8 and Figure 9.14.

Listing 9.8. Retrieving all items.

```
1:      void getAllItemsBtn_Clicked(java.awt.event.ActionEvent
2:          event) {
3:          String items[] = imgList.getListItems();
4:
5:          if (items.length > 0) {
6:              // blank the results text area
7:              results.setText("Items:\r\n");
8:
9:              // display each selected item
10:             for(int i = 0; i < items.length; i++)
11:                 results.appendText(items[i] + "\r\n");
12:         }
13:         else
14:             results.setText("Nothing selected!");
15:     }
```

Figure 9.14.

All items can be retrieved with `getListItems`.

Other Useful Methods

In addition to the methods already described, there are a few other useful member methods of `ImageListBox`. These are shown in Table 9.5.

Table 9.5. Other useful methods of `ImageListBox`.

Method	Purpose
`changeImage(int, Image)`	Set a new image for the specified row.
`changeText(int, String)`	Sets new text for the specified row.
`clear()`	Removes all rows in the list.
`countItems()`	Returns the number of items in the list.
`isVisibleIndex(int)`	Returns `true` if the specified row is currently visible.
`makeVisible(int)`	Makes the specified row visible.
`setTopRow(int)`	Makes the specified row the top visible row.

Do	Don't

DO allow your users to make multiple selections whenever possible. It is normally much easier for a user to select multiple items from a list at once than to revisit a dialog numerous times, selecting one item at a time.

DO make sure to use `getSelectedItems` and `getSelectedIndexes` if working with a list that has enabled multiple selection.

The Spinner Components

As shown in Figure 9.15, Visual Café includes four nonabstract spinner-type classes: `NumericSpinner`, `ListSpinner`, `DaySpinner`, and `MonthSpinner`. A numeric spinner can be used for gathering integer input and can be limited to operate within a specific range. A list spinner is useful when you want the user to choose among alternatives. Two perfect examples of list spinners are the day spinner and month spinner classes. These classes allow the user to choose between the days of the week or the months of the year. Figure 9.16 shows an example of each of these spinner types as they appear on an applet.

Figure 9.15.
The Spinner *inheritance tree.*

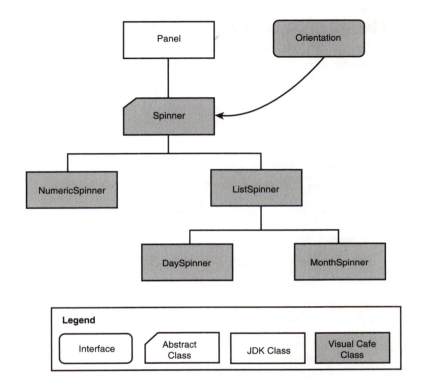

Figure 9.16.
A sample applet illustrating the four spinner types.

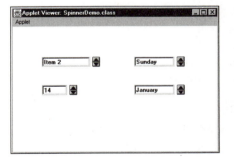

The Spinner Class

Because each of the four spinner classes is derived from the abstract class Spinner, most of the functionality of these classes is contained in Spinner. Each spinner knows the item number that is currently displayed. A spinner's item number can be set or retrieved with these methods:

```
int getCurrent()
```

```
void setCurrent(int item)
```

Sometimes you want to know the text that the user has selected rather than the item number he selected. This can be done with getCurrentText, which returns a String. For most spinners, you will not want to let users edit the contents; however, you can allow them to do so if you wish. You can set or evaluate a spinner's editable flag with the following methods:

```
boolean getEditable()
```

```
void setEditable(boolean editableFlag)
```

Each spinner can be given a minimum and a maximum value. For example, if you have a spinner that is used to gather an employee's age, you might want to limit its values to 16–65. You can work with a spinner's minimum and maximum values with the following methods:

```
void setMax(int maxValue)
```

```
int getMax()
```

```
void setMin(int minValue)
```

```
int getMin()
```

When a spinner reaches its maximum value, you can have it either wrap around to its minimum value or stop at the maximum. Similarly, an attempt to spin past a spinner's minimum value can optionally wrap to the maximum value. You can set or determine whether a spinner will wrap with the following methods:

```
void setWrappable(int wrappable)
```

```
boolean getWrappable()
```

You can also set the orientation of a spinner. Doing so changes the appearance of the arrows. Spinners can be oriented horizontally or vertically. Figure 9.16 showed four vertically oriented spinners. Figure 9.17 shows the same four spinners oriented horizontally.

You set a spinner's orientation with setOrientation, passing it either ORIENTATION_HORIZONTAL or ORIENTATION_VERTICAL. By default, spinners are oriented vertically. You can determine a spinner's orientation with getOrientation.

Figure 9.17.

Spinners can be oriented horizontally as well as vertically.

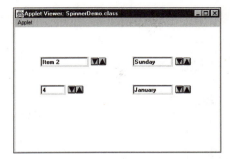

The `ListSpinner` **Class**

The `ListSpinner` class extends `Spinner` by providing methods for adding and retrieving lists of text items. You can add a single item to a list spinner with `addItem`. For example, the following code from the `SpinnerDemo` sample applet (included on the MCP Web site) will add four items to a list spinner and then select the second item:

```
void addListItems() {
    listSpinner.addItem("Item 1");
    listSpinner.addItem("Item 2");
    listSpinner.addItem("Item 3");
    listSpinner.addItem("Item 4");

    listSpinner.setCurrent(1);
}
```

If you are adding multiple rows, the easiest way is with `setListItems`, whose signature is as follows:

```
void setListItems(String[])
```

To use this method, create an array of strings and pass it to `setListItems`, as shown in the following example:

```
void addListItems() {
    String items[] = {  "Item 1",
                        "Item 2",
                        "Item 3",
                        "Item 4"
    };

    try {
        listSpinner.setListItems(items);
    }
    catch (java.beans.PropertyVetoException e) {
    }
}
```

You can retrieve the current or all strings from a list spinner with the following methods:

```
String getCurrentText()

String[] getListItems()
```

WARNING

> Keep in mind that `getCurrentText` could return a string that is not a part of the list if the spinner is editable.

DaySpinner **and** MonthSpinner

The two primary examples of list spinners are `DaySpinner` and `MonthSpinner`. These classes are very simple extensions of `ListSpinner`. No new public member methods are provided. Each adds only a constructor that uses successive calls to `addItem` to populate the list with the necessary strings.

The NumericSpinner **Class**

The `NumericSpinner` class extends `Spinner` by adding methods to set and get the amount by which the spinner will increment or decrement. The following two methods are provided:

```
int getIncrement()

void setIncrement(int newIncrement)
```

DirectionButton

In some ways, the `DirectionButton` class is similar to the `Spinner` class. You can use two `DirectionButton` objects to create your own spinners or you can combine direction buttons in other ways to customize a program's user interface. A `DirectionButton` is a button that contains an arrow that faces either up, down, left, or right, as can be seen in Figure 9.18.

Figure 9.18.

A `DirectionButton` *can face in any of four directions.*

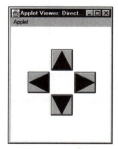

As you can see in Figure 9.19, `DirectionButton` extends the abstract class `ButtonBase`, which is a subclass of `Canvas`.

Figure 9.19.
`DirectionButton`
extends `ButtonBase`.

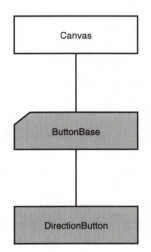

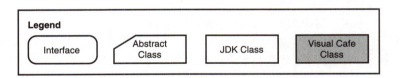

To create a new direction button, drag one from the Component palette to the Form Designer or use either of the following constructors:

```
DirectionButton()
```

```
DirectionButton(int direction)
```

The first constructor will create a left-facing direction button. The second constructor will orient the arrow based on the *direction* parameter, which can be set to any of the following values:

```
DirectionButton.LEFT
```

```
DirectionButton.RIGHT
```

```
DirectionButton.UP
```

```
DirectionButton.DOWN
```

After a direction button object is constructed, the direction of its arrow can be set or retrieved with the following methods:

```
void setDirection(int direction)
```

```
int getDirection()
```

You can alter the appearance of a direction button's arrow with any of the following methods:

```
void setArrowIndent(int indentAmount)
```

```
void shrinkTriangle(int left, int right, int top, int bottom)
```

The `shrinkTriangle` method is passed the number of pixels by which the arrow should be reduced on each side.

Because `DirectionButton` is a subclass of `ButtonBase`, a direction button can be made to generate continuous events while the button is held down. You saw this earlier today with `LabelButton`. The following example illustrates how to use `setNotifyWhilePressed` and `setNotifyDelay` to make a direction button generate a new event every second while depressed:

```
leftButton.setNotifyWhilePressed(true);
leftButton.setNotifyDelay(1000);
```

An Example

As an example of working with direction buttons, the `DirectionButtonDemo` applet is shown in Listing 9.9 and is included on the MCP Web site. This applet displays four buttons, one in each direction. The user is allowed to click these buttons to navigate between rows 0 and 9 and columns 0 and 9. As buttons are clicked, the location is written to a text area to the right of the buttons, as shown in Figure 9.20.

Listing 9.9. `DirectionButtonDemo.java`.

```
1:    import java.awt.*;
2:    import java.applet.*;
3:
4:    public class DirectionButtonDemo extends Applet {
5:        void leftButton_Action(java.awt.event.ActionEvent event){
6:            if (col > 0)
7:                col--;
8:            ShowLocation("Left ");
9:        }
10:
```

9

```
11:    void rightButton_Action(java.awt.event.ActionEvent event){
12:       if (col < 9)
13:          col++;
14:       ShowLocation("Right ");
15:    }
16:
17:    void upButton_Action(java.awt.event.ActionEvent event) {
18:       if (row > 0)
19:          row--;
20:       ShowLocation("Up ");
21:    }
22:
23:    void downButton_Action(java.awt.event.ActionEvent event){
24:       if (row < 9)
25:          row++;
26:       ShowLocation("Down ");
27:    }
28:
29:     void ShowLocation(String where) {
30:        results.appendText(where + " to (" +
31:               String.valueOf(row) + "," +
32:               String.valueOf(col) + ")\r\n");
33:     }
34:
35:    public void init() {
36:       // Call parents init method.
37:       super.init();
38:    }
39:
40:    public void addNotify() {
41:       // Call parents addNotify method.
42:       super.addNotify();
43:
44:       //{{INIT_CONTROLS
45:       setLayout(null);
46:       resize(426,266);
47:       downButton = new symantec.itools.awt.DirectionButton();
48:       downButton.reshape(84,144,45,45);
49:       add(downButton);
50:       try {
51:          downButton.setDirection(
52:                 symantec.itools.awt.DirectionButton.DOWN);
53:       }
54:       catch (java.beans.PropertyVetoException veto) { }
55:       upButton = new symantec.itools.awt.DirectionButton();
56:       upButton.reshape(84,48,45,45);
57:       add(upButton);
58:       try {
59:          upButton.setDirection(
60:                 symantec.itools.awt.DirectionButton.UP);
```

continues

Listing 9.9. continued

```
 61:          }
 62:          catch (java.beans.PropertyVetoException veto) { }
 63:          rightButton = new symantec.itools.awt.DirectionButton();
 64:          rightButton.reshape(132,96,45,45);
 65:          add(rightButton);
 66:          try {
 67:              rightButton.setDirection(
 68:                      symantec.itools.awt.DirectionButton.RIGHT);
 69:          }
 70:          catch (java.beans.PropertyVetoException veto) { }
 71:          leftButton = new symantec.itools.awt.DirectionButton();
 72:          leftButton.reshape(36,96,45,45);
 73:          add(leftButton);
 74:          results = new java.awt.TextArea();
 75:          results.reshape(228,36,174,195);
 76:          add(results);
 77:          results.disable();
 78:          //}}
 79:
 80:          //{{REGISTER_LISTENERS
 81:          Action lAction = new Action();
 82:          downButton.addActionListener(lAction);
 83:          upButton.addActionListener(lAction);
 84:          rightButton.addActionListener(lAction);
 85:          leftButton.addActionListener(lAction);
 86:          //}}
 87:      }
 88:
 89:      int row = 0, col = 0;
 90:
 91:      //{{DECLARE_CONTROLS
 92:      symantec.itools.awt.DirectionButton downButton;
 93:      symantec.itools.awt.DirectionButton upButton;
 94:      symantec.itools.awt.DirectionButton rightButton;
 95:      symantec.itools.awt.DirectionButton leftButton;
 96:      java.awt.TextArea results;
 97:      //}}
 98:
 99:      class Action implements java.awt.event.ActionListener {
100:          public void actionPerformed(java.awt.event.ActionEvent
101:                  event) {
102:              Object object = event.getSource();
103:              if (object == downButton)
104:                  downButton_Action(event);
105:              else if (object == upButton)
106:                  upButton_Action(event);
107:              else if (object == rightButton)
108:                  rightButton_Action(event);
109:              else if (object == leftButton)
110:                  leftButton_Action(event);
111:          }
112:      }
113: }
```

Figure 9.20.

*As the user clicks the
direction buttons,
the text area indicates
the current row and
column.*

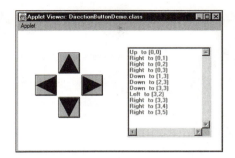

StateCheckBox

The Abstract Windowing Toolkit (AWT) includes a Checkbox component that can be either checked or unchecked. Usually this is adequate, but in some cases, it is important to indicate that the checkbox retains its default value. With Visual Café, this can be done with the StateCheckBox component. As can be seen in Figure 9.21, StateCheckBox extends Canvas, rather than Checkbox as you might have expected.

Figure 9.21.
StateCheckBox
extends Canvas.

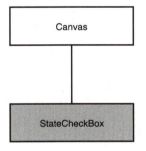

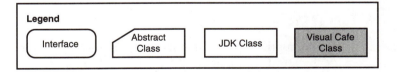

Figure 9.22 shows three separate StateCheckBox components in action. The first is in the default state, the second is checked, and the third is unchecked. The shading behind the checkmark distinguishes the default state from checked state.

Figure 9.22.
The three states of a
`StateCheckBox`
object.

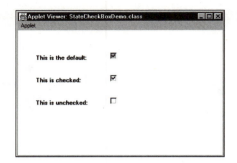

A state checkbox can be created in a two-state or three-state style. A two-state checkbox will behave exactly like an AWT checkbox. A three-state checkbox will include the initial default state. The style is set with `setStyle`, which is passed either of the following values:

`StateCheckBox.TWO_STATE`

`StateCheckBox.THREE_STATE`

A state checkbox's style can be retrieved with `getStyle`.

To get or set the state of a state checkbox, use the following methods:

`int getState()`

`void setSetState(int `*newState*`)`

These methods return or can be passed the following values:

`StateCheckBox.STATE_DEFAULT`

`StateCheckBox.STATE_CHECKED`

`StateCheckBox.STATE_UNCHECKED`

Summary

Today you continued your exploration of the Visual Café Object Library. You learned how to use the `MultiList` component to create grid-like lists. You saw how `LabelButton` offers a more powerful alternative to the AWT `Button` class and how `ImageListBox` allows you to mix images and text within the same list. You learned about the `DirectionButton` and `Spinner` components and how these components simplify item selection. Finally, you saw how `StateCheckBox` improves the AWT checkbox by including a default state.

Additional components from the Object Library are described on Days 16 and 17.

Q&A

Q **I have enabled multiple selection on a `MultiList` object and need to know which one of many items was selected last. How can I do this?**

A Use `getSelectedRow`. This method will return the last selected row in the list.

Q **I would like to use a spinner that has the decrement arrow to the left of a text field and the increment arrow to the right of the text field. Is there a way to do this with `ListSpinner`?**

A No, there isn't. However, it can be done with two `DirectionButtons`. This is one of the exercises at the end of this lesson.

Q **I would like to write an applet that can be run in English or Spanish and need to use a day spinner, but I can't because the `DaySpinner` component only works in English. Is there a way to change `DaySpinner` to support international languages?**

A No, you would have to write your own version of `DaySpinner`. Again, this is an exercise at the end of this lesson.

Workshop

The workshop includes quiz questions to help you gauge your understanding of the material in this chapter. The workshop also includes exercises to provide hands-on experience with what you've learned in this chapter. Answers to quiz questions can be found in Appendix D, "Answers."

Quiz

1. What is the column number of the first column in a multilist?
2. Name two ways in which `LabelButton` improves upon `Button`.
3. What is the purpose of the `setNotifyWhilePressed` method?
4. If the statement `setNotifyWhilePressed(true)` has been executed, how often will a component receive subsequent events if the user holds the mouse button down over the component?
5. Which component allows multiple selections: `MultiList` or `ImageListBox`?
6. What happens when a spinner reaches its maximum value?
7. What is the difference between a two-state and a three-state state checkbox?

Exercises

1. Use a multilist to write a program that displays the name, age, and gender of a handful of your friends, relatives, or co-workers. Allow users to add, edit, or delete entries. Include a button in the applet that increments everyone's age.

2. Write a class that is similar to `ListSpinner` but has a left-facing arrow at the left of the text and a right-facing arrow at the right of the text. Allow the user to change the contents of your spinner with these arrows.

3. Write a `BilingualDaySpinner` class that can be used to display the days of the week in English or Spanish.

4. Write an applet that uses `BilingualDaySpinner` and a state checkbox. Whenever the checkbox is at its default or checked value, display days in English. When unchecked, display days in Spanish.

Day 10

Windows, Frames, and Dialogs

In the last few days, you have learned a great deal about the AWT classes and classes in the Visual Café Object Library. So far you've placed these components directly onto the applet window. In this lesson, you'll learn how to create standalone windows, frames, and dialogs. By placing AWT and Object Library components on standalone windows, you can create more powerful user interfaces.

Windows

Because windows, frames, and dialogs are similar concepts, they are implemented using inheritance. Figure 10.1 shows the hierarchy of these classes.

Because Window is the superclass of Frame and Dialog, and therefore a superclass of the many Dialog class derivatives, it makes sense to begin an exploration of these classes with Window. The Window class is used to create free-standing windows that appear outside the screen area of an applet. Windows have neither borders nor a menu bar.

Figure 10.1.
The Window,
Dialog, *and* Frame
class hierarchy.

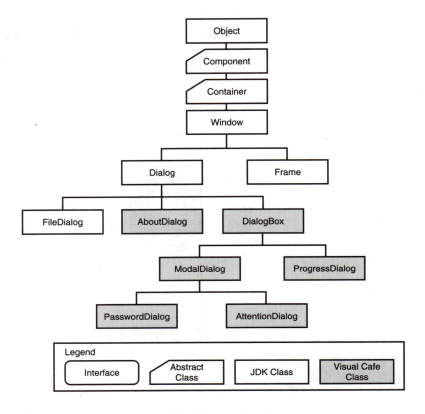

Each window must have an onscreen parent, which is passed to the Window constructor, as follows:

```
Window(Frame parent)
```

Despite the fact that Frame is a subclass of Window, each Window object must have a Frame as its onscreen parent. This chicken-before-the-egg contradiction can be considered evidence that Java's developers occasionally drank something stronger than java while designing the class library.

Fortunately, the Frame class includes a constructor that requires no parameters. This means that a window can be constructed as follows:

```
Frame dummyFrame = new Frame();
MyWindow wnd = new MyWindow(dummyFrame);
```

Constructing a window does not cause it to be displayed. To display a constructed window, you must use the show method, as shown in the following:

```
Frame dummyFrame = new Frame();
MyWindow wnd = new MyWindow(dummyFrame);
wnd.show();
```

In addition to the show method, the Window class also includes the methods shown in Table 10.1.

Table 10.1. Nonprivate methods of the Window class.

Method	Purpose
addNotify()	Creates a peer for the component
dispose()	Disposes of resources in use by the window
getToolkit()	Returns the toolkit in use by the window
getWarningString()	Returns a warning string that is displayed in nonsecure windows
pack()	Packs the components on the window
show()	Makes the window visible
toBack()	Moves the window behind other windows
toFront()	Moves the window in front other windows

10

Adding a Window to a Program

To add a window to a Visual Café program, select Form from the Insert menu. This displays the Insert Form dialog, shown in Figure 10.2. This dialog can be used to add a variety of windows and dialogs to Visual Café programs. Each of the Window, Frame, and Dialog classes shown on this dialog is described in this lesson.

Figure 10.2.

The Insert Form dialog.

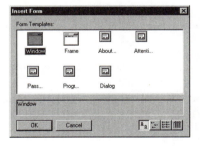

To add a window, select Window and click the OK button. This adds a new class, Window1, to your open project. Because Window1 is fairly nondescript, use the Property List to rename the new window SimpleWindow. Next, place whatever controls you like on the window. For this example, I've placed a lone Label and set its Text property to an appropriate message. At this point, the MyWindow class will appear as follows:

```
import java.awt.*;

public class SimpleWindow extends Window {
```

```
public SimpleWindow(Frame parent) {
    super(parent);
}

public void addNotify() {
    // Call parents addNotify method.
    super.addNotify();

    //{{INIT_CONTROLS
    setLayout(null);
    resize(insets().left + insets().right + 430,insets().top
            + insets().bottom + 270);
    label1 = new java.awt.Label("This is the window!");
    label1.reshape(insets().left + 72,insets().top + 48,
            262,76);
    add(label1);
    //}}
}

//{{DECLARE_CONTROLS
java.awt.Label label1;
//}}
}
```

To display the window, place a button named windowButton on the applet and add an event handler for the Click event for this button. Complete the windowButton_Clicked method as follows:

```
void windowButton_Clicked(Event event) {
    Frame dummyFrame = new Frame();
    Window wnd = new SimpleWindow(dummyFrame);
    wnd.show();
}
```

You are now ready to compile and execute this applet. Figure 10.3 illustrates the applet's appearance when it is run.

What happened here? This is a pretty ugly window: It's just a gray area on the screen without borders, a title, or a menu bar. This is because Window is intended as a minimalist class. Because of this, most Java programs never directly create a Window object. Instead, they create Frame and Dialog objects. The Window class is available, however, so that you can base your own classes on it and add whatever special features you desire.

TIP

> Because a Window object does not include borders or a menu bar, it is usually better to use Frame or Dialog.

Figure 10.3.

Running the
SimpleWindowApplet.

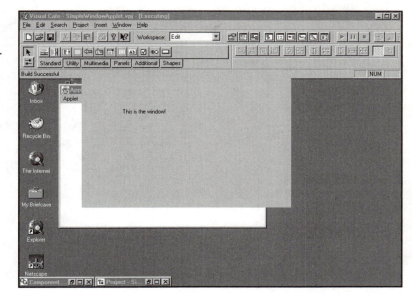

Frames

The Frame class extends Window and provides a class that can be used whenever you want to create a window with borders, a title, and a menu bar. Frames, like windows, are free-standing windows that are not part of the browser in which an applet is being run. Figure 10.4 illustrates a simple frame that has been moved outside the browser's borders.

Creating a Frame object is as simple as using one of the constructors shown in Table 10.2. If you use the Frame() constructor, a default title of untitled will be used. So unless the frame will be used to display untitled books, albums, or symphonies, you probably want to use the Frame(String) constructor. As examples of constructing new frames, consider the following:

```
Frame untitledFrame = new Frame();
Frame noTitleFrame = new Frame("");
Frame titledFrame = new Frame("Hi Mom, Send Cash");
```

Table 10.2. Constructors for the Frame class.

Constructor	Purpose
Frame()	Creates a frame with a default title
Frame(String)	Creates a frame with the specified title

Figure 10.4.

*A frame exists outside
the browser window.*

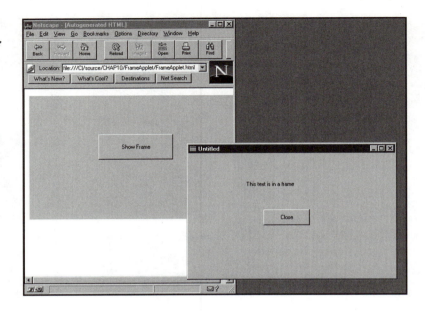

After a frame is constructed, you can treat it like any other container. By default, a `Frame`
object uses the `BorderLayout` layout manager. You can specify a different layout manager and
can add components, including `Panel` objects, using `add`. Of course, `Frame` offers its own
features beyond those available to other containers. A `Frame` object can have a menu, use a
variety of different cursors, and have an icon placed on its title bar. In addition to the menu
that can be added to the `Frame` object, each `Frame` object has a control menu located in the
top left of the frame, as shown in Figure 10.5.

Figure 10.5.

*A frame with its
control menu dropped
down.*

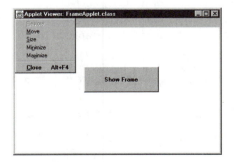

To support these features, the `Frame` class includes the nonprivate member methods shown
in Table 10.3.

Table 10.3. Nonprivate methods of the `Frame` class.

Method	Purpose
addNotify()	Creates a peer for the component
dispose()	Disposes of resources (for example, menu bars) in use by the frame
getCursorType()	Returns the cursor type that is displayed when the mouse pointer is over the frame
getIconImage()	Returns the image used as the frame's icon
getMenuBar()	Gets the frame's menu bar
getTitle()	Returns the frame's title
isResizable()	Returns true if the frame is resizable
paramString()	Returns the frame's parameter string
remove(MenuComponent)	Removes the specified item from the frame's menu
setCursor(int)	Sets the cursor that will be displayed when the mouse pointer is over the frame
setIconImage(Image)	Sets the image to be used as the frame's icon
setMenuBar(MenuBar)	Sets the frame's menu bar
setResizable(boolean)	Makes the frame resizable or not, depending on the specified parameter
setTitle(String)	Sets the dialog's title

To use a frame, perform the following steps:

1. Add the frame to the Visual Café project by selecting Form from the Insert menu, just as you did to add a window. However, select Frame instead of Window on the Insert Form dialog.

2. Place components (buttons, text fields, and so on) on the frame.

3. Use `resize` to set the frame to the correct dimensions.

4. Create the frame using `new`.

5. Make the frame visible with a call to `show`.

6. When done with the frame, call `dispose` to release resources. Even though Java includes garbage collection, it is necessary to call the `dispose` method to release graphics resources allocated by the underlying toolkit.

10

A Frame Example

The following example creates an applet and adds the frame shown in Figure 10.4.

When you add a Frame object to a project, Visual Café creates a class for the new Frame. Listing 10.1 shows this class.

Listing 10.1. MyFrame.java **as generated by Visual Café.**

```
1:    /*
2:        A basic extension of the java.awt.Frame class
3:     */
4:
5:    import java.awt.*;
6:
7:    public class MyFrame extends Frame {
8:
9:        void MyFrame_WindowClosing(java.awt.event.WindowEvent
10:           event) {
11:        hide();              // hide the Frame
12:        }
13:
14:        public MyFrame() {
15:
16:        }
17:
18:        public MyFrame(String title) {
19:            this();
20:            setTitle(title);
21:        }
22:
23:        public synchronized void show() {
24:            move(50, 50);
25:            super.show();
26:        }
27:
28:        public void addNotify() {
29:
30:            // Call parents addNotify method.
31:            super.addNotify();
32:
33:            // This code is automatically generated by Visual Café
34:            // when you add components to the visual environment.
35:            // It instantiates and initializes the components. To
36:            // modify the code, only use code syntax that matches
37:            // what Visual Café can generate, or Visual Café may
38:            // be unable to back parse your Java file into its
39:            // visual environment.
40:            //{{INIT_CONTROLS
41:            setLayout(null);
42:            resize(insets().left + insets().right+400,insets().top
43:                  + insets().bottom + 300);
44:            setTitle("A Simple Frame");
45:            //}}
46:
```

10

```
47:        //{{INIT_MENUS
48:        //}}
49:
50:        //{{REGISTER_LISTENERS
51:        Window lWindow = new Window();
52:        addWindowListener(lWindow);
53:        //}}
54:    }
55:
56:    //{{DECLARE_CONTROLS
57:    //}}
58:
59:    //{{DECLARE_MENUS
60:    //}}
61:
62:    class Window extends java.awt.event.WindowAdapter {
63:        public void windowClosing(java.awt.event.WindowEvent
64:            event) {
65:          Object object = event.getSource();
66:          if (object == Frame1.this)
67:              MyFrame_WindowClosing(event);
68:        }
69:    }
70: }
```

ANALYSIS As you can see from Listing 10.1, the generated code includes a constructor that takes no parameters (lines 14–16), a constructor that takes a title string as a parameter (lines 18–21), a show method (23–26), and it registers a listener class (lines 51–52 and 62–69). As you add components to the frame with the Visual Café Form Designer, code will be generated to create these components and their interactions.

Of course, this frame is pretty useless so far because no components have been placed on it. To remedy this, use the Form Designer to add some components. First, add a Label to display the message Text in a frame. Next, add an AWT button with a label of Close and a name of closeButton. Because you want to use this button to close the frame, you need to add code that will respond to a click of the button. Create the closeButton_Clicked method as shown in Listing 10.2.

Listing 10.2. The handleEvent method of MyFrame.

```
1:    void closeButton_Clicked(java.awt.event.ActionEvent event) {
2:        dispose();
3:        hide();
4:    }
```

To display a frame, you must declare it, allocate it with new, and then call show to make the frame visible. These actions are normally performed by the class that is causing the frame to be displayed. Frequently, this will be an applet class, as shown in Listing 10.3.

Listing 10.3. `FrameApplet.java.`

```
1:   import java.awt.*;
2:   import java.applet.*;
3:
4:   public class FrameApplet extends Applet {
5:       void button1_Clicked(java.awt.event.ActionEvent event) {
6:           frame.show();
7:       }
8:
9:       public void init() {
10:          // Call parents init method.
11:          super.init();
12:
13:          frame = new MyFrame();
14:      }
15:
16:      public void addNotify() {
17:          // Call parents addNotify method.
18:          super.addNotify();
19:
20:          //{{INIT_CONTROLS
21:          setLayout(null);
22:          resize(426,266);
23:          button1 = new java.awt.Button("Show Frame");
24:          button1.reshape(144,84,155,54);
25:          add(button1);
26:          //}}
27:
28:          //{{REGISTER_LISTENERS
29:          Action lAction = new Action();
30:          button1.addActionListener(lAction);
31:          //}}
32:      }
33:
34:      MyFrame frame;
35:
36:      //{{DECLARE_CONTROLS
37:      java.awt.Button button1;
38:      //}}
39:
40:      class Action implements java.awt.event.ActionListener {
41:          public void actionPerformed(java.awt.event.ActionEvent
42:              event) {
43:            Object object = event.getSource();
44:            if (object == button1)
45:              button1_Clicked(event);
46:          }
47:      }
48: }
```

ANALYSIS   Line 34 of Listing 10.3 declares the variable `frame`, which is of type `MyFrame`. In the `init` method (lines 9–14), `frame` is allocated with `new`. A button labeled Show Frame is also added to the applet and a listener is registered (line 30). If the button click is detected, `frame.show` (line 6) is used to display the frame.

TIP

Don't forget to resize the frame or it will be made only large enough to display the title bar.

Working with Cursors and Titles

As Table 10.3 shows, you can control the appearance of a frame at runtime in a number of ways. One common way is to change its title; another is to change the cursor used in the frame. In this section, you will learn how to create an applet that allows the user to manipulate both of these aspects of an applet. The applet you will create is called `CursorDemoApplet` and is shown in Figure 10.6.

Figure 10.6.

Running `CursorDemoApplet.`

To create this applet, perform the following steps:

1. Start with a new applet.

2. Place a button on the applet. Configure that button to construct and display the frame by writing the following code to execute when the button is clicked:

```
void button1_Clicked(java.awt.event.ActionEvent
        event) {
    frame = new CursorDemoFrame();
    frame.show();
}
```

3. Add a new frame by using the Insert Form dialog.

4. Place the New Title and Cursor Style labels on the frame.

5. Place a `TextField` named `title` next to the New Title label.

6. Place a `Choice` component named `choiceCursor` next to the Cursor Style label.

7. Add Default, Crosshair, Hand, Move, Text, and Wait to the `Items` property of `choiceCursor`.

8. Add the event-handling methods shown in Listing 10.4 to the `CursorDemoFrame` class.

Listing 10.4. The event-handling methods of `CursorDemoFrame`.

```
1:  void closeButton_Clicked(java.awt.event.ActionEvent event) {
2:      hide();
3:      dispose();
4:  }
5:
6:  void applyButton_Clicked(java.awt.event.ActionEvent event) {
7:      setTitle(title.getText());
8:
9:      int Cursors[]={DEFAULT_CURSOR, CROSSHAIR_CURSOR,
10:             HAND_CURSOR, MOVE_CURSOR, TEXT_CURSOR,
11:              WAIT_CURSOR };
12:
13:     setCursor(Cursors[choiceCursor.getSelectedIndex()]);
14:  }
```

ANALYSIS   In Listing 10.4, clicking the Close button hides and then disposes of the frame (lines 1–4). More interesting is what happens when the Apply button is clicked. The method `applyButton_Clicked` uses `setTitle(title.getText)` to take the string entered by the user and make it the title of the frame. Similarly, a call to `setCursor` causes the frame to use the cursor selected by the user in `choiceCursor`, the drop-down list of cursor styles.

Do	Don't

DO remember that you can assign a layout manager to a frame.

DON'T forget that frames can have menus. See Day 11, "Menus and Toolbars," for details.

DO remember to set the size of the frame before displaying it.

Dialogs

The Java `Dialog` class is similar to the `Frame` class. Just like a frame, a dialog can hold components and accept user input. A dialog can be constructed using either of the constructors shown in Table 10.4.

Table 10.4. Constructors for the `Dialog` class.

Constructor	Purpose
`Dialog(Frame, boolean)`	Creates a dialog with the specified parent frame and modality
`Dialog(Frame, String, boolean)`	Creates a dialog with the specified parent frame, title string, and modality

As with the Window class, each Dialog must have a Frame as its parent. Because an applet is not a frame, you cannot create a dialog with an applet as its parent. This isn't much of an inconvenience, however, because it is simple to create a frame, and you don't really need to do anything with the frame other than use it as the dialog's parent in the dialog constructor. For example, you can create a dialog that uses a dummy frame as follows:

```
Frame dummyFrame = new Frame();
dummyFrame.resize(250, 250);
Dialog d = new Dialog(dummyFrame, false);
```

A key difference between a frame and a dialog is found in the final parameter to each of the Dialog constructors. This boolean parameter specifies the modality of the dialog. A dialog can be either *modal* or *modeless*.

 A *modal* dialog requires user input before allowing the user to interact with other parts of the program. A *modeless* dialog is simply another window on the screen that the user can ignore.

A modal dialog forces users to respond to it before they can continue working with other parts of the applet. Because of this, a modal dialog is perfect for displaying error messages or for gathering necessary user input. A modeless dialog does not require that the user close the dialog before continuing.

Another difference between a frame and a dialog is that a menu can only be attached directly to a frame. Menus are described in detail on Day 11.

Because a dialog is closely related to a frame, a dialog's set of nonprivate methods should be familiar. These are shown in Table 10.5.

Table 10.5. Nonprivate methods of the Dialog class.

Method	Purpose
addNotify()	Creates a peer for the component
getTitle()	Returns the dialog's title
isModal()	Returns true if the dialog is modal
isResizable()	Returns true if the dialog is resizable
paramString()	Returns the dialog's parameter string
setResizable(boolean)	Makes the dialog resizable or not, depending on the specified parameter
setTitle(String)	Sets the dialog's title

A `Dialog` **Example**

The example `ResizableDialogApplet`, provided on the MCP Web site (`www.mcp.com/info/`
`1-57521/1-57521-303-6`), shows how to use many of the `Dialog` class methods shown in Table
10.5. This example includes an applet window with a button that displays a dialog. The
dialog, shown in Figure 10.7, includes buttons labeled Toggle and Close. The Toggle button
changes the dialog from resizable to not resizable. The dialog also includes a label that
contains the current state of the dialog.

Figure 10.7.

Running
`ResizableDialogApplet.`

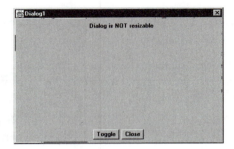

Because the dialog can be resized, all the components (the two buttons and the label) are first
placed into panels. This allows the components to be properly positioned whenever the
dialog is resized (see Figure 10.8).

Figure 10.8.

The components on the
`ResizableDialog`
remain correctly placed
after the dialog has been
resized.

To create this applet, perform the following steps:

1. Start with a new applet.

2. Place a button on the applet. Configure that button to construct and display the
frame by writing the following event handler for it:

```
void button1_Clicked(java.awt.event.ActionEvent event) {
    Frame dummyFrame = new Frame();
    dummyFrame.resize(250, 250);
    Dialog dlg = new ResizableDialog(dummyFrame, false);
    dlg.show();
}
```

10

3. Add a new dialog, named `ResizableDialog`, by using the Insert Form dialog.

4. Use the Property List to change the layout for the dialog to `BorderLayout`.

5. Place two AWT panels on the dialog. Use the Property List to set the `Placement` property for one to `North` and the other to `South`. This places one panel across the top of the dialog and the other across the bottom. For each panel, set the value of the `Layout` property to `FlowLayout`.

6. Drag a label onto the top panel and name it `resizeLabel`.

7. Drag two buttons onto the bottom panel. Assign them the labels Toggle and Close and the names `toggleButton` and `closeButton`.

8. In the `ResizableDialog` class, outside of any member methods, add the following declaration:

```
String labelText [] = {
    "Dialog is NOT resizable",
    "Dialog is resizable"
};
```

The two strings in this array will be placed into `resizeLabel` based on the current resizable state of the dialog.

9. Immediately before the `REGISTER_LISTENERS` section of `addNotify`, add the following code:

```
// make the dialog not resizable
setResizable(false);

// correctly initialize the text in the label
resizeLabel.setText(labelText[0]);
resizeLabel.resize(resizeLabel.preferredSize());
```

The call to `setResizable` is used so that the dialog will not be resizable initially. Because this corresponds with `labelText[0]`, as declared earlier, `setText` is used to place this string in the label. Because the strings in `labelText` are not of the same size, the label is then resized to its preferred size.

10. Add event-handling methods for the Toggle and Close buttons so they appear as shown in Listing 10.5. If the Close button is clicked, the frame is hidden and then disposed of (lines 12–13). However, if the Toggle button is clicked, the method `isResizable` is used to determine the current state of the dialog. Based on the value returned from `isResizable`, the label is set to the proper text. In all cases, the label is resized and `setResizable` is used to toggle the state of the dialog.

Listing 10.5. The event-handling methods of `ResizableDialogApplet.java`**.**

```
 1:   void toggleButton_Clicked(java.awt.event.ActionEvent event) {
 2:      if (isResizable())
 3:         resizeLabel.setText(labelText[0]);
 4:      else
 5:         resizeLabel.setText(labelText[1]);
 6:      resizeLabel.resize(resizeLabel.preferredSize());
 7:
 8:      setResizable(!isResizable());
 9:   }
10:
11:   void closeButton_Clicked(java.awt.event.ActionEvent event) {
12:      hide();
13:      dispose();
14:   }
```

The `FileDialog` Class

The `FileDialog` class is included in the Java AWT libraries to provide a simple way for creating dialogs that can be used to open or save files. Figures 10.9 and 10.10 show `FileDialog` being used in SAVE and OPEN mode, respectively.

Figure 10.9.

The FileDialog *in* SAVE *mode under Windows 95.*

Figure 10.10.

The FileDialog *in* OPEN *mode under Windows 95.*

An instance of `FileDialog` can be constructed using either of two constructors, as shown in the following three examples:

```
FileDialog dlg1 = new FileDialog(frame, "Save");
```

```
FileDialog dlg2 = new FileDialog(frame, "Save", FileDialog.SAVE);

FileDialog dlg3 = new FileDialog(frame, "Open", FileDialog.OPEN);
```

Each `FileDialog` is created in either OPEN or SAVE mode, depending on whether it will be used to open an existing file or write to a file. These modes are identified by `FileDialog.SAVE` and `FileDialog.OPEN`. By default, a new instance of `FileDialog` is created in SAVE mode. Therefore, `dlg1` and `dlg2` will be in SAVE mode, but `dlg3` will be in OPEN mode.

Because `FileDialog` is a subclass of `Dialog`, it is necessary for each `FileDialog` to have a parent frame. The parent frame is passed as the first parameter to either `FileDialog` constructor. As with other dialogs, it is not necessary for the frame to be displayed.

WARNING

> You cannot use `FileDialog` when programming applets due to Java's security restrictions. Because applets cannot access files, there is no need to open or close them.

Once constructed, a `FileDialog` is displayed with the `show` method. The entire purpose of displaying a `FileDialog` usually is to get a filename from the user. Naturally, there are member methods in `FileDialog` that enable you to retrieve this information after the user has entered it. The `getDirectory` method can be used to retrieve the directory name selected by the user. Similarly, `getFile` returns the filename. Combined, they give you the fully qualified filename.

As an example, the following code creates a `FileDialog` in SAVE mode, displays it, and then prints the full path and filename entered by the user:

```
Frame f = new Frame();
f.resize(250, 250);

FileDialog d = new FileDialog(f, "Save a File", FileDialog.SAVE);
d.show();

System.out.println("Picked: " + d.getDirectory() + d.getFile());
```

NOTE

> To add a `FileDialog` to a project, select Component from the Insert menu. From there, scroll into the Forms section, where you can select either Open File Dialog or Save File Dialog. In either case, a `FileDialog` is placed on the selected form and the value for Mode in the Property List controls whether the dialog is for opening or saving files. You can also use the Property List to set values for the `Default Directory` and `Default Filename`.
>
> After a `FileDialog` has been added to a form, you can use the Interaction wizard as for any other onscreen control.

10

Table 10.6 lists the nonprivate methods of the `FileDialog` class.

Table 10.6. Nonprivate methods of the `FileDialog` class.

Method	Purpose
addNotify()	Creates a peer for the component
getDirectory()	Returns the directory selected in the dialog
getFile()	Returns the filename selected in the dialog
getFilenameFilter()	Returns the `FilenameFilter` in use for the dialog
getMode()	Returns whether the dialog is in SAVE or OPEN mode
setDirectory(String)	Sets the active directory for the dialog
setFile(String)	Sets the current filename for the dialog
setFilenameFilter(FilenameFilter)	Sets the `FilenameFilter` to use for the dialog
paramString()	Returns the dialog's parameter string

 NOTE For additional examples of using `FileDialog`, see Day 13, "Using Streams for Input and Output."

Using Visual Café's Canned Dialogs

Many of the dialogs you'll use in one program will be similar to those you've used in other programs. For example, how many times have you created a dialog to display a warning message, display an about message, show the progress of a lengthy operation, or get the user's name and password? Because dialogs such as these are used every day by programmers, Visual Café has made using these dialogs easier by including canned dialogs to perform these functions. Visual Café includes the following dialog classes:

- [ ] AboutDialog
- [ ] AttentionDialog
- [ ] PasswordDialog
- [ ] ProgressDialog

You can easily add these dialogs to a Visual Café project by selecting either Form or Component from the Insert menu and then selecting the desired dialog class.

The `AboutDialog` **Class**

The `AboutDialog` class is useful for displaying short messages that convey information about a program. Typically, this type of dialog displays things such as the program name, its version number, a serial number, the technical support phone number, or a copyright notice.

A sample `AboutDialog` is shown in Figure 10.11. When you add an `AboutDialog` to a project, it includes a label you can customize in the Property List and an OK button that closes the dialog when clicked. The dialog shown in Figure 10.11 was created with the following code:

```
Frame dummyFrame = new Frame();
dummyFrame.resize(250, 250);
AboutDialog dlg = new AboutDialog(dummyFrame, false);
dlg.show();
```

Figure 10.11.

A simple
`AboutDialog`.

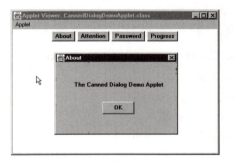

There are two different constructors available for creating an `AboutDialog`, as shown in Table 10.7.

Table 10.7. Constructors for the `AboutDialog` class.

Constructor	Purpose
`AboutDialog(Frame, boolean)`	Creates a dialog with the specified parent and modal status
`AboutDialog(Frame, String, boolean)`	Creates a dialog with the specified parent, title, and modal status

The `AttentionDialog` **Class**

The `AttentionDialog` class is used to create dialogs that present short pieces of information to the user. Likely uses could include informational messages ("This is your 10th visit to this Web page"), warning messages ("You are running low on system resources"), or error messages ("The URL you entered could not be found"). A sample `AttentionDialog` is shown in Figure 10.12.

Figure 10.12.

An AttentionDialog *can include a graphic.*

As you can see from Figure 10.12, an AttentionDialog can include a simple graphic. In this case, a warning message that includes a bullet hole graphic is displayed. There are four different constructors available for creating an AttentionDialog, as shown in Table 10.8.

Table 10.8. Constructors for the AttentionDialog **class.**

Constructor	Purpose
AttentionDialog(Frame)	Creates a dialog with the specified parent.
AttentionDialog(Frame, boolean)	Creates a dialog with the specified parent. The boolean parameter is ignored.
AttentionDialog(Frame, String, boolean)	Creates a dialog with the specified parent and message string. The boolean parameter is ignored.
AttentionDialog(Frame, String, String, URL)	Creates a dialog with the specified parent, title string, message string, and graphic.

NOTE

Two of the AttentionDialog constructors include boolean parameters. The Visual Café Interaction wizard requires that these parameters be present in order to generate interactions for attention dialogs. However, the value used for these parameters will have no impact.

As an example of how to create an `AttentionDialog` that includes a graphic, consider the following code:

```
Frame dummyFrame = new Frame();
dummyFrame.resize(250, 250);
URL myURL;
try {
    myURL=symantec.itools.net.RelativeURL.getURL("bullethole.gif");
    AttentionDialog dlg = new AttentionDialog(dummyFrame, "",
            "Something Nasty Happened", myURL);
    dlg.show();
}
catch (java.net.MalformedURLException error) {
}
```

As usual, a dummy frame is constructed. Next, a URL is created using Symantec's `RelativeURL` class. Because the `getURL` method can throw an exception, it must be enclosed in a `try…catch` block. If `myURL` is successfully constructed, it is passed as a parameter to the `AttentionDialog` constructor and the dialog is shown.

Unlike the `AboutDialog`, the `AttentionDialog` class does not provide code that will automatically handle a click of the OK button. This is because the authors of Visual Café have no idea what you want to happen when the OK button is clicked on an attention dialog. You could be displaying a message that says "Click OK to reformat your hard drive" for all they know. Because of this, you must write your own code to handle the OK button click.

The `PasswordDialog` Class

The `PasswordDialog` can be used to easily gather a username and password, as can be seen in Figure 10.13. There are four constructors for the `PasswordDialog` class. These are shown in Table 10.9.

Figure 10.13.

The `PasswordDialog`
in action.

Table 10.9. Constructors for the PasswordDialog class.

Constructor	Purpose
PasswordDialog(Frame)	Creates a dialog with the specified parent.
PasswordDialog(Frame, String)	Creates a dialog with the specified parent and title.
PasswordDialog(Frame, boolean)	Creates a dialog with the specified parent. The boolean parameter is ignored.
PasswordDialog(Frame, String, boolean)	Creates a dialog with the specified parent and title. The boolean parameter is ignored.

NOTE

As with AttentionDialog, two of the PasswordDialog constructors include boolean parameters. The Visual Café Interaction wizard requires that these parameters be present in order to generate interactions for attention dialogs. However, the value used for these parameters will have no impact.

In addition to its constructors and other methods it inherits, PasswordDialog includes the four methods shown in Table 10.10. These methods can be used to set and retrieve values for the username and password fields. The following example illustrates how to create a password dialog and set the default username to Mike:

```
Frame dummyFrame = new Frame();
dummyFrame.resize(250, 250);
PasswordDialog dlg = new PasswordDialog(dummyFrame);

dlg.setUserName("Mike");
dlg.show();
```

Table 10.10. Nonprivate methods in the PasswordDialog class.

Method	Purpose
getPassword()	Returns the password
getUserName()	Returns the user's name
setPassword(String)	Sets the password
setUserName(String)	Sets the user's name

The `ProgressDialog` Class

The final type of canned dialog included with Visual Café is the `ProgressDialog`. Progress dialogs are a staple in the world of install programs and can be used any time the system is performing a lengthy operation. An example of a Visual Café progress dialog is shown in Figure 10.14.

Figure 10.14.

A ProgressDialog *at 50% complete.*

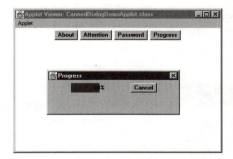

A progress dialog can be created with any of the four constructors shown in Table 10.11. As with all other dialogs, a frame must be used as the dialog's parent. In addition to its constructors, the `ProgressDialog` class also includes a public method, `setProgress`. The `setProgress` method is passed an integer from 0 to 100 to indicate how much of the operation is complete. As an example of creating a progress dialog and updating progress through an operation, consider the following:

```
Frame dummyFrame = new Frame();
dummyFrame.resize(250, 250);
ProgressDialog dlg = new ProgressDialog(dummyFrame);
dlg.show();

for (int progress=1; progress<=100; progress++) {
    // do 1% of whatever must be done here
    dlg.setProgress(progress);
}
```

Table 10.11. Constructors for the `ProgressDialog` class.

Constructor	Purpose
`ProgressDialog(Frame)`	Creates a dialog with the specified parent
`ProgressDialog(Frame, boolean)`	Creates a dialog with the specified parent and modal value

continues

Table 10.11. continued

Constructor	Purpose
ProgressDialog(Frame, String, boolean)	Creates a dialog with the specified parent, title, and modal value
ProgressDialog(Frame, String, String, boolean)	Creates a dialog with the specified parent, title, button label, and modal value

Do	Don't

DON'T forget to create a dummy frame if you want to create a dialog whose parent is an applet.

DO save yourself work by creating your own reusable dialogs. See Day 22, "Reusable Packages, Forms, and Projects," for details on doing this.

Summary

Today you learned about windows, frames, and dialogs. You learned that windows are of limited practical use because they do not include borders or a title bar. You learned how to create standalone frames and how to manipulate a frame at runtime by changing its title and cursor. You learned about the Dialog class and how it can be created in both modal and modeless forms. Finally, you learned about the canned dialogs that are included with Visual Café to simplify program development.

Q&A

Q I am using a dummy frame as the parent of a dialog, but when I display the dialog, only a portion of the dialog appears. What's wrong?

A You have either forgotten to resize the frame or have made it a size that is too small. If you forget to resize the frame, the dialog will be only large enough to display the title bar.

Q Why is the Window class included with Java if it doesn't have borders or a title bar?

A Although the Window class itself is probably of limited use in most programs, it serves as the superclass of both Frame and Dialog. Additionally, you can derive your own sublclasses from Window to create your own custom user interfaces. Because you may not always need a title bar or borders, Window provides a useful starting point.

Q I like the ability to reuse the canned dialogs that come with Visual Café. Is there a way to add canned dialogs of my own to Visual Café?

A Yes, there is. Doing so is described in detail in Day 22.

Workshop

The workshop includes quiz questions to help you gauge your understanding of the material in this chapter. The workshop also includes exercises to provide hands-on experience with what you've learned in this chapter. Answers to the quiz questions can be found in Appendix D, "Answers."

Quiz

1. Correctly draw an inheritance tree showing Frame, Container, Window, and Dialog.
2. What method is used to release the resources in use by a window, frame, or dialog?
3. Why are you unlikely to use a Window directly in a Java program?
4. What must always be done before a Dialog is constructed?
5. Explain the difference between modal and modeless.
6. Describe an example in which you would use the FileDialog class in an applet.
7. Name the four canned dialogs provided with Visual Café.
8. What happens when the OK button on an AttentionDialog is clicked?

Exercises

1. Use PasswordDialog to validate a user logging on to an applet. If the password is the same as the reversed username, allow the user to log on. Otherwise, use an AttentionDialog to warn the user that he could not be logged on.
2. Write a program that counts from 1–100,000. Use a ProgressDialog to keep the user aware of the program's progress.

Day 11

Menus and Toolbars

In this chapter, you will learn how to create menus and toolbars. Visual Café includes a Menu editor that greatly simplifies menu creation. You will learn how to use the Menu editor to create menu bars, menus, menu items, separators, submenus, and checkbox menu items.

Toolbars are often used instead of or in addition to menus, and Visual Café's Object library includes classes that aid in creating toolbars. In this chapter, you will learn how easy it is to create a fully functional toolbar without writing a single line of code.

Menus

Many Java applets do not require a menu. However, as the uses of Java move beyond simple Web-based animations, menus will become more prevalent in Java applets and applications. In this section, you will learn about the classes that are used to create Java menus. You will also see how much of the work involved in creating menus is automated by Visual Café.

The hierarchy of Java classes involved in creating menus is shown in Figure 11.1. The `MenuComponent` class serves as an abstract base class for `MenuBar` and `MenuItem`; as such, you will never construct an actual instance of `MenuComponent`.

Figure 11.1.

The Java Menu *classes.*

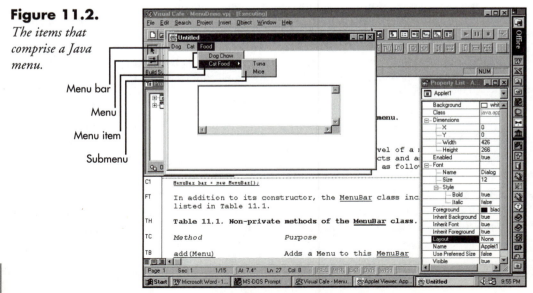

Menus in Java are created by combining three items: a menu bar, one or more menus, and one or more menu items on each of the menus. Each of these items is labeled in Figure 11.2, which is a sample menu that will be built later in this chapter.

Figure 11.2.

The items that comprise a Java menu.

The MenuBar **Class**

The MenuBar class represents the top-most level of a menu. After creating a menu bar, you can create Menu objects and assign those objects to the menu bar. A menu bar is created as follows:

```
MenuBar bar = new MenuBar();
```

In addition to its constructor, the MenuBar class includes the methods listed in Table 11.1.

Table 11.1. Nonprivate methods of the MenuBar class.

Method	Purpose
add(Menu)	Adds a menu to this menu bar
addNotify()	Creates a peer for the object
countMenus()	Returns the number of menus on this menu bar
getHelpMenu()	Returns the menu that has been identified as the Help menu for this menu bar
getMenu(int)	Returns the menu at the specified index
remove(int)	Removes the menu at the specified index
remove(MenuComponent)	Removes the specified MenuComponent from this menu bar
removeNotify()	Removes the object's peer
setHelpMenu(Menu)	Indicates the Help menu for this menu bar

In Java, menus are added to a class that implements the MenuContainer interface. In most cases, this will be a class you define and base on Frame because Frame is the only Java container that implements MenuContainer. Unless you are defining your own menu-style classes, it is usually sufficient to add menus to a frame object. The following code adds a menu bar to a frame:

```
MenuBar bar = new MenuBar();
// add menus to the MenuBar
myFrame.setMenuBar(bar);
```

Because a menu bar can only be added to a frame, you cannot add a menu bar directly to an applet.

The Menu **Class**

A menu bar without any menus is as worthless as a pizza without any pepperoni. This can be easily rectified by creating Menu objects. To create a new menu, simply provide the name of the menu to the constructor, as follows:

```
Menu catMenu = new Menu("Cat");
Menu dogMenu = new Menu("Dog");
```

After creating a menu, you must add it to the menu bar. Menus will be displayed across the menu bar in the order in which they are added to it. For example, the following code will create a Cat menu followed by a Dog menu:

```
Menu catMenu = new Menu("Cat");
menuBar.add(catMenu);
Menu dogMenu = new Menu("Dog");
menuBar.add(dogMenu);
```

A second `Menu` constructor with the following signature is provided:

```
Menu(String label, boolean tearOff)
```

In addition to these constructors, the `Menu` class includes the methods listed in Table 11.2.

Table 11.2. Nonprivate methods of the `Menu` class.

Method	Purpose
add(MenuItem)	Adds the specified `MenuItem` to the menu
add(String)	Adds an item with the specified label to the menu
addNotify()	Creates a peer for the object
addSeparator()	Adds a separator line to the menu
countItems()	Returns the number of items in the menu
getItem(int)	Returns the `MenuItem` at the specified index
isTearOff()	Returns `true` if the menu can be torn off
remove(int)	Removes the `MenuItem` at the specified index
remove(MenuComponent)	Removes the specified `MenuComponent` from the menu
removeNotify()	Removes the object's peer

The `MenuItem` Class

The menu still isn't useful, however, because no menu items have been added. A new menu item can be created by passing a string to the menu item constructor. For example, the following code illustrates all that is needed to create a menu bar, a Dog menu on the menu bar, and three items on the Dog menu:

```
MenuBar menuBar = new MenuBar();
Menu dogMenu = new Menu("Dog");
dogMenu.add(new MenuItem("Labrador"));
dogMenu.add(new MenuItem("Poodle"));
dogMenu.add(new MenuItem("Spaniel"));
menuBar.add(dogMenu);
myFrame.setMenuBar(menuBar);
```

By default, MenuItems are *enabled*. This means that the user can select them from the menu on which they appear. It is possible to disable a MenuItem. This can be done using either the disable method or by passing false to the enable method. A MenuItem can be enabled by passing true to enable or by using enable without any parameters. These methods are illustrated in the following:

```
MenuItem item = new MenuItem("Big Dog");
item.disable();          // disable the MenuItem
item.enable();           // enable the MenuItem
item.enable(false);      // disable the MenuItem
item.enable(true);       // enable the MenuItem
```

The enable and disable methods are not the only ones available for a MenuItem. Table 11.3 describes each of the nonprivate members of MenuItem.

Table 11.3. Nonprivate methods of the MenuItem class.

Method	Purpose
addNotify()	Creates a peer for the object
disable()	Disables selection of this menu item
enable()	Enables selection of this menu item
enable(boolean)	Enables or disables selection of the menu item based on the specified boolean
getLabel()	Returns the label for this menu item
isEnabled()	Returns true if the menu item is selectable
paramString()	Returns a parameter string for this menu item
setLabel(String)	Sets the label of the menu item to the specified string

The CheckboxMenuItem Class

The CheckboxMenuItem class is a subclass of MenuItem that can be used to display a checkmark next to the item when desired. A CheckboxMenuItem is used in a manner almost identical to a regular MenuItem. It provides the additional getState and setState(boolean) methods, but is constructed and added to a menu as though it were a MenuItem. For example, the following code will create a new CheckboxMenuItem with the menu text Checkbox, set it to its checked state, and then add it to the menu:

```
CheckboxMenuItem checkbox = new CheckboxMenuItem("Checkbox");
checkbox.setState(true);
menu.add(checkbox);
```

In addition to its constructor, the CheckboxMenuItem class includes the methods listed in Table 11.4.

Table 11.4. Nonprivate methods of the `CheckboxMenuItem` **class.**

Method	Purpose
`addNotify()`	Creates a peer for the object
`getState()`	Returns `true` if `CheckboxMenuItem` is checked or `false` otherwise
`paramString()`	Returns a parameter string for this `MenuItem`
`setState(boolean)`	Checks or unchecks `CheckboxMenuItem` depending on the specified `boolean`

The Visual Café Menu Editor

Although it is important to understand the `MenuBar`, `Menu`, `MenuItem`, and `CheckboxMenuItem` classes, much of the basic work required to use these classes is automated by the Visual Café Menu editor. Using the Menu editor, you can visually design a menu. You can create submenus, add checkbox items, and even attach code to menu commands.

To use the Menu editor, place a `MenuBar` component on the frame to which you wish to attach the menu. The easiest way to do this is to open the Component Library window, select the `MenuBar` component from the Menus & Menu Items section, and drag the component onto the frame. If you are starting with an otherwise empty frame, the frame will appear as shown in Figure 11.3.

Figure 11.3.

Placing a `MenuBar` *component on a frame.*

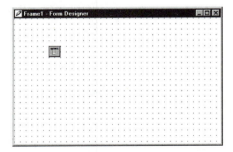

To activate the Menu editor, double click the `MenuBar` component. The Menu editor will appear as shown in Figure 11.4. At this point, you will have an empty menu and you can begin adding items to it.

11

Figure 11.4.

The Menu editor before menu items are added.

Adding Menus and Menu Items

As you can see in Figure 11.4, the Menu editor starts out with an empty menu, but contains an outlined rectangle that serves as a placeholder for where the first menu will be located. To convert the placeholder into a menu, click it and then type the label of the new menu. If the Property List is visible, you will notice that as you enter the label, it will also appear in the Label property on the Property List.

After you type the menu label, press Enter. Doing so will create two new placeholders: one to the right of the first menu and one underneath it (see Figure 11.5). The placeholder to the right is for the next menu; the placeholder below is for the first menu item of the first menu. This placeholder is already selected, so you can immediately begin typing a label for the first menu item.

Figure 11.5.

Creating the first menu creates two new placeholders.

TIP

> When labeling a menu or menu item, you can indicate a selection character by prefacing it with the ampersand character (&). For example, &File creates a File menu with an underlined F. Similarly, &Open and Save &As create menu items with the O and A characters underlined. By providing selection characters, you allow users to invoke menus and menu items by typing the characters instead of using the mouse or navigation keys.

Adding Separators

Separators are horizontal lines that can be placed between menu items in a menu. For example, Figure 11.6 shows the Help menu of Visual Café. This menu includes two separators to help visually distinguish the types of items on this menu.

Figure 11.6.

Separators can be added to help visually distinguish items on a menu.

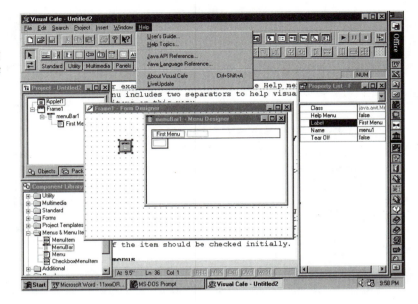

To add a separator to a menu, create a new menu item; instead of entering a label for the item, use the Property List to change the value of the Separator property to true.

TIP

> You can create a separator by setting a menu item's Label property to −.

Adding CheckboxMenuItems

Add a CheckboxMenuItem to a menu by dragging it from the Component Library window to the desired location on the menu. When there, you can set the item's label as with any other menu item. Additionally, you can set the Enabled property to true or false to indicate whether the item should be checked initially.

Adding Submenus

To create a submenu, create a menu item and then change the menu item into a submenu. To do this, select the desired menu item and then click the right mouse button. This displays a context menu that includes the option Create Submenu. Selecting this option turns the menu item into a submenu by adding a placeholder to the right of the item (see Figure 11.7). At this point the new placeholder can be changed to a menu item, checkbox menu item, or separator.

Figure 11.7.

A menu item can be converted into a submenu.

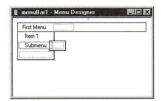

TIP

You are not limited to a single level of submenu. Submenus can have sub-submenus, and so on, as deeply as necessary.

Attaching Code to Menu Items

Visual Café makes it easy to attach code to menu items. You can invoke the Interaction wizard by right-clicking the desired menu item. This gives you full access to the power of the Interaction wizard to connect a menu selection to other components.

Additionally, each of the menus, menu items, separators, and submenus is listed in the Objects drop-down list of the source-code editing window. Even better, the menu items are appropriately indented, making it easy to determine which menu items can be selected from which menus and submenus (see Figure 11.8).

Figure 11.8.

All menu components are shown in the object list and are appropriately indented.

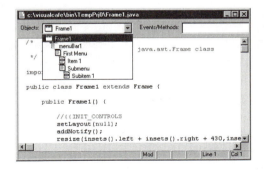

To create code that will handle a menu selection in this way, select the desired menu label in the Objects list and then select Action in the Events/Methods drop-down list.

WARNING

At the time this chapter was written, there was a bug in Visual Café related to the generation of menu-handling code. If, after generating code to handle the selection of a menu item, you used the Menu editor to change the label of the menu item, the generated code was not updated to use the new label. For example, if the `Save` menu item was changed to `Save As` in the code listed previously, you would need to manually change the following line to compare against `Save As`:

```
if (label.equalsIgnoreCase("Save")) {
```

An Example

In this section, you will create a menu system that includes a menu bar, multiple menus and menu items, a checkbox menu item, and a submenu. The menu bar includes three menus: a Dog menu, a Cat menu, and a Food menu that includes a Cat Food submenu as well as a Dog Chow submenu. These menus are shown in Figures 11.9, 11.10, and 11.11.

Figure 11.9.

The Dog menu.

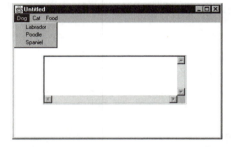

Figure 11.10.

The Cat menu.

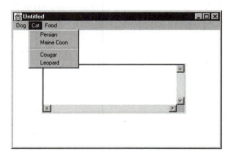

Figure 11.11.

The Food menu and Cat Food submenu.

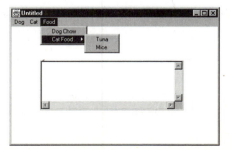

To create this applet start, perform the following steps:

1. Start with a new applet.

2. Place a button named `menuButton` on the applet and have that button construct and display the frame. Do this by adding the following action event handler for the `menuButton` object:

```
void menuButton_Clicked(java.awt.event.ActionEvent event) {
    frame = new MenuDemoFrame();
    frame.show();
}
```

3. Add the following declaration immediately above the `DECLARE_CONTROLS` section of the class:

```
MenuDemoFrame frame;
```

4. Add a new frame by using the Insert Form dialog. Name the frame `MenuDemoFrame`.

5. Drag a `MenuBar` from the Component Library onto the frame and invoke the Menu editor by double-clicking the Menu Bar icon.

6. Create a menu of dog breeds by adding a new menu named `dogMenu`. Then add menu items for `Labrador`, `Poodle`, and `Spaniel`.

7. Create a menu of cat breeds by adding a new menu named `catMenu`. Then add menu items for `Persian`, `Maine Coon`, `Cougar`, and `Leopard`. Add a separator between `Maine Coon` and `Cougar`.

8. Create a menu with the label of `Food` and a name of `foodMenu`. Add a checkbox menu item with a label of `Dog Chow`. Add a menu item named `catFoodMenu` with a label of `Cat Food`. Use the right-mouse button to convert this to a submenu. For the new submenu, create items called `Tuna` and `Cat Chow`.

9. Add a `TextArea` component named `info` to the frame (the component should resemble the one in Figure 11.12).

10. Open the source code window for `MenuDemoFrame`. Select Persian in the Objects list and Action in the Events/Methods list to create an event handler for when Persian is selected from the menu. Write the `Persian_Action` method so that it appears as follows:

```
void Persian_Action(java.awt.event.ActionEvent event) {
    info.setText("A big furry cat\r\n");
    info.appendText("that I'm allergic to.");
}
```

11. Repeat this process for Maine Coon, using the following code for the `MaineCoon_Action` method:

```
void MaineCoon_Action(java.awt.event.ActionEvent event) {
    info.setText("A really ferocious cat that\r\n");
    info.appendText("my Grandmother thinks is\r\n");
    info.appendText("a house cat.");
}
```

11

12. Ensure that the `Action` listener class calls the `Persian_Action` and `MaineCoon_Action` methods as shown in the following code:

```
class Action implements java.awt.event.ActionListener {
  public void actionPerformed(java.awt.event.ActionEvent event) {
    String str = event.getActionCommand();
    if (str.equals("Persian"))
      Persian_Action(event);
    else if (str.equals("Maine Coon"))
      MaineCoon_Action(event);
  }
}
```

Figure 11.12.

A text area is placed on the frame along with the menu bar.

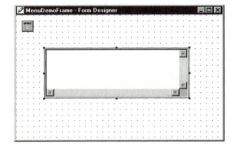

At this point, you are ready to run the `MenuDemo` applet. If you have not followed each of the steps listed previously, you can find this applet on the MCP Web site (`www.mcp.com/info/1-57521/1-57521-303-6`). This applet is an excellent example of how Visual Café streamlines Java development. You were able to create the `MenuDemoFrame` class, the heart of the applet, and only had to write the code that placed the descriptions of the cats in the text area. Everything else was done automatically by Visual Café. It is worth taking a quick look at exactly what code was generated for `MenuDemoFrame` (Listing 11.1 contains the complete source).

Listing 11.1. The `MenuDemoFrame` class.

```
1:   import java.awt.*;
2:
3:   public class MenuDemoFrame extends Frame {
4:      void MaineCoon_Action(java.awt.event.ActionEvent event) {
5:         info.setText("A really ferocious cat that\r\n");
6:         info.appendText("my Grandmother thinks is\r\n");
7:         info.appendText("a house cat.");
8:      }
9:
10:     void Persian_Action(java.awt.event.ActionEvent event) {
11:        info.setText("A big furry cat\r\n");
12:        info.appendText("that I'm allergic to.");
13:     }
```

```
14:
15:    void MenuDemoFrame_WindowClosing(java.awt.event.WindowEvent
16:          event) {
17:      hide();              // hide the Frame
18:    }
19:
20:    public MenuDemoFrame() {
21:
22:    }
23:
24:    public MenuDemoFrame(String title) {
25:        this();
26:        setTitle(title);
27:    }
28:
29:     public synchronized void show() {
30:        move(50, 50);
31:        super.show();
32:     }
33:
34:     public void addNotify() {
35:
36:        // Call parents addNotify method.
37:        super.addNotify();
38:
39:        //{{INIT_CONTROLS
40:        setLayout(null);
41:        resize(insets().left + insets().right + 430,
42:              insets().top + insets().bottom + 270);
43:        info = new java.awt.TextArea();
44:        info.reshape(insets().left + 60,insets().top + 72,
45:            299,107);
46:        add(info);
47:        setTitle("Untitled");
48:        //}}
49:
50:        //{{INIT_MENUS
51:        menuBar1 = new java.awt.MenuBar();
52:
53:        dogMenu = new java.awt.Menu("Dog");
54:        dogMenu.add("Labrador");
55:        dogMenu.add("Poodle");
56:        dogMenu.add("Spaniel");
57:        menuBar1.add(dogMenu);
58:
59:        catMenu = new java.awt.Menu("Cat");
60:        catMenu.add("Persian");
61:        catMenu.add("Maine Coon");
62:        catMenu.addSeparator();
63:        catMenu.add("Cougar");
64:        catMenu.add("Leopard");
65:        menuBar1.add(catMenu);
66:
```

11

continues

Listing 11.1. continued

```
67:        foodMenu = new java.awt.Menu("Food");
68:        foodMenu.add(new java.awt.CheckboxMenuItem("Dog Chow"));
69:
70:        menu1 = new java.awt.Menu("Cat Food");
71:        menu1.add("Tuna");
72:        menu1.add("Mice");
73:        foodMenu.add(menu1);
74:        menuBar1.add(foodMenu);
75:        setMenuBar(menuBar1);
76:        //$$ menuBar1.move(12,12);
77:        //}}
78:
79:        //{{REGISTER_LISTENERS
80:        Window lWindow = new Window();
81:        addWindowListener(lWindow);
82:        Action lAction = new Action();
83:        catMenu.addActionListener(lAction);
84:        //}}
85:    }
86:
87:    //{{DECLARE_CONTROLS
88:    java.awt.TextArea info;
89:    //}}
90:
91:    //{{DECLARE_MENUS
92:    java.awt.MenuBar menuBar1;
93:    java.awt.Menu dogMenu;
94:    java.awt.Menu catMenu;
95:    java.awt.Menu foodMenu;
96:    java.awt.Menu menu1;
97:    //}}
98:
99:    class Window extends java.awt.event.WindowAdapter {
100:       public void windowClosing(java.awt.event.WindowEvent
101:           event) {
102:          Object object = event.getSource();
103:          if (object == MenuDemoFrame.this)
104:             MenuDemoFrame_WindowClosing(event);
105:       }
106:    }
107:
108:    class Action implements java.awt.event.ActionListener {
109:       public void actionPerformed(java.awt.event.ActionEvent
110:           event) {
111:          String str = event.getActionCommand();
112:          if (str.equals("Persian"))
113:             Persian_Action(event);
114:          else if (str.equals("Maine Coon"))
115:             MaineCoon_Action(event);
116:       }
117:    }
118: }
```

ANALYSIS As you can see, Visual Café and the Menu editor took care of quite a few details for you. You should be able to examine the INIT_MENUS section (lines 50–77) and see how these lines correspond with the actions you took in the Menu editor.

Do	Don't

DO try to limit your submenus to only two levels. If you use more levels than that, it can become confusing for your users.

DON'T forget to use the ampersand character (&) to indicate selection characters for menu items.

Toolbars

Of course, a menu is not the only way to present your user with choices. A toolbar is an excellent alternative when there are few enough actions that they will all fit on a toolbar. Alternatively, a toolbar can be used in conjunction with a menu to present the user with easy access to the most common actions. A significant advantage of toolbars over menus is that toolbars can also hold components such as text fields and choices. For example, Figure 11.13 shows a toolbar that includes three buttons and a choice component.

Figure 11.13.
A toolbar with three image buttons and a choice component.

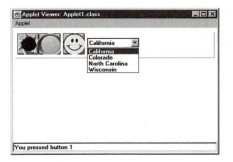

The `ToolBarPanel` and `ToolBarSpacer` Classes

Visual Café includes two classes, `ToolBarPanel` and `ToolBarSpacer`, that make creating a toolbar a very simple process. `ToolBarPanel` is a subclass of `Container` and is used to hold the components you wish to place in a toolbar. `ToolBarSpacer` can be used to fine-tune the spacing of components on the toolbar.

11

> **TIP**
>
> A toolbar can be placed directly onto an applet, unlike a menu bar, which must be placed on a frame. This makes a toolbar an especially attractive option when creating applets.

To create the toolbar shown in Figure 11.13, perform the following steps:

1. Start with a new applet. Set the Layout property of the applet to BorderLayout.

2. Add a ToolBarPanel to the applet and set its Placement property to North.

3. Drag an image button component onto the toolbar panel. Using the Property List, select a valid GIF file for the URL property. The sample applet ToolbarDemo, included on the MCP Web site, uses bullethole.gif, which is located in the same directory as the applet.

4. Drag a second image button onto the toolbar panel and select a valid URL. ToolbarDemo uses doorbell.gif.

5. Drag a toolbar spacer onto the toolbar and position it to the right of the second image button.

6. Drag a third image button onto the toolbar panel and select a valid URL. ToolbarDemo uses smiley.gif.

7. Drag another toolbar spacer onto the toolbar and position it to the right of the last image button.

8. Drag a choice component onto the toolbar and position it to the right of the second spacer. Use the Property List to set the width to 100. Add three or four strings to the Items property so you can see that it works properly.

9. Drag a text field onto the applet. Set its Placement property to South and its name to status.

10. Use the Objects and Events/Methods lists in a source-code editing window to add the following event-handling methods for the button clicks:

    ```java
    void imageButton1_Action(java.awt.event.ActionEvent event) {
       status.setText("You pressed button 1");
    }

    void imageButton2_Action(java.awt.event.ActionEvent event) {
       status.setText("You pressed button 2");
    }

    void imageButton3_Action(java.awt.event.ActionEvent event) {
       status.setText("You pressed button 3");
    }
    ```

At this point, you are ready to execute the ToolbarDemo applet. It doesn't do anything truly useful yet; but, on the other hand, you have created a fully functional toolbar with very minimal coding.

Summary

In this chapter you learned about Java's menu classes: MenuBar, Menu, MenuItem, and CheckboxMenuItem. You learned how to combine these to create menus and submenus that can be attached to a frame. You learned how to use the Menu editor to allow you to visually create a menu. You stepped through a detailed example that used the Menu editor to create a menu that included multiple menus, menu items, checkbox menu items, separators, and submenus. Finally, you learned about the ToolBarPanel and ToolBarSpacer classes. You learned how to combine these classes with ImageButton to create a functional toolbar without writing a single line of code.

Tomorrow you'll get a break from user-interface programming and will learn about the classes in the java.util package.

Q&A

Q Can I place a toolbar panel on items other than an applet?

A Yes. Because ToolBarPanel is a distant subclass of Component, it can be placed anywhere a component can be placed. This includes frames, dialogs, windows, and even other panels.

Q In the Menu editor, I created menu items named 1 and 2. When I tried to add event-handling code for these methods, I got an error message. What happened?

A When Visual Café creates an event handler for a menu item, it uses a naming convention of MenuItemLabel_Action. For example, line two in Listing 11.1 is MaineCoon_Action. This method name was automatically generated because the menu item's label was Maine Coon. In your case, Visual Café attempted to create methods named 1_Action and 2_Action. Because method names in Java cannot begin with digits, this caused an error. One obvious workaround for the problem is to change your menu item labels. However, if you can't do that, you can rename these methods in your source code. Be sure to change their names where they are called in the Action method generated by Visual Café.

Workshop

The workshop includes quiz questions to help you gauge your understanding of the material in this chapter. The workshop also includes exercises to provide hands-on experience with what you've learned in this chapter. Answers to the quiz questions can be found in Appendix D, "Answers."

Quiz

1. On a piece of paper, draw a menu and label the following items: menu bar, menu item, checkbox menu item, submenu, and separator.

2. To what Java classes can a menu be attached?

3. What methods are available in `CheckboxMenuItem` that are not available in `MenuItem`?

4. How do you create a submenu in the Menu editor?

5. What is the maximum allowable number of nested submenus?

6. What two classes are provided with Visual Café specifically for creating a toolbar?

7. Why might you want to use a toolbar instead of a menu?

Exercises

1. Write a program that uses a vertical toolbar instead of the horizontal toolbar demonstrated in this chapter.

2. Write a program that includes a menu and a toolbar. On the toolbar, include a combo box that includes the label of each menu item. Also include an Enable button and a Disable button on the toolbar. When either of the buttons on the toolbar is clicked, enable or disable the menu item selected in the combo box.

3. Write an application that uses a Most Recently Used (MRU) list. An example of an MRU list can be seen at the bottom of the File menu in Visual Café. Most commonly, an MRU list keeps track of the most recently opened files. However, an MRU list could be used to keep track of anything. Use a simple text field to gather a name from the user. When the user clicks a button, add the name to the top of the MRU list. Only allow four entries in the MRU list. Naturally, keep only the most recently used items!

4. Extra Credit: Change your MRU list example to use the `FileDialog` class that was described in Chapter 10, "Windows, Frames, and Dialogs."

11

Day 12

The Java Utility Classes

Today you'll learn about the `java.util` package. This package provides some very useful Java classes on which you will come to rely. This lesson introduces the following classes and interfaces:

```
BitSet
Date
Enumeration
Hashtable
Properties
Observable
Random
Vector
Stack
StringTokenizer
```

The `BitSet` class is useful for storing and manipulating arbitrarily long sets of bits. The `Date` class can be used to represent dates and times, and provides methods for converting dates to and from strings. The `Enumeration` interface is useful for retrieving sets of values from other classes. The `Hashtable` class can be used for creating an array of keys and values and allowing elements to be looked up by either key or value. The `Properties` class extends `Hashtable` by allowing elements to be streamed into or out of the class. The `Observable` class can be extended, and enables you to create new classes that will notify other classes when they change. It works in conjunction with the `Observer` interface, which is also part of the `java.util` package.

The `Random` class is a pseudo-random number generator that can return integer, floating-point, or Gaussian-distributed values. The `Stack` class is an extension of `Vector` and supplies a last-in-first-out (LIFO) data structure. The `Vector` class can be used to store any objects and can store objects of more than one type in the same vector. The `StringTokenizer` class provides a flexible mechanism for parsing strings.

The `BitSet` Class

The `BitSet` class represents a dynamically sized set of bits. Two constructors are provided: one that creates an empty set of an unspecified size, and one that creates a set of a specified size. The `set` method can be used to set an individual bit, and `clear` can be used to clear an individual bit. The first bit in a bit set is the zero bit, so `myBitset.set(0)` is a valid statement.

The logical functions `AND`, `OR`, and `XOR` are all supported and combine the bit set with another set. Bit sets can be compared for equality using `equals` and can be converted to strings using `toString`. For the purpose of converting a bit set to a string, a set bit is represented by the value `1`, and a clear bit is represented by `0`.

The available constructor and nonprivate methods for `BitSet` are shown in Table 12.1.

Table 12.1. Nonprivate constructors and methods of `BitSet`.

Member	Purpose
`BitSet()`	Constructs an empty bit set.
`BitSet(int)`	Constructs an empty bit set with the specified number of bits.
`and(BitSet)`	Performs a logical `AND` operation on two bit sets, placing the result in the object invoking the method.
`clear(int)`	Clears the specified bit.
`clone()`	Creates a duplicate copy of the bit set.
`equals(Object)`	Returns `true` if two bit sets are equal.
`get(int)`	Returns the value of the specified bit.
`hashCode()`	Returns a hash code for the bit set.
`or(BitSet)`	Performs a logical `OR` operation on two bit sets, placing the result in the object invoking the method.

Member	Purpose
set(int)	Sets the specified bit.
size()	Returns the size of the bit set in bits.
toString()	Formats the bit set as a string.
xor(BitSet)	Performs a logical XOR operation on two bit sets, placing the result in the object invoking the method.

An Example

As an example of how to use BitSet, consider Listing 12.1, which shows the method bitSetTestButton_Clicked from the BitSetTest applet. This applet, which is included on the MCP Web site (www.mcp.com/info/1-57521/1-57521-303-6), includes a text area named results and a button. When the button is clicked, the code in Listing 12.1 executes and demonstrates various BitSet methods by writing to the text area. The results of executing BitSetTest are shown in Figure 12.1.

Listing 12.1. bitSetTestButton_Clicked **from the** BitSetTest **applet.**

```
1:     void bitSetTestButton_Clicked(java.awt.event.ActionEvent
2:           event) {
3:         // create a BitSet and set items 1 and 4
4:         BitSet bits1 = new BitSet(10);
5:         bits1.set(1);
6:         bits1.set(4);
7:
8:         // create a BitSet and set items 4 and 5
9:         BitSet bits2 = new BitSet(10);
10:         bits2.set(4);
11:         bits2.set(5);
12:
13:         // display the contents of these two BitSets
14:         results.appendText("Bits 1=" + bits1.toString()+"\r\n");
15:         results.appendText("Bits 2=" + bits2.toString()+"\r\n");
16:
17:         // test for equality of the two BitSets
18:         if(bits1.equals(bits2))
19:             results.appendText("bits1 == bits2\r\n");
20:         else
21:             results.appendText("bits1 != bits2\r\n");
22:
23:         // create a clone and then test for equality
24:         BitSet clonedBits = (BitSet)bits1.clone();
25:         if(bits1.equals(clonedBits))
26:             results.appendText("bits1 == clonedBits\r\n");
27:         else
28:             results.appendText("bits1 != clonedBits\r\n");
29:
```

continues

12

Listing 12.1. continued

```
30:        // logically AND the first two BitSets
31:        bits1.and(bits2);
32:        results.appendText("ANDing bits1 and bits2\r\n");
33:        // and display the resulting BitSet
34:        results.appendText("bits1=" + bits1.toString() + "\r\n");
35:    }
```

Figure 12.1.

*The results of
executing*
BitSetTest.

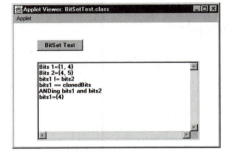

ANALYSIS　In the BitSetTest method, two bit sets are constructed (lines 4 and 9). The first,
bits1, has bits 1 and 4 set (lines 5–6). The second, bits2, has bits 4 and 5 set (lines
10–11). The toString method is used to display the contents of the bit sets (lines 14–15).
The bit sets are then compared using equals (lines 18–21). Next, a clone of bits1 is created
(line 24). To show that the clone method was successful, the bit sets are compared and a
message is displayed (lines 25–28). Finally, the and method is used to logically AND two bit
sets and the result is displayed using toString (lines 31–34).

NOTE　Because the BitSet class is contained in the package java.util, be sure
to import java.util.*.

The Date Class

The Date class stores a representation of a date and time and provides methods for
manipulating the date and time components. As summarized in Table 12.2, constructors are
provided that create a new Date instance based on the current date and time, on the number
of milliseconds since midnight on January 1, 1970, on a string, or from integers representing
the year, month, day, hours, minutes, and seconds.

Table 12.2. Constructors for the Date class.

Constructor	Purpose
Date()	Creates a date using today's date.
Date(long)	Creates a date using the specified number of milliseconds since January 1, 1970.
Date(int,int,int)	Creates a date using the specified year, month, and day.
Date(int,int,int,int,int)	Creates a date using the specified year, month, day, hours, and minutes.
Date(int,int,int,int,int,int)	Creates a date using the specified year, month, day, hours, minutes, and seconds.
Date(String)	Creates a date using the specified string. Strings must be in a format acceptable to the parse method (described later in this section).

As examples of how these constructors can be used to create new dates, consider the following:

```
Date date1 = new Date();
Date date2 = new Date(95, 10, 14);
Date date3 = new Date(95, 10, 14, 13, 16, 45);
Date date4 = new Date("14 November 1995 13:16:45");
```

In this case, date1 is set to the current date and time. The date2 variable is set to November 14, 1995 (months are zero-based in the Date class, so 10 is passed as a parameter to indicate the eleventh month). The third example adds more exactness to the second example. While date2 represents the stroke of midnight on November 14, 1995, date3 is explicitly set to 13:16:45 (45 seconds after 1:16 p.m.). Finally, date4 stores the same time as date3, but constructs the date from a string.

Many methods are also provided for manipulating Date instances. For example, Date objects can be compared with the before, after, and equals methods. Methods are also provided for converting a date into various formatted strings. The nonprivate instance methods of the Date class are shown in Table 12.3.

Table 12.3. Nonprivate instance methods of the Date class.

Method	Purpose
after(Date)	Returns true if the object's date occurs after the specified date.
before(Date)	Returns true if the object's date occurs before the specified date.
equals(Object)	Returns true if two dates are equal.

continues

Table 12.3. continued

Method	Purpose
getDate()	Returns the day (1–31) portion of the date.
getDay()	Returns the day of the week (Sunday is 0) indicated by the date.
getHours()	Returns the hours (0–23) portion of the date.
getMinutes()	Returns the minutes (0–59) portion of the date.
getMonth()	Returns the month (0–11) portion of the date.
getSeconds()	Returns the seconds (0–59) portion of the date.
getTime()	Returns the number of milliseconds since midnight on January 1, 1970.
getTimezoneOffset()	Returns the offset in minutes for the current time zone from UTC (Coordinated Universal Time, similar to GMT, Greenwich Mean Time).
getYear()	Returns the number of years since 1900.
hashCode()	Returns a hash code for the date.
setDate(int)	Sets the day of the month.
setHours(int)	Sets the hours.
setMinutes(int)	Sets the minutes.
setMonth(int)	Sets the month.
setSeconds(int)	Sets the seconds.
setTime(long)	Sets the time to the specified number of milliseconds since midnight on January 1, 1970.
setYear(int)	Sets the year to be the specified number of years since 1900.
toGMTString()	Returns a formatted string of the date in the GMT time zone.
toLocaleString()	Returns a formatted string of the date in the current time zone.
toString()	Returns a formatted string of the date, including the day of the week.

In addition to the instance methods shown in Table 12.3, the Date class includes two static methods. Static methods can be invoked without an instance of the class. The static methods of the Date class can be used to determine the number of seconds since midnight on January 1, 1970, based on a string or on integer values representing the date and time. These are summarized in Table 12.4, and examples of their use are as follows:

```
long temp = Date.parse("14 November 1996");
Date date1 = new Date(temp);
temp = Date.UTC(96, 10, 14, 13, 16, 45);
Date date2 = new Date(temp);
```

Table 12.4. Static methods of the `Date` class.

Method	Purpose
`UTC(int,int,int,int,int,int)`	Returns the milliseconds since midnight on January 1, 1970 based on the year, month, day, hours, minutes, and seconds parameters.
`parse(String)`	Returns the milliseconds since midnight on January 1, 1970 based on parsing the supplied string.

The parse method can accept strings in a variety of formats, including standard date syntax such as `Fri, 14 Nov 1997 13:16:00 GMT+0800 PST` or `Fri, 14 Nov 1997 13:16:00 PST`.

An Example

As an example of how to use the `Date` class, consider Listing 12.2, which shows the method `DateDemo` from `DateDemoApplet`, which is included on the MCP Web site. This applet includes a text area named `results`. The `init` method of `DateDemoApplet` invokes `DateDemo`.

Listing 12.2. The method `DateDemo` from `DateDemoApplet`.

```
 1:   void DateDemo() {
 2:       Date today = new Date();     // today
 3:
 4:       // display the current date in a couple of different
 5:       // formats
 6:       results.appendText("Today is:"+today.toString()+"\r\n");
 7:       results.appendText("Locale Time:"+today.toLocaleString()
 8:           + "\r\n");
 9:       results.appendText("GMT:"+today.toGMTString() + "\r\n");
10:
11:       // store Bastille Day (July 14th) in an instance
12:       Date BastilleDay = new Date(92, 6, 14);    // 7-14-96
13:
14:       // set Bastille Day to be in the current year
15:       BastilleDay.setYear(today.getYear());
16:
17:       // see if we've already missed Bastille Day
18:       if (today.after(BastilleDay))
19:           results.appendText("You missed Bastille Day!\r\n");
20:       else
21:           results.appendText("Bastille Day is coming!\r\n");
22:   }
```

12

ANALYSIS In `DateDemo`, a date is created based on the current date (line 2). The `toString`, `toLocaleString`, and `toGMTString` methods are used to display the current date in various formats (lines 6–9). A `Date` object named `BastilleDay` is then constructed using the date of that holiday in 1992 (line 12). Next, the year value for `BastilleDay` is set to the current year using the `setYear` and `getYear` methods (line 15). Finally, `after` is used to determine whether Bastille Day has already occurred this year, or whether there is still time to shop for presents for your French friends (lines 18–21). The results of executing this class are shown in Figure 12.2.

Figure 12.2.

The results of executing `DateDemoApplet` *before Bastille Day.*

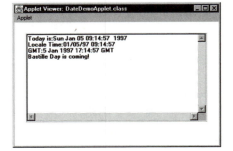

The `Enumeration` **Interface**

The `Enumeration` interface defines methods that can be used to iterate through a set of objects. It provides only two methods: `hasMoreElements` and `nextElement`. These are typically used in a loop that visits each item in the set. For example, the following code iterates through each item in a vector, calling the method `DoSomething` for each element:

```
for (Enumeration e = myVector.elements() ; e.hasMoreElements() ;)
DoSomething(e.nextElement());
```

You will see the `Enumeration` interface used later today; the `Hashtable`, `Properties`, `Vector`, and `StringTokenizer` classes all make use of this interface.

The `Hashtable` **Class**

The `Hashtable` class extends the `Dictionary` class that is defined in the `java.util` package. `Dictionary` is an abstract class that forms the basis of data structures that support the looking up of an element based on a key value. A hash table is used for mapping keys to values. For example, it could be used to map names to ages, programmers to projects, job titles to salaries, and so on.

A hash table expands in size as elements are added to it. When creating a new hash table, you can specify an initial capacity and a load factor. The hash table will increase in size whenever the addition of a new element would enlarge the hash table past its threshold. A hash table's threshold is its capacity multiplied by its load factor. For example, a hash table with a capacity of 100 and a load factor of 0.75 would have a threshold of 75 items. The constructors for Hashtable are shown in Table 12.5.

Table 12.5. Constructors for the Hashtable class.

Constructor	Purpose
Hashtable(int)	Constructs a new hash table with the specified initial capacity.
Hashtable(int, float)	Constructs a new hash table with the specified initial capacity and load factor.
Hashtable()	Constructs a new hash table using default values for initial capacity and load factor.

As an example of how to construct a new hash table, consider the following:

```
Hashtable hash1 = new Hashtable(500, .80);
```

In this case, a hash table that will hold 500 elements is constructed. When the hash table becomes 80% full (a load factor of .80), its maximum size will be increased.

Each element in a hash table consists of a key and value. Elements are added to a hash table using the put method and are retrieved using get. You can delete elements from a hash table by using remove. The contains and containsKey methods can be used to look up a value or key in the hash table. These and other Hashtable methods are summarized in Table 12.6.

Table 12.6. Nonprivate methods of the Hashtable class.

Method	Purpose
clear()	Removes all elements from the hash table.
clone()	Creates a clone of the hash table.
contains(Object)	Returns true if the hash table contains the specified object.
containsKey(Object)	Returns true if the hash table contains the specified key.
elements()	Returns an enumeration of the elements in the hash table.
get(Object)	Retrieves the object associated with the specified key.
isEmpty()	Returns true if the hash table is empty.
keys()	Returns an enumeration of the keys in the hash table.
put(Object, Object)	Adds a new element to the hash table using the specified key and value.

continues

Table 12.6. continued

Method	Purpose
rehash()	Rehashes the hash table into a larger hash table.
remove(Object)	Removes the object given by the specified key.
size()	Returns the number of elements in the hash table.
toString()	Returns a formatted string representing the hash table.

NOTE

When a hash table is rehashed, it is placed in a table that is one item more than twice the size of the current table. Of course, because this is coded within a protected member of the Hashtable class, it is subject to change in subsequent releases of the Java Development Kit.

An Example

The applet HashtableDemoApplet, included on the MCP Web site, illustrates the use of many of the methods in Hashtable. The method HashtableDemo, shown in Listing 12.3, creates a hash table that is used to store the five best albums by Pink Floyd.

Listing 12.3. The method HashtableDemo from HashtableDemoApplet.

```
1:    void HashtableDemo() {
2:        // create a new Hashtable
3:        Hashtable ht = new Hashtable();
4:
5:        // add Pink Floyd's best albums
6:        ht.put("Pulse", new Integer(1995));
7:        ht.put("Dark Side of the Moon", new Integer(1973));
8:        ht.put("Wish You Were Here", new Integer(1975));
9:        ht.put("Animals", new Integer(1977));
10:       ht.put("Ummagumma", new Integer(1969));
11:
12:       // display the Hashtable
13:       results.appendText("Initailly: "+ht.toString()+ "\r\n");
14:
15:       // test for any album from 1969
16:       if (ht.contains(new Integer(1969)))
17:           results.appendText("An album from 1969 exists\r\n");
18:
19:       // test for the Animals album
20:       if (ht.containsKey("Animals"))
21:           results.appendText("Animals was found\r\n");
22:
```

12

```
23:        // find out what year Wish You Were Here was released
24:        Integer year = (Integer)ht.get("Wish You Were Here");
25:        results.appendText("Wish You Were Here was released in "+
26:              year.toString() + "\r\n");
27:
28:        // remove an album
29:        results.appendText("Removing Ummagumma\r\n");
30:        ht.remove("Ummagumma");
31:
32:        // move through an enumeration of all keys in the table
33:        results.appendText("Remaining:\r\n");
34:        for (Enumeration enum=ht.keys();enum.hasMoreElements() ;)
35:           results.appendText((String)enum.nextElement()+"\r\n");
36:    }
```

ANALYSIS After the hash table is created (line 3), it is loaded with the names and release dates of five albums (lines 6–10). The initial contents of the table are then displayed to the results text area using toString (line 13). For each item in the hash table, the name of the album is used as the key, and the year is used as the element. Therefore, to determine whether any albums were released in 1969, contains is used to search the hash table's elements (line 16). Similarly, containsKey (line 20) is used to search for the key Animals to see whether that album made the list.

Next, the get method is used to see whether Wish You Were Here is in the hash table (lines 24–26). Because get returns the element associated with the key, both the name and year are displayed at this point. This can be seen in Figure 12.3.

Figure 12.3.

The results of executing HashtableDemo- Applet.

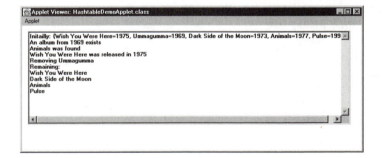

I had some second thoughts about including "Ummagumma" in a list of best albums, so I used remove to delete it from the hash table (lines 29–30). Finally, I used the keys method to create an enumeration of the keys stored in the hash table, and the applet then iterates through the enumeration using enum.hasMoreElements and enum.nextElement (lines 34–35).

Do	Don't

DO specify a sufficiently large initial capacity to prevent excessive reallocation of the hash table.

DON'T confuse elements and keys. Elements are retrieved by their keys.

The `Properties` Class

The `Properties` class extends `Hashtable` and adds the capability to read and write a hash table to a stream. Because an applet cannot access files, the `Properties` class is useful only for applications.

Like `Hashtable`, this class can be used to store keys and associated values. Through its `save` and `load` methods, properties can be written to disk, making this class an excellent mechanism for storing configuration information between runs of a program. An example of a properties file written by the `save` method is as follows:

```
#This is a header comment
#Sat Sep 14 15:55:15 Pacific Daylight Time 1996
prop3=put three
prop2=put two
prop1=put one
```

Because `Properties` is a subclass of `Hashtable`, new key/value pairs are added using the `put` method of `Hashtable`. The constructors and nonprivate methods of `Properties` are shown in Table 12.7.

Table 12.7. Nonprivate constructors and methods of the `Properties` class.

Member	Purpose
`Properties()`	Creates a new `Properties` object.
`Properties(Properties)`	Creates a new `Properties` object based on the specified default values.
`getProperty(String)`	Returns the property value associated with the specified key.
`getProperty(String,String)`	Returns the property value associated with the specified key. If the key is not found, the specified default is returned.
`list(PrintStream)`	Lists all the properties to the specified `PrintStream`.

Member	Purpose
load(InputStream)	Reads a set of properties from the specified InputStream.
propertyNames()	Returns an enumeration of all property names.
save(OutputStream, String)	Saves the Properties object and a header string to the specified OutputStream.

An Example

As an example of how to use the Properties class, consider Listing 12.4, which shows the method TestProperties from the PropertiesDemo applet, which is included on the MCP Web site. This example creates an instance of Properties, puts three key/value pairs into it, saves the properties, and then reloads them into a different instance.

Listing 12.4. The TestProperties method from PropertiesDemo.

```
1:    static void TestProperties() {
2:        // create a new instance
3:        Properties props1 = new Properties();
4:
5:        // put three properties into it
6:        props1.put("prop1", "put one");
7:        props1.put("prop2", "put two");
8:        props1.put("prop3", "put three");
9:
10:       // retrieve each of the three properties
11:       String prop1 = props1.getProperty("prop1", "one");
12:       String prop2 = props1.getProperty("prop2", "two");
13:       String prop3 = props1.getProperty("prop3");
14:
15:       // save the properties to a file
16:       try
17:       {
18:           props1.save(new FileOutputStream("test.ini"),
19:                   "My header");
20:       }
21:        catch (IOException e) {
22:           return;
23:       }
24:
25:       // create a new instance and read the file in from
26:       // the file
27:       Properties props2 = new Properties();
28:       try
29:       {
30:           FileInputStream inStr = new
31:                   FileInputStream("test.ini");
32:           props2.load(inStr);
```

continues

Listing 12.4. continued

```
33:        }
34:        catch (IOException e) {
35:            return;
36:        }
37:
38:        // retrieve a property from the second instance
39:        String prop = props2.getProperty("prop2", "two");
40:    }
```

 A `Properties` object, `props1`, is created on line 3, and values are placed into it using `put` (lines 6–8). Lines 11–13 illustrate how to retrieve values using the `getProperty` methods.

The save method is used to write the properties to a file (lines 16–23). A `FileOutputStream` object is created and passed as the only parameter to save. (Streams are described on Day 13, "Using Streams for Input and Output.") To verify that the properties were successfully written, the `props2` object is created and `load` is used to read the properties from the file to which they were written (lines 27–36).

The Random Class

The `Random` class represents a pseudo-random number generator. A pseudo-random number generator does not generate truly random numbers; it does, however, generate numbers that can be used to approximate truly random numbers in most circumstances. A pseudo-random number generator works by using an algorithm that generates a sequence of random numbers based on an initial *seed value*.

The seed value tells the random number generator where to start. The chief problem with this is that the generator always generates the same sequence of numbers for a specific seed value. For example, a pseudo-random number generator seeded with the value `1234` might generate the following sequence of integers: 13, 42, 75, 18, and 91. If the same generator is seeded six months later with `1234`, it will generate the exact same sequence of numbers. However, if the generator is seeded with a different number, a different sequence of values will be generated.

Two constructors are provided for the `Random` class: one taking a seed value as a parameter, and the other taking no parameters and using the current time as a seed. Constructing a random number generator with a seed value is a good idea unless you want the random number generator to always generate the same set of values. On the other hand, sometimes it is useful to generate the same sequence of "random" numbers. This is frequently useful while debugging a program.

After the random number generator is created, a value can be retrieved from it using any of the following methods:

```
nextDouble
nextFloat
nextGaussian
nextInt
nextLong
```

The constructors and methods of `Random` are summarized in Table 12.8. Use of the `Random` class is very simple, so no example is presented here. However, `ObserverDemoApplet`, shown in the following discussion about the `Observer` class, also uses `Random`.

Table 12.8. Nonprivate constructors and methods of the `Random` class.

Method	Purpose
`Random()`	Creates a new random number generator.
`Random(long)`	Creates a new random number generator based on the specified seed value.
`nextDouble()`	Returns the next double value between 0.0D and 1.0D from the random number generator.
`nextFloat()`	Returns the next float value between 0.0F and 1.0F from the random number generator.
`nextGaussian()`	Returns the next Gaussian-distributed double from the random number generator. Generated Gaussian values will have a mean of 0 and a standard deviation of 1.0.
`nextInt()`	Returns the next integer value from the random number generator.
`nextLong()`	Returns the next long value from the random number generator.
`setSeed(long)`	Sets the seed value for the random number generator.

12

Do   **Don't**

DON'T forget that the `Random` class is a pseudo-random number generator. Whenever it is seeded with the same value, it generates the same sequence of numbers.

DO take advantage of this when testing your program. You can use the same seed value to produce predictable behavior in a program that would otherwise act randomly.

Observers and Observables

An `Observable` class may be watched or monitored by another class that implements the `Observer` interface. Associated with each `Observable` instance is a list of observers. Whenever the `Observable` instance changes, it can notify each of its observers. By using `Observable` and `Observer` classes, you can achieve a better partitioning of your code by decreasing the reliance of one class on another.

The `Observable` Class

The `Observable` class includes a single constructor that takes no parameters. It also includes a number of methods for managing its list of observers. These are summarized in Table 12.9.

Table 12.9. Nonprivate constructors and methods of the `Observable` class.

Member	Purpose
`Observable()`	Creates a new `Observable` instance.
`addObserver(Observer)`	Adds an observer to the list of objects observing this instance.
`clearChanged()`	Clears the internal flag used to indicate that an observable object has changed.
`countObservers()`	Returns the number of observers of this object.
`deleteObserver(Observer)`	Deletes an observer from the list of observers of this object.
`deleteObservers()`	Deletes all observers of this object.
`hasChanged()`	Returns `true` if the object has changed.
`notifyObservers()`	Notifies all observers that a change has occurred in the observable object.
`notifyObservers(Object)`	Notifies all observers that a change has occurred and passes them the specified argument.
`setChanged()`	Sets the internal flag to indicate that a change has occurred.

The `Observer` Interface

The `Observer` interface defines an `update` method that is invoked by an observable object whenever that object changes and wants to notify its observers. The signature of `update` is as follows:

```
public abstract void update(Observable o, Object arg);
```

This method is called whenever an Observable instance that is being observed invokes either of its notifyObservers methods. It is passed the observable object that changed and an optional additional parameter.

An Example

As an example of how Observable can be used, consider the declaration of the Obsable class in Listing 12.5. The Obsable class stores a secret number that is generated by a random number generator. Whenever the secret number changes, all observers are notified.

Listing 12.5. The Obsable class extends Observable and is used in ObservableDemoApplet.

```
 1:    class Obsable extends Observable {
 2:        private int secretNumber;
 3:        private Random generator;
 4:
 5:        public Obsable(int seed) {
 6:            // create a random number generator that will
 7:            // make the "secret numbers"
 8:            generator = new Random(seed);
 9:        }
10:
11:        public void GenerateNumber() {
12:            // generate a new secret number
13:            secretNumber = generator.nextInt();
14:            // indicate to Observable that the instance
15:            // has changed
16:            setChanged();
17:            // notify all of the observers and pass the new number
18:            notifyObservers(new Integer(secretNumber));
19:        }
20:    }
```

ANALYSIS The Obsable class stores a private variable, secretNumber (line 2), that is randomly generated based on the random number generator created on line 8. Whenever the method GenerateNumber (lines 11–19) is called, the next random number is retrieved (line 13). Then, setChanged is used to indicate that the observable class has changed (line 16). Finally, all observers of this instance are notified of the change (line 18).

No Observable class is complete without an observer, so Listing 12.6 shows ObservableDemoApplet, which extends Applet and implements the Observer interface. This applet is included on the MCP Web site. The results of executing this applet are shown in Figure 12.4.

12

Listing 12.6. The `ObservableDemoApplet` class implements the `Observer` interface.

```
1:    public class ObservableDemoApplet extends Applet implements
2:          Observer {
3:        public ObservableDemoApplet() {
4:            // create a new instance of the observable class
5:            obs = new Obsable(12);
6:            // indicate that "this" is an observer
7:            obs.addObserver(this);
8:        }
9:
10:       void changeButton_Clicked(java.awt.event.ActionEvent
11:             event) {
12:           obs.GenerateNumber();
13:       }
14:
15:       public void init() {
16:           // Call parents init method.
17:           super.init();
18:       }
19:
20:       // this method is invoked when the observable object
21:       // notifies its observers
22:       public void update(Observable o, Object arg) {
23:           // store the secret number and display it
24:           secretNumber = (Integer)arg;
25:           textField.setText(String.valueOf(secretNumber));
26:       }
27:
28:       public void addNotify() {
29:           // Call parents addNotify method.
30:           super.addNotify();
31:
32:           // This code is automatically generated by Visual Café
33:           // when you add components to the visual environment.
34:           // It instantiates and initializes the components. To
35:           // modify the code, only use code syntax that matches
36:           // what Visual Café can generate, or Visual Café may
37:           // be unable to back parse your Java file into its
38:           // visual environment.
39:           //{{INIT_CONTROLS
40:           setLayout(null);
41:           resize(426,266);
42:           label1 = new java.awt.Label("Secret Number:");
43:           label1.reshape(60,48,108,25);
44:           add(label1);
45:           textField = new java.awt.TextField();
46:           textField.setEditable(false);
47:           textField.reshape(180,48,167,23);
48:           add(textField);
49:           changeButton = new java.awt.Button("Change");
50:           changeButton.reshape(60,96,119,24);
51:           add(changeButton);
52:           //}}
```

12

```
53:
54:        //{{REGISTER_LISTENERS
55:        Action lAction = new Action();
56:        changeButton.addActionListener(lAction);
57:        //}}
58:    }
59:
60:    Integer secretNumber;
61:    Obsable obs;
62:
63:    //{{DECLARE_CONTROLS
64:    java.awt.Label label1;
65:    java.awt.TextField textField;
66:    java.awt.Button changeButton;
67:    //}}
68:
69:    class Action implements java.awt.event.ActionListener {
70:        public void actionPerformed(java.awt.event.ActionEvent event) {
71:            Object object = event.getSource();
72:            if (object == changeButton)
73:                changeButton_Clicked(event);
74:        }
75:    }
76: }
```

Figure 12.4.

The results of executing ObservableDemo-Applet.

12

ANALYSIS The ObservableDemoApplet constructor (lines 3–8) creates an instance of Obsable, the Observable class defined in Listing 12.5. The constructor also adds the applet as an observer of the observable object.

As shown in Figure 12.4, the user interface of ObservableDemoApplet includes a button and a read-only text field. When the button is clicked, the random number generator in Obsable generates a new random number. Because the applet is an observer of the Obsable instance, the applet is notified of the change and the text field is updated. The Action listener class (lines 69–75) and the changeButton_Clicked method (lines 10–13) are responsible for calling the GenerateNumber method in Obsable.

Whenever a new random number is generated, it results in a call to the update method in any observing classes. This method (lines 22–26) is passed an observable item and an object as parameters. As shown in the declaration of Obsable, the object is an integer. Therefore, update casts the object into Integer, stores it in the instance variable secretNumber, and then updates the text field.

The Vector Class

One of the problems with an array is that you must know how big it must be when you create it. This is not always practical, and is rarely easy. Imagine what would have happened if the founding fathers of the United States were programmers and they used a 13-element array to hold the names of all the states. Even if the lead programmer on this project (Thomas Jefferson, if I remember my eighth-grade history correctly) had the foresight to double or triple the array size to allow for future growth, it still would not have been enough.

The Java Vector class solves this problem by providing a form of resizable array that can grow as more elements are added to it. A vector stores items of type Object so that it can be used to store instances of any Java class. A single vector may store different elements that are instances of different classes.

At any point in time, a vector has the capacity to hold a certain number of elements. When a vector reaches its capacity, its capacity is incremented by an amount specific to that vector. The Vector class provides three different constructors that enable you to specify the initial capacity and increment quantity of a vector when it is created. These constructors are summarized in Table 12.10.

Table 12.10. Constructors for the Vector class.

Constructor	Purpose
Vector(int)	Creates a new vector with the specified initial capacity.
Vector(int, int)	Creates a new vector with the specified initial capacity and increment quantity.
Vector()	Creates a new vector with defaults for the initial capacity and increment quantity.

You add an item to a vector by using addElement. Similarly, an element can be replaced using setElementAt. A vector can be searched using the contains method, which simply looks for an occurrence of an object. The elements method is useful because it returns an enumeration of the objects stored in Vector. These and other member methods of Vector are summarized in Table 12.11.

Table 12.11. Nonprivate methods of the Vector class.

Method	Purpose
addElement(Object)	Inserts the specified element into a vector.
capacity()	Returns the number of elements that will fit into the currently allocated portion of the vector.
clone()	Clones the vector, but not its elements.
contains(Object)	Returns true if the vector contains the specified object.
copyInto(Object [])	Copies the elements of the vector into the specified array.
elementAt(int)	Retrieves the element located at the specified index.
elements()	Returns an enumeration of the elements in the vector.
ensureCapacity(int)	Ensures that the vector can hold at least the specified minimum capacity.
firstElement()	Returns the first element in the vector.
indexOf(Object)	Searches the vector and returns the zero-based index of the first matching object.
indexOf(Object, int)	Searches the vector beginning at the specified index number and returns the zero-based index of the next matching object.
insertElementAt(Object, int)	Adds the specified object at the specified index.
isEmpty()	Returns true if the vector has no elements.
lastElement()	Returns the last element in the vector.
lastIndexOf(Object)	Searches the vector and returns the zero-based index of the last matching object.
lastIndexOf(Object, int)	Searches the vector beginning at the specified index number and returns the zero-based index of the prior matching object.
removeAllElements()	Removes all elements from the vector.
removeElement(Object)	Removes the specified object from the vector.
removeElementAt(int)	Removes the object at the specified index.
setElementAt(Object, int)	Replaces the object at the specified index with the specified object.

continues

12

Table 12.11. continued

Method	Purpose
setSize(int)	Sets the size of the vector to the specified new size.
size()	Returns the number of elements currently in the vector.
toString()	Returns a formatted string representing the contents of the vector.
trimToSize()	Removes any excess capacity in the vector by resizing it.

An Example

As an example of using `Vector`, consider the sample class `VectorDemoApplet`, which is included on the MCP Web site. The `VectorDemo` method of this applet is shown in Listing 12.7. This example uses a text area to display the results of various operations.

Listing 12.7. The `VectorDemo` method from `VectorDemoApplet`.

```
1:      void VectorDemo() {
2:          // create a new Vector to hold 10 elements
3:          // and to increase by 4 each time it's necessary
4:          Vector v1 = new Vector(10, 4);
5:
6:          // add elements, both Integer and String, to the Vector
7:          v1.addElement(new Integer(1));
8:          v1.addElement(new Integer(2));
9:          v1.addElement(new Integer(3));
10:         v1.addElement("Four");
11:         v1.addElement(new Integer(5));
12:
13:         // display the entire Vector
14:         results.appendText("Entire Vector\r\n    ");
15:         results.appendText(v1.toString() + "\r\n");
16:
17:         // see if the Vector contains this Integer
18:         if (v1.contains(new Integer(2)))
19:             results.appendText("It contains 2\r\n");
20:
21:         // see if the Vector contains this String
22:         if (v1.contains("Four"))
23:             results.appendText("It contains Four\r\n");
24:
25:         // Display the capacity of the Vector
26:         int capacity = v1.capacity();
27:         results.appendText("Can hold " +
28:                 String.valueOf(capacity) + "\r\n");
29:
```

12

```
30:          // Display the element at index number 3
31:          results.appendText("ElementAt 3 = " +
32:                  (String)v1.elementAt(3) + "\r\n");
33:
34:          // clear out the Vector
35:          v1.removeAllElements();
36:          results.appendText("Vector has been emptied\r\n");
37:
38:          // add the names of five Pink Floyd albums
39:          v1.addElement("Piper At The Gates of Dawn");
40:          v1.addElement("Saucerful of Secrets");
41:          v1.addElement("Ummagumma");
42:          v1.addElement("Meddle");
43:          v1.addElement("The Dark Side of the Moon");
44:
45:          // use an enumeration to display each of the album titles
46:          results.appendText("Enumerating album titles\r\n");
47:          for (Enumeration enum = v1.elements();
48:                  enum.hasMoreElements(); )
49:            results.appendText("   " + (String)enum.nextElement()
50:                    + "\r\n");
51:    }
```

ANALYSIS In this example, a vector, v1, is constructed (line 4). Initially, enough space is reserved for 10 elements, and the vector will increase its capacity by four whenever there is no room for a new element. Initially, five elements—four Integers and one String—are added to the vector (lines 7–11). This illustrates the capability to store objects of different types in the same vector. Next, the toString method is used to display the entire vector (line 15). This, along with the other messages displayed by VectorDemoApplet, is shown in Figure 12.5.

Figure 12.5.

The result of executing VectorDemoApplet.

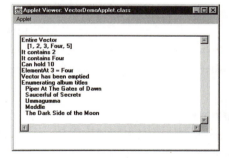

Next, the contains method is used to determine whether the vector contains Integer 2 and the string "Four" (lines 18–23). The capacity of the vector is then displayed (lines 26–28) and the item at index number three is retrieved and displayed (31–32). Because vectors are zero-based, this will retrieve the fourth element in the vector.

The method `removeAllElements` is then used to remove the current elements (line 35). The names of five Pink Floyd five albums are added to the vector. Finally, the `elements` method is used to return an enumeration of the elements, and the `hasMoreElements` and `nextElement` methods are used in a loop that displays each of the album titles (lines 47–50).

The `Stack` Class

The `Stack` class extends `Vector` and implements a simple last-in-first-out stack. A program adds an item to a stack by pushing it onto the stack. An item may subsequently be popped off the stack and used. The item popped off a stack will always be the most recently pushed item.

Because `Stack` extends the `Vector` class, no size is associated with a `Stack` instance. The stack will continue to grow in size as new items are pushed onto it. In addition to methods to push and pop items, a `peek` method is provided for looking at the next item, a `search` method is provided for scanning the stack for a specific item, and an `empty` method is provided determining whether more items are stored in the stack.

The single constructor as well as the nonprivate methods of `Stack` are summarized in Table 12.12.

Table 12.12. Constructors and nonprivate methods of the `Stack` class.

Member	Purpose
`Stack()`	Creates a new stack.
`empty()`	Returns `true` if the stack is empty.
`peek()`	Returns the last object added to the stack but does not remove it from the stack.
`pop()`	Returns the last object added to the stack and removes it.
`push(Object)`	Adds the specified object to the stack.
`search(Object)`	Searches for the specified object in the stack.

An Example

As an example of how to use the `Stack` class, consider Listing 12.8, which shows the method `StackDemo` from `StackDemoApplet`, which is included on the MCP Web site. Like many other examples in this lesson, this applet includes a text area named `results` to which status messages are written.

Listing 12.8. The `StackDemo` method from `StackDemoApplet`.

```
 1:    void StackDemo() {
 2:        add(results);
 3:
 4:        // create a new Stack
 5:        Stack stk = new Stack();
 6:
 7:        // add three items to the Stack
 8:        stk.push("1");
 9:        stk.push("2");
10:        stk.push("3");
11:
12:        // display the entire Stack
13:        results.appendText("Stack=" + stk.toString() + "\r\n");
14:
15:        // peek at what's next off the stack
16:        String str = (String)stk.peek();
17:        results.appendText("Peeked at: " + str + "\r\n");
18:
19:        // see if there's a "2" anywhere in the Stack
20:        if (stk.search("2") != -1)
21:            results.appendText("Found 2\r\n");
22:
23:        // pop an item off the Stack
24:        str = (String)stk.pop();
25:        results.appendText("Popped: " + str + "\r\n");
26:
27:        // display the entire Stack
28:         results.appendText("Stack=" + stk.toString() + "\r\n");
29:    }
```

ANALYSIS In this example, a stack is created and three items are added to it (lines 5–10). The `toString` method is used to display the stack's initial contents (line 13). The `peek` method (line 16) is used to look at the last object added to the stack but does not actually remove the object.

Next, `search` is used to look for an occurrence of 2 within the stack (line 20). Finally, `pop` (line 24) is used to remove an object from the stack, and `toString` is used to redisplay its contents (line 28). The results of executing this applet are shown in Figure 12.6.

Figure 12.6.

The result of executing
`StackDemoApplet`.

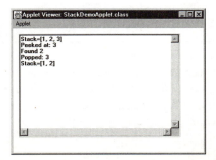

The `StringTokenizer` Class

A `StringTokenizer` can be used to parse a string into its constituent tokens. For example, each word in a sentence could be considered a token. But the `StringTokenizer` class goes beyond the parsing of sentences. You can create a fully customized tokenizer by specifying the set of token delimiters when the `StringTokenizer` is created. For parsing text, the default whitespace delimiters are usually sufficient, but you could use the set of arithmetic operators (+, *, /, and -) if parsing an expression.

The delimiter characters can be specified when a new `StringTokenizer` object is constructed. Table 12.13 summarizes the three available constructors. Following are examples of these constructors in use:

```
StringTokenizer st1 = new StringTokenizer("A stream of words");
StringTokenizer st2 = new StringTokenizer("4*3/2-1+4", "*+/-", true);
StringTokenizer st3 = new StringTokenizer("aaa,bbbb,ccc", ",");
```

In the first example, the `st1` `StringTokenizer` will be constructed using the supplied string and the default delimiters. The default delimiters are the space, tab, newline, and carriage-return characters. These delimiters are useful when parsing text, as with `st1`. The second example constructs a `StringTokenizer` for tokenizing arithmetic expressions using the *, +, /, and - symbols as supplied. Finally, the third `StringTokenizer`, `st3`, tokenizes the supplied string using only the comma character as a delimiter.

Table 12.13. Constructors for the `StringTokenizer` class.

Constructor	Purpose
`StringTokenizer(String)`	Creates a new `StringTokenizer` based on the specified string to be tokenized.
`StringTokenizer(String, String)`	Creates a new `StringTokenizer` based on the specified string to be tokenized and a set of delimiters.
`StringTokenizer(String,String,boolean)`	Creates a new `StringTokenizer` based on the specified string to be tokenized, a set of delimiters, and a flag that indicates whether delimiters should be returned as tokens.

Because `StringTokenizer` implements the `Enumeration` interface, it includes the `hasMoreElements` and `nextElement` methods. Additionally, the methods `hasMoreTokens` and `nextToken` are provided and perform the same operations. The nonprivate methods of `StringTokenizer` are summarized in Table 12.14.

Table 12.14. Nonprivate methods of the `StringTokenizer` **class.**

Method	Purpose
`countTokens()`	Returns the number of remaining tokens.
`hasMoreElements()`	Returns `true` if there are more elements in the string being tokenized. It is identical to `hasMoreTokens`.
`hasMoreTokens()`	Returns `true` if there are more tokens in the string being tokenized. It is identical to `hasMoreElements`.
`nextElement()`	Returns the next element in the string. It is identical to `nextToken`.
`nextToken()`	Returns the next token in the string. It is identical to `nextElement`.
`nextToken(String)`	Changes the set of delimiters to the specified string and then returns the next token in the string.

An Example

As an example of how to use `StringTokenizer`, consider Listing 12.9, which shows the method `StringTokenizerDemo` from `StringTokenizerDemoApplet`. This applet is included on the MCP Web site.

Listing 12.9. The `StringTokenizerDemo` **method from** `StringTokenizerDemoApplet`.

```
 1:    void StringTokenizerDemo() {
 2:        // put an arithmetic expression in a string
 3:        // and create a tokenizer for the string
 4:        String mathExpr = "4*3+2/4";
 5:        StringTokenizer st1 = new StringTokenizer(mathExpr,
 6:            "*+/-", true);
 7:        // while there are tokens left, display each token
 8:        results.appendText("Tokens of mathExpr:\r\n");
 9:        while (st1.hasMoreTokens())
10:            results.appendText(st1.nextToken() + "\r\n");
11:
12:        // create a String of comma-delimited fields
13:        // and create a tokenizer for the string
14:        String commas = "field1,field2,field3,and field 4";
15:        StringTokenizer st2=new StringTokenizer(commas,",",false);
16:
17:        // while there are tokens left, display each token
18:        results.appendText("Comma-delimited tokens:\r\n");
19:        while (st2.hasMoreTokens())
20:            results.appendText(st2.nextToken() + "\r\n");
21:    }
```

12

ANALYSIS In this example, two StringTokenizer objects are created and used to tokenize different types of strings. The first, st1, is used to parse an arithmetic expression. The second, st2, parses a line of comma-delimited fields. For both tokenizers, hasMoreTokens and nextToken are used to iterate through the set of tokens, displaying each token in the results text area, as shown in Figure 12.7.

Figure 12.7.

The result of executing StringTokenizer- DemoApplet.

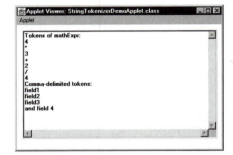

Summary

This lesson has given you a thorough overview of the classes in the java.util package. You have learned how to use the BitSet class to store large amounts of Boolean data, how to manipulate dates and times with the Date class, how to generate random numbers, and how to tokenize strings. You have learned how the Observable class works in conjunction with the Observer interface to allow you to decouple your code. The Hashtable is described here, and you have learned how the Properties class can be used in applications to stream data to and from files. Finally, you have learned how the Vector class can be used as a resizable array and how the Stack class extends Vector.

Q&A

Q Why would I use BitSet? It seems like I could use an array of Boolean values to do the same thing.

A That's almost true. You could use an array of Booleans to hold true and false values like a bit set does. However, the BitSet class includes many methods (such as AND, OR, and XOR) that you would have to write to operate on two arrays. Even if you won't need these methods, a bit set is still a better choice than an array because a bit set requires much less memory. Because a bit set uses each bit in a byte to represent one element in the set, it is much more memory efficient than the one byte per element used by an array of Booleans.

12

Q Can I ever run out of random numbers?

A No, a random number generator will continue generating numbers as long as you ask it to.

Q How do I know what is a good load factor for a hash table?

A There is no set answer for this because it depends on the data being hashed. Generally, a load factor of 50% to 75% works well.

Q What do I do if I need to retrieve a value in a stack that wasn't the most recently added?

A You use a vector! You cannot retrieve any value from a stack other than the most recently added value. You can use the `search` method to determine whether a value exists in a stack, but you cannot remove the element from the stack after it is found.

Workshop

The workshop includes quiz questions to help you gauge your understanding of the material in this chapter, and also includes exercises to provide hands-on experience with what you've learned in this chapter. You can find the answers to the quiz questions in Appendix D, "Answers."

Quiz

1. When using the constructor `Date(long milliseconds)`, the `milliseconds` parameter represents the number of milliseconds since a particular date. What date is that?

2. In the `Date` class, are months numbered from 0–11 or from 1–12? Are days numbered from 0–30 or 1–31?

3. What is the difference between the `contains` and `containsKey` methods of `Hashtable`?

4. What is the difference between `Hashtable` and `Properties`?

5. What happens if you use the same seed value to create two random number generators?

6. What causes the `update` method to be called for a class implementing the `Observer` interface?

7. What's the difference between a stack and a vector?

8. In the `StringTokenizer` class, what's the difference between the methods `nextElement` and `nextToken`?

12

Exercises

1. Bits 1, 2, 8, 9, and 10 are set in `bitset1`, and bits 1, 2, and 3 are set in `bitset2`. What is the result of using AND, OR, and XOR on these two bit sets?

2. Write an applet that displays a frame. On the frame, include a text area and a button that allow the user to change the name of the frame. Have the applet observe the frame and display a message whenever the title changes.

3. Write a program that seeds a random number generator with the number of seconds between now and November 14, 1995.

4. Write an applet that allows the user to add, remove, and edit words in a vector.

5. Write a simple postfix calculator that can interpret equations using digits, +, -, /, and *. (In a postfix calculator, the operands are entered before the operator. Therefore, `4 3 + 2 *` represents 4 plus 3 and that sum multiplied by 2.)

6. Modify your postfix calculator to use a stack.

12

Day 13

Using Streams for Input and Output

In this chapter, you will learn how to move data into and out of your Visual Café programs through the use of streams. Along the way, you will learn about Java's byte streams, character streams, and object streams. You will see how you can use streams to write to and read from files and strings. You will see how to improve the performance of streams by buffering them, and you will see some special-purpose streams that add features such as line numbering and the capability to push data back into a stream.

Input and Output Streams

The `java.io` package includes a rich hierarchy of classes for reading from and writing to streams. Streams are a popular and convenient abstraction of how programs receive data from external devices such as files, other programs, and networks. If you've done programming prior to Java, especially on a UNIX machine, you have probably already encountered streams.

NEW TERM A *stream* is a source from which data is read or to which data is written.

The obvious mental image of a stream is of gently flowing water. In most cases, this is a very appropriate way to think about data streams. You can think of each drop of water flowing down the stream as a piece of data. Also, just as streams of water have a direction, so do data streams. Some data streams flow as input into a program, others flow as output from a program.

Input Streams

Because all input streams share a common set of core operations, these operations are collected in the abstract class `InputStream`. Figure 13.1 shows the extensive hierarchy of classes descended from `InputStream`.

Figure 13.1.

`InputStream` *serves as the superclass of a vast hierarchy of classes.*

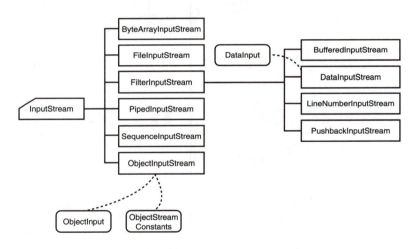

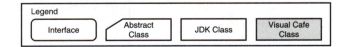

Reading

The `InputStream` class includes three different `read` methods:

```
int read()
```

```
int read(byte dest[])
```

```
int read(byte dest[], int offset, int length)
```

13

The first method reads a single byte from the stream and returns it as an int. The second method reads as many bytes as are currently available from the stream and places them into an array. It returns the number of bytes read, or –1 if the end of the stream has been reached. If no bytes are available, this method blocks until bytes become available.

 Blocking means that a method suspends execution of its thread until some condition is met. In the case of read(byte[]), the method blocks until input is available.

The final read method also reads an array of bytes but starts reading at the specified *offset* and reads only *length* number of bytes. It returns the number of bytes read or, if at the end of the stream, –1. This method blocks until bytes are available.

One simple way to avoid having a thread become blocked is to use the available method. This parameterless method returns the number of bytes that can currently be read before the method blocks. For example, the following loop uses available to verify that a byte is available before reading it:

```
// assume input has already been opened as a stream
while (input.available() > 0) {
    int temp = input.read());
    // use temp
}
```

Marking Input Streams

Sometimes you find a part of a stream that is so interesting that you want to return to it. Java supports this by allowing you to mark input steams. The following three methods are associated with marking streams:

```
boolean markSupported()
```

```
void mark(int readlimit)
```

```
void reset()
```

The method markSupported is used to determine whether a particular stream supports marking. Because not all streams support marking, you should always use this method before placing a mark. To place a mark in a stream, use the mark method, passing it the number of bytes that can be read before the mark is lost. Larger values for *readLimit* cause the stream to allocate more memory. When you are ready to return to a placed mark, use reset. A stream can have only one mark at a time. If mark is called on an already marked stream, the first mark will be replaced.

13

 Because reset can throw the exception IOException, it must be enclosed in a try...catch block.

WARNING

Sometimes you don't want to mark a stream, but you know that you want to quickly jump ahead in the stream. You can do this with `skip`. This method allows you to move forward through a stream without reading the intervening bytes. To use `skip`, pass it a `long` representing the number of bytes to move forward. For example, the following will move ahead 64 bytes:

```
myStream.skip(64);
```

Closing an Input Stream

To close an input stream, use the `close` method. This releases any resources allocated by the stream. Alternatively, you can wait for the garbage collector to notice that the stream is no longer in use. However, because many streams are based on limited resources (such as file handles), you should close them rather than wait for the garbage collector.

Output Streams

The natural counterpart to the input stream is the output stream. Naturally, Java includes an `OutputStream` abstract class. Just as `InputStream` sits at the top of a hierarchy of classes, so does `OutputStream`, as shown in Figure 13.2.

Figure 13.2.

`OutputStream` *is the superclass of its own hierarchy of classes.*

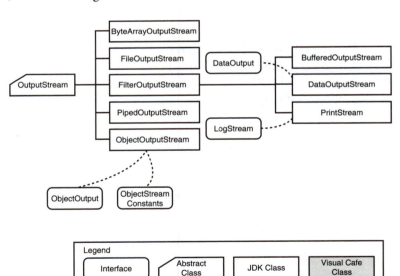

Writing

The `OutputStream` class includes three different `write` methods:

```
void write(int b)
```

```
void write(byte b[])
```

```
void write(byte b[], int offset, int length)
```

The first method writes a single integer to the stream, while the second writes an array of bytes. The third writes an array of *length* bytes beginning at the specified *offset*. Each of the write methods blocks until the data is written. Additionally, each can throw the exception IOException, so each must be enclosed in try...catch blocks.

Flushing and Closing Streams

Some streams buffer data before sending it on its way. To force the stream to send buffered data, use the flush method as follows:

```
myStream.write(myBuffer);
myStream.flush();
```

Most disk writes are buffered to improve performance. This means data is not written to disk until the buffer is full, the stream is flushed, or the stream is closed. Periodically calling flush is a good way to ensure that a stream contains the data you think it does.

 TIP Many years ago, when I was a C programmer, I learned the importance of flushing streams. In the predebugger era, I was debugging a program that was crashing. My plan was to write debug information to a file and examine the contents of that file after the program crashed, but when I did this, the file was empty. After I read the manuals, I discovered that my file writes were being buffered and that the program was crashing before actually writing the buffered data. The solution was to flush the stream.

Just as InputStream includes a close method, so does OutputStream. You should call close whenever you are finished with the stream rather than wait for the garbage collector.

File Streams

Disk-based files are one of the most common sources of streamed data. Although Java applets are prevented from having low-level access to a machine's file system, they can use streams to store and retrieve data. The classes FileInputStream and FileOutputStream allow you to read and write bytes.

The FileInputStream Class

Three constructors are provided for FileInputStream:

```
FileInputStream(String filename)

FileInputStream(File file)

FileInputStream(FileDescriptor fd)
```

The first of these constructors is the easiest to use because it allows you to create a new `FileInputStream` from a string. The second constructor creates a `FileInputStream` from a `File` object. The final constructor is passed a `FileDescriptor`. In Java, you do not explicitly create `FileDescriptor` objects. However, file descriptor objects are contained in some Java classes, including `FileInputStream`, `FileOutputStream`, and `RandomAccessFile`. To get a `FileDescriptor`, use the `getFD` method of these classes. As examples of constructing a `FileInputStream` consider the following code:

```
// construct with a String
FileInputStream input = new FileInputStream("C:/test.txt");

// construct with a File
File f = new File("C:/test.txt");
FileInputStream input2 = new FileInputStream(f);
```

TIP

> To open a file in the same directory as the applet, do not include any path information when using the `FileInputStream(String)` constructor.

An Example

As an example of using `FileInputStream`, consider the `FileInputDemo` applet, shown in Figure 13.3. This applet is included on the MCP Web site (www.mcp.com/info/1-57521/1-57521-303-6). When the View button is clicked, the applet's source code is read and placed into the text area that takes up most of the applet. The method `viewButton_Clicked` is shown in Listing 13.1.

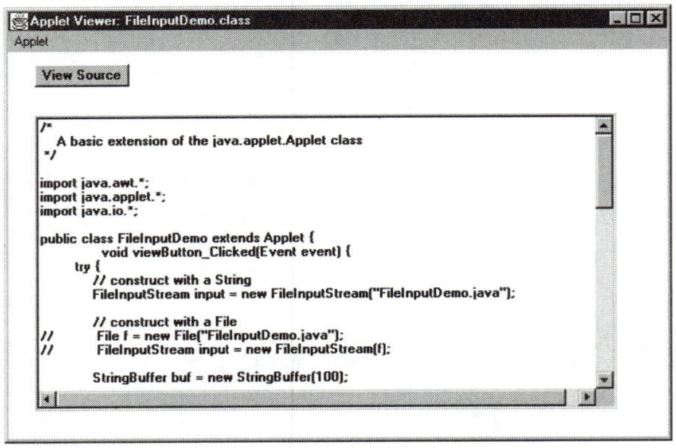

Figure 13.3.

A `FileInputStream`
is used to read an
applet's source code.

```
Applet Viewer: FileInputDemo.class                        _ □ ×
Applet

  View Source

  /*
     A basic extension of the java.applet.Applet class
  */

  import java.awt.*;
  import java.applet.*;
  import java.io.*;

  public class FileInputDemo extends Applet {
          void viewButton_Clicked(Event event) {
     try {
           // construct with a String
           FileInputStream input = new FileInputStream("FileInputDemo.java");

           // construct with a File
  //       File f = new File("FileInputDemo.java");
  //        FileInputStream input = new FileInputStream(f);

           StringBuffer buf = new StringBuffer(100);
```

Listing 13.1. The `viewButton_Clicked` method from `FileInputDemo.java`.

```
 1:    void viewButton_Clicked(java.awt.event.ActionEvent event) {
 2:        try {
 3:            // construct with a String
 4:            FileInputStream input = new FileInputStream(
 5:                    "FileInputDemo.java");
 6:
 7:            StringBuffer buf = new StringBuffer(100);
 8:            while (input.available() > 0) {
 9:                buf.append((char)input.read());
10:            }
11:            source.appendText(buf.toString());
12:        }
13:        catch (Exception e) {
14:            source.setText("Exception:\r\n");
15:            source.appendText(e.toString());
16:        }
17:    }
```

ANALYSIS   Lines 4 and 5 of Listing 13.1 construct a new `FileInputStream` using a string containing the applet's filename. Next, a string buffer is allocated (line 7) that will initially hold 100 bytes. A loop then moves through the stream (lines 8–10). A call to `available` is performed to verify that more data can be read from the stream. Then, `read` is used to read a byte from the stream. The byte is cast to a `char` and then appended to the string buffer. After the loop completes, the contents of the string buffer are placed in the text area.

NOTE
Be sure to import the `java.io` package. You can do this as follows:

```
import java.io.*;
```

The `FileOutputStream` Class

The `FileOutputStream` class is the counterpart of `FileInputStream`. A `FileOutputStream` can be constructed with any of the following constructors:

```
FileOutputStream(String filename)
```

```
FileOutputStream(String filename, boolean append)
```

```
FileOutputStream(File file)
```

```
FileOutputStream(FileDescriptor fd)
```

Each of these constructors (except the second) has an equivalent in `FileInputStream`. The second constructor uses a string and a Boolean. The Boolean indicates whether data should be appended to the file if the file is not empty.

13

An Example

FileOutputDemo, included on the MCP Web site, illustrates the use of both FileOutputStream and FileInputStream. When this applet is run, it will appear as shown in Figure 13.4. After the user enters text in the top text area and clicks the Write button, text is written to a file named TEST.TXT. When the Read button is clicked, an input stream is opened that reads this file and displays it in the lower file area to verify that the write was successful. Listing 13.2 shows the relevant code from FileOutputDemo.

Figure 13.4.

Clicking Write saves the text to a file that is reread when Read is clicked.

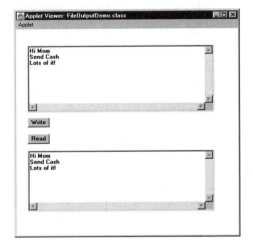

Listing 13.2. Event-handling methods of FileOutputDemo.java.

```
 1:    String fileName = "test.txt";
 2:
 3:    void writeButton_Clicked(java.awt.event.ActionEvent event) {
 4:        try {
 5:            FileOutputStream outStream = new FileOutputStream(
 6:                    fileName);
 7:
 8:            String str = textArea1.getText();
 9:
10:            byte [] buffer;
11:            buffer = new byte[str.length()];
12:
13:            str.getBytes(0, str.length(), buffer, 0);
14:
15:            outStream.write(buffer);
16:        }
17:        catch (Exception e) {
18:            textArea2.setText("Exception:\r\n");
19:            textArea2.appendText(e.toString());
20:        }
21:    }
22:
23:    void readButton_Clicked(java.awt.event.ActionEvent event) {
24:        try {
```

13

```
25:            // construct with a String
26:            FileInputStream input=new FileInputStream(fileName);
27:
28:            StringBuffer buf = new StringBuffer(100);
29:            while (input.available() > 0)
30:                buf.append((char)input.read());
31:            textArea2.appendText(buf.toString());
32:        }
33:        catch (Exception e) {
34:            textArea2.setText("Exception:\r\n");
35:            textArea2.appendText(e.toString());
36:        }
37:    }
```

Buffered Streams

Some streams flow as quickly as the Mississippi; others run as slowly and consistently as the toilet in a cheap motel. When working with a slow stream, you can improve performance by buffering the stream. Both input and output streams can be buffered. When a program needs data from a buffered input stream, it looks first in the stream's buffer. If that is empty, the stream itself is read.

For example, suppose you are working with a FileInputStream and need to read a single byte. It is very inefficient to read data from a disk one byte at a time. A buffered stream solves this problem by reading more bytes than necessary (perhaps 1,024 bytes) and caching these bytes. As the program requests to read each byte, it is retrieved from the cache. When the cache is empty, the stream will once again read 1,024 bytes to refill the buffer.

Java includes the BufferedInputStream and BufferedOutputStream classes. Each of these includes two constructors as follows:

```
BufferedInputStream(InputStream stream)

BufferedInputStream(InputStream stream, int bufSize)

BufferedOutputStream(OutputStream stream)

BufferedOutputStream(OutputStream stream, int bufSize)
```

The *bufSize* parameter is used to specify the size of the buffer. When not specified, a default value will be used to create the buffer.

What is most interesting and useful about the BufferedInputStream and BufferedOutputStream constructors is that they are passed streams as parameters. This means you can link them with other stream constructors to create a stream that combines the behavior of both stream types. For example, Listing 13.1 showed you how to use FileInputStream to read the contents of a Java source code file. In that example, the stream was unbuffered. The buffered equivalent of Listing 13.1 is shown in Listing 13.3. This code is taken from the BufferedInputDemo sample applet that is included on the MCP Web site.

13

Listing 13.3. Constructing a buffered file input stream.

```
1:    void viewButton_Clicked(java.awt.event.ActionEvent event) {
2:      try {
3:        BufferedInputStream bis = new BufferedInputStream(
4:            new FileInputStream("BufferedInputDemo.java"));
5:
6:        StringBuffer buf = new StringBuffer(100);
7:        while (bis.available() > 0) {
8:          buf.append((char)bis.read());
9:        }
10:       results.appendText(buf.toString());
11:     }
12:     catch (Exception e) {
13:       results.setText("Exception:\r\n");
14:       results.appendText(e.toString());
15:     }
15:   }
```

ANALYSIS As you can see on lines 3 and 4, a new `FileInputStream` is constructed and passed as a parameter to the constructor for `BufferedInputStream`. This results in a file-based stream that supports buffering.

Do	Don't

DO chain stream constructors together to take advantage of the features in multiple stream classes.

DON'T use overly large buffer sizes when constructing new buffered streams. Doing so could negate the speed benefits you're looking for.

The `DataInputStream` and `DataOutputStream` Classes

So far, the streams you've examined have worked with bytes cast to characters. Because the world isn't limited to characters, Java includes classes for working with other primitive types. The `DataInputStream` and `DataOutputStream` classes can read and write all of the Java primitive types.

The `DataOutputStream` Class

A `DataOutputStream` can be created by using the one provided constructor:

```
DataOutputStream(OutputStream)
```

As with buffered streams, a `DataOutputStream` is created from an existing stream. `DataOutputStream` includes the following methods for writing Java primitives to a stream:

```
write(byte buffer[], int offset, int length)
```

```
write(int value)
```

```
writeBoolean(boolean value)
```

```
writeByte(int value)
```

```
writeBytes(String str)
```

```
writeChar(int value)
```

```
writeChars(String str)
```

```
writeDouble(double value)
```

```
writeFloat(float value)
```

```
writeInt(int value)
```

```
writeLong(long value)
```

```
writeShort(short value)
```

```
writeUTF(String unicodeString)
```

In addition, `DataOutputStream` includes a `flush` method that flushes the stream and a `size` method that returns an `int` indicating the number of bytes written to the stream.

The `DataInputStream` Class

Like `DataOutputStream`, `DataInputStream` has only one constructor:

```
DataInputStream(InputStream)
```

`DataInputStream` includes a wide variety of methods for reading from a stream. The following methods are provided for reading bytes:

```
int read(byte buffer[])
```

```
int read(byte buffer[], int offset, int length)
```

```
byte readByte()
```

Each of the `read` methods returns the number of bytes that were read or -1 if the end of the stream was reached. The `readByte` method reads a single byte and returns that value.

13

Reading Numeric Values

The following methods are provided for reading numeric values from the stream:

```
double readDouble()
```

```
float readFloat()
```

```
int readInt()
```

```
long readLong()
```

```
short readShort()
```

```
int readUnsignedByte()
```

```
int readUnsignedShort()
```

Each of these methods returns the value retrieved from the stream.

Reading the Full Stream

`DataInputStream` includes the `readFully` method, which can be used to read until all bytes are read from the stream. This method is overloaded to have the following two signatures:

```
void readFully(byte buffer[])
```

```
void readFully(byte buffer[], int offset, int length)
```

Naturally, these methods block the thread until the end of the stream is reached or the desired number of bytes is read.

Other Methods

The `DataInputStream` class also includes the following methods:

```
boolean readBoolean()
```

```
char readChar()
```

```
String readUTF()
```

```
String readUTF(DataInput stream)
```

```
int skipBytes(int quantity)
```

The `readBoolean` and `readChar` methods can be used to read variables of these types. Similarly, the `readUTF` methods can be used to write UTF (Unicode Text Format) strings. The `skipBytes` method can be used to quickly move forward through a stream without reading all intervening bytes. This method blocks until all desired bytes have been skipped.

An Example

As an example of how to use `DataInputStream` and `DataOutputStream`, consider listing 13.4, which shows the `DataInputOutputDemo` applet that is included on the MCP Web site. This applet writes information about three Pink Floyd albums to a `DataOutputStream`. It then reads the information back through a `DataInputStream` and displays the results in a text area. When the applet is run, it appears as shown in Figure 13.5.

Listing 13.4. `DataInputOutputDemo.java.`

```
 1:     import java.awt.*;
 2:     import java.applet.*;
 3:     import java.io.*;
 4:
 5:     public class DataInputOutputDemo extends Applet {
 6:         void writeAllCDs() {
 7:             try {
 8:                 DataOutputStream out = new DataOutputStream(
 9:                         new FileOutputStream(fileName));
10:
11:                 writeOneCD(out, false, "Ummagumma", 1969);
12:                 writeOneCD(out, true,  "Dark Side of the Moon", 1973);
13:                 writeOneCD(out, true,  "Pulse", 1994);
14:
15:                 out.close();
16:             }
17:             catch (Exception e) {
18:                 results.setText("Exception: " + e);
19:             }
20:         }
21:
22:         void writeOneCD(DataOutputStream out, boolean good,
23:                 String title, int year) {
24:             try {
25:                 out.writeBoolean(good);
26:                 out.writeInt(title.length());
27:                 out.writeBytes(title);
28:                 out.writeInt(year);
29:             }
30:             catch (Exception e) {
31:                 results.appendText("Exception: " + e);
32:             }
33:         }
34:
35:         void readAllCDs() {
36:             try {
37:                 DataInputStream in = new DataInputStream(
38:                         new BufferedInputStream(
39:                 new FileInputStream(fileName)));
40:
41:                 while(in.available() > 0)
42:                     readOneCD(in);
43:
44:                 in.close();
45:             }
46:             catch (Exception e) {
47:                 results.setText("Exception: " + e);
48:             }
49:         }
50:
```

13

continues

Listing 13.4. continued

```
51:     void readOneCD(DataInputStream in) {
52:         try {
53:             boolean good = in.readBoolean();
54:             int length = in.readInt();
55:
56:             byte [] buf;
57:             buf = new byte[length];
58:             in.read(buf, 0, length);
59:
60:             String title = new String(buf);
61:
62:             int year = in.readInt();
63:
64:             results.appendText(title);
65:             results.appendText(
66:                     " (" + String.valueOf(year) + ") ");
67:
68:             results.appendText("is a " + (good ? "good":"bad")
69:                     + " CD\r\n");
70:         }
71:         catch (Exception e) {
72:             results.appendText("Exception: " + e);
73:         }
74:     }
75:
76:     public void init() {
77:         // Call parents init method.
78:         super.init();
79:
80:         writeAllCDs();
81:         readAllCDs();
82:     }
83:
84:     public void addNotify() {
85:         // Call parents addNotify method.
86:         super.addNotify();
87:
88:         // This code is automatically generated by Visual Café
89:         // when you add components to the visual environment.
90:         // It instantiates and initializes the components. To
91:         // modify the code, only use code syntax that matches
92:         // what Visual Cafe can generate, or Visual Cafe may
93:         // be unable to back parse your Java file into its
94:         // visual environment.
95:         //{{INIT_CONTROLS
96:         setLayout(null);
97:         resize(426,266);
98:         results = new java.awt.TextArea();
99:         results.reshape(24,12,370,181);
100:        add(results);
101:        //}}
102:    }
103:
104:    String fileName = "PinkFloyd.CD";
105:    //{{DECLARE_CONTROLS
```

13

```
106:     java.awt.TextArea results;
107:     //}}
108: }
```

Figure 13.5.

The result of executing the application in Listing 13.4.

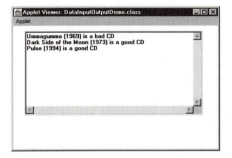

ANALYSIS The methods writeAllCDs (lines 6–20) and writeOneCd (22–33) take care of writing the information to the stream. The constructors on lines 8 and 9 create a file-based DataOutputStream. This stream is then passed as a parameter to writeOneCD, which is called one time for each of the three CDs being written. The remaining parameters to writeOneCD represent whether the CD is good, its title, and the year it was released.

Within writeOneCD, these values are written to the stream. First, writeBoolean is used to write whether the CD is good (line 25). Next, the length of the title is written with writeInt (line 26) and the title is written with writeBytes (line 27). The length of the title is written so that when the stream is read back in, the program can know how many bytes to read for the title. Finally, writeInt writes the year the CD was released (line 28).

The methods readAllCDs (lines 35–49) and readOneCD (lines 51–74) are the counterparts of writeAllCDs and writeOneCD. When the DataInputStream is constructed (lines 37–38), you should notice that the stream is also buffered. The output stream was not buffered but could have been. The distinction was made in this code only to illustrate the way streams can be combined. Although the input stream has more data available, calls are made to readOneCD (lines 41–42) to read the details of each CD.

In readOneCD, the data elements written to the stream are read back. This method is careful to read each item in the same order it was written. After the details for a CD are read, a message is appended to the results text area to prove that the streaming happened successfully.

Character-Oriented Streams

Each of the streams presented thus far has operated on streams of bytes. The Java Development Kit also includes support for 16-bit character streams. Because streams are often sent character data, there are advantages to using Java's character streams. For example, because character streams are 16-bit instead of 8-bit, they are compatible with Java's unicode strings. This allows you to create programs with internationalizable strings. A second advantage of Java's character streams is that they will, in most cases, outperform byte streams. Java's character streams use buffer-based read and write operations rather than the byte-based operations of byte streams.

NOTE

The character stream classes are new to Java Development Kit version 1.1.

Figure 13.6.

The character-based input stream classes.

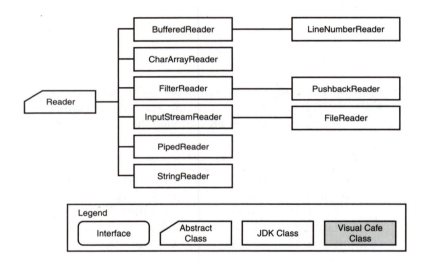

Character Input Streams

Because all character input streams share a common set of core operations, these operations are collected in the abstract class Reader. This class corresponds to the byte stream method InputStream. Figure 13.6 shows the hierarchy of classes descended from Reader.

The methods of the abstract Reader class can be seen in Table 13.1. Because Reader is so similar to InputStream, you should recognize most of these methods from prior descriptions.

Table 13.1. Methods of the abstract class Reader.

Method	Purpose
close	Closes the stream
mark(int)	Marks the stream, allowing the specified read-ahead limit
markSupported()	Returns true if marking is supported; false, otherwise
read()	Reads a character from the stream

Method	Purpose
read(char[])	Reads an array of characters from the stream
read(char[], int, int)	Reads an array of characters from the stream, starting at the specified offset and continuing for the specified length
ready()	Returns true if the stream is ready to be read; false, otherwise
reset()	Resets the stream either to its marked position or to some other position meaningful to the specific type of stream
skip(long)	Skips past the specified number of characters

Character Output Streams

The class Writer is an abstract class that serves as a superclass for all character output streams. The hierarchy of classes descended from Writer can be seen in Figure 13.7. The methods of Writer are shown in Table 13.2.

Figure 13.7.

The character-based output stream classes.

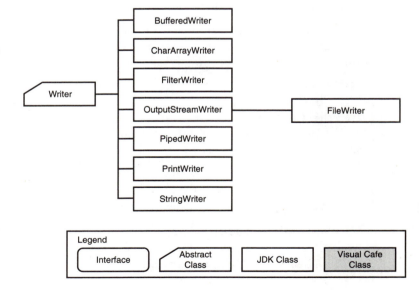

Table 13.2. Methods of the abstract class Writer.

Method	Purpose
close	Closes the stream
flush()	Flushes the stream

continues

Table 13.2. continued

Method	Purpose
write(char [])	Writes an array of characters to the stream
write(char [], int, int)	Writes the specified range of characters to the stream
write(int)	Writes a single character to the stream
write(String)	Writes a string to the stream
write(String, int, int)	Writes the specified portion of the string to the stream

Buffered Streams

The BufferedReader and BufferedWriter classes can be used to create buffered character streams. Each of these classes has two constructors, as follow:

```
BufferedReader(Reader input)

BufferedReader(Reader input, int bufSize)

BufferedWriter(Writer output)

Buffered Writer(Writer output, int bufSize)
```

When specified, the *bufSize* parameter indicates the size of the buffer to allocate for the stream. Each of these constructors is passed another stream so that the constructors can be chained together, as in the following example:

```
BufferedReader bufReader = new BufferedReader(
        new FileReader("input.txt"));
```

BufferedReader offers only one method not included in Reader: readLine. This method is passed no parameters but returns a string containing all the characters up to the next carriage return (\r), line feed (\n), or carriage return and line feed pair (\r\n).

Likewise, BufferedWriter includes only one method not included in Writer: newLine. This method writes a line separator to the stream. The exact line separator that is used is defined by the system property line.separator, but it is usually \n.

The LineNumberReader Class

LineNumberReader, a subclass of BufferedReader, automatically keeps track of the number of lines that have been read. LineNumberReader has two constructors that correspond with the BufferedReader constructors:

```
LineNumberReader(Reader input)

LineNumberReader(Reader input, int bufSize)
```

Additionally, two new methods are provided to manipulate line numbers:

```
int getLineNumber()
```

```
void setLineNumber(int lineNum)
```

WARNING

The method `setLineNumber` sets only a private member variable that tracks the current line number. It does not reposition the stream to a specific line within the stream.

Reading and Writing Files

The classes `FileWriter` and `FileReader` can be used to stream characters into and out of files. These classes correspond to the byte stream classes `FileInputStream` and `FileOutputStream`. `FileReader` supports the following three constructors:

```
FileReader(String fileName)
```

```
FileReader(File file)
```

```
FileReader(FileDescriptor fd)
```

There are four constructors for `FileWriter`:

```
FileWriter(String fileName)
```

```
FileWriter(String fileName, boolean append)
```

```
FileWriter(File file)
```

```
FileWriter(FileDescriptor fd)
```

The `FileWriter` and `FileReader` classes include no additional member methods beyond those they inherit from their superclasses.

WARNING

Each of the `FileReader` constructors other than the one that is passed a `FileDescriptor` can throw `FileNotFoundException`. Similarly, each of the `FileWriter` methods other than the one passed a `FileDescriptor` can throw `IOException`.

An Example

As an example of using `FileWriter`, `FileReader`, and `LineNumberReader`, consider the `FileWriterDemo` applet, shown in Listing 13.5. This applet, which is included on the

13

MCP Web site, writes two lines of text to a file and then reads the same file and displays the contents in a text area. The results of executing `FileWriterDemo` are shown in Figure 13.8.

Listing 13.5. `FileWriterDemo.java.`

```
1:   import java.awt.*;
2:   import java.applet.*;
3:   import java.io.*;
4:
5:   public class FileWriterDemo extends Applet {
6:       void writeTest() {
7:           try {
8:               // construct with a String
9:               FileWriter fw = new FileWriter("char.txt");
10:
11:              fw.write("Hello World\r\n");
12:              fw.write("Goodbye World\r\n");
13:              fw.flush();
14:              fw.close();
15:          }
16:          catch (Exception e) {
17:              ta.appendText(e.toString());
18:          }
19:      }
20:
21:      void readTest() {
22:          try {
23:              LineNumberReader lnr = new LineNumberReader(
24:                      new FileReader("char.txt"));
25:
26:              String str;
27:              while((str = lnr.readLine()) != null) {
28:                  int lineNum = lnr.getLineNumber();
29:                  ta.appendText(String.valueOf(lineNum) +
30:                      ": " + str + "\r\n");
31:              }
32:          }
33:          catch (Exception e) {
34:              ta.appendText(e.toString());
35:          }
36:      }
37:
38:      public void init() {
39:          // Call parents init method.
40:          super.init();
41:
42:          writeTest();
43:          readTest();
44:      }
45:
46:      public void addNotify() {
47:          // Call parents addNotify method.
48:          super.addNotify();
49:
50:          // This code is automatically generated by Visual Café
51:          // when you add components to the visual environment.
52:          // It instantiates and initializes the components. To
```

```
53:        // modify the code, only use code syntax that matches
54:        // what Visual Cafe can generate, or Visual Cafe may
55:        // be unable to back parse your Java file into its
56:        // visual environment.
57:        //{{INIT_CONTROLS
58:        setLayout(null);
59:        resize(426,266);
60:        ta = new java.awt.TextArea();
61:        ta.reshape(24,36,369,196);
62:        add(ta);
63:        //}}
64:    }
65:
66:        //{{DECLARE_CONTROLS
67:        java.awt.TextArea ta;
68:        //}}
69:  }
```

Figure 13.8.

*The results of
executing the*
FileWriterDemo
applet.

ANALYSIS In the method writeTest (lines 6–19), a new FileWriter object, fw, is constructed
from a filename. The write method is used to write two strings to the stream. The
stream is then flushed and closed. In readTest (lines 21–36), a new LineNumberReader stream
is opened for the same filename. A while loop (lines 27–31) then calls readLine until it returns
null. In this way, each line is retrieved. As each line is displayed, its line number is placed at
the front of the display through the use of getLineNumber.

Using Strings as Streams

You may occasionally find it useful to treat a string as though it is a stream. This can be done
with the StringReader and StringWriter classes. StringReader allows characters to be read
from the string as though they are being read from a stream. StringReader supports the
methods of its Reader superclass and has a single constructor:

```
StringReader(String str)
```

To stream characters into a string, use StringWriter, which offers two constructors:

```
StringWriter()
```

```
StringWriter(int bufferSize)
```

13

The difference between these constructors is the optional *bufferSize* parameter. When specified, *bufferSize* indicates the size of the buffer to allocate for the string. If not specified, a default buffer size is used. In addition to the usual methods it inherits from `Writer`, `StringWriter` includes two additional methods for accessing its contents:

```
StringBuffer getBuffer()
```

```
String toString()
```

An Example

As an example of how the `StringReader` and `StringWriter` classes can be used, consider the `StringReaderDemo` applet, shown in Listing 13.6. This applet, which is included on the MCP Web site, streams data into a string in the `writeTest` method (lines 5–10) and then reads the data back from a different stream in the `readTest` method (lines 12–24). The results of executing this applet can be seen in Figure 13.9.

Listing 13.6. `StringReaderDemo.java.`

```
 1:    import java.awt.*;
 2:    import java.applet.*;
 3:    import java.io.*;
 4:
 5:    public class StringReaderDemo extends Applet {
 6:        void writeTest() {
 7:            StringWriter writer = new StringWriter();
 8:            writer.write("Hello ");
 9:            writer.write("xxxWorldxxx", 3, 8);
10:            theString = writer.toString();
11:        }
12:
13:        void readTest() {
14:            StringReader reader = new StringReader(theString);
15:            try {
16:                int curChar;
17:                while((curChar = reader.read()) != -1) {
18:                    ta.appendText(String.valueOf((char)curChar));
19:                }
20:            }
21:            catch(Exception e) {
22:                ta.appendText("Exception: " + e);
23:            }
24:        }
25:
26:        public void init() {
27:            // Call parents init method.
28:            super.init();
29:
30:            writeTest();
31:            readTest();
32:        }
33:
34:        public void addNotify() {
35:            // Call parents addNotify method.
```

13

```
36:        super.addNotify();
37:
38:        // This code is automatically generated by Visual Café
39:        // when you add components to the visual environment.
40:        // It instantiates and initializes the components. To
41:        // modify the code, only use code syntax that matches
42:        // what Visual Cafe can generate, or Visual Cafe may
43:        // be unable to back parse your Java file into its
44:        // visual environment.
45:        //{{INIT_CONTROLS
46:        setLayout(null);
47:        resize(426,266);
48:        ta = new java.awt.TextArea();
49:        ta.reshape(12,12,402,220);
50:        add(ta);
51:        //}}
52:    }
53:
54:    String theString;
55:
56:    //{{DECLARE_CONTROLS
57:    java.awt.TextArea ta;
58:    //}}
59: }
```

Figure 13.9.

The results of
executing
StringReaderDemo.

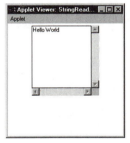

The PushbackReader Class

Imagine you've overindulged at the Mexican bar of an all-you-can-eat buffet. Unfortunately, you can't undo what you ate; the best you can do is pop a few antacids. But if you were a PushbackReader stream and you read a few too many characters, you could undo your actions.

In addition to the normal read methods, the PushbackReader class includes the following unread methods:

```
void unread(int c)

void unread(char buffer[], int offset, int length)

void unread(char buffer[])
```

Each PushbackReader contains a buffer that holds characters that are pushed backed into the streams. When a read occurs, characters are retrieved first from the buffer and then, when the buffer is empty, from the stream itself. To create a `PushbackReader`, either use the default buffer size or specify your own. To create a `PushbackReader` object, use either of the following two constructors:

```
PushbackReader(Reader stream)
```

```
PushbackReader(Reader stream, int bufferSize)
```

As an example of how to use `PushbackReader`, consider Listing 13.7, which shows the `pushbackTest` method from the `PushbackReaderDemo` applet, which is included on the MCP Web site. You should be able to examine this method and convince yourself that, although the stream starts out containing `Hello World`, it displays `Goodbye World`.

Listing 13.7. The `pushbackTest` method from `PushbackReaderDemo.java`.

```
 1:  void pushbackTest() {
 2:      StringReader reader = new StringReader("Hello World");
 3:      PushbackReader pbr = new PushbackReader(reader, 20);
 4:
 5:      char charBuf[];
 6:      charBuf = new char[20];
 7:
 8:      try {
 9:          pbr.read(charBuf, 0, 5);
10:
11:          char pushBack[] = {'G', 'o', 'o', 'd', 'b', 'y', 'e'};
12:          pbr.unread(pushBack, 0, 7);
13:
14:          char charBuf2[];
15:          charBuf2 = new char[20];
16:
17:          pbr.read(charBuf2, 0, 20);
18:          ta.appendText(String.valueOf(charBuf2));
19:      }
20:      catch(Exception e) {
21:          ta.appendText("Exception: " + e);
22:      }
23:  }
```

Do   **Don't**

DO use character streams if you expect to internationalize your program. Unlike English, not all languages can be represented with a single byte per character.

DON'T forget that character streams are new to the 1.1 release of the Java Development Kit.

Object Streams

Sometimes it isn't enough to be able to write Java primitives to a stream. Sometimes you want to write an entire object to a stream. Fortunately, Java supports object streams through its ObjectInputStream and ObjectOutputStream classes.

The `ObjectOutputStream` Class

ObjectOutputStream is a subclass of OutputStream, and as such is a byte stream. To create a new ObjectOutputStream, pass the constructor any OutputStream object, as in the following:

```
ObjectOutputStream out = new ObjectOutputStream(
        new FileOutputStream("objects.out"));
```

You can write a variable to an ObjectOutputStream using any of the following methods:

```
void write(byte buf[])
```

```
void write(byte buf[], int offset, int length)
```

```
void write(int data)
```

```
void writeBoolean(boolean data)
```

```
void writeByte(int data)
```

```
void writeBytes(String data)
```

```
void writeChar(int data)
```

```
void writeChars(String data)
```

```
void writeDouble(double data)
```

```
void writeFloat(float data)
```

```
void writeInt(int data)
```

```
void writeObject(Object data)
```

```
void writeShort(int data)
```

```
void writeUTF(String data)
```

The writeObject method is the most generic in this list because it allows you to write objects of any type to the stream. In addition to the methods for writing, ObjectOutputStream includes two other commonly used methods:

```
void close()
```

```
void flush()
```

As an example of using ObjectOutputStream, consider Listing 13.8, which shows the writeObjects method of the ObjectStreamDemo applet that is included on the MCP Web site:

13

Listing 13.8. The `writeObjects` method from `ObjectStreamDemo.java`.

```
1:    void writeObjects() {
2:        try {
3:            ObjectOutputStream out = new ObjectOutputStream(
4:                    new FileOutputStream("objects.out"));
5:
6:            out.writeDouble(3.14159);
7:            out.writeObject("Hi Mom");
8:            out.writeObject(new Date());
9:            out.flush();
10:           out.close();
11:       }
12:       catch(Exception e) {
13:           ta.setText("Exception:\r\n");
14:           ta.appendText(e.toString());
15:       }
16:   }
```

This example creates an object stream from the filename `objects.out` and then writes the value of pi, a message to my mother, and today's date to the stream. The stream is then flushed and closed.

The `ObjectInputStream` Class

`ObjectInputStream` is essentially a mirror image of `ObjectOutputStream`. An `ObjectInputStream` is created by passing its constructor an `OutputStream` object, as shown in the following:

```
ObjectInputStream in = new ObjectInputStream(
        new FileInputStream("objects.out"));
```

Similarly, for each of the methods for writing data in `ObjectOutputStream`, `ObjectInputStream` includes a method for reading data. This means the following methods are available for reading data from the stream:

```
int read()
```

```
int read(byte buf[], int offset, int len)
```

```
boolean readBoolean()
```

```
byte readByte()
```

```
char readChar()
```

```
double readDouble()
```

```
float readFloat()
```

```
int readInt()
```

```
String readLine()
```

```
long readLong()
```

13

```
Object readObject()
```

```
short readShort()
```

```
int readUnsignedByte()
```

```
int readUnsignedShort()
```

```
String readUTF()
```

The readObjects method of the ObjectStreamDemo applet, shown in Listing 13.9, illustrates the use of these methods to read the objects written by writeObjects in Listing 13.8. As you can see in Listing 13.9, the objects are read in the same order in which they were written.

Listing 13.9. The readObjects method from ObjectStreamDemo.java.

```
 1:    void readObjects() {
 2:        try {
 3:            ObjectInputStream in = new ObjectInputStream(
 4:                    new FileInputStream("objects.out"));
 5:            double pi = in.readDouble();
 6:            String hello = (String)in.readObject();
 7:            Date date = (Date)in.readObject();
 8:            in.close();
 9:
10:            ta.appendText(String.valueOf(pi) + "\r\n");
11:            ta.appendText(hello + "\r\n");
12:            ta.appendText(date.toString());
13:        }
14:        catch(Exception e) {
15:            ta.setText("Exception:\r\n");
16:            ta.appendText(e.toString());
17:        }
18:    }
```

Streaming Your Own Objects

These examples worked well for streaming objects that come with Java, but what about streaming your own objects? Unfortunately, this fits into the "There's no such thing as a free lunch" category. Fortunately, however, there is such a thing as a very cheap lunch. For an object to be streamable, it must simply implement the Serializable interface. This interface requires that the class include the following two methods:

```
void writeObject(ObjectOutputStream stream)
```

```
void readObject(ObjectInputStream stream)
```

These methods are responsible for reading and writing whatever information you wish to pass the stream. This will often be each of an object's member variables, but this is not always case. For example, if a class includes DateOfBirth and CurrentAge members, you might opt to stream only `DateOfBirth` because the receiving stream can calculate `CurrentAge` from `DateOfBirth` if necessary.

> You must be careful to ensure that each value written in `writeObject` is read back in by `readObject`.

The `writeObject` and `readObject` methods can be written using the `read` and `write` methods described in prior sections. For example, the following code illustrates the use of `writeObject` and `readObject`:

```
private void writeObject(ObjectOutputStream out)
      throws IOException {
   out.writeObject(name);
   out.writeObject(DOB);
}

private void readObject(ObjectInputStream in)
      throws IOException, ClassNotFoundException {
   name = (String)in.readObject();
   DOB = (Date)in.readObject();
}
```

Additionally, `ObjectOutputStream` and `ObjectInputStream` each provide a method that can simplify this process. The `defaultReadObject` method of `ObjectInputStream` reads all nonstatic, nontransient members of the class. This means you could have written `readObject` as follows, assuming that `name` and `DOB` are the only nonstatic, nontransient members:

```
private void readObject(ObjectInputStream in)
      throws IOException, ClassNotFoundException {
   in.defaultReadObject();
}
```

Similarly, you could rewrite `writeObject` using `defaultWriteObject` as follows:

```
private void writeObject(ObjectOutputStream out)
      throws IOException {
   out.defaultWriteObject();
}
```

> You can only call `defaultReadObject` from within a class's `readObject` method. Similarly, you can only call `defaultWriteObject` from within a class's `writeObject` method.

An Example

When you work with an inheritance hierarchy of classes, there usually is some useful information in more than one class in the hierarchy. For example, an applet for the local animal shelter might include an Animal class that contains generic information such as the name and date of birth of an animal. The same application might include subclasses of Animal, such as Cat and Dog. These classes would hold specifics about each type of animal, such as how many of its nine lives a certain cat has remaining and whether a certain dog is a suitable guard dog.

This type of situation is interesting because to accurately stream information about a cat or dog, information must also be streamed from the Animal superclass. As an example of how this works, consider Listing 13.10. This listing shows the Animal, Cat, and Dog classes from the AnimalObjectStream sample applet, which is included on the MCP Web site.

Listing 13.10. The Animal, Cat, and Dog classes from AnimalObjectStream.java.

```
 1:    class Animal implements Serializable
 2:    {
 3:        private String name;
 4:        private Date DOB;
 5:
 6:        String getInfo() {
 7:            return "No info available.";
 8:        }
 9:
10:        Animal(String str) {
11:            name = str;
12:        }
13:
14:        String getName() {
15:            return name;
16:        }
17:
18:        void setDOB(Date date) {
19:            DOB = date;
20:        }
21:
22:        String getDOBString() {
23:        if (DOB == null)
24:            return "";
25:        else
26:            return "(" + DOB.toString() + ")";
27:        }
28:
29:        private void writeObject(ObjectOutputStream out)
30:                throws IOException {
31:            out.writeObject(name);
32:            out.writeObject(DOB);
33:        }
34:
35:        private void readObject(ObjectInputStream in)
36:                throws IOException, ClassNotFoundException {
37:            name = (String)in.readObject();
38:            DOB = (Date)in.readObject();
```

continues

Listing 13.10. continued

```
39:        }
40:    }
41:
42:    class Cat extends Animal implements Serializable
43:    {
44:        int remainingLives;
45:
46:        String getInfo() {
47:            return getName() + " has " +
48:                    String.valueOf(remainingLives) +
49:                    " lives left " + getDOBString();
50:        }
51:
52:        Cat(String str, int lives) {
53:            super(str);
54:            remainingLives = lives > 9 ? 9 : lives;
55:        }
56:
57:        private void writeObject(ObjectOutputStream out)
58:                throws IOException {
59:          // write remainingLives
60:            out.writeInt(remainingLives);
61:        }
62:
63:        private void readObject(ObjectInputStream in)
64:                throws IOException, ClassNotFoundException {
65:          // read remainingLives
66:            remainingLives = in.readInt();
67:        }
68:    }
69:
70:    class Dog extends Animal implements Serializable
71:    {
72:        boolean guardDog;
73:
74:        String getInfo() {
75:            return getName() + " is " +
76:                (guardDog ? "" : "not ") + "a guard dog " +
77:            getDOBString();
78:        }
79:
80:        Dog(String str, boolean guard) {
81:            super(str);
82:            guardDog = guard;
83:        }
84:
85:        private void writeObject(ObjectOutputStream out)
86:                throws IOException {
87:            out.defaultWriteObject();
88:        }
89:
90:        private void readObject(ObjectInputStream in)
91:                throws IOException, ClassNotFoundException {
92:            in.defaultReadObject();
93:        }
94:    }
```

ANALYSIS As you can see in Listing 13.10, each of these classes implements the `Serializable` interface. The `Animal` class includes a `writeObject` method (lines 29–33) that uses `ObjectOutputStream.writeObject` to write the name and date of birth of the animal. It also includes a `readObject` method that uses `ObjectOutputStream.readObject` to retrieve each of these values.

The `Cat` class implements `writeObject` (lines 57–61) and `readObject` (lines 63–67) by using `writeInt` and `readInt`. However, whenever a `Cat` is streamed, the data in its parent class (`Animal`) will be automatically streamed as well.

The `Dog` class takes a slightly different approach. Its `writeObject` method (lines 85–88) calls `defaultWriteObject`, and its `readObject` (lines 90–93) calls `defaultReadObject`. This automatically takes care of streaming the nonstatic, nontransient member variables of `Dog`.

To verify that these classes are correctly streaming their data, the `AnimalObjectStream` applet includes the `writePets` and `readPets` methods. These are shown in Listing 13.11.

Listing 13.11. The `writePets` and `readPets` methods from `AnimalObjectStream.java`.

```
 1:     void writePets() {
 2:         try {
 3:             Animal[] pet = new Animal[4];
 4:
 5:             pet[0] = new Cat("Muffy", 3);
 6:             pet[1] = new Dog("Rebel", false);
 7:             pet[1].setDOB(new Date());
 8:             pet[2] = new Cat("Bagheera", 12);
 9:             pet[2].setDOB(new Date());
10:             pet[3] = new Dog("Moose", true);
11:
12:             ObjectOutputStream oStream = new
13:                     ObjectOutputStream(
14:                     new FileOutputStream("animals.txt"));
15:             oStream.writeObject(pet);
16:             oStream.close();
17:         }
18:         catch(Exception e) {
19:             ta.setText("Exception:\r\n");
20:             ta.appendText(e.toString());
21:         }
22:     }
23:
24:     void readPets() {
25:         try {
26:             ObjectInputStream iStream = new
27:                     ObjectInputStream(
28:                     new FileInputStream("animals.txt"));
29:             Animal[] pet = (Animal[])iStream.readObject();
30:
```

continues

13

Listing 13.11. continued

```
31:                for(int count=0; count<pet.length; count++)
32:                    ta.appendText(pet[count].getInfo() + "\r\n");
33:            }
34:        catch(Exception e) {
35:            ta.setText("Exception:\r\n");
36:            ta.appendText(e.toString());
37:        }
38:    }
```

ANALYSIS AnimalObjectStream first calls writePets to stream four pets into a file named animals.txt. An array of Animal objects is allocated on line 3 and is then loaded with specific Cat and Dog objects (lines 5–10). The date of birth is known only for Rebel and Bagheera, and setDOB is used for these pets. The ObjectOutputStream is constructed by passing it a FileOutputStream (lines 12–14). Next, writeObjects is passed the array of pets (line 15) and the stream is closed.

To read the stream, an ObjectInputStream is created from a FileInputStream on lines 26–28 of readPets (lines 24–38). Then the array of pets is read from the stream with readObject (line 29). Finally, a loop moves through the array of pets and calls the getInfo method for each pet. The information returned from getInfo is displayed in a text area, ta. The results of executing AnimalObjectStream are shown in Figure 13.10. From this figure, you can see that the appropriate getInfo method in Dog or Cat was called for each pet, even though all dogs and cats were retrieved from the stream as generic animals.

Figure 13.10.

The results of executing the AnimalObjectStream *applet.*

Do   **Don't**

DON'T forget that you can use transient when declaring a variable to instruct defaultReadObject and defaultWriteObject to ignore that member.

DON'T forget that, because static members are not instance members, they are not streamed.

13

Summary

In this chapter, you learned quite a bit about Java streams. You learned how the abstract classes InputStream and OutputStream sit at the top of the byte stream hierarchy. You also learned that there are character stream equivalents, Reader and Writer. You worked through many examples of using streams to write to and read from files. You learned how streams can be chained together to create streams that offer the combined features of more than one stream class. You learned how to use the ObjectInputStream and ObjectOutputStream classes to create object streams. Finally, you learned about the Serializable interface and how you can use it to make your own classes streamable.

Q&A

Q **Why are there two different class hierarchies, one for byte streams and one for character streams? It seems like a better design would have been to have all stream types share a common base class.**

A When the 1.0 version of the Java Development Kit (JDK) was released, it included support for byte streams only. It was quickly discovered that 8-bit byte streams were inadequate in an environment that uses 16-bit characters. JDK release 1.1 remedied the situation by adding character streams.

Included in the original versions of the JDK were classes and methods that assumed byte-size characters. For example, the class LineNumberInputStream (similar to LineNumberReader) was intended to support line-oriented operations based on the occurrence of bytes denoting the end of each line. However, because the end-of-line indicator can be a 16-bit character, an 8-bit byte stream was a shaky foundation for such a class. For this reason, LineNumberInputStream was deprecated and the character-oriented LineNumberReader was added.

Q **I thought I read that Java applets couldn't write to files on a user's local hard drive. However, it seems that a FileOutputStream can be used to do just that. Is this a security risk?**

A Java applets are prevented from having low-level access to a user's disk. This means applets do not have the same set of functions available to them that a typical C or other language program might. However, as you saw in this chapter, streams represent a very powerful mechanism for writing data to and reading data from files. Streaming does not present any security risks because it all happens under the control of the Java Virtual Machine.

13

Workshop

The workshop includes quiz questions to help you gauge your understanding of the material in this chapter. The workshop also includes exercises to provide hands-on experience with what you've learned in this chapter. Answers to the quiz questions can be found in Appendix D, "Answers."

Quiz

1. How would you construct a new `InputStream` object at runtime?
2. What is the meaning of the integer parameter passed to `InputStream.mark(int)`?
3. What is blocking?
4. What do `InputStream` and `Reader` have in common? Why do both classes exist?
5. Give an example of chaining the `FileInputStream` and `BufferedInputStream` constructors.
6. What character stream class allows you to unread characters?
7. If you want to make a class streamable, what interface must the class implement? What methods must be written for the class?
8. Which member variables in a class are written when `defaultWriteObject` is used?

Exercises

1. Use a `PushbackReader` to write an applet that allows the user to enter text into one text field, click a button, and have the text redisplayed with a space character between each pair of characters in the original string.
2. Write a simple editor. When loaded, the editor should open a specific file and then allow the user to edit the text and save the file.
3. Extra credit: Modify the editor to use the `FileDialog` class that was described on Day 10, "Windows, Frames, and Dialogs."
4. Write an inventory applet that reads and writes `Part` objects in an object stream. Each `Part` object should include a name, product code, price, and quantity. Have the applet stream out the initial inventory, stream the inventory back in, sell a few items (to reduce inventory), and then stream out the closing inventory.

Day 14

Multithreading

Today you will learn how to work with Java threads. By using threads, you can write programs that give the appearance of doing more than one task at a time. For example, a multithreaded program might be downloading graphics in one thread, connecting to a database in another, and interacting with the user in a third.

Working with Simple Threads

There is nothing more frustrating than having to wait for a program to complete a lengthy, time-consuming task. In an age where 32-bit operating systems and powerful processors are the norm, it is not only rude to make your users wait, it is unacceptable. In fact, making your users wait will probably cause them to look elsewhere. Of course, this problem is nothing new; programmers have fought this battle for many years.

One of the ways the battle has been fought is by using add-on libraries that supply a language with the capability to execute multiple threads.

A *thread* is an independent path of execution through a program. A *multithreaded program* contains more than one thread of execution.

If you allow a program to execute multiple threads, the program can break its work into simultaneously executing pieces. For example, in a word processor, a thread can be started to print a document while a second thread allows the user to continue typing. Although threads turned out to be an excellent solution for handling lengthy tasks such as printing, supporting threads through add-on libraries turned out to be inadequate.

Without thread support built directly into the language, threads were difficult to work with, difficult to debug, inconsistently supported by different vendors, and prone to error. Java avoids all of these problems by incorporating support for threads directly into the language. Incidentally, Java is not the first language to do this.

Running a Single Thread

The easiest way to create a new thread in Java is to create a subclass of `Thread`. The only method you need to override is run, as follows:

```
Class MyThread extends Thread {
    public void run() {
        // processing code goes here
    }
}
```

Within the run method, write the main processing code for the thread. Earlier in this chapter you saw an example of using a thread to print a document. In that case, the code to print the document would be placed in run.

When a thread is constructed, it does not automatically start running. To start running a thread that has already been constructed, call the start method, as follows:

```
class MyThread extends Thread {
    public void run() {
        // processing code goes here
    }
}

public class MyApplet extends Applet {
    public void button_Clicked() {
        MyThread thread = new MyThread();
        thread.start();
    }
}
```

The start method takes care of calling run. You should never call run directly.

WARNING

14

In addition to starting a method, you can also pause the thread for a specified duration. To do this, use the `sleep` method, whose signature is as follows:

```
void.sleep(long milliseconds)
```

TIP

The `sleep` method is static. This means you can use it even when you are not working with explicit threads. For example, to pause a program for one second, use `Thread.sleep(1000)`.

As an example of running a thread in response to a button click, consider the `SimpleThreadDemo` applet. The code for this applet is shown in Listing 14.1.

Listing 14.1. `SimpleThreadDemo.java.`

```
 1:    import java.awt.*;
 2:    import java.applet.*;
 3:    import java.util.*;
 4:
 5:    public class SimpleThreadDemo extends Applet {
 6:        void startButton_Clicked(java.awt.event.ActionEvent
 7:              event) {
 8:          int width  = mainPanel.size().width;
 9:          int height = mainPanel.size().height;
10:
11:          CircleThread t = new CircleThread(
12:              mainPanel.getGraphics(), width, height);
13:          t.start();
14:        }
15:
16:        public void init() {
17:          // Call parents init method.
18:           super.init();
19:        }
20:
21:        public void addNotify() {
22:          // Call parents addNotify method.
23:          super.addNotify();
24:
25:          //{{INIT_CONTROLS
26:          setLayout(null);
27:          resize(426,266);
28:          buttonPanel = new java.awt.Panel();
29:          buttonPanel.setLayout(new FlowLayout(
30:              FlowLayout.CENTER,5,5));
31:          buttonPanel.reshape(0,235,426,31);
32:          add(buttonPanel);
```

continues

14

Listing 14.1. continued

```
33:            startButton = new java.awt.Button("Start");
34:            startButton.reshape(193,5,39,23);
35:            buttonPanel.add(startButton);
36:            mainPanel = new java.awt.Panel();
37:            mainPanel.setLayout(null);
38:            mainPanel.reshape(0,0,426,235);
39:            add(mainPanel);
40:            //}}
41:
42:            //{{REGISTER_LISTENERS
43:            Action lAction = new Action();
44:            startButton.addActionListener(lAction);
45:            //}}
46:        }
47:
48:        //{{DECLARE_CONTROLS
49:        java.awt.Panel buttonPanel;
50:        java.awt.Button startButton;
51:        java.awt.Panel mainPanel;
52:        //}}
53:
54:        class Action implements java.awt.event.ActionListener {
55:            public void actionPerformed(java.awt.event.ActionEvent
56:                    event) {
57:                Object object = event.getSource();
58:                if (object == startButton)
59:                    startButton_Clicked(event);
60:            }
61:        }
62: }
63:
64: class CircleThread extends Thread {
65:        protected Graphics graphics;
66:        protected Random r = new Random();
67:        protected int width, height;
68:
69:        public CircleThread(Graphics g, int w, int h) {
70:            width    = w;
71:            height   = h;
72:            graphics = g;
73:
74:            graphics.setColor(Color.red);
75:        }
76:
77:        public void run() {
78:            while (true) {
79:                try {
80:                    sleep(50);
81:                }
82:                catch (InterruptedException e) {
83:                }
84:
```

14

```
85:                graphics.fillOval(getCoordinate(width),
86:                    getCoordinate(height), 15, 15);
87:        }
88:    }
89:
90:    int getCoordinate(int maxValue)    {
91:        return (int)(r.nextInt() % maxValue + 1);
92:    }
93: }
```

ANALYSIS   This applet includes two classes: `SimpleThreadDemo`, which extends `Applet`, and `CircleThread`, which extends `Thread`. `CircleThread` continuously displays small red circles at random locations on the screen. This is done by run (lines 77–88). This method is a never-ending loop that starts by pausing for 50 milliseconds (line 80) and then uses `fillOval` to draw a circle (lines 85–85). The location of the circle is determined by using the `getCoordinate` method (lines 90–91), which uses a pseudo-random number generator to pick a coordinate. The results of running `SimpleThreadDemo` can be seen in Figure 14.1.

No instances of `CircleThread` are started until the user selects the Start button. This invokes `startButton_Clicked` (lines 6–14). This method determines the width and height of the panel on which the circles are drawn (lines 8–9), then constructs a new `CircleThread` object. The object doesn't start running, however, until start is called on line 13.

Figure 14.1.

`SimpleThreadDemo` *creates one thread that draws circles randomly on the screen.*

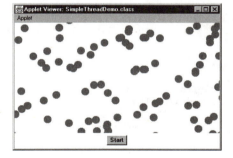

Running Multiple Threads

You may have noticed that `SimpleThreadDemo` does not do anything to prevent a user from clicking the Start button more than one time. In the event a user clicks the Start button more than once, a new `CircleThread` object is created for each click. This means there will be two threads drawing circles on the screen. Rerun `SimpleThreadDemo` and click the Start button multiple times. You should notice that circles are being drawn more quickly. This is because there are more threads running; even though each thread still sleeps for 50 milliseconds after each circle, there are plenty of other threads to keep up the work.

14

Just because the circles are being drawn more quickly isn't necessarily proof that multiple threads are at work. Perhaps Java has detected that the user requested to run the same thread twice, and is running the thread at double speed. To see that multiple threads are actually running, consider the `ColoredCircleDemo` applet. The `ColoredCircleThread` class from this applet is shown in Listing 14.2.

Listing 14.2. The `ColoredCircleThread` class from `ColoredCircleDemo.java`.

```
1:    class ColoredCircleThread extends Thread {
2:        protected Graphics graphics;
3:        protected Random r = new Random();
4:        protected int width, height;
5:        static int threadQty=0;
6:
7:        public ColoredCircleThread(Graphics g, int w, int h) {
8:            width   = w;
9:            height  = h;
10:           graphics = g;
11:
12:           switch(threadQty++) {
13:               case 0:
14:                   g.setColor(Color.red);
15:                   break;
16:               case 1:
17:                   g.setColor(Color.cyan);
18:                   break;
19:               default:
20:                   g.setColor(Color.yellow);
21:                   break;
22:           }
23:       }
24:
25:       public void run() {
26:           while (true) {
27:               try {
28:                   sleep(50);
29:               }
30:               catch (InterruptedException e) {
31:               }
32:
33:               graphics.fillOval(getCoordinate(width),
34:                       getCoordinate(height), 15, 15);
35:           }
36:       }
37:
38:       int getCoordinate(int maxValue)     {
39:           return (int)(r.nextInt() % maxValue + 1);
40:       }
41:   }
```

14

ANALYSIS The key difference between `ColoredCircleThread` and `CircleThread` is in their constructors. The `ColoredCircleThread` constructor chooses to draw the circles in red, cyan, or yellow, based on how many threads have already been created (lines 12–22). The first thread always draws red circles, and the second thread always draws cyan circles. All higher-numbered threads draw yellow circles. This makes it very easy to see how many threads are executing.

After loading this applet, click the Start button three times. You will see red, cyan, and yellow circles being drawn at the same frequency. Now click the Start button a dozen or so more times. This will start that many new threads. Each of these threads will create yellow circles. After a few seconds, you should notice that yellow overwhelms red and cyan.

Suspending and Resuming Threads

Sometimes you need to temporarily stop a thread. This is known as *suspending* the thread. When a suspended thread is restarted, this is known as *resuming*. You can suspend or resume a thread with the following methods of the `Thread` class:

```
void suspend()

void resume()
```

Think about how you could apply this to either of the sample applets you've worked with in this chapter. In these samples, when a thread was constructed, no reference to it was retained. As you recall from Listing 14.1, the `startButton_Clicked` method simply stored the thread object reference in a local variable that went out of scope after the thread was started, as follows:

```
void startButton_Clicked(java.awt.event.ActionEvent event) {
    int width  = mainPanel.size().width;
    int height = mainPanel.size().height;

    CircleThread t = new CircleThread(
            mainPanel.getGraphics(), width, height);
    t.start();
}
```

If you want to give the user the ability to suspend and then resume `CircleThread` objects, the applet must store references to these objects somewhere so they can be used later to call `suspend` and `resume`. A likely solution would be to use either an array or a vector. However, the Java `ThreadGroup` class offers an additional solution.

Thread Groups

The `ThreadGroup` class offers a way of working with a collection of threads as though they are a single thread. You can suspend or resume all of the threads in a thread group with a single command. To create a `ThreadGroup`, use one of the following two constructors:

```
ThreadGroup(String name)

ThreadGroup(ThreadGroup parent, String name)
```

14

The string passed to these constructors as the name of the group can be any arbitrary string. The name of a thread group can be retrieved by calling getName, which returns a String containing the name of the group.

If no parent is specified when a ThreadGroup is constructed, the parent of the newly constructed group is the parent of the thread constructing the group. Knowing the parent of a group is important because when the suspend and resume methods are used, they act on all threads in the group and all threads for which the group is a parent. This means that suspending a thread group will also suspend the children of the group.

To add a thread to a thread group when the thread is constructed, specify the thread group as a parameter to the constructor. This can be done using the following Thread constructor:

```
Thread(ThreadGroup group, String name)
```

To determine the parent of a group, use getParent. This method returns a ThreadGroup representing the parent of the group. To determine how many threads are active in a group, use activeCount, which returns an integer value.

The SuspendDemo applet is an example of how to use the suspend and resume methods and how to work with thread groups. It allows the user to create, suspend, and resume threads that display circles or squares on an applet. Figure 14.2 shows what SuspendDemo looks like when run. Listing 14.3 shows the GraphicThread, CircleThread, and SquareThread classes from SuspendDemo.

Figure 14.2.

The SuspendDemo *applet allows the user to create, suspend, and resume threads.*

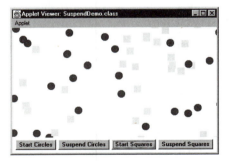

Listing 14.3. The GraphicThread, CircleThread, **and** SquareThread **classes from** SuspendDemo.java.

```
1:    abstract class GraphicThread extends Thread {
2:        protected Graphics graphics;
3:        protected static Random r = new Random();
4:        protected int width, height;
5:        static int count=0;
6:
```

```
7:        public GraphicThread(Graphics g, int w, int h,
8:                ThreadGroup grp) {
9:            super(grp, String.valueOf(count++));
10:
11:            width  = w;
12:            height = h;
13:            graphics = g;
14:        }
15:
16:        public void run() {
17:            while (true) {
18:                try {
19:                    sleep(50);
20:                }
21:                catch (InterruptedException e) {
22:                }
23:
24:                draw(graphics, getCoordinate(width),
25:                        getCoordinate(height));
26:            }
27:        }
28:
29:        int getCoordinate(int maxValue) {
30:            return (int)(r.nextInt() % maxValue + 1);
31:        }
32:
33:        abstract void draw(Graphics g, int x, int y);
34:    }
35:
36: class CircleThread extends GraphicThread {
37:        static ThreadGroup group = new ThreadGroup("circles");
38:
39:        public CircleThread(Graphics g, int width,int height) {
40:            super(g, width, height, group);
41:            g.setColor(Color.blue);
42:        }
43:
44:        void draw(Graphics g, int x, int y) {
45:            g.fillOval(x, y, 15, 15);
46:        }
47:    }
48:
49:    class SquareThread extends GraphicThread {
50:        static ThreadGroup group = new ThreadGroup("squares");
51:
52:        public SquareThread(Graphics g,int width,int height) {
53:                super(g, width, height, group);
54:            g.setColor(Color.yellow);
55:        }
56:
57:        void draw(Graphics g, int x, int y) {
58:            g.fillRect(x, y, 15, 15);
59:        }
60:    }
```

14

ANALYSIS Because SuspendDemo draws both circles and squares, the essential aspects of these classes have been collected into an abstract base class, GraphicThread (lines 1–34) The classes CircleThread (lines 36–47) and SquareThread (lines 49–60) are each subclasses of GraphicThread.

The constructor for GraphicThread (lines 7–14) is passed the graphics device, width, and height of the display area, and the ThreadGroup to which the new thread will belong. On line 9, this constructor uses super to create Thread as a member of the specified thread group.

As a result of adding the abstract base class GraphicThread, the CircleThread class is much simpler. It contains a static ThreadGroup member, group, that is initialized on line 37. This member is passed to the GraphicThread constructor through the call to super on line 40.

The SquareThread class is completely analogous to CircleThread. The only two differences are the name of the thread group (line 50) and the use of fillRect (line 58) instead of fillOval.

Of course, these methods are useless without the code that gets them running. This is done in the event-handling methods shown in Listing 14.4.

Listing 14.4. The event-handling methods of the SuspendDemo class.

```
 1:  void circleButton_Clicked(java.awt.event.ActionEvent event) {
 2:      int width  = mainPanel.size().width;
 3:      int height = mainPanel.size().height;
 4:
 5:      CircleThread t = new CircleThread(
 6:          mainPanel.getGraphics(), width, height);
 7:      t.start();
 8:  }
 9:
10:  void suspendCircleButton_Clicked(java.awt.event.ActionEvent
11:          event) {
12:      if(suspendCircleButton.getLabel().equals(
13:          "Suspend Circles")) {
14:          CircleThread.group.suspend();
15:          suspendCircleButton.setLabel("Resume Circles");
16:      }
17:      else {
18:          CircleThread.group.resume();
19:          suspendCircleButton.setLabel("Suspend Circles");
20:      }
21:  }
22:
23:  void squareButton_Clicked(java.awt.event.ActionEvent event) {
24:      int width  = mainPanel.size().width;
25:      int height = mainPanel.size().height;
26:
27:      SquareThread t = new SquareThread(
28:          mainPanel.getGraphics(), width, height);
29:      t.start();
30:  }
31:
```

14

```
32:   void suspendSquareButton_Clicked(java.awt.event.ActionEvent
33:        event) {
34:     if(suspendSquareButton.getLabel().equals(
35:         "Suspend Squares")) {
36:       SquareThread.group.suspend();
37:       suspendSquareButton.setLabel("Resume Squares");
38:     }
39:     else {
40:       SquareThread.group.resume();
41:       suspendSquareButton.setLabel("Suspend Squares");
42:     }
43:   }
```

ANALYSIS The circleButton_Clicked method (lines 1–8) starts a new thread. This method is identical to startButton_Clicked in Listing 14.1. The suspendCircleButton_Clicked method checks whether the button's label is Suspend Circles. If so, suspend is called and the button's label is changed to Resume Circles. If the button's label already equals Resume Circles, resume is called and label is changed to Suspend Circles.

Do	Don't

DO put a thread to sleep momentarily if it has finished its work so that other threads can do their jobs.

DON'T forget that you must call start before a thread will actually run.

DO design the classes you derive from Thread so they can be run as multiple threads.

DO use thread groups whenever you wish to control more than one thread as though it were a single thread.

DON'T forget to use suspend and resume.

Working with Multiple Threads

You've seen multiple threads used in some of the previous examples, but in each of those examples, the threads worked independently of each other. One thread drew circles, and the other drew squares. The square-drawing thread did not need to draw squares only where the circle-drawing thread had not drawn circles. Each thread went about its business in an entirely autonomous manner. This is not always the case. Usually, two or more threads need to access a common variable, stream, or system resource.

Suppose you have one thread that increments a variable and a second thread that decrements the same variable. You would think that these two threads would take turns and that the variable would retain its initial value. Unfortunately, with the PriorityDemo applet (shown in Listing 14.5), this is not the case.

14

Listing 14.5. `PriorityDemo.java.`

```
1:    import java.awt.*;
2:    import java.applet.*;
3:
4:    public class PriorityDemo extends Applet {
5:        void startButton_Clicked(java.awt.event.ActionEvent
6:                event) {
7:            CountThread upThread = new CountThread(1, results);
8:            upThread.setPriority(Thread.MIN_PRIORITY);
9:            upThread.start();
10:
11:           CountThread downThread = new CountThread(-1, results);
12:           downThread.setPriority(Thread.MAX_PRIORITY);
13:           downThread.start();
14:
15:           startButton.enable(false);        // only run once
16:       }
17:
18:       public void init() {
19:           // Call parents init method.
20:           super.init();
21:       }
22:
23:       public void addNotify() {
24:           // Call parents addNotify method.
25:           super.addNotify();
26:
27:           //{{INIT_CONTROLS
28:           setLayout(null);
29:           resize(426,266);
30:           buttonPanel = new java.awt.Panel();
31:           buttonPanel.setLayout(new FlowLayout(
32:                   FlowLayout.CENTER,5,5));
33:           buttonPanel.reshape(0,240,426,31);
34:           add(buttonPanel);
35:           startButton = new java.awt.Button("Start");
36:           startButton.reshape(192,5,42,23);
37:           buttonPanel.add(startButton);
38:           mainPanel = new java.awt.Panel();
39:           mainPanel.setLayout(null);
40:           mainPanel.reshape(0,0,426,235);
41:           add(mainPanel);
42:           results = new java.awt.TextArea();
43:           results.reshape(96,60,255,105);
44:           mainPanel.add(results);
45:           //}}
46:
47:           //{{REGISTER_LISTENERS
48:           Action lAction = new Action();
49:           startButton.addActionListener(lAction);
50:           //}}
51:       }
52:
```

14

```
53:        //{{DECLARE_CONTROLS
54:        java.awt.Panel buttonPanel;
55:        java.awt.Button startButton;
56:        java.awt.Panel mainPanel;
57:        java.awt.TextArea results;
58:        //}}
59:
60:        class Action implements java.awt.event.ActionListener {
61:            public void actionPerformed(java.awt.event.ActionEvent
62:                    event) {
63:                Object object = event.getSource();
64:                if (object == startButton)
65:                    startButton_Clicked(event);
66:            }
67:        }
68:    }
69:
70:    class CountThread extends Thread {
71:        static int value = 1000;
72:        int increment;
73:        static TextArea results;
74:        int useCount = 0;
75:
76:        CountThread(int i, TextArea ta) {
77:            if (results == null)
78:                results = ta;
79:
80:            increment = i;
81:        }
82:
83:        public  void run() {
84:            while (value > 0 && value < 2000) {
85:                value += increment;
86:                useCount++;
87:            }
88:
89:            results.appendText("Final Value = " + String.valueOf(
90:                    value)+ "\r\n");
91:            results.appendText("Done with " + String.valueOf(
92:                    increment) + ", used " + String.valueOf(useCount)
03:                    + " times\r\n");
94:        }
95:    }
```

ANALYSIS The PriorityDemo applet includes the CountThread class (lines 70–95). The CountThread constructor is passed an amount by which the static member variable value will be changed. The constructor is also passed a TextArea variable. The text area is also stored in a static member, results, if it has not already been set. As the thread runs, it can display information in results.

14

The run method of CountThread (lines 83–94) continues to loop as long as value (which is initially set to 1000) stays between 0 and 2000. For each pass through the loop, value is changed by the amount of increment. Additionally, useCount is incremented to track how many times the loop executes. When the loop terminates, information is displayed in the results text area.

When the applet's Start button is clicked, the startButton_Clicked method (lines 5–16) creates two instances of this class. The first, upThread, adds one to value. The second, downThread, subtracts one. The results of running this applet are shown in Figure 14.3.

Figure 14.3.

The results of running the PriorityDemo *applet.*

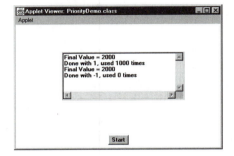

NOTE

Do not worry if you run the applets in the next few sections and they appear differently from the figures in this book. When working with multiple threads, it can be important to synchronize the threads. Thread synchronization is discussed in the section later in this chapter titled "Synchronized Threads." In that section, you will learn why the next few sample applets may sometimes look different from the figures.

As you can see in Figure 14.3, when value reached 2000, the loop terminated. Before running this applet, it would have been reasonable to assume that the threads would each run an equal number of times through the run method's loop. However, Figure 14.3 shows that the loop that adds one ran 1,000 times and the loop that subtracts one never ran at all. This happened because once upThread started and entered its loop, downThread never got a chance to take over. This problem didn't show up in previous examples because the threads in those examples used sleep periodically. When they did, a different thread assumed control.

Thread Priorities

One way to remedy this situation is by setting the priority at which each thread executes. The setPriority method can be used to do this. You can set a thread's priority anywhere between

Thread.MIN_PRIORITY and Thread.MAX_PRIORITY. By default, threads are assigned Thread.NORM_PRIORITY. The Thread class defines these to be 1, 10, and 5. What happens if the startButton_Clicked method of PriorityDemo is changed to be the following:

```
void startButton_Clicked(java.awt.event.ActionEvent event) {
    CountThread upThread = new CountThread(1, results);
    upThread.setPriority(Thread.MIN_PRIORITY);
    upThread.start();

    CountThread downThread = new CountThread(-1, results);
    downThread.setPriority(Thread.MAX_PRIORITY);
    downThread.start();

    startButton.enable(false);     // can only run once
}
```

Here, upThread is given the lowest allowable priority and downThread is given the highest. This method is included in PriorityDemo2, and the results of executing it are shown in Figure 14.4. As you can see, this didn't quite have the desired effect of upThread and downThread sharing time. Because it was given the higher priority, downThread took control and ran to completion.

Figure 14.4.

In PriorityDemo2, *the thread with the highest priority takes control.*

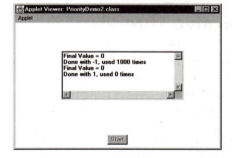

This is because Java allows the highest priority runnable thread to execute. Because downThread is never put to sleep or suspended, it remains the highest priority thread until it completes. After it completes, upThread finally gets a chance to run, but isn't allowed to do much because the condition of the run method's while loop evaluates to false. To convince yourself of this, change the CountThread run method to use a do...while loop instead of a while loop, as follows:

```
public  void run() {
    do {
        value += increment;
        useCount++;
    } while (value > 0 && value < 2000);
```

14

```
        results.appendText("Final Value = " +
            String.valueOf(value)+ "\r\n");
        results.appendText("Done with " + String.valueOf(increment) +
            ", used " + String.valueOf(useCount) + " times\r\n");
}
```

The result of running PriorityDemo2 with a do…while loop is shown in Figure 14.5. As you can see, the high priority downThread took initial control and ran 1,000 times until value equaled 0. Then upThread got its chance and ran 2,000 times.

Figure 14.5.

After the high priority thread completes, the low priority thread is allowed to run.

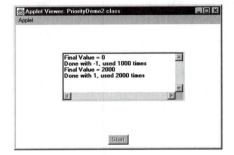

Cooperative Threads

Clearly, you could solve this problem by adding a call to sleep in the loop in the run method. However, this would cause the applet to run much more slowly than necessary. Alternatively, you can use yield. This method tells a thread to stop processing and let other threads have a chance. After other threads are sleeping, suspended, or yielding, the thread will have another chance to run. To add yield to the run method of CountThread, use the following code:

```
public  void run() {
    while (value > 0 && value < 2000 && useCount < 10000) {
        value += increment;
        useCount++;
        yield();
    }

    results.appendText("Final Value = " +
            String.valueOf(value) + "\r\n");
    results.appendText("Done with " + String.valueOf(increment) +
            ", used " + String.valueOf(useCount) + " times\r\n");
}
```

In run, you will also notice that the loop now terminates when a maximum value for useCount is reached. This is to prevent the loop from executing endlessly. The result of executing the YieldDemo sample applet, from which this version of run is taken, is shown in Figure 14.6. From this figure you can see that value was equal to 1,268 when upThread terminated. This means that downThread had run 268 times fewer than upThread by the time upThread ran 10,000 times. With upThread out of the way, downThread ran to completion and value was back where it started.

Figure 14.6.

When yield *is used, neither thread assumes complete control.*

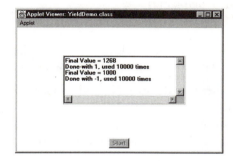

Synchronized Threads

If you've been running the applets in the previous sections, you probably noticed that they didn't always look like the screen captures in the figures. You probably saw a screen or two that looked like Figure 14.7.

Figure 14.7.

Without synchronization, two threads can each write to a text area at the same time.

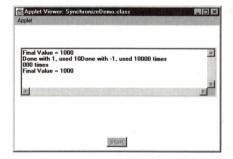

What happened here is that two threads tried to write to the text area at the same time. The first thread wrote the first line and then Done with 1, used 10 on the second line before being interrupted by the second thread. The second thread wrote the rest of the second line. The first thread then wrote the third line, and the second thread wrote the fourth line.

To rectify this, synchronize the threads. This is done using the synchronized keyword. When a program attempts to execute code that is marked as synchronized, it attempts to acquire a lock on the object and will only execute the code if the lock was acquired. In this way, you can ensure that only one thread has access to the desired object.

14

Synchronized Blocks

You can synchronize an entire method or a block of code. When you synchronize a block of code, you enclose the it as follows:

```
synchronize (object) {
    // synchronized code
}
```

This prevents the block of code from executing if any other thread has already acquired a lock on object. This could occur for two reasons:

☐ Another thread is executing this same block of code and has already acquired the lock

☐ Another thread is executing an entirely different block of code (or an entire method) that is locked on the same object.

To solve the problem illustrated in Figure 14.7, you can synchronize on the block that writes to the text area. This could be done with the run method shown in Listing 14.6.

Listing 14.6. The run method using a synchronized block in
SynchronizeDemo.java.

```
1:    public void run() {
2:        while (value>0 && value<2000 && useCount < 10000) {
3:            value += increment;
4:            useCount++;
5:            yield();
6:        }
7:        synchronized (this) {
8:            results.appendText("Final Value = " +
9:                    String.valueOf(value)+ "\r\n");
10:           results.appendText("Done with " +
11:                   String.valueOf(increment) + ", used " +
12:                   String.valueOf(useCount) + " times\r\n");
13:       }
14:   }
```

ANALYSIS In this case, lines 7–13 are synchronized on the current object (this in line 7). This prevents any other thread from acquiring a lock on this object and entering this block of code. However, there is nothing preventing a different class from writing to the results text area without acquiring a lock. Because of this, a better solution would be to synchronize on results, as follows:

```
synchronized (this) {
    results.appendText("Final Value = " +
            String.valueOf(value)+ "\r\n");
```

```
results.appendText("Done with " +
        String.valueOf(increment) + ", used " +
        String.valueOf(useCount) + " times\r\n");
}
```

Synchronized Methods

Sometimes you need to mark an entire method as synchronized. This can be done using synchronized in the method declaration, as shown in the declaration of showResults in Listing 14.7.

Listing 14.7. The `run` method calls the synchronized method `showResults`.

```
 1:    public void run() {
 2:        while (value > 0 && value<2000 && useCount < 10000) {
 3:            value += increment;
 4:            useCount++;
 5:            yield();
 6:        }
 7:        showResults();
 8:    }
 9:
10:    synchronized void showResults() {
11:        results.appendText("Final Value = " +
12:                String.valueOf(value)+ "\r\n");
13:        results.appendText("Done with " +
14:                String.valueOf(increment) + ", used " +
15:                String.valueOf(useCount) + " times\r\n");
16:    }
```

ANALYSIS The only difference between Listings 14.7 and 14.6 is that the showResults method has been created from the code that was contained within the synchronized block of Listing 14.6. When a method is synchronized, it locks on the object of which it is a member. This means that Listings 14.6 and 14.7 are equivalent and that there is no way for showResults to synchronize on the results object.

Do	Don't
DO declare methods and code blocks as synchronized whenever multiple threads may access the same resource, including the user interface (as you saw in Figure 14.7).	

DO set the priority of threads to control how often each will execute.

DON'T sleep in the subway, darling.

DO use yield to break up large processing blocks and allow other threads an opportunity to run.

14

The Runnable Interface

What do you do if you need to create a thread out of an existing class? Because Thread is a class without multiple inheritance, you cannot derive a new class from Thread and a second class, such as Applet. Fortunately, Java includes an interface, Runnable, that is intended to solve precisely this problem.

To implement the Runnable interface, simply override the run method. This can be seen in Listing 14.8, which shows the code for the RunnableDemo sample applet.

Listing 14.8. RunnableDemo.java.

```
 1:    import java.awt.*;
 2:    import java.applet.*;
 3:
 4:    public class RunnableDemo extends Applet implements Runnable{
 5:
 6:        public void init() {
 7:            // Call parents init method.
 8:            super.init();
 9:        }
10:
11:        public void run() {
12:            for(int i=0; i< 10; i++)
13:                results.appendText(String.valueOf(i));
14:        }
15:
16:        public void start() {
17:            mainThread = new Thread(this);
18:            mainThread.start();
19:        }
20:
21:        public void addNotify() {
22:            // Call parents addNotify method.
23:            super.addNotify();
24:
25:            //{{INIT_CONTROLS
26:            setLayout(null);
27:            resize(426,204);
28:            buttonPanel = new java.awt.Panel();
29:            buttonPanel.setLayout(new FlowLayout(
30:                    FlowLayout.CENTER,5,5));
31:            buttonPanel.reshape(0,240,426,31);
32:            add(buttonPanel);
33:            startButton = new java.awt.Button("Start");
34:            startButton.reshape(192,5,42,23);
35:            buttonPanel.add(startButton);
36:            mainPanel = new java.awt.Panel();
37:            mainPanel.setLayout(null);
38:            mainPanel.reshape(0,0,426,235);
39:            add(mainPanel);
```

```
40:          results = new java.awt.TextArea();
41:          results.reshape(84,60,254,107);
42:          mainPanel.add(results);
43:          //}}
44:      }
45:
46:      Thread mainThread;
47:
48:      //{{DECLARE_CONTROLS
49:      java.awt.Panel buttonPanel;
50:      java.awt.Button startButton;
51:      java.awt.Panel mainPanel;
52:      java.awt.TextArea results;
53:      //}}
54:  }
```

ANALYSIS   The RunnableDemo class extends Applet and implements Runnable (line 4). It includes an overridden run method (lines 11–14) that writes the values zero through nine to a text area. This can be seen in Figure 14.8. To get things rolling, the applet's start method (lines 16–19) constructs a new thread, mainThread, and starts it.

Figure 14.8.

The Runnable
interface provides
thread support as well.

Summary

In this chapter, you learned about threads and writing multithreaded programs. You learned about the Thread class and the Runnable interface. You learned how to suspend and resume threads and how to work with thread groups. You saw examples of simple threads that can run autonomously and examples of threads that need to cooperate with other threads. For creating cooperative threads, this chapter described how to set the priority of a thread and how to have a thread temporarily yield control. You also learned about the synchronized keyword and how to use it to lock a method or block of code from being interrupted by another thread.

14

Q&A

Q **I declared a new subclass of `Thread` and have constructed an instance of it, but it doesn't run. What's wrong?**

A Either your computer is turned off or you forgot to call `start`. Even though you constructed a new thread, it will not run until you call `start`.

Q **I've heard about daemon threads. What are they and does Java support them?**

A Daemon threads are worker threads that exist to help other threads. The Java garbage collector is a perfect example of a daemon thread. It serves no useful purpose on its own, but does serve the purpose of cleaning up after other threads. When a program consists entirely of daemon threads, it stops running. The Java `Thread` class does support daemon threads. You can mark a thread as a daemon with `setDaemon(boolean)`. Additionally, `getDaemon` can be used to determine whether a thread is a daemon.

Q **Is there any limit to the number of threads a program can use?**

A Not really. Java will let you create as many threads as you want. However, there is a practical limit that will be influenced by the speed of the user's machine, the user's operating system (different operating systems implement threads differently), and the complexity of the threads you create. The only way to effectively determine the practical limit is by experimentation. Most programs err on the side of too few threads because most programmers are inexperienced with them.

Workshop

The workshop includes quiz questions to help you gauge your understanding of the material in this chapter. The workshop also includes exercises to provide hands-on experience with what you've learned in this chapter. Answers to the quiz questions can be found in Appendix D, "Answers."

Quiz

1. In what two ways can you add threading support to a new class?
2. What must you do before a new thread instance will run?
3. What is the difference between `yield`, `sleep`, and `suspend`?
4. What values are assigned to `Thread.MIN_PRIORITY`, `Thread.NORM_PRIORITY`, and `Thread.MAX_PRIORITY`?
5. When `synchronized` is used to synchronize a block of code, why is an object reference enclosed in parentheses as is the case with `synchronized(myObj)`?

14

6. Why is no object reference specified when synchronizing an entire method?

7. What is the only method that must be overriden for a class to implement the `Runnable` interface?

Exercises

1. Write an applet similar to `SuspendDemo` but allow the user to set the priority of the threads to high or low.

2. Write an applet similar to `SimpleThreadDemo` but implement the `Runnable` interface instead of creating a subclass of `Thread`.

3. Write an applet that simulates water flowing into a storage tank. Water can be let out through one valve or added by three valves. Automatically shut off the inflow valves when the tank is full.

14

In Review

On Day 8, "Using the Object Library," you learned about some of the components in the Visual Café Object Library. You learned how to improve your Java programs with the WrappingLabel, Label3d, TreeView, slider, InvisibleButton, HTML link, StatusBar, ProgressBar, Timer, Calendar, ComboBox, and formatted text field components.

On Day 9, "More Object Library Components," you continued your exploration of the Visual Café Object Library. You learned how to use the MultiList component to create grid-like lists. You saw how LabelButton offers a more powerful alternative to the AWT Button class and how ImageListBox allows you to mix images and text within the same list. You learned about the DirectionButton and Spinner components and how they simplify item selection. Finally, you saw how StateCheckBox improves the AWT checkbox by including a default state.

On Day 10, "Windows, Frames, and Dialogs," you learned about windows, frames, and dialogs. You learned that windows are of limited practical use because they do not include borders or a title bar. You learned how to create standalone frames and how to manipulate a frame at runtime by changing its title and cursor. You learned about the `Dialog` class and how it can be created in both modal and modeless forms. Finally, you learned about the canned dialogs that are included with Visual Café to simplify program development.

On Day 11, "Menus and Toolbars," you learned about Java's menu classes: `MenuBar`, `Menu`, `MenuItem`, and `CheckboxMenuItem`. You learned how to combine these to create menus and submenus that can be attached to a frame. You learned how to use the Menu editor to allow you to visually create a menu. You stepped through a detailed example that used the Menu editor to create a menu that included multiple menus, menu items, checkbox menu items, separators, and submenus. Finally, you learned about the `ToolBarPanel` and `ToolBarSpacer` classes. You learned how to combine these classes with `ImageButton` to create a functional toolbar without writing a single line of code.

Day 12, "The Java Utility Classes," gave you a thorough overview of the classes in the `java.util` package. You learned how to use the `BitSet` class to store large amounts of Boolean data, how to manipulate dates and times with the `Date` class, how to generate random numbers, and how to tokenize strings. You learned how the `Observable` class works in conjunction with the `Observer` interface to allow you to decouple your code. The `Hashtable` class was described, and you learned how the `Properties` class can be used in applications to stream data to and from files. Finally, you learned how the `Vector` class can be used as a resizable array and how the `Stack` class extends `Vector`.

On Day 13, "Using Streams for Input and Output," you learned quite a bit about Java streams. You learned how the abstract classes `InputStream` and `OutputStream` sit at the top of the byte stream hierarchy. You also learned that there are character stream equivalents, `Reader` and `Writer`. You worked through many examples of using streams to write to and read from files. You learned how streams can be chained together to create streams that offer the combined features of more than one stream class. You learned how to use the `ObjectInputStream` and `ObjectOutputStream` classes to create object streams. Finally, you learned about the `Serializable` interface and how you can use it to make your own classes streamable.

On Day 14, "Multithreading," you learned about threads and writing multithreaded programs. You learned about the `Thread` class and the `Runnable` interface. You learned how to suspend and resume threads and how to work with thread groups. You saw examples of simple threads that can run autonomously and examples of threads that need to cooperate with other threads. For creating cooperative threads, this chapter described how to set the priority of a thread and how to have a thread temporarily yield control. You also learned about the `synchronized` keyword and how to use it to lock a method or block of code from being interrupted by another thread.

WEEK 3

15
16
17
18
19
20
21

At A Glance

During your final week you will encounter a variety of more advanced Java and Visual Café topics, including client/server programming with sockets, graphics, multimedia, Java Beans, native methods, and database access.

On Day 15, "Client/Server Programming with Sockets," you will learn how to use sockets to write client/server programs. Much of this day builds on the knowledge you gained in the two previous days about streams and multithreading. You will first learn how to write a single-threaded server that can respond to requests from a generic client application. In doing so you will learn how to use streams to easily exchange messages with a client. Building on this experience, you will see how to create a multithreaded server and then how to write a client applet that can communicate with your server. The remainder of the day includes a detailed example of how to design and write a client and server that communicate through prolonged conversations.

On Day 16, "Working with Graphics," you will learn how to augment the appearance of your Java programs by using graphics. You will learn how to use the AWT `Graphics` class to draw lines and geometric shapes such as arcs, ovals, rectangles, and polygons. You will see how to use the `Canvas` class to control the placement of these shapes. Visual Café provides its own set of classes for drawing shapes, and you will learn how to use these visual components. You will also learn how to display and manipulate images. You will learn about Java's classes for filtering, cropping, and modifying images. You will also learn about the `ImageObserver` interface, which allows an applet to monitor the progress of an image that is being retrieved for display.

On Day 17, "Multimedia Programming," you will learn how Visual Café simplifies multimedia programming through some of the components in its Object Library. You will learn how to use the `SlideShow` component to display a series of images and how to create animations with `Animator` and `MovingAnimation`. You will also learn about the `Firework`, `Plasma`, and `NervousText` components. Although you will probably use these components less frequently than `SlideShow`, `Animator`, and `MovingAnimation`, they are appropriate for some programs. You will also learn how to add sound to your programs with the `SoundPlayer` component. Finally, you will learn about the `MediaTracker` class, which will be useful if you wish to program your own multimedia classes.

On Day 18, "Java Beans," you will learn about the Java Beans approach to reusable software components. You will learn how to create your own Beans components and how to add them directly into the Visual Café environment.

On Day 19, "Adding Native Methods," you will learn how to augment Java by writing methods in other languages, especially C and C++. Occasionally you must write a Java application that uses existing legacy code in another language. The techniques you learn today make this possible. In the parlance of Java, when a method is written in a different language it is known as a *native method*. The Java Native Interface is a set of functions that allows you to write native methods that become part of your Java classes.

On Day 20, "The Visual Café Database Tools," you will learn about the following database tools that are provided with the Database Development Edition of Visual Café for database programming:

- ☐ The dbNAVIGATOR
- ☐ The dbAware project wizard
- ☐ The dbAware template wizard
- ☐ The Add Table wizard
- ☐ The dbANYWHERE workgroup server
- ☐ Sybase's SQL Anywhere database

On Day 21, "Using the dbAWARE Components," you will learn how to write code to take advantage of the database capabilities inherent in Visual Café Pro. You will first see how to work with a dbANYWHERE data source by writing code. After you master that, you will see how Visual Café streamlines the process by including visual, database-aware components in the Component Library.

Day 15

Client/Server Programming with Sockets

Today you will learn how to use sockets to write client/server programs. Much of this day builds on the knowledge you gained in the two previous days about streams and multithreading. You will first learn how to write a single-threaded server that can respond to requests from a generic client application. In doing so you will learn how to use streams to easily exchange messages with a client.

Building on this experience, you will see how to create a multithreaded server and then how to write a client applet that can communicate with your server. The remainder of the day includes a detailed example of how to design and write a client and server that communicate through prolonged conversations.

Overview of Client/Server Architecture

The term *client/server* has become one of the buzzwords of the 1990s, and before you spend an entire day on the subject, exactly what "client/server" means needs to be defined. Naturally, a client/server application consists of two parts—a client and a server. Client applications submit requests to servers, and servers fulfill client requests and usually return data in response.

A typical client/server environment is shown in Figure 15.1, which illustrates three client machines connected to a single server. In this environment, each of the three client machines submits requests that are serviced by the single server. The server, typically because it is running an operating system such as UNIX or Windows NT, can easily respond to concurrent requests from more than one client. After the server has performed the requested function, it responds to the client. Depending on what the server was asked to do, it might respond with an answer or simply with a response that indicates that an operation was successful.

Figure 15.1.

Three clients connected to one server.

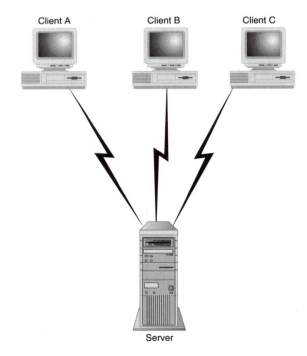

Although common, it is not necessary for the client and server to be on different machines. Figure 15.2 shows a local client/server architecture. In this figure, the client and server are the same machine. Even though the client and server both reside on the same computer, they will usually be separate programs.

Figure 15.2.
A local client/server architecture.

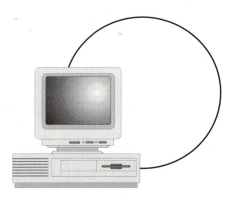

   TIP

A local server can be an ideal application development environment. This allows you to develop and test your client and server programs on a single computer. You then move them to separate computers for more complete testing after the initial development is complete.

Of course, nothing limits a client from submitting requests to multiple servers. Just as a server can fulfill requests from many clients, a client can submit requests to many servers. Figure 15.3 illustrates this by showing four clients and two servers. Clients A and B access both servers, but client C accesses only server 2, and client D accesses only server 1.

A Single-Threaded Server

In this section you will see how to use Java's socket classes to write the server side of a client/server system. To do this you will use the Socket and ServerSocket classes.

The first thing a socket-based server must know how to do is listen for client requests to connect. This is handled very simply by ServerSocket. To create a new ServerSocket, pass the constructor the port number on which to base the socket. For example, to use port 2000, you would do the following:

```
ServerSocket server = new ServerSocket(2000);
```

After the socket has been created, your program needs to listen for client requests to connect through the socket. This is done with the accept method. This method listens through the server socket and blocks until it receives a connection request. After a request is received, accept returns a Socket object, which can be used to communicate over the socket. For example, the following illustrates how to wait for a connection through port 2000:

```
ServerSocket server = new ServerSocket(2000);
Socket inSocket = server.accept();
```

Figure 15.3.

A two-server architecture.

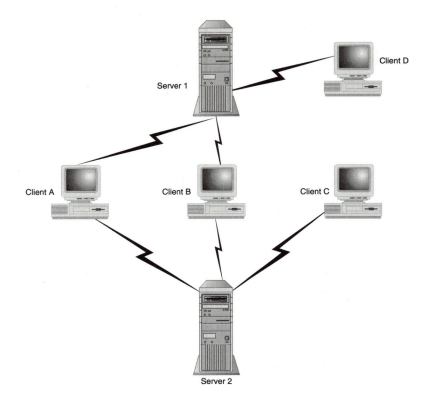

After a socket has been created, you can create both input and output streams from it and then communicate through these streams. The methods getInputStream and getOutputStream return objects of type InputStream and OutputStream, respectively. These methods can be used to create communication streams between a client and a server, as follows:

```
BufferedReader inStream = new BufferedReader(
        new InputStreamReader(
        inSocket.getInputStream()));
PrintWriter outStream = new PrintWriter(
        inSocket.getOutputStream(), true);
```

From here, the server can send messages to a client through the print writer, as follows:

```
outStream.println("Welcome to my server!");
```

And the server can read messages sent to it from a client through the BufferedReader, as follows:

```
String str = inStream.readLine();
```

A Sample Server

Suppose you want to write a server to which users can connect to look up information about different programming languages. After connecting to the server, users can enter the name of a language, and the server responds with information about that language. The user interface of such a server can be seen in Figure 15.4.

Figure 15.4.

The minimal user interface of the Internet Language Dictionary.

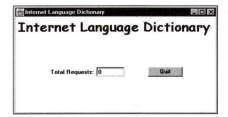

As you can tell from Figure 15.4, the user interface of a server can be very minimal. After all, even though users are connected to a server, they do not see the server's user interface. In fact, it is possible to write a server that has no user interface whatsoever. (For an example, see the exercises at the end of this chapter.)

The class `LanguageDictionary`, shown in Listing 15.1, creates the Internet Language Dictionary that is shown in Figure 15.4.

Listing 15.1. `LanguageDictionary.java`.

```
 1:    import java.awt.*;
 2:    import java.net.*;
 3:    import java.io.*;
 4:
 5:    public class LanguageDictionary extends Frame {
 6:        public static void main(String[] args) {
 7:            LanguageDictionary dict = new LanguageDictionary();
 8:            dict.ProcessRequests();
 9:        }
10:
11:        void quitButton_Clicked(java.awt.event.ActionEvent event){
12:            System.exit(0);
13:        }
14:
15:        void WindowClosing(java.awt.event.WindowEvent event) {
16:            hide();          // hide the Frame
17:        }
18:
19:        public LanguageDictionary() {
20:
21:        }
22:
```

continues

Listing 15.1. continued

```
23:     public LanguageDictionary(String title) {
24:         this();
25:         setTitle(title);
26:     }
27:
28:     void ProcessRequests() {
29:         show();
30:
31:         try {
32:             ServerSocket server = new ServerSocket(2000);
33:             Socket inSocket = server.accept();
34:             BufferedReader inStream = new BufferedReader(
35:                     new InputStreamReader(
36:                         inSocket.getInputStream())));
37:             PrintWriter outStream = new PrintWriter(
38:                     inSocket.getOutputStream(), true);
39:
40:             outStream.println(
41:                     "Welcome to the Language Dictionary");
42:
43:             boolean more = true;
44:             do {
45:                 String str = inStream.readLine();
46:                 if (str == null)
47:                     more = false;
48:                 else {
49:                     totalRequests++;
50:
51:                     String trimStr = str.trim().toUpperCase();
52:                     if (trimStr.equals("QUIT")) {
53:                         outStream.println(
54:                                 "Y'all come back now...");
55:                         more = false;
56:                     }
57:                     else if (trimStr.equals("C++"))
58:                         outStream.println(
59:                                 "My former favorite language");
60:                     else if (trimStr.equals("JAVA"))
61:                         outStream.println("My favorite language");
62:                     else if (trimStr.equals("COBOL"))
63:                         outStream.println("Eek!");
64:                     else
65:                         outStream.println("Are you sure " + str +
66:                                 " is a language?");
67:
68:                     totalRequestsField.setText(
69:                             String.valueOf(totalRequests));
70:
71:                 }
72:             } while (more);
73:             inSocket.close();
74:         }
75:         catch (Exception e) {
76:             System.out.println;
```

```
77:          }
78:      }
79:
80:      public synchronized void show() {
81:          move(50, 50);
82:          super.show();
83:      }
84:
85:       public void addNotify() {
86:
87:          // Call parents addNotify method.
88:          super.addNotify();
89:
90:          //{{INIT_CONTROLS
91:          setLayout(null);
92:          resize(insets().left + insets().right + 509,
93:                  insets().top + insets().bottom + 271);
94:          imageViewer1 = new
95:                  symantec.itools.multimedia.ImageViewer();
96:          imageViewer1.reshape(insets().left + 0,
97:                  insets().top + 0,509,52);
98:          add(imageViewer1);
99:          try {
100:             imageViewer1.setURL(new java.net.URL(
101:      "file:/C:/source/CHAP15/LanguageDictionary/logo.JPG"));
102:         }
103:         catch (java.net.MalformedURLException error) { }
104:         catch (java.beans.PropertyVetoException veto) { }
105:         panel1 = new java.awt.Panel();
106:         panel1.setLayout(null);
107:         panel1.reshape(insets().left + 0,insets().top + 48,
108:             509,200);
109:         add(panel1);
110:         label1 = new java.awt.Label("Total Requests:");
111:         label1.reshape(60,60,105,21);
112:         panel1.add(label1);
113:         totalRequestsField = new java.awt.TextField();
114:         totalRequestsField.setText("0");
115:         totalRequestsField.reshape(168,60,60,21);
116:         panel1.add(totalRequestsField);
117:         quitButton = new java.awt.Button("Quit");
118:         quitButton.reshape(276,60,72,21);
119:         panel1.add(quitButton);
120:         setTitle("Internet Language Dictionary");
121:         //}}
122:
123:         //{{INIT_MENUS
124:         //}}
125:
126:         //{{REGISTER_LISTENERS
127:         Window lWindow = new Window();
128:         addWindowListener(lWindow);
129:         Action lAction = new Action();
130:         quitButton.addActionListener(lAction);
131:         //}}
132:      }
```

continues

Listing 15.1. continued

```
133:
134:    int totalRequests = 0;
135:
136:    //{{DECLARE_CONTROLS
137:    symantec.itools.multimedia.ImageViewer imageViewer1;
138:    java.awt.Panel panel1;
139:    java.awt.Label label1;
140:    java.awt.TextField totalRequestsField;
141:    java.awt.Button quitButton;
142:    //}}
143:
144:    //{{DECLARE_MENUS
145:    //}}
146:
147:    class Window extends java.awt.event.WindowAdapter {
148:        public void windowClosing(java.awt.event.WindowEvent
149:            event) {
150:            Object object = event.getSource();
151:            if (object == LanguageDictionary.this)
152:                WindowClosing(event);
153:        }
154:    }
155:
156:    class Action implements java.awt.event.ActionListener {
157:        public void actionPerformed(java.awt.event.ActionEvent
158:            event) {
159:            Object object = event.getSource();
160:            if (object == quitButton)
161:                quitButton_Clicked(event);
162:        }
163:    }
164: }
```

ANALYSIS From Listing 15.1, you can see that LanguageDictionary is an application, not an applet. The main method (lines 6–9) creates a new LanguageDictionary object. Because LanguageDictionary extends Frame (line 5), it is allowed to display the normal user interface components. The user interface is created by the code generated by Visual Café in addNotify (lines 85–132).

After main constructs a new instance of LanguageDictionary, it calls that object's ProcessRequests method (lines 28–78). ProcessRequests begins by using show to display the frame (line 29). Then a new ServerSocket is created on port 2000 (line 32). Line 33 uses accept to wait for a client to attempt to connect to the server. This method will block until a client attempts to connect.

After a client has connected, a BufferedReader (inStream) and a PrintWriter (outStream) are constructed (lines 34–38). These streams will be used to communicate with the client. The first example of communication with the client occurs on lines 40–41, where outStream.println is used to welcome the new client.

After the client has been welcomed, a lengthy do…while loop is entered (lines 44–71). This loop will continue to execute until the client sends the string QUIT to the server. First, a string is read from the client (line 45). If the string is null, more is set to false, causing the loop to end.

If the string is not null, the number of total requests is incremented (line 49) and a trimmed, uppercase version of the string is stored (line 51). This version of the string is then compared to a variety of predefined strings (QUIT, C++, JAVA, and COBOL). If the string matches QUIT, a good-bye message is streamed back to the client. If the string matches the language names, a very brief comment on the language is streamed back to the client. If the string does not match anything, a message is streamed back to the client asking whether he is sure it is a language. At the end of the do…while loop, the onscreen text field is updated to show the correct number of total requests (lines 68–69). After the loop exits, the socket is closed (line 73) and communication with the client ceases.

Testing the Server

Of course, to test your new server, you need a client. Fortunately, a generic client, Telnet, is available on just about every computer. Before starting Telnet, go ahead and start the LanguageDictionary application. Now start Telnet. If you are using Windows 95 or Windows NT, you can run Telnet by typing telnet on the Start | Run menu. After starting Telnet, connect to a server by selecting Remote System from the Connect menu. This will display the Connect dialog shown in Figure 15.5.

Figure 15.5.

The Connect dialog of the Windows 95 version of Telnet.

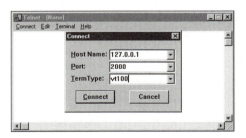

In the Connect dialog, enter the name of the host running the LanguageDictionary application and the port on which it is running. The terminal type will default to vt100 and can be left alone. If you want to run LanguageDictionary and Telnet on the same computer, you can specify 127.0.0.1 as the hostname. This is a special loopback value that instructs Telnet to use the local machine as the host. Because LanguageDictionary will look for requests coming on port 2000, make certain you instruct Telnet to also use port 2000.

If you've entered everything correctly, your Telnet client will at this point connect to your language dictionary server. If connected, the Telnet window should include the message Welcome to the Language Dictionary. From Telnet, you can now enter the name of various languages. Press Enter after entering the name of a language, and that name will be sent to the server. The server will respond with a comment about the language. To quit the language dictionary, enter quit instead of entering a language. A sample session with the language dictionary is shown in Figure 15.6.

Figure 15.6.

A sample session using the language dictionary.

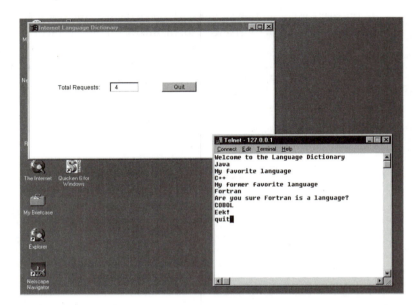

NOTE

If Telnet is not echoing your commands to the screen, make certain that Local Echo is selected on the screen displayed when Terminal | Preferences is selected.

A Multithreaded Server

If you attempted to connect to the Internet language dictionary server more than once without shutting down the server between attempts, you might have noticed that the server did not respond to connections after the first. This problem is solved by using multiple threads and is the topic of this section. Listing 15.2 shows the main and ProcessRequests methods from the class MultiThreadedDictionary.

Listing 15.2. Selected methods from MultiThreadedDictionary.java.

```
1:     public class MultiThreadedDictionary extends Frame {
2:         public static void main(String[] args) {
```

```
 3:                    MultiThreadedDictionary dict = new
 4:                            MultiThreadedDictionary();
 5:                    dict.ProcessRequests();
 6:            }
 7:
 8:        void ProcessRequests() {
 9:            show();
10:
11:            try {
12:                ServerSocket socket = new ServerSocket(2000);
13:
14:                for(;;) {
15:                    Socket incoming = socket.accept();
16:
17:                    status.appendText("New logon at " +
18:                            (new Date()).toString() + "\r\n");
19:                    new DictionaryThread(incoming).start();
20:                }
21:            }
22:            catch (Exception e) {
23:                status.appendText(e.toString() + "\r\n");
24:            }
25:        }
26:
27:        // other methods not shown
28:
29:    }
```

ANALYSIS   Similar to the LanguageDictionary application's main method, the main method of Listing 15.2 creates a new instance of the class and calls ProcessRequests (lines 2–6). ProcessRequests displays the frame (line 9)and then creates a new server socket based on port 2000 (line 12). Next, an infinite loop (line 14–20) waits for incoming requests. Requests are accepted and result in the creation of a new Socket (line 15). The time of the new logon is written to a text area named status (line 17–18). On line 19, a new DictionaryThread object is constructed by passing it the socket. This thread is then started.

Because this needs to be a multithreaded application, DictionaryThread extends Thread. The DictionaryThread class is shown in Listing 15.3.

Listing 15.3. DictionaryThread.java.

```
 1:    import java.net.*;
 2:    import java.io.*;
 3:
 4:    public class DictionaryThread extends Thread {
 5:        private Socket inSocket;
 6:
 7:        public DictionaryThread(Socket s) {
 8:            inSocket = s;
 9:        }
10:
```

continues

Listing 15.3. continued

```
11:     public void run() {
12:         try {
13:             BufferedReader inStream = new BufferedReader(
14:                 new InputStreamReader(
15:                 inSocket.getInputStream()));
16:             PrintWriter outStream = new PrintWriter(
17:                 inSocket.getOutputStream(), true);
18:
19:             outStream.println(
20:               "Welcome to the Multithreaded Dictionary");
21:
22:             boolean more = true;
23:             do {
24:                 String str = inStream.readLine();
25:                 if (str == null)
26:                     more = false;
27:                 else {
28:                     String trimStr = str.trim().toUpperCase();
29:                     if (trimStr.equals("QUIT")) {
30:                         outStream.println(
31:                             "Y'all come back now...");
32:                         more = false;
33:                     }
34:                     else if (trimStr.equals("C++"))
35:                         outStream.println(
36:                             "My former favorite language");
37:                     else if (trimStr.equals("JAVA"))
38:                         outStream.println(
39:                             "My favorite language");
40:                     else if (trimStr.equals("COBOL"))
41:                         outStream.println("Eek!");
42:                     else
43:                         outStream.println("Are you sure " + str
44:                             + " is a language?");
45:                 }
46:             } while (more);
47:             inSocket.close();
48:         }
49:         catch (Exception e) {
50:             System.out.println(e);
51:         }
52:     }
53: }
```

ANALYSIS DictionaryThread includes only two member methods: a constructor (lines 7–9) and run (lines 11–52). The constructor simply stores the socket it is passed. The run method should appear similar to the bulk of the ProcessRequests method of LanguageDictionary in Listing 15.1. Input and output streams are created, a welcome message is displayed, a loop reads input and compares to it a set of known languages or QUIT, and the socket is closed.

Although the run method of DictionaryThread is similar to ProcessRequests of LanguageDictionary, an application that uses DictionaryThread will be able to work with more than one client at a time because DictionaryThread extends Thread. This can be seen in Figure 15.7, which illustrates the simultaneous use of the multithreaded dictionary by two client copies of Telnet.

Figure 15.7.

The multithreaded dictionary can work with more than one concurrent client.

Writing the Client

Unfortunately, you can't always use Telnet as your client. Now that you know how to write a multithreaded server, let's take a look at what is involved in writing a client applet that is tailored for use with that server. This client will replace the generic Telnet client. The client applet you will write in this section is shown in Figure 15.8.

The basic premise of the applet shown in Figure 15.8 is that the user connects to the dictionary server by clicking the Connect button. When connected, the user can enter the name of a language and click the Submit button. Information about the language will be returned in the Answer field. Information about the status of the applet or connection can be displayed in the Status field.

Writing a client is not all that different from writing a server: The client connects to the server through a socket and then uses input and output streams to communicate with the server. This can be seen in Listing 15.4.

Figure 15.8.

A client that has been written specifically for use with the language dictionary.

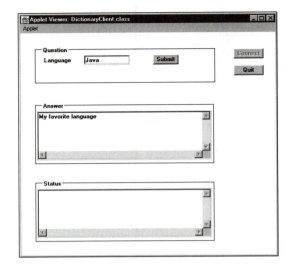

Listing 15.4. `DictionaryClient.java.`

```
1:    import java.awt.*;
2:    import java.applet.*;
3:    import java.io.*;
4:    import java.net.*;
5:
6:    public class DictionaryClient extends Applet {
7:        void submitButton_Clicked(java.awt.event.ActionEvent
8:              event) {
9:            outStream.println(languageField.getText());
10:
11:           String line;
12:           try {
13:               line = inStream.readLine();
14:               answer.setText(line);
15:           }
16:           catch (IOException e) {
17:               status.appendText(e.toString() + "\r\n");
18:           }
19:       }
20:
21:       void quitButton_Clicked(java.awt.event.ActionEvent event){
22:           outStream.println("QUIT");
23:           System.exit(0);
24:       }
25:
26:       void connectButton_Clicked(java.awt.event.ActionEvent
27:             event) {
28:           try {
29:               socket = new Socket(getCodeBase().getHost(), PORT);
30:               inStream  = new BufferedReader(
```

15

```
31:                    new InputStreamReader(socket.getInputStream()));
32:                outStream=new PrintWriter(socket.getOutputStream(),
33:                    true);
34:                connectButton.enable(false);
35:                submitButton.enable(true);
36:
37:                // read the welcome message from the server
38:                String line = inStream.readLine();
39:                answer.appendText(line);
40:            }
41:        catch (IOException e) {
42:            status.appendText("Error connecting\r\n");
43:        }
44:    }
45:
46:    public void init() {
47:        // Call parents init method.
48:        super.init();
49:    }
50:
51:    public void addNotify() {
52:        // method generated by Visual Café and not shown here
53:    }
54:
55:    public static final int PORT = 2000;
56:    Socket socket;
57:    BufferedReader inStream;
58:    PrintWriter outStream;
59:
60:    //{{DECLARE_CONTROLS
61:    symantec.itools.awt.BorderPanel borderPanel1;
62:    java.awt.TextArea answer;
63:    symantec.itools.awt.BorderPanel borderPanel3;
64:    java.awt.TextArea status;
65:    symantec.itools.awt.BorderPanel borderPanel2;
66:    java.awt.Button submitButton;
67:    java.awt.TextField languageField;
68:    java.awt.Label label1;
69:    java.awt.Button connectButton;
70:    java.awt.Button quitButton;
71:    //}}
72:
73:    class Action implements java.awt.event.ActionListener {
74:        public void actionPerformed(java.awt.event.ActionEvent
75:            event) {
76:            Object object = event.getSource();
77:            if (object == connectButton)
78:                connectButton_Clicked(event);
79:            else if (object == quitButton)
80:                quitButton_Clicked(event);
81:            else if (object == submitButton)
82:                submitButton_Clicked(event);
83:        }
84:    }
85: }
```

ANALYSIS   When the Connect button is clicked, the `connectButton_Clicked` method (lines 26–44) will execute. This method creates a new socket on port 2000 and then creates input and output streams for the new socket. Once connected to a server, the Connect button is disabled (line 34) and the Submit button is enabled (line 35).

The user sends requests to the server by clicking the Submit button, which is handled by the method `submitButton_Clicked` (lines 7–19). This method streams out the current contents of the `languageField` text field (line 9). It then uses `inStream.readLine` to retrieve a response from the server (line 13). The response is then placed in the `answer` text area with `setText` (line 14).

Your clients should always tell their servers when they are disconnecting. In the `DictionaryClient` applet, this is done when the Quit button is clicked and `QUIT` is streamed out to the server (line 22). When the server receives this message, it knows that the client has disconnected and can execute any necessary server-side code.

Conversational Client/Server Systems

So far, the sample client and server programs discussed today have all involved relatively simple interactions between the client and the server. Transactions have been limited to request/response pairs: A client makes a request, the server responds. Not all client/server applications are this simple. This section builds on the prior discussion of client/server Java programming with a conversational client/server system.

A conversational client/server system is one in which the client and server carry on a more substantial interaction than request and response. In particular, you will see how to write a client/server system for playing Tic Tac Toe. The system will include a server application and a client applet. Two users running the applet can connect to the server and play a game across the Internet. An example of this is shown in Figure 15.9.

Design

In designing this type of client/server system, one of the first things you should do is determine the messages that can be sent between the clients and the server. For each message you must also determine the syntax of the message. For example, you know that a client will need to send a message to the server indicating where the player wishes to make his next move. This can be handled by sending a message in the format `PLAY[X¦O][0-2][0-2]`. The `[X¦O]` represents the shape being played; the first digit represents the row; the second digit represents the column. So `PLAYX01` indicates that X is playing in the top row's middle column.

Another decision that must be made is whether the client or server will be responsible for detecting conditions such as invalid moves, playing out of turn, won games, and drawn games. In this case the decision was made to have the Tic Tac Toe server be responsible for detecting these special conditions. The server can then notify the clients as necessary.

Figure 15.9.

Two clients playing Tic Tac Toe while connected to a server.

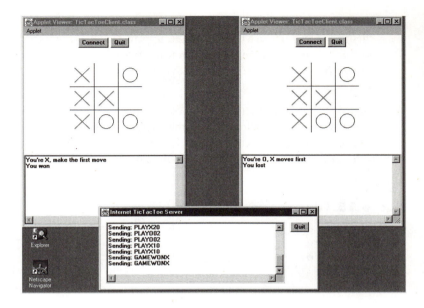

The messages that can be sent from client to server and from server to client are shown in Tables 15.1 and 15.2, respectively.

Table 15.1. Messages sent to the server.

Message	Description
DISCONNECT	Indicates that the client is disconnecting.
PLAY[X¦O][row][column]	Indicates a play by the specified shape in the specified row and column.

Table 15.2. Messages sent to the clients.

Message	Description
GAMEDRAWN	Indicates that the game is a draw.
GAMEWON[X¦O]	Indicates that the game has been won by the player with the specified shape.
PLAY[X¦O][row][column]	Indicates a play by the specified shape in the specified row and column.
SIDE[X¦O]	Indicates whether the client will be playing as X or O.
START	Indicates that two players have connected and the server is ready for X to make the initial play.

In addition to these formal messages, the server can also send informative messages to the clients. For example, if a client attempts to play when it is not its turn, the server will respond with It's not your turn. The best way to understand how the clients use these messages to interact is by drawing an event trace for one or more games. Figure 15.10 shows an event trace for a typical game.

Figure 15.10 illustrates two clients connecting to a server. When a client connects to the server, it does not need to send a formal message to the server; the connection itself serves as notification that a new client exists. The server responds by sending SIDEX to the first client to connect and SIDEO to the second client. The clients will use these messages to know which shape each is drawing.

Figure 15.10.

An event trace for a typical game played by two clients on a server.

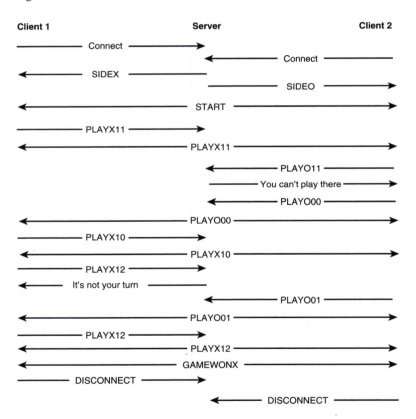

After there are two connected clients, the server sends the START message to each. The X player then submits his initial move. He submits PLAYX11, indicating that he wishes to play in the center square. When the server receives this message, it checks to make sure the center square

15

is available. Since it is, the server sends PLAYX11 to both clients. This informs the clients that a move has been made. Notice that even though X knew about this move when he submitted it, the move is not valid until the server approves the move.

After the PLAYX11 message is received by both clients, the O player attempts to play in the same square. The server responds with a message saying You can't play there. O changes his move to the top-left square (PLAYO00), and this move is accepted and broadcasted back to both clients. The X player then plays in the first column of the middle row (PLAYX10). X then tries to cheat with PLAYX12, but the server knows that it is not X's turn and responds with It's not your turn.

O then takes his turn and X closes out the game with PLAYX12. The server detects that this move wins the game for X and sends GAMEWONX to both clients. Both clients then disconnect; X to attend his victory celebration and O to seek solace in a bottle of beer.

The Internet Tic Tac Toe Server

Having designed the messages that will be passed between the clients and the server, it is now time to write the code. As always, the server is an application rather than an applet. The code for the TicTacToeServer application is shown in Listing 15.5.

Listing 15.5. TicTacToeServer.java.

```
1:    import java.awt.*;
2:    import java.net.*;
3:
4:    public class TicTacToeServer extends Frame {
5:        void quitButton_Clicked(java.awt.event.ActionEvent event){
6:            // shut down the threads
7:            if(game != null) {
8:                if(game.xThread!=null && game.xThread.isAlive()) {
9:                    status.appendText("Shutting Down X\r\n");
10:                   game.xThread.suspend();
11:               }
12:               if(game.oThread!=null && game.oThread.isAlive()) {
13:                   status.appendText("Shutting Down O\r\n");
14:                   game.oThread.suspend();
15:               }
16:           }
17:           System.exit(0);
18:       }
19:
20:       public static void main(String[] args) {
21:           new TicTacToeServer();
22:       }
23:
24:       void WindowClosing(java.awt.event.WindowEvent event) {
25:           System.exit(0);
```

continues

Listing 15.5. continued

```
26:        }
27:
28:        public TicTacToeServer() {
29:            show();
30:            play();
31:        }
32:
33:        private void play() {
34:            game = new Game();
35:
36:            try {
37:                ServerSocket socket = new ServerSocket(2000);
38:
39:                for(;;) {
40:                    Socket incoming = socket.accept();
41:
42:                    currentClients++;
43:                    status.appendText("Connecting to #" +
44:                            String.valueOf(currentClients) + "\r\n");
45:                    new TicTacToeServerThread(incoming,
46:                            currentClients, this).start();
47:                    if(currentClients == 2)
48:                        game.start();
49:                }
50:            }
51:            catch (Exception e) {
52:                status.appendText(e.toString() + "\r\n");
53:            }
54:        }
55:
56:        public synchronized void show() {
57:            move(50, 50);
58:            super.show();
59:        }
60:
61:        public void addNotify() {
62:
63:            // Call parents addNotify method.
64:            super.addNotify();
65:
66:            //{{INIT_CONTROLS
67:            setLayout(null);
68:            resize(insets().left + insets().right + 451,
69:                    insets().top + insets().bottom + 156);
70:            quitButton = new java.awt.Button("Quit");
71:            quitButton.reshape(insets().left + 396,insets().top
72:                    + 12,38,21);
73:            add(quitButton);
74:            status = new java.awt.TextArea();
75:            status.reshape(insets().left + 12,insets().top + 12,
76:                    372,132);
77:            add(status);
78:            setTitle("Internet TicTacToe Server");
79:            //}}
```

15

```
80:
81:         //{{INIT_MENUS
82:         //}}
83:
84:         //{{REGISTER_LISTENERS
85:         Window lWindow = new Window();
86:         addWindowListener(lWindow);
87:         Action lAction = new Action();
88:         quitButton.addActionListener(lAction);
89:         //}}
90:     }
91:
92:     public void clientDisconnected() {
93:         currentClients--;
94:     }
95:
96:     int currentClients=0;
97:     Game game;
98:
99:     //{{DECLARE_CONTROLS
100:    java.awt.Button quitButton;
101:    java.awt.TextArea status;
102:    //}}
103:
104:    //{{DECLARE_MENUS
105:    //}}
106:
107:    class Window extends java.awt.event.WindowAdapter {
108:        public void windowClosing(java.awt.event.WindowEvent
109:             event) {
110:            Object object = event.getSource();
111:            if (object == TicTacToeServer.this)
112:                WindowClosing(event);
113:        }
114:    }
115:
116:    class Action implements java.awt.event.ActionListener {
117:        public void actionPerformed(java.awt.event.ActionEvent
118:             event) {
119:            Object object = event.getSource();
120:            if (object == quitButton)
121:                quitButton_Clicked(event);
122:        }
123:    }
124: }
```

ANALYSIS As you saw in Figure 15.10, the server has a very minimal user interface. It includes a Quit button and a text area that is used to display messages. To aid in debugging and understanding how the server works, each message sent to a client will also be displayed in the text area.

Because TicTacToeServer is an application, it begins with the main method (lines 20–22). As always, the addNotify method (lines 61–90) places the components on the form. The constructor (lines 28–31) shows the server's frame and then calls the play method (line 30).

The play method (lines 33–54) starts by constructing a new Game object. Next, a ServerSocket on port 2000 is created (line 37) and the program loops while waiting for connections (lines 39–49). After a new connection is made, a new TicTacToeServer thread is constructed (line 45–46) and started. This thread will maintain the socket connection with the client and will handle all communication. If play detects that the current client is the second client to connect, the game is started on line 48.

The Game Class

The Game object that was constructed at the start of the play method is responsible for keeping track of which client is playing as X and which is playing as O and for properly routing messages to these clients. Game is also responsible for detecting won or drawn games. The code for Game is shown in Listing 15.6.

Listing 15.6. Game.java.

```
 1:    public class Game {
 2:        String whoseTurn = "X";        // X goes first
 3:        TicTacToeServerThread xThread;
 4:        TicTacToeServerThread oThread;
 5:
 6:        char positions[][] = {
 7:            {' ',' ',' '},
 8:            {' ',' ',' '},
 9:            {' ',' ',' '}
10:        };
11:
12:        public void setXThread(TicTacToeServerThread t) {
13:            xThread = t;
14:        }
15:
16:        public void setOThread(TicTacToeServerThread t) {
17:            oThread = t;
18:        }
19:
20:        public void sendMessageToX(String str) {
21:            if(xThread != null)
22:                xThread.sendMessage(str);
23:        }
24:
25:        public void sendMessageToO(String str) {
26:            if(oThread != null)
27:                oThread.sendMessage(str);
28:        }
29:
30:        public void sendMessageToBoth(String str) {
31:            if(xThread != null)
32:                xThread.sendMessage(str);
33:            if(oThread != null)
34:                oThread.sendMessage(str);
35:        }
36:
```

```
37:        boolean setCellShape(int row, int col, char shape) {
38:            boolean retval = false;
39:
40:            if(positions[row][col] == ' ') {
41:                positions[row][col] = shape;
42:                retval = true;
43:            }
44:            return retval;
45:        }
46:
47:        public void setNextPlayer() {
48:            if (whoseTurn.equals("X"))
49:                whoseTurn = "O";
50:            else
51:                whoseTurn = "X";
52:        }
53:
54:        // Returns true if the game was won
55:        public boolean isWon(char shape) {
56:            int winners[] = {
57:                // winners across the rows
58:                (1<<0 | 1<<1 | 1<<2),
59:                (1<<3 | 1<<4 | 1<<5),
60:                (1<<6 | 1<<7 | 1<<8),
61:
62:                // winners down the columns
63:                (1<<0 | 1<<3 | 1<<6),
64:                (1<<1 | 1<<4 | 1<<7),
65:                (1<<2 | 1<<5 | 1<<8),
66:
67:                // diagonal winners
68:                (1<<0 | 1<<4 | 1<<8),
69:                (1<<2 | 1<<4 | 1<<6)
70:            };
71:
72:            int currentValue = calcBoardValue(shape);
73:            boolean retval = false;
74:
75:            for(int i=0; i<winners.length; i++) {
76:                if ((currentValue & winners[i]) == winners[i])
77:                    retval=true;
78:            }
79:
80:            return retval;
81:        }
82:
83:        private int calcBoardValue(char shape) {
84:            int value = 0;
85:
86:            for(int row=0; row<3; row++) {
87:                for(int col=0; col<3; col++) {
88:                    if(positions[row][col] == shape)
89:                        value |= (1 << (row * 3 + col));
90:                }
91:            }
92:            return value;
```

continues

Listing 15.6. continued

```
93:        }
94:
95:        // return true if the game is a draw (all cells full)
96:        public boolean isDrawn() {
97:            for(int row=0; row<3; row++) {
98:                for(int col=0; col<3; col++) {
99:                    if(positions[row][col] == ' ')
100:                        return false;
101:                }
102:            }
103:            return true;
104:        }
105:
106:        void start() {
107:            sendMessageToBoth("START");
108:            sendMessageToX("You're X, make the first move");
109:            sendMessageToO("You're O, X moves first");
110:            blankAllPositions();
111:            whoseTurn = "X";
112:        }
113:
114:        private void blankAllPositions() {
115:            for(int row=0; row<3; row++)
116:                for(int col=0; col<3; col++)
117:                    positions[row][col] = ' ';
118:        }
119:    }
```

ANALYSIS   The Game class includes a member variable, whoseTurn, that holds either X or O to indicate which player moves next. Players are alternated with the method setNextPlayer (lines 47–52). Game also includes member variables, xThread and oThread, that identify the threads being used to communicate with each player. The methods sendMessageToX (lines 20–23), sendMessageToO (lines 25–28), and sendMessageToBoth (lines 30–35) are used to send messages to these threads.

Game also includes an array of characters, positions (lines 6–10), that stores the contents of each cell. Initially, all cells are blank; as plays are made, the members of this array will be filled with X and O characters. The method setCellShape (lines 37–45) is used to place one of these characters into the positions array.

The method isWon (lines 55–70) is used whenever a play is made to determine whether that play wins the game. This method first creates an array of all eight possible winning positions. Each position is turned into an integer by shifting a bit by the number of each cell in the winning position. For example, a game is won if a player occupies the entire first row (cell positions 0, 1, and 2). This is represented by line 58, which uses ¦ to OR bits that are shifted by these values, as follows:

```
1 << 0                    1
1 << 1                    2
1 << 2                    4
```

So a winning position across the top row is represented by the integer value 7. The method `calcBoardValue` (line 83–93) calculates the value of the cells occupied by the specified shape in a similar manner. The loop between lines 75 and 78 then compares the current value of the board to each known winning position.

It is much easier to detect a draw than it is to detect a win. The `isDrawn` method simply looks to see whether every element in the `positions` array is occupied. If so (and if the game wasn't already won), the game is a draw.

As you saw in Listing 15.5, a new game is begun when the `start` method of `Game` is called. This method (lines 106–112) sends each client a `START` message. It then reminds X that he goes first and O that he needs to wait until X makes the first move. All positions are then blanked and `whoseTurn` is set to X.

The `TicTacToeServerThread` Class

The `TicTacToeServerThread` class is an extension of `Thread`. This class is responsible for listening for commands from a client and for streaming information to the client. Each client will have its own instance of `TicTacToeServerThread` with which to communicate. The code for this class is shown in Listing 15.7.

Listing 15.7. `TicTacToeServerThread.java`.

```
1:   import java.io.*;
2:   import java.net.*;
3:
4:   public class TicTacToeServerThread extends Thread {
5:       private Socket inSocket;
6:       private int shape;
7:       TicTacToeServer server;
8:       BufferedReader inStream;
9:       PrintWriter outStream;
10:      Game game;
11:      public final static int Cross = 1;
12:      public final static int Circle = 2;
13:
14:      public TicTacToeServerThread(Socket s, int n,
15:          TicTacToeServer bs) {
16:          inSocket = s;
17:          shape = n;
18:          server = bs;
19:          game = server.game;
20:
21:          if(n == Cross)
```

continues

Listing 15.7. continued

```
22:              game.setXThread(this);
23:          else
24:              game.setOThread(this);
25:      }
26:
27:      public void run() {
28:          try {
29:              inStream  = new BufferedReader(
30:                      new InputStreamReader(
31:                      inSocket.getInputStream())));
32:              outStream = new PrintWriter(
33:                      inSocket.getOutputStream(), true);
34:
35:              // tell the client which shape he is
36:              if(shape == Cross)
37:                  outStream.println("SIDEX");
38:              else
39:                  outStream.println("SIDEO");
40:
41:              // enter a loop to play the game
42:              boolean done = false;
43:              while(!done) {
44:                  String str = inStream.readLine();
45:                  if (str == null)
46:                      done = true;
47:                  else if (str.startsWith("PLAY"))
48:                      makePlay(str);
49:                  else if (str.startsWith("DISCONNECT"))
50:                      done = true;
51:                  else
52:                      server.status.appendText(str + "\r\n");
53:              }
54:
55:              inSocket.close();
56:
57:              // tell the server that the client disconnected
58:              server.clientDisconnected();
59:
60:          }
61:          catch(Exception e) {
62:              server.status.appendText(e.toString() + "\r\n");
63:          }
64:      }
65:
66:      void sendMessage(String str) {
67:          server.status.appendText("Sending: " + str + "\r\n");
68:          outStream.println(str);
69:      }
70:
71:      private void makePlay(String str) {
72:          // str is in format PLAY[X|0][row][col]
73:          char curPlayer = game.whoseTurn.charAt(0);
74:
75:          // make sure the right player is attempting to move
```

15

```
76:            if (str.charAt(4) == curPlayer) {
77:
78:                // check to make sure the cell can be played in
79:                int row = Integer.parseInt(str.substring(5,6));
80:                int col = Integer.parseInt(str.substring(6,7));
81:
82:                if(game.setCellShape(row, col, curPlayer)) {
83:                    game.sendMessageToBoth(str);
84:                    game.setNextPlayer();
85:
86:                    // check to see if this player just won the game
87:                    if(game.isWon(curPlayer))
88:                        game.sendMessageToBoth("GAMEWON" +
89:                                String.valueOf(curPlayer));
90:
91:                    // check to see if all cells are filled
92:                    else if(game.isDrawn())
93:                        game.sendMessageToBoth("GAMEDRAWN");
94:                }
95:                else
96:                    sendMessage("You can't play there");
97:            }
98:            else
99:                sendMessage("It's not your turn!!");
100:    }
101: }
```

ANALYSIS The constructor for TicTacToeServerThread (lines 14–25) is passed a socket, an integer value, and a reference to the TicTacToeServer that is creating the thread. These parameters are stored for later use by other class methods. The integer value is used to determine whether the thread will represent a player using X or a player using O. The first player to connect for any game is always given X and will move first.

Because TicTacToeServerThread extends Thread, it must include a run method (lines 27–64). This method creates the familiar BufferedReader and PrintWriter variables. Next, a message is sent to the client via outStream indicating whether the client is playing X or O (lines 36–39). You should be able to look back at the event trace of Figure 15.10 to see that this is appropriate.

Next, run enters a continuous loop (lines 43–53) that reads messages from inStream. The loop terminates if an empty message or a message containing DISCONNECT is received. At that point, the socket is closed (line 55) and the server is told that the client has disconnected (line 58). If a message is received within the loop that starts with PLAY, the makePlay method is called (line 48).

The makePlay method (lines 71–100) is passed a string in the format PLAY[X¦O][row][column]. First, makePlay verifies that the play has been submitted by the player whose turn it is (line 73–76). If someone is attempting to move out of turn, that player is sent a message (line 99).

However, if the correct player is attempting a move, the row and column are parsed from the string (lines 79–809). Next, `game.setCellShape` is used to determine whether that cell is empty. If the cell is not empty, a message will be sent back to the client attempting the move (line 96).

However, if the player is able to play in the desired cell, the message is forwarded to both clients (line 83). This notifies them that the play is valid. Next, the current player is switched (line 84). Finally, the server calls `game.isWon` to find out whether the game was just won (line 87). If so, a GAMEWON[X¦O] message is sent to both clients. If not, `game.isDrawn` is used to find out whether the game is a draw.

A Tic Tac Toe Client

Figure 15.11 shows the classes that comprise the `TicTacToeClient` applet. Three new classes are introduced: `TicTacToeClient`, `TicTacToeCanvas`, and `TicTacToeReader`.

Figure 15.11.

The classes of the
`TicTacToeClient`
applet.

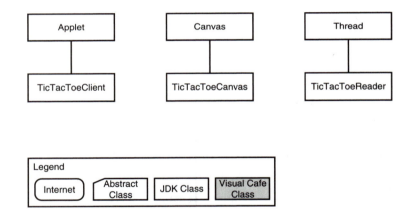

`TicTacToeClient` is the applet class and as such is responsible for getting things started and for managing the overall user interface. The most frequently used portion of the user interface is the actual Tic Tac Toe grid itself. The mechanics of the grid are encapsulated in the `TicTacToeCanvas` class. `TicTacToeCanvas` knows how to draw the grid and can also detect mouse clicks within cells of the grid. Finally, `TicTacToeReader` monitors the input stream from the server and dispatches the relevant messages to the client.

The `TicTacToeReader` Class

The `TicTacToeReader` class, shown in Listing 15.8, is an extension of `Thread` and is responsible for reading commands from the server through the input stream. The constructor for this class (lines 8–13) stores references to the stream being read and the client that created the reader object. The constructor finishes by starting the thread.

Listing 15.8. `TicTacToeReader.java`.

```
 1:   import java.io.*;
 2:   import java.net.*;
 3:
 4:   public class TicTacToeReader extends Thread {
 5:       BufferedReader inStream;
 6:       TicTacToeClient client;
 7:
 8:       public TicTacToeReader(BufferedReader in,
 9:               TicTacToeClient c) {
10:          inStream = in;
11:          client = c;
12:          start();
13:       }
14:
15:       public void run() {
16:          String line;
17:          try {
18:              boolean more = true;
19:              do {
20:                  line = inStream.readLine();
21:
22:                  if(line==null)
23:                      more = false;
24:                  else if(line.startsWith("PLAY"))
25:                      client.makePlay(line);
26:                  else if(line.startsWith("SIDE"))
27:                      client.assignSide(line);
28:                  else if(line.startsWith("START"))
29:                      client.startGame();
30:                  else if(line.startsWith("GAMEWON"))
31:                      client.gameWon(line);
32:                  else if(line.startsWith("GAMEDRAWN"))
33:                      client.gameDrawn();
34:                  else
35:                      client.status.appendText(line + "\r\n");
36:              } while (more = true);
37:          }
38:          catch (IOException e) {
39:              client.status.appendText(e.toString() + "\r\n");
40:          }
41:          finally {
42:              client.status.appendText(
43:                      "Connection closed by server\r\n");
44:          }
45:       }
46:   }
```

ANALYSIS   The only other method in `TicTacToeReader` is run (lines 15–45). This method consists mostly of a do...while loop (lines 19–36) that reads a line from the input stream and then executes a callback method in the client that created the stream. For example, if the line starts with PLAY, the method `client.makePlay` is invoked (lines 24–25).

The `TicTacToeClient` Class

The code to `TicTacToeClient` is shown in Listing 15.9. The action within the client really begins when the user clicks the Connect button. This executes the `connectButton_Clicked` method (lines 7–28). This method performs the usual actions of creating a new `Socket`, a `BufferedReader`, and a `PrintWriter` (lines 10–16). It also creates a new `TicTacToeReader` object based on the input stream (line 18). Before returning, the button is disabled (because the user is already connected), the canvas is cleared and repainted, and the `canMove` flag is set to `false`. This flag is used to indicate whether the client can submit moves to the server.

Listing 15.9. `TicTacToeClient.java`.

```
1:   import java.awt.*;
2:   import java.applet.*;
3:   import java.io.*;
4:   import java.net.*;
5:
6:   public class TicTacToeClient extends Applet {
7:       void connectButton_Clicked(java.awt.event.ActionEvent
8:               event) {
9:           try {
10:              socket = new Socket(getCodeBase().getHost(),
11:                      PORT);
12:              inStream  = new BufferedReader(
13:                      new InputStreamReader(
14:                      socket.getInputStream()));
15:              outStream = new PrintWriter(
16:                      socket.getOutputStream(), true);
17:
18:              tttReader = new TicTacToeReader(inStream, this);
19:              connectButton.enable(false);
20:              canMove = false;
21:
22:              tttCanvas.clear();
23:              tttCanvas.repaint();
24:          }
25:          catch (IOException e) {
26:              status.appendText("Error connecting to server\r\n");
27:          }
28:      }
29:
30:      void disconnect() {
31:          outStream.println("DISCONNECT");
32:      }
33:
34:      void quitButton_Clicked(java.awt.event.ActionEvent event){
35:          // if connected, disconnect first
36:          if(connectButton.isEnabled() == false)
37:              disconnect();
38:          System.exit(0);
39:      }
40:
41:      public void init() {
```

15

```
42:         // Call parents init method.
43:         super.init();
44:
45:         tttCanvas = new TicTacToeCanvas(this);
46:         panel2.add("Center", tttCanvas);
47:     }
48:
49:     public void addNotify() {
50:         // Call parents addNotify method.
51:         super.addNotify();
52:
53:         //{{INIT_CONTROLS
54:         setLayout(null);
55:         resize(334,411);
56:         buttonPanel = new java.awt.Panel();
57:         buttonPanel.setLayout(new FlowLayout(
58:             FlowLayout.CENTER,5,5));
59:         buttonPanel.reshape(0,0,334,31);
60:         add(buttonPanel);
61:         connectButton = new java.awt.Button("Connect");
62:         connectButton.reshape(116,5,60,23);
63:         buttonPanel.add(connectButton);
64:         quitButton = new java.awt.Button("Quit");
65:         quitButton.reshape(181,5,36,23);
66:         buttonPanel.add(quitButton);
67:         statusPanel = new java.awt.Panel();
68:         statusPanel.setLayout(new BorderLayout(0,0));
69:         statusPanel.reshape(0,252,334,154);
70:         add(statusPanel);
71:         status = new java.awt.TextArea();
72:         status.setEditable(false);
73:         status.reshape(0,0,334,154);
74:         statusPanel.add("Center", status);
75:         panel1 = new java.awt.Panel();
76:         panel1.setLayout(null);
77:         panel1.reshape(0,36,334,226);
78:         panel1.setBackground(new Color(16777215));
79:         add(panel1);
80:         panel2 = new java.awt.Panel();
81:         panel2.setLayout(new BorderLayout(0,0));
82:         panel2.reshape(96,24,150,150);
83:         panel2.setBackground(new Color(16777215));
84:         panel1.add(panel2);
85:         //}}
86:
87:         //{{REGISTER_LISTENERS
88:         Action lAction = new Action();
89:         quitButton.addActionListener(lAction);
90:         connectButton.addActionListener(lAction);
91:         //}}
92:     }
93:
94:     public void submitPlay(int row, int col) {
95:         outStream.println("PLAY"   + sideString +
96:                 String.valueOf(row) + String.valueOf(col));
97:     }
```

continues

Listing 15.9. continued

```
98:
99:      // store the shape that this client is playing
100:     public void assignSide(String line) {
101:         // line is in format of SIDE[X¦O]
102:         sideString = line.substring(4,5);
103:     }
104:
105:     public void makePlay(String line) {
106:         // line is in format of PLAY[X¦O][nn]
107:
108:         char shape = 'O';
109:         if (line.charAt(4) == 'X')
110:             shape = 'X';
111:
112:         int row = Integer.parseInt(line.substring(5,6));
113:         int col = Integer.parseInt(line.substring(6,7));
114:
115:         tttCanvas.setCellShape(row, col, shape);
116:         tttCanvas.repaint();
117:     }
118:
119:     public void startGame() {
120:         enableAllCells(true);
121:     }
122:
123:     public void endGame() {
124:         // disable all cell buttons since the game is over
125:         enableAllCells(false);
126:
127:         // disconnect from the server
128:         disconnect();
129:
130:         // allow user to reconnect
131:         connectButton.enable(true);
132:     }
133:
134:     public void gameWon(String line) {
135:         // line is in format of GAMEWON[X¦O][nn]
136:
137:         if (sideString.equals(line.substring(7,8)))
138:             status.appendText("You won\r\n");
139:         else
140:             status.appendText("You lost\r\n");
141:
142:         endGame();
143:     }
144:
145:     public void gameDrawn() {
146:         status.appendText("Drawn game\r\n");
147:
148:         endGame();
149:     }
150:
151:     void enableAllCells(boolean state) {
152:         canMove = state;
```

```
153:       }
154:
155:       public static final int PORT = 2000;
156:       Socket socket;
157:       BufferedReader inStream;
158:       PrintWriter outStream;
159:       TicTacToeReader tttReader;
160:       String sideString;
161:       TicTacToeCanvas tttCanvas;
162:       boolean canMove = false;
163:
164:       //{{DECLARE_CONTROLS
165:       java.awt.Panel buttonPanel;
166:       java.awt.Button connectButton;
167:       java.awt.Button quitButton;
168:       java.awt.Panel statusPanel;
169:       java.awt.TextArea status;
170:       java.awt.Panel panel1;
171:       java.awt.Panel panel2;
172:       //}}
173:
174:       class Action implements java.awt.event.ActionListener {
175:           public void actionPerformed(java.awt.event.ActionEvent
176:               event) {
177:             Object object = event.getSource();
178:             if (object == quitButton)
179:                quitButton_Clicked(event);
180:             else if (object == connectButton)
181:                connectButton_Clicked(event);
182:           }
183:       }
184: }
```

ANALYSIS The methods makePlay (lines 105–117), assignSide (lines 100–103), startGame (lines 119–121), gameWon (lines 134–143), and gameDrawn (lines 145–1490) are each callback methods that are called from within the run method of the TicTacToeReader created for each client.

The TicTacToeCanvas Class

The final new class introduced in the TicTacToeClient applet is TicTacToeCanvas. This class, shown in Listing 15.10, handles drawing the game grid and watching for mouse clicks within the grid.

Listing 15.10. TicTacToeCanvas.java.

```
1:     import java.awt.*;
2:
3:     public class TicTacToeCanvas extends Canvas {
4:
5:         char positions[] = {
```

continues

Listing 15.10. continued

```
 6:          ' ',' ',' ',' ',' ',' ',' ',' ',' '
 7:      };
 8:
 9:      public TicTacToeCanvas(TicTacToeClient client) {
10:          this.client = client;
11:      }
12:
13:      void TicTacToeCanvas_MouseClick(java.awt.event.MouseEvent
14:              event) {
15:          // determine the row and column the click occurred in
16:          int row = event.getY() / cellDim;
17:          int col = event.getX() / cellDim;
18:
19:          client.submitPlay(row, col);
20:      }
21:
22:      public void setCellShape(int row, int col, char shape) {
23:          // store the shape
24:          positions[row * 3 + col] = shape;
25:      }
26:
27:      public void clear() {
28:          for (int i=0; i<positions.length; i++)
29:              positions[i] = ' ';
30:      }
31:
32:      public void paint(Graphics g) {
33:          int firstLine = cellDim;
34:          int secondLine = cellDim * 2;
35:          int width = cellDim * 3;
36:          int height = width;
37:
38:          // draw horizontal lines
39:          g.drawLine(0, firstLine, width, firstLine);
40:          g.drawLine(0, secondLine, width, secondLine);
41:
42:          // draw vertical lines
43:          g.drawLine(firstLine, 0, firstLine, height);
44:          g.drawLine(secondLine, 0, secondLine, height);
45:
46:          // draw the X and O symbols
47:          for(int i=0; i<positions.length; i++) {
48:              if (positions[i] == 'X') {
49:                  int x = i % 3;
50:                  int y = i / 3;
51:
52:                  drawX(g, x, y);
53:              }
54:              else if (positions[i] == 'O') {
55:                  int x = i % 3;
56:                  int y = i / 3;
```

```
57:
58:                    drawO(g, x, y);
59:                }
60:            }
61:        }
62:
63:        private void drawO(Graphics g, int x, int y) {
64:            int topLeftX  = x * cellDim + shapeInsets;
65:            int topLeftY  = y * cellDim + shapeInsets;
66:
67:            int shapeDim = cellDim - (2 * shapeInsets);
68:            g.drawOval(topLeftX, topLeftY, shapeDim, shapeDim);
69:        }
70:
71:        private void drawX(Graphics g, int x, int y) {
72:            int topLeftX  = x * cellDim + shapeInsets;
73:            int topLeftY  = y * cellDim + shapeInsets;
74:            int btmRightX = x * cellDim + cellDim - shapeInsets;
75:            int btmRightY = y * cellDim + cellDim - shapeInsets;
76:
77:            g.drawLine(topLeftX, topLeftY, btmRightX, btmRightY);
78:
79:            int topRightX = x * cellDim + cellDim - shapeInsets;
80:            int topRightY = y * cellDim + shapeInsets;
81:            int btmLeftX = x * cellDim + shapeInsets;
82:            int btmLeftY = y * cellDim + cellDim - shapeInsets;
83:
84:            g.drawLine(topRightX, topRightY, btmLeftX, btmLeftY);
85:        }
86:
87:        private TicTacToeClient client;
88:        private final int cellDim     = 50;
89:        private final int shapeInsets = 10;
90:    }
```

ANALYSIS The member array positions (lines 5–7) stores the character that is to be displayed in each cell of the grid. Each element in the array is initially set to a space character; as moves are made, the elements are replaced with X or O by calls to setCellShape (lines 22–25). The array can be reset to spaces by a call to clear (lines 27–30).

The paint method of TicTacToeCanvas (lines 32–61) begins by drawing the grid with two horizontal lines (lines 39–40) and two vertical lines (lines 43–44). Next, a loop (lines 47–60) looks at each element of positions and then calls drawX or drawO to draw the individual shapes.

The TicTacToeCanvas_MouseClick method (lines 13–20) is called whenever a mouse button is clicked while over the canvas. The row and column indicated by the click are calculated and then passed as parameters to the client's submitPlay method.

Summary

Today you learned how to use the `Socket` and `ServerSocket` classes to write client/server programs. You started by writing a simple, single-threaded server and used Telnet as the client. From there you enhanced the server to use multiple threads and then added your own custom client.

Because of the extensive use of threads and streams in today's lesson, it helped to reinforce what you learned in the preceding two chapters. The bulk of this chapter described a detailed sample client/server system for playing Tic Tac Toe. This involved writing a multithreaded server and a custom client.

Q&A

Q I tried unsuccessfully to convert some of the server applications in this chapter into applets. What did I do wrong?

A Unfortunately, nothing. A Java applet cannot be a server. Servers are only supported in applications.

Q In all of the examples in this chapter, only strings were sent through the communication streams. Can other types of data be sent?

A Yes, if you create the appropriate types of streams. You can even stream objects if you use `ObjectOutputStream` and `ObjectInputStream`.

Workshop

The workshop includes quiz questions to help you gauge your understanding of the material in this chapter. The workshop also includes exercises to provide hands-on experience with what you've learned in this chapter. Answers to the quiz questions can be found in Appendix D, "Answers."

Quiz

1. What is the maximum number of clients a server can support?
2. What is the purpose of the `accept` method in `ServerSocket`?
3. What happens to the following code if no client attempts to connect to the server?
   ```
   ServerSocket server = new ServerSocket(2000);
   Socket inSocket = server.accept();
   ```
4. What is the significance of specifying `127.0.0.1` as the hostname in Telnet?

5. What member method of `Socket` can be used to return the input stream of the socket?

6. Why can't line 76 in Listing 15.6 be replaced with a simple test for equality, as in `if (currentValue == winners[i])`?

Exercises

1. Rewrite the `LanguageDictionary` application so that it has no user interface.

2. Enhance the Tic Tac Toe client and server to allow the players to send messages to each other.

3. Write an additional client for the Tic Tac Toe system that allows a user to observe a game played by two other players, rather than play the game himself.

4. Extra Credit: Enhance the Tic Tac Toe observer client so that an observer can begin observing a game already in progress. (Tip: The server will need to send a message to the client for each cell that is already occupied at the time the client connects.)

5. Enhance the `TicTacToeClient` applet to draw images instead of lines and circles.

Day 16

Working with Graphics

Today you will learn how to augment the appearance of your Java programs by using graphics. You will learn how to use the AWT Graphics class to draw lines and geometric shapes such as arcs, ovals, rectangles, and polygons. You will see how to use the Canvas class to control the placement of these shapes. Visual Café provides its own set of classes for drawing shapes, and you will learn how to use these visual components.

You will also learn how to display and manipulate images. You will learn about Java's classes for filtering, cropping, and modifying images. You will also learn about the ImageObserver interface, which allows an applet to monitor the progress of an image that is being retrieved for display.

The AWT Graphics Class

In this section you will learn about the Graphics class that is included in the java.awt package. You've already seen the Graphics class used in some of the examples in this book. For example, the following code can be used to display Hello World on the screen:

```
public void paint(Graphics g)
{
    g.drawString("Hello World", 10, 10);
}
```

As you would expect of a class named Graphics, it can be used to do much more than draw strings. The Graphics class can be used to draw a variety of shapes. Figure 16.1 illustrates a very simple screen that was created with member methods of the Graphics class.

Figure 16.1.

A very simple example of drawing filled and outlined shapes.

The Graphics class includes methods for drawing both filled and outlined shapes. An outlined shape, as its name suggests, is just the outline of the shape; a filled shape is the outline plus the area bounded by the outline. The bounded area is painted in the color that has been previously selected for the Graphics object.

A variety of shapes can be drawn using the Graphics class, as shown in Table 16.1. As you can see from this table, all shapes except a line can be drawn both filled and outlined. Because a line always has a width of one pixel, there is no need to draw filled lines.

Table 16.1. Shapes that can be drawn by the Graphics class.

Shape	Filled	Outlined
Arc	Yes	Yes
Line	No	Yes
Oval	Yes	Yes
Polygon	Yes	Yes

16

Shape	Filled	Outlined
Rectangle	Yes	Yes
Round rectangle	Yes	Yes
3D rectangle	Yes	Yes

When you use any of these methods to draw a shape, you pass it the coordinates at which the shape is to be drawn. As far as the Graphics class is concerned, coordinate numbering starts at 0,0 in the top left and increases down and to the right. This can be seen in Figure 16.2.

Figure 16.2.

The Graphics
*coordinate system
places 0,0 in the top
left and increases
down and to the right.*

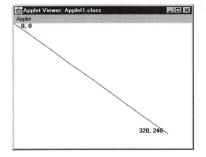

Lines

One of the simplest shapes to draw is a line. A line can be drawn using the drawLine member of the Graphics class. The signature of drawLine is as follows:

```
public abstract void drawLine(int x1, int y1, int x2, int y2);
```

This method will draw a line between the points given by (x1, y1) and (x2, y2). As an example, imagine you have been asked to display the image shown in Figure 16.3. This drawing can be created with the paint method shown in Listing 16.1. This method is taken from the Puzzle sample applet that is included on the MCP Web site (www.mcp.com/info/1-57521/1-57521-303-6).

Figure 16.3.

*A simple figure
created with*
drawLine.

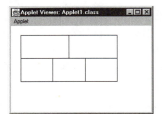

Listing 16.1. The `paint` method of `Puzzle.java`.

```
 1:    public void paint(Graphics g)
 2:    {
 3:        // draw the three horizontal lines
 4:        g.drawLine(20,  20, 220,  20);
 5:        g.drawLine(20,  70, 220,  70);
 6:        g.drawLine(20, 120, 220, 120);
 7:
 8:        // draw the vertical lines at each end
 9:        g.drawLine(20,  20,  20, 120);
10:        g.drawLine(220, 20, 220, 120);
11:
12:        // draw the vertical line in the top half
13:        g.drawLine(120, 20, 120, 70);
14:
15:        // draw two vertical lines in the bottom half
16:        g.drawLine( 86, 70,  86, 120);
17:         g.drawLine(154, 70, 154, 120);
18:    }
```

NOTE

The drawing in Figure 16.3 was first presented to me in the form of a puzzle: Starting from a point inside or outside the figure, draw a single line that crosses each and every line segment of the figure exactly once. On a day when I must have been a particularly annoying seven-year-old, my dad drew this puzzle for me and offered me $20 if I could solve it. I couldn't, even though I occasionally returned to it for nearly 15 more years. It wasn't until college, when I learned about Euler and the Bridges of Konigsberg, that I discovered the puzzle was unsolvable. However, it did solve my dad's problem of keeping a seven-year-old quiet in the back of a car.

Rectangles

There are more methods for drawing rectangles than I have fingers on one hand: There are six. Fortunately, I could count them all on two hands and didn't need to use my toes or this book would have had an unpleasant odor. Of the six methods for drawing rectangles, three draw filled rectangles and three draw outlined rectangles. Methods whose names begin with draw are used to create outlined rectangles; methods whose names begin with fill are used to create filled rectangles. The following methods are available:

```
public void drawRect(int x, int y, int width, int height);
```

```
public abstract void fillRect(int x, int y, int width, int height);
```

```
public void draw3DRect(int x, int y, int width, int height,
        boolean raised);
public void fill3DRect(int x, int y, int width, int height,
        boolean raised);
public abstract void drawRoundRect(int x, int y, int width,
        int height, int arcWidth, int arcHeight);
public abstract void fillRoundRect(int x, int y, int width,
        int height, int arcWidth, int arcHeight);
```

A simple rectangle, as drawn by drawRect and fillRect, requires only parameters for the starting x and y coordinates and the width and height of the rectangle. You can paint a three-dimensional rectangle with draw3DRect or fill3DRect by specifying an additional parameter that indicates whether the rectangle should appear raised or lowered. You achieve the three-dimensional effect by brightening or darkening the color of the rectangle when it is drawn. Because of this, you must use setColor prior to painting the rectangle or the three-dimensional effect will not be apparent.

Finally, a rectangle with rounded corners can be painted with drawRoundRect or fillRoundRect. These methods require two additional parameters that specify the width and height of the arc that is used to draw the corners. Larger values for these parameters will create more rounded corners.

As an example of how these methods can be used, consider the code in Listing 16.2, which is from the RectangleDemo sample applet included on the MCP Web site. This code will create the screen shown in Figure 16.4.

Listing 16.2. The paint method of RectangleDemo.java.

```
 1:     public void paint(Graphics g)
 2:     {
 3:         // draw an outlined rectangle
 4:         g.drawRect(10, 10, 200, 200);
 5:         g.drawString("drawRect", 10, 225);
 6:
 7:         // draw a filled rectangle
 8:         g.fillRect(15, 15, 30, 60);
 9:         g.drawString("fillRect", 15, 90);
10:
11:         // set a color so that the 3D rectangles
12:         // are displayed as raised or indented
13:         g.setColor(Color.cyan);
14:
15:         // draw an outlined 3D rectangle
16:         g.draw3DRect(60, 15, 40, 10, false);
17:         g.drawString("draw3DRect", 60, 40);
18:
19:         // draw a filled 3D rectangle
20:         g.fill3DRect(140, 15, 30, 20, true);
```

continues

Listing 16.2. continued

```
21:        g.drawString("fill3DRect", 140, 50);
22:
23:        // draw an outlined round rectangle
24:        g.drawRoundRect(20, 110, 40, 60, 20, 40);
25:        g.drawString("drawRoundRect", 20, 185);
26:
27:        // draw a filled round rectangle
28:        g.fillRoundRect(120, 110, 60, 60, 20, 20);
29:        g.drawString("fillRoundRect", 120, 185);
30:    }
```

Figure 16.4.

Examples of the various rectangle methods.

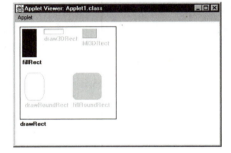

Arcs

You've already used arcs to create the rounded corners of a rectangle drawn with `drawRoundRect` or `fillRoundRect`. You can also create an arc on its own. Arcs are created with the `drawArc` or `fillArc` methods, whose signatures are as follows:

```
public abstract void drawArc(int x, int y, int width, int height,
        int startAngle, int arcAngle);

public abstract void fillArc(int x, int y, int width, int height,
        int startAngle, int arcAngle);
```

As with the rectangle methods, the method whose name begins with `draw` paints an outlined shape, and the method whose name begins with `fill` paints a filled shape. To paint an arc, you specify the position and size of an imaginary rectangle that binds the arc. You also specify the starting angle of the arc and the number of degrees in the arc. This can be seen in Figure 16.5.

Figure 16.5 shows an arc and also uses `drawRectangle` to explicitly paint the invisible rectangle that surrounds the arc. The rectangle and arc of this example were created with the following two statements:

```
g.drawArc(60, 30, 100, 200, 45, 180);

g.drawRect(60, 30, 100, 200);
```

16

Figure 16.5.

Specify an arc by describing an imaginary rectangle surrounding it.

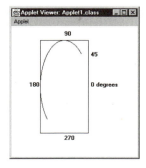

The first four parameters to drawArc indicate a rectangle that starts at (60, 30), is 100 pixels wide, and 200 pixels high. These same values are passed to drawRect to explicitly draw the rectangle. The final two parameters to drawArc indicate that the arc should begin at 45 degrees and end 180 degrees later (at 225 degrees). As you can see in Figure 16.5, the 0 degree position is at three o'clock. Because the final parameter is a positive number, the arc will be drawn in a counter-clockwise direction. A negative number causes the arc to be drawn in a clockwise direction. This can be seen in Figure 16.6, which shows the same arc when drawn in the opposite direction with the following code:

```
g.drawArc(60, 30, 100, 200, 45, -180);
```

Figure 16.6.

The same arc when drawn in a clockwise direction.

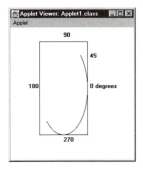

The ArcDemo applet, which is included on the MCP Web site and shown in Listing 16.3, demonstrates how to use drawArc and fillArc. Three rows of arcs are painted, as can be seen in Figure 16.7. The first row shows four arcs drawn with counter-clockwise angles. The second row shows the same four arcs drawn in a clockwise direction. The final row shows two filled arcs with starting angles other than 0.

Listing 16.3. The `paint` method of `ArcDemo.java`.

```
1:     public void paint(Graphics g)
2:     {
3:         // draw arcs with counter-clockwise angles
4:         g.drawArc(10, 60, 20, 50, 0, 90);
5:         g.drawArc(60, 60, 20, 50, 0, 180);
6:         g.drawArc(110, 60, 20, 50, 0, 270);
7:         g.drawArc(160, 60, 20, 50, 0, 360);
8:
9:         // draw arcs with clockwise angles
10:         g.drawArc(10, 120, 20, 50, 0, -90);
11:         g.drawArc(60, 120, 20, 50, 0, -180);
12:         g.drawArc(110, 120, 20, 50, 0, -270);
13:         g.drawArc(160, 120, 20, 50, 0, -360);
14:
15:         // draw filled arcs that don't start at 0
16:         g.fillArc(10, 180, 20, 50, 45, 180);
17:         g.fillArc(60, 180, 20, 50, 0, 135);
19:     }
```

Figure 16.7.

Sample arcs painted with drawArc *and* fillArc.

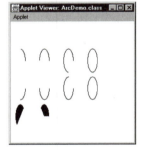

Ovals

Drawing an oval is very similar to drawing a regular rectangle. An oval can be painted using either of the following methods:

```
public abstract void drawOval(int x, int y,int width,int height);

public abstract void fillOval(int x, int y,int width,int height);
```

As is consistent with the other member methods of `Graphics`, `drawOval` paints an outlined oval and `fillOval` paints a filled oval. As with arcs, the parameters passed to these methods describe an imaginary rectangle surrounding the oval. As an example of painting ovals, the `OvalDemo` applet is shown in Listing 16.4 and is included on the MCP Web site. This class paints a large outlined oval and then paints a smaller filled oval inside the larger oval. The results of executing this class can be seen in Figure 16.8.

16

Listing 16.4. The `paint` method of `OvalDemo.java`.

```
1:    public void paint(Graphics g)
2:    {
3:        // draw an outlined oval
4:        g.drawOval(10, 10, 225, 300);
5:        g.drawString("drawOval", 102, 323);
6:
7:        // draw a filled oval within the outlined oval
8:        g.fillOval(73, 120, 100, 100);
9:        g.drawString("fillOval", 105, 233);
10:   }
```

Figure 16.8.

Sample ovals painted with drawOval *and* fillOval.

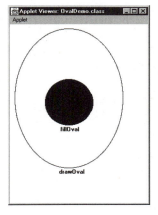

Polygons

If what you really want to draw is a nonstandard shape that can't be painted with one of the methods described so far, you might be able to use the polygon drawing methods. As usual, methods are provided for painting outlined and filled shapes. The following four methods can be used to paint polygons:

```
public abstract void fillPolygon(int xPoints[], int yPoints[],
        int nPoints);

public abstract void drawPolygon(int xPoints[], int yPoints[],
        int nPoints);

public void fillPolygon(Polygon p);

public void drawPolygon(Polygon p);
```

The first two of these methods are each passed two arrays that represent the x and y positions of the points on the polygon and an integer. As an example of how this works, consider the following:

```
int xPoints[] = new int[4];
int yPoints[] = new int[4];
```

```
xPoints[0] = 150;
xPoints[1] = 150;
xPoints[2] = 250;
xPoints[3] = 150;

yPoints[0] = 150;
yPoints[1] = 250;
yPoints[2] = 250;
yPoints[3] = 150;

g.fillPolygon(xPoints, yPoints, 4);
```

In this case, two arrays are allocated to hold four items each. The corners of the polygon are given by the matched pairs of the arrays. For example, (xPoints[0], yPoints[0]) and (xPoints[1], yPoints[1]) identify the first two of four corners on the polygon.

The other two methods for drawing polygons are passed a polygon as their lone parameter. These methods are more convenient if you already have a Polygon object. The following code is equivalent to the prior example, but passes a Polygon to fillPolygon instead of passing the arrays:

```
int xPoints[] = new int[4];
int yPoints[] = new int[4];

xPoints[0] = 150;
xPoints[1] = 150;
xPoints[2] = 250;
xPoints[3] = 150;

yPoints[0] = 150;
yPoints[1] = 250;
yPoints[2] = 250;
yPoints[3] = 150;

Polygon p = new Polygon(xPoints, yPoints, 4);
g.fillPolygon(p);
```

As a further example of how the fillPolygon and drawPolygon methods can be used, look at Listing 16.5, which shows code taken from the PolygonDemo applet included on the MCP Web site. This example draws three shapes: a four-sided polygon and two triangles, as can be seen in Figure 16.9.

Listing 16.5. A portion of PolygonDemo.java.

```
1:    public void paint(Graphics g)
2:    {
3:        drawFirstPolygon(g);
4:        drawSecondPolygon(g);
5:        drawThirdPolygon(g);
6:    }
7:
```

16

```
8:     private void drawFirstPolygon(Graphics g)
9:     {
10:        int xPoints[] = new int[5];
11:        int yPoints[] = new int[5];
12:
13:        xPoints[0] = 60;
14:        xPoints[1] = 100;
15:        xPoints[2] = 150;
16:        xPoints[3] = 110;
17:        xPoints[4] = 60;
18:
19:        yPoints[0] = 10;
20:        yPoints[1] = 70;
21:        yPoints[2] = 30;
22:        yPoints[3] = 170;
23:        yPoints[4] = 10;
24:
25:        g.drawPolygon(xPoints, yPoints, 5);
26:     }
27:
28:     private void drawSecondPolygon(Graphics g)
29:     {
30:        int xPoints[] = new int[4];
31:        int yPoints[] = new int[4];
32:
33:        xPoints[0] = 150;
34:        xPoints[1] = 150;
35:        xPoints[2] = 250;
36:        xPoints[3] = 150;
37:
38:        yPoints[0] = 150;
39:        yPoints[1] = 250;
40:        yPoints[2] = 250;
41:        yPoints[3] = 150;
42:
43:        g.fillPolygon(xPoints, yPoints, 4);
44:     }
45:
46:     private void drawThirdPolygon(Graphics g)
47:     {
48:        int xPoints[] = new int[4];
49:        int yPoints[] = new int[4];
50:
51:        xPoints[0] = 250;
52:        xPoints[1] = 300;
53:        xPoints[2] = 200;
54:        xPoints[3] = 250;
55:
56:        yPoints[0] = 300;
57:        yPoints[1] = 350;
58:        yPoints[2] = 350;
59:        yPoints[3] = 300;
60:
61:        Polygon p = new Polygon(xPoints, yPoints, 4);
62:
63:        g.drawPolygon(p);
64:     }
```

16

Figure 16.9.

Sample polygons
painted with
`drawPolygon` *and*
`fillPolygon`.

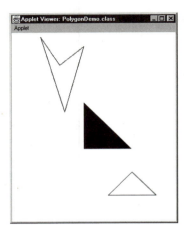

Using a Canvas

In the examples you've seen so far in this chapter, the graphics have been drawn directly onto the applet's window. This was done in the `paint` method of the class derived from `Applet`. There are two problems inherent with this approach:

☐ Because shape locations are specified in exact coordinates, it is difficult to combine shapes with layout managers. Because layout managers work by positioning components at runtime based on their sizes and the relative placement of other components, layout managers are not very compatible with shapes that are drawn at specific positions.

☐ When shapes are coded to be drawn at specific locations, they affect the ability of a user to resize the window. For example, go back and run any of the sample applets shown so far in this chapter. When the applet appears, resize the window and observe how the shapes are left in their fixed positions and become truncated if the size of the window is reduced.

The easiest way to solve both of these problems is to use the `Canvas` class. `Canvas` is a subclass of `Component`, and is meant to be subclassed and have its `paint` method overridden. When you use a canvas, you place it on the form as you would any other component and then draw shapes on the canvas rather than on the form itself. As an example of using `Canvas`, consider the `CanvasDemo` applet, shown in Listing 16.6. This applet is also included on the MCP Web site.

Listing 16.6. `CanvasDemo.java`.

```
 1:    import java.awt.*;
 2:    import java.applet.*;
 3:
 4:    class MyCanvas extends Canvas {
 5:        public void paint(Graphics g) {
 6:            g.fillOval(1, 1, size().width-2, size().height-2);
 7:        }
 8:    }
 9:
10:    public class CanvasDemo extends Applet {
11:
12:        public void init() {
13:            // Call parents init method.
14:            super.init();
15:
16:            canvas[0] = new MyCanvas();
17:            canvas[1] = new MyCanvas();
18:            canvas[2] = new MyCanvas();
19:            canvas[3] = new MyCanvas();
20:
21:            for(int i=0; i<4; i++)
22:                add(canvas[i]);
23:        }
24:
25:        public void addNotify() {
26:            // Call parents addNotify method.
27:            super.addNotify();
28:
29:            //{{INIT_CONTROLS
30:            setLayout(new GridLayout(2,2,0,0));
31:            resize(426,266);
32:            //}}
33:        }
34:
35:        MyCanvas canvas[] = new MyCanvas[4];
36:
37:        //{{DECLARE_CONTROLS
38:        //}}
39:    }
```

16

ANALYSIS The class MyCanvas is defined as a subclass of Canvas (lines 4–8) and the paint method is overridden. This method uses fillOval to draw an oval that is nearly the full height and width of the canvas. The CanvasDemo applet class declares an array of four MyCanvas objects (line 35) and then constructs each (lines 16–19). Each is then added to the applet form. Because the applet is using a 2×2 row column grid layout (line 30), each Canvas object fills one of these grid cells.

When the applet is painted, the paint method of MyCanvas is called to paint each of the four Canvas objects. Because the Canvas objects are placed according to a layout manager, they will stretch and resize themselves as necessary. This can be seen in Figures 16.10 and 16.11, which show the CanvasDemo applet before and after being resized.

Figure 16.10.

The CanvasDemo *applet at its original size.*

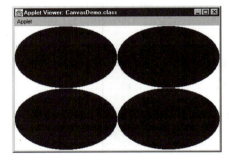

Figure 16.11.

The CanvasDemo *applet after being resized.*

Do	Don't

DO paint on a canvas instead of directly on the applet whenever possible.

DON'T forget that a form's paint method can be called quite often, including when the form is moved or resized. Take care to optimize the code you write in this method.

The Visual Café Shape Package

In addition to the java.awt.Graphics package, Visual Café includes its own package for drawing shapes. The Visual Café Shape package includes the following classes:

- ☐ Circle
- ☐ Ellipse
- ☐ HorizontalLine
- ☐ Rect

16

☐ Shape

☐ Square

☐ VerticalLine

The Shape class is abstract, so you cannot create instances of it, but the other six classes are available for direct use. Each of these six classes is available on the Shapes tab of the Component palette, and you can drag them onto the Form Designer. The sample applet ShapeDemo, which is included on the MCP Web site and shown in Figure 16.12, illustrates these classes.

Figure 16.12.

The ShapeDemo *applet illustrates the Visual Café Shape package.*

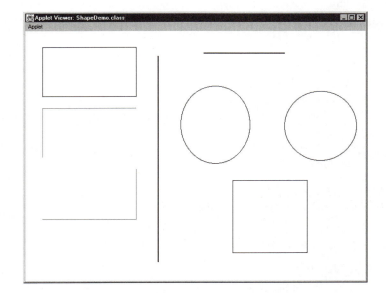

Each of these shapes allows you to set three additional properties beyond those that normally appear in the Property List. The additional properties are Border Style, Fill Color, and Fill Mode. Border Style can be set to control whether the shape appears to be raised above or lowered below the form and can be set to BEVEL_LINE, BEVEL_NONE, BEVEL_LOWERED, or BEVEL_RAISED.

Fill Mode is either true or false, and is used to specify whether the shape is filled or empty. If the shape is filled, the value of the Fill Color property specifies what color to use.

Images

In addition to geometric shapes and lines, you can also use the Graphics class to display images, such as JPG or GIF files. To do this, you use any of the four provided drawImage methods, whose signatures are as follows:

```
public abstract boolean drawImage(Image img, int x, int y,
    ImageObserver observer);

public abstract boolean drawImage(Image img, int x, int y,
    int width, int height, ImageObserver observer);

public abstract boolean drawImage(Image img, int x, int y,
    Color bgcolor, ImageObserver observer);

public abstract boolean drawImage(Image img, int x, int y,
    int width, int height,Color bgcolor,ImageObserver observer);
```

The first of these methods is passed the image itself, the coordinates of its top-left corner, and an ImageObserver. ImageObserver is an interface that is implemented by the Component class. Because Applet is a subclass of Component, you can use any class you derive from Applet as an ImageObserver. ImageObserver objects are useful because they can be sent information about the image as it is being loaded. Because Applet implements the ImageObserver interface, you can pass this as the ImageObserver parameter. This can be seen in the following code fragment:

```
public class MyClass extends Applet
{
    // ...other methods here
    public void paint(Graphics g)
    {
        g.drawImage(myImage, 100, 100, this);
    }
}
```

The second drawImage method is passed parameters for width and height. This causes the image to be scaled so that it appears in the specified rectangle. The final two drawImage methods are the same as the first two, with the addition of being able to specify a background color for the image.

Loading an Image

Before you can use drawImage you must have an Image object to draw. This can be done with either of the Applet class's getImage methods:

```
Image getImage(URL url)
```

```
Image getImage(URL url, String name)
```

Because each of these methods is passed a URL (Uniform Resource Locator), you must first create an instance of a URL. This can be done by using the following URL constructor:

```
public URL(String spec) throws MalformedURLException
```

This constructor is simply passed the URL as a string, as in the following example:

```
myURL = new URL("http://mtngoat/java/test.jpg");
```

However, because the constructor can throw MalformedURLException, the constructor must be enclosed in a try...catch block that catches the exception. This could be done as follows:

```
try {
    myURL = new URL("http://mtngoat/java/test.jpg");
}
catch (MalformedURLException e) {
    // handle error
}
```

Alternatively, because the methods getCodeBase and getDocumentBase each return a URL, either of these can be used in conjunction with getImage. To retrieve the URL of the applet, use getCodeBase. To retrieve the URL of the document from which the applet was loaded, use getDocumentBase.

Typically, an applet will call getImage from within the init method, as follows:

```
public class MyClass extends Applet
{
    Image myImage;

    // ...other methods here

    public void init()
    {
        // ... other code here
        myImage = getImage(getDocumentBase(), "savannah.jpg");
    }
}
```

As an example of displaying images, consider the ImageDemo applet, as shown in Listing 16.7. This applet is included on the MCP Web site.

Listing 16.7. The ImageDemo applet displays the same image at two different sizes.

```
1:    import java.awt.*;
2:    import java.applet.*;
3:    import java.awt.image.*;
4:
5:    public class ImageDemo extends Applet {
6:        public void paint(Graphics g) {
7:            // paint the image in the specified rectangle
8:            g.drawImage(myImage, 0, 0, 162, 244, this);
9:
```

continues

Listing 16.7. continued

```
10:        // paint the image on the screen
11:        g.drawImage(myImage, 180, 0, this);
12:    }
13:
14:    public void init() {
15:        // Call parents init method.
16:        super.init();
17:
18:        // create the image
19:        myImage = getImage(getDocumentBase(), "park2.jpg");
20:    }
21:
22:    public void addNotify() {
23:        // Call parents addNotify method.
24:        super.addNotify();
25:
26:        //{{INIT_CONTROLS
27:        setLayout(null);
28:        resize(485,368);
29:        //}}
30:    }
31:
32:    private Image myImage;
33:
34:    //{{DECLARE_CONTROLS
35:    //}}
36: }
```

ANALYSIS Note that because the Image class is in java.awt.image, this package must be imported (line 3). In the init method (lines 14–20), getImage is used to create the Image object, myImage, that is declared on line 32. In the paint method (lines 6–12), this image is displayed twice. The first use of drawImage specifies a square from point (0, 0) to point (162, 244). The image will be resized and displayed in this area. This can be seen in Figure 16.13. The second use of drawImage specifies only the coordinates of the top left of the image. In this case, the image will be drawn at its full size.

Filtering Images

It is also possible to create and use filters on images before they are displayed. The class CropImageFilter is provided in the java.awt.image package, and is a useful filter that enables you to display only a portion of the image. The CropImageDemo sample applet, shown in Listing 16.8 and included on the MCP Web site, illustrates how to use CropImageFilter.

16

Figure 16.13.

*The same image
displayed with two
different* drawImage
methods.

Listing 16.8. `CropImageDemo.java.`

```
1:    import java.awt.*;
2:    import java.applet.*;
3:    import java.awt.image.*;
4:
5:    public class CropImageDemo extends Applet {
6:        public void paint(Graphics g) {
7:            // paint the cropped image
8:            g.drawImage(croppedImage, 0, 0, this);
9:
10:           // paint the original image to the right of
11:           // the cropped one
12:           g.drawImage(myImage, 160, 0, this);
13:       }
14:
15:       public void init() {
16:           // Call parents init method.
17:           super.init();
18:
19:           myImage = getImage(getDocumentBase(), "savannah.jpg");
20:
21:           // create a filter that will crop the image to the
22:           // area starting at point (195, 0) with a width of 140
23:           // and a height of 150
24:           CropImageFilter myCropFilter = new CropImageFilter(
25:               195, 0, 140, 150);
26:
```

continues

Listing 16.8. continued

```
27:         // create a new image source based on the original image
28:         // and using the newly created filter
29:         FilteredImageSource imageSource = new
30:             FilteredImageSource(myImage.getSource(),
31:             myCropFilter);
32:
33:         // create the cropped image
34:         croppedImage = createImage(imageSource);
35:     }
36:
37:     public void addNotify() {
38:         // Call parents addNotify method.
39:         super.addNotify();
40:
41:         //{{INIT_CONTROLS
42:         setLayout(null);
43:         resize(586,578);
44:         //}}
45:     }
46:
47:     private Image myImage;
48:     private Image croppedImage;
49:
50:     //{{DECLARE_CONTROLS
51:     //}}
52: }
```

ANALYSIS   After using getImage to create the Image object (line 19), the init method constructs a new CropImageFilter object named myCropFilter (lines 24–25). This constructor is passed the x and y coordinates, and the width and height of where to start cropping the image. In this case, a rectangle 140 pixels wide and 150 high will be cropped beginning at point (195, 0). Next, the constructor for FilteredImageSource is used to create a new image source (lines 29–31). The image source is based on the original image and myCropFilter. Finally, createImage is used to return the actual Image object (line 34).

This work is put to use in the paint method (lines 6–13). This method uses drawImage first to display the cropped image and then to display the original image for comparison. The results can be seen in Figure 16.14.

Writing Your Own Image Filter

It is also possible to create your own filters. To do so, you create a subclass of either ImageFilter or RGBImageFilter and override methods to provide the filtering you want. The RGBImageFilter class is a subclass of ImageFilter, and makes it very easy to write a filter that manipulates the colors of the individual pixels in an image.

Figure 16.14.

The `CropImageFilter` *can be used to crop images.*

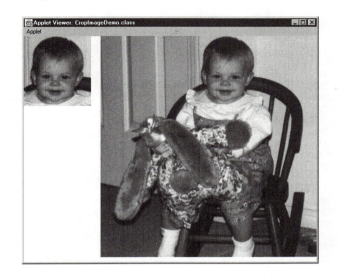

As an example of how you can create your own filter based on `RGBImageFilter`, imagine you need to write a filter that will remove part of an image. This could be very useful in a litigation support system for processing documents. In this type of system, it is important to be able to redact, or black-out, text. Or, as you'll see in this example, a redaction filter is useful for hiding the eyes of a Mafia informant. Listing 16.9 shows the `CustomFilterDemo` applet, which is included on the MCP Web site. This example illustrates the use of a redaction filter, as can be seen in Figure 16.15.

Listing 16.9. `CustomFilterDemo.java` **illustrates the creation of a custom filter.**

```
1:    import java.awt.*;
2:    import java.applet.*;
3:    import java.awt.image.*;
4:
5:    class RedactFilter extends RGBImageFilter {
6:        int startX, startY, endX, endY;
7:
8:        // the constructor is passed the coordinates of the area
9:        // to redact and stores these values
10:       public RedactFilter(int x, int y, int width,int height) {
11:           startX = x;
12:           startY = y;
13:           endX   = startX + width;
14:           endY   = startY + height;
15:       }
16:
```

continues

Listing 16.9. continued

```
17:     public int filterRGB(int x, int y, int rgb) {
18:         // if the (x,y) position is in the redacted area
19:         // return red, otherwise return the same color that
20:         // was passed in
21:         if (x>=startX && x<=endX && y >= startY && y <= endY)
22:             return 0xff0000ff;
23:         else
24:             return rgb;
25:     }
26: }
27:
28: public class CustomFilterDemo extends Applet {
29:     public void paint(Graphics g) {
30:         // paint the redacted image
31:         g.drawImage(redactedImage, 0, 0, this);
32:     }
33:
34:     public void init() {
35:         // Call parents init method.
36:         super.init();
37:
38:         // get the original image
39:         myImage = getImage(getDocumentBase(), "savannah.jpg");
40:
41:         // create a filter and specify the range to be redacted
42:         ImageFilter filter = new RedactFilter(220, 80, 80, 15);
43:
44:         // create a new image source based on the original
45:         // image and the new filter
46:         FilteredImageSource imageSource=new FilteredImageSource(
47:                 myImage.getSource(), filter);
48:
49:         // create the redacted image from the image source
50:         redactedImage = createImage(imageSource);
51:     }
52:
53:     public void addNotify() {
54:         // Call parents addNotify method.
55:         super.addNotify();
56:
57:         //{{INIT_CONTROLS
58:         setLayout(null);
59:         resize(562,469);
60:         //}}
61:     }
62:
63:     private Image myImage;
64:     private Image redactedImage;
65:
66:     //{{DECLARE_CONTROLS
67:     //}}
68: }
```

ANALYSIS The class RedactFilter (lines 5–26) is defined as a subclass of RGBImageFilter. Its constructor (lines 10–15) is passed values that indicate the area to be redacted. The method filterRGB (lines 17–25) is an overridden member of RGBImageFilter. This method is called once for each pixel in the image. Its x and y parameters indicate the location of the pixel being passed. Its rgb parameter indicates the current color of the pixel. The value returned by filterRGB is the color that will be displayed for this pixel. To alter the image, return something different from the current value in rgb. In this case, RedactFilter checks whether the pixel is within the specified area (line 21). If so, red is returned. If not, the unchanged rgb value is returned.

Figure 16.15.

The RedactFilter *can be used to conceal the identity of a Mafia informant.*

The RedactFilter is used in a manner very similar to how CropImageFilter was used in the prior example. In the init method of CustomFilterDemo (lines 34–51), getImage is used to create the image (line 39). Next, a new instance of RedactFilter is constructed and a new image source is created based on the original image and the filter (lines 42–47). Finally, createImage is used to create the redacted image from the image source (line 50). The paint method (lines 29–32) uses drawImage as it would with any other image.

The ImageObserver Interface

As you might recall, when the drawImage method was introduced, you needed to pass this as the final parameter to it, as in the following example:

```
g.drawImage(redactedImage, 0, 0, this);
```

This parameter represents an `ImageObserver` and because the `Applet` class implements the `ImageObserver` interface through the `Component` class, you can use an `Applet` object's `this` variable. So far you've been asked to take this parameter on faith. Now it's time to see what an `ImageObserver` can do.

The `ImageObserver` interface includes a single method. This method, `imageUpdate`, is called whenever additional information about an image becomes available. For example, it might take time to retrieve a large image across the Internet. The `ImageObserver` interface can monitor the progress of an image retrieval. An applet could then display a progress message, an estimated time to complete, or take any other useful action. The signature of `imageUpdate` is as follows:

```
public abstract boolean imageUpdate(Image img, int infoflags,
        int x, int y, int width, int height);
```

The first parameter represents the image being updated. The second parameter represents a combination of various flags that give information about the image. These flags are described in Table 16.2. The remaining parameters usually represent a rectangle indicating the portion of the image that has been retrieved so far. Depending on the values in the `infoflags` parameter, some of these parameters might be invalid. The `imageUpdate` method should return `true` if you want to continue receiving updates, or `false` otherwise.

Table 16.2. Flags used in the `imageUpdate` method.

Flag	Description
ABORT	Retrieval of the image was aborted.
ALLBITS	All bits of the image have been retrieved.
ERROR	An error occurred while the image was retrieved.
FRAMEBITS	A frame that is part of a multiframe image has been completely retrieved.
HEIGHT	The `height` parameter now represents the final height of the image.
PROPERTIES	The properties of the image have been retrieved.
SOMEBITS	More bits have been retrieved.
WIDTH	The `width` parameter now represents the final width of the image.

As an example of how `imageUpdate` can be used, consider the `ImageObserverDemo` applet, shown in Listing 16.10 and included on the MCP Web site. In this example, a text area is created that will be used to display status messages. The `imageUpdate` method compares the value in the `infoflags` parameter against `ImageObserver.ERROR` and `ImageObserver.ALLBITS`. When one of these flags is set, a message is appended to the text area.

Listing 16.10. The `ImageObserverDemo` **applet illustrates the use of the**
`ImageObserver` **interface.**

```
1:    import java.awt.*;
2:    import java.applet.*;
3:    import java.awt.image.*;
4:
5:    public class ImageObserverDemo extends Applet {
6:
7:        public void init() {
8:            // Call parents init method.
9:            super.init();
10:
11:           // create the image
12:           myImage = getImage(getDocumentBase(), "savannah.jpg");
13:       }
14:
15:       public void addNotify() {
16:           // Call parents addNotify method.
17:           super.addNotify();
18:
19:           //{{INIT_CONTROLS
20:           setLayout(null);
21:           resize(625,411);
22:           status = new java.awt.TextArea();
23:           status.reshape(420,12,180,252);
24:           add(status);
25:           //}}
26:       }
27:
28:       public void paint(Graphics g) {
29:           // paint the image in the specified rectangle
30:           g.drawImage(myImage, 10, 10, 350, 350, this);
31:       }
32:
33:       public synchronized boolean imageUpdate(Image img,
34:               int infoflags, int x,int y,int width,int height) {
35:           // if an error occurs, display the message
36:           if ((infoflags & ImageObserver.ERROR) != 0)
37:               status.appendText("Error\r\n");
38:
39:           // once all the bits have been received display
40:           // a message and repaint the applet
41:           if ((infoflags & ImageObserver.ALLBITS) != 0) {
42:               status.appendText("Allbits\r\n");
43:               repaint();
44:           }
45:           return true;
46:       }
47:
48:       private Image myImage;
49:
```

continues

Listing 16.10. continued

```
50:      //{{DECLARE_CONTROLS
51:      java.awt.TextArea status;
52:      //}}
53:  }
```

Do	Don't

DO use an `ImageObserver` when possible to monitor the status of an image.

DON'T use too many large images at any one time. Some of an applet's users might be using 14.4 modems that are too slow for effective image retrieval.

The `ImageViewer` Component

Visual Café includes a component, `ImageViewer`, that simplifies some aspects of working with images. The `ImageViewer` component is on the Multimedia tab of the Component palette, and can be dragged onto the Form Designer. You can also create an `ImageViewer` by using one of the following constructors:

```
ImageViewer()

ImageViewer(Image src) throws MalformedURLException

ImageViewer(String src) throws MalformedURLException

ImageViewer(URL src) throws MalformedURLException
```

Within the Property List you can set two properties beyond the normal ones. The `Center Mode` property, which can be set to true or false, indicates whether the image will be centered in the area allocated for it. The `URL` property can be used to specify the URL of an image that will be displayed when the component is first shown. You can enter a filename in this property to display a file.

Because an `ImageViewer` can be created from an image, string, or URL, the `ImageViewer` class includes methods for manipulating each of these components, as shown in Table 16.3.

Table 16.3. Additional public methods of `ImageViewer`.

Method	Purpose
getFileName()	Returns a string containing the filename of the image.
getImage()	Returns the image that is being displayed.
getURL()	Returns the URL of the image that is being displayed.

Method	Purpose
setFileName(String)	Sets the filename of the image to display.
setImage(Image)	Sets the image to display.
setURL(URL)	Sets the URL of the image to display.

The ImageViewerDemo applet, shown in Listing 16.11 and included on the MCP Web site, illustrates the use of the ImageViewer component. The centerButton_Clicked method (lines 2–12) allows the user to adjust the image from centered to not centered. When not centered, the image is placed in the top left. The result of running ImageViewerDemo is shown in Figure 16.16.

Listing 16.11. `ImageViewerDemo.java.`

```
 1:  import java.awt.*;
 2:  import java.applet.*;
 3:
 4:  public class ImageViewerDemo extends Applet {
 5:      void centerButton_Clicked(java.awt.event.ActionEvent
 6:              event) {
 7:          try {
 8:              if(centerButton.getLabel().equals("Center")) {
 9:                  imgViewer.setCenterMode(true);
10:                  centerButton.setLabel("Uncenter");
11:              }
12:              else {
13:                  imgViewer.setCenterMode(false);
14:                  centerButton.setLabel("Center");
15:              }
16:              imgViewer.repaint();
17:          }
18:          catch (java.beans.PropertyVetoException e) {
19:          }
20:      }
21:
22:      public void init() {
23:          // Call parents init method.
24:          super.init();
25:      }
26:
27:      public void addNotify() {
28:          // Call parents addNotify method.
29:          super.addNotify();
30:
31:          //{{INIT_CONTROLS
32:          setLayout(null);
33:          resize(437,313);
```

continues

Listing 16.11. continued

```
34:        centerButton = new java.awt.Button("Center");
35:        centerButton.reshape(288,48,84,21);
36:        add(centerButton);
37:        borderPanel1 = new symantec.itools.awt.BorderPanel();
38:        borderPanel1.setLayout(new BorderLayout(0,0));
39:        borderPanel1.reshape(24,24,228,264);
40:        add(borderPanel1);
41:        imgViewer = new symantec.itools.multimedia.ImageViewer();
42:        imgViewer.reshape(0,0,207,238);
43:        borderPanel1.add("Center", imgViewer);
44:        try {
45:            imgViewer.setCenterMode(false);
46:        }
47:        catch (java.beans.PropertyVetoException veto) { }
48:        try {
49:            imgViewer.setURL(
50:    symantec.itools.net.RelativeURL.getURL("Vclogo.gif"));
51:        }
52:        catch (java.net.MalformedURLException error) { }
53:        catch (java.beans.PropertyVetoException veto) { }
54:        //}}

55:
56:        //{{REGISTER_LISTENERS
57:        Action lAction = new Action();
58:        centerButton.addActionListener(lAction);
59:        //}}
60:    }
61:
62:    //{{DECLARE_CONTROLS
63:    java.awt.Button centerButton;
64:    symantec.itools.awt.BorderPanel borderPanel1;
65:    symantec.itools.multimedia.ImageViewer imgViewer;
66:    //}}
67:
68:    class Action implements java.awt.event.ActionListener {
69:        public void actionPerformed(java.awt.event.ActionEvent
70:            event) {
71:          Object object = event.getSource();
72:          if (object == centerButton)
73:              centerButton_Clicked(event);
74:        }
75:    }
76: }
```

 TIP

> If you are working with images retrieved from a database, you should consider using the database-aware ImageViewer class. This class is described in Chapter 21, "Using the dbAWARE Components."

16

Figure 16.16.

The result of running
`ImageViewerDemo`.

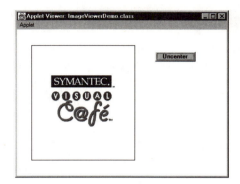

Summary

This chapter gave you an in-depth look at the `Graphics` class and how you can use the methods of this class to enhance the appearance of your Java programs. In this chapter, you learned how to draw outlined and filled shapes such as lines, arcs, ovals, rectangles, and polygons. You learned how to use the `Canvas` class to better control the placement of drawn figures. You saw how the Visual Café `Shape` classes offer an alternative to the AWT's `Graphics` class.

You also learned about the `Image` class. You learned how to filter, crop, and modify images prior to display. Finally, you saw how the `ImageObserver` interface allows an applet to monitor the progress of an image that is being retrieved. In the next chapter you will learn how to further improve your Java programs by using Visual Café's multimedia capabilities.

Q&A

Q Why does Visual Café let me draw shapes both through the `java.awt.Graphics` class and through its own Shape package?

A Each approach has its advantages. The methods in the `Graphics` class are more flexible in that you can draw many more shapes (largely through the polygon methods). However, you cannot use the `Graphics` class in the Form Designer. For this you need the Visual Café Shape package.

Q How can I animate an image?

A Animation is covered in the next chapter.

Q I'd like to use the `ImageViewer` component, but I also need to filter the image. Filtering appears to be available only if I use the `Image` class instead of `ImageViewer`. Is there a way to use both?

A Yes, there is. Since one of the constructors for `ImageViewer` is passed an `Image` object, simply filter the image and pass the result to the `ImageViewer` constructor.

Workshop

The workshop includes quiz questions to help you gauge your understanding of the material in this chapter. The workshop also includes exercises to provide hands-on experience with what you've learned in this chapter. Answers to the quiz questions can be found in Appendix D, "Answers."

Quiz

1. What are the seven shapes that can be drawn by the `Graphics` class?

2. What is the difference between `drawRect` and `fillRect`?

3. The `Graphics` class does not include a `drawCircle` method. How would you draw a circle?

4. What is the main advantage of using the `Canvas` class?

5. What provided class can you use to display only a portion of an image?

6. If you create your own filter by extending `RGBImageFilter`, you override the method `public int filterRGB(int x, int y, int rgb)`. How often is this method called and what value should it return?

7. What must you do to have your `Applet` subclass implement the `ImageObserver` interface?

Exercises

1. Create a subclass of `Graphics` that can be used to paint squares and circles.

2. Write an applet that displays only the top-left quarter of an image.

3. Use `ImageViewer` to write an applet that allows the user to enter the name of an image file to view.

4. Do ten situps. After all, there's no sense dying of a heart attack now that you're almost done with the book.

5. Create a custom filter that lightens an image.

16

Day **17**

Multimedia Programming

In this chapter you will learn how Visual Café simplifies multimedia programming through some of the components in its Object Library. You will learn how to use the SlideShow component to display a series of images and how to create animations with Animator and MovingAnimation. You will also learn about the Emblaze20, Firework, Plasma, and NervousText components. Although you will probably use these components less frequently than SlideShow, Animator, and MovingAnimation, they are appropriate for some programs. You will also learn how to add sound to your programs with the SoundPlayer component. Finally, you will learn about the MediaTracker class, which will be useful if you want to program your own multimedia classes.

SlideShow

The SlideShow component can be used to easily display a sequence of images with a Visual Café program. As shown in Figure 17.1, SlideShow is simply an extension of Panel. The SlideShow class is actually very similar to the ImageViewer class you learned about in Chapter 16, "Working with Graphics." However, SlideShow goes beyond ImageViewer by adding methods that facilitate the use of multiple images.

Figure 17.1.
SlideShow *extends*
Panel.

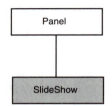

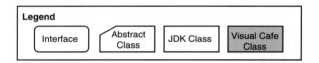

To create a SlideShow object, drag one onto the Form Designer or use its parameterless constructor as in the following example:

```
SlideShow myShow = new SlideShow();
```

Slide shows are composed with images, and each image may have a description. To add an image and its description to the show, use the method addImageAndDescription, whose signature is as follows:

```
int addImageAndDescription(URL location, String desc)
```

The *location* parameter indicates where the image is located. The *desc* parameter is a description of the image. You can pass an empty string if a program does not use descriptions, but image descriptions can be useful for a variety of reasons: Users can search for an image by description, or a description can simply be displayed adjacent to the image. The return value of addImageAndDescription will be the image's index number in the slide show; the first image is assigned an index of 0.

Displaying Images

The following methods can be used to display an image in the slide show:

```
void display()
```

```
int nextImage()
```

```
int previousImage()
```

```
int setImage(int index)
```

To start the show and display the first image, use `display`. After that, you can use `nextImage` and `previousImage` to navigate sequentially through the show. Alternatively, you can use `setImage` to move to a specific index number. The integer returned by `nextImage`, `previousImage`, and `setImage` represents the index number of the image that is displayed by the slide show after the call to these methods completes.

Setting and Getting Information

You can set or get an image's description by using the following methods:

```
String getDescription(int index)
```

```
void setDescription(int index, String desc)
```

For example, the following will set the description of the second image to `I Am Image Two`:

```
mySlideShow.setDescription(1, "I Am Image Two");
```

If you would rather know the URL of a specific image index, you can determine that by using `getURL(int index)`, as shown in the following example:

```
URL theURL = getURL(2);
```

The following four methods are provided for working with index numbers:

```
int getCurrentImageIndex()
```

```
int getNumberOfImages()
```

```
boolean isAtFirstImage()
```

```
boolean isAtLastImage()
```

The `getCurrentImageIndex` method returns the index of the image currently being displayed. To find out how many images are in the show, use `getNumberOfImages`. `isAtFirstImage` and `isAtLastImage` can be used to determine whether the show is displaying its first or last image.

17

An Example

The `SlideShowDemo` sample applet is provided on the MCP Web site (`www.mcp.com/info/ 1-57521/1-57521-303-6`). This applet displays a `SlideShow` component that displays the four images shown in Figures 17.2 through 17.5. The source code for this applet is shown in Listing 17.1.

Figure 17.2.

The first image in `SlideShowDemo` *is a bullet hole.*

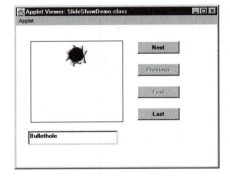

Figure 17.3.

The second image in `SlideShowDemo` *is a light bulb.*

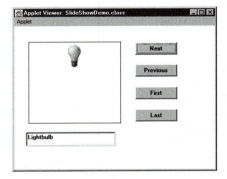

Figure 17.4.

The third image in `SlideShowDemo` *is a smiley face.*

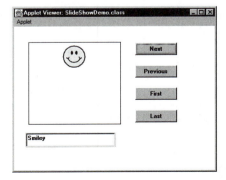

Figure 17.5.

The fourth image in SlideShowDemo *is a sphere.*

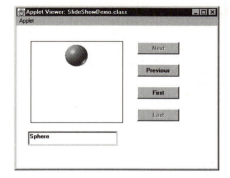

Listing 17.1. `SlideShowDemo.java.`

```
1:   import java.awt.*;
2:   import java.applet.*;
3:   import symantec.itools.awt.*;
4:   import java.net.*;
5:
6:   public class SlideShowDemo extends Applet {
7:       void prevButton_Clicked(java.awt.event.ActionEvent
8:               event) {
9:         slideShow.previousImage();
10:        UpdateButtons();
11:        ShowDescription();
12:      }
13:
14:      void firstButton_Clicked(java.awt.event.ActionEvent
15:              event) {
16:        slideShow.setImage(0);
17:        UpdateButtons();
18:        ShowDescription();
19:      }
20:
21:      void lastButton_Clicked(java.awt.event.ActionEvent
22:              event) {
23:        int qty = slideShow.getNumberOfImages();
24:        slideShow.setImage(qty - 1);
25:        UpdateButtons();
26:        ShowDescription();
27:      }
28:
29:      void nextButton_Clicked(java.awt.event.ActionEvent
30:              event) {
31:        slideShow.nextImage();
32:        UpdateButtons();
33:        ShowDescription();
34:      }
35:
36:      void UpdateButtons() {
```

continues

17

Listing 17.1. continued

```
37:            if(slideShow.isAtLastImage()) {
38:                nextButton.enable(false);
39:                lastButton.enable(false);
40:            }
41:            else {
42:                nextButton.enable(true);
43:                lastButton.enable(true);
44:            }
45:            if(slideShow.isAtFirstImage()) {
46:                firstButton.enable(false);
47:                prevButton.enable(false);
48:            }
49:            else {
50:                firstButton.enable(true);
51:                prevButton.enable(true);
52:            }
53:        }
54:
55:     private void ShowDescription() {
56:         int current = slideShow.getCurrentImageIndex();
57:         descField.setText(slideShow.getDescription(current));
58:     }
59:
60:     private void LoadImages() {
61:         try {
62:             slideShow.addImageAndDescription(new URL(
63:     "file:/C:/source/CHAP17/SlideShowDemo/bullethole.gif"),
64:     "Bullethole");
65:             slideShow.addImageAndDescription(new URL(
66:     "file:/C:/source/CHAP17/SlideShowDemo/lightbulb.gif"),
67:     "Lightbulb");
68:             slideShow.addImageAndDescription(new URL(
69:     "file:/C:/source/CHAP17/SlideShowDemo/smiley.gif"),
70:     "Smiley");
71:             slideShow.addImageAndDescription(new URL(
72:     "file:/C:/source/CHAP17/SlideShowDemo/sphere.gif"),
73:     "Sphere");
74:             slideShow.display();
75:         }
76:         catch (MalformedURLException e) {
77:         }
78:
79:         ShowDescription();
80:         UpdateButtons();
81:     }
82:
83:     public void init() {
84:         // Call parents init method.
85:         super.init();
86:
87:         LoadImages();
88:     }
89:
90:     public void addNotify() {
91:         // Call parents addNotify method.
```

17

```
92:          super.addNotify();
93:
94:          //{{INIT_CONTROLS
95:          setLayout(null);
96:          resize(418,306);
97:          borderPanel1 = new symantec.itools.awt.BorderPanel();
98:          borderPanel1.setLayout(new BorderLayout(0,0));
99:          borderPanel1.reshape(24,24,204,192);
100:         add(borderPanel1);
101:         slideShow = new symantec.itools.multimedia.SlideShow();
102:         slideShow.reshape(0,0,183,166);
103:         borderPanel1.add("Center", slideShow);
104:         nextButton = new java.awt.Button("Next");
105:         nextButton.reshape(252,36,87,26);
106:         add(nextButton);
107:         prevButton = new java.awt.Button("Previous");
108:         prevButton.reshape(252,84,87,26);
109:         add(prevButton);
110:         firstButton = new java.awt.Button("First");
111:         firstButton.reshape(252,132,87,26);
112:         add(firstButton);
113:         lastButton = new java.awt.Button("Last");
114:         lastButton.reshape(252,180,87,26);
115:         add(lastButton);
116:         descField = new java.awt.TextField();
117:         descField.reshape(24,228,187,31);
118:         add(descField);
119:         //}}
120:
121:         //{{REGISTER_LISTENERS
122:         Action lAction = new Action();
123:         nextButton.addActionListener(lAction);
124:         lastButton.addActionListener(lAction);
125:         firstButton.addActionListener(lAction);
126:         prevButton.addActionListener(lAction);
127:         //}}
128:     }
129:
130:     //{{DECLARE_CONTROLS
131:     symantec.itools.awt.BorderPanel borderPanel1;
132:     symantec.itools.multimedia.SlideShow slideShow;
133:     java.awt.Button nextButton;
134:     java.awt.Button prevButton;
135:     java.awt.Button firstButton;
136:     java.awt.Button lastButton;
137:     java.awt.TextField descField;
138:     //}}
139:
140:     class Action implements java.awt.event.ActionListener {
141:         public void actionPerformed(java.awt.event.ActionEvent
142:             event) {
143:             Object object = event.getSource();
144:             if (object == nextButton)
145:                 nextButton_Clicked(event);
146:             else if (object == lastButton)
147:                 lastButton_Clicked(event);
```

continues

Listing 17.1. continued

```
148:                 else if (object == firstButton
149:                     firstButton_Clicked(event)
150:                 else if (object == prevButton
151:                     prevButton_Clicked(event)
152:
153:
154:
```

 The first thing you should notice in Listing 17.1 is that line 4 imports the `java.ne` package. Because the program will be constructing URLs, it will use the `java.ne` package

The `LoadImages` method (lines 60–81) uses four calls to `addImageAndDescription` to add th four images to the slide show. Because the `URL` constructor can throw `MalformedURLException` this exception is caught on lines 76–77. After the images have been loaded, the slide sho is started with `display` on line 74. `LoadImages` completes by calling `ShowDescription` an `UpdateButtons`

`ShowDescription` (lines 55–58) uses `getCurrentImageIndex` and `getDescription` to retriev the description of the currently selected image. The description is then displayed in a text fiel on the form

`UpdateButtons` (lines 36–53) ensures that buttons are enabled only when they have an actio to perform. For example, if the user is looking at the first image, it makes no sense to give hi the option of moving to a previous image. For this reason, these buttons are disabled i `isAtFirstImage` (line 45) is `true`. A similar test is done with `isAtLastImage` for the Next an Last buttons

The event-handling methods `prevButton_Clicked` (lines 7–12) and `nextButton_Clicke` (lines 29–34) use `previousImage` and `nextImage` to change images. After the image is changed they call `UpdateButtons` and `ShowDescription` to change these components on the form.

To move to the first image in the show, `firstButton_Clicked` uses `slideShow.setImage(0)` Moving to the last image is only trivially more complicated: In order to determine the valu to pass `setImage`, a call is made to `getNumberOfImages`. Because image indexes are zero-based one less than this value represents the last image in the show; this value is passed to `setImage`

Animato

There might be times when you will want to go beyond a slide show and include an animate sequence in one of your Visual Café programs. The `Animator` class makes this very simple t do. As shown in Figure 17.6, `Animator` extends `Canvas` and implements the `Runnabl` interface

Figure 17.6.
Animator *extends*
Canvas *and*
implements
Runnable.

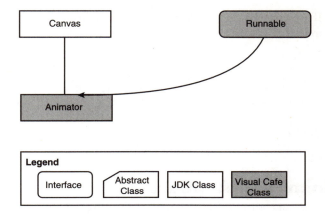

To create an Animator object, drag one onto the Form Designer or use the parameterless constructor, as in the following example:

```
Animator myAnimation = new Animator();
```

Like SlideShow, Animation works with a list of images. You can add images to an animation by using the following methods:

```
void addImage(URL location)
```

```
void setImageList(URL[] locations)
```

If you are starting with an empty animation and want to add a set of images, this is most easily accomplished with setImageList. The following example, from the AnimationDemo sample applet that is included on the MCP Web site, shows how to use setImageList to place 10 images into an animation:

```
private void LoadImages() {
    try {
        URL[] tempURL = new URL[10];
        tempURL[0] = new URL("file:/C:/AnimatorDemo/Bean1.gif");
        tempURL[1] = new URL("file:/C:/AnimatorDemo/Bean2.gif");
        tempURL[2] = new URL("file:/C:/AnimatorDemo/Bean3.gif");
        tempURL[3] = new URL("file:/C:/AnimatorDemo/Bean4.gif");
        tempURL[4] = new URL("file:/C:/AnimatorDemo/Bean5.gif");
        tempURL[5] = new URL("file:/C:/AnimatorDemo/Bean6.gif");
        tempURL[6] = new URL("file:/C:/AnimatorDemo/Bean7.gif");
        tempURL[7] = new URL("file:/C:/AnimatorDemo/Bean8.gif");
        tempURL[8] = new URL("file:/C:/AnimatorDemo/Bean9.gif");
        tempURL[9] = new URL("file:/C:/AnimatorDemo/Bean10.gif");
    } catch (MalformedURLException e) {
}
```

If you need to add an image to the end of an animation sequence, use addImage, as in the following example:

```
try {
    myAnimation.addImage(new URL("file:/C:end1.gif"));
    myAnimation.addImage(new URL("file:/C:end2.gif"));
    myAnimation.addImage(new URL("file:/C:end3.gif"));
} catch (MalformedURLException e) {
}
```

To determine what images are used by an Animation object, use the getImageList method:

```
URL[] getImageList();
```

Animation Appearance

You can control the appearance of an animation by using the following four methods:

```
void setClearFrame(boolean clear)
```

```
void setDelay(int milliseconds)
```

```
void setNumLoops(int loopCount)
```

```
void setRepeatMode(boolean repeat)
```

Use setClearFrame to specify whether the canvas should be erased before each image in the animation is drawn. If the frame is not cleared, the images will be drawn on top of each other. The setDelay method can be used to specify how many milliseconds should pass before each new image is drawn. To specify a 1-second delay between each image, use the following:

```
myAnimation.setDelay(1000);
```

The setNumLoops method specifies how many loops through the image sequence will be performed. If you want the animation to execute endlessly rather than for a particular number of loops, use setRepeatMode(true). This causes the animation to repeat an infinite number of times.

Naturally, there are methods that retrieve the value of each of these properties:

```
boolean getClearFrame()
```

```
int getDelay()
```

```
int getNumLoops()
```

```
boolean getRepeatMode()
```

17

Starting and Stopping

You can start and stop an animation by using the following methods:

```
void startAnimation()
```

```
void stopAnimation()
```

MovingAnimation

As shown in Figure 17.7, MovingAnimation is a subclass of Animator that also implements the Runnable interface. MovingAnimation gives Animator the capability to move an object across a form by drawing each image at a slightly different location.

Figure 17.7.

MovingAnimation *extends* Animator *and implements* Runnable.

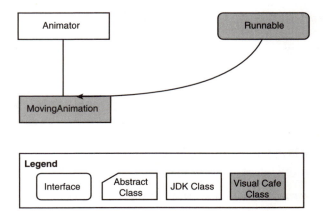

This type of animation is frequently used to give the impression of movement. In the MovingAnimationDemo sample applet (included on the MCP Web site), this type of animation is used to make Duke appear to tumble across the screen, as shown in Figures 17.8, 17.9, and 17.10.

Figure 17.8.

Duke begins to tumble in the MovingAnimationDemo *applet.*

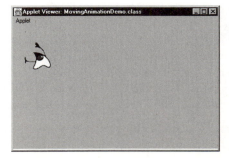

Figure 17.9.

Duke is midway through his tumble in the MovingAnimationDemo *applet.*

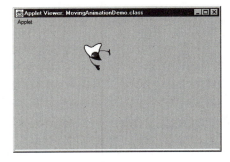

Figure 17.10.

Duke has nearly completed his tumble in the MovingAnimationDemo *applet.*

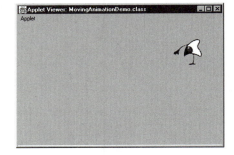

To create a MovingAnimation object, drag one onto the Form Designer or use the parameterless constructor, as in this example:

```
MovingAnimation myAnimation = new MovingAnimation();
```

Because MovingAnimation draws so heavily on the capabilities of Animator, it adds few methods of its own. When each image is drawn, it is shifted a specifiable number of pixels to the right. To set or get the shift amount, use the following methods:

```
void setShiftOffset(int offset)
```

```
int getShiftOffset()
```

Emblaze

Another option for adding animation to your Visual Café programs is to use the Emblaze20 component. This component displays animations that have been created with the Emblaze Creator product from the GEO Interactive Media Group. For more information about Emblaze or GEO, go to http://www.emblaze.com.

To create an Emblaze20 object, drag one onto the Form Designer. In the Property List, set the URL property of the object.

Firework

The Firework component is not terribly useful in real programs, but you might be able to use it to enliven an otherwise dull-looking page. As shown in Figure 17.11, the Firework component paints a series of rocket-like bursts on a canvas. To do this, Firework extends Canvas and implements the Runnable interface. This is shown in Figure 17.12.

Figure 17.11.

The Firework
component in action.

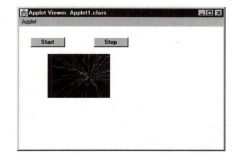

Figure 17.12.

Firework *extends*
Canvas *and*
implements the
Runnable *interface.*

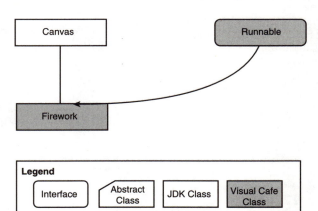

To create a new Firework component, drag one onto the Form Designer or use the parameterless constructor as follows:

```
Firework myFireworks = new Firework();
```

When the component is added to the form, it automatically starts running. You can stop or start the launching of additional fireworks by using the following methods:

```
freezeRockets()
```

```
unfreezeRockets()
```

TIP

> The Firework component is an excessive hog of CPU when used in the
> Form Designer. Because Firework is so easy to use, you will generally
> be better off creating it and adding it to a form in code rather than in
> the Form Designer. For example, the following creates a Firework
> object of the specified size and places it on the form:
>
> ```
> firework1 = new Firework();
> firework1.reshape(60,60,130,96);
> add(firework1);
> ```

Plasma

Similar to Firework in usefulness is the Plasma component. This component can be used to
place a multicolored blob on a form. The blob gradually changes as the program is run.
Although black-and-white doesn't do it justice, it can be seen in Figure 17.13. Like Firework,
Plasma extends Canvas and implements the Runnable interface, as shown in Figure 17.14.

Figure 17.13.

The Plasma *compo-
nent as it oozes across
a form.*

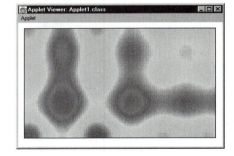

Figure 17.14.

Plasma *extends*
Canvas *and
implements the*
Runnable *interface.*

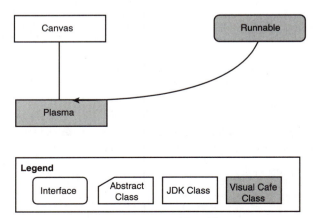

To add a `Plasma` component to a form, drag one onto the Form Designer or use the parameterless constructor, as follows:

```
Plasma myPlasma = new Plasma();
```

A `Plasma` object will begin oozing when the form is loaded, but you can start or stop the plasma at runtime with the following methods:

```
startPlasma()
```

```
stopPlasma()
```

TIP

If you add a `Plasma` component to a form in the Form Designer, it will not automatically begin oozing. To see the `Plasma` component ooze in the Form Designer, you must set its Preview Component property to `true`.

NervousText

The `NervousText` component can be used to display text that appears to dance or bounce around the canvas on which it is drawn. Figure 17.15 displays the message `This is nervous text`. Like `Firework` and `Plasma`, `NervousText` extends `Canvas` and implements the `Runnable` interface. This is shown in Figure 17.16.

Figure 17.15.
The NervousText
component in action.

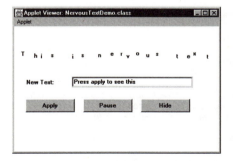

To use a `NervousText` component, drag one onto the Form Designer or use the constructor as in the following example:

```
NervousText myNervousText = new NervousText();
```

Figure 17.16.

`NervousText` *extends*
`Canvas` *and*
implements the
`Runnable` *interface.*

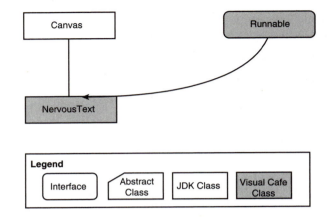

You can set or get the text that will be displayed by using these methods:

```
String getText()
```

```
void setText(String newText)
```

The following method from the `NervousTextDemo` applet, which is included on the MCP Web site, sets the nervous text to a string the user entered in a text field:

```
void applyButton_Clicked(Event event) {
   nervousText.setText(newText.getText());
}
```

To temporarily hide or show a hidden `NervousText` component, use the following methods:

```
void hide()
```

```
void show()
```

This is shown in the following method:

```
void hideButton_Clicked(java.awt.event.ActionEvent event) {
    if (hideButton.getLabel().equals("Hide")) {
        nervousText.hide();
        hideButton.setLabel("Show");
    }
    else {
        nervousText.show();
        hideButton.setLabel("Hide");
    }
}
```

This method checks a button's label to see whether the user wants to hide or show the nervous text. If the user wants to hide the text, `Hide` is used and the button's label is toggled to `Show`. If the user wants to show already hidden nervous text, `Show` is used and the button's label is toggled to `Hide`.

Sometimes you don't want to hide nervous text but do want to stop it from jumping around. Fortunately, you can pause nervous text; it remains in place until it is unpaused. Pausing is supported by the following methods:

```
boolean isPaused()

void pause(boolean)
```

SoundPlayer

The SoundPlayer component is a nonvisual component, meaning that it will not appear on a form at runtime. You can, however, work with it visually in the Form Designer while programming. Because SoundPlayer has no visual aspects, it does not derive from Canvas as do many other multimedia components. Instead, as shown in Figure 17.17, SoundPlayer is a direct subclass of Object.

Figure 17.17.

SoundPlayer *is a direct subclass of* Object.

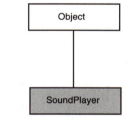

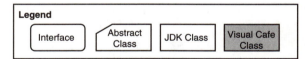

To create a new SoundPlayer object, drag one onto the Form Designer or use the constructor, as shown in this example:

```
SoundPlayer mySounds = new SoundPlayer();
```

Adding Sounds

A SoundPlayer object plays sounds that are stored in Sun's AU file format. A sound player can play more than one sound and can play the sound files either simultaneously or in sequence. You can use the following methods to work with a SoundPlayer's sound list:

```
void setURLList(URL[] urlList)

URL[] getURLList()
```

```
void addURL(URL url)

void addStringURL(String string)
```

The easiest way to add multiple sounds to a SoundPlayer is through the setURLList method. This method is passed an array of URL objects, as shown in the following method from the SoundPlayerDemo sample applet that is included on the MCP Web site:

```
private void LoadSounds() {
    try {
        URL[] tempURL = new URL[2];
        tempURL[0] = new URL("file:/C:/gong.au");
        tempURL[1] = new URL("file:/C:/woof.au");

        soundPlayer.setURLList(tempURL);
    }
    catch (java.net.MalformedURLException error) {
    }
}
```

 TIP

Don't forget that when working with the URL class, you need to import java.net.

If you want to add a single sound, you can do so by using addURL. The following example loads the same files as the preceding example:

```
private void LoadURLSounds() {
    try {
        URL gongURL = new URL("file:/C:/gong.au");
        soundPlayer.addURL(gongURL);

        URL woofURL = new URL("file:/C:/woof.au");
        soundPlayer.addURL(woofURL);
    }
    catch (java.net.MalformedURLException error) {
    }
}
```

Alternatively, if you would prefer to work with strings instead of URLs, you can use addStringURL. The two files can be added to a SoundPlayer with this code:

```
private void LoadStringSounds() {
    soundPlayer.addStringURL("file:/C:/gong.au");
    soundPlayer.addStringURL("file:/C:/woof.au");
}
```

> **TIP**
>
> In Microsoft Windows, the easiest way to create Sun AU files is to use the Microsoft Sound Recorder to record a WAV file and then convert the WAV file to an AU file. A great shareware program for doing this is GoldWave, which can be downloaded over the Internet from `http://www.zdnet.com`.

Playing and Stopping

You can start or stop a sound player by using the following methods:

```
void play()
```

```
void stop()
```

```
void stop(int delay)
```

The `delay` parameter can be used to specify a number of milliseconds to wait before stopping the sound. If `delay` is not specified, the sound will be stopped immediately.

Repeating and Synchronizing

By default, a sound player plays each of the sounds in its list one time. You can, however, instruct it to repeat the sounds as many times as necessary. The following methods are provided for working a sound player's repeat status:

```
void setRepeat(int repeatQuantity)
```

```
int getRepeat()
```

If you want the sounds to be repeated endlessly, pass `SoundPlayer.INFINITE` to `setRepeat`.

You can also tell a sound player to play all the sounds simultaneously or in succession. When a sound player is in *synchronized mode*, it plays each sound after the preceding sound completes. When a sound player is not in synchronized mode, all sounds are started at the same time. You can get or set a sound player's synchronized mode by using the following methods:

```
void setSyncMode(boolean synchMode)
```

```
boolean getSyncMode()
```

As an example of how these methods work together, consider what happens when the Play button of the `SoundPlayerDemo` applet is clicked. This applet is shown in Figure 17.18, and the `playButton_Clicked` method is shown in Listing 17.2.

Figure 17.18.

The
`SoundPlayerDemo`
sample applet.

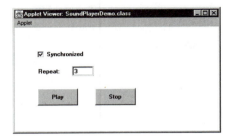

Listing 17.2. A portion of `SoundPlayerDemo.java.`

```
 1:    void playButton_Clicked(java.awt.event.ActionEvent event) {
 2:        boolean sync = syncCheckbox.getState();
 3:
 4:        int repeat;
 5:        try {
 6:            repeat = Integer.parseInt(repeatQty.getText());
 7:        }
 8:        catch (NumberFormatException e) {
 9:            repeat = 1;
10:        }
11:
12:        soundPlayer.setSyncMode(sync);
13:        soundPlayer.setRepeat(repeat);
14:
15:        soundPlayer.play();
16:    }
```

The `MediaTracker` Class

If you want to write your own multimedia classes, you need to be aware of how Java loads images. When an `Image` object is created (commonly with a call to `Applet.getImage`), the image is not loaded from the given URL at that time. The image, which Java assumes to be most likely located on a different machine across an intranet or the Internet, is not loaded until it is actually used. If you are writing your own animation class and want to quickly display images in succession, you will have annoying delays between images while the image is retrieved across the network.

Fortunately, Java provides a solution to this problem with its `MediaTracker` class. A `MediaTracker` object can be used to ensure that all necessary images are loaded before starting a process that uses them. To create a new `MediaTracker` object, use the following constructor:

`MediaTracker(Component component)`

The *component* parameter designates the component that will use the images that are to be tracked. In most cases, you can simply pass `this`.

Adding Images

The images that a MediaTracker object tracks must be added to the media tracker with one of the following methods:

```
void addImage(Image img, int id)

void addImage(Image img, int id, int width, int height)
```

The first method adds an image and assigns it the indicated identification number. This can be any number you desire. The same identification number can be assigned to multiple images, allowing you to query the MediaTracker about those images as a set. Other MediaTracker methods use this number to allow you to track the status of the image. The second addImage method adds the image and converts it to the specified width and height.

For an example of using addImage, consider the following code that adds two images to a MediaTracker object:

```
MediaTracker tracker = new MediaTracker(this);
Image blueImage = getImage(getDocumentBase(), "blue.gif");
tracker.addImage(blueImage, 0);

Image greenImage = getImage(getDocumentBase(), "green.gif");
tracker.addImage(greenImage, 1);
```

Waiting for Images to Load

After you add all the images to the media tracker, you can start the loading process and wait for it to complete by using the following methods:

```
void waitForAll() throws InterruptedException

public waitForAll(long milliseconds) throws InterruptedException

waitForID(int id) throws InterruptedException

waitForID(int id, long milliseconds) throws InterruptedException
```

The two waitForAll methods wait until all images are loaded. If the milliseconds parameter is specified, waitForAll waits that many milliseconds before stopping and returning control to the next line in the program. The parameterless version of waitForAll waits until all images load or cannot load due to errors.

The waitForId methods are similar to waitForAll, except these methods wait only until a specific image has been loaded.

Similarly, you can use the following methods to check on the load status of one or all of the images:

```
int statusAll(boolean load)

int statusID(int id, boolean load)
```

If the *load* parameter is true, it instructs these methods to begin loading the images. These methods return one of the following values:

- [ ] LOADING
- [ ] ABORTED
- [ ] ERRORED
- [ ] COMPLETE

There are still more options: You can use the following methods to determine whether one or all of the images have been loaded:

```
boolean checkAll()
```

```
boolean checkAll(boolean load)
```

```
boolean checkID(int id)
```

```
boolean checkID(int id, boolean load)
```

These methods are simpler than the status methods in that they return Boolean values instead of integer values that indicate status information. The optional *load* parameter can be used to start image loading if passed as true.

Handling Errors

If an error occurs while images are being retrieved, the errors can be checked with the following methods:

```
Object[] getErrorsAny()
```

```
Object[] getErrorsID(int id)
```

```
boolean isErrorAny()
```

```
boolean isErrorID(int id)
```

The getErrorsAny method returns an array of objects for which errors occurred. The method getErrorsId returns a similar array, but only looks at images with the specified ID. The isErrorAny and isErrorID methods are similar, except they return less specific information. These methods return true if any error occurred or false if not.

Summary

In this chapter, you learned about the multimedia components in Visual Café's Object Library. You saw how to use SlideShow to display a series of images and how to create animations by using Animator, MovingAnimation, and Emblaze20. You learned about the novelty components—Firework, Plasma, and NervousText. You also learned how to add sound to your programs by using the SoundPlayer component. Finally, you learned about the MediaTracker class and how you can use it as an aid in creating your own multimedia classes.

Q&A

Q I like the SlideShow component, but would like to have my images dissolve into each other rather than always have each new image simply replace the existing image. Can this be done?

A No, you can't do this with the SlideShow component that comes with Visual Café. To create this type of effect, you must create your own image filters. This is discussed in the section titled "Writing Your Own Image Filter" in Chapter 16.

Q What in the world are the Plasma, Fireworks, and NervousText components for?

A These are novelty components that you are unlikely to use in any real-world programs. The NervousText component duplicates one of Sun's original Java demos. The Plasma and Fireworks components offer limited abilities to add simple animation to Web pages. Although you are unlikely to use these components, you might find it useful to examine their source code if you plan to create your own similar classes.

Q I would like to use MovingAnimation to create an image that moves vertically rather than horizontally. How do I do this?

A Unfortunately, MovingAnimation supports only horizontal movement. However, you should be able to easily write your own class to do this, especially if you use the source to MovingAnimation as a guide.

Workshop

The workshop includes quiz questions to help you gauge your understanding of the material in this chapter, and also includes exercises to provide hands-on experience with what you've learned in this chapter. You can find the answers to the quiz questions in Appendix D, "Answers."

Quiz

1. What methods can you use to move between images in a slide show?
2. What happens if myAnimation.setClearFrame(false) is executed and the animation is then started?
3. In what way does MovingAnimation enhance the Animator class?
4. The Animator, Firework, Plasma, and NervousText components all extend the same class and implement the same interface. Name their immediate superclass and the interface they implement.

5. What does it mean to say that a sound player is in synchronized mode?

6. What sound formats are supported by the `SoundPlayer` class?

7. What does the `MediaTracker.waitForAll` method do?

Exercises

1. Write a class called `BetterMovingAnimation` that allows an image to move in both a vertical and horizontal direction.

2. Write a class called `ScrollingText` that will display a piece of text and allow it to scroll across its canvas.

3. Think of a real-world use for the `Plasma` class. If we all put our heads together, we might find one. Send your answers to mcohn@spider.innercite.com. The best answers will be posted at http://spider.innercite.com/~mcohn.

4. Write a program that allows the user to add sounds to a `SoundPlayer` object and then play back the sounds.

Day 18

Java Beans

Today you will learn about Java Beans. You've probably heard quite a bit about beans and, whether you knew it or not, you have already worked with them. The components in Visual Café's Component Library are beans. Today you will learn how to write your own beans and how to add them into the Component Library where they can be reused in other programs.

What Is a Bean?

A Java Bean is a reusable software component that can be visually manipulated in a development environment. Each of these attributes—reusability and visual manipulation—work together to provide a proven approach to writing better software.

Reusability

Java Beans are meant to be reusable. In fact, this is the primary purpose behind a bean's existence. If a Java class will not be reused, there is no reason to write it as a bean. This is why items such as checkboxes, radio buttons, and labels are excellent candidates to be written as beans, but a component that deletes the entry for John Smith in an employee database is not. However, a component that deletes from a database an employee whose name is passed to the component could be a useful bean.

One of the biggest and most perpetual criticisms of those who write software is that we always take too long to do it. Ever since Adam and Eve sat down with the earliest version of COBOL, people have sought ways of creating new software more quickly. These efforts saw the creation of new languages, new approaches to analysis and design, new procedures, more highly caffeinated colas, and new development tools. Eventually, programmers realized that writing new software more quickly was one thing but reusing existing code was even better. Because existing code has already been tested and proven to work in one project, it offers a tremendous time-saving opportunity if it can be reused in subsequent projects.

The motivation behind Java Beans is to provide a mechanism for writing reusable software components that can provide this type of time-saving opportunities.

Visual Manipulation

For a long time, it has been possible to create libraries of common methods or functions and then link these libraries into new programs. This is still a suitable approach for many tasks, but it doesn't work well within today's visual development environments. Programmers have learned they can be more productive in a visual environment that allows them to drag and drop components into a program. For example, Figure 18.1 shows how a user can visually manipulate a button component in Visual Café.

Figure 18.1.

Visually manipulate a button component in Visual Café.

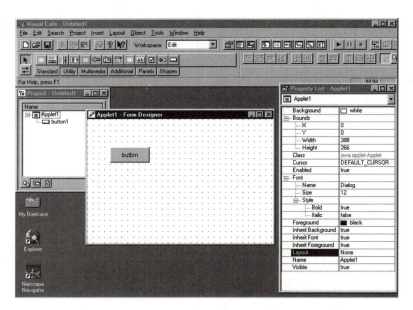

For a software component to be truly reusable, it must fit with how programmers work. Because programmers have become accustomed to visually manipulating components, you must write components that can be manipulated visually. Through its support for Java Beans, Visual Café allows you to write your own components and add them directly to Visual Café's Component Library. In this way, your components are fully integrated into Visual Café and are highly reusable.

Dissecting a Sample Bean

There is a common misperception among those who have not written a bean that doing so is complicated and difficult. I suspect some of this is the result of naming them *Java Beans* instead of simply *reusable components* without any capital letters. Because beans have been given a name, they take on the aura of being something more complicated than they are. Fortunately, writing a bean class is no more difficult than writing any other Java class. There are some standard naming conventions that must be followed and some additional code that must be written but, as you will see today, none of this is any more difficult than what you've already done throughout this book.

Listing 18.1 shows a very simple bean. When added to an applet and run, this bean will appear as shown in Figure 18.2. As you can see from the figure, this bean draws a small circle on the screen. As you can't see from the figure, when the mouse button is pressed while the pointer is on the circle, the circle changes color until the mouse button is released.

18

Figure 18.2.

The results of executing the simple bean of Listing 18.1.

Listing 18.1. A very simple bean and its `BeanInfo` class.

```
1:   import java.awt.*;
2:   import java.awt.event.*;
3:   import java.beans.*;
4:
5:   public class JavaBean extends Canvas implements
6:           java.io.Serializable {
7:      public JavaBean() {
8:         super();
9:         setSize(40,40);
10:        enableEvents(MouseEvent.MOUSE_EVENT_MASK);
11:     }
12:
```

continues

Listing 18.1. continued

```
13:        public void paint(Graphics context) {
14:            if (down && hasFocus) {
15:                context.setColor(pressedColor);
16:            }
17:            else {
18:                context.setColor(releasedColor);
19:            }
20:            context.fillArc(5, 5, getSize().width - 10,
21:                    getSize().height-10,0,360);
22:        }
23:
24:        protected void processMouseEvent (MouseEvent e) {
25:            switch(e.getID()) {
26:                case MouseEvent.MOUSE_PRESSED:
27:                    down = true;
28:                    repaint();
29:                    break;
30:                case MouseEvent.MOUSE_RELEASED:
31:                    down = false;
32:                    repaint();
33:                    break;
34:                case MouseEvent.MOUSE_ENTERED:
35:                    hasFocus = true;
36:                    repaint();
37:                    break;
38:                case MouseEvent.MOUSE_EXITED:
39:                    hasFocus = false;
40:                    repaint();
41:                    break;
42:            }
43:            super.processMouseEvent(e);
44:        }
45:
46:        public synchronized Color getReleasedColor() {
47:            return releasedColor;
48:        }
49:
50:        public void setReleasedColor (Color newColor) {
51:            releasedColor = newColor;
52:            repaint();
53:        }
54:
55:        public synchronized Color getPressedColor() {
56:            return pressedColor;
57:        }
58:
59:        public void setPressedColor (Color newColor) {
60:            pressedColor = newColor;
61:            repaint();
62:        }
63:
64:        private Color pressedColor = Color.black;
65:        private Color releasedColor = Color.red;
66:        transient boolean down = false;
67:        transient boolean hasFocus = false;
68:    }
```

18

ANALYSIS   The first thing you should notice in Listing 18.1 is that line 3 imports the java.beans package. This package contains some of the class and interface definitions that will be used by the classes declared in this file. The class JavaBean is declared on line 5 as an extension of Canvas. This will be your bean class. You might have expected it to be an extension of a bean class, but there is no common base class or interface that must be used by all beans.

Looking through the JavaBean class (lines 5–68), you will not find anything that identifies this class as a bean. There are no special methods such as DoBeanStuff or GetBeanId. This class looks just like any other class you have written in your study of Java. It includes a paint method (lines 13–22) that draws the circle (using fillArc) in the appropriate color. The class includes processMouseEvents (lines 24–44), which handles the various mouse events. Finally, it includes methods for getting and setting the color to use when the mouse button is released or pressed.

Accompanying the JavaBean class is the JavaBeanInfo class, which is shown in Listing 18.2. Because beans can be visually manipulated in development tools such as Visual Café, a BeanInfo class can be written to accompany each bean. Among other possibilities, the BeanInfo class that accompanies a bean is used to specify the name of an icon file used to represent the bean, the properties contained within the bean, and the methods supported by the bean.

18

Listing 18.2. JavaBeanInfo.java.

```
 1:   class JavaBeanInfo extends SimpleBeanInfo {
 2:      public java.awt.Image getIcon(int iconKind) {
 3:         if (iconKind == BeanInfo.ICON_COLOR_16x16 ||
 4:               iconKind == BeanInfo.ICON_MONO_16x16) {
 5:            java.awt.Image img = loadImage("JavaBeanIcon16.gif");
 6:            return img;
 7:         }
 8:         if (iconKind == BeanInfo.ICON_COLOR_32x32 ||
 9:               iconKind == BeanInfo.ICON_MONO_32x32) {
10:            java.awt.Image img = loadImage("JavaBeanIcon32.gif");
11:            return img;
12:         }
13:         return null;
14:      }
15:
16:      public PropertyDescriptor[] getPropertyDescriptors() {
17:         try  {
18:            PropertyDescriptor background = new
19:                  PropertyDescriptor("background", beanClass);
20:            PropertyDescriptor foreground = new
21:                  PropertyDescriptor("foreground", beanClass);
22:            background.setBound(true);
23:            foreground.setBound(true);
24:
```

continues

Listing 18.2. continued

```
25:           PropertyDescriptor rv[] = {background, foreground};
26:           return rv;
27:       }
28:       catch (IntrospectionException e) {
29:           throw new Error(e.toString());
30:       }
31:   }
32:
33:   private final static Class beanClass = JavaBean.class;
34: }
```

ANALYSIS The getIcon method (lines 2–14) of JavaBeanInfo returns an Image object that is the appropriate size based on what was requested. The other method shown in JavaBeanInfo is getPropertyDescriptors, which creates and returns an array of PropertyDescriptor objects. Each PropertyDescriptor describes one property of the bean. For example, the PropertyDescriptor created on lines 18 and 19 describes the background property of the bean. Because the property name is given as background on line 19, the methods getBackground and setBackground are used to get and set the values of this property. This is a naming convention expected of bean accessor methods and, if you look at the Component class (on which JavaBean is based through its immediate superclass, Canvas), you will see that it contains methods called getBackground and setBackground.

To use your new bean in an applet, simply construct it and use it like you would any other component. This can be seen in Listing 18.3. Later today you'll learn how to add a new bean to the Component Library. Once a component is in the Component Library, you can drag it onto the Form Designer and visually manipulate it.

Listing 18.3. Using the sample bean, JavaBean, in an applet.

```
1:    import java.awt.*;
2:    import java.applet.*;
3:    import java.awt.event.*;
4:    import JavaBean;
5:
6:    public class BeanApp extends Applet {
7:        JavaBean bean;
8:
9:        public void init() {
10:           super.init();
11:           setLayout(new FlowLayout());
12:           resize(200,100);
13:
14:           bean = new JavaBean();
15:           add("Center",bean);
```

```
16:        //{{INIT_CONTROLS
17:        addNotify();
18:        setLayout(new FlowLayout(FlowLayout.CENTER,5,5));
19:        setSize(104,0);
20:        //}}
21:     }
22:   //{{DECLARE_CONTROLS
23:   //}}
24:  }
```

Describing Bean Properties

Because you want to be able to visually manipulate the properties of a bean from within Visual Café, the BeanInfo class associated with a bean needs to describe the properties of that bean. A bean's BeanInfo class is always given the same name as the bean class but with BeanInfo appended (for example, the BullsEye class will be associated with a BullsEyeBeanInfo class). A bean's properties are the values displayed in the Visual Café Property List and can be set via that window. For example, Figure 18.2 shows the Property List for the BullsEye component that will be created in this section. As you can see, you can set all the usual properties (Bounds, Font, Enabled, Foreground, and so on). Additionally, you can set three properties that are specific to this component: Indent, Inner Color, and Outer Color.

Through the magic of inheritance, a bean receives all the properties of its parents. Each of these properties will be displayed in the Visual Café Property List. A bean can also be augmented with new properties. The bean's BeanInfo class then describes the new properties by using the PropertyDescriptor class. You can create a new PropertyDescriptor object by using any of the following constructors:

```
PropertyDescriptor(String propertyName, Class beanClass)

PropertyDescriptor(String propertyName, Class beanClass,
     String getterName, String setterName)

PropertyDescriptor(String propertyName, Method getter,
     Method setter)
```

If you follow the preferred naming convention for accessor methods of get*Property* and set*Property*, you can use the first of these constructors. If you used different method names, you can use either alternative constructor. The following example illustrates how to create new PropertyDescriptor objects:

```
PropertyDescriptor indent = new PropertyDescriptor("indent",
     beanClass);
PropertyDescriptor outdent = new PropertyDescriptor("outdent",
     beanClass, "getTheOutdent", "setTheOutdent");
```

After creating a new `PropertyDescriptor` object, you should call its `setDisplayName` method. This method is passed the name that will appear in the Visual Café Property List for the bean. For example, the following creates a new `PropertyDescriptor` object for the `indent` property and uses the label `Indent Amount` in the Property List:

```
PropertyDescriptor indent = new PropertyDescriptor("indent",
    beanClass);
indent.setDisplayName("Indent Amount");
```

The `BullsEye` Bean Example

As an example of describing a bean's properties, consider the `BullsEye` bean shown in Figure 18.3. This bean shows two concentric, different-colored circles. When the user clicks the component, the circles switch colors. The source code of this bean is shown in Listing 18.4.

Figure 18.3.

The `BullsEye` bean.

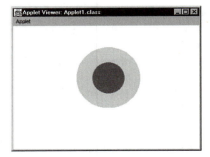

Listing 18.4. `BullsEye.java.`

```
1:  import java.awt.*;
2:  import java.awt.event.*;
3:  import java.beans.*;
4:
5:  public class BullsEye extends Canvas implements
6:          java.io.Serializable {
7:      public BullsEye() {
8:          super();
9:          setSize(40,40);
10:         enableEvents(MouseEvent.MOUSE_EVENT_MASK);
11:
12:         indent = 0;
13:         innerColor = Color.red;
14:         outerColor = Color.cyan;
15:     }
16:
17:     public void setIndent(int indent) {
18:         this.indent = indent;
19:         repaint();
20:     }
21:
22:     public int getIndent() {
23:         return indent;
```

```
24:     }
25:
26:     public void paint(Graphics g) {
27:         // get the object's dimensions
28:         Dimension d = size();
29:
30:         // since the bullseye needs to be a circle, use the
31:         // lesser of the width and the height
32:         int diameter=d.width < d.height ? d.width : d.height;
33:
34:         // reduce the diameter by the amount of the
35:         // indent (on each side)
36:         diameter -= 2 * indent;
37:
38:         // the starting x,y coordinates for the outer circle
39:         // are indented by the specified amount
40:         int outerXY = indent;
41:
42:         // select the desired outer color, use the inner color
43:         // as the outer color if the mouse is held down over
44:         // the component
45:         if(down && hasFocus)
46:             g.setColor(innerColor);
47:         else
48:             g.setColor(outerColor);
49:
50:         // draw the outer circle
51:         g.fillOval(outerXY, outerXY, diameter, diameter);
52:
53:         // make the inner circle 1/2 the size of the outer
54:         int innerDiameter = diameter / 2;
55:         int innerXY = indent + (innerDiameter / 2);
56:
57:         // select the desired inner color, use the outer color
58:         // as the inner color if the mouse is held down over
59:         // the component
60:         if(down && hasFocus)
61:             g.setColor(outerColor);
62:         else
63:             g.setColor(innerColor);
64:
65:         g.fillOval(innerXY, innerXY, innerDiameter, innerDiameter);
66:     }
67:
68:     protected void processMouseEvent (MouseEvent e) {
69:         switch(e.getID()) {
70:             case MouseEvent.MOUSE_PRESSED:
71:                 down = true;
72:                 repaint();
73:                 break;
74:             case MouseEvent.MOUSE_RELEASED:
75:                 down = false;
76:                 repaint();
77:                 break;
78:             case MouseEvent.MOUSE_ENTERED:
```

18

continues

Listing 18.4. continued

```
79:             hasFocus = true;
80:             repaint();
81:             break;
82:          case MouseEvent.MOUSE_EXITED:
83:             hasFocus = false;
84:             repaint();
85:             break;
86:       }
87:       super.processMouseEvent(e);
88:    }
89:
90:    public synchronized Color getInnerColor() {
91:       return innerColor;
92:    }
93:
94:    public void setinnerColor (Color newColor) {
95:       innerColor = newColor;
96:       repaint();
97:    }
98:
99:    public synchronized Color getOuterColor() {
100:       return outerColor;
101:    }
102:
103:    public void setOuterColor (Color newColor) {
104:       outerColor = newColor;
105:       repaint();
106:    }
107:
108:    transient boolean down = false;
109:    transient boolean hasFocus = false;
110:
111:    protected int indent;
112:    protected Color innerColor;
113:    protected Color outerColor;
114: }
```

ANALYSIS Not much is special about BullsEye.java. Three properties—indent, innerColor, and outerColor—are defined on lines 111–113. The accessor methods for indent are setIndent (lines 17–20) and getIndent (lines 22–24). Similarly named accessor methods for innerColor and outerColor are defined between lines 90 and 106.

The paint method (lines 26–66) is the meat of the BullsEye class. This method calculates the diameter of the outer circle and then adjusts it for the indent (line 36). It then sets the color and draws the outer circle (lines 45–51). The diameter of the inner circle is calculated (lines 54–55) and that circle is then drawn (lines 60–65).

Listing 18.5 shows the BullsEyeBeanInfo class that accompanies the BullsEye bean.

18

Listing 18.5. `BullsEyeBeanInfo.java`.

```
 1:   public class BullsEyeBeanInfo extends SimpleBeanInfo {
 2:      public PropertyDescriptor[] getPropertyDescriptors() {
 3:         try {
 4:            PropertyDescriptor indent = new PropertyDescriptor(
 5:               "indent", beanClass);
 6:            indent.setDisplayName("Indentation");
 7:
 8:            PropertyDescriptor innerColor = new
 9:                  PropertyDescriptor("innerColor", beanClass);
10:            innerColor.setDisplayName("Inner Color");
11:
12:            PropertyDescriptor outerColor = new
13:                  PropertyDescriptor("outerColor", beanClass);
14:            outerColor.setDisplayName("Outer Color");
15:
16:            PropertyDescriptor[] rv = {
17:                  indent,
18:                  innerColor,
19:                  outerColor};
20:
21:               return rv;
22:         }
23:         catch (IntrospectionException e) {
24:            throw new Error(e.toString());
25:         }
26:      }
27:
28:      private final static Class beanClass = BullsEye.class;
29:   }
```

ANALYSIS BullsEyeBeanInfo extends `SimpleBeanInfo`, as you also saw in Listing 18.2. When you are creating a `BeanInfo` class, you can either implement the `BeanInfo` interface yourself or you can create a subclass of `SimpleBeanInfo` as is done here. In most cases it is simpler to subclass `SimpleBeanInfo` because this allows you to provide method bodies for only those methods the bean requires. In the case of `BullsEyeBeanInfo`, only a single method, `getPropertyDescriptors`, is necessary.

 TIP

A quick, efficient way to start your own bean is to create a new Visual Café project and select Basic Java Bean from the New Project menu. This creates a sample bean and `BeanInfo` class to which you can add.

Because three properties were added to the `BullsEye` bean, `getPropertyDescriptors` creates and returns an array of three `PropertyDescriptor` objects. First, a new `PropertyDescriptor` for the `indent` property is created on lines 4–5. The display name of this property is then set to `Indentation` on line 6. This process is repeated for the `innerColor` and `outerColor` properties (lines 8–14). Lines 16–19 create an array of the `PropertyDescriptor` objects and this array is returned on line 21.

Testing the Bean Visually

Having created the bean, it is now time to add it to the Visual Café Component Library and see how it can be manipulated with the Property List. To add a bean to the Component Library, take the following steps:

1. Write the bean and its `BeanInfo` class.
2. Create a Java Archive (JAR) from the bean.
3. Add the bean to the Component Library.

You already know how to do the first step, so you're ready to create a Java Archive. Because a Java Bean can contain more than one file, you must create a Java Archive file that contains the necessary files before you use a bean. A Java Archive file is more commonly called a JAR file.

To create a JAR file, open your bean project and select Project | JAR from the Visual Café menu. You will be presented with the screen shown in Figure 18.4. Here you can enter the name of the JAR file to use. When you click the OK button, the JAR file is created.

Figure 18.4.

Creating a JAR file for the `BullsEye` *bean.*

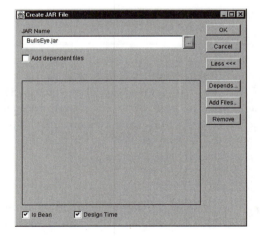

Next you must add the JAR file to the Visual Café Component Library. You can do this in either of the following ways:

☐ Select Insert | Component into Library from the menu.

☐ Place the JAR file in the `bin\components` subdirectory of the directory in which you install Visual Café.

NOTE

If you place the JAR file in the `bin\components` directory, you must restart Visual Café for the bean to be added to the Component Library.

At this point you are ready to test your new bean. To do so, display the Component Library by selecting Window | Component Library from the main menu. As shown in Figure 18.5, the Component Library window should include an entry for the `BullsEye` bean.

Figure 18.5.

The Component Library includes the new `BullsEye` *bean.*

To verify that the properties you added work correctly, drag a `BullsEye` component onto an empty form in the Form Designer. When the `BullsEye` component is selected in the Form Designer, the Property List will display its properties. These should appear as shown in Figure 18.6.

Figure 18.6.

Working with a `BullsEye` *component in the Form Designer and Property List.*

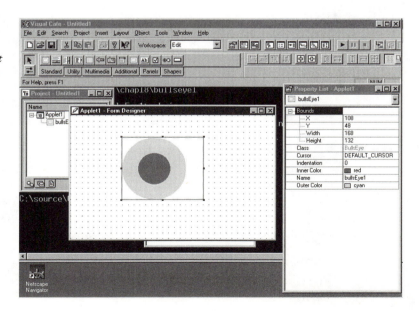

18

Adding an Icon

As you can see in Figure 18.5, when the BullsEye bean is added to the Component Library, Visual Café provides it with a default image. Usually you should create a custom, more descriptive image to accompany your beans. To do this, you need to implement the getIcon method in the BeanInfo class. Listing 18.6 shows how to do this for the BullsEye bean.

Listing 18.6. Adding a custom image to the BullsEye bean.

```
 1:    public class BullsEyeBeanInfo extends SimpleBeanInfo {
 2:        public java.awt.Image getIcon(int iconKind) {
 3:            if (iconKind == BeanInfo.ICON_COLOR_16x16 ||
 4:                iconKind == BeanInfo.ICON_MONO_16x16) {
 5:                java.awt.Image img = loadImage("BullsEye16.gif");
 6:                return img;
 7:            }
 8:            if (iconKind == BeanInfo.ICON_COLOR_32x32 ||
 9:                iconKind == BeanInfo.ICON_MONO_32x32) {
10:                java.awt.Image img = loadImage("BullsEye32.gif");
11:                return img;
12:            }
13:            return null;
14:        }
15:
16:        // other methods not shown
17:    }
```

ANALYSIS The getIcon method is passed an integer that indicates the type of icon being requested. In this example, BullsEyeBeanInfo checks whether a 16×16-pixel color or monochrome icon is being requested. If so, an image based on BullsEye16.gif is created and returned (lines 3–7). A similar test is performed to see whether a 32×32-pixel icon is being requested (lines 8–12).

NOTE For its Component Library and Component palette, Visual Café uses 32×32-pixel images. However, Visual Café displays only the top-left 16×16 pixels. This is similar to a Windows icon (ICO) file.

To see the effect of the new BeanInfo class, compile it, make a new JAR file, and add the JAR file to the Component Library using Insert | Component into Library. Your Component Library should look like the one shown in Figure 18.7.

Figure 18.7.

*The Component
Library with a custom
icon for the* BullsEye
component.

Adding a Bean to the Component Palette

The next step in making a bean more useful is putting it on the Component palette. Do this
by providing an implementation for the method getBeanDescription in your BeanInfo class.
As an example, consider the following:

```
public BeanDescriptor getBeanDescriptor() {
    SymantecBeanDescriptor bd=new SymantecBeanDescriptor(beanClass);
    bd.setFolder("My Beans");
    bd.setToolbar("My Beans");

    return (BeanDescriptor) bd;
}
```

NOTE

> The class SymantecBeanDescriptor is located in the package
> symantec.itools.beans. Therefore, if you use this class, you must
> include the following import statement:
>
> import symantec.itools.beans.*;

You create a SymantecBeanDescriptor object by passing its constructor the bean class. Then
the SymantecBeanDescriptor methods setFolder and setToolbar are used to indicate where
in the Component Library the new component should appear. You use setFolder to indicate
which folder within the Component Library will display the bean. Similarly, setToolbar is
used to indicate which tab on the Component palette will display this component. This
example places the BullsEye component in the My Beans folder of the Component Library
(see Figure 18.8) and the My Beans tab of the Component palette (see Figure 18.9).

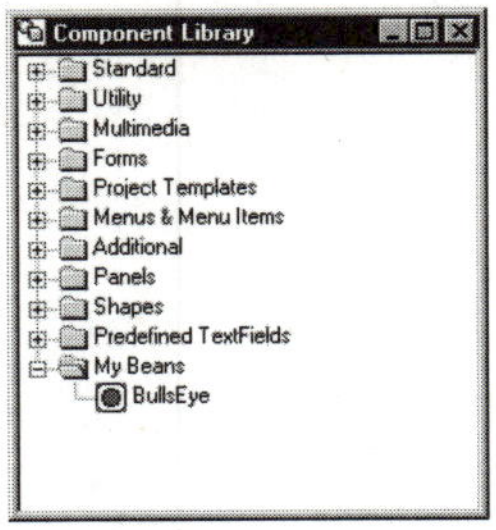

Figure 18.8.

The BullsEye
*component has been
added to the My
Beans folder of the
Component Library.*

Figure 18.9.

The BullsEye
*component has been
added to the My
Beans tab of the
Component palette.*

Enumerating Property Values

The BullsEye bean you've been working today added three properties to those it inherited: indent, innerColor, and outerColor. When shown in the Visual Café Property List, the indent property could be set by the user entering a numeric value. The innerColor and outerColor parameters could be set by making a selection from a drop-down list of colors. What if instead of entering a number for the indent property, you wanted to let the user choose from a list of valid indent amounts? This is entirely possible with Visual Café.

Each of the properties that can be set in the Visual Café Property List invokes a *Property editor* that is used to enter or select a value for the property. Each type of property (string, integer, or color) has a default Property editor. With the BullsEye component, you have already seen how the default Property editors for integer and color properties work. If you want the user to select from a list of valid choices instead of entering a value, all you need to do is replace the Property editor that will be used for a property.

This is done in the getPropertyDescriptors method of the BeanInfo class that you have already seen. Listing 18.7 illustrates how to use an enumerated list Property editor for the indent property. Figure 18.10 shows how the list will appear when displayed in Visual Café's Property List.

Listing 18.7. Using an enumerated list for a Property editor.

```
1:    public PropertyDescriptor[] getPropertyDescriptors() {
2:       try {
3:          PropertyDescriptor indent = new PropertyDescriptor(
4:                "indent", beanClass);
```

18

```
 5:              indent.setDisplayName("Indentation");
 6:              indent.setValue("ENUMERATION",
 7:                   "NONE=0, A_LITTLE=5, ALOT=10");
 8:
 9:              PropertyDescriptor innerColor = new PropertyDescriptor(
10:                   "innerColor", beanClass);
11:              innerColor.setDisplayName("Inner Color");
12:
13:              PropertyDescriptor outerColor = new PropertyDescriptor(
14:                   "outerColor", beanClass);
15:              outerColor.setDisplayName("Outer Color");
16:
17:              PropertyDescriptor[] rv = {
18:                   indent,
19:                   innerColor,
20:                   outerColor};
21:
22:           return rv;
23:           }
24:           catch (IntrospectionException e) {
25:               throw new Error(e.toString());
26:           }
27: }
```

Figure 18.10.

*Using an enumerated
list to edit the* indent
property of the
BullsEye
component.

18

ANALYSIS   The only change to getPropertyDescriptors comes in lines 6 and 7. The setValue method is used to specify the strings that will appear in the drop-down list and the numeric value associated with each string. To create an enumerated list, the first value passed to setValue must always be ENUMERATION. The second parameter is a string that contains a series of comma-delimited elements. Each element contains the text to display in the list followed by an assignment operator (=) followed by the value to use if that item is selected. In this case, if the user selects NONE, the indent property will be set to 0. If the user selects A_LITTLE, the indent property will be set to 5. If the user selects ALOT, the indent property will be set to 10.

DO use setValue whenever possible to ensure that a property can only be set to a valid range of values.

DO take the time to create or find custom icons for your beans. It will make locating them in the Component Library or Component palette easier.

Custom Events and Listeners

Sometimes you want a bean to generate custom events that are specific to that bean. Using the BullsEye bean you've been building today as an example, suppose you want to let other objects know whenever the user has pressed the mouse button while the pointer is over the bean. To do this, create a new event type and have the bean send it whenever it detects a mouse press.

With the event model introduced with version 1.1 of the Java Development Kit, creating custom event classes is very simple. You can create a custom event by subclassing EventObject. Listing 18.8 shows the BullsEyeEvent class, which is created in this way.

Listing 18.8. BullsEyeEvent.java is a custom event class.

```
 1:    import java.util.*;
 2:
 3:    public class BullsEyeEvent extends EventObject {
 4:       public static final int PRESSED=0, RELEASED=1;
 5:       protected int id;
 6:
 7:       public BullsEyeEvent(Object obj, int id) {
 8:          super(obj);
 9:          this.id = id;
10:       }
11:
12:       public int getID() {
13:          return id;
14:       }
15:    }
```

ANALYSIS BullsEyeEvent contains a static enumeration (line 4) that will be used to distinguish between the two types of events this class will manage: mouse-button presses and mouse-button releases. The constructor (lines 7–10) stores the type of event in the object's id member (line 9).

For other objects to receive the events generated by a BullsEye object, they must listen for the events. The easiest way to do this is by defining an interface that will listen for the new events. Any class that wants to receive the new events can then implement the listener interface. The BullsEyeListener interface is defined as follows:

```
public interface BullsEyeListener extends java.util.EventListener {
    public void BullsEyeEventHandler(BullsEyeEvent bel);
}
```

Having created new event and listener classes, the next step is to put them to use by incorporating them in the BullsEye class, which is shown in Listing 18.9.

Listing 18.9. BullsEye.java as modified to generate custom events.

```
1:    import java.awt.*;
2:    import java.awt.event.*;
3:    import java.beans.*;
4:    import java.util.*;
5:
6:    public class BullsEye extends Canvas implements
7:            java.io.Serializable {
8:        public BullsEye() {
9:            super();
10:           setSize(40,40);
11:           enableEvents(MouseEvent.MOUSE_EVENT_MASK);
12:
13:           indent = 0;
14:           innerColor = Color.red;
15:           outerColor = Color.cyan;
16:       }
17:
18:       public void paint(Graphics g) {
19:           // get the object's dimensions
20:           Dimension d = size();
21:
22:           // since the bullseye needs to be a circle, use the
23:           // lesser of the width and the height
24:           int diameter=d.width < d.height ? d.width : d.height;
25:
26:           // reduce the diameter by the amount of the
27:           // indent (on each side)
28:           diameter -= 2 * indent;
29:
30:           // the starting x,y coordinates for the outer circle
31:           // are indented by the specified amount
32:           int outerXY = indent;
33:
34:           // select the desired outer color, use the inner color
35:           // as the outer color if the mouse is held down over
36:           // the component
37:           if(down && hasFocus)
38:               g.setColor(innerColor);
39:           else
40:               g.setColor(outerColor);
```

continues

Listing 18.9. continued

```
41:
42:            // draw the outer circle
43:            g.fillOval(outerXY, outerXY, diameter, diameter);
44:
45:            // make the inner circle 1/2 the size of the outer
46:            int innerDiameter = diameter / 2;
47:            int innerXY = indent + (innerDiameter / 2);
48:
49:            // select the desired inner color, use the outer color
50:            // as the inner color if the mouse is held down over
51:            // the component
52:            if(down && hasFocus)
53:                g.setColor(outerColor);
54:            else
55:                g.setColor(innerColor);
56:
57:            g.fillOval(innerXY, innerXY, innerDiameter, innerDiameter);
58:        }
59:
60:        protected void processMouseEvent (MouseEvent e) {
61:            switch(e.getID()) {
62:                case MouseEvent.MOUSE_PRESSED:
63:                    down = true;
64:                    sendEvent(new BullsEyeEvent(this,
65:                        BullsEyeEvent.PRESSED));
66:                    repaint();
67:                    break;
68:                case MouseEvent.MOUSE_RELEASED:
69:                    down = false;
70:                    sendEvent(new BullsEyeEvent(this,
71:                        BullsEyeEvent.RELEASED));
72:                    repaint();
73:                    break;
74:                case MouseEvent.MOUSE_ENTERED:
75:                    hasFocus = true;
76:                    repaint();
77:                    break;
78:                case MouseEvent.MOUSE_EXITED:
79:                    hasFocus = false;
80:                    repaint();
81:                    break;
82:            }
83:            super.processMouseEvent(e);
84:        }
85:
86:        public int getIndent() {
87:            return indent;
88:        }
89:
90:        public void setIndent(int indent) {
91:            this.indent = indent;
92:            repaint();
93:        }
94:
95:        public synchronized Color getInnerColor() {
```

```
 96:        return innerColor;
 97:    }
 98:
 99:    public void setInnerColor(Color newColor) {
100:        innerColor = newColor;
101:        repaint();
102:    }
103:
104:    public synchronized Color getOuterColor() {
105:        return outerColor;
106:    }
107:
108:    public void setOuterColor(Color newColor) {
109:        outerColor = newColor;
110:        repaint();
111:    }
112:
113:    public void addBullsEyeListener(BullsEyeListener bel) {
114:        listeners.addElement(bel);
115:    }
116:
117:    public void removeBullsEyeListener(BullsEyeListener bel) {
118:        listeners.removeElement(bel);
119:    }
120:
121:    public void sendEvent(BullsEyeEvent event) {
122:
123:        for (Enumeration enum = listeners.elements();
124:             enum.hasMoreElements(); ) {
125:          BullsEyeListener bel = (BullsEyeListener)
126:               enum.nextElement();
127:
128:          bel.BullsEyeEventHandler(event);
129:        }
130:    }
131:
132:    transient boolean down = false;
133:    transient boolean hasFocus = false;
134:
135:    protected int indent;
136:    protected Color innerColor;
137:    protected Color outerColor;
138:    protected Vector listeners = new Vector();
139: }
```

ANALYSIS Because the BullsEye class will need to send events to its listeners, it must keep track of who these listeners are. This is done by storing them in a vector called listeners, which is created on line 138. An object can be added to the listeners vector through a call to addBullsEyeListener (lines 113–115) or removed through a call to removeBullsEyeListener (lines 117–119).

Events are generated when the processMouseEvent method (lines 60–84) detects that the mouse button has been pressed or released. On these conditions, the method sendEvent is called (lines 64–65 and 70–71) and is passed a newly constructed BullsEyeEvent object. The BullsEyeEvent object is created with the constant BullsEyeEvent.PRESSED or BullsEyeEvent.RELEASED, depending on which type of mouse event was captured.

The sendEvent method (lines 121–130) uses an enumeration over the listeners vector and calls the BullsEyeEventHandler method in each listener. Because each listener has implemented the BullsEyeListener interface, you know it will contain a BullsEyeEventHandler method.

At this point, you are ready to compile the new version of the BullsEye bean. Before testing it, be sure to create a JAR file and add the JAR to the Component Library.

To test the new BullsEye bean, create an applet that will listen for BullsEyeEvent objects. Figure 18.11 shows an applet that does exactly this. This applet includes a BullsEye component and a text field. The applet listens for events; when one is received, it updates the text field with an appropriate message. The code for this applet is shown in Listing 18.10.

Figure 18.11.

An applet listening for
BullsEyeEvent
objects.

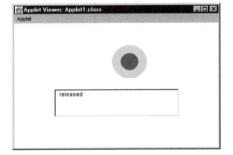

Listing 18.10. An applet that listens for BullsEyeEvent objects.

```
1:     import java.awt.*;
2:     import java.applet.*;
3:     import BullsEye;
4:
5:     public class Applet1 extends Applet implements
6:          BullsEyeListener {
7:
8:       public void BullsEyeEventHandler(BullsEyeEvent event) {
9:         if(event.getID() == BullsEyeEvent.PRESSED)
10:           status.setText("pressed");
11:         else if(event.getID() == BullsEyeEvent.RELEASED)
12:           status.setText("released");
13:       }
14:
15:       public void addNotify() {
16:         // Call parents addNotify method.
```

```
17:         super.addNotify();
18:
19:         setLayout(null);
20:         setSize(426,266);
21:         status = new java.awt.TextField();
22:         status.setBounds(84,144,259,60);
23:         add(status);
24:         status.setCursor(new Cursor(Cursor.TEXT_CURSOR));
25:         bullsEye1 = new BullsEye();
26:         bullsEye1.setBounds(204,48,120,72);
27:         add(bullsEye1);
28:
29:         bullsEye1.addBullsEyeListener(this);
30:     }
31:
32:     java.awt.TextField status;
33:     BullsEye bullsEye1;
34: }
```

ANALYSIS This applet contains a `TextField` object named `status` and a `BullsEye` object (declared on lines 32 and 33). Lines 5 and 6 show that the applet implements the `BullsEyeListener` interface. This means the class will provide a `BullsEyeEventHandler` method and this method can be found on lines 8–13. This method uses the `getID` method of `BullsEyeEvent` to determine whether the mouse button was pressed or released over the `BullsEye` component. In either case, `setText` is used to change the contents of the text field.

Bound and Constrained Properties

From their names, you might suspect that bound and constrained properties are properties that have been kidnapped and are being held for ransom. This, however, is not the case.

NEW TERM A *bound property* sends an event to any registered listeners whenever its value is changed. A *constrained property* sends an event to any registered listeners whenever an attempt is made to change the property's value. The listeners have the option of vetoing, or canceling, the proposed change.

The first step in creating a bound or constrained property is to modify the `PropertyDescriptor` object in the `BeanInfo` class. This is done by using the following two methods:

```
setBound(boolean boundState)
```

```
setConstrained(boolean constrainedState)
```

Listing 18.11 shows the `getPropertyDescriptors` method from `BullsEye` after it has been modified to make the `indent` property both bound and constrained. On lines 6 and 7 of this listing, you can see how `setBound` and `setConstrained` were used.

Listing 18.11. The `getPropertyDescriptors` **method from**
`BullsEyeBeanInfo.java`.

```
 1:    public PropertyDescriptor[] getPropertyDescriptors() {
 2:        try {
 3:            PropertyDescriptor indent = new PropertyDescriptor(
 4:                    "indent", beanClass);
 5:            indent.setDisplayName("Indentation");
 6:            indent.setBound(true);
 7:            indent.setConstrained(true);
 8:
 9:             PropertyDescriptor innerColor = new PropertyDescriptor(
10:                    "innerColor", beanClass);
11:            innerColor.setDisplayName("Inner Color");
12:
13:            PropertyDescriptor outerColor = new PropertyDescriptor(
14:                    "outerColor", beanClass);
15:            outerColor.setDisplayName("Outer Color");
16:
17:            PropertyDescriptor[] rv = {
18:                    indent,
19:                    innerColor,
20:                    outerColor};
21:
22:            return rv;
23:        }
24:        catch (IntrospectionException e) {
25:            throw new Error(e.toString());
26:        }
27:    }
```

Modifying the Bean

The next step in supporting bound or constrained properties is to add the necessary code to the bean class itself. Listing 18.12 shows the portion of the `BullsEye` class that has been modified to support bound and constrained properties.

Listing 18.12. A portion of `BullsEye.java`.

```
 1:    import symantec.itools.beans.VetoableChangeSupport;
 2:    import symantec.itools.beans.PropertyChangeSupport;
 3:
 4:    public class BullsEye extends Canvas implements
 5:            java.io.Serializable {
 6:        public void setIndent(int newIndent) throws
 7:                PropertyVetoException {
 8:            if (indent != newIndent) {
 9:                Integer oldIndentInt = new Integer(indent);
10:                Integer newIndentInt = new Integer(newIndent);
11:
12:                vetos.fireVetoableChange("Indent", oldIndentInt,
13:                        newIndentInt);
```

```
14:
15:            indent = newIndent;
16:            repaint();
17:
18:            changes.firePropertyChange("Indent", oldIndentInt,
19:                newIndentInt);
20:        }
21:    }
22:
23:    public void addPropertyChangeListener(
24:            PropertyChangeListener listener) {
25:        changes.addPropertyChangeListener(listener);
26:    }
27:
28:    public void removePropertyChangeListener(
29:            PropertyChangeListener listener) {
30:        changes.removePropertyChangeListener(listener);
31:    }
32:
33:    public void addVetoableChangeListener(
34:            VetoableChangeListener listener) {
35:        vetos.addVetoableChangeListener(listener);
36:    }
37:
38:    public void removeVetoableChangeListener(
39:            VetoableChangeListener listener) {
40:        vetos.removeVetoableChangeListener(listener);
41:    }
42:
43:    private VetoableChangeSupport vetos =
44:            new VetoableChangeSupport(this);
45:    private PropertyChangeSupport changes =
46:            new PropertyChangeSupport(this);
47:
48:    // a portion of the class is not shown
49:
50:    }
```

ANALYSIS Because the BullsEye class is responsible for notifying listeners when the value of a bound or constrained property changes, it must keep track of its listeners. In the section "Custom Events and Listeners" earlier today, you added a vector to the BullsEye class and used this vector to store listener objects. A very similar approach is used to track listeners who are listening to bound or constrained objects.

Lines 43–44 declare a VetoableChangeSupport object. Think of this object as a vector that will hold references to any object that wants to listen for attempts to change a constrained property. Listener objects are added to this vector with calls to addVetoableChangeListener (lines 33–36) and removeVetoableChangeListener (lines 38–41). You will need to write these methods for any bean that contains constrained properties.

Similarly, lines 45–46 declare a PropertyChangeSupport object that will hold references to any object listening for changes to a bound property. Listeners are added to this vector with calls to addPropertyChangeListener (lines 23–26) and removePropertyChangeListener (lines 28–31). You must write these methods for any bean that contains bound properties.

You must also change the setIndent method (lines 6–21) so that it generates the appropriate events at the necessary times. The body of setIndent is now wrapped in an if statement so that events are not generated unless an actual change occurs. Lines 12–13 call fireVetoableChange, passing it the name of the property and its old and new values. This causes a message to be sent to any object that has registered as a listener with addVetoableChangeListener.

If any listener objects at this point, the listener will throw a PropertyVetoException exception; otherwise, execution will continue with line 15, which sets the new indent value. After the component is repainted, firePropertyChange is used on lines 18–19 to notify the listeners who registered with addPropertyChangeListener.

NOTE

Because support for bound and constrained properties requires the use of the PropertyChangeSupport and VetoableChangeSupport classes, you must import two additional packages into the bean class, as follows:

```
import symantec.itools.beans.VetoableChangeSupport;
import symantec.itools.beans.PropertyChangeSupport;
```

Listening for the Changes

To register as a listener for vetoable change events, an object must implement the VetoableChangeListener interface. This interface requires the class to provide a method body for the vetoableChange method, whose signature is as follows:

```
public void vetoableChange(PropertyChangeEvent event)
        throws PropertyVetoException
```

The vetoableChange method is called whenever an object that is being listened to calls fireVetoableChange (as was done on lines 12–13 of Listing 18.12). The vetoableChange method can look at the PropertyChangeEvent object that it is passed to find out information about the event. PropertyChangeEvent contains the following useful methods:

```
public Object getNewValue()
```

```
public Object getOldValue()
```

```
public String getPropertyName()
```

To find out the proposed new value, use getNewValue. Use getOldValue to find out the property's current value and use getPropertyName to find out the name of the property being changed. If your vetoableChange method determines that the proposed new value is not acceptable, it can throw the exception PropertyVetoException to stop the change.

TIP

> If a `vetoableChange` method throws `PropertyVetoException`, there is no guarantee that the property will not be changed anyway. The author of the bean might have chosen to ignore vetoes under some circumstances or he might have incorrectly coded the bean so that the property is changed even if vetoed.

Listening for nonvetoable property changes is very similar, but even easier. Any object that wants to listen for this type of event must implement the `PropertyChangeListener` interface. This interface includes a single method that must be provided in the listener class as follows:

```
public void propertyChange(PropertyChangeEvent event)
```

The `propertyChange` method is called whenever an object that is being listened to calls `firePropertyChange` (as was done on lines 18–19 of Listing 18.12). Like `vetoableChange`, `propertyChange` is passed a `PropertyChangeEvent` object that can be examined for specific information about the event.

An Example

As an example of how to write an applet that listens for vetoable and nonvetoable property changes, consider Listing 18.13. The main screen for this applet is shown in Figure 18.12. This applet consists of a `BullsEye` component, a text area for displaying messages, and a text field and button used to set new values for the `indent` property of the `BullsEye` component.

Figure 18.12.

This applet demonstrates the use of bound and constrained properties.

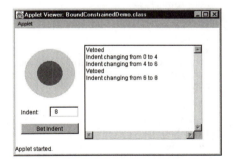

Listing 18.13. `BoundConstrainedDemo.java.`

```
1:  import java.awt.*;
2:  import java.applet.*;
3:  import BullsEye;
4:  import java.beans.*;
5:
```

continues

Listing 18.13. continued

```
6:    public class BoundConstrainedDemo extends Applet
7:         implements PropertyChangeListener,
8:                    VetoableChangeListener {
9:
10:       // if the button is pressed, set the indent to the
11:       // entered value
12:       void indentButton_Action(java.awt.event.ActionEvent event){
13:           try {
14:               bullsEye1.setIndent(Integer.parseInt(
15:                   indentAmount.getText())));
16:           }
17:           catch (PropertyVetoException e) {
18:           }
19:       }
20:
21:       public void addNotify() {
22:           super.addNotify();
23:
24:           setLayout(null);
25:           setSize(426,266);
26:
27:           // create a text area to hold status messages
28:           status = new java.awt.TextArea();
29:           status.setBounds(144,36,247,204);
30:           add(status);
31:           status.setCursor(new Cursor(Cursor.TEXT_CURSOR));
32:
33:           // create a label
34:           label1 = new java.awt.Label("Indent:");
35:           label1.setBounds(12,168,48,24);
36:           add(label1);
37:
38:           // create a text field in which the user
39:           // can enter the desired indent amount
40:           indentAmount = new java.awt.TextField();
41:           indentAmount.setBounds(72,168,60,22);
42:           add(indentAmount);
43:           indentAmount.setCursor(new Cursor(Cursor.TEXT_CURSOR));
44:
45:           // create a button that will set the indent amount
46:           indentButton = new java.awt.Button();
47:           indentButton.setActionCommand("Set Indent");
48:           indentButton.setLabel("Set Indent");
49:           indentButton.setBounds(12,204,120,23);
50:           add(indentButton);
51:
52:           // create the bulls eye
53:           bullsEye1 = new BullsEye();
54:           bullsEye1.setBounds(12,36,120,120);
55:           add(bullsEye1);
56:
57:           // register the property listeners
58:           bullsEye1.addPropertyChangeListener(this);
59:           bullsEye1.addVetoableChangeListener(this);
60:
61:           // register a listener for a button click
```

```
62:            Action lAction = new Action();
63:            indentButton.addActionListener(lAction);
64:        }
65:
66:        // this method is called as notification that a
67:        // property is changing value
68:        public void propertyChange(PropertyChangeEvent event) {
69:            Integer oldValue = (Integer)event.getOldValue();
70:            Integer newValue = (Integer)event.getNewValue();
71:
72:            status.appendText(event.getPropertyName() +
73:                " changing from " +
74:                String.valueOf(oldValue) +
75:                " to " +
76:                String.valueOf(newValue) +
77:                "\n");
78:        }
79:
80:        // this method is called and can veto a property
81:        // value change
82:        public void vetoableChange(PropertyChangeEvent event)
83:                throws PropertyVetoException {
84:            Integer oldValue = (Integer)event.getOldValue();
85:            Integer newValue = (Integer)event.getNewValue();
86:
87:            // veto attempts to set the indent to an odd number
88:            if (newValue.intValue() % 2 == 1) {
89:                status.appendText("Vetoed\n");
90:                throw new PropertyVetoException(
91:                    "Only Odd Values Allowed", event);
92:            }
93:        }
94:
95:        java.awt.TextArea status;
96:        java.awt.Label label1;
97:        java.awt.TextField indentAmount;
98:        java.awt.Button indentButton;
99:        BullsEye bullsEye1;
100:
101:        class Action implements java.awt.event.ActionListener {
102:            public void actionPerformed(java.awt.event.ActionEvent
103:                event) {
104:                Object object = event.getSource();
105:                if (object == indentButton)
106:                    indentButton_Action(event);
107:            }
108:        }
109: }
```

18

ANALYSIS   On lines 6–8, the applet implements both the PropertyChangeListener and the VetoableChangeListener interfaces. It implements PropertyChangeListener by providing the propertyChange method (lines 68–78). This method gets the old and new values from the event and casts each as an integer. It then calls status.appendText to display a message about the property change to the text area.

`VetoableChangeListener` is implemented by providing the `vetoableChange` method (lines 82–93). This method also retrieves the old and new values from the event. It then checks whether the proposed new value is an odd number. If it is, an informational message is displayed and it throws the exception `PropertyVetoException`.

Before the applet can listen for property changes, it must register as a listener. This is done on lines 58–59 with calls to `addPropertyChangeListener` and `addVetoableChangeListener`.

Do	Don't

DO err on the side of creating too many bound or constrained properties when creating a bean. It takes very little work for a bean to support bound and constrained properties, and you never know when some other object is going to want to have this capability.

DON'T forget that you need to register listeners with `addPropertyChangeListener` or `addVetoableChangeListener`. It is a common mistake to create a listener class and then forget to register the class.

Summary

Today you stopped working with other people's beans and learned how to write your own. You learned how to write both a bean class and a `BeanInfo` class. You learned how to describe the properties of a bean in order to control how it is displayed in Visual Café's Property List. You learned how to assign an icon to a bean and how to add a bean to the Component Library and the Component palette. Then you learned how to create custom event classes and listeners that work in conjunction with your new beans. Finally, you learned about bound and constrained properties.

Q&A

Q Do all beans have to be user-interface components?

A No. Many beans do have a user-interface, or visual, aspect to them, but this is not a requirement. You can also create *nonvisual beans*, which do not appear on the screen when they are included in a program.

Q How do I get rid of a bean that I've added to the Component Library?

A To remove a bean that was added by selecting Insert | Component into Library from the main menu, display the Component Library window (select Window | Component Library), highlight the desired bean, and press the Delete key. To remove a bean whose JAR file you have placed in the `bin\components` directory, close Visual Café, delete the JAR file, and restart Visual Café.

Workshop

The workshop includes quiz questions to help you gauge your understanding of the material in this chapter. The workshop also includes exercises to provide hands-on experience with what you've learned in this chapter. Answers to quiz questions can be found in Appendix D, "Answers."

Quiz

1. What is the difference between adding a component to the Component Library by using Insert | Component into Library and placing the JAR file in the `bin\components` directory?

2. What is the purpose of a JAR file?

3. What method of the `PropertyDescriptor` class is used to restrict a property to an enumerated set of values?

4. What class is typically subclassed when creating a custom event? What interface is typically subclassed when creating a custom event listener?

5. What interface must a class implement if it wishes to listen for vetoable property change events?

6. What is the difference between a bound property and a constrained property?

Exercises

1. Create a bean and `BeanInfo` class for a `ReverseLabel` class. This class should behave like a normal label (including a property for setting the alignment of the label). However, when the user clicks a mouse button over the label, have the string reverse itself so that `hello` becomes `olleh`. Each subsequent mouse click should reverse the string so that every second click returns the string to its original state.

2. Create a nonvisual bean, including its `BeanInfo` class for keeping track of the current user of a program.

3. Create a bean that is an error message dialog. The dialog needs to include buttons labeled `Abort`, `Retry`, and `Ignore` but allow the user to change these either through code or through the Property List. Have the bean send a custom event when the dialog is closed indicating whether the user clicked the Abort, Retry, or Ignore button.

18

Day 19

Adding Native Methods

Today you will learn how to augment Java by writing methods in other languages, especially C and C++. Occasionally you must write a Java application that uses existing legacy code in another language. The techniques you learn today make this possible. In the parlance of Java, when a method is written in a different language it is known as a *native method*. The Java Native Interface is a set of functions that allows you to write native methods that become part of your Java classes.

A First Example

At first glance, Java Native Interface (JNI) programming appears complicated. And with good reason: By definition, it involves Java plus an additional language. Any time you write a program that combines more than one language, you introduce an extra bit of complexity. Fortunately, the JNI abstracts many of the details of multilanguage programming and makes the task relatively painless. In order to present an overview of the process of writing a native method to show how simple the task can be, this chapter starts with an example. Because it is assumed that most readers will use either C or C++ for any native methods they write, these languages are used throughout today.

To create a native method in C or C++, you must take the following steps:

1. Write and compile the Java application.
2. Create a header file.
3. Write and compile the native method.

Write the Java Application

The first step in writing an application that uses a native method is to write the application itself. Listing 19.1 shows the class NativeHello. This class includes a native method, sayHello (line 2). This method will be implemented in C and will write Hello From C on the screen. As you can see in Listing 19.1, no method body is provided for sayHello; instead, it is simply terminated with a semicolon.

NOTE

> Because of security restrictions, native methods are not available to applets at this time. To use a native method, you must write a Java application.

Listing 19.1. NativeHello.java.

```
1:    public class NativeHello {
2:        public native void sayHello();
3:
4:        static {
5:            System.loadLibrary("hello");
6:        }
7:
8:        public static void main(String[] args) {
9:            new NativeHello().sayHello();
10:       }
11:   }
```

ANALYSIS NativeHello also includes a block of static code (lines 4–6). This causes the code to be executed when the class is first loaded. Inside the static block, the method System.loadLibrary is used to load the dynamically linked library (DLL) that contains the native method implementation. Because the sayHello method will be implemented in HELLO.DLL, hello is passed to loadLibrary. Finally, NativeHello includes a public main method (lines 8–10) that creates a new instance of the class and calls the sayHello method.

Before moving to the next step, you must also compile the class. Because the native method is not yet written, you cannot run the class.

NOTE

Under Windows NT and Windows 95, native methods are placed in dynamically linked libraries, which end with the `.dll` extension. Under Solaris, native methods are stored in shared libraries, which end with the `.so` extension. For simplicity, dynamically linked library and DLL will be used throughout the rest of today, but can be thought to encompass both the dynamically linked libraries of Windows and the shared libraries of Solaris.

Create a Header File

After you have written a class that uses a native method, the next step is to create a header that can be included in the C file. The header file tells the C file the signatures of the native methods. The header is created by running the javah utility. This program reads the `.class` file (not the source, or `.java`, file) and from it knows what methods must be implemented natively. You run javah from the command line by giving it the name of the class file to process (without the `.class` extension). The following example will create a header from `NativeHello.class`:

```
javah -jni NativeHello
```

WARNING

Because javah reads the `.class` file and not the `.java` file, you must compile the class before running javah.

Listing 19.2 shows the header file that was created by javah. The name of the header file is the same as the `.class` file except the extension is replaced with the C standard `.h`.

19

Listing 19.2. `NativeHello.h` **as generated by** `javah.exe`.

```
1:    /* DO NOT EDIT THIS FILE - it is machine generated */
2:    #include <jni.h>
3:    /* Header for class NativeHello */
4:
5:    #ifndef _Included_NativeHello
6:    #define _Included_NativeHello
7:    #ifdef __cplusplus
8:    extern "C" {
9:    #endif
10:   /*
11:    * Class:     NativeHello
12:    * Method:    sayHello
```

continues

Listing 19.2. continued

```
13:     * Signature: ()V
14:     */
15:   JNIEXPORT void JNICALL Java_NativeHello_sayHello
16:     (JNIEnv *, jobject);
17:
18:   #ifdef __cplusplus
19:   }
20:   #endif
21:   #endif
```

 Lines 15–16 of Listing 19.2 are the prototype of the native method. The name of the native method is based on the name of the member method that was given in the Java file. The function name in the C file also includes the class and package name according to the following naming convention:

Java[_PackageName][_ClassName][_MethodName]

This indicates that a native method will always begin with Java; then, the package, class, and method names are concatenated, each with a leading underscore character. If the class containing a native method is not placed in a package (and is therefore in the default package), the package name is omitted. Therefore, the sayHello method of Listing 19.1 is referenced as Java_NativeHello_sayHello in the C file on lines 15–16 of Listing 19.2.

The JNIEXPORT and JNICALL macros that are included as part of the prototype of the native method are used to ensure that the native method code is compilable.

Every native method you write will have at least the two parameters that are passed to Java_NativeHello_sayHello in this example. The JNIEnv parameter is a pointer to the JNI interface. As you will see throughout later examples in this chapter, this pointer can be used to reference additional JNI methods. The jobject parameter is a reference to the object invoking the native method. It is analogous to the C++ this pointer.

NOTE The NativeHello applet, including both the Java and C++ portions, can be found on the MCP Web site (www.mcp.com/info/1-57521/ 1-57521-303-6).

Write the Native Method

The next step is to write the actual native method. Listing 19.3 shows the C source code that does this.

Listing 19.3. The native method is implemented in `NativeHello.c`.

```
1:    #include <jni.h>
2:    #include "NativeHello.h"
3:    #include <stdio.h>
4:
5:    JNIEXPORT void JNICALL
6:    Java_NativeHello_sayHello(JNIEnv *env, jobject obj) {
7:        printf("Hello from C!\n");
8:    }
```

ANALYSIS Listing 19.3 starts by including three header files. The first, `jni.h`, is the generic Java Native Interface (JNI) header file that you will include for every native method file you write. The second, `NativeHello.h`, is the header that was created by running javah in the previous step. The third included file, `stdio.h`, is included because this particular native method uses `printf`, which is prototyped in `stdio.h`.

Lines 5–8 are the native method itself. You should recognize the signature as matching the one generated by javah and placed in `NativeHello.h`. The actual body of the method (line 7) is nothing more than a standard C `printf` statement.

You can write and compile this function into a Windows DLL with Visual C++ by taking the following steps:

1. Create a new project workspace, selecting Dynamic Link Library as the type.

2. Write the C file and add it to the project.

3. Add the necessary include directories to Visual C++. This can be accomplished by selecting Tools | Options | Directories and adding the paths to `jni.h` and `jni_md.h`. If you installed Visual Café into `C:\VisualCafe`, these can be found in `C:\VisualCafe\Java\Include` and `C:\VisualCafe\Java\Include\Win32`.

4. Compile the native method and copy the DLL into the directory with your Java class file.

After you've created the DLL, you can test the application from within Visual Café or from a command-line prompt as follows:

```
java NativeHello
```

You should see the message `Hello World` written to the screen exactly as though you had done so directly from within a Java program without a native method.

Parameters and Return Values

In the `NativeHello` example you saw how to invoke a method in a C program, but you didn't pass any of your own parameters to it, nor did you get a return value back from it. Naturally, there is a way to do both of these things. Because there is no guarantee that Java and the language in which a native method will be written use the same sizes for their primitive types, the JNI provides a mapping between Java primitives and native types. This mapping is shown in Table 19.1.

Table 19.1. Mapping between Java primitives and native types.

Java primitive	Native type	Size in bits	Signed
boolean	jboolean	8	No
byte	jbyte	8	Yes
char	jchar	16	No
double	jdouble	64	Yes
float	jfloat	32	Yes
int	jint	32	Yes
long	jlong	64	Yes
short	jshort	16	Yes
void	void	N/A	N/A

From Table 19.1 you can see that a variable that is declared as a byte in a Java program will be received as a jbyte by the native method. As an example of how this works, consider Listing 19.4, which shows the code to the ParameterDemo sample application, which appears on the MCP Web site.

Listing 19.4. ParameterDemo.java.

```
1:    public class ParameterDemo {
2:        public native float Multiply(float f, int i);
3:
4:        static {
5:            System.loadLibrary("ParameterDemo");
6:        }
7:
8:        public static void main(String[] args) {
9:            ParameterDemo app = new ParameterDemo();
10:           float result = app.Multiply(3.14f, 7);
11:           System.out.println("Result is " +
12:                   String.valueOf(result));
13:       }
14:   }
```

ANALYSIS The ParameterDemo class includes a native method Multiply, which is passed a float and an int. It also returns a float, which will be the product of its two parameters.

The Multiply method is invoked on line 10 and its return value is stored and then displayed. Listing 19.5 shows the contents of ParameterDemo.c, which includes the native implementation of Multiply.

Listing 19.5. ParameterDemo.c.

```
1:      #include <jni.h>
2:      #include "ParameterDemo.h"
3:      #include <stdio.h>
4:
5:      JNIEXPORT jfloat JNICALL
6:      Java_ParameterDemo_Multiply(JNIEnv *env, jobject obj,
7:              jfloat f, jint i) {
8:          return f * i;
9:      }
```

WARNING

Don't forget that before you write the native method, you need to run javah to create the header file. This can be done with

```
javah -jni ParameterDemo
```

ANALYSIS In Listing 19.5 you can see that the signature for Multiply includes the JNIEnv and jobject parameters that were passed to sayHello in the previous example. However, Multiply is also passed a jfloat and a jint. The values of these parameters are simply multiplied and returned on line 8.

Strings as Parameters

Passing primitive types as parameters and receiving them as return values is a step in the right direction. However, because Java is an object-oriented language, it is important that programs are able to pass objects to native methods as well. Because the Java String class is one of the more commonly used classes, it is an excellent choice to use for demonstrating how to pass objects.

Because Java stores unicode strings, you must convert them to C-style strings before you can use them in a C or C++ program. To convert a string for use in a C or C++ program, use GetStringUTFChars, whose signature is as follows:

```
const jbyte* GetStringUTFChars(JNIEnv *env, jstring string,
        jboolean *isCopy);
```

The *env* parameter is the pointer to the JNI environment that is passed as the first parameter to the native method. The *isCopy* parameter can be used to determine whether a copy of the string was made when it was converted. In most cases, this doesn't matter within the native method and you can pass a null value instead of a jboolean object.

Because the GetStringUTFChars method is implemented in the Java Virtual Machine (JVM) but is being called from the native method, the native method needs a way to invoke this method through the JVM. This is the main purpose of the JNIEnv parameter that is passed to each native method. Through this object, a native method can access methods that live on the Java side of the native method boundary. Each method is invoked through the JNIEnv object as a function pointer. Therefore, a sample call to GetStringUTFChars appears as follows:

```
const char *str = (*env)->GetStringUTFChars(env, myJstring, 0);
```

If you just want to get the length of a jstring parameter, you can do so with the following method:

```
jsize GetStringUTFLength(JNIEnv *env, jstring string);
```

An Example

As an example of passing strings to and from a native method, consider the StringDemo sample application, whose Java code is shown in Listing 19.6 and whose result is shown in Figure 19.1. This application, which can be found on the MCP Web site, can be used to look up information on the gods and goddesses of Greek mythology. The Java application passes the name of a god or goddess to a C function that returns a string containing information about the deity.

TIP

The StringDemo application is a perfect example of how a legacy C or C++ application can be wrapped in Java methods. In this example, the strings returned by the native method are hard-coded into the C function. However, the information could be retrieved from a legacy database or file system.

Listing 19.6. StringDemo.java.

```
1:     import java.awt.*;
2:
3:     public class StringDemo {
4:         public native String Lookup(String name);
5:
6:         static {
7:             System.loadLibrary("StringDemo");
8:         }
9:
10:        void Run() {
11:            String [] gods = { "Pan",
12:                               "Helios",
13:                               "Lisaus",
```

```
14:                                   "Aphrodite"
15:                               };
16:
17:          OutputFrame results = new OutputFrame();
18:          results.setVisible(true);
19:
20:          for(int i=0; i<gods.length; i++) {
21:              String text = Lookup(gods[i]);
22:              results.addString(gods[i] + " is the " + text);
23:          }
24:      }
25:
26:      public static void main(String[] args) {
27:          StringDemo app = new StringDemo();
28:          app.Run();
29:      }
30:  }
31:
32:  class OutputFrame extends Frame {
33:      void WindowClosing(java.awt.event.WindowEvent event) {
34:          hide();
35:          System.exit(0);
36:      }
37:
38:      public OutputFrame() {
39:      }
40:
41:      public synchronized void show() {
42:          move(50, 50);
43:          super.show();
44:      }
45:
46:      void addString(String s) {
47:          results.append(s + "\n");
48:      }
49:
50:      public void addNotify() {
51:
52:          // Call parents addNotify method.
53:          super.addNotify();
54:
55:          //{{INIT_CONTROLS
56:          setLayout(null);
57:          resize(insets().left + insets().right + 500,
58:                  insets().top + insets().bottom + 250);
59:          results = new java.awt.TextArea();
60:          results.reshape(insets().left + 30,insets().top + 30,
61:                  450,126);
62:          add(results);
63:          setTitle("A Simple Frame");
64:          //}}
65:
66:          //{{INIT_MENUS
67:          //}}
68:
```

continues

Listing 19.6. continued

```
69:          //{{REGISTER_LISTENERS
70:          Window lWindow = new Window();
71:          addWindowListener(lWindow);
72:          //}}
73:      }
74:
75:      //{{DECLARE_CONTROLS
76:      java.awt.TextArea results;
77:      //}}
78:
79:      //{{DECLARE_MENUS
80:      //}}
81:
82:      class Window extends java.awt.event.WindowAdapter {
83:          public void windowClosing(java.awt.event.WindowEvent
84:              event) {
85:          Object object = event.getSource();
86:          if (object == OutputFrame.this)
87:              WindowClosing(event);
88:          }
89:      }
90:  }
```

Figure 19.1.

Output of the
StringDemo
application.

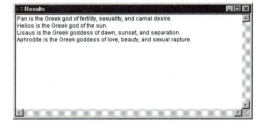

ANALYSIS In the StringDemo class, a native method named Lookup is declared (line 4). Lookup is passed a String and will return a String. The OutputFrame class (lines 32–90) is used to create a place for the application to display information about the deities that are passed to Lookup.

The Run method (lines 10–24) creates an array containing the names of four deities. A loop (lines 20–23) then iterates through this array, passing each name to Lookup (line 21) and then displaying the string that is returned (line 22).

Listing 19.7 shows a C language implementation of the Lookup native method that is called on line 21 of Listing 19.6. As you can see from its signature (lines 7–8), it returns and is passed

19

a jstring. The method GetStringUTFChars is used on line 10 to convert the jstring name into a C-style, null-terminated string pointed to by str.

Listing 19.7. `StringDemo.c.`

```
1:    #include <jni.h>
2:    #include "StringDemo.h"
3:    #include <stdio.h>
4:    #include <string.h>
5:
6:    JNIEXPORT jstring JNICALL
7:    Java_StringDemo_Lookup(JNIEnv *env, jobject obj,
8:           jstring name) {
9:       char buf[128];
10:       const char *str=(*env)->GetStringUTFChars(env, name, 0);
11:
12:       if(!stricmp(str, "Pan")) {
13:          strcpy(buf, "Greek god of fertility, sexuality, "
14:          strcat(buf, "and carnal desire.");
15:       }
16:       else if (!stricmp(str, "Aphrodite")) {
17:          strcpy(buf, "Greek goddess of love, beauty, "
18:          strcat(buf, "and sexual rapture.");
19:       }
20:       else if (!stricmp(str, "Lisaus")) {
21:          strcpy(buf, "Greek goddess of dawn, sunset, "
22:          strcat(buf, "and separation.");
23:       }
24:       else if (!stricmp(str, "Helios"))
25:          strcpy(buf, "Greek god of the sun.");
26:
27:       (*env)->ReleaseStringUTFChars(env, name, str);
28:
29:       return (*env)->NewStringUTF(env, buf);
30:    }
```

ANALYSIS After the string has been placed into str, it is tested against a pantheon of four gods and the appropriate text is placed into the local variable buf. Line 27 uses ReleaseStringUTFChars to tell the Java Virtual Machine that you are finished with the memory that was allocated by GetStringUTFChars. For every call to GetStringUTFChars, you must eventually call ReleaseStringUTFChars. If you do not, your program will gradually leak memory.

Because the native method needs to return a Java String object, it must allocate one. This is done by calling back into the Java Virtual Machine through the JNIEnv parameter passed to the native method. Line 29 of Listing 19.7 calls NewStringUTF in this manner, passing it the JNIEnv parameter and the C string from which to create the Java string.

> **TIP**
>
> If you are writing a native method in C++, you have an option to pass the JNIEnv parameter to every JNI method. For example, instead of writing
>
> ```
> (*env)->ReleaseStringUTFChars(env, name, str);
> ```
>
> in C++, you can write the more succinct
>
> ```
> env->ReleaseStringUTFChars(name, str);
> ```
>
> This works because a series of inline functions are defined in JNI.H that map the C++ style function calls into the more verbose style.

Do	Don't

DO call ReleaseStringUTFChars to tell the Java Virtual Machine that you are finished with memory allocated by a call to GetStringUTFChars.

DO be careful to pass variables of the proper type when writing native methods in C.

Invoking Java Methods

NEW TERM Sometimes you want to invoke a Java method from within a native method. A method invoked in this way is often referred to as a callback method. A Java *callback method* is a method that is invoked from a native method that has been called from Java. (Note: The term *callback method* is not unique to Java and can have a broader meaning than the one just given.)

To call a nonstatic method, you must take the following steps within a native method:

1. Use GetObjectClass to retrieve the Java class object for the object that contains the method.

2. Use GetMethodID to find the desired method within the class.

3. Invoke the method with one of the methods such as CallVoidMethod, CallDoubleMethod, or CallBooleanMethod.

An Example

As an example of how to call a Java method from within a native method, consider the MethodCallDemo sample application that appears on the MCP Web site. In this application, a Java method passes a string to a C function. The C function capitalizes the string and then calls a Java method to display the string. The results of running this application can be seen in Figure 19.2. Listing 19.8 shows the Java portion of the code from MethodCallDemo.

Figure 19.2.

Output of the
`MethodCallDemo`
application.

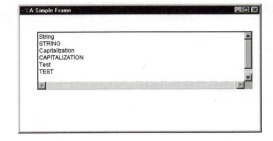

Listing 19.8. `MethodCallDemo.java.`

```
 1:    import java.awt.*;
 2:
 3:    public class MethodCallDemo {
 4:        public native void NativeStringToCaps(String name);
 5:
 6:        static {
 7:            System.loadLibrary("MethodCallDemo");
 8:        }
 9:
10:        void Run() {
11:            String [] strings = { "String",
12:                                  "Capitalization",
13:                                  "Test"
14:                                };
15:
16:            results = new OutputFrame();
17:            results.setVisible(true);
18:
19:            for(int i=0; i<strings.length; i++) {
20:                DisplayString(strings[i]);
21:                NativeStringToCaps(strings[i]);
22:            }
23:        }
24:
25:        public void DisplayString(String s) {
26:            results.textArea.append(s + "\n");
27:        }
28:
29:        public static void main(String[] args) {
30:            MethodCallDemo app = new MethodCallDemo();
31:            app.Run();
32:        }
33:        OutputFrame results;
34:    }
35:
36:    class OutputFrame extends Frame {
37:        void WindowClosing(java.awt.event.WindowEvent event) {
38:            hide();
39:            System.exit(0);
40:        }
41:
```

continues

Listing 19.8. continued

```
42:     public OutputFrame() {
43:     }
44:
45:     public synchronized void show() {
46:         move(50, 50);
47:         super.show();
48:     }
49:
50:     void addString(String s) {
51:         textArea.append(s + "\n");
52:     }
53:
54:     public void addNotify() {
55:
56:         // Call parents addNotify method.
57:         super.addNotify();
58:
59:         //{{INIT_CONTROLS
60:         setLayout(null);
61:         resize(insets().left + insets().right + 500,
62:                insets().top + insets().bottom + 250);
63:         textArea = new java.awt.TextArea();
64:         textArea.reshape(insets().left + 36,insets().top +
65:                36,450,126);
66:         add(textArea);
67:         setTitle("A Simple Frame");
68:         //}}
69:
70:         //{{INIT_MENUS
71:         //}}
72:
73:         //{{REGISTER_LISTENERS
74:         Window lWindow = new Window();
75:         addWindowListener(lWindow);
76:         //}}
77:     }
78:
79:     //{{DECLARE_CONTROLS
80:     java.awt.TextArea textArea;
81:     //}}
82:
83:     //{{DECLARE_MENUS
84:     //}}
85:
86:     class Window extends java.awt.event.WindowAdapter {
87:         public void windowClosing(java.awt.event.WindowEvent
88:                event) {
89:             Object object = event.getSource();
90:             if (object == OutputFrame.this)
91:                 WindowClosing(event);
92:         }
93:     }
94: }
```

ANALYSIS In Listing 19.8, a native method, `NativeStringToCaps`, is declared on line 4 and the native library containing this method is loaded on line 7. `DisplayString` (lines 25–27) writes a string to a text area that was created in the `OutputFrame` class (lines 36–94). The `for` loop between lines 19 and 22 uses `DisplayString` to display each string before it is capitalized (line 20). The loop then passes each string to `NativeStringToCaps`, which calls back into `DisplayString` to write the capitalized string.

Listing 19.9 shows the C side of the `MethodCallDemo` application. In the signature of `NativeStringToCaps` (lines 7–8), you can see that this function is passed a `jstring` parameter. This parameter is then converted, using `GetStringUTFChars` on line 10, to a C-style, null-terminated string. It is capitalized on line 12 with a call to `strupr`.

Listing 19.9. `MethodCallDemo.c`.

```
 1:  #include <jni.h>
 2:  #include "MethodCallDemo.h"
 3:  #include <stdio.h>
 4:  #include <string.h>
 5:
 6:  JNIEXPORT void JNICALL
 7:  Java_MethodCallDemo_NativeStringToCaps(JNIEnv *env,
 8:      jobject obj, jstring jstr) {
 9:    char buf[128];
10:    const char *str=(*env)->GetStringUTFChars(env, jstr, 0);
11:
12:    char *newStr = strupr((char *)str);
13:
14:    jclass cls = (*env)->GetObjectClass(env, obj);
15:    jmethodID methodID = (*env)->GetMethodID(env, cls,
16:        "DisplayString", "(Ljava/lang/String;)V");
17:
18:    if (methodID == 0) {
19:      (*env)->ReleaseStringUTFChars(env, jstr, str);
20:      return;
21:    }
22:
23:    (*env)->CallVoidMethod(env, obj, methodID,
24:        (*env)->NewStringUTF(env, newStr));
25:
26:    (*env)->ReleaseStringUTFChars(env, jstr, str);
27:  }
```

ANALYSIS Line 14 uses `GetObjectClass`, passing it the `JNIEnv` pointer and the `jobject` that were passed to this function. `GetObjectClass` returns the class of the object in the form of a `jclass` variable. This corresponds to a `Class` object in Java code. Next, `GetMethodID` is used on lines 15–16 to locate the desired method. `GetMethodID` is passed the `JNIEnv` pointer, the `jclass` variable returned by `GetObjectClass`, the name of the method, and a signature string representing the method's parameter and return types.

The signature string is of the form

```
(argument-types)return-type
```

TIP

Because constructors do not really have method names, you must pass `<init>` to GetMethodID when looking up the method identifier of a constructor.

Signature strings are created through the use of a shorthand encoding scheme as shown in Table 19.2. From Table 19.2 you can tell that the signature string (Ljava/lang/String;)V of line 16 in Listing 19.9 indicates that the method takes a String parameter and has no return value (in other words, is void).

Table 19.2. Symbols for method signature encoding.

Signature	Java Type
Z	boolean
B	byte
C	char
D	double
F	float
I	int
J	long
S	short
Lfully-qualified-class;	Fully qualified class
[type	type []

Because encoding method signatures can be tedious and prone to error, the javap.exe program is provided to automate this task. To run javap, use the following command line:

```
javap -s -private filename
```

NOTE

The -s that is passed to javap instructs it to display the signature strings. -private instructs it to display all class members. There are additional command-line parameters to javap that can be found by running javap at the command line without specifying any parameters.

The results of running javap on MethodCallDemo.java can be seen in Listing 19.10. As you can see, the encoded signature string for each method is placed on the line following the method.

Listing 19.10. The output of running javap on MethodCallDemo.java.

```
 1:    Compiled from MethodCallDemo.java
 2:    public synchronized class MethodCallDemo extends java.lang.Object
 3:        /* ACC_SUPER bit set */
 4:    {
 5:        OutputFrame results;
 6:        /*    LOutputFrame;    */
 7:        public native void NativeStringToCaps(java.lang.String);
 8:        /*    (Ljava/lang/String;)V    */
 9:        void Run();
10:        /*    ()V    */
11:        public void DisplayString(java.lang.String);
12:        /*    (Ljava/lang/String;)V    */
13:        public static void main(java.lang.String[]);
14:        /*    ([Ljava/lang/String;)V    */
15:        public MethodCallDemo();
16:        /*    ()V    */
17:        static static {};
18:        /*    ()V    */
19:    }
```

ANALYSIS After calling GetMethodID, it is important that you check to see whether a valid method identifier was returned. This check is done on line 18 of Listing 19.9. If GetMethodID returns 0, the method was not found. The native method should return immediately, which will cause the exception NoSuchMethodError to be thrown in the Java code.

Finally, after having identified the class and the method, the native method is able to invoke the method. In Listing 19.9, this is accomplished through a call to CallVoidMethod on lines 23–24. CallVoidMethod is used because the Java method being called, DisplayString, is void. There are a series of CalltypeMethod methods that can be used, depending on the return value of the method being called. The signatures of these methods are as follows:

```
jboolean CallBooleanMethod(JNIEnv *env, jobject obj,
        jmethodID methodID, ...)

jbyte CallByteMethod(JNIEnv *env, jobject obj,
        jmethodID methodID, ...)

jchar CallCharMethod(JNIEnv *env, jobject obj,
        jmethodID methodID, ...)

jdouble CallDoubleMethod(JNIEnv *env, jobject obj,
        jmethodID methodID, ...)
```

```
jfloat CallFloatMethod(JNIEnv *env, jobject obj,
        jmethodID methodID, ...)

jint CallIntMethod(JNIEnv *env, jobject obj,
        jmethodID methodID, ...)

jlong CallLongMethod(JNIEnv *env, jobject obj,
        jmethodID methodID, ...)

void CallVoidMethod(JNIEnv *env, jobject obj,
        jmethodID methodID, ...)

jobject CallObjectMethod(JNIEnv *env, jobject obj,
        jmethodID methodID, ...)

jshort CallShortMethod(JNIEnv *env, jobject obj,
        jmethodID methodID, ...)
```

After the *methodID* parameter is passed to these methods, you can specify the parameters that will be passed to the Java method. For example, the call to CallVoidMethod on lines 23–24 of Listing 19.9 passes newStr as the lone parameter to the Java DisplayString method.

Calling Static Methods

You can call a static method, rather than an instance method, in an almost identical manner. To call a static method, take the following steps within a native method:

1. Use GetObjectClass to retrieve the Java class object.

2. Use GetStaticMethodID (instead of GetMethodID) to find the desired method within the class.

3. Invoke the method with one of the methods such as CallStaticVoidMethod, CallStaticDoubleMethod, or CallStaticBooleanMethod.

The parameters passed to GetStaticMethodID are identical to those passed to GetMethodID. However, the parameters passed to the CallStatic*type*Method methods differ from those passed to the Call*type*Method methods. Because the Call*type*Method methods were used to invoke an instance method, one of the parameters passed to these methods was an object instance. Because the CallStatic*type*Method methods are invoking class (static) methods rather than instance methods, a jclass parameter is passed instead of a jobject parameter. The following CallStatic*type*Method methods are available:

```
jboolean CallStaticBooleanMethod(JNIEnv *env, jclass clazz,
        jmethodID methodID, ...)

jbyte CallStaticByteMethod(JNIEnv *env, jclass clazz,
        jmethodID methodID, ...)

jchar CallStaticCharMethod(JNIEnv *env, jclass clazz,
        jmethodID methodID, ...)

jdouble CallStaticDoubleMethod(JNIEnv *env, jclass clazz,
        jmethodID methodID, ...)
```

19

```
jfloat CallStaticFloatMethod(JNIEnv *env, jclass clazz,
     jmethodID methodID, ...)

jint CallStaticIntMethod(JNIEnv *env, jclass clazz,
     jmethodID methodID, ...)

jlong CallStaticLongMethod(JNIEnv *env, jclass clazz,
     jmethodID methodID, ...)

void CallStaticVoidMethod(JNIEnv *env, jclass clazz,
     jmethodID methodID, ...)

jobject CallStaticObjectMethod(JNIEnv *env, jclass clazz,
     jmethodID methodID, ...)

jshort CallStaticShortMethod(JNIEnv *env, jclass clazz,
     jmethodID methodID, ...)
```

Using Global References

When you use a method such as GetMethodID or GetStaticMethodID to look up a method identifier, Java returns a local reference to the desired method. The existence of the local reference will prevent the Java Virtual Machine's garbage collector from releasing the memory used by the object. However, after the native method call returns control to the Java code, these objects can be garbage collected, even if references to their method identifiers have been stored in global variables in the native code.

This means that the method identifier returned by GetMethodID or GetStaticMethodID can be safely used during the native method call in which it is retrieved, but you cannot store a method identifier in one native method call and use it in a subsequent native method call. For example, the following code will not work:

```
jclass cls = 0;
jmethodID methodID = 0;

JNIEXPORT void JNICALL
Java_MyClass_BadCode(JNIEnv *env, jobject obj) {
    if (cls == 0) {
        cls = (*env)->GetObjectClass(env, obj);
        methodID = (*env)->GetMethodID(env, cls, "DisplayString",
                "(Ljava/lang/String;)V");
    }
}
```

The first time the native method Java_MyClass_BadCode is called, the global variables cls and methodID will be equal to 0. Because of this, GetObjectClass will be used to find the class and GetMethodID will be used to find the method identifier of DisplayString. The next time Java_MyClass_BadCode is called, cls will hold a nonzero value. However, both cls and methodID can reference an object that has already been garbage collected by the Java Virtual Machine.

However, it will improve performance if you can somehow look up a method identifier one time and then continue to use this identifier on subsequent native method calls. Fortunately, the JNI provides a way to do this. You can use the method `NewGlobalRef` to create a global reference to an object. An object will not be garbage collected as long as it has any global references. A correct version of the previous code appears as follows:

```
jclass cls = 0;
jmethodID methodID = 0;

JNIEXPORT void JNICALL
Java_MyClass_BadCode(JNIEnv *env, jobject obj) {
    jclass tempCls;
    if (cls == 0) {
        tempCls = (*env)->GetObjectClass(env, obj);
        cls = (*env)->NewGlobalRef(env, tempCls);
        methodID = (*env)->GetMethodID(env, cls, "DisplayString",
                "(Ljava/lang/String;)V");
    }
}
```

When you have finished with the global reference, you must tell the Java Virtual Machine that you no longer need the global reference. This is accomplished with the following method:

```
void DeleteGlobalRef(JNIEnv *env, jobject globalRef)
```

WARNING

> If you do not delete a global reference, the object will never be garbage collected.

Do	**Don't**

DO be careful to pass an object to the `Call`*type*`Method` methods and a class to the `CallStatic`*type*`Method` methods.

DO use javap to determine method signature strings. It is much easier, and less error prone, than figuring them out yourself.

DON'T attempt to keep a method identifier between calls to native methods unless you have created a global reference to its object.

Accessing Member Variables

A native method can also access the member variables of a Java class. The approach for doing so is very similar to how member methods are accessed. A native method can either set or retrieve the value of member variables. The basic steps for doing so are as follows:

1. Use `GetObjectClass` to retrieve the Java class object for the object that contains the variable.

2. Use `GetFieldID` or `GetStaticFieldID` to find the desired variable.

3. To retrieve a value, use one of the methods such as `GetIntField`, `GetBooleanField`, or `GetStaticLongField`.

4. To set the value of the variable, use one of the methods such as `SetIntField`, `SetBooleanField`, or `SetStaticLongField`.

The signatures for `GetFieldID` and `GetStaticFieldID` are

```
jfieldID GetFieldID(JNIEnv *env, jclass cls, const char *name,
        const char *sig);
jfieldID GetStaticFieldID(JNIEnv *env, jclass cls,
        const char *name, const char *sig);
```

Each is passed a pointer to the JNI environment, the class, the name of the member variable, and a string representing the method signature. This string is in the same format as the method signatures that are passed to `GetMethodID` and `GetStaticMethodID`. The same encoding symbols shown in Table 19.2 are used to encode variable signatures. For example, consider the following:

```
jfieldID stringField = (*env)->GetFieldID(env, cls, "myStr",
        "Ljava/lang/String");
jfieldID staticIntField = (*env)->GetStaticFieldID(env, cls,
        "myStaticInt", "I");
```

The first example references the `String` instance variable `myStr`. The second example references a static `int` variable, `myStaticInt`.

After getting the field identifier, you can then set or retrieve the field's contents. To retrieve the contents of an instance variable, use one of the `GetTypeField` methods, whose signatures are as follow:

```
jboolean GetBooleanField(JNIEnv *env, jobject obj, jfieldID fid)

jbyte GetByteField(JNIEnv *env, jobject obj, jfieldID fid)

jchar GetCharField(JNIEnv *env, jobject obj, jfieldID fid)
```

19

```
jdouble GetDoubleField(JNIEnv *env, jobject obj, jfieldID fid)

jfloat GetFloatField(JNIEnv *env, jobject obj, jfieldID fid)

jint GetIntField(JNIEnv *env, jobject obj, jfieldID fid)

jlong GetLongField(JNIEnv *env, jobject obj, jfieldID fid)

jobject GetObjectField(JNIEnv *env, jobject obj, jfieldID fid)

jshort GetShortField(JNIEnv *env, jobject obj, jfieldID fid)
```

To retrieve the contents of a static variable, use one of the GetStatic*Type*Field methods, whose signatures are as follow:

```
jboolean GetStaticBooleanField(JNIEnv *env, jclass cls, jfieldID fid)

jbyte GetStaticByteField(JNIEnv *env, jclass cls, jfieldID fid)

jchar GetStaticCharField(JNIEnv *env, jclass cls, jfieldID fid)

jdouble GetStaticDoubleField(JNIEnv *env, jclass cls, jfieldID fid)

jfloat GetStaticFloatField(JNIEnv *env, jclass cls, jfieldID fid)

jint GetStaticIntField(JNIEnv *env, jclass cls, jfieldID fid)

jlong GetStaticLongField(JNIEnv *env, jclass cls, jfieldID fid)

jobject GetStaticObjectField(JNIEnv *env, jclass cls, jfieldID fid)

jshort GetStaticShortField(JNIEnv *env, jclass cls, jfieldID fid)
```

To set the contents of an instance variable, use one of the following Set*Type*Field methods:

```
jboolean SetBooleanField(JNIEnv *env, jobject obj, jfieldID id,
        jboolean newValue)

jbyte SetByteField(JNIEnv *env, jobject obj, jfieldID id,
        jbyte newValue)

jchar SetCharField(JNIEnv *env, jobject obj, jfieldID id,
        jchar newValue)

jdouble SetDoubleField(JNIEnv *env, jobject obj, jfieldID id,
        jdouble newValue)

jfloat SetFloatField(JNIEnv *env, jobject obj, jfieldID id,
        jfloat newValue)

jint SetIntField(JNIEnv *env, jobject obj, jfieldID id,
        jint newValue)

jlong SetLongField(JNIEnv *env, jobject obj, jfieldID id,
        jlong newValue)
```

19

```
jobject SetObjectField(JNIEnv *env, jobject obj, jfieldID id,
        jobject newValue)

jshort SetShortField(JNIEnv *env, jobject obj, jfieldID id,
        jshort newValue)
```

Similarly, a native method can set the contents of a static variable with the following SetStatic*Type*Field methods:

```
jboolean SetStaticBooleanField(JNIEnv *env, jclass cls,
        jfieldID id, jboolean newValue)

jbyte SetStaticByteField(JNIEnv *env, jclass cls,
        jfieldID id, jbyte newValue)

jchar SetStaticCharField(JNIEnv *env, jclass cls,
        jfieldID id, jchar newValue)

jdouble SetStaticDoubleField(JNIEnv *env, jclass cls,
        jfieldID id, jdouble newValue)

jfloat SetStaticFloatField(JNIEnv *env, jclass cls,
        jfieldID id, jfloat newValue)

jint SetStaticIntField(JNIEnv *env, jclass cls,
        jfieldID id, jint newValue)

jlong SetStaticLongField(JNIEnv *env, jclass cls,
        jfieldID id, jlong newValue)

jobject SetStaticObjectField(JNIEnv *env, jclass cls,
        jfieldID id, jobject newValue)

jshort SetStaticShortField(JNIEnv *env, jclass cls,
        jfieldID id, jshort newValue)
```

WARNING

Field identifiers, like method identifiers, cannot be safely used between native method calls. In order to use a field identifier in subsequent native method calls, you must first create a global reference. Details on doing so were given in the section "Using Global References," earlier today.

An Example

The FieldDemo application, which can be found on the MCP Web site, is an example of using the methods for accessing variables from within native methods. This application declares two integer variables: an instance variable and a static variable. A native method is then called, which changes the values of these variables. The values are displayed before and after the call to the native method, as shown in Figure 19.3. Listing 19.11 shows the Java code for the FieldDemo application.

Figure 19.3.

Output of the
FieldDemo
application.

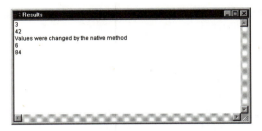

Listing 19.11. `FieldDemo.java.`

```
 1:    import java.awt.*;
 2:
 3:    public class FieldDemo {
 4:        public int publicInt;
 5:        public static int staticInt = 42;
 6:
 7:        public native void ChangeValues();
 8:
 9:        static {
10:            System.loadLibrary("FieldDemo");
11:        }
12:
13:        void Run() {
14:            publicInt = 3;
15:
16:            results = new OutputFrame();
17:            results.setVisible(true);
18:
19:            DisplayString(String.valueOf(publicInt));
20:            DisplayString(String.valueOf(staticInt));
21:
22:            ChangeValues();
23:            DisplayString("Values changed by the native method");
24:
25:            DisplayString(String.valueOf(publicInt));
26:            DisplayString(String.valueOf(staticInt));
27:        }
28:
29:        public void DisplayString(String s) {
30:            results.textArea.append(s + "\n");
31:        }
32:
33:        public static void main(String[] args) {
34:            FieldDemo app = new FieldDemo();
35:            app.Run();
36:        }
37:        OutputFrame results;
38:    }
39:
40:    class OutputFrame extends Frame {
41:        void WindowClosing(java.awt.event.WindowEvent event) {
42:            hide();
```

```
43:            System.exit(0);
44:        }
45:
46:     public OutputFrame() {
47:     }
48:
49:     public synchronized void show() {
50:         move(50, 50);
51:         super.show();
52:     }
53:
54:     void addString(String s) {
55:         textArea.append(s + "\n");
56:     }
57:
58:     public void addNotify() {
59:
60:         // Call parents addNotify method.
61:         super.addNotify();
62:
63:         //{{INIT_CONTROLS
64:         setLayout(null);
65:         resize(insets().left + insets().right + 500,
66:                 insets().top + insets().bottom + 250);
67:         textArea = new java.awt.TextArea();
68:         textArea.reshape(insets().left + 36,insets().top +
69:                 36,450,126);
70:         add(textArea);
71:         setTitle("A Simple Frame");
72:         //}}
73:
74:         //{{INIT_MENUS
75:         //}}
76:
77:         //{{REGISTER_LISTENERS
78:         Window lWindow = new Window();
79:         addWindowListener(lWindow);
80:         //}}
81:     }
82:
83:     //{{DECLARE_CONTROLS
84:     java.awt.TextArea textArea;
85:     //}}
86:
87:     //{{DECLARE_MENUS
88:     //}}
89:
90:     class Window extends java.awt.event.WindowAdapter {
91:         public void windowClosing(java.awt.event.WindowEvent
92:                 event) {
93:             Object object = event.getSource();
94:             if (object == OutputFrame.this)
95:                 WindowClosing(event);
96:         }
97:     }
98: }
```

ANALYSIS The method ChangeValues (line 7) is declared as a native method. The Run method (lines 13–27) displays the values of publicInt and staticInt, calls ChangeValues, and then redisplays the values of publicInt and staticInt.

Listing 19.12 shows FieldDemo.c, the C language implementation of the native method ChangeValues.

Listing 19.12. FieldDemo.c.

```
 1:    #include <jni.h>
 2:    #include "FieldDemo.h"
 3:    #include <string.h>
 4:
 5:    JNIEXPORT void JNICALL
 6:    Java_FieldDemo_ChangeValues(JNIEnv *env, jobject obj) {
 7:          jfieldID staticIntFld;
 8:        jfieldID publicIntFld;
 9:        int staticIntValue;
10:        int publicIntValue;
11:
12:        // get the class of this object
13:        jclass cls = (*env)->GetObjectClass(env, obj);
14:
15:        // get the static int field
16:        staticIntFld = (*env)->GetStaticFieldID(env, cls,
17:            "staticInt", "I");
18:        staticIntValue = (*env)->GetStaticIntField(env, cls,
19:            staticIntFld);
20:
21:        // and then set it back in Java with double the value
22:        (*env)->SetStaticIntField(env, cls, staticIntFld,
23:            staticIntValue * 2);
24:
25:        // get the public int field
26:        publicIntFld = (*env)->GetFieldID(env, cls, "publicInt",
27:            "I");
28:        publicIntValue = (*env)->GetIntField(env, obj,
29:            publicIntFld);
30:
31:        // and then set it back in Java with double the value
32:        (*env)->SetIntField(env, obj, publicIntFld, publicIntValue * 2);
33:    }
```

ANALYSIS The first thing the ChangeValues method does is call GetObjectClass (line 13) to get the class of the object calling ChangeValues. Next, GetStaticFieldID, GetStaticIntField, and SetStaticIntField are called (lines 16–23). These methods get the field identifier, the field's current value, and then assign a new value that is twice the current value. Similar method calls are then used to double the value of the instance variable on lines 26–32.

19

Do	Don't

DON'T forget to pass a `jobject` variable to the `GetTypeField` and `SetTypeField` methods but pass a `jclass` variable to the `GetStaticTypeField` and `SetStaticTypeField` methods.

DON'T attempt to keep a field identifier between calls to native methods unless you have created a global reference to its object.

Arrays

Java allows a native method to easily access an array of either primitives or objects. When accessing an array of objects, the native method retrieves a single object at a time from the array. However, when accessing an array of primitives, the native method can access either the entire array or a region of it all at once. The following methods are provided for accessing an entire array:

```
jboolean *GetBooleanArrayElements(JNIEnv *env, jbooleanArray array,
        jboolean *isCopy)

jbyte *GetByteArrayElements(JNIEnv *env, jbyteArray array,
        jboolean *isCopy)

jchar *GetCharArrayElements(JNIEnv *env, jCharArray array,
        jboolean *isCopy)

jdouble *GetDoubleArrayElements(JNIEnv *env, jDoubleArray array,
        jboolean *isCopy)

jfloat *GetFloatArrayElements(JNIEnv *env, jFloatArray array,
        jboolean *isCopy)

jint *GetIntArrayElements(JNIEnv *env, jIntArray array,
        jboolean *isCopy)

jlong *GetLongArrayElements(JNIEnv *env, jLongArray array,
        jboolean *isCopy)

jshort *GetShortArrayElements(JNIEnv *env, jShortArray array,
        jboolean *isCopy)
```

For example, to access an array of `int` variables, you would do the following:

```
jint *item = (*env)->GetIntArrayElements(env, myArray, 0);
```

The return value of the `GetTypeArrayElements` methods will point to the first item in the array. The native method can then access specific items in the array just as though the array exists in the native language. This can be seen in the following example, which also illustrates the use of `GetArrayLength` to determine the number of elements in an array:

```
int i;
jsize numElems = (*env)->GetArrayLength(env, myArray);

jint *item = (*env)->GetIntArrayElements(env, myArray, 0);
for(i=0; i<numElems; i++)
    printf("%d\n", item[i]);
```

Because the Java garbage-collection process could possibly move an array from one location in memory to another, the `GetTypeArrayElements` methods instruct the Java Virtual Machine to either lock the array in its current memory location or move it to a nonmovable memory location. When a native method has finished with an array, it needs to call the appropriate `ReleaseTypeArrayElements` method to inform the Virtual Machine that the array must no longer be locked in place. The following `ReleaseTypeArrayElements` are available:

```
void ReleaseBooleanArrayElements(JNIEnv *env, jbooleanArray array,
        jboolean *elems, jint mode)

void ReleaseByteArrayElements(JNIEnv *env, jbyteArray array,
        jbyte *elems, jint mode)

void ReleaseCharArrayElements(JNIEnv *env, jcharArray array,
        jchar *elems, jint mode)

void ReleaseDoubleArrayElements(JNIEnv *env, jdoubleArray array,
        jdouble *elems, jint mode)

void ReleaseFloatArrayElements(JNIEnv *env, jfloatArray array,
        jfloat *elems, jint mode)

void ReleaseIntArrayElements(JNIEnv *env, jintArray array,
        jint *elems, jint mode)

void ReleaseLongArrayElements(JNIEnv *env, jlong array,
        jlong *elems, jint mode)

void ReleaseShortArrayElements(JNIEnv *env, jshortArray array,
        jshort *elems, jint mode)
```

Array Regions

The `GetTypeArrayElements` methods lock and make available all of the items in an array of primitive types. If you want to work with only a subset of an array's element, this can be overkill. For these situations there are JNI methods that allow you to work with a subset of an array or primitives. The following `GetTypeArrayRegion` methods can be used to access a subset of items in an array:

```
void GetBooleanArrayRegion(JNIEnv *env, jbooleanArray array,
        jsize start, jsize len, jboolean *buf)

void GetByteArrayRegion(JNIEnv *env, jbyteArray array,
        jsize start, jsize len, jbyte *buf)

void GetCharArrayRegion(JNIEnv *env, jcharArray array,
        jsize start, jsize len, jchar *buf)
```

```
void GetDoubleArrayRegion(JNIEnv *env, jdoubleArray array,
        jsize start, jsize len, jdouble *buf)

void GetFloatArrayRegion(JNIEnv *env, jfloatArray array,
        jsize start, jsize len, jfloat *buf)

void GetIntArrayRegion(JNIEnv *env, jintArray array,
        jsize start, jsize len, jint *buf)

void GetLongArrayRegion(JNIEnv *env, jlongArray array,
        jsize start, jsize len, jlong *buf)

void GetShortArrayRegion(JNIEnv *env, jshortArray array,
        jsize start, jsize len, jshort *buf)
```

Each of these methods is passed a pointer to the JNI environment, the primitive array, a starting point within the array, the number of elements to get, and a pointer to the buffer where the elements will be placed. For example, the following will copy the second array element into the dest variable:

```
long dest;
(*env)->GetLongArrayRegion(env, myLongArray, 1, 1, &dest);
```

In addition to retrieving the values of array elements, a native method must also be able to set the values of array elements. This is accomplished with the Set*Type*ArrayRegion methods, whose signatures are as follow:

```
void SetBooleanArrayRegion(JNIEnv *env, jbooleanArray array,
        jsize start, jsize len, jboolean *buf)

void SetByteArrayRegion(JNIEnv *env, jbyteArray array,
        jsize start, jsize len, jbyte *buf)

void SetCharArrayRegion(JNIEnv *env, jcharArray array,
        jsize start, jsize len, jchar *buf)

void SetDoubleArrayRegion(JNIEnv *env, jdoubleArray array,
        jsize start, jsize len, jdouble *buf)

void SetFloatArrayRegion(JNIEnv *env, jfloatArray array,
        jsize start, jsize len, jfloat *buf)

void SetIntArrayRegion(JNIEnv *env, jintArray array,
        jsize start, jsize len, jint *buf)

void SetLongArrayRegion(JNIEnv *env, jlongArray array,
        jsize start, jsize len, jlong *buf)

void SetShortArrayRegion(JNIEnv *env, jshortArray array,
        jsize start, jsize len, jshort *buf)
```

An Example

The sample application ArrayDemo, which is provided on the MCP Web site, is an example of how to use the Get*Type*ArrayElements, Release*Type*ArrayElements, Get*Type*ArrayRegion, and Set*Type*ArrayRegion methods. Figure 19.4 shows the results of executing this applet. Listing 19.13 shows ArrayDemo.java, the Java side of the ArrayDemo sample application.

19

Figure 19.4.

Output of the
ArrayDemo
application.

Listing 19.13. `ArrayDemo.java.`

```
 1:    import java.awt.*;
 2:
 3:    public class ArrayDemo {
 4:        public native void ChangeAges(int [] ages);
 5:        public native void ChangeAnAge(int [] ages, int which);
 6:
 7:        static {
 8:            System.loadLibrary("ArrayDemo");
 9:        }
10:
11:        void Run() {
12:            results = new OutputFrame();
13:            results.setVisible(true);
14:
15:            results.textArea.append("Starting ages:\n");
16:            ShowAges();
17:
18:            ChangeAges(ages);
19:            results.textArea.append("Everyone got older:\n");
20:            ShowAges();
21:
22:            ChangeAnAge(ages, 1);
23:            results.textArea.append("Second person got older:\n");
24:            ShowAges();
25:        }
26:
27:        void ShowAges() {
28:            for(int i=0; i<ages.length; i++) {
29:                results.textArea.append(String.valueOf(ages[i]) +
30:                    "\n");
31:            }
32:        }
33:
34:        public static void main(String[] args) {
35:            ArrayDemo app = new ArrayDemo();
36:            app.Run();
37:        }
38:
39:        int [] ages = {21, 32, 14};
40:        OutputFrame results;
41:    }
42:
43:    class OutputFrame extends Frame {
44:        void WindowClosing(java.awt.event.WindowEvent event) {
```

```
45:          hide();
46:          System.exit(0);
47:      }
48:
49:      public OutputFrame() {
50:      }
51:
52:      public synchronized void show() {
53:          move(50, 50);
54:          super.show();
55:      }
56:
57:      void addString(String s) {
58:          textArea.append(s + "\n");
59:      }
60:
61:      public void addNotify() {
62:
63:          // Call parents addNotify method.
64:          super.addNotify();
65:
66:          //{{INIT_CONTROLS
67:          setLayout(null);
68:          resize(insets().left + insets().right + 500,
69:              insets().top + insets().bottom + 250);
70:          textArea = new java.awt.TextArea();
71:          textArea.reshape(insets().left + 36,insets().top +
72:              36,450,126);
73:          add(textArea);
74:          setTitle("A Simple Frame");
75:          //}}
76:
77:          //{{INIT_MENUS
78:          //}}
79:
80:          //{{REGISTER_LISTENERS
81:          Window lWindow = new Window();
82:          addWindowListener(lWindow);
83:          //}}
84:      }
85:
86:      //{{DECLARE_CONTROLS
87:      java.awt.TextArea textArea;
88:      //}}
89:
90:      //{{DECLARE_MENUS
91:      //}}
92:
93:      class Window extends java.awt.event.WindowAdapter {
94:          public void windowClosing(java.awt.event.WindowEvent
95:              event) {
96:              Object object = event.getSource();
97:              if (object == OutputFrame.this)
98:                  WindowClosing(event);
99:          }
100:     }
101: }
```

ANALYSIS Two native methods are declared in the `ArrayDemo` class on lines 4 and 5. This application uses an array of ages (declared on line 39). The `Run` method (lines 11–25) displays the values in the array (line 16) and then calls the native method `ChangeAges` (line 18) before redisplaying the ages. As you can see in Figure 19.4, the second time each age is displayed it has been increased by one. Next, the native method `ChangeAnAge` is called (line 22) to update only the second age, and the ages are redisplayed for a final time.

Listing 19.14 shows `ArrayDemo.c`, the C language implementation of `ArrayDemo`'s native methods.

Listing 19.14. `ArrayDemo.c`

```
1:    #include <jni.h>
2:    #include "ArrayDemo.h"
3:    #include <string.h>
4:
5:    JNIEXPORT void JNICALL
6:    Java_ArrayDemo_ChangeAges(JNIEnv *env, jobject obj,
7:          jintArray ages) {
8:       int i;
9:       jsize numElems = (*env)->GetArrayLength(env, ages);
10:
11:       jint *item = (*env)->GetIntArrayElements(env, ages, 0);
12:       for(i=0; i<numElems; i++)
13:          item[i]++;
14:
15:       (*env)->ReleaseIntArrayElements(env, ages, item, 0);
16:    }
17:
18:    JNIEXPORT void JNICALL
19:    Java_ArrayDemo_ChangeAnAge(JNIEnv *env, jobject obj,
20:          jintArray ages, jint which) {
21:       int currentAge;
22:       (*env)->GetIntArrayRegion(env, ages, which, which,
23:          &currentAge);
24:
25:       currentAge++;
26:
27:       (*env)->SetIntArrayRegion(env, ages, which, which,
28:          &currentAge);
29:    }
```

ANALYSIS The `ChangeAges` (lines 5–16) method increments the value in each item in the array (simulating the effects of a full year passing and everyone in the array being a year older). This is accomplished by getting the number of items in the array on line 9, locking the entire array on line 11, updating the array contents in the loop on lines 12–13, and then releasing the locked array on line 15.

The other native method shown in Listing 19.14 is ChangeAnAge (lines 18–29). This method updates only a single array element. ChangeAnAge is passed the array as well as a jint variable indicating which value to increase. GetIntArrayRegion (lines 22–23) is then used to retrieve the value of a single array element. The value is incremented on line 25 and then placed back into the array with SetIntArrayRegion (lines 27–28).

Arrays of Objects

So far, all the array-handling methods that have been described work with Java's primitive types, such as int, float, boolean, and double. Arrays of objects are handled with different methods. Unlike the methods for working with arrays of primitives, the methods for working with arrays of Java objects work on a single array element at a time. The following methods are provided to retrieve or set a single object array element:

```
jobject GetObjectArrayElement(JNIEnv *env, jobjectArray array,
        jsize index);

void SetObjectArrayElement(JNIEnv *env, jobjectArray array,
        jsize index, jobject value);
```

For example, the following code will retrieve the first object in an array and copy it over the second object:

```
if ((*env)->GetArrayLength(env, ages) > 1) {
    jobject jobj = (*env)->GetObjectArrayElement(env, myArray, 0);
    (*env)->SetObjectArrayElement(env, myArray, 1, jobj);
}
```

Exception Handling

It is possible to catch and throw exceptions in native methods. The ExceptionDemo sample application, which appears on the MCP Web site, illustrates how a native method can catch an exception and how it can generate an exception and throw it back to the Java code. Listing 19.15 shows the Java code to ExceptionDemo.

Listing 19.15. ExceptionDemo.java.

```
 1:    public class ExceptionDemo {
 2:        public native void GenerateException();
 3:
 4:        static {
 5:            System.loadLibrary("ExceptionDemo");
 6:        }
 7:        public static void main(String[] args) {
 8:            try {
 9:                new ExceptionDemo().GenerateException();
10:            }
```

continues

19

Listing 19.15. continued

```
11:          catch (Exception e) {
12:              System.out.println(e);
13:          }
14:      }
15:  }
```

ANALYSIS In this listing, you can see that the ExceptionDemo class includes a native method, GenerateException (line 2). The main method (lines 7–14) executes GenerateException within a try...catch block. If an exception is caught, it is written to System.out (line 12).

Listing 19.16 shows the C language native method implementation of the ExceptionDemo class. It includes a single method, Java_ExceptionDemo_GenerateException, which corresponds to GenerateException in Listing 19.15. The call to GetFieldID (lines 13–14) attempts to find a variable that does exist in ExceptionDemo. This results in an exception being thrown. Because the JNI is intended to work with many languages, it must support exceptions even in languages (such as C) that do not have any form of built-in exception handling. This is accomplished by allowing a native method to call ExceptionOccurred, which returns a jthrowable object if an exception occurred. In Listing 19.16, line 15 calls ExceptionOccurred and stores the result in except. Line 17 tests except to determine whether an exception occurred.

Listing 19.16. ExceptionDemo.c.

```
1:   #include <jni.h>
2:   #include "ExceptionDemo.h"
3:   #include <stdio.h>
4:
5:   JNIEXPORT void JNICALL
6:   Java_ExceptionDemo_GenerateException(JNIEnv *env,
7:        jobject obj) {
8:      jclass newException;
9:
10:      // get the class of this object
11:      jclass cls = (*env)->GetObjectClass(env, obj);
12:
13:      jfieldID fid= (*env)->GetFieldID(env, cls,
14:          "NotThere", "I");
15:      jthrowable except = (*env)->ExceptionOccurred(env);
16:
17:      if(except) {
18:          printf("---------Exception Report---------\n");
19:          (*env)->ExceptionDescribe(env);
20:          printf("--------------------------------\n");
21:          (*env)->ExceptionClear(env);
22:
23:          newException = (*env)->FindClass(env,
```

```
24:                "java/lang/NullPointerException");
25:        if(newException == 0)
26:            return;
27:        (*env)->ThrowNew(env, newException,
28:            "brought to you by a native method.");
29:    }
30: }
```

ANALYSIS   If except is non-null, the test on line 17 will be true. The function `ExceptionDescribe` (line 19) is used to display information about the exception. `ExceptionClear` must be called when a native method is finished with an exception. Many of the JNI methods will automatically fail if the environment includes an uncleared exception.

Lines 23–28 of Listing 19.16 take care of throwing a new exception back to the calling Java code. First, `FindClass` is used to return a `jclass` object. If the `jclass` object equals 0, the class could not be found and the native method simply returns. If, however, the class is found, `ThrowNew` is used to throw a new exception.

When the `ExceptionDemo` application is run, the following text is displayed:

```
---------Exception Report---------
Exception in thread "main" java.lang.NoSuchFieldError: NotThere
        at ExceptionDemo.main(ExceptionDemo.java:11)
----------------------------------
java.lang.NullPointerException: brought to you by a native method
```

Summary

This chapter showed you how to add native methods to your Java applications. You learned how to write native methods in C and C++ that can pass parameters and return values across language boundaries. You saw how to write native methods that can invoke methods and access variables on the Java side of the boundary. Finally, you learned how to work with arrays, objects, and exceptions within native methods.

Q&A

Q Why can't I use native methods in applets?

A The designers of Java considered this to be a security risk. Because applets are downloaded over the Internet, usually without the user being aware that an applet is starting, it would be too easy for an applet to carry out destructive behavior if it could access native methods. For example, with native methods, it would become very simple to write an applet that would delete all the files on a user's hard drive.

Q **My Java application uses multiple threads. Are there any special concerns of which I should be aware in writing native methods?**

A Yes, there are. The JNIEnv pointer that is passed to each native method is valid only in the thread that called the native method. You should not pass this pointer to another thread. Local references to field and method identifiers are also valid within only the thread in which they are retrieved. You should create global references to them with NewGlobalRef if they will be used in multiple threads. Finally, be very careful about the use of any global variables that are declared in the native language. These globals could be accessed simultaneously by more than one Java thread.

Workshop

The workshop includes quiz questions to help you gauge your understanding of the material in this chapter. The workshop also includes exercises to provide hands-on experience with what you've learned in this chapter. Answers to the quiz questions can be found in Appendix D, "Answers."

Quiz

1. How do you create the header file that gets included in C or C++ native method implementation source files?

2. What is the purpose of the System.loadLibrary method?

3. What naming convention does Java follow when naming the native language function that implements a native method?

4. What two parameters are always passed to a native method? What do these parameters represent?

5. If a native method uses GetStringUTFChars, what other method must eventually be called? Why?

6. What are the three basic steps involved in calling a Java method from within a native method?

7. How does the Java Virtual Machine ever find out a native method is finished with an array that was locked in place by a call to one of the GetTypeArrayElements methods?

8. How many objects (not primitives) can be retrieved from an array at a time?

9. Why can't a native method throw an exception that is caught in Java code?

19

Exercises

1. Write a native method that reverses a string that is passed to it.

2. Write a native method that reverses an array of strings that is passed to it.

3. Write a native method that invokes a Java callback method that reverses a string that is passed between the methods.

4. Write a native method that accesses two integer variables in the Java code. Divide one variable by the other and return the value as a floating-point value. If a divide-by-zero error occurs, be sure to throw an exception back to the Java program.

19

Day 20

The Visual Café
Database Tools

The Database Development edition of Visual Café includes the following tools for working with databases. These tools work together to simplify Java database programming.

☐ The dbNAVIGATOR

☐ The dbAware project wizard

☐ The dbAware template wizard

☐ The Add Table Wizard

☐ The dbANYWHERE Workgroup Server

☐ A copy of Sybase's SQL Anywhere database

This chapter describes each of these tools and how they can be combined to quickly and easily provide solutions to your database programming challenges.

dbANYWHERE

dbANYWHERE is a middleware component that facilitates the creation of three-tiered database architectures. Figure 20.1 illustrates this by showing three clients attached to a dbANYWHERE server that performs database requests against a database server.

Figure 20.1.

A three-tiered dbANYWHERE architecture.

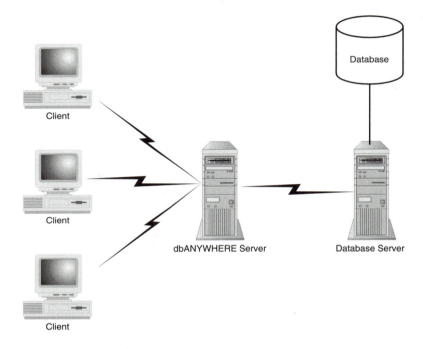

dbANYWHERE also allows you to create a self-hosted architecture, meaning that dbANYWHERE resides on the same machine as the client. In fact, using dbANYWHERE, it is possible in some cases to completely combine the three tiers shown in Figure 20.1 (client, middleware, database server) onto a single machine. Although this is not a particularly effective end-user solution (why would you need a Web browser to access a database on your local hard drive?), it can be a highly productive development environment. As you'll see later today, Sybase's SQL Anywhere product (a version of which is provided with Visual Café Pro) also operates in a self-hosted mode and is an ideal complement to dbANYWHERE.

With dbANYWHERE, you can connect to any of the following databases:

- ☐ Oracle
- ☐ Sybase
- ☐ Microsoft SQL Server

20

☐ Microsoft Access

☐ any ODBC data source

Running dbANYWHERE

To start dbANYWHERE, run DBAW.EXE (normally installed in a folder named dbAnywhere). When dbANYWHERE loads it will resemble the screen shown in Figure 20.2. As dbANYWHERE continues to run, its status and informational messages will be written to this window.

Figure 20.2.

The main screen of dbANYWHERE.

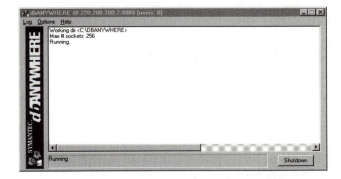

You can control what information is logged to the dbANYWHERE screen by selecting Properties from the Options menu and then choosing the Logging tab. When you begin working with dbANYWHERE, you might find it useful to enable the logging of SQL statements and connection statistics (these options are shown as enabled in Figure 20.3). Additionally, in some cases you might find it valuable to enable file logging of dbANYWHERE activity.

Figure 20.3.

The logging properties of dbANYWHERE.

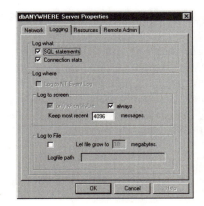

The remainder of the tabbed pages on the dbANYWHERE Server Properties dialog box can be used to set other options. For example, you can limit the amount of time a user can remain logged on or the amount of idle time before a connection is automatically terminated.

NOTE

dbANYWHERE is not automatically installed when you install Visual Café. To install it, run the setup program on the Visual Café CD-ROM and select dbANYWHERE from the menu of installation options.

Sybase SQL Anywhere

Sybase SQL Anywhere is a full-scale relational database that is ideal for self-hosted applications or application development. SQL Anywhere has also been targeted at developers writing portable applications such as for sales force automation. For this type of application, the software must be written so that it can work when the computer is connected over a network to a centralized database or when the computer is disconnected from the network and database. SQL Anywhere excels at this type of application because of its replication and synchronization features, which allow changes made to SQL Anywhere data to be merged back into a centralized database when the computer is again connected to the network. Similarly, changes to the data in the centralized database are replicated back to the version of the database on the remote computer.

The Database Development edition of Visual Café includes a copy of SQL Anywhere, which you can use in conjunction with dbANYWHERE. The combination of these packages gives you an excellent head start on most database projects.

Starting the Database Engine

Start the SQL Anywhere database engine by running the DBENG50.EXE file, which is normally found in the C:\SQLANY50\WIN32 directory. To start the database engine, you must specify the name of a SQL Anywhere database file. Database files end with a .DB extension. SQL Anywhere includes a sample database named SADEMO.DB, which will be placed in the base directory on which you installed the product (usually C:\SQLANY50). The name of the database file to be started is specified as a command-line parameter to the database engine. The following example will start the sample database:

```
C:\sqlany50\win32\dbeng50.exe c:\sqlany50\sademo.db
```

20

When SQL Anywhere loads, it displays a status screen similar to the one shown in Figure 20.4. Notice on the next-to-last line that SQL Anywhere says it is now accepting requests. This is your indication that startup has gone well and the database is ready for use.

Figure 20.4.

The SQL Anywhere status screen immediately after the program is started.

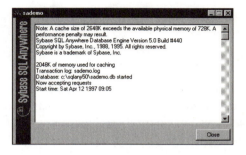

 SQL Anywhere is not automatically installed when you install Visual Café. To install it, run the setup program on the Visual Café CD-ROM, and select SQL Anywhere from the menu of installation options to invoke the SQL Anywhere setup program.

Using SQL Central

SQL Anywhere includes more than the database engine; it includes a set of tools that help you manage and manipulate databases. One of the most useful of these is SQL Central. SQL Central can be used to perform routine tasks such as the following:

☐ Create a database

☐ Back up a database

☐ Compress a database

☐ Add tables to a database

☐ Add indexes to a database

☐ Specify column constraints

Instructions for performing the most common of these tasks will be given in the following sections.

Connecting to a Database

To connect to a database, select Tools | Connect. You will be presented with a logon screen like the one shown in Figure 20.5. If the screen you see includes only the User ID and Password fields, click the More button to see the additional fields.

20

Figure 20.5.

The SQL Anywhere Logon screen.

On the logon screen, enter DBA in the User ID field, sql in the Password field, and the name of the database file where you installed the sample database in the Database File field (these values are shown in Figure 20.5). After you successfully log on, the desired database (in this case, sademo) is shown as an item in the tree that makes up the left panel of the SQL Central desktop. By clicking the plus icons to the right of the items in the tree, you can expand the items. Figure 20.6 shows what the tree looks like when partially expanded.

Figure 20.6.

The tree for the sademo *database has been partially expanded to reveal the database's components.*

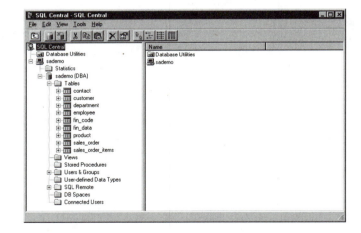

Creating a Database

If you select the Database Utilities item in the tree, the right panel of the SQL Central desktop will display a list of available options, as shown in Figure 20.7. From this list, you can perform any of the following operations:

☐ Create a new SQL Anywhere database

☐ Upgrade from a Watcom database to a SQL Anywhere database

☐ Back up an existing database

☐ Compress a database

☐ Uncompress a compressed database

☐ Create a write file for the database

☐ Translate a SQL Anywhere transaction log

☐ Change the log file used by a database

☐ Unload a database

☐ Create and synchronize a remote database

☐ Erase a database

NOTE

Many of these operations are beyond the scope of this chapter; for more information, refer to the SQL Anywhere documentation. The purpose of this chapter is to provide a starting point for using SQL Anywhere and to provide enough information for you to use SQL Anywhere to create simple test databases that allow you to learn about dbANYWHERE and the data-aware components of Visual Café.

Figure 20.7.

When Database Utilities is selected on the left, a set of database commands is displayed on the right.

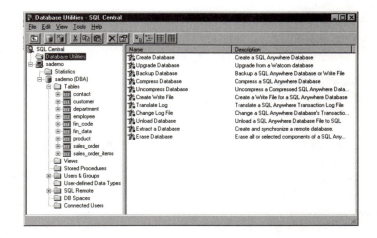

To create a new database, double-click Create Database in the right panel. This invokes the SQL Anywhere Database Creation wizard. This seven-screen wizard steps you through the database-creation process, asking for information such as the name of the database file, whether you want to maintain a transaction log, whether you want to mirror the transaction log, whether the database is encrypted, and the name of the user who owns the system objects. Unless you have a reason to change any of these values from their defaults, you should leave them as set by Visual Café. When you click the Finish button on the final page of the wizard, a database will be created in the filename you specified.

Creating Tables

To create a new table, select the Tables item in the tree underneath the database to which you want to add the table. Then, in the right panel, double-click Add Table (see Figure 20.8).

Figure 20.8.

Select Add Table to create a new table within the selected database.

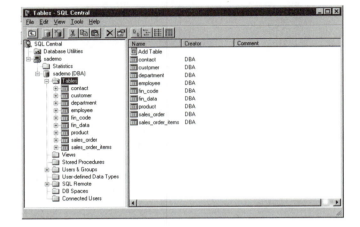

Double-clicking Add Table displays the New Table Properties dialog. This dialog, shown in Figure 20.9, allows you to enter the name of the table, the name of the creator, the database space for the new table, and a comment about the table.

 A *database space* is a file in which a database is stored. Each table resides in a single database space, but a database can span multiple database spaces (as long as each table is in only one space).

Figure 20.9.

The New Table Properties dialog is displayed when you create a new table.

20

Adding Columns

Of course, a table without any columns is about as useful as an apple pie without apples. To add a new column, expand the desired table in the left panel of the SQL Central desktop. Beneath the table you will see tree items for the following:

- ☐ Columns
- ☐ Foreign Keys
- ☐ Referenced By
- ☐ Indexes
- ☐ Triggers

Select Columns in the right panel, and then double-click Add Column. This displays the General tab of the New Column Properties dialog, as shown in Figure 20.10. Here you can enter the name of the new column and a brief description of it. You can select the column type, size, and some additional properties by selecting the Data Type tab. The contents of this tab are shown in Figure 20.11.

Figure 20.10.

The General tab of the New Column Properties dialog.

Figure 20.11.

The Data Type tab of the New Column Properties dialog.

20

From the Data Type tab you can also set a column's advanced properties. Do this by clicking the Edit button in the Advanced properties panel (refer to Figure 20.11). This will display the Advanced Column Properties dialog, shown in Figure 20.12.

Figure 20.12.

The Advanced Column Properties dialog is accessed by clicking the Edit button on the Data Type tab.

On this dialog, you can specify a default value for the column. Figure 20.12 shows that the first_name column will default to Mike. The Constraints fields can be used to indicate whether entries in this column must be unique and whether null values are allowed.

On the Advanced Column Properties dialog, you can also specify a check constraint for the column. A check constraint might be used to ensure that the column's value fits within a certain range or contains an item from an approved list of values. For details on the syntax for writing check constraints, see the SQL Anywhere documentation.

TIP

> If you are creating multiple columns, click the Apply button rather than the OK button to create each column. This creates a column using the currently entered values, and also leaves the New Column Properties dialog displayed with all values intact. This allows you to change only the different properties before clicking Apply to create a second column.

After you have created one or more columns, you can indicate which column or columns constitute a table's *primary key*.

NEW TERM

A *primary key* is the column or columns that uniquely identify each row in a table. For example, in a table containing information about employees, a Social Security number would make a good candidate for the table's primary key.

A *compound primary key* is a primary key that is made from more than one column. For example, in a database of all the compact discs I own, it would be insufficient to use disc title or artist alone as the primary key. I have more than one CD with the title "Greatest Hits" and I certainly have more than one Jimmy Buffett CD. In this case, a compound primary key is created by using the title and artist columns.

To add a column to a table's primary key, highlight the column when viewing the tree in SQL Central and click the right mouse button. This will display a context menu for the selected column. If you choose Add to Primary Key, the column will become part of the primary key for the table.

Using ISQL

In addition to SQL Central, SQL Anywhere includes an ISQL (Interactive SQL) program that you will probably use frequently. You can use ISQL to test the behavior of any SQL statements against your database. By using SQL's data manipulation commands, you can even create new tables in ISQL if you prefer it over SQL Central.

NOTE For information on SQL, see Day 24, "Bonus Day: An Introduction to SQL."

ISQL, like SQL Central, asks you to enter your username and password at startup. After that, you are presented with a an empty screen that resembles the one shown in Figure 20.13.

Figure 20.13.

The initial ISQL screen awaits your command.

20

The screen in Figure 20.13 is split into the following windows:

☐ Data

☐ Statistics

☐ Command

When you enter a SQL statement into the Command window and click the Execute button, the results of that statement are displayed in the Data window. Statistics about the execution of the statement are displayed in the Statistics window. This can be seen in Figure 20.14, which shows the results of the execution of a simple select statement.

Figure 20.14.

The results of the execution of a SQL statement are shown in the Data window.

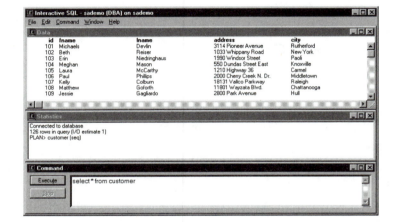

 TIP

You can enter more than one SQL statement in the Command window by starting each statement on its own line.

ISQL Shortcuts

ISQL provides a few time-saving shortcuts of which you should be aware. First, you can easily recall a previous SQL statement by selecting Recall from the Command menu. This displays the Command Recall dialog (shown in Figure 20.15). To recall a command, highlight the command and click the Recall button. The command will be pasted into the Command window but not executed. This allows you to edit the command before clicking the Execute button.

Figure 20.15.

Previously executed commands can be easily recalled.

An additional convenience of ISQL is that you can select table and column names from lists rather than typing them. When working with a database with many tables, it is easy to forget the exact name of a column or table. To take advantage of this feature in ISQL, position the cursor in the Command window at the point where you would like to insert a table or column name. Then select Insert Table from the Edit menu. The Tables dialog, shown in Figure 20.16, will be displayed. On the Tables dialog, you can either add a table name to the SQL statement you are building by clicking the Insert button, or you can select a column name by clicking the Columns button.

Figure 20.16.

You can add a table or column name to a SQL statement from the Tables dialog.

Creating a dbAware Project

When you create a new Visual Café project, you can use the dbAware project wizard to quickly add database support to the project. If you select dbAware Project Wizard on the New Project dialog, you will be stepped through a series of screens that allow you to customize the project to your needs. For example, you must first determine the type of project you wish to create: an applet or an application. Enter your decision in the Project Type screen of the dbAware project wizard (shown in Figure 20.17).

20

Figure 20.17.

Enter the project type.

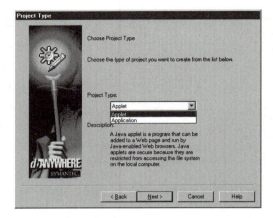

NOTE
> Because the dbAware project wizard uses dbANYWHERE to communicate with the database, you must start dbANYWHERE before starting the project wizard. Additionally, if the database you use requires a database server (such as SQL Anywhere, Oracle, or SQL Server), you must start the database server prior to starting the project wizard.

After clicking the Next button, you will be asked to identify the dbANYWHERE server you wish to use. Information about the dbANYWHERE server is entered in the wizard on the screen shown in Figure 20.18. First, you are asked to give the server a name. This can be any string you want and is not related to any configuration setting in the server. Next, you are asked to enter the IP address or the name of the host machine running the server. If you are running a self-hosted database server such as SQL Anywhere, you can leave this value as localhost. Finally, you are asked to enter the port number that is used by the dbANYWHERE server. This value must correspond with the port number entered on the Network tab of the dbANYWHERE properties page. By default, port 8889 is used.

On the next screen of the project wizard, select the data source to which the program will connect. Do so by choosing one from the drop-down list, as shown in Figure 20.19.

Figure 20.18.

You must tell the project wizard which dbANYWHERE server to use.

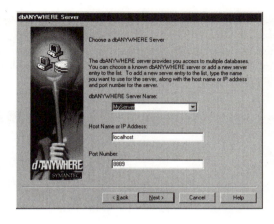

NOTE

You should create an ODBC data source that represents the SQL Anywhere sample database. To do so, start the 32-bit ODBC manager from the Control Panel and add a new data source. On the ODBC configuration screen, set the user ID to DBA, the password to sql, and the database file to C:\SQLANY50\SADEMO.DB (or wherever you installed SQL Anywhere). You can use whatever value you want for the Data Source Name field, but the examples in this chapter and the next assume you have used My SQLAnywhere Source.

Figure 20.19.

Tell the dbAware project wizard which data source you want to connect to.

20

After you select a data source and click the Next button, you will be asked to log on to the database if you have not already done so. You are required to log on to the database because, at this point, the project wizard will query the database to find out what tables are available. The next step in the project wizard requires you to select which table you wish to work with (see Figure 20.20).

Figure 20.20.

The project wizard asks you which table you want to work with.

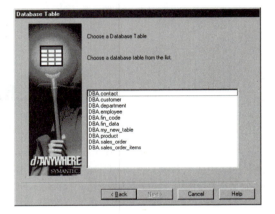

After you select the desired table and click the Next button, the project wizard will display the Database Columns screen. This screen shows the columns that are available in the table you selected and allows you to choose the columns that will be displayed in the project you are creating. Figure 20.21 shows how the Database Columns screen appears for the Customer table of the sample SQL Anywhere database. All checked columns will be displayed on the form created by the project wizard. To remove a column, uncheck it.

Figure 20.21.

You can select the columns that will be displayed.

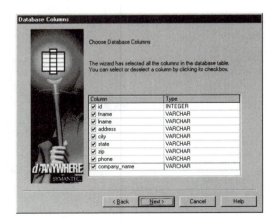

After you check only the desired columns, clicking the Next button will move you to the Components and Labels screen (shown in Figure 20.22). On this screen, you can select the Visual Café component and the label that will be used for each column. A column can be displayed as any of the following component types:

- ☐ `TextArea`
- ☐ `TextField`
- ☐ `List`
- ☐ `ImageViewer`

Figure 20.22.

In the dbAware project wizard, you are asked to choose a component and label for each database column.

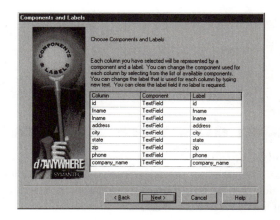

The final screen of the dbAware project wizard on which you need to make selections is the Database Operations screen, which is shown in Figure 20.23.

Figure 20.23.

On the Database Operations screen, select which actions will be available on the form.

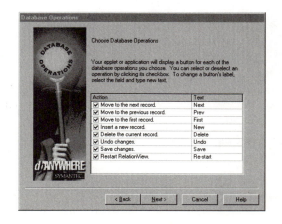

Each selected action on the Database Operations screen becomes a button on the finished form. This can be seen in Figure 20.24, which shows the applet that was generated by following the steps in this description of the dbAware project wizard.

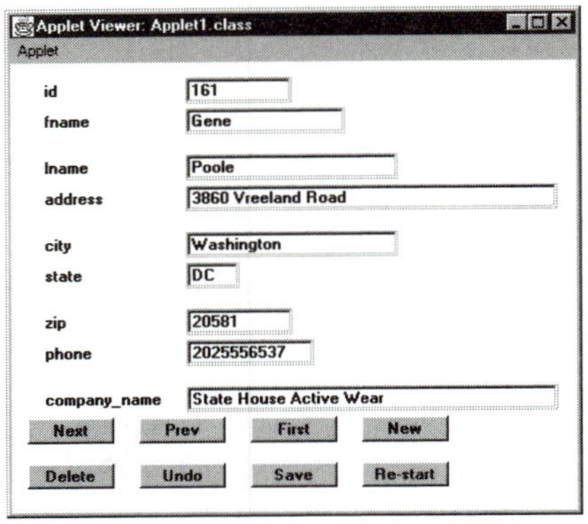

Figure 20.24.

The completed applet generated by the dbAware project wizard.

Using a dbAware Template

In addition to the dbAware project wizard, Visual Café includes the dbAware template wizard. If you select this wizard when creating a new project, it will step you through the creation of a database project and will also create a new database table based on the selected template. This project wizard is nearly identical to the dbAware project wizard, except that you can select one of the following table templates:

- [ ] Personal contact information
- [ ] Submit Web site feedback
- [ ] Software feedback
- [ ] Web site suggestions
- [ ] Software registration
- [ ] Classroom registration
- [ ] Customer support registration
- [ ] Web site registration
- [ ] Event registration
- [ ] Political registration
- [ ] Product enhancements
- [ ] Bug reports

- ☐ Contest entry
- ☐ Guest book
- ☐ User profile survey
- ☐ Sports survey
- ☐ Music CDs
- ☐ Video library
- ☐ Personal inventory
- ☐ Favorite quotes

The table you select from this list will be added to the data source you select in the project wizard. If one of these templates matches your needs completely or partially, you should base your new project on it.

TIP

Using the database administration tools provided for the database you are using (for example, SQL Central for SQL Anywhere), you can add columns to or delete columns from the table created by the dbAware template wizard.

Adding Database Support to an Existing Project

The dbAware project wizards are great timesavers when you are adding database support to a new project, but Visual Café provides a similar capability for adding database support to an existing project. If you select Add Table Wizard from the Insert menu, you will be able to step through a series of wizard screens identical to those of the dbAware project wizard. When you complete this wizard, the fields and buttons created will be placed on the form that is currently displayed in the Form Designer.

The dbNAVIGATOR

When working in Visual Café, you frequently need information about the structure of the database you are working with. The dbNAVIGATOR window fulfills this need by allowing you to browse your dbANYWHERE data sources, their databases, tables, and columns. Access the dbNAVIGATOR by selecting it from the Window menu. The dbNAVIGATOR window will appear as shown in Figure 20.25.

20

Figure 20.25.

The dbNAVIGATOR window.

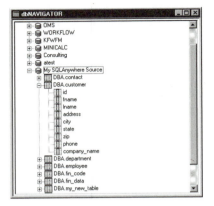

Figure 20.25 shows that the dbANYWHERE data source, My SQLAnywhere Source, has been expanded and beneath it are its tables and their owners: DBA.contact, DBA.customer, DBA.department, and so on. Furthermore, the DBA.customer table has been expanded to show its columns: id, fname, lname, address, and so on.

As items are highlighted in the dbNAVIGATOR tree, the Property List displays information about the selected item. For example, Figure 20.26 shows the information that is displayed when the fname column of the DBA.customer table is highlighted.

Figure 20.26.

The Property List displays information about the item highlighted in the dbNAVIGATOR.

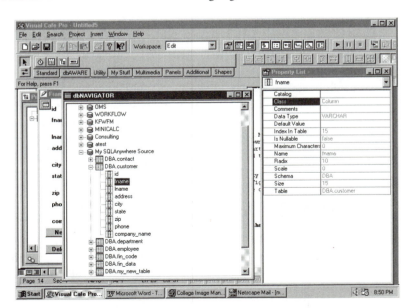

20

Summary

In this chapter, you learned about the database tools included with Visual Café Pro. You learned how dbANYWHERE simplifies the creation of three-tiered database programs and how Sybase SQL Anywhere provides the features of a full-scale relational database in a package small enough to run in a self-hosted environment. You saw how to take advantage of Visual Café's powerful dbAware project wizards to create a new database project or to create a project from a database template. Additionally, you saw how to use the Add Table wizard to add database support to an existing project. Finally, you learned how to use the dbNAVIGATOR to examine the structure of a dbANYWHERE data source. Tomorrow you will be able to put this knowledge to work by writing your own code to manipulate a database.

Q&A

Q **How do I know which database product I should use for a particular database project?**

A To determine which database to use, you must assess a variety of project requirements. For example, consider how many users will use the system concurrently, how many tables will comprise the database, what types of data will be stored in the database, what type of record locking and transaction control are needed, and so on. For many simple desktop-style applications, you do not need the power of a full relational database and can get by with a product such as Access or Paradox. For other projects, you might need the additional capabilities of a full relational database and should focus your selection efforts on Oracle, Sybase, SQL Anywhere, and Microsoft SQL Server. Another huge consideration will always be the cost of these products, as it varies tremendously.

Q **You mentioned that I can use ISQL to create databases and tables for SQL Anywhere. Why would I use ISQL instead of SQL Central?**

A This is a matter of personal preference. A visual tool such as SQL Central is great when you begin experimenting with a database, but nothing beats the long-term convenience of a database-creation script. For example, you can store hundreds of database definition commands in a single file, load that file into ISQL, and execute it to create the database. If you will create a database more than once (or if you are redistributing the database to customers or other sites), it is impractical to suggest that other users enter hundreds of point-and-click operations instead of providing them with a script.

20

Workshop

The workshop includes quiz questions to help you gauge your understanding of the material in this chapter. The workshop also includes exercises to provide hands-on experience with what you've learned in this chapter. Answers to the quiz questions can be found in Appendix D, "Answers."

Quiz

1. What is a self-hosted architecture?
2. What databases are supported by dbANYWHERE?
3. What is the difference between the dbAware project wizard and the dbAware template wizard?
4. What SQL Anywhere tool allows you to create a new database with visual tools?
5. How can you easily add database support to an existing project?
6. What is the purpose of the ISQL program?
7. Without leaving Visual Café, how can you find out what columns are in a table in a database?
8. How can you activate the dbNAVIGATOR?

Exercises

1. Use SQL Anywhere to create a new database space, create a database in that space, and create a table that will hold your golf scores. Include columns for the name of the course, the date, and your score.
2. Configure an ODBC data source that uses the SQL Anywhere database you created in the prior step.
3. Use the dbNAVIGATOR to examine the structure of your new database table.
4. Use ISQL to insert a few rows into your new table. (If you don't know SQL, see Day 24.)
5. Create a new Visual Café project that allows you to browse this table, enter new records, and delete records.

Day 21

Using the dbAWARE Components

In Day 20, "The Visual Café Database Tools," you learned about the database tools included with Visual Café Pro. In this chapter, you will learn how to write code to take advantage of the database capabilities inherent in Visual Café Pro. You will first see how to work with a dbANYWHERE data source by writing code. After you master that, you will see how Visual Café streamlines the process by including visual database-aware components in the Component Library.

Retrieving Data from a Table

One of the most common database tasks you'll perform is retrieving data from a table. Not only is this a common task, it also provides an excellent overview of the steps involved in working with a dbANYWHERE database. The following steps are required to retrieve data from a dbANYWHERE database:

1. Connect to the dbANYWHERE server.
2. Connect to the database.

3. Formulate a request for data.

4. Create a view that shows the result set.

5. Bind fields to the result set.

Connecting to dbANYWHERE

To connect to a dbANYWHERE server, create a new instance of the Session object that is in the symantec.itools.db.pro package. You do so by passing the Session object a single string parameter that indicates the URL of the server. The Session constructor can throw SQLException, so you must catch this exception. The following example illustrates this:

```
Session session;

try {
    session = new Session("dbaw://localhost:8889");
}
catch (symjava.sql.SQLException e) {
    // handle exception here
}
```

The URL passed to the constructor is in the following format:

```
dbaw://server_name_or_address:port_number
```

The name of the server can be an Internet domain, a TCP/IP address, or the string localhost, which indicates that the dbANYWHERE server is found on the local machine.

Connecting to a Database

After connecting to a dbANYWHERE server, you need to connect to a specific database. This is done by using a ConnectionInfo object. A new ConnectionInfo object may be created using any of the following four constructors:

```
ConnectionInfo(String dbname)

ConnectionInfo(String dbname, String user, String password)

ConnectionInfo(String dbname, boolean autoDisconnect)

ConnectionInfo(String dbname, String user, String password,
        boolean autoDisconnect)
```

The dbname parameter is the name of the database to which you wish to connect. This is the same name you specified when you created the ODBC data source. For example, when I added an ODBC data source to my system for SQL Anywhere, I did so with the ODBC configuration screen shown in Figure 21.1. On this screen, I assigned the new data source the name My SQLAnywhere Source.

Figure 21.1.

Configuring the ODBC data source My SQLAnywhere Source.

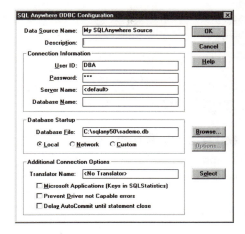

The *user* and *password* parameters can be used to identify the username and password that will be used to log on to the database. The *autoDisconnnect* parameter can be set to *true* if you wish to have the program disconnect from the database server after each transaction. For most purposes, you should use *false* for *autoDisconnect* or use one of the constructors that does not require this parameter.

Instead of specifying the database name, automatic disconnection value, username, and password when you construct the ConnectionInfo object, you can specify these values with other methods, as shown in Table 21.1. This table also shows methods that can be used to retrieve the values of these properties for a ConnectionInfo object.

Table 21.1. Methods of the ConnectionInfo class.

Method	Purpose
getAutoDisconnect()	Returns the value of the object's automatic disconnection flag.
getDBString()	Returns the object's database name.
getPassword()	Returns the password.
getUser()	Returns the username.
setAutoDisconnect(boolean)	Sets the value of the object's automatic disconnection flag.
setDBString(String)	Sets the object's database name.
setPassword(String)	Sets the password.
setUser(String)	Sets the username.

21

As an example of how to construct a `ConnectionInfo` object and set the parameter values individually, consider the following:

```
ConnectionInfo connection;

connection = new ConnectionInfo("My SQLAnywhere Source");
connection.setUser("DBA");
connection.setPassword("sql");
connection.setAutoDisconnect(false);
```

Formulating a Request

After you connect to a dbANYWHERE server and a database, you can create a request for data. This is done using the `Request` object, which can be created with the following constructor:

```
Request(Session session, ConnectionInfo connectionInfo)
```

After you construct a `Request` object, you can use the `setSQL` method to specify the SQL statement that will be executed. For example, if you want to retrieve the `emp_fname` and `emp_lname` columns from the `DBA.employee` table of the SQL Anywhere sample database, you could do the following:

```
request.setSQL("Select emp_fname, emp_lname from DBA.employee");
```

 NOTE

> If you are unfamiliar with SQL, see Day 24, "Bonus Day: An Introduction to SQL."

To select which record should be initially retrieved by the SQL statement, use `setInitialRecordPosition`. This method is passed one of the following values:

- ☐ `REC_POS_FIRST`
- ☐ `REC_POS_NEW`
- ☐ `REC_POS_NOPOS`

Specifying `REC_POS_FIRST` positions the result set created from this request on the first row. `REC_POS_NEW` positions the result set on a new record, and `REC_POS_NOPOS` indicates that the initial position is not specified. The following example illustrates how to create a new `Request` object, give it a SQL statement, and specify that the result set be positioned on the first retrieved record:

```
Request request;

request = new Request(session, connection);
request.setSQL("Select emp_fname, emp_lname from DBA.employee");
request.setInitialRecordPosition(Request.REC_POS_FIRST);
```

Creating a View

Visual Café uses the `RelationView` class to create a view into the results created by executing the SQL in a `Request` object. One way to create a new `RelationView` object is to use the constructor, passing it a `Request` object, as shown in the following:

```
RelationView relationView = new RelationView(request);
```

Another way is to use the `executeRequest` member method of `Request`. If the SQL statement is successful, this method constructs and returns a `RelationView` object. Both approaches can throw `SQLException`, so you must enclose the attempt in a `try...catch` block. This can be seen in the following example, which creates a `RelationView` by using `executeRequest`:

```
try {
    Request request = new Request(session, connection);
    request.setSQL("Select emp_fname, emp_lname from employee");

    relationView = request.executeRequest();
}
catch (symjava.sql.SQLException e) {
    // handle exception here
}
```

Bind Fields

The final step is to display the results. Visual Café includes a variety of database-aware components that can be bound to the contents of a `RelationView`. By binding an onscreen component (such as a text field) to a `RelationView`, the component will be automatically updated whenever the contents of the `RelationView` change.

The most commonly used database-aware component is the `TextField` that is part of the package `symantec.itools.db.awt`. Although this is a different `TextField` class than the one provided in the `java.awt` package, it provides many of the same features.

WARNING

Because `symantec.itools.db.awt.TextField` shares the same class name with `java.awt.TextField`, you must explicitly reference the Symantec class whenever you also use AWT classes in your program.

To bind a text field to a `RelationView`, use the method `setBinding`, whose signature is as follows:

```
void setBinding(RelationView relation, String columnName)
```

21

The following example illustrates how to bind the emp_fname column of a RelationView to a text field:

```
symantec.itools.db.awt.TextField fname;

fname = new symantec.itools.db.awt.TextField();
fname.setBinding(relationView, "emp_fname");
fname.setDynamicUpdate(false);
fname.setTreatBlankAs("Default");
fname.reshape(132, 72, 160, 20);
add(fname);
```

An Example

Listing 21.1 is a partial listing of the source code to the FirstDemo sample applet, which is included on the MCP Web site (www.mcp.com/info/1-57521/1-57521-303-6). This applet opens the Employee table from the SQL Anywhere sademo database. It then reads and displays two columns from the first record in the database.

Listing 21.1. FirstDemo.java.

```
1:   import java.awt.*;
2:   import java.applet.*;
3:   import symantec.itools.db.pro.*;
4:   import symantec.itools.db.awt.*;
5:
6:   public class FirstDemo extends Applet {
7:
8:       // ...
9:
10:      private void ConnectToDatabase() {
11:          try {
12:              session = new Session("dbaw://localhost:8889");
13:              logonFrame=new symantec.itools.db.awt.LogonFrame();
14:              session.setLogonObject(logonFrame);
15:          }
16:          catch (symjava.sql.SQLException e) {
17:              status.setText(e.getMessage());
18:              return;
19:          }
20:
21:          connection = new ConnectionInfo("My SQLAnywhere Source");
22:          connection.setUser("DBA");
23:          connection.setPassword("sql");
24:          connection.setAutoDisconnect(false);
25:
26:          try {
27:              request = new Request(session, connection);
28:              request.setSQL(
29:                  "Select emp_fname, emp_lname from employee");
30:              request.setOptimisticConcurrency("All");
31:              request.setInitialRecordPosition(
32:                      Request.REC_POS_FIRST);
33:              relationView = request.executeRequest();
34:          }
```

```
35:            catch (symjava.sql.SQLException e) {
36:                status.setText(e.getMessage());
37:                return;
38:            }
39:        }
40:
41:        private void AddFields() {
42:            // add a label for the first name field
43:            java.awt.Label fnameLabel =
44:                    new java.awt.Label("First Name");
45:            fnameLabel.reshape(42, 72, 80, 20);
46:            add(fnameLabel);
47:
48:            // add the first name field
49:            fname = new symantec.itools.db.awt.TextField();
50:            fname.setBinding(relationView, "emp_fname");
51:            fname.reshape(132,72, 160, 20);
52:            add(fname);
53:
54:            // add a label for the last name field
55:            java.awt.Label lnameLabel =
56:                    new java.awt.Label("Last Name");
57:            lnameLabel.reshape(42, 112, 80, 20);
58:            add(lnameLabel);
59:
60:            // add the last name field
61:            lname = new symantec.itools.db.awt.TextField();
62:            lname.setBinding(relationView, "emp_lname");
63:            lname.reshape(132, 112, 160, 20);
64:            add(lname);
65:        }
66:
67:        Session session;
68:        LogonFrame logonFrame;
69:        ConnectionInfo connection;
70:        Request request;
71:        RelationView relationView;
72:        symantec.itools.db.awt.TextField fname;
73:        symantec.itools.db.awt.TextField lname;
74:    }
```

ANALYSIS Lines 3 and 4 of Listing 21.1 import the two Visual Café packages that provide database support. The symantec.itools.db.pro package contains classes related to accessing and manipulating databases. The symantec.itools.db.awt package contains the database-aware, user-interface classes.

The ConnectToDatabase and AddFields methods add database support to this applet. ConnectToDatabase (lines 10–39) creates a new session with the local dbANYWHERE host (line 12). It then creates an instance of the LogonFrame class. The LogonFrame object is then passed to session.setLogonObject. This establishes a generic logon window that the program will display if the user needs to log on to the database. The generic logon frame is shown in Figure 21.2.

21

Figure 21.2.

The generic logon frame.

A connection to the data source is established on lines 21–24 and the query is formed between lines 27 and 32. In this case, the emp_fname and emp_lname columns will be retrieved from the Employee table. Finally, a RelationView object is created through a call to executeRequest on line 33.

The AddFields method (lines 41–65) is responsible for placing fields on the form that will display the data retrieved from the database. For each column, a label and a text field are created. A text field is constructed and bound to the emp_fname column on lines 49 and 50. Similarly, a second text field is constructed and bound to emp_lname on lines 61 and 62.

The results of executing the FirstDemo sample applet are shown in Figure 21.3.

Figure 21.3.

The results of the execution of the FirstDemo sample applet.

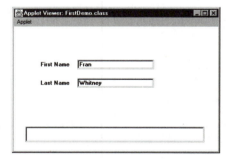

NOTE

Remember to start both SQL Anywhere and dbANYWHERE prior to running FirstDemo.

Do   **Don't**

DON'T specify a username or password for the ConnectionInfo object if you want to require the user to fill these in. In an environment where security is an issue, you should rely on the user to enter his name and password.

Navigating Through a Result Set

Because FirstDemo displays only the first record in a query's result set, it is of limited practical use. It would be more useful if buttons were added to allow the user to move between records, as shown in Figure 21.4.

Figure 21.4.

The NavigationDemo *applet allows the user to move between records.*

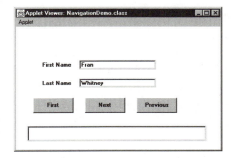

In the NavigationDemo sample applet shown in Figure 21.4, the user can click a button to move to the first, next, or previous record in the result set. As the user moves between records, the contents of the text fields are updated. You would think that the code for changing records would include reading the new record and then placing the new values into each of the onscreen text fields. Fortunately, Visual Café's database-aware components make it even simpler than that.

The NavigationDemo applet is identical to FirstDemo except for the code to create and respond to the navigational buttons. Listing 21.2 shows the event-handling methods from NavigationDemo.

Listing 21.2. Three methods from NavigationDemo.java.

```
1:   void firstButton_Clicked(java.awt.event.ActionEvent event) {
2:      try {
3:         relationView.first();
4:      }
5:      catch (symjava.sql.SQLException e) {
6:         status.setText(e.getMessage());
7:      }
8:   }
9:
10:  void nextButton_Clicked(java.awt.event.ActionEvent event) {
11:     try {
12:        relationView.next();
13:     }
14:     catch (symjava.sql.SQLException e) {
15:        status.setText(e.getMessage());
16:     }
```

21

continues

Listing 21.2. continued

```
17:    }
18:
19:    void prevButton_Clicked(java.awt.event.ActionEvent event) {
20:        try {
21:            relationView.prev();
22:        }
23:        catch (symjava.sql.SQLException e) {
24:            status.setText(e.getMessage());
25:        }
26:    }
```

ANALYSIS   As you can see in Listing 21.2, you don't have to write any code to directly manage the database-aware text fields. In firstButton_Clicked, relationView.first is used on line 3 to position the RelationView object to its first record. The database-aware components automatically update themselves after this happens. Similarly, the next and prev methods of RelationView are used to move forward and backward through the result set.

Adding and Deleting Records

Of course, retrieving data is not the only thing you'll want to do with a database. Many of the database programs you'll write will allow users to add or delete records. To delete the current record of a RelationView, use the method deleteRecord, as follows:

```
try {
    relationView.deleteRecord();
}
catch (symjava.sql.SQLException e) {
    // handle exception
}
```

Adding a record is only slightly more complicated. First, you must allocate space for a new record in the RelationView. This is done with getNewRecord, as shown in the following:

```
try {
    relationView.getNewRecord();
}
catch (symjava.sql.SQLException e) {
    // handle exception
}
```

When getNewRecord is executed, it blanks all fields bound to the RelationView. After allocating a new record, a typical program allows the user to interact with the user-interface fields to enter new values. After the user finishes, the record must be saved to the RelationView. This is done with saveMultiView as follows:

```
try {
    relationView.saveMultiView();
```

```
}
catch (symjava.sql.SQLException e) {
    // handle exception
}
```

TIP

There may be cases where you want to prefill some of the user-interface fields with default values in order to save the user time. You can do this by including code after the call to getNewRecord that places these values in the appropriate fields.

As an example of how these methods can be used together in a real program, consider the AddDeleteDemo sample applet shown in Figure 21.5. This example is similar to the NavigationDemo applet, except it works with the Department table instead of the Employee table and includes three new buttons: New, Save, and Delete. Listing 21.3 shows the relevant methods from AddDeleteDemo.

Figure 21.5.

AddDeleteDemo *allows users to enter and delete departments.*

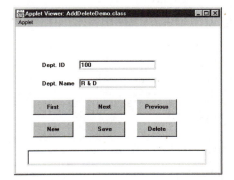

Listing 21.3. Selected methods from the AddDeleteDemo sample applet.

```
 1:    private void ConnectToDatabase() {
 2:        try {
 3:            session = new Session("dbaw://localhost:8889");
 4:            logonFrame = new symantec.itools.db.awt.LogonFrame();
 5:            session.setLogonObject(logonFrame);
 6:        }
 7:        catch (symjava.sql.SQLException e) {
 8:            status.setText(e.getMessage());
 9:            return;
10:        }
11:
12:        connection=new ConnectionInfo("My SQLAnywhere Source");
13:        connection.setUser("DBA");
```

continues

Listing 21.3. continued

```
14:        connection.setPassword("sql");
15:        connection.setAutoDisconnect(false);
16:
17:        try {
18:            request = new Request(session, connection);
19:            request.setSQL(
20:                "Select dept_id, dept_name from DBA.department");
21:            request.setInitialRecordPosition("First");
22:
23:            relationView = request.executeRequest();
24:        }
25:        catch (symjava.sql.SQLException e) {
26:            status.setText(e.getMessage());
27:            return;
28:        }
29:    }
30:
31:    private void AddFields() {
32:        // add a label for the department id field
33:        java.awt.Label idLabel =
34:            new java.awt.Label("Dept. ID");
35:        idLabel.reshape(42, 72, 80, 20);
36:        add(idLabel);
37:
38:        // add the department id field
39:        deptID = new symantec.itools.db.awt.TextField();
40:        deptID.setBinding(relationView, "dept_id");
41:        deptID.setDynamicUpdate(false);
42:        deptID.setTreatBlankAs("Default");
43:        deptID.reshape(132, 72, 160, 20);
44:        add(deptID);
45:
46:        // add a label for the department name field
47:        java.awt.Label nameLabel =
48:            new java.awt.Label("Dept. Name");
49:        nameLabel.reshape(42, 112, 80, 20);
50:        add(nameLabel);
51:
52:        // add the department name field
53:        deptName = new symantec.itools.db.awt.TextField();
54:        deptName.setBinding(relationView, "dept_name");
55:        deptName.setDynamicUpdate(false);
56:        deptName.setTreatBlankAs("Default");
57:        deptName.reshape(132, 112, 160, 20);
59:        add(deptName);
60:    }
61:
62:    void newButton_Clicked(java.awt.event.ActionEvent event) {
63:        try {
64:            relationView.getNewRecord();
65:        }
66:        catch (symjava.sql.SQLException e) {
67:            status.setText(e.getMessage());
68:        }
```

21

```
69:  }
70:
71:  void saveButton_Clicked(java.awt.event.ActionEvent event) {
72:      try {
73:          relationView.saveMultiView();
74:      }
75:      catch (symjava.sql.SQLException e) {
76:          status.setText(e.getMessage());
77:      }
78:
79:  void deleteButton_Clicked(java.awt.event.ActionEvent event) {
80:      try {
81:          relationView.deleteRecord();
82:      }
84:      catch (symjava.sql.SQLException e) {
85:          status.setText(e.getMessage());
86:      }
87:  }
```

Using the dbAWARE Components

So far, you've had to write code for all database access tasks. The Database Development edition of Visual Café includes a series of components that simplify database development by allowing you to work with them visually in the Form Designer. These components are located on the dbAWARE tab of the Component palette, and are therefore known as the dbAWARE components. The dbAWARE user-interface components include the following:

- [ ] TextField
- [ ] TextArea
- [ ] ImageViewer
- [ ] RecordStateLabel
- [ ] RecordNumberLabel
- [ ] Label
- [ ] CheckBox
- [ ] RadioButton
- [ ] List
- [ ] Grid

Additionally, there are dbAWARE components for managing connections to dbANYWHERE servers and databases. The following components can be used for these purposes:

- [ ] Session
- [ ] ConnectionInfo
- [ ] RelationView

21

An Example

The dbAwareDemo sample applet that is included on the MCP Web site is an example of how to use the dbAWARE components. This applet is shown in Figure 21.6. The rest of this section describes how to create this applet in the Form Designer.

Figure 21.6.

The dbAwareDemo *applet was created by dragging dbAWARE components onto the Form Designer.*

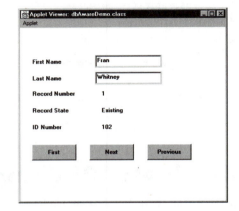

Place the Nonvisual Components

The first thing you need to do is place the nonvisual components on the form. Start with an empty applet and drag a Session component from the Component palette to the form. The Session object has two properties that you can set: Name and URL. Change the Name property to session and set URL to indicate the correct dbANYWHERE server. For a self-hosted server on the default port, use dbaw://localhost:8889.

Next, drag a ConnectionInfo component onto the form. It has the following properties:

- ☐ AutoDisconnect
- ☐ Data Source Name
- ☐ Name
- ☐ Password
- ☐ User Name

The meanings of these properties are the same as the equivalent parameters that can be passed to the ConnectionInfo constructor described earlier in this chapter. For the purposes of this example, leave AutoDisconnect at its default of false. Set the Data Source Name to the name of the ODBC data source you configured for the SQL Anywhere sademo database. Change the name of the component to connection. Finally, set Password to sql and User Name to DBA.

TIP   If you cannot see the nonvisual components in the Form Designer, it is because you have disabled viewing of invisible components. Make sure there is checkmark next to Invisibles on the Layout menu.

The last nonvisual component you need to add is `RelationView`. Add one to the applet form by dragging it from the Component palette. Set the name of the new component to `relationView`. Set its `ConnectionInfo` property to `connection`, the name of the `ConnectionInfo` component that you dropped on the form. Then set its `Session` property to `session`, the name of the `Session` component you added. Next, enter an SQL statement into the `Select Clause` property. When you click the `Select Clause` property to edit it, the SQL Statement window will be displayed, as shown in Figure 21.7.

Figure 21.7.

Editing an SQL statement in the SQL Statement window.

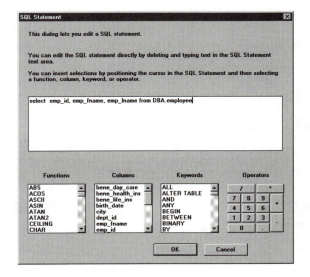

In the SQL Statement window, you can simply enter the text of an SQL statement or you can use the lists at the bottom of the window to help create the SQL. If you double-click a function, column, keyword, or operator, the selected item will be added at the current cursor location in the SQL statement. For the purposes of this example, enter the following SQL statement:

```
select emp_id, emp_fname, emp_lname from DBA.employee
```

21

Place the Visual Components

You are now ready to place the visual, or user-interface, components. From the dbAWARE tab of the Component palette, drag a TextField component and place it where the first name is displayed in Figure 21.6. Set the Name property of this component to fnameField. If the Binding property is collapsed, expand it so that its subproperties are visible. In the RelView Name property, enter the name of the RelationView to which this field is to be bound. For this example, the RelationView object that was dropped on the form was named relationView, so enter this value in the RelView Name property. Finally, for the Projection Name property, enter the name of the column you wish to display. To display the first name column of the Employee table, enter emp_fname.

 The term *projection* is used throughout Visual Café to mean a column within a RelationView.

Add a second text field that will display the last name. Repeat these steps, except specify emp_lname for the Projection Name property. Finally, from the Standard tab of the Component palette, add two AWT labels that say First Name and Last Name.

 TIP At this point, the applet is runnable. Even though it won't do much yet, you may want to run it to verify that you have successfully completed the steps thus far. Remember to start both dbANYWHERE and the SQL Anywhere sample database. If everything is successful, you should see a screen resembling the one shown in Figure 21.8.

Figure 21.8.

The partially completed dbAwareDemo *applet.*

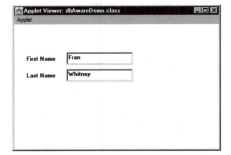

The RecordStateLabel and RecordNumberLabel components can be used to display information about the record being displayed through a RelationView. RecordStateLabel displays text that indicates the state of the current record. The following record states are possible:

- [ ] Existing
- [ ] Modified

☐ New

☐ Marked for Deletion

☐ Deleted

☐ New Modified

☐ Invalid

RecordNumberLabel displays the sequence number of the record within the RelationView. Record numbering begins with 1.

To add these components to the sample applet, drag them from the Component palette and position them as shown in Figure 21.6. Each of these components has a RelView Name property that you need to set to the name of the RelationView object that is being displayed. In this case, enter relationView for this property of each component.

The last dbAWARE component to be added is Label. Drag a Label component from the dbAWARE tab of the Component palette and place it at the appropriate position on the form. As usual, set its RelView Name property to relationView. Set the Projection Name property to the name of the column to be displayed. For this example, use emp_id.

Finishing Touches

If you haven't already done so, you should place the Record Number, Record State, and ID Number labels on the form in the positions shown in Figure 21.6. Each of these is simply an AWT label. Also, add the First, Next, and Previous buttons. Use the methods shown in Listing 21.4 as event handlers for clicks on these buttons.

Listing 21.4. Event-handling methods for the dbAwareDemo applet.

```
 1:   void firstButton_Clicked(java.awt.event.ActionEvent event) {
 2:      try {
 3:          relationView.first();
 4:      }
 5:      catch (symjava.sql.SQLException e) {
 6:      }
 7:   }
 8:
 9:   void nextButton_Clicked(java.awt.event.ActionEvent event) {
10:      try {
11:          relationView.next();
12:      }
13:      catch (symjava.sql.SQLException e) {
14:      }
15:   }
16:
17:   void prevButton_Clicked(java.awt.event.ActionEvent event) {
18:      try {
19:          relationView.prev();
20:      }
```

continues

Listing 21.4. continued

```
21:    catch (symjava.sql.SQLException e) {
22:    }
23:  }
```

At this point, you are ready to run the applet. Although it doesn't do anything you haven't already been able to do by writing code, you were able to create this applet almost entirely in the Form Designer.

The dbAWARE Grid Component

The dbAWARE Grid component is particularly powerful. As can be seen in Figure 21.9, a Grid object displays each record as a row and each selected column as a column in the grid. Additionally, a Grid object can optionally display a series of buttons that will initiate common activities. You can optionally enable any or all of the following buttons:

- ☐ Insert
- ☐ Go to a specific record number
- ☐ Undo
- ☐ Restart
- ☐ Delete
- ☐ Undelete
- ☐ Save

Figure 21.9.

The Grid *component is one of the most powerful dbAWARE components.*

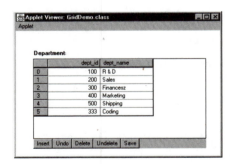

The following list summarizes the steps necessary to add a Grid component to a form:

1. Add Session, ConnectionInfo, and RelationView components to the form as usual. The columns selected in the Select Clause property of the RelationView object will become the columns displayed in the grid.

2. Drag a Grid component from the Component palette to the form.

3. Set the `RelView Name` property of the grid to the name of the `RelationView` component.

4. Enable or disable display of each of the grid's buttons by setting the button subproperties of the `Binding` property.

The `GridDemo` sample applet, which was shown in Figure 21.9, was created by following these steps and is included on the MCP Web site.

Working with More Than One Table

You must frequently display data from more than one table. When two or more tables are combined into a single logical view for the user, the tables are usually combined into one of two types of relationships:

☐ A simple join

☐ A master-detail relationship

Each of these relationship types can be easily handled with the dbAWARE components of Visual Café.

Simple Joins

A simple join can be used when you want to combine information from two or more tables and display it to the user as though the information came from a single source. For example, suppose you want to program the applet form shown in Figure 21.10. This form displays the name of a department and the last name of the department manager.

Figure 21.10.

A form can display joined data from two tables.

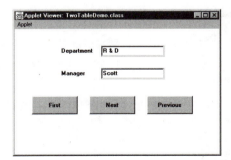

The Department table contains the following columns:

☐ `dept_id`

☐ `dept_name`

☐ `dept_head_id`

21

Clearly, `dept_name` can be displayed as the department name, but the name of the manager is not stored in the Department table. However, `dept_head_id` is the employee ID number of the manager. The program can find this value in the Employee table and, from there, retrieve the manager's name. The SQL statement to perform this join is as follows:

```
select dept_name, emp_lname from department, employee
       where dept_head_id = emp_id
```

NOTE

> If you are unfamiliar with SQL, see Day 24.

The only difference in creating a program that displays data retrieved from more than one table and a program that displays data from a single table is in the SQL statement you use. The `TwoTableDemo` sample applet included on the MCP Web site creates the screen shown in Figure 21.9. It was created using the following steps:

1. Drag a `Session` component onto the form and set its `URL` property.

2. Drag a `ConnectionInfo` component onto the form and set its properties.

3. Drag a `RelationView` component onto the form and set its `Session`, `ConnectionInfo`, and `Select Clause` properties. For the `Select Clause` property, use the SQL shown earlier.

4. Drag a dbAWARE `TextField` component onto the form and bind it to the `dept_name` projection of the `RelationView` you added.

5. Drag a dbAWARE `TextField` component onto the form and bind it to `emp_lname` projection of the `RelationView` you added.

6. Add labels and navigation buttons.

Master-Detail Relationships

The other type of relationship that frequently exists between two tables is a master-detail relationship.

In a *master-detail* relationship, the current record in the master table determines which rows are selected from the detail table.

As an example of a master-detail relationship, consider Figure 21.11, which is taken from the `MasterDetailDemo` sample applet provided on the MCP Web site. In this example, the user can move through a series of departments. Within each department, the user can move through a list of employees. Naturally, the list of employees varies based on the department that is selected. In this case, the department is the *master* and the employees are the *detail*.

Figure 21.11.

A master-detail relationship exists between a department and the employees of that department.

With Visual Café's dbAWARE components, you can easily create screens that show master-detail relationships. The following list summarizes the steps necessary to show a master-detail relationship on a form:

1. Add `Session`, `ConnectionInfo`, and `RelationView` components to the form exactly as you would to create a form with a single table.

2. Add to the form any dbAWARE user interface components that you want to display data from the master table.

3. Add a second `RelationView` component to the form. Set its `Session`, `ConnectionInfo`, and `Select Clause` properties as normal.

4. Set the `ParentRelView` property (a subproperty of `Join` in the Property List). Set it to the name of the first `RelationView` object you added to the form (the master `RelationView`).

5. Set the `Join Columns` property by clicking the property and invoking the Join Definition screen, as shown in Figure 21.12. On this screen, you can select column names and the relationship between them. The selections you make here determine how the master and detail `RelationView` objects will be related.

Figure 21.12.

The join definition screen.

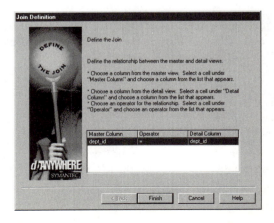

21

6. Add to the form any dbAWARE components that will be bound to the detail `RelationView`. In their `Binding` properties, be sure to specify the name of the second `RelationView` you added to the form.

The dbAWARE `List` Component

Another convenient way to display a master-detail relationship is by using the dbAWARE `List` component. Figure 21.13 shows how this component can be used to display the last names of all employees in the selected department.

Figure 21.13.

Use the `List`
*component to display
a master-detail
relationship.*

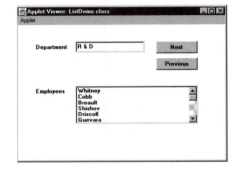

To add a `List` component to a form, perform the following steps:

1. Add `Session`, `ConnectionInfo`, and `RelationView` components to the form exactly as you would to create a form with a single table.

2. Add to the form any dbAWARE user-interface components that you want to display data from the master table.

3. Drag a `List` component from the Component palette onto the form.

4. Set the `ConnectionInfo` subproperty of the `Lookup` property to the name of the `ConnectionInfo` component on the form.

5. Set the `Select Clause` subproperty of the `Lookup` property to the SQL statement that will select the one column that will be displayed in the list. (Only a single column may be displayed.)

6. Set the `Lookup RelView` subproperty of the `Lookup` property to the name of the `RelationView` component on the form.

7. Set the `Join Columns` subproperty of the `Lookup` property to establish the proper join.

The `ListDemo` sample applet, which was shown in Figure 21.13, was created by following these steps and is included on the MCP Web site.

21

Do	**Don't**

DO use only one `Session` and `ConnectionInfo` component for both the master and detail `RelationView` objects you add to a form.

Summary

In this chapter, you learned about the dbAWARE components that are provided with Visual Café Pro. You learned about the nonvisual components—`Session`, `ConnectionInfo`, and `RelationView`. You learned how to combine these with the visual components such as `TextField`, `Label`, `Grid`, and `List`. You first learned how to manipulate these components by writing your code and then saw how to accomplish the same tasks visually in the Form Designer. You are now ready to apply this new knowledge by writing your own three-tier database applications with Visual Café.

Q&A

Q **I need to write a screen that has a master-detail-detail relationship. Based on the selection in the first level of detail, more detail from a third table is displayed. How can I do this?**

A This can be easily done by repeating the process that you followed to create the first level of detail. Add a third `RelationView` component to the form and set its `ParentRelView` property to the second `RelationView` object (which represents the first level of detail).

Q **Is there any limit to the number of columns that should be specified when joining two tables?**

A Generally no, but the specific database engine you are using may impose one. If it does, it should be well beyond what you are likely to encounter. Keep in mind that joining more than two or three columns is likely to result in a performance penalty that may affect the usefulness of the program or the form.

Workshop

The workshop includes quiz questions to help you gauge your understanding of the material in this chapter. The workshop also includes exercises to provide hands-on experience with what you've learned in this chapter. Answers to the quiz questions can be found in Appendix D, "Answers."

21

Quiz

1. What are the three dbAWARE nonvisual components?
2. In what two ways can you construct a new `RelationView` object?
3. To what does a `ConnectionInfo` component connect?
4. What is a projection?
5. What is the difference between `RecordStateLabel` and `RecordNumberLabel`?
6. Give an example of a master-detail relationship other than the one described in this chapter.

Exercises

1. Write a form that displays all the columns in the `employee` table of the SQL Anywhere sample database. Allow the user to add, view, navigate, and delete.
2. The Employee table of the SQL Anywhere sample database includes a column named `manager_id`. This column refers back to the Employee table and can be used to determine an employee's manager. Write a form that displays a manager and shows each of his employees in a dbAWARE `List`. Allow the user to navigate among managers.
3. Modify the previous program by replacing `List` with individual fields that show four or five pieces of information about one employee. Allow the user to navigate through employees as well as managers (similar to the `MasterDetailDemo` applet).

In Review

On Day 15, "Client/Server Programming with Sockets," you learned how to use the Socket and ServerSocket classes to write client/server programs. You started by writing a simple, single-threaded server and used Telnet as the client. From there you enhanced the server to use multiple threads and then added your own custom client. The bulk of this chapter described a detailed sample client/server system for playing Tic Tac Toe. This involved writing a multithreaded server and a custom client.

Day 16, "Working with Graphics," gave you an in-depth look at the Graphics class and how you can use the methods of this class to enhance the appearance of your Java programs. In this chapter, you learned how to draw outlined and filled shapes such as lines, arcs, ovals, rectangles, and polygons. You learned how to use the Canvas class to better control the placement of drawn figures. You saw how the Visual Café Shape classes offer alternatives to AWT's Graphics class. You also learned about the Image class. You learned how to filter, crop, and modify images prior to display. Finally, you saw how the ImageObserver interface allows an applet to monitor the progress of an image that is being retrieved.

On Day 17, "Multimedia Programming," you learned about the multimedia components in Visual Café's Object library. You saw how to use SlideShow to display a series of images and how to create animations by using Animator and MovingAnimation. You learned about the novelty components: Firework, Plasma, and NervousText. You also learned how to add sound to your programs by using the SoundPlayer component. Finally, you learned about the MediaTracker class and how you can use it as an aid in creating your own multimedia classes.

On Day 18, "Java Beans," you learned how to create reusable software components known as Java Beans. You learned how to create your own Beans components and how to add them directly into the Visual Café environment.

Day 19, "Adding Native Methods," showed you how to add native methods to your Java applications. You learned how to write native methods in C and C++ that can pass parameters and return values across language boundaries. You saw how to write native methods that can invoke methods and access variables on the Java side of the boundary. Finally, you learned how to work with arrays, objects, and exceptions within native methods.

On Day 20, "The Visual Café Database Tools," you learned about the database tools included with Visual Café Pro. You learned how dbANYWHERE simplifies the creation of three-tiered database programs and how Sybase SQL Anywhere provides the features of a full-scale relational database in a package small enough to run in a self-hosted environment. You saw how to take advantage of Visual Café's powerful dbAware project wizards to create a new database project or to create a project from a database template. Additionally, you saw how to use the Add Table wizard to add database support to an existing project. Finally, you learned how to use the dbNAVIGATOR to examine the structure of a dbANYWHERE data source. In the next chapter, you will be able to put this knowledge to work by writing your own code to manipulate a database.

On Day 21, "Using the dbAWARE Components," you learned about the dbAWARE components that are provided with Visual Café Pro. You learned about the nonvisual components—Session, ConnectionInfo, and RelationView. You learned how to combine these with the visual components such as TextField, Label, Grid, and List. You first learned how to manipulate these components by writing your code and then saw how to accomplish the same tasks visually in the Form Designer.

Day **22**

Reusable Packages, Forms, and Projects

Today you will learn how to write reusable code and how to use Java packages to create collections of classes that are easily shareable by multiple programmers or projects. You will also learn how to create reusable forms and project templates.

Packaging Your Code

Throughout this book, you have used packages provided for you by others. You've used packages that are common to all Java environments such as `java.util`, `java.awt`, and `java.io`, as well as packages such as `symantec.itools.awt` that are specific to Visual Café. Packages are a convenient way to provide code to others so that it can be reused. In this section, you will learn how to create your own packages. By creating your own packages, you can more easily reuse code from one project with another. Also, you can distribute packages to others, either free of charge or for profit.

What Is a Package?

When you write a Java program, you store your source code in files with the .java extension. The Java compiler then creates one .class file for each class it finds in a .java file. Because a .java file may include more than one class, compiling it may create more than one .java file, as shown in Figure 22.1.

Figure 22.1.

The Java compiler creates one .class file for each class.

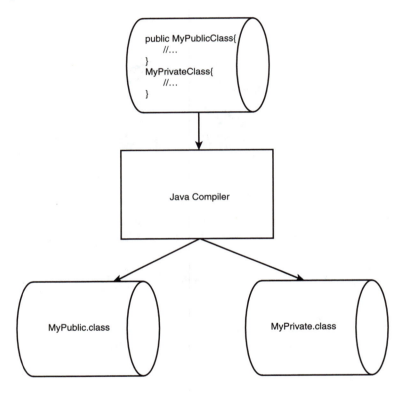

```
public MyPublicClass{
    //...
}
MyPrivateClass{
    //...
}
```

Java Compiler

MyPublic.class   MyPrivate.class

A public class must be stored in a file that has the same name as the class. For example, the public Person class must be defined in Person.java. When Person.java is compiled, it creates Person.class. If more than one class is defined in the .java file, only one of these classes can be defined as public.

A Java package is analogous to the directories in which the .class files are stored. When Visual Café generates code, it typically includes the fully qualified class name, as in the following example:

```
button1 = new java.awt.Button("button");
```

This line creates a new instance of the Button class, which is part of the java.awt package. When Java needs to find this class, it does so by looking in a directory whose name is made up of the period-separated components of the package name. This means that Java will expect to find the Button class in the java\awt directory.

How Java Locates Packages

Java searches for the java\awt directory as a subdirectory of the starting points you specify. Visual Café looks for subdirectories beginning with the directories specified in the CLASSPATH variable in the SC.INI file. SC.INI is located in the bin directory beneath the directory in which you installed Visual Café. Normally, this means it can be found in C:\VisualCafe\bin\sc.ini or C:\VisualCafePro\bin\sc.ini.

As an example, suppose the CLASSPATH line of your SC.INI file contained the following entries:

```
CLASSPATH=C:\MyCode;F:\Users\Tom\Code;F:\Users\Mary\Code
```

WARNING

The CLASSPATH line in SC.INI must also include references to the directories where the Java and Visual Café libraries are located. When you install Visual Café, these pathnames are automatically placed in the CLASSPATH line. For simplicity and readability, the examples given in this section do not show these pathnames. You should be careful when editing SC.INI to add directory names to the end of the line, separating each directory with a semicolon (;). Do not delete any directories from CLASSPATH that you did not add.

Further, suppose you create a new instance of the OKButton class (which is in the standards package) as follows:

```
button = new standards.OKButton();
```

In this case, Visual Café will look in the following places for the OKButton class file:

- ☐ C:\MyCode\OKButton.class
- ☐ F:\Users\Tom\Code\OKButton.class
- ☐ F:\Users\Mary\Code\OKButton.class

TIP

You can include the current directory in CLASSPATH by using a single period as a directory. Similarly, you can specify relative pathnames using two periods (..). For example, the following will look for classes

> in the current directory, the MyCode directory that is a subdirectory of the current directory's parent (that is, a sibling of the current directory), and in C:\CommonClasses:
>
> CLASSPATH=.;..\MyCode;C:\CommonClasses

The CLASSPATH Environment Variable

If you are running a Java application or applet outside the Visual Café development environment, Java will look at the contents of your CLASSPATH environment variable rather than the CLASSPATH line in SC.INI. Be sure to add the names of your package directories to this environment variable if you will be running Java programs outside Visual Café (for example, standalone applications or applets loaded in Internet Explorer or Navigator).

TIP

The easiest way to synchronize your CLASSPATH environment variable with Visual Café's CLASSPATH line in SC.INI is to use %CLASSPATH% in Visual Café. This tells Visual Café to append the environment CLASSPATH. This can be done as follows:

CLASSPATH=%PATH%

You may wish to use additional package directories while developing new programs. You can do this by listing those directories in SC.INI along with %PATH%, as follows:

CLASSPATH=\MyNewClasses;%PATH%

Naming Your Java Packages

What all of this means for you as a package designer, instead of just a package user, is that you must place your files in a directory whose name corresponds to the package name. If you want to make a package named CommonClasses, you will need a directory named CommonClasses that can be found as a subdirectory of a directory in your CLASSPATH statement.

An Experiment

To better understand this, create a directory named \MyCompany\Java\OurClasses. In this directory, create a new project that includes a file named Person.java that consists of the following code:

```
public class Person extends Object {
    private String firstName;
    private String lastName;
```

```
public Person(String f, String l) {
    firstName = f;
    lastName  = l;
}

public String getFirstName() {
    return firstName;
}

public String getLastName() {
    return lastName;
}
}
```

Compile this code to create the file `Person.class`. Now edit the `SC.INI` file so that the `CLASSPATH` line ends with the following:

```
;\MyCompany\Java\OurClass
```

Restart Visual Café so that the change to `SC.INI` takes effect. Next, create a sample applet and place a button and text field on the applet. Name them `startButton` and `textField`. Create an event handler for the Start button using the following code that executes when the button is clicked:

```
void startButton_Clicked(Event event) {
    Person p = new Person("Herman", "Melville");

    textField.setText(p.getFirstName() + " " + p.getLastName());
}
```

NOTE

> An applet that does exactly this is provided on the MCP Web site (www.mcp.com/info/1-57521/1-57521-303-6). The applet is named `PackageDemo`. After you load the applet into Visual Café, look at the top of the file. You will see a series of import statements. Make sure all are commented out. You will use these lines later in this experiment.

Compile and run the applet. When you click the button, the name `Herman Melville` should be written to the text field.

Because no package statement was included in `Person.java`, it was necessary to include a reference to the class's directory location in `SC.INI`. An alternative is to use packages. Continue the experiment by taking the following three steps:

1. Add `package OurClasses;` as the first line of `Person.java` and recompile this class.

2. Edit `SC.INI` so that `CLASSPATH` ends with `;\MyCompany\Java` (no `\OurClasses` at the end). Close and restart Visual Café after you make this change.

3. Add `import OurClasses;` at the top of the sample applet.

Now compile and run this applet. You should not receive any compile errors and when the button is clicked, it should once again write `Herman Melville` to the text field. In this case, you have created a package named `OurClasses`. Because it is located beneath the `\MyCompany\Java` directory, it was necessary to add that directory name to the `CLASSPATH`.

Finally, try one more variation on this experiment. Take the following steps:

1. In `Person.java`, change the package statement to `package Java.OurClasses` and then recompile the class.

2. Edit `SC.INI` so that `CLASSPATH` ends with `;\MyCompany`. Close and then restart Visual Café.

3. Change the import statement at the top of the applet to read `import Java.OurClasses;`.

Compile and run the applet as before to ensure that it works.

Table 22.1 summarizes the `CLASSPATH` directory and package names that you were able to successfully combine. As you can see from this table, when the class path and package name are combined (substituting \ for .), each entry results in `\MyCompany\Java\OurClasses`.

Table 22.1. Combinations of CLASSPATH directories and package names.

CLASSPATH directory	Package
`\MyCompany\Java\OurClasses`	(None)
`\MyCompany\Java`	`OurClasses`
`\MyCompany`	`Java.OurClasses`

Do	Don't

DO collect your code into packages.

DO make code reuse a daily goal. The more you can free yourself from the drudgery of rewriting code, the more time you can spend on the truly creative aspects of your programming.

DO be careful where you place files when creating your own packages. Make sure you completely understand Table 22.1 before you create a package.

DON'T wait until you start working on a medium or large project to use packages.

DON'T forget that you must restart Visual Café for any changes to `SC.INI` to take effect.

22

Creating Reusable Forms

In addition to creating reusable components, you can also create entire forms that can be reused. These forms can be added to the Insert Form dialog so they are completely integrated into Visual Café. Creating a reusable form is a simple, three-step process:

1. Create the form.
2. Add the form to the Component Library.
3. Reuse the form in another program.

Create the form exactly as you would any other form. You will usually want to do this from within the applet or application in which you first encounter the need for the form. For example, suppose you plan to write a series of programs that collect demographic information such as name and gender. When you write the first of these programs, you can create the form you intend to reuse and then add that form to the Component Library.

Figure 22.2 shows a form built as part of the FormDemo sample applet included on the MCP Web site. This form was created using the following steps:

1. Open a new applet.
2. Select Form from the Insert menu and then select Frame.
3. Place the components on the new form.
4. Modify the applet so it displays the form when a button is clicked.

Figure 22.2.

A simple demographic collection form that can be reused.

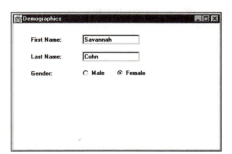

Step 3 has nothing to do with actually creating a reusable form, but is very convenient for testing the form. If you don't need or want to test your forms, you can skip that step.

To add this form to the Component Library, right-click the form and select Add to Library; this displays the dialog shown in Figure 22.3. In this dialog, enter a name for the new form and select the Forms group in the list of available groups. The name you enter will be the name that is displayed for this form in the Insert Form dialog. If you name the new form MyForm, it will appear that way on the Insert Form dialog, as shown in Figure 22.4.

Figure 22.3.

The Add to Library dialog.

Figure 22.4.

The Insert Form dialog displays the form name you chose when adding the form.

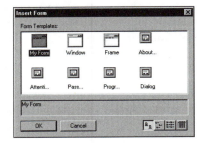

That's it. The form has been added to the Component Library. To verify that it can be reused successfully, close the current project and start a new applet. Select Form from the Insert menu and choose the new form. To display the form, place code similar to the following at the end of the applet's `init` method:

```
MyForm f = new MyForm();
f.show();
```

 TIP

Although this example illustrated the addition of a new form that was based on `Frame`, you can use the same process to add a new form based on `Dialog`, `PasswordDialog`, or any available form class.

Creating Project Templates

With Visual Café, it is even possible to reuse entire projects by creating a *project template*.

 NEW TERM A *project template* is a complete ready-to-run project that can include forms, components, and custom code.

22

You are already very familiar with using project templates. Every time you select New Project from the File menu, you are asked to select a project template. In this section, you will learn how easy it is to create your own project template.

Suppose you are a big fan of the Visual Café plasma control and find yourself using it in every applet you write. If this is the case, using a project template could save you a lot of time. To create the project template, create the application or applet just as you normally would. For example, you could modify the applet form to look like Figure 22.5. Then you could add a form to the project that is displayed when the user clicks the Show Me the Plasma button. This form could appear as shown in Figure 22.6.

Figure 22.5.

An applet form that has been customized for use in a project template.

Figure 22.6.

A form that has been added to an applet. The form and its components are included in the project template.

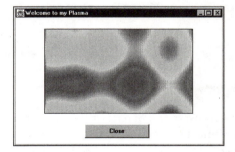

At this point, the applet consists of an applet form that uses Label, TextField, and Button components, and an additional form that uses the Plasma and Button components. To turn this applet into a project template, select Create Project Template from the Project menu. This displays the Create Project Template dialog, shown in Figure 22.7.

In the Create Project Template dialog, enter a name and description for the project. When the New Project dialog is displayed, the name will appear beneath the project icon (if icons are displayed), and the description will appear below the project list.

Figure 22.7.

*The Create Project
Template dialog.*

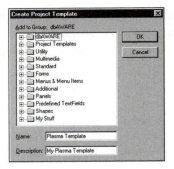

At this point, you have created a new project template. Whenever you create a new project, one of your options will be the newly created template, as can be seen in Figure 22.8.

Figure 22.8.

*The New Project
dialog.*

Summary

This chapter covers a lot of territory related to writing reusable code. Writing reusable code is a commitment you must choose to undertake. In the day-to-day rush to complete tasks, it is often easier to finish a piece of code and tell yourself that you'll come back to it later to make it more reusable. Normally, you don't ever make it back. As you encounter opportunities to create reusable code—whether in the form of packages, components, forms, or project templates—you should spend the extra effort to save yourself time in the future.

Q&A

Q I am following your instructions for creating a reusable form, but it doesn't work. I'm doing everything exactly the way you say, except I am basing my new form on `Dialog` instead of `Frame`. What's going wrong?

A You've probably forgotten that a dialog must have a `Frame` object as its parent. You learned this on Day 10, "Windows, Frames, and Dialogs." If you want to display a

dialog, you must pass it a frame as its parent. Because an `Applet` is not a `Frame`, you must create a dummy frame. On Day 10, you learned how to do this as follows:

```
Frame dummyFrame = new Frame();
dummyFrame.resize(250, 250);
Dialog d = new Dialog(dummyFrame, false);
```

Q I am the only programmer in my company. Should I still be concerned with using packages and writing reusable code?

A Yes, you should. After you get familiar with packages, you will find it easier to use them to group logically related pieces of code. For example, you may end up creating one package for your database access classes, another package for parsing input files you receive from clients, and a third package for sending reports via e-mail to system users.

Workshop

The workshop includes quiz questions to help you gauge your understanding of the material in this chapter. The workshop also includes exercises to provide hands-on experience with what you've learned in this chapter. Answers to the quiz questions can be found in Appendix D, "Answers."

Quiz

1. When running a program in the Visual Café development environment, where does Visual Café look to find class files?

2. How can you ensure that the `CLASSPATH` entry in `SC.INI` stays synchronized with your environment's `CLASSPATH` variable?

3. If a file is located in `C:\Projects\Reusable\Utilities` and the class is in the `Reusable.Utilities` package, what must be in the `CLASSPATH` entry for the class to be located?

4. What three steps must you follow to create a reusable form?

Exercises

1. Create a set of simple animal classes such as `Human`, `Pig`, `Cow`, and `Dog` (a single method or two in each class is sufficient). Place these classes in the `C:\MyCode\Java\Animals` subdirectory. Create a package called `Animals` from these classes. Use this package in a program. Change the package to `Java.Animals` and make any necessary changes to the program to use the new package.

2. Turn the preceding applet into a project template.

Day **23**

Using JavaDoc

One of the problems that maintenance programmers have faced through the years has been the horrible documentation left behind by the original programmers. The original programmers usually included comments in the source code, but generally didn't comment as thoroughly as they should have. Then an ambitious project manager recognized the inadequacy of inline comments and forced programmers to write a lengthy document about the software. This document was handed over to the maintenance programmers, who used it to continue supporting and enhancing the software. Even if the maintenance programmers kept the inline comments current, the other documentation fell out of date because it was just too hard to maintain. And besides, the maintenance programmers asked, "Why should we keep the document up to date if we're also documenting the code?"

This is a very good question, and one that the Java developers must have asked themselves. Imagine you're on the Java team. You've been working long hours, writing the hundreds of classes that comprise Java, and then you wake up one morning, hands still trembling from the previous night's caffeine bender, and realize, "Darn! Now we've got to document all that code." The solution the Java developers came up with actually made it possible for them to avoid writing a separate document describing each class, interface, and method. Instead, they wrote a program that would extract specially formatted source code comments and create class documentation from the embedded comments. The tool they developed to do this is called JavaDoc, and it is included in the Java Development Kit.

Overview

JavaDoc reads a `.java` file and creates a set of HTML files that can be read by a Web browser. As an example, consider the documentation for the `Employee` class shown in Figure 23.1. At the top of the documentation shown in this figure is an inheritance tree showing that `Employee` is a subclass of `Person`, which is a subclass of `java.lang.Object`.

Figure 23.1.

A sample documentation page generated by JavaDoc.

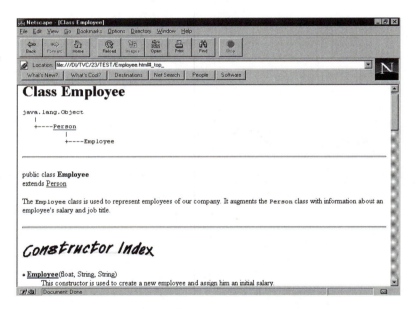

In addition to the class's inheritance tree, Figure 23.1 shows that an overall class description can be provided as well as a constructor index. Figure 23.1 shows only one screen of the documentation that will be created for the `Employee` class later today. There are many more areas and types of documentation that can be generated, and they are described later today.

In addition to generating documentation for a single class, JavaDoc can generate system-level documentation. For example, Figure 23.2 shows an `AllNames.html` file generated by JavaDoc. This file lists all nonprivate members, both methods and variables, processed by JavaDoc.

23

Figure 23.2.

Viewing the contents of `AllNames.html`.

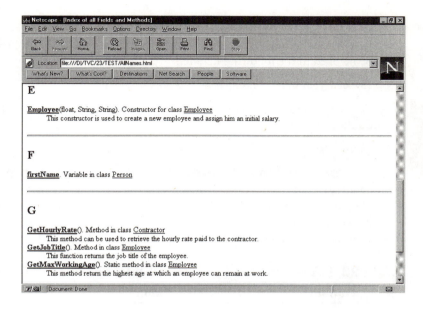

Similarly, JavaDoc can create `tree.html`. This file depicts the complete Java inheritance hierarchy, as shown in Figure 23.3.

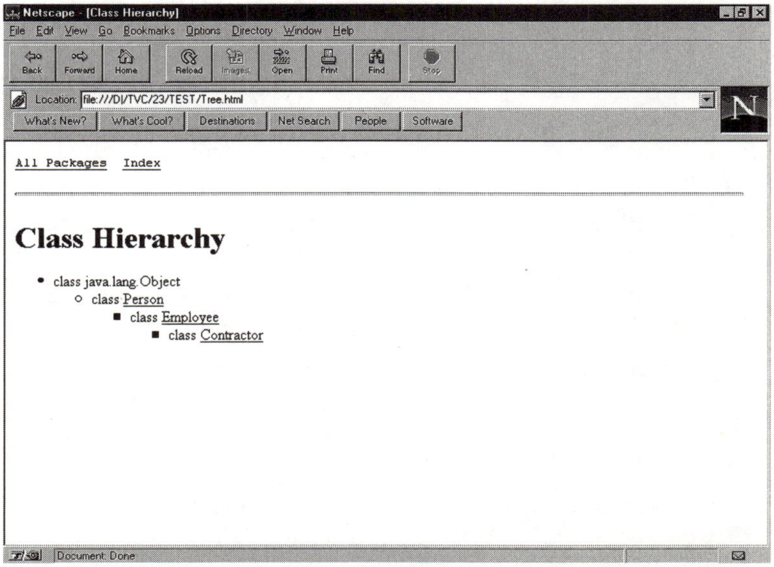

Figure 23.3.

Viewing the Java class hierarchy in `tree.html` *generated by JavaDoc.*

Running JavaDoc

JavaDoc is a command-line program that is supplied with the Java Development Kit. It can be invoked in the following manner:

```
javadoc [options] PackageName ¦ FileName.java
```

For example, to use JavaDoc to create documentation on a class named Employee, you would do the following:

```
javadoc employee.java
```

Command-Line Arguments and Environment Variables

The [options] parameter shown as part of the JavaDoc command line can be included if desired. It can be used to specify which directories should be searched for input files, the directory in which to put the generated HTML files, whether JavaDoc should run in a special verbose mode, and other options as summarized in Table 23.1.

Table 23.1. The JavaDoc command-line options.

Option	Description
-authors	An undocumented option that, when specified, will generate HTML based on the @author tag.
-classpath *path*	Specifies the path to be searched for files ending with the .java extension. If specified, it overrides the CLASSPATH environment variable.
-d *directory*	Specifies the target directory for writing HTML files.
-doctype [MIF ¦ HTML]	An undocumented option that specifies the type of file to create. By default, HTML files are created, but FrameMaker MIF files can also be generated.
-noindex	An undocumented option that suppresses creation of the AllNames.html file.
-notree	An undocumented option that suppresses creation of the tree.html file.
-verbose	Instructs JavaDoc to run in a special mode that displays additional information as the files are parsed. This option is most useful if you have a class for which the documentation appears incorrect.
-version	An undocumented option that, when specified, will generate HTML based on the @version tag.

The only environment variable used by JavaDoc is CLASSPATH. This variable, if set in your environment, informs JavaDoc of the directories in which it should search for .java files. For example, to search the current directory, C:\MYJAVA\SOURCE, and C:\YOURJAVA\SOURCE, you would set CLASSPATH to the following:

```
.;C:\myjava\source;C:\yourjava\source
```

NOTE JavaDoc is included as part of the Java Development Kit (JDK) as released by Sun Microsystems and is included in the JAVA\BIN subdirectory of the directory into which you install Visual Café.

23

Adding JavaDoc Comments

Unfortunately, JavaDoc is only as smart as the information you give it. It gets its information by parsing source code files and looking for comments enclosed within the /** and */ delimiters. JavaDoc comments are placed immediately above the class or member that they are meant to describe. For example, consider the following class definition and associated comment:

```
/** This is a comment that describes MyClass in general. */
public class MyClass {
    /** The DoSomething method is used to do something. */
    public int DoSomething() {
        // method source goes here
    }
    // remaining class source code
}
```

In this example, JavaDoc comments have been placed above the class and above the DoSomething member method. Leading spaces and asterisk (*) characters are stripped from JavaDoc comment lines. This makes it possible for you to start each line with an asterisk, as shown in the following example:

```
/**
  * This is a comment that describes MyClass
  * in general. The leading * characters and
  * spaces will be removed. */
public class Contractor extends Employee {
    // class body
}
```

Doing so is, of course, a matter of personal preference, but this style is common among many Java programmers.

Documenting Classes

When documenting a class (in the comment immediately preceding the class definition), you can add class documentation tags to enhance the usability of the documentation. Class documentation tags each begin with an @ symbol to distinguish them. The following class documentation tags are available:

```
@author author-name
```

```
@see classname
```

```
@see fully-qualified-classname
```

```
@see fully-qualified-classname#method-name
```

```
@version version-text
```

As an example of how these tags work, consider the following definitions of an `Employee` class and a `Contractor` class:

```
/**
 * The Employee class is used to represent employees
 * of our company. It augments the Person class with
 * information about an employee's salary and job
 * title.
 * @author Mike Cohn
 * @version 1.0.0
 * @see Contractor
 */
public class Employee extends Person {
    // class body
}

/**
 * The Contractor class is used to represent
 * contract employees. Contract employees are
 * paid by the hour.
 * @author Mike Cohn
 * @version 1.0.0
 */
public class Contractor extends Employee {
    // class body
}
```

The comment preceding the `Employee` class describes the class and then shows the use of three of the class documentation tags. The author and version are only included in the generated documentation if you specify -`authors` and -`version` on the command line. The `@see` `Contractor` line in the `Employee` comment will inform readers that they may want to see a related class. Because the `@see` tag is used, JavaDoc will generate a link to the `Contractor` class documentation. This can be seen in Figure 23.4.

As you can see in Figure 23.4, a link is provided for all superclasses of `Employee` (`java.lang.Object` and `Person`) and the `@see` tag has created a link to `Contractor` in a "See Also" section. If you click this link, you will jump directly to the `Contractor` documentation, as shown in Figure 23.5. The `Contractor` documentation does not need an `@see` tag back to `Employee` because `Employee` is a superclass of `Contractor` and already appears as a link in the inheritance hierarchy.

23

Figure 23.4.

Class documentation for Employee, *including a link to* Contractor.

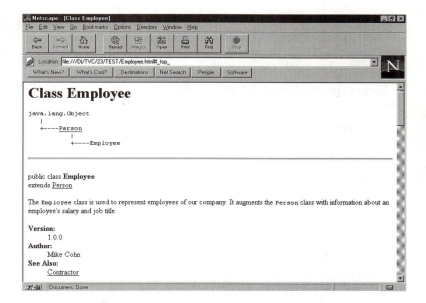

Figure 23.5.

Class documentation for Contractor.

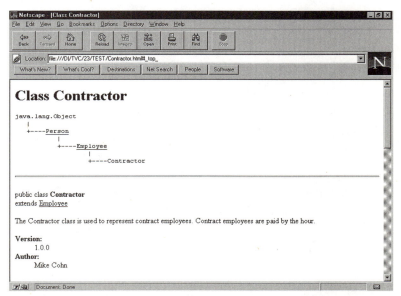

The link from Employee to Contractor positions your Web browser at the top of the documentation for the Contractor class. Sometimes you'd prefer to have a link jump to a specific place within the target class. You can link directly to a method by specifying the name of the method after the target class. For example, the following tag would jump directly to the `GetHourlyRate` method in the `Contractor` class:

```
@see Contractor#GetHourlyRate
```

Documenting Methods

Like its class documentation tags, JavaDoc also supports method documentation tags. Method documentation tags are optional and can be placed in a JavaDoc comment directly above the method they describe. Like class documentation tags, method tags begin with the @ symbol. The following method documentation tags are available:

```
@param parameter-name description
```

```
@return description
```

```
@exception fully-qualified-class-name description
```

To see how these tags can be used, consider the following definition of the `Contractor` class:

```java
public class Contractor extends Employee {
    public Contractor(float sal, String fName, String lName) {
        super(sal, fName, lName);
    }
    private float hourlyRate;
/**
 * This method can be used to retrieve the hourly rate
 * paid to the contractor.
 * @return The contractor's hourly rate, excluding
 *         exceptional circumstances such as holidays
 *         and overtime.
 */
    public float GetHourlyRate() {
        return hourlyRate;
    }
/**
 * This method calculates how much is due to
 * a contractor based on how much he's worked
 * and his hourly rate.
 * @param hours The number of hours worked by the
 *         contractor during this pay period.
 * @return The amount of money due the contractor.
 */
    public float CalculatePayCheck(int hours) {
        return hours * hourlyRate;
    }
}
```

The `Contractor` class includes two nonconstructor methods—`GetHourlyRate` and `CalculatePayCheck`. Each of these uses the `@return` tag to describe its return value. Additionally, `GetHourlyRate` uses `@param` to describe its input parameters. The results of this documentation can be seen in Figure 23.6.

Figure 23.6.

Using @param *and* @return *to document* Contractor.

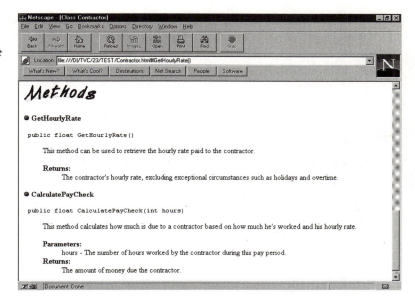

As you can see from Figure 23.6, the @return and @param tags nicely format the descriptions entered in the JavaDoc comments. If a method receives more than one parameter, the @param tag can be repeated as often as necessary. Although the @exception tag is not shown in this example, it behaves identically to @return and @param.

Enhancing Your Documentation with HTML

By using the class and method documentation tags that you can embed within JavaDoc comments, you can make huge strides toward improving the way you document your code. However, because JavaDoc produces HTML files, you can go much further. By embedding HTML commands within your JavaDoc comments, you have almost infinite control over how your documentation will appear when viewed in a browser.

By using HTML tags, you can enhance your documentation by drawing attention to bold or italicized text, including numbered and bulleted lists, images, preformatted text, or even links to other documentation files or Web-based resources. Table 23.2 shows the HTML tags that you will probably find most useful in documenting your Java code.

Table 23.2. Useful HTML tags for documenting Java code.

Tag	Purpose
`<A>…</A>`	Indicates a link anchor.
`<B>…</B>`	Formats marked text with bold font.
`<BLOCKQUOTE>…</BLOCKQUOTE>`	Formats marked text as a lengthy quotation.
`<CITE>…</CITE>`	Formats marked text as a citation.
`<CODE>…</CODE>`	Formats marked text as source code.
`<EM>…</EM>`	Adds emphasis to marked text.
`<I>…</I>`	Formats marked text in italics.
`<IMG>`	Inserts a named image file.
`<LI>`	Indicates a list item within an ordered or unordered list.
`<OL>…</OL>`	Indicates an ordered (numbered) list.
`<P>`	Indicates the end of a paragraph.
`<PRE>…</PRE>`	Indicates preformatted text. Spacing and layout is preserved by using a monospaced font.
`<STRONG>…</STRONG>`	Adds maximum-strength emphasis to marked text.
`<TT>…</TT>`	Formats marked text in a typewriter font.
`<UL>…</UL>`	Indicates an unordered (bulleted) list.

WARNING

> Because JavaDoc makes its own assumptions about how it will format text, you cannot use HTML tags like `<H1>` that are used to define headings.

An Example

This section demonstrates the use of JavaDoc, including class documentation tags, method documentation tags, and embedded HTML tags. Assume you have the following class definition that you need to document:

```java
public class Employee extends Person {
    private float salary;
    private String job;
    public Employee(float sal, String fName, String lName) {
        super(fName, lName);
        salary = sal;
```

23

```
    }
    public void AssignJob(String newJob) {
        job = newJob;
    }
    public String GetJobTitle() {
        return job;
    }
    public static int GetMaxWorkingAge() {
        return 64;
    }
    private float GetMaxSalary() {
        return 200000f;
    }
    public boolean ChangeSalary(float newSalary) {
        if (newSalary < salary)
            return false;
        if (newSalary > GetMaxSalary())
            return false;
        salary = newSalary;
        return true;
    }
}
```

First, you need to document the class itself. You do this with the following comment:

```
/**
 * The <TT>Employee</TT> class is used to represent
 * employees of our company. It augments the <TT>Person</TT>
 * class with information about an employee's salary and
 * job title.<P>
 * This class was written by:
 * <BLOCKQUOTE>
 * <IMG src=logo.gif width=300 height=100>
 * </BLOCKQUOTE>
 * @author Mike Cohn
 * @version 1.0.0
 * @see Contractor
 */
public class Employee extends Person {
```

This will create the documentation screen shown in Figure 23.7. You can see that the `<TT>`...`</TT>` tags were used to set the names of other classes in a distinctive typewriter-style font. The `<P>` tag is used to indicate the end of a paragraph. If this tag had not been used, the text on the following line would have merged with the text prior to the tag. The `<BLOCKQUOTE>` and `<IMG>` tags were used to include a graphic image indicating the author of the class.

Next you need to document the constructor. This is done with the following comment, which will produce the documentation shown in Figure 23.8:

```
/** This constructor is used to create a new employee and
  * assign him an initial salary. <EM>It does not verify that
  * salary is less than the company's maximum salary.</EM>
  * You could use this method as follows:
  * <CODE><PRE>
  * Employee Emp = new Employee(35000f,"Mike","Cohn");
```

```
 * </PRE></CODE>
 * @param sal The starting salary of the new employee.
 * @param fName The employee's first name.
 * @param lName The employee's last name.
 */
public Employee(float sal, String fName, String lName) {
```

Figure 23.7.

Class documentation for Employee, *including an embedded graphic.*

In this case, the <CODE>…</CODE> and <PRE>…</PRE> tags were used to indicate a preformatted block of source code. Also, the <EM>…</EM> tags were used to apply emphasis to the statement that the employee's salary must be less than a company maximum. Finally, because this constructor is passed three parameters, each parameter is documented with the @param method tag.

In addition to the full documentation shown in Figure 23.8, JavaDoc creates a constructor index and a method index for the class. The method index lists each of a class's nonprivate methods. These indexes appear as separate sections in the HTML document, as shown in Figure 23.9.

23

Figure 23.8.

Documentation for the Employee *constructor.*

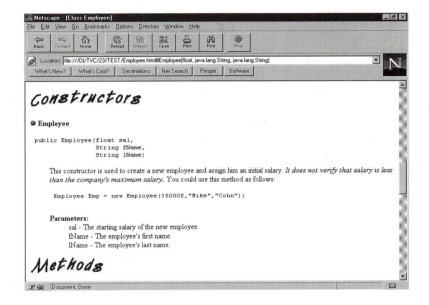

Figure 23.9.

The constructor and method indexes for the Employee *class.*

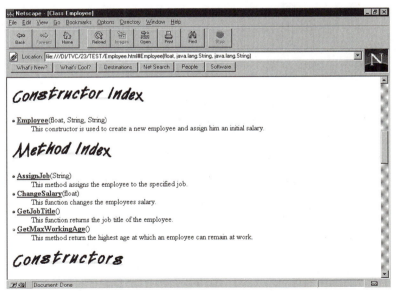

The `AssignJob` method is documented by adding the following comment:

```
/**
 * This method assigns the employee to the
 * specified job. This method does not verify the
 * <I>job title</I> against the list of <I>approved
 * job titles</I> created by <B>Human Resources</B>.
 * Likely job titles you may want to pass include:
 * <UL>
 * <LI>Programmer
 * <LI>Analyst
 * <LI>QA
 * <LI>Tech Writer
 * <LI>Project Manager
 * <LI>Database Administrator
 * <LI>Database Engineer
 * </UL>
 * Reminder: All positions must be approved by the
 * <B>Manager of Human Resources</B> according to
 * the company's <CITE>Employee Hiring Guidelines.
 * </CITE>
 * @param newJob This is the new job title.
 * @see #GetJobTitle
 */
public void AssignJob(String newJob) {
```

The result of this documentation can be seen in Figure 23.10. This example demonstrates the use of `<B>`…`</B>` and `<I>`…`</I>` to bold and italicize text. Additionally, the use of an unordered (bulleted) list is demonstrated. The `<UL>`…`</UL>` tags indicate the beginning and end of the list, and the `<LI>` tags indicate each of the list items. This example also demonstrates the use of `<CITE>`…`</CITE>` to indicate a citation. Finally, the @see method tag is used. In this example, no class name appears to the left of the #. This will create a link to a method within the current class.

Next, the following comment is written for `GetJobTitle`:

```
/**
 * This function returns the job title of the employee.
 * @return A string representing the job title (for
 * example, "programmer").
 * @see #AssignJob
 */
public String GetJobTitle() {
```

The method `GetMaxWorkingAge` is defined as static, meaning that it is associated with the class itself rather than with instances of the class. However, because it is a public method, it can be documented as shown in the following comment:

```
/**
 * This method returns the highest age at which
 * an employee can remain at work. <STRONG>
 * After this age, an employee must retire and
 * move to Florida.</STRONG>
 * @return The last allowable working year before
 * mandatory retirement.
 */
public static int GetMaxWorkingAge() {
```

23

Figure 23.10.

Documentation for the AssignJob *method.*

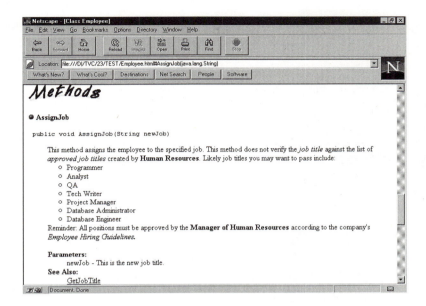

The documentation for GetJobTitle and GetMaxWorkingAge will appear as shown in Figure 23.11. As you can see from this figure, the use of the <STRONG>...</STRONG> tag places heavy emphasis on the need for retirees to move to Florida.

Figure 23.11.

Documentation for GetJobTitle *and* GetMaxWorkingAge.

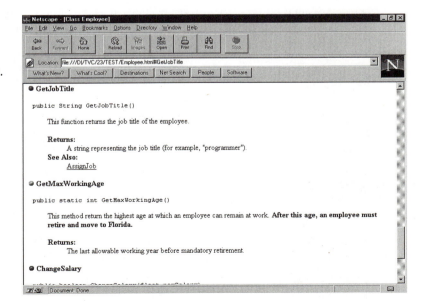

Next, the method `GetMaxSalary` is documented, as follows:

```
/**
 * This comment will not show up in JavaDoc because
 * it is private.
 */
private float GetMaxSalary() {
```

However, `GetMaxSalary` is declared as `private`, so it will not be documented by JavaDoc. Because private functions are not usable outside the class in which they are declared, there is no need to document them for use by others in the same way that exists for externally visible methods.

At this point, the only method left to document is `ChangeSalary`, which is documented as follows:

```
/**
 * This function changes the employee's salary.
 * A salary change can occur only after the two following
 * tests have been applied:
 * <OL>
 * <LI>The new salary is higher than the current salary.
 * <LI>The new salary is less than the maximum salary.
 * </OL>
 * @return <B>true</B> if the salary change is approved,
 *         <B>false</B> otherwise.
 * @param newSalary The proposed new salary.
 */
public boolean ChangeSalary(float newSalary) {
```

The documentation for `ChangeSalary` will appear as shown in Figure 23.12. This example demonstrates the use of `<OL>…</OL>` and `<LI>` to introduce an ordered list and its items. Ordered lists are like unordered lists except that instead of bullets, they have numbers to the left of each item. Additionally, this example shows that some HTML tags can be embedded with class or method documentation tags. In this case, `<B>…</B>` is embedded within the `@return` tag.

For clarity and completeness, Listing 23.1 shows the complete source to the `Employee` class and Listing 23.2 shows the complete source to the `Contractor` class. These files can be found on the MCP Web site (`www.mcp.com/info/1-57521/1-57521-303-6`).

Listing 23.1. `Employee.java`.

```
1:    /**
2:     * The <TT>Employee</TT> class is used to represent
3:     * employees of our company. It augments the <TT>Person</TT>
4:     * class with information about an employee's salary and
5:     * job title.<P>
6:     * This class was written by:
7:     * <BLOCKQUOTE>
8:     * <IMG src=logo.gif width=300 height=100>
```

23

```
 9:      * </BLOCKQUOTE>
10:      * @author Mike Cohn
11:      * @version 1.0.0
12:      * @see Contractor
13:     */
14:    public class Employee extends Person {
15:        private float salary;
16:        private String job;
17:
18:        /** This constructor is used to create a new employee and
19:         * assign him an initial salary. <EM>It does not verify
20:         * that salary is less than the company's maximum
21:         * salary.</EM> You could use this method as follows:
22:         * <CODE><PRE>
23:         * Employee Emp = new Employee(35000f,"Mike","Cohn");
24:         * </PRE></CODE>
25:         * @param sal The starting salary of the new employee.
26:         * @param fName The employee's first name.
27:         * @param lName The employee's last name.
28:         */
29:        public Employee(float sal, String fName, String lName) {
30:            super(fName, lName);
31:            salary = sal;
32:        }
33:
34:        /**
35:         * This method assigns the employee to the
36:         * specified job. This method does not verify the
37:         * <I>job title</I> against the list of <I>approved
38:         * job titles</I> created by <B>Human Resources</B>.
39:         * Likely job titles you may want to pass include:
40:         * <UL>
41:         * <LI>Programmer
42:         * <LI>Analyst
43:         * <LI>QA
44:         * <LI>Tech Writer
45:         * <LI>Project Manager
46:         * <LI>Database Administrator
47:         * <LI>Database Engineer
48:         * </UL>
49:         * Reminder: All positions must be approved by the
50:         * <B>Manager of Human Resources</B> according to
51:         * the company's <CITE>Employee Hiring Guidelines.
52:         * </CITE>
53:         * @param newJob This is the new job title.
54:         * @see #GetJobTitle
55:         */
56:        public void AssignJob(String newJob) {
57:            job = newJob;
58:        }
59:
60:        /**
61:         * This function returns the job title of the employee.
62:         * @return A string representing the job title (for
63:         * example, "programmer").
```

23

continues

Listing 23.1. continued

```
64:          * @see #AssignJob
65:          */
66:         public String GetJobTitle() {
67:             return job;
68:         }
69:
70:        /**
71:         * This method returns the highest age at which
72:         * an employee can remain at work. <STRONG>
73:         * After this age, an employee must retire and
74:         * move to Florida.</STRONG>
75:         * @return The last allowable working year before
76:         * mandatory retirement.
77:         */
78:         public static int GetMaxWorkingAge() {
79:             return 64;
80:         }
81:
82:        /**
83:          * This comment will not show up in JavaDoc because
84:          * it is private.
85:          */
86:         private float GetMaxSalary() {
87:             return 200000f;
88:         }
89:
90:        /**
91:         * This function changes the employee's salary.
92:         * A salary change can occur only after the two
93:         * following tests have been applied:
94:         * <OL>
95:         * <LI>The new salary is higher than the current salary.
96:         * <LI>The new salary is less than the maximum salary.
97:         * </OL>
98:         * @return <B>true</B> if the salary change is approved,
99:         *          <B>false</B> otherwise.
100:        * @param newSalary The proposed new salary.
101:        */
102:        public boolean ChangeSalary(float newSalary) {
103:            if (newSalary < salary)
104:                return false;
105:            if (newSalary > GetMaxSalary())
106:                return false;
107:            salary = newSalary;
108:            return true;
109:        }
110: }
```

Figure 23.12.

Documentation for the ChangeSalary *method.*

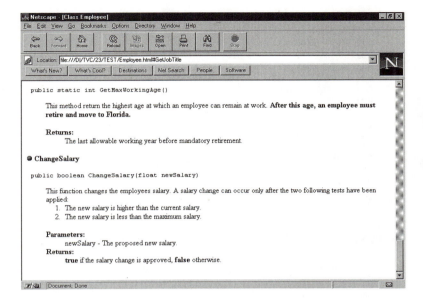

Listing 23.2. Contractor.java.

```
1:    /**
2:     * The Contractor class is used to represent
3:     * contract employees. Contract employees are
4:     * paid by the hour.
5:     * @author Mike Cohn
6:     * @version 1.0.0
7:     */
8:    public class Contractor extends Employee {
9:        public Contractor(float sal,String fName,String lName) {
10:           super(sal, fName, lName);
11:       }
12:       private float hourlyRate;
13:       /**
14:        * This method can be used to retrieve the hourly rate
15:        * paid to the contractor.
16:        * @return The contractor's hourly rate, excluding
17:        *          exceptional circumstances such as holidays
18:        *          and overtime.
19:        */
20:       public float GetHourlyRate() {
21:           return hourlyRate;
```

continues

Listing 23.2. continued

```
22:        }
23:        /**
24:         * This method calculates how much is due to
25:         * a contractor based on how much he's worked
26:         * and his hourly rate.
27:         * @param hours The number of hours worked by the
28:         *         contractor during this pay period.
29:         * @return The amount of money due the contractor.
30:         */
31:        public float CalculatePayCheck(int hours) {
32:            return hours * hourlyRate;
33:        }
34:    }
```

Summary

Today you learned how JavaDoc can simplify the job of documenting your classes. You saw how class documentation tags can be used to link classes by providing jumps between related classes. You also learned how to use method documentation tags to document the parameters, return values, and exceptions of each method. Even with this much power and flexibility, it only scratched the surface of what can be done. By embedding HTML commands directly into your comments, you learned how to enhance your documentation by using formatted text, numbered and bulleted lists, and embedded images. Finally, you saw an extensive example that put all of these pieces together to document a single class.

Q&A

Q **I've included an @authors tag in my class documentation, but when I run JavaDoc this tag is ignored. What am I doing wrong?**

A The @authors tag is ignored by JavaDoc unless you specify the -authors option on the JavaDoc command line.

Q **I've included an @version tag in my class documentation, but when I run JavaDoc this tag is ignored. What am I doing wrong?**

A This is the same problem as with the @authors tag. The @version tag is ignored by JavaDoc unless you specify the -version option on the JavaDoc command line.

Workshop

The workshop includes quiz questions to help you gauge your understanding of the material in this chapter. The workshop also includes exercises to provide hands-on experience with what you've learned in this chapter. Answers to quiz questions can be found in Appendix D, "Answers."

Quiz

1. What tag is used to document the parameters used by a method?

2. What tag must you add to a class's documentation in order to include the name of the programmer who wrote the class?

3. What documentation will be generated for the following method comment?

```
/**
     * This is a two-line comment
     * for GetMaxSalary.
  */
    public float GetMaxSalary() {
```

4. What documentation will be generated for the following method comment?

```
/**
     * This is a comment for GetMaxSalary.
  */
    private float GetMaxSalary() {
```

Exercise

Thoroughly comment all the classes and methods in the Tic Tac Toe programs of Day 15, "Client/Server Programming with Sockets."

Day 24

An Introduction to SQL

SQL (pronounced either "ess-queue-ell" or "sequel") is a language for manipulating relational databases. SQL grew out of work done at IBM during the early 1970s, debuted as a commercial product in 1979, gained acceptance throughout the 1980s, and by the end of that decade had become a standard. In this bonus day, you get a solid introduction to the basics of SQL and a hint of the power and flexibility found in its more complicated features. Today's lesson cannot teach you everything there is to know about SQL; that would easily take an entire book. This lesson does, however, cover the central concepts of SQL and provides more than enough information to write many database programs.

A Short History of SQL

SQL has always been closely associated with relational databases. The idea behind the relational database was first presented in Dr. E. F. Codd's "A Relational Model of Data for Large Shared Data Banks" in *Communications of the Association for Computing Machinery* in 1970. Codd's work encouraged IBM to begin the System/R project to create a workable relational database. As part of the System/R project, a query language—SEQUEL—was designed. SEQUEL was an acronym for Structured English Query Language. IBM eventually changed the name of its database query language to SQL, an acronym for Structured Query Language.

By the late 1970s, companies other than IBM were beginning to look at the commercial prospects of relational databases. The first company to market a relational database was Relational Software in 1979. Relational Software later changed its name to Oracle Corporation. In 1983, IBM finally released its relational database, DB2.

SQL and relational databases grew in popularity during the 1980s with initial ANSI standardization coming in 1986 and ISO standardization in 1987. Since then, the SQL-92 standard was approved by the ANSI committee in 1992, and work has begun on a SQL3 standard.

In the 1990s, efforts began to extend SQL by creating a *call-level interface,* which is similar to a functional-level API (application programming interface). The effort to create a standard call-level interface was begun by the SQL Access Group, and a CLI specification was published in 1992. Microsoft's ODBC (Open Database Connectivity) is an example of a popular call-level interface.

Overview of SQL

Despite the fact that SQL is generally considered to be an acronym for Structured Query Language, SQL is neither particularly structured nor a query language. Without support for structured programming concepts like loops, SQL cannot be considered a structured language. On the other hand, to call SQL a query language is to do it a severe injustice. SQL is as full a language as you could want for manipulating a relational database, one that goes beyond querying to include inserting, updating, and deleting. It is even possible to create new tables and indexes with SQL.

After you've created your database, probably 90% of the SQL you write will begin with one of SQL's four most common verbs: `select`, `insert`, `update`, or `delete`. As an example, suppose you've built a database for storing rental prices at the apartment buildings in town. In order to find the rent at a specific apartment building, you would use the following simple `select` statement:

```
select rent from property where name="Oceanside"
```

This statement will create the following result set:

```
rent
800
```

From this query, you know it costs $800 to rent an apartment in the Oceanside complex. All SQL statements consist of elements similar to those used in this query: keyword verbs (select), column names (rent), table names (property), and clauses (select… and where…).

Result Sets

 All query statements in SQL return a result set. A *result set* is a set of rows that match the criteria given in the SQL query.

A query can return anywhere from zero to millions of rows, depending on the size of the tables being searched and the selection criteria. All SQL statements operate on relational tables, and each query statement will return a table as its result set.

Null Values

In a Java program, you typically must identify a value you will use to indicate a condition of no value. In many cases, you will use the Java keyword null. SQL supports null values that can be used when a column's value is missing or unknown. For example, if you are using a database that stores birthdates and you don't know a particular birthdate, you could store the value null instead. In SQL, as in Java, null is not synonymous with zero; selecting all rows with a null value in a specific column will create a different result set than selecting all rows with zero in that column.

Column and Table Names

Database tables and columns are each assigned a unique name. Although the SQL standard specifies a maximum length of 128 characters for these names, the practical limits imposed by commercial SQL products are significantly lower. Oracle, for example, supports 30-character names.

SQL assumes that when you reference a table, you are referring to a table you own. In this case, all you need to do is include the table's name in the statement. If you are referencing a table you don't own, you can prefix the table name with the owner name followed by a period. Like referencing a Java class member, you can refer to the property table owned by Steve as follows:

```
steve.property
```

Because a table cannot have two columns with the same name, you can reference a column by name alone in a simple, one-table SQL statement. However, when two or more tables are used in a single SQL statement, sometimes you need to qualify the field names by preceding them with the table name and a period. For example, husband.lastname could be used in a SQL statement to distinguish it from wife.lastname, if both the Husband and Wife tables were used in the same statement.

NOTE

> It is also possible and occasionally necessary to fully qualify a column name by prefixing the name of the table owner, as in `steve.husband.lastname`.

Simple Queries

It is possible to use the select statement without referencing a table at all. This can be seen in the following example:

```
select "hello, world"
```

This statement will result in the traditional `hello, world`.

Because this simple `select` statement doesn't even reference a table or database, it is worth moving on to more useful examples. To do so, use the Property table shown in Table 24.1. Each row in this table represents an apartment complex and stores its name, the part of town in which it is located, and the monthly rent.

Table 24.1. All rows of the Property table.

Name	Location	Rent
Claremont Oaks	South	600
Hillsdale Village	North	700
Oceanside	East	800
Pacific Gardens	East	1200
Pinewood Apts.	East	550
Pinewood Estates	North	700
Pine Lake Apts.	West	600
Pine Lake Towers	West	650
Seaview Apts.	North	750
Suncreek Apts.	South	800
Windsor Apts.	East	2800

If you want to select the name of all properties in the database, you could use the following:

```
select name from property
```

24

This SQL statement would generate the following result set:

Name
Claremont Oaks
Hillsdale Village
Oceanside
Pacific Gardens
Pinewood Apts.
Pinewood Estates
Pine Lake Apts.
Pine Lake Towers
Seaview Apts.
Suncreek Apts.
Windsor Apts.

24

Selecting Multiple Columns

Of course, selecting a single column is of limited use. If you want to select multiple columns from a table, you can list the field names separated by commas (,). The following SQL statement creates the result set shown in Table 24.2:

```
select name, rent from property
```

Table 24.2. Selecting the name and rent columns.

Name	Rent
Claremont Oaks	600
Hillsdale Village	700
Oceanside	800
Pacific Gardens	1200
Pinewood Apts.	550
Pinewood Estates	700
Pine Lake Apts.	600
Pine Lake Towers	650
Seaview Apts.	750
Suncreek Apts.	800
Windsor Apts.	2800

Selecting All Columns

Sometimes in SQL you want to select all the columns in a table. When working with a small table such as the Property table, it's fairly easy to list them all, as in `select name, location, rent from property`. However, if a table has ten, twenty, or even more columns, typing each column name can become quite laborious and result in typing errors. SQL facilitates selecting all columns in a table by using the asterisk (*) character in place of the column names. To select all columns in the Property table, you could use the following:

```
select * from property
```

In effect, the asterisk character can be thought of as a wildcard that matches all columns. This SQL statement is synonymous with `select name, location, rent from property`; both will generate the results shown in Table 24.3.

Table 24.3. Result set from `select * from property`.

Name	Location	Rent
Claremont Oaks	South	600
Hillsdale Village	North	700
Oceanside	East	800
Pacific Gardens	East	1200
Pinewood Apts.	East	550
Pinewood Estates	North	700
Pine Lake Apts.	West	600
Pine Lake Towers	West	650
Seaview Apts.	North	750
Suncreek Apts.	South	800
Windsor Apts.	East	2800

WARNING

Although it's easier to use the asterisk (*) to select columns, you are better off doing so only during interactive SQL sessions. If you have used the asterisk, your program is more prone to changes in the underlying database than it needs to be. For example, if you have written your program to expect two integer columns and the table is rearranged to either include a new column or change the column order, it is likely your program will fail.

Calculated Columns

If you've ever rented an apartment, you know that rent is bound to go up. So how do you determine the rent on each of these apartments if you assume a likely 10% rent increase? It's actually quite simple, and can be achieved with the following SQL statement for which the result set is shown in Table 24.4:

```
select name, (rent * 1.1) from property
```

Table 24.4. Calculating proposed rent.

Name	Rent * 1.1
Claremont Oaks	660
Hillsdale Village	760
Oceanside	860
Pacific Gardens	1320
Pinewood Apts.	605
Pinewood Estates	770
Pine Lake Apts.	660
Pine Lake Towers	715
Seaview Apts.	825
Suncreek Apts.	880
Windsor Apts.	3080

One problem with these results is that it isn't clear that the second column indicates the proposed rent. It would be nice to replace the column heading Rent * 1.1 with the more informative column heading Proposed Rent. This can be done as follows:

```
select name, (rent * 1.1) "Proposed Rent" from property
```

This will generate the same result set as shown in Table 24.4, but the second column will have the more descriptive heading, Proposed Rent.

TIP Most SQL statements allow you to use the column selection asterisk (*) with calculated fields, as in the following:

```
select *, (rent * 1.1) "Proposed Rent" from property
```

This will give you a result set with four columns: Name, Location, Rent, and Proposed Rent.

Restricting Results

Now that you know how to retrieve one or more columns from a table, it is time to learn how to write more discriminating `select` statements. All the `select` statements covered so far have returned all rows in a table. Luckily, with SQL it is easy to extend a basic `select` statement to return only rows that match certain criteria.

Comparisons

SQL supports the standard six comparison operators shown in Table 24.5. Each of these symbols has a direct analog in Java, with the only syntactic difference being that SQL uses <> instead of Java's != to express inequality.

Table 24.5. SQL comparison operators.

Operator	Comparison
<	Less than
<=	Less than or equal
=	Equal
>=	Greater than or equal
>	Greater than
<>	Greater than or equal

A SQL `select` statement can select a subset of rows in a table by using a `where` clause with one of the comparison operators. For example, to select all rows with rent greater than $700 in the Property table, the following SQL statement could be used:

```
select name, rent from property where rent > 700
```

This will generate the result set shown in Table 24.6.

Table 24.6. Properties whose rent is greater than $700.

Name	Rent
Oceanside	800
Pacific Gardens	1200
Seaview Apts.	750
Suncreek Apts.	800
Windsor Apts.	2800

Notice that because the > operator was used instead of the >= operator, the result set did not include Hillsdale Village and Pinewood Estates.

24

If you want to select all properties that cost exactly $600, use the following:

```
select name from property where rent = 600
```

This results in the following:

Name
Claremont Oaks
Pine Lake Apts.

Using comparison operators does not limit you to numeric fields. If you want to select all properties whose names start with *S* or any subsequent letter, you could use the following SQL statement:

```
select * from property where name >= 'S'
```

This creates the result set shown in Table 24.7.

Table 24.7. Properties whose names start with *S* or a subsequent letter.

Name	Location	Rent
Seaview Apts.	North	750
Suncreek Apts.	South	800
Windsor Apts.	East	2800

Even better, it is possible to create a compound where clause. To select all properties that start with *S* or a subsequent letter and cost less than $1,000, you could use the following:

```
select * from property where name >= 'S' and rent < 1000
```

This creates the result set shown in Table 24.8.

Table 24.8. Properties whose names start with *S* or a subsequent letter and cost less than $1,000.

Name	Location	Rent
Seaview Apts.	North	750
Suncreek Apts.	South	800

Ranges

SQL facilitates range testing with its between and not between predicates. A between clause is formed as follows:

```
value between low and high
```

The between predicate is inclusive on both ends of the range, so the following query will create the result set shown in Table 24.9.

```
select * from property where rent between 500 and 750
```

Table 24.9. Properties that rent for between $500 and $750.

Name	Location	Rent
Claremont Oaks	South	600
Hillsdale Village	North	700
Pinewood Apts.	East	550
Pinewood Estates	North	700
Pine Lake Apts.	West	600
Pine Lake Towers	West	650
Seaview Apts.	North	750

On the other hand, the not between predicate is noninclusive. Table 24.10 shows the result set created by the following SQL statement:

```
select * from property where rent not between 500 and 750
```

Table 24.10. Properties not renting for between $500 and $750.

Name	Location	Rent
Oceanside	East	800
Pacific Gardens	East	1200
Suncreek Apts.	South	800
Windsor Apts.	East	2800

Set Membership

Occasionally, you want to select rows that have a column matching a member of a set of values. For example, if you want to find all properties that cost either $600, $700, or $800, use the in predicate, as shown in the following SQL statement:

```
select * from property where rent in (600, 700, 800)
```

Just as the between predicate had its not between counterpart, in has its counterpart: not in. The not in predicate will return the complementary result set, selecting every row not matched by the value list. For example, to select all properties that cost anything other than $600, $700, or $800, use the following:

```
select * from property where rent not in (600, 700, 800)
```

Pattern Matching

Although it doesn't provide the flexibility of dedicated pattern-matching languages like AWK, sed, or any other regular-expression parser, SQL does support a reasonable set of pattern-matching features. Pattern-matching support is provided through the percent-sign (%) and underline (_) characters. The % character is used to represent zero or more characters; the _ character is used to represent exactly one character. Table 24.11 shows examples of SQL pattern matching.

Table 24.11. Pattern-matching examples.

Pattern	Matches
Pine %	Pine followed by anything; for example, Pine Lake Apts. and Pine Lake Towers but not Pinewood Estates or Pinewood Apts..
Pine%Apts.	Pine followed by anything but ending with Apts.; for example, Pinewood Apts. and Pine Lake Apts..
_____ Apts.	Any seven-letter word followed by a space and the word Apts.; for example, Seaview Apts. and Windsor Apts..
%Apts.	Anything that ends in Apts..

WARNING

Spaces are significant when performing like comparisons. Although spaces are ignored when using the six standard comparison operators shown in Table 24.11, spaces are compared when using like. Keep the following truths in mind:

```
"Pinewood" = "Pinewood"
"Pinewood" = "Pinewood   "
"Pinewood" like "Pinewood"
"Pinewood" not like "Pinewood   "
```

To make use of pattern matching in SQL, use the like predicate. For example, to select all properties that start with *S*, you could use the following statement:

```
select * from property where name like 'S%'
```

This will generate the result set shown in Table 24.12.

Table 24.12. Selecting all properties whose names start with *S* through the use of pattern matching.

Name	Location	Rent
Seaview Apts.	North	750
Suncreek Apts.	South	800

Just as there are `not between` and `not in` predicates, there is, of course, a `not like` predicate that will return a result set of all rows that do not match a given pattern. To select, for example, all properties that do not end with `Apts.`, you could use the following SQL statement to get the result set shown in Table 24.13:

```
select * from property where name not like '% Apts.'
```

Table 24.13. Properties that are not like `'% Apts.'`.

Name	Location	Rent
Claremont Oaks	South	600
Hillsdale Village	North	700
Oceanside	East	800
Pacific Gardens	East	1200
Pinewood Estates	North	700
Pine Lake Towers	West	650

TIP

Although you might be tempted to liberally use pattern matching in many of your SQL queries, be aware of the impact of doing so. Although a simple select statement, such as `select * from property where name = 'Oceanside'`, will probably use an index (it will if one was made on the name column), your SQL engine will not be able to use any indexes if you use anything other than simple pattern matching. Because SQL databases are usually built around B-trees or B*-trees, there is no efficient way to search if the first character (at least) isn't given. Searching for `% Apts.` in the previous example will most likely invoke a full-table scan, in which all rows of the database are read and compared against the pattern to select those that match. When performance is a consideration, you will probably want to limit yourself to queries in which the first few characters are given, as in `Pine%`.

One problem that can occur in pattern-matching searches is searching for patterns that include the percent and underline characters used as SQL's pattern tokens. For example, if you are searching a table of Java variable names, you might want to search for a variable name that included the underline character. How could you search for all variables that start with `find_me`?

Luckily, SQL allows for the use of escape characters, the way Java uses the backslash character (\) as an escape character. To search for all variables that start with `find_me`, you could use the following SQL:

```
select * from variables where name like 'find$_me%' escape '$'
```

The last part of this statement indicates that the dollar character ($) will function as an escape character for that statement. Anywhere the $ character is used in this statement, it will be ignored and the character following it will be treated as a literal character. In this case, the $ is treated as a single, actual underline character.

Case Sensitivity

Most SQL databases allow you to compare string fields without regard to case by using either the upper or lower keywords. For example, to search for Oceanside without knowing whether it's stored as OCEANSIDE, OceanSide, or Oceanside, you could use either of the following SQL statements:

```
select * from property where upper(name) = 'OCEANSIDE'
```

```
select * from property where lower(name) = 'oceanside'
```

WARNING

In some SQL searches, using the upper and lower commands can cause the database to switch from an indexed search to a full-table scan, causing query responsiveness to slow down dramatically. Consult your database documentation about how to determine whether this problem exists with your RDBMS, or experiment by using a query on a table with many rows.

Handling Duplicate Rows

Occasionally, you might want to prevent an SQL statement from returning duplicate rows. For example, if you want to determine the range of costs for living in an apartment on the north side of town, you could use the following SQL statement:

```
select rent from property where location = "North"
```

If this query is run, it will generate the following result set:

Rent
700
700
750

These results certainly answer the question—apartments in the north side of town rent for between $700 and $750—but it is redundant to return 700 twice when you're determining a range. In SQL, you can suppress duplicate rows by using the `distinct` keyword, as shown below:

```
select distinct rent from property where location = "North"
```

This query will generate the following desired result set:

Rent
700
750

Column Functions

You will frequently need to perform simple calculations for a column across all rows of a result set. For example, you might want to find the average value of a column, its highest or lowest value, or the sum of a column for all rows. SQL makes this type of calculation simple.

The keywords avg, sum, min, and max will select a column's average (mean), sum, minimum value, and maximum value, respectively. If you want to find out how much it would cost to rent an apartment in each building on the north side of town, you could use the following SQL:

```
select sum(rent) from property where location = "North"
```

This will generate the following simple one-row result set:

Sum(Rent)
2150

If, instead, you want to know the average rent on the north side of town, you could use the following:

```
select avg(rent) from property where location = "North"
```

This statement generates the following one-row result set:

Avg(Rent)
716.67

Earlier you queried the database for the highest and lowest rental costs for a location by using the `distinct` keyword; however, even that solution was flawed because all it told you was the prices, not which were the highest and the lowest. By using the SQL `min` and `max` keywords, you can get one step closer to the ideal answer. These keywords will find the minimum and maximum values from a column, as shown in the following statement:

```
select min(rent), max(rent) from property
where location = "North"
```

This statement will generate the result set shown in Table 24.14.

Table 24.14. Minimum and maximum values in the north side of town.

Min(Rent)	Max(Rent)
700	750

TIP

Although `min` and `max` are most frequently used on numeric columns, you can use them on character-type columns. For example, if you need to find the first and last names from the Property table in alphabetical order, use the following statement:

```
select min(name), max(name) from property
```

This will return the following result set:

Min(Name)	Max(Name)
Claremont Oaks	Windsor Apts.

Column Aliases

You can further enhance your attempt to find the highest and lowest rental costs on the north side of town by improving the column labels. Although a result set like that shown in Table 24.14 certainly answers the question posed by the query, it is not as clear as it could be.

With SQL, it is possible to assign aliases to columns to clarify the output. To do so, just list a column alias after the field in the `select` list, as shown in the following:

```
select min(rent) "Cheapest", max(rent) "Most Expensive"
from property where location = "North"
```

This will result as shown in Table 24.15.

Table 24.15. Assign aliases to clarify output.

Cheapest	Most Expensive
700	750

TIP

It is not always necessary to enclose the column label in quotes (`" "`), as shown in the preceding example. If the column label is only one word, the quotes can be omitted. For example, the preceding statement could have been written without quotes:

```
select min(rent) Cheapest, max(rent) "Most Expensive"
from property where location = "North"
```

Sorting

Because SQL is based on the concepts of sets, each of the queries examined so far makes no guarantees about the order in which rows will be returned into a result set. For example, consider the following statement:

```
select name, rent from property where location = "North"
```

This statement will always generate a single set of rows; however, the order in which those rows are returned in the result set, and are then presumably examined by the program, can vary. By default, SQL makes no guarantees about the order in which the rows will be returned, and the rows might be returned as shown in either Table 24.16 or Table 24.17.

Table 24.16. One possible result set.

Name	Rent
Hillsdale Village	700
Pinewood Estates	700
Seaview Apts.	750

Table 24.17. A second possible result set.

Name	Rent
Seaview Apts.	750
Pinewood Estates	700
Hillsdale Village	700

24

In most cases, you want to retrieve results in a defined order, so SQL provides an `order by` clause. If you want to retrieve all properties on the north side of town, you could use the following:

```
select name, rent from property where location = "North"
order by name
```

This will create the result set shown in Table 24.18.

Table 24.18. Retrieve all properties on the north side of town.

Name	Rent
Hillsdale Village	700
Pinewood Estates	700
Seaview Apts.	750

As you can see, the rows are returned in ascending alphabetical order. What if you had wanted to retrieve them in descending order? SQL takes care of this by allowing you to append either `asc` or `desc` after the field name to specify the sort order. The following would retrieve rows in descending order:

```
select name, cost from property where location = "North"
order by name desc
```

As you've seen, you can use SQL to generate calculated columns. The following statement was used earlier to select the name and proposed rent for each apartment:

```
select name, (rent * 1.1) from property
```

Unfortunately, it created a randomly ordered result set. How can you sort this query by proposed rent, given that proposed rent is calculated? As is usually the case with SQL, there are several ways to do this. The most obvious is as follows:

```
select name, (rent * 1.1) from property order by (rent * 1.1)
```

The problem with this statement is that the calculation must be repeated. If it's used in a program, the redundancy increases the likelihood that the two calculations might inadvertently become different over time. With the calculation used twice in the same SQL statement, you would have to remember to make the change twice. This might seem trivial in this example, but you can easily imagine the problems encountered in a lengthy SQL statement.

An alternative to repeating the calculation is using a one-based integer to indicate the column number. For example, the following SQL statement will sort on the second column (the mortgage value):

```
select name, (rent * 1.1) from property order by 2
```

Finally, you can use a column alias and then sort on the alias. This can be done as follows:

```
select name, (rent * 1.1) "Proposed Rent" from property
order by "Proposed Rent"
```

WARNING

> Although the SQL-92 standard still supports specifying a sort column by number, it paves the way for future versions of the standard to remove support for doing so. Because of this, you should always sort on a named column or column alias.

Sorting on one field is a start, but how do you handle the inevitable need to sort on two fields? You can think of a two-field sort (or any n-field sort where *n* is greater than one) as being comprised of a series of tie-breaking sorts. For example, sort on column x; if the values in column x are the same, break the tie by sorting on column y; if the values in column y are the same... and so forth.

Fortunately, SQL supports this by allowing you to create compound order by clauses. As an example, think of how you would write an SQL statement to create the result set shown in Table 24.19.

Table 24.19. Use of a compound order by clause.

Location	Name
West	Pine Lake Towers
West	Pine Lake Apts.
South	Suncreek Apts.
South	Claremont Oaks
North	Seaview Apts.
North	Pinewood Estates
North	Hillsdale Village
East	Windsor Apts.
East	Pinewood Apts.
East	Pacific Gardens
East	Oceanside

Table 24.19 shows all properties sorted in descending alphabetical order, first by location and then by name. This result set can be created with the following SQL statement:

```
select location, name from property order by
location desc, name desc
```

There is no practical limit to the number of columns on which a query can be sorted; however, there is usually limited value in sorting much beyond a second column. One limit imposed by SQL is that in order to sort on a column, you must include that column in the column list of the `select` statement. For example, you could not do the following because the `location` column is not selected:

```
select name from property order by location desc, name desc
```

WARNING

When ordering by multiple columns, you do not always need to specify the `asc` or `desc` keyword for each sort column. By default, columns will sort in ascending order; however, the `asc` and `desc` keywords change the sort order from the point of use until either the end of that SQL statement or `asc` or `desc` is used again. For example, even though ascending order is the default, the following statement will sort both `location` and `name` in descending order:

```
select location, name from property order by
location desc, name
```

If you want to sort `name` in ascending order, `asc` would have to be explicitly appended to this statement. Consider the following SQL statement that performs a three-column ordering:

```
select location, rent, name from property
order by location desc, rent, name asc
```

In this case, because it is explicitly declared, the `location` and `rent` columns will be ordered in descending order and the `name` column will be sorted in ascending order. If a fourth column were added to the end of this `order by` clause and didn't include a sort direction, it would sort in the same order as the `name` column (ascending).

24

Multitable Queries

All the query statements examined so far involve only one table. Although querying a single table can demonstrate the basic syntax of SQL, it does little to show off SQL's power and flexibility. If all the world's database applications consisted of single tables, SQL would probably never have achieved its popularity, and programmers would still be using nothing but record-oriented APIs.

Fortunately, it is not much more difficult to retrieve results from two or more tables than from a single table. As a demonstration of joining two tables, consider the two tables shown in Tables 24.20 and 24.21.

Table 24.20. The Book table.

Title	Author
Moby Dick	Herman Melville
The Sign of Four	Arthur Conan Doyle

Table 24.21. The Character table.

Title	Character
Moby Dick	Queequeg
Moby Dick	Ishmael
The Sign of Four	Sherlock Holmes
The Sign of Four	Dr. Watson

The Book and Character tables are clearly related through the `Title` column. From these two tables, you should be able to construct a query telling you that Sherlock Holmes and Dr. Watson are characters in *The Sign of Four,* and Ishmael and Queequeg are characters in *Moby Dick.* A join operation in SQL allows you to combine two or more tables into a single virtual table by using the familiar `select` statement. An example of joining the Book and Character tables can be seen in the result set shown in Table 24.22, which was created from the following SQL statement:

```
select * from book, character
```

Table 24.22. Simple join of the Book and Character tables.

Title	Author	Title	Character
Moby Dick	Herman Melville	Moby Dick	Queequeg
Moby Dick	Herman Melville	Moby Dick	Ishmael
Moby Dick	Herman Melville	Moby Dick	Sherlock Holmes
Moby Dick	Herman Melville	Moby Dick	Dr. Watson
The Sign of Four	Arthur Conan Doyle	The Sign of Four	Queequeg
The Sign of Four	Arthur Conan Doyle	The Sign of Four	Ishmael
The Sign of Four	Arthur Conan Doyle	The Sign of Four	Sherlock Holmes
The Sign of Four	Arthur Conan Doyle	The Sign of Four	Dr. Watson

24

NEW TERM Although this ability to rewrite literature and suddenly make Sherlock Holmes a major character in *Moby Dick* is interesting, it is clearly not what you intended with this SQL statement. What happened here is that SQL has created the Cartesian product of the two tables and created a virtual table (your result set) containing each row of the first table joined with each row of the second table. What you want is to have rows from the first table joined with rows from the second table only when both rows agree on the title of the book. In SQL, this is known as an equi-join. An *equi-join* makes use of a `where` clause in the `select` statement to ensure that only roles meeting some test of equivalence are joined.

Equi-Joins

As an example of an equi-join, the result set shown in Table 24.23 can be achieved with the following SQL statement:

```
select * from book, character where
book.title = character.title
```

Table 24.23. Equi-join of the Book and Character tables.

Title	Author	Title	Character
Moby Dick	Herman Melville	Moby Dick	Queequeg
Moby Dick	Herman Melville	Moby Dick	Ishmael
The Sign of Four	Arthur Conan Doyle	The Sign of Four	Sherlock Holmes
The Sign of Four	Arthur Conan Doyle	The Sign of Four	Dr. Watson

By forming an equi-join, you have instructed SQL to limit the rows created in the virtual result set table to only those rows meeting the criteria in the `where` clause. Of course, because each table contained a `Title` column, the result set shown in Table 24.23 contains two `Title` columns. You can avoid this problem by explicitly naming columns in the `select` list instead of using the asterisk to select all columns. A first try at solving this problem would be to list each of the column names, as shown in the following SQL statement:

```
select title, author, character from book, character
where book.title = character.title
```

Unfortunately, if you were to execute this statement, you would generate an error message saying something like `title is an ambiguous column name`. This is because a column named `Title` appears in both tables, so you must identify the specific `Title` column you want to access. To do this, use the table name followed by a period, as you do for a class member reference. For columns appearing in only one table, it is not necessary to precede their names with a table name. The following SQL statement will achieve the desired output, as shown in Table 24.24:

```
select book.title, author, character from book, character
where book.title = character.title
```

Table 24.24. Explicit column selection.

Book	Author	Character
Moby Dick	Herman Melville	Queequeg
Moby Dick	Herman Melville	Ishmael
The Sign of Four	Arthur Conan Doyle	Sherlock Holmes
The Sign of Four	Arthur Conan Doyle	Dr. Watson

TIP When joining two or more tables, you can precede the asterisk all-field selection operator with a table name. The asterisk will then be scoped only for that table. For example, the following SQL statement will select all columns from the Book table and only the `Character` column from the Character table:

```
select book.*, character from book, character where
book.title = character.title
```

Comparison Joins

Not all joins must be based on comparing columns in separate tables for equivalence (for example, equi-joins). Any other comparison operator is valid in the `where` clause of a join; you can see this by extending the Book table to include a `Pages` column and a few more books, as shown in Table 24.25. The Character table is also extended to include new rows associated with the new books and appears in Table 24.26.

Table 24.25. The Book table with additional entries.

Title	Author	Pages
Moby Dick	Herman Melville	615
The Sign of Four	Arthur Conan Doyle	47
A Study in Scarlet	Arthur Conan Doyle	76
The Final Problem	Arthur Conan Doyle	11
The Trial	Franz Kafka	229

Table 24.26. The Character table with additional entries.

Title	Character
Moby Dick	Queequeg
Moby Dick	Ishmael
The Sign of Four	Sherlock Holmes
The Sign of Four	Dr. Watson
A Study in Scarlet	Sherlock Holmes
A Study in Scarlet	Dr. Watson
The Final Problem	Sherlock Holmes
The Final Problem	Dr. Watson
The Final Problem	Professor Moriarty
The Trial	Joseph K.

Using these new Book and Character tables, you can generate a query such as the following:

```
select book.title, character from book, character where
book.title = character.title and pages > 40
```

This query will select all characters and any books they appeared in that were more than forty pages long. The results are shown in Table 24.27.

Table 24.27. Characters in books with more than 40 pages.

Title	Character
Moby Dick	Queequeg
Moby Dick	Ishmael
The Sign of Four	Sherlock Holmes
The Sign of Four	Dr. Watson
A Study in Scarlet	Sherlock Holmes
A Study in Scarlet	Dr. Watson

Of course, all the normal syntax of a single-table `select` statement is still available when processing a join. For example, the `distinct` keyword could be used in a join to select the names of all characters who appeared in books by Arthur Conan Doyle, as shown in Listing 24.1.

Listing 24.1. Characters of Arthur Conan Doyle.

```
select distinct character from book, character
where book.title = character.title
and book.author = "Arthur Conan Doyle"
```

This SQL will generate the following result set:

Character
Dr. Watson
Professor Moriarty
Sherlock Holmes

Joining Three or More Tables

Joining three tables is only a little more difficult than joining two, and is achieved by adding to the where clause of the select statement. To demonstrate a three-table join, add a third table that can be joined to the Book and Character tables. By introducing the ReadBy table shown in Table 24.28, your database can now be used to track the books read by students in a literature class.

Table 24.28. The ReadBy table.

Title	Student
Moby Dick	Phoebe
Moby Dick	Alan
Moby Dick	Laura
The Sign of Four	Phoebe
The Sign of Four	Laura
The Sign of Four	Savannah
A Study in Scarlet	Savannah
A Study in Scarlet	Alan
The Final Problem	Robert

If you want to query the database to find out which students have read anything about Sherlock Holmes that was longer than 40 pages, that will involve three tables: the ReadBy table to give the student's name, the Book table to make sure it was longer than 40 pages, and the Character table to see whether Sherlock Holmes appears as a major character. The SQL shown in Listing 24.2 will perform this query and generate the result set shown in Table 24.29.

24

Listing 24.2. Query to see who has read which long stories about Sherlock Holmes.

```
select readby.* from readby, book, character
where readby.title = book.title
and book.title = character.title
and character = 'Sherlock Holmes'
and book.pages > 40
```

Table 24.29. Students and the long stories they've read about Sherlock Holmes.

Title	Student
The Sign of Four	Phoebe
The Sign of Four	Laura
The Sign of Four	Savannah
A Study in Scarlet	Savannah
A Study in Scarlet	Alan

You'll notice from Table 24.28 that Robert read the Sherlock Holmes story *The Final Problem*. However, because this story is only 11 pages long, it was not placed in the result set shown in Table 24.29.

As an additional example of how the various SQL commands you've learned in this chapter can be combined into more powerful queries, you could select just the names of students who've read long Sherlock Holmes stories with the SQL shown in Listing 24.3.

Listing 24.3. Query to see who has read a long story about Sherlock Holmes.

```
select distinct student from readby, book, character
where readby.title = book.title
and book.title = character.title
and character = 'Sherlock Holmes'
and book.pages > 40
```

This query will generate the following result set:

Student
Phoebe
Laura
Savannah
Alan

TIP

> Because a high level of performance is almost always a design require-
> ment of any database project, you must consider the impact of joining
> many tables. Although a well-designed, fully normalized database
> might minimize data dependencies and redundancies, it might also lead
> to queries that join a large number of tables. For most applications, a
> practical guideline is that no more than four or five tables should be
> joined together. Of course, this depends mostly on the allowable query
> time, the size of the individual tables, the particular database manage-
> ment system (DBMS) being used, and the platform (operating system
> and processor) on which the database is running.

Recursive Joins

 NEW TERM   Sometimes you will need to join a table to itself. This is referred to as either a recursive
join or a self join. A *recursive* or *self join* is a join between a table and itself.

Table 24.30 introduces the Programmer table, which contains a list of programmers, their
primary languages, and the names of their team leaders.

Table 24.30. Programmers, their languages, and their team leaders.

Name	Language	Team_Leader
Laura	null	null
Savannah	Java	Laura
Alan	Java	Laura
Jay	Java	null
Mark	Java	Jay
Randy	Java	Jay

How would you go about writing a query that shows every programmer's name, primary
language, team leader's name, and team leader's primary language? One attempt might be
as follows:

```
select name, language, team_leader from programmer
where name = team_leader
```

The problem with this, however, is that it will select only rows into the result set for which
the Name and Team_Leader columns contain the same name. In other words, it will select only
those programmers who are also their own team leaders. In this sample data, this statement
would generate an empty result set.

The key to forming the desired SQL statement is to use table aliases to make it seem as though there are two duplicate copies of the same table: one called *coders* and another called *leaders*. After you know the "trick," this type of query is fairly straightforward, as shown in Listing 24.4. This query acts on named copies of each table and is therefore able to join the Name column of one copy (the *coder* copy) to the Team_Leader column of the other copy (the *leader* copy). The result set created by this query is shown in Table 24.31.

NOTE

> Although it is convenient to think of the database as having made "copies" of a table, the analogy is imperfect. No physical copy of the table is made and there should be no additional runtime performance penalty imposed on a self join, other than what is incurred by all joins.

24

Listing 24.4. Retrieving programmers' and team leaders' languages.

```
select coder.name, coder.language, leader.name,
leader.language "Leader's Language"
from programmer coder, programmer leader
where coder.team_leader = leader.name
```

Table 24.31. Coders and their team leaders' languages.

Name	Language	Team_Leader	Leader's Language
Savannah	Java	Laura	null
Alan	Java	Laura	null
Mark	Java	Jay	Java
Randy	Java	Jay	Java

Grouping Results

It's often useful to look at rows in an input table as a group while considering them for selection into a result set. For example, you might be asked to find the average page length by author for entries in the Book table. You can't do the simple select avg(pages) from book because it will average the page counts across the entire table. Another reasonable approach would be to use the following:

```
select author, avg(pages) from book
```

However, this won't work and is an illegal SQL statement. It is illegal because there will be one value for the avg(pages) column, but there will be multiple rows for the author column (one row in the result set for each row in the input Book table). To solve this dilemma, you have to introduce a new SQL clause. The group by clause instructs an SQL statement to consider subsets of the input table in discrete groups while being considered for selection into the result set. To determine each individual author's total and average page counts, as shown in Table 24.32, use the following SQL statement:

```
select author, sum(pages) Total, avg(pages) Average
from book group by author
```

Table 24.32. Total and average pages by author.

Author	Total	Average
Arthur Conan Doyle	134	44
Herman Melville	615	615
Franz Kafka	229	229

Counting Rows

It is common when grouping records to be interested in the number of records in each group. For example, continuing with the Book database, it would be reasonable to want to know how many students have read each book. The result set that answers this query is shown in Table 24.33, and can be achieved with the count keyword, as follows:

```
select title, count(student) "Count" from readby
group by title
```

Table 24.33. Count of students having read each book.

Title	Count
A Study in Scarlet	2
Moby Dick	3
The Final Problem	1
The Sign of Four	3

NOTE

> Although it is generally not necessary to put column aliases in quotes, it was necessary to do so in the preceding SQL statement because count is an SQL keyword. Any time you want to use a reserved SQL keyword as a column alias, you must enclose it in quotes.

Because the count keyword actually counts the number of rows rather than something specific to the field being counted, the column name given to count is not important. In fact, SQL acknowledges this by allowing a shorthand notation. Rather than specifying a column name, the asterisk can be used by count as follows:

```
select title, count(*) "Count" from readby group by title
```

This will generate the same result set, shown in Table 24.33, as did count(student).

Restricting Groups

A basic group by clause is sufficient when you want to query across all groups. Sometimes, however, you want to include only those groups possessing certain attributes. Continuing with the example of counting the number of students reading each book, how can you formulate a query that will select only those items read by more than one student?

The solution can be found by using the group by clause's optional having parameter. By using having, you can specify that only certain groups will be selected. This can be seen in Listing 24.5, which creates the result set shown in Table 24.34.

Listing 24.5. Selecting popular books.

```
select title, count(*) "Count" from readby
group by title
having count(*) > 1
order by "Count"
```

Table 24.34. Count of students having read popular books.

Title	Count
A Study in Scarlet	2
Moby Dick	3
The Sign of Four	3

Subqueries

NEW TERM Even with everything you've already seen that can be done with an SQL statement, it isn't always enough. Sometimes you need to write a where or having clause that is more specific than what can be done with the normal selection syntax discussed so far. SQL accommodates this by allowing you to effectively concatenate queries so that the result set of a statement is determined by a select statement that depends on the result set of a subsidiary select statement, and so on. These types of SQL statements are known as subqueries. A *subquery* is a query in which one `select` statement is embedded within another `select` statement.

Comparisons

One form of subquery is a *comparison subquery,* in which the result of the main query depends on the result of a subquery using one of the six comparison operators (<, <=, =, >=, >, <>). An example of this can be found in the Book database by querying for authors who have written more than the average number of pages. The SQL to perform this query is shown in Listing 24.6, and the results are shown in Table 24.35.

Listing 24.6. Comparison subquery to select prolific authors.

```
select author, sum(pages) Pages from book
group by author
having sum(pages) >
(select avg(pages) from book)
```

Table 24.35. Prolific authors.

Author	Pages
Franz Kafka	229
Herman Melville	615

This query works by selecting the author and total page counts grouped by author, as shown earlier. This first part of the query creates a virtual result set table with three rows: one each for Kafka, Melville, and Doyle. The subquery then selects which of these three rows will appear in the final result set by removing those rows that do not meet the condition expressed in the subquery. In this case, the Arthur Conan Doyle row is removed because his total page count is less than the average.

Existence

Another type of subquery is based on testing for *existence.* Conceptually, this type of query works by making a preliminary virtual table based on the primary `select` statement and then performing a subquery for each row in that result set. If the subquery doesn't select any rows, the row in the preliminary virtual table is removed. An example of an existence test would be to find all books that have been read. The following SQL can be used to answer this query:

```
select title from book where exists
(select title from readby where readby.title = book.title)
```

24

This query will return a result set as follows:

Title
Moby Dick
The Sign of Four
A Study in Scarlet
The Final Problem

Because the subquery is executed once for each row in the main query, a row will be included in the result set only if the subquery returns a non-null result set. In this case, the subquery is searching the ReadBy table to see whether `book.title` matches the title column for any row in ReadBy. Because no one has read *The Trial*, the subquery for that row is null, and *The Trial* does not appear in the final result set.

Subqueries can be as long and complex as a primary query. Subqueries can even have their own subqueries or `having` clauses. An example of a subquery that uses a `having` clause is shown in Listing 24.7. This query selects all books read by more than two students and generates the following result set:

Title
Moby Dick
The Sign of Four

Listing 24.7. All books with more than two readers.

```
select title from book
where exists
(select count(*) from readby
where readby.title = book.title
having count(*) > 2)
```

TIP

There is also a `not exists` test that can be performed using analogous syntax. To find all books that have not been read, you could use the following:

```
select title from book where not exists
(select title from readby where readby.title = book.title)
```

Using the sample data, only *The Trial* will be selected.

Quantification

NEW TERM Sometimes, with a subquery, you want to compare a value to a column of values in the subquery. For example, you might want to find out whether any book a student has read was longer than 40 pages, or you might want to find out whether all books that a student read were longer than 100 pages. In SQL, these are known as *quantifier tests*. SQL includes predicates for *existential quantification* (does any value exist that satisfies the test?) and *universal quantification* (does every value satisfy the test?).

Existential Quantification

If you want to construct a query that will find all students who have read at least one book longer than 40 pages, it can be done with existential quantification by using the any keyword, as shown in Listing 24.8.

Listing 24.8. Students who've read more than 40 pages.

```
select distinct student from readby
where 40 < any
(select pages from book
where readby.title = book.title)
```

This SQL statement selects students from the ReadBy table and then processes a subquery for each student. The subquery selects the pages column from the Book table. For each student, the subquery will be a result set with a single column (Pages) that has zero or more rows, depending on how many books the student read. The comparison is then made between 40 and each row in the subquery. If, for any row, 40 is less than the pages value, the subquery is satisfied and the row in the primary query is selected. The result set from executing the SQL in Listing 24.8 is as follows:

Student
Alan
Laura
Phoebe
Savannah

Universal Quantification

Universal quantification is very similar to existential quantification, except the subquery is satisfied only if all rows of the subquery pass the comparison test. A good example is shown in Listing 24.9, which queries the database for students who have read only books longer than 100 pages.

24

Listing 24.9. Students who've read only books longer than 100 pages.

```
select distinct student from readby
where 100 < all
(select pages from book
where readby.title = book.title)
```

The only difference between this query and the previous one is that it uses `all` instead of `any`. For this query, all books read by a student must be longer than 100 pages for the student's name to appear in the result set. The results of this query are as follows:

Student
Alan
Laura
Phoebe

Set Membership

A final type of subquery tests for set membership. This type of subquery is done with the `in` predicate. Using the `in` predicate can be seen in an example of a query for all programmers who work for a team leader who knows Java. The result set shown in Table 24.36 is generated from the SQL shown in Listing 24.10.

Listing 24.10. Programmers who work for a leader who knows Java.

```
select * from programmer
where team_leader in
(select name from programmer
where language = 'Java')
```

Table 24.36. Programmers who work for a leader who knows Java.

Name	Language	Team_Leader
Mark	Java	Jay
Randy	Java	Jay

24

Inserting New Data

Even though selecting data with SQL is not particularly difficult, inserting new rows of data is even simpler. The basic syntax of an SQL `insert` statement is as follows:

```
insert into tablename [(columns)] values (constants)
```

For example, to insert a new book into your database, you could do the following:

```
insert into book (title, author, pages)
values ("Goldfinger", "Ian Fleming", 284)
```

This would insert the 284-page book *Goldfinger* by Ian Fleming as a new row in the Book table. Because all columns of the Book table are being added, you could have omitted the column names and instead used the following:

```
insert into book values ("Goldfinger", "Ian Fleming", 284)
```

In this case, the column values are listed in order and all must be given. The following statement will not work:

```
insert into book values ("Goldfinger", 284)
```

If you do not know the value for a specific column, you can use `null` to indicate that no value is available, as follows:

```
insert into book values ("Goldfinger", null, 284)
```

Here you're indicating that you don't know the author of *Goldfinger*.

WARNING

When an SQL database is created, the creator can normally indicate for each column whether it can contain `null` values. If, in the previous example, the database creator had created the author field so that it must store a non-`null` value, the `insert` statement would fail.

In general, it is good practice not to use the default column list and to explicitly list each of the fields for which you're inserting values. This will prevent problems from showing up in your programs later, when someone adds a new column to the table.

Inserting Multiple Rows

Adding data one row at a time gets the job done, but can become labor intensive if you need to insert lots of rows. You can use the multiple-row `insert` statement to solve this problem by selecting rows from a table in the database and inserting them into a (probably different) table. Although it might seem unlikely that you would ever want to do this, you'll find occasions for doing so quite often.

24

As an example, suppose you have created a new table called Bonuses and want to copy into it the names of all programmers who know Java. This can be achieved with the SQL shown in Listing 24.11.

Listing 24.11. Programmers deserving bonuses.

```
insert into bonuses (name)
select name from programmer
where language = 'Java'
```

The Bonuses table after executing this SQL is as follows:

Name
Savannah
Alan
Jay
Mark
Randy

Naturally, a `select` statement used to insert multiple rows can be as complex as you'd like. It can join multiple tables, include test conditions, use groupings, and even contain a subquery.

TIP
A common use of a multiple-row insert is to select rows into a temporary table with a complicated query. The temporary table can then be processed further until you get the final result set.

Updating Data

The `update` statement is used to modify data already in the database. A single `update` statement can modify one or more columns in one or more rows of a table. Each `update` statement includes a `set` clause that identifies the columns to be updated and the values to which each column is to be set. An optional `where` clause can be used to restrict the update so that it acts on a subset of the table. You can write SQL statements that update either one or more specific rows in a table or that update every row in a table.

Updating Specific Rows

As an example of a statement that updates a specific row, suppose you've decided that the 615-page edition of *Moby Dick* is just too long and you are going to use the condensed, 112-page version. To update the database, you could use the following SQL:

```
update book set pages=112 where title="Moby Dick"
```

As a similar example, suppose you realize that the author of the Sherlock Holmes books was Sir Arthur Conan Doyle, not just Arthur Conan Doyle. There are a few ways you could apply this update to your database. The easiest SQL to do this is shown in Listing 24.12.

Listing 24.12. Updating an author's name.

```
update book set author = "Sir Arthur Conan Doyle"
where author = "Arthur Conan Doyle"
```

This statement will quite simply replace every occurrence of `Arthur Conan Doyle` with `Sir Arthur Conan Doyle`. For your database, this is completely correct and would be the most efficient SQL for updating the database. However, suppose the Book table also includes *The White Company* and *Micah Clarke*, as shown in Table 24.37.

Table 24.37. The revised Book table.

Title	Author	Pages
Moby Dick	Herman Melville	615
The Sign of Four	Arthur Conan Doyle	47
A Study in Scarlet	Arthur Conan Doyle	76
The Final Problem	Arthur Conan Doyle	11
The Trial	Franz Kafka	229
The White Company	Arthur Conan Doyle	437
Micah Clarke	Arthur Conan Doyle	512

These last two entries were also written by Doyle but were not Sherlock Holmes adventures. Now, further assume that (for some reason) you want your database to show that Sir Arthur Conan Doyle was the author of the Sherlock Holmes adventures but that Arthur Conan Doyle was the author of *The White Company* and *Micah Clarke*. You know you can't use the approach shown in Listing 24.12 because that will update every occurrence of the author's name. You can, however, solve the problem by using a test of set membership with the `in` keyword, as shown in Listing 24.13.

24

Listing 24.13. Updating the author of specific works.

```
update book set author = "Sir Arthur Conan Doyle"
where title in ("The Sign of Four", "A Study in Scarlet",
"The Final Problem")
```

Although this SQL statement solves the problem, it isn't very general purpose because you've had to hard-code the names of the books to update. It would be easier to maintain if you could just tell the database to update the author column for any book in which Sherlock Holmes is a character. As shown in Listing 24.14, this can be done by using an existential quantification subquery.

Listing 24.14. Updating the author of any book about Sherlock Holmes.

```
update book set author = "Sir Arthur Conan Doyle"
where book.title = any
(select title from book
where 'Sherlock Holmes' in
(select character from character
where character.title = book.title))
```

The SQL statement shown in Listing 24.14 works by updating the author column whenever the primary query's `book.title` column equals any title selected by the subquery. Because the subquery will select only books in which Sherlock Holmes is a character, this achieves your goal.

Updating All Rows

Updating all rows in a table is made simple because no `where` clause is necessary. As an example, if you want to double the rent of all entries in your Property table, you can do so as follows:

```
update property set rent = rent * 2
```

Deleting

Just as it is important to be able to add data to a database, it is also important to be able to delete data. SQL's `delete` statement can be used to delete either specific rows or all rows in a table.

Deleting All Rows

To delete all rows, simply use the following syntax:

```
delete from tablename
```

As an example, if you are starting a new semester and want to remove all entries from the ReadBy table, this can be done as follows:

```
delete from readby
```

After executing this statement, the ReadBy table will be empty and ready for new inserts.

Deleting Specific Rows

In most cases, you will not want to remove all rows from a table, just selected rows. This can be done by attaching a where clause onto a delete statement. For example, suppose you want to delete *The Trial* from the book database because no one has read it. You could do this as follows:

```
delete from book where title = "The Trial"
```

Of course, there might be other books that no one has read and this statement wouldn't delete those. You would have to write a series of similar statements or use a subquery to select books that haven't been read.

Summary

Today's lesson has introduced you to the SQL programming language. You have learned that SQL is a full-featured, database-manipulation language that allows for selecting, inserting, updating, and deleting records from a database. You have started with simple, one-table queries and progressed to performing column calculations, record groupings, and sorts. From there, you have learned how to join multiple tables and perform complicated, real-life selections from them. Combined with its discussion of inserting, updating, and deleting, this lesson provides a solid introduction to SQL.

Q&A

Q I am used to writing database programs with dBASE or one of the variants on that language. Why don't I see functions in SQL to get the next record or the previous record? How do I do this in SQL?

A Unlike dBASE, which is oriented around records, the SQL language is oriented around sets. The SQL select keyword returns a result set that can be interpreted by your programs. In SQL you do not act on a single record at a time, you act on

24

an entire result set. Of course, a result set may contain only a single record. To navigate through a result set, you can use methods such as `RelationView.first` and `RelationView.next`, which were described on Day 21, "Using the dbAWARE Components."

Q If I don't specify an `order by` clause for a `select` statement, in what order are the rows returned?

A This can vary from one database vendor to another, but the rows usually will be returned in the same order in which they were added to the database.

Workshop

The workshop includes quiz questions to help you gauge your understanding of the material in this chapter. The workshop also includes exercises to provide hands-on experience with what you've learned in this chapter. Answers to the quiz questions can be found in Appendix D, "Answers."

Quiz

1. What are SQL's four most common verbs?
2. How would you select only the `name` column from a table named Employee?
3. How would you retrieve these employee names in alphabetical order?
4. How would you retrieve only those employees whose last name is Smith?
5. What will the following code do?

   ```
   select * from book, character where book.title = character.title
   ```

6. What is meant by the terms *existential quantification* and *universal quantification*?

Exercises

1. Using any SQL database product you own (for example, SQL Anywhere if you are using Visual Café Pro), create a database that contains a table named Account with columns for `Name`, `Phone`, and `AccountNumber`. Create a second table named Invoice with columns for `Date`, `Amount`, and `AccountNumber`.

2. Write a series of `insert` statements to create three new accounts. Write `insert` statements to create between zero and five invoices for each account.

3. Write an SQL statement that displays each account and the total amount of its associated invoices. Display this result set in descending order of invoice amount.

4. Write an SQL statement that displays the name of only the account with the highest dollar amount of invoices.

24

5. Write an SQL statement that displays the name of only the account with the greatest number of invoices.

6. Write an SQL statement to double the amount of all invoices that are more than 30 days old.

7. Write an SQL statement to delete all of the invoices for the account that has the fewest number of invoices.

APPENDIX

A

Java Operator Precedence

Table A.1 shows the precedence of the Java operators.

Table A.1. Java operator precedence.

Operator	Operation	Example
++	Increment	a++
--	Decrement	a--
+	Unary plus	+4
-	Unary minus	-4
~	Bitwise logical negation	~a
!	Negation	!a
*	Multiplication	a * b
/	Division	a / b
%	Modulus	a % b
+	Addition	a + b
-	Subtraction	a - b
+	String concatenation	"Hello " + "World"
<<	Left shift	a << b
>>	Right shift	a >> b
>>>	Right shift with zero fill	a >>> b
<	Less than	a < b
<=	Less than or equal to	a <= b
>	Greater than	a > b
>=	Greater than or equal to	a >= b
instanceof	Type comparison	a instanceof b
==	Equality	a == b
!=	Inequality	a != b
&	Bitwise/logical AND	a & b
^	Bitwise/logical XOR	a ^ b
¦	Bitwise/logical OR	a ¦ b
&&	Conditional AND	a && b

Operator	Operation	Example
¦¦	Conditional OR	a ¦¦ b
?:	Conditional	a ? expr1 : expr2
=	Assignment	a = b
*=	Multiply and assign	a *= b
/=	Divide and assign	a /= b
%=	Modulus and assign	a %= b
+=	Add and assign	a += b
-=	Subtract and assign	a -= b
<<=	Left shift and assign	a <<= b
>>=	Right shift and assign	a >>= b
>>>=	Right shift, fill, and assign	a >>>= b
&=	AND and assign	a &= b
^=	XOR and assign	a ^= b
¦=	OR and assign	a ¦= b

APPENDIX B

Java Classes

This appendix includes a complete list of all public classes in the Java Development Kit (JDK) version 1.1. Classes that were introduced in version 1.1 appear in bold.

The `java.acl` Package

Acl

AclEntry

AclNotFoundException

Group

LastOwnerException

NotOwnerException

Owner

Permission

The `java.applet` Package

Applet

AppletContext

AppletStub

AudioClip

The `java.awt` Package

Adjustable

AWTError

AWTEvent

AWTEventMulticaster

AWTException

BorderLayout

Button

Canvas

B

CardLayout

Checkbox

CheckboxGroup

CheckboxMenuItem

Choice

Color

Component

Container

Cursor

Dialog

Dimension

Event

EventQueue

FileDialog

FlowLayout

Font

FontMetrics

Frame

Graphics

GridBagConstraints

GridBagLayout

GridLayout

IllegalComponentStateException

Image

Insets

ItemSelectable

Label

LayoutManager

LayoutManager2

List

MediaTracker

Menu

MenuBar

MenuComponent

MenuContainer

MenuItem

MenuShortcut

Panel

Point

Polygon

PopupMenu

PrintGraphics

PrintJob

Rectangle

Scrollbar

ScrollPane

Shape

SystemColor

TextArea

TextComponent

TextField

Toolkit

Window

The `java.awt.datatransfer` Package

Clipboard

ClipboardOwner

DataFlavor

StringSelection

Transferable

UnsupportedFlavorException

The `java.awt.event` Package

ActionEvent

ActionListener

AdjustmentEvent

AdjustmentListener

ComponentAdapter

ComponentEvent

ComponentListener

ContainerAdapter

ContainerEvent

ContainerListener

FocusAdapter

FocusEvent

FocusListener

InputEvent

ItemEvent

ItemListener

KeyAdapter

KeyEvent

B

KeyListener

MouseAdapter

MouseEvent

MouseListener

MouseMotionAdapter

MouseMotionListener

PaintEvent

TextEvent

TextListener

WindowAdapter

WindowEvent

WindowListener

The `java.awt.image` Package

AreaAveragingScaleFilter

ColorModel

CropImageFilter

DirectColorModel

FilteredImageSource

ImageConsumer

ImageFilter

ImageObserver

ImageProducer

IndexColorModel

MemoryImageSource

PixelGrabber

ReplicateScaleFilter

RGBImageFilter

The `java.beans` Package

BeanDescriptor

BeanInfo

Beans

Customizer

EventSetDescriptor

FeatureDescriptor

IndexedPropertyDescriptor

IntrospectionException

Introspector

MethodDescriptor

ParameterDescriptor

PropertyChangeEvent

PropertyChangeListener

PropertyChangeSupport

PropertyDescriptor

PropertyEditor

PropertyEditorManager

PropertyEditorSupport

PropertyVetoException

SimpleBeanInfo

VetoableChangeListener

VetoableChangeSupport

Visibility

The `java.io` Package

BufferedInputStream

BufferedOutputStream

BufferedReader

BufferedWriter

ByteArrayInputStream

ByteArrayOutputStream

CharArrayReader

CharArrayWriter

CharConversionException

DataInput

DataInputStream

DataOutput

DataOutputStream

EOFException

Externalizable

File

FileDescriptor

FileInputStream

FilenameFilter

FileNotFoundException

FileOutputStream

FileReader

FileWriter

FilterInputStream

FilterOutputStream

FilterReader

FilterWriter

InputStream

InputStreamReader

InterruptedIOException

InvalidClassException

InvalidObjectException

IOException

LineNumberInputStream

LineNumberReader

NotActiveException

NotSerializableException

ObjectInput

ObjectInputStream

ObjectInputValidation

ObjectOutput

ObjectOutputStream

ObjectStreamClass

ObjectStreamException

OptionalDataException

OutputStream

OutputStreamWriter

PipedInputStream

PipedOutputStream

PipedReader

PipedWriter

PrintStream

PrintWriter

PushbackInputStream

PushbackReader

RandomAccessFile

B

Reader

SequenceInputStream

Serializable

StreamCorruptedException

StreamTokenizer

StringBufferInputStream

StringReader

StringWriter

SyncFailedException

UnsupportedEncodingException

UTFDataFormatException

WriteAbortedException

Writer

The `java.lang` Package

AbstractMethodError

ArithmeticException

ArrayIndexOutOfBoundsException

ArrayStoreException

Boolean

Byte

Character

Class

ClassCastException

ClassCircularityError

ClassFormatError

ClassLoader

ClassNotFoundException

Cloneable

CloneNotSupportedException

Compiler

Double

Error

Exception

ExceptionInInitializerError

Float

IllegalAccessError

IllegalAccessException

IllegalArgumentException

IllegalMonitorStateException

IllegalStateException

IllegalThreadStateException

IncompatibleClassChangeError

IndexOutOfBoundsException

InstantiationError

InstantiationException

Integer

InternalError

InterruptedException

LinkageError

Long

Math

NegativeArraySizeException

NoClassDefFoundError

NoSuchFieldError

NoSuchFieldException

B

NoSuchMethodError

NoSuchMethodException

NullPointerException

Number

NumberFormatException

Object

OutOfMemoryError

Process

Runnable

Runtime

RuntimeException

SecurityException

SecurityManager

Short

StackOverflowError

String

StringBuffer

StringIndexOutOfBoundsException

System

Thread

ThreadDeath

ThreadGroup

Throwable

UnknownError

UnsatisfiedLinkError

VerifyError

VirtualMachineError

Void

The `java.lang.reflect` Package

Array

Constructor

Field

InvocationTargetException

Member

Method

Modifier

The `java.math` Package

BigDecimal

BigInteger

The `java.net` Package

BindException

ConnectException

ContentHandler

ContentHandlerFactory

DatagramPacket

DatagramSocket

DatagramSocketImpl

FileNameMap

HttpURLConnection

InetAddress

MalformedURLException

MulticastSocket

NoRouteToHostException

B

ProtocolException

ServerSocket

Socket

SocketException

SocketImpl

SocketImplFactory

UnknownHostException

UnknownServiceException

URL

URLConnection

URLEncoder

URLStreamHandler

URLStreamHandlerFactory

The `java.rmi` Package

AccessException

AlreadyBoundException

ConnectException

ConnectIOException

MarshalException

Naming

NoSuchObjectException

NotBoundException

Remote

RemoteException

RMISecurityException

RMISecurityManager

ServerError

ServerException

ServerRuntimeException

StubNotFoundException

UnexpectedException

UnknownHostException

UnmarshalException

B

The `java.rmi.dgc` Package

dgc.DGC

dgc.Lease

dgc.VMID

The `java.rmi.registry` Package

LocateRegistry

Registry

RegistryHandler

The `java.rmi.server` Package

ExportException

LoaderHandler

LogStream

ObjID

Operation

RemoteCall

RemoteObject

RemoteRef

RemoteServer

RemoteStub

RMIClassLoader

RMIFailureHandler

RMISocketFactory

ServerCloneException

ServerNotActiveException

ServerRef

Skeleton

SkeletonMismatchException

SkeletonNotFoundException

SocketSecurityException

UID

UnicastRemoteObject

Unreferenced

The `java.security` Package

Certificate

DigestException

DigestInputStream

DigestOutputStream

Identity

IdentityScope

InvalidKeyException

InvalidParameterException

Key

KeyException

KeyManagementException

KeyPair

KeyPairGenerator

MessageDigest

NoSuchAlgorithmException

NoSuchProviderException

Principal

PrivateKey

Provider

ProviderException

PublicKey

SecureRandom

Security

Signature

SignatureException

Signer

The `java.security.interfaces` Package

DSAKey

DSAKeyPairGenerator

DSAParams

DSAPrivateKey

DSAPublicKey

The `java.sql` Package

CallableStatement

Connection

DatabaseMetaData

DataTruncation

Date

Driver

DriverManager

DriverPropertyInfo

PreparedStatement

ResultSet

ResultSetMetaData

SQLException

SQLWarning

Statement

Time

Timestamp

Types

The `java.text` Package

BreakIterator

CharacterIterator

ChoiceFormat

CollationElementIterator

CollationKey

Collator

DateFormat

DateFormatSymbols

DecimalFormat

DecimalFormatSymbols

FieldPosition

Format

MessageFormat

NumberFormat

ParseException

ParsePosition

RuleBasedCollator

SimpleDateFormat

StringCharacterIterator

The `java.util` **Package**

BitSet

Calendar

Date

Dictionary

EmptyStackException

Enumeration

EventListener

EventObject

GregorianCalendar

Hashtable

ListResourceBundle

Locale

MissingResourceException

NoSuchElementException

Observable

Observer

Properties

PropertyResourceBundle

Random

ResourceBundle

B

SimpleTimeZone

Stack

StringTokenizer

TimeZone

TooManyListenersException

Vector

The `java.util.zip` Package

Adler32

CheckedInputStream

CheckedOutputStream

Checksum

CRC32

DataFormatException

Deflater

DeflaterOutputStream

GZIPInputStream

GZIPOutputStream

Inflater

InflaterInputStream

ZipEntry

ZipException

ZipFile

ZipInputStream

ZipOutputStream

APPENDIX

C

Java Reserved Words

This appendix provides a definition of each of the Java reserved words. Examples are provided with many definitions.

abstract

This keyword indicates that a class or method is not implemented. An abstract method can be implemented in a subclass. An abstract method cannot also be defined as private, final, or static. For example, an abstract class can be declared as follows:

```
abstract class myClass {
    // ...
}
```

An abstract method can be defined as follows:

```
abstract class MyClass {
    abstract void myMethod(int x, int y);
}
```

boolean

The boolean keyword is used to indicate a Java primitive type that can hold the values true or false. Examples of how to use boolean can be seen in the following method:

```
boolean myMethod(int x, int y, boolean update) {
    boolean returnValue = true;
    if (update == false)
        returnValue = false;
    return returnValue;
}
```

In this example, myMethod is passed a boolean parameter (update), returns a boolean value, and declares a local boolean variable (returnValue).

break

A break statement is used to transfer control to the end of a loop or switch statement. For example, the following illustrates how to use break to exit a loop:

```
for(int i=0; i<10; i++) {
    if (i == 5)
        break;
}
// break will transfer control to here
```

byte

The byte keyword represents an 8-bit signed Java primitive. It can hold values between –128 and 127.

byvalue

This keyword is reserved for future use.

case

The case keyword is used to select alternative code blocks within a switch statement, as shown in the following example:

```
switch(today) {
    case 0:
        System.out.println("Sunday");
        break;
    case 1:
        System.out.println("Monday");
        break;
}
```

In this example, if today is equal to 0, Sunday will be displayed. If today is equal to 1, Monday will be displayed.

cast

This keyword is reserved for future use.

catch

The catch keyword indicates a block of exception-handling code that follows a try statement. If a try…catch block is followed by a finally block, the code in the finally block is always executed. The following example illustrates the interaction of these keywords:

```
public void paint(Graphics g) {
    String [] stringArray = {"A", "Four", "Element", "Array"};

    try {
        for(int i=0;i<5;i++)
            g.drawString(stringArray[i], 10, 30+10*i);
    }
    catch (ArrayIndexOutOfBoundsException e) {
        g.drawString("oops: array too small", 10, 10);
    }
    finally {
        g.drawString("Always executed", 10, 70);
    }
}
```

In this case, the catch block will execute when the exception ArrayIndexOutOfBoundsException is generated. This exception will be generated on the fifth pass through the for loop because there are only four elements in the array in this example.

char

The char keyword represents a 16-bit unicode character.

class

The `class` keyword is used to declare a new type of object. The following example illustrates the creation of a new class named `MyClass` that is based on the `Applet` class.

```
public class MyClass extends Applet {
    private String aString;
    private int xPosition;

    public void init() {
        xPosition = 32;
        aString = "This is a string";
    }

    public void paint(Graphics g) {
        g.drawString(aString, xPosition, 10);
    }
}
```

const

This keyword is reserved for future use.

continue

The `continue` statement is used in a `do`, `for`, or `while` loop to pass control back to the top of the loop. For example, consider the following loop:

```
for(int count=0; count<10; count++) {
    if (count == 3)
        continue;
    System.out.println(String.valueOf(count) + "\r\n");
}
```

When the `continue` statement is encountered, the flow of control will pass back to the top of the loop (skipping the `println` statement) and `count` will be incremented and the next pass through the loop will begin.

A `continue` statement may include an optional label, as in

```
continue there;
```

In this case the program will resume execution at the location specified by the label. This can be seen in the following example:

```
public void paint(Graphics g) {
    int line=1;

    outsideLoop:
    for(int out=0; out<3; out++) {
        g.drawString("out = " + out, 5, line * 20);
        line++;
```

```
    for(int inner=0;inner < 5; inner++) {
        double randNum = Math.random();
        g.drawString(Double.toString(randNum), 15, line*20);
        line++;
        if (randNum < .60)
            continue outsideLoop;
    }
  }
}
```

In this case, the outer loop will execute three times and the inner loop will execute five times. However, if a random number is less than 0.60, a `continue` statement will exit the inner loop and revert control to the outer loop. This will cause the inner loop to execute possibly fewer than five times.

default

The `default` keyword is used to indicate a block of code to execute in a `switch` statement if no other block is matched by a `case` statement. This can be seen in the following example:

```
switch(x) {
    case 0:
        System.out.println("Sunday");
        break;
    case 6:
        System.out.println("Saturday");
        break;
    default:
        System.out.println("Weekday");
        break;
}
```

do

The `do` keyword is used to initiate a `do...while` loop, the syntax of which is as follows:

```
do {
    statement
} while (booleanExpression);
```

This is illustrated by the following example:

```
do {
    System.out.println("Hello\r\n");
} while (count++ < 5);
```

double

The `double` keyword represents a 64-bit floating-point number.

else

The `else` keyword can be optionally used following an `if` statement to provide code that will execute whenever the `if` statement evaluates to `false`. This can be seen in the following example:

```
int x = AskUserForANumber();

if (x < 10)
    System.out.println("Number is less than 10.");
else
    System.out.println("Number is greater than 10.");
```

extends

The `extends` keyword is used to indicate that a class or interface is a subclass of another class. This can be seen in the following examples:

```
public class MyClass extends Applet {
    // class definition goes here
}
public interface MyInterface extends Observable {
    // interface definition goes here
}
```

final

The `final` keyword is an access modifier that can be used with variables, methods, and classes. When applied to a variable, `final` indicates that the variable holds a constant value. When applied to a method, `final` indicates that the method may not be overridden. When applied to a class, `final` indicates that the class may not be subclassed. These uses can all be seen in the following example:

```
public final class MyClass {
    public final int SECRET_CODE = 1234;
    public final boolean compareCode(int code) {
        return (code == SECRET_CODE);
    }
}
```

finally

The `finally` keyword indicates a block of code that will always execute regardless of any exceptions thrown or caught in the preceding try...catch block. The following example illustrates this:

```
public void paint(Graphics g) {
    String [] stringArray = {"A", "Four", "Element", "Array"};

    try {
        for(int i=0;i<5;i++)
            g.drawString(stringArray[i], 10, 30+10*i);
    }
    catch (ArrayIndexOutOfBoundsException e) {
        g.drawString("oops: array too small", 10, 10);
    }
    finally {
        g.drawString("Always executed", 10, 70);
    }
}
```

float

The float keyword represents a 32-bit floating-point number.

for

The for keyword is used to create a loop. The first line of a for loop enables you to specify a starting value for a loop counter, specify the test condition that will exit the loop, and indicate how the loop counter should be incremented after each pass through the loop, as shown in the following example:

```
for (int count=0; count<100; count++) {
    YourMethod(count);
    System.out.println("Count = " + count);
}
```

future

This keyword is reserved for future use.

generic

This keyword is reserved for future use.

goto

This keyword is reserved for future use.

if

A Java if statement is a test of any Boolean expression. If the Boolean expression evaluates to true, the statement following the if is executed. On the other hand, if the Boolean expression evaluates to false, the statement following the if is not executed. For example, consider the following code fragment:

```
int x = AskUserForANumber();

if (x < 10)
    System.out.println("Number is less than 10.");
```

The if statement can be combined with an else statement that will execute whenever the if statement evaluates to false, as shown in the following example:

```
int x = AskUserForANumber();

if (x < 10)
    System.out.println("Number is less than 10.");
else
    System.out.println("Number is greater than 10.");
```

implements

The implements keyword is used to indicate that a class implements one or more interfaces, as shown in the following example:

```
class Watch implements Clock  {
    // class definition goes here
}

class HotDog implements Furnace, Canine  {
    // class definition goes here
}
```

import

The import keyword is used to make the code of a Java class more readable by allowing it to reference other classes without fully specifying the class name. The following examples illustrate the most common uses of import:

```
import java.util.*;

import java.util.Date;
```

In the first example, all classes in the package java.util will be available within the class file that contains this statement. In the second example, only the class java.util.Date can be used without fully qualifying the class name.

inner

This keyword is reserved for future use.

instanceof

The instanceof keyword is a Java operator that can be used to determine whether an object is a subclass of a specific class or whether the object implements a specific interface. This is illustrated in the following example:

```
interface Barker {
    // interface definition goes here
}

class Dog {
    // class definition goes here
}

class BassettHound extends Dog implements Barker {
    // class definition goes here
}

public class Program {
    public void main(String[] args) {
        BassetHound cleo = new BassettHound();
```

```
            if(cleo instanceof BassettHound)
                // true if Cleo is a bassett hound
            if(cleo instanceof Dog)
                // true if Cleo is a dog
            if(cleo instanceof Barker)
                // true if Cleo barks
        }
    }
```

int

The int keyword represents a 32-bit signed number that can hold a value between −2,147,483,648 and 2,147,483,647.

interface

The interface keyword is used to define a Java interface. An interface is an entirely abstract class. A class may implement an interface by providing method bodies for the interface's methods. The following example illustrates an interface definition and two classes that implement the interface:

```
interface Clock {
    public String GetTime(int hour);
}

class Cuckoo implements Clock  {
    public String GetTime(int hour) {
        StringBuffer str = new StringBuffer();
        for (int i=0; i < hour; i++)
            str.append("Cuckoo ");
        return str.toString();
    }
}

class Watch implements Clock  {
    public String GetTime(int hour) {
        return new String("It is " + hour + ":00");
    }
}
```

long

The long keyword represents a 64-bit signed number that can hold a value between −9,223,372,036,854,775,808 and 9,223,372,036,854,775,807.

native

The native keyword is used to indicate that a method is implemented in a different language (such as C). When a native method is declared in a class, a semicolon is used instead of a method body. As an example, consider the following:

```
public class NativeHello {
    public native void sayHello();
```

```
        public int foo() {
            return 23;
        }
    }
```

The native method sayHello is terminated with a semicolon (unlike the non-native method foo, for which a method body is defined).

new

The new keyword is used to construct new objects. It can be used to create an individual object or an array of objects, as shown in the following examples:

```
Date date = new Date();

MyObject myObject = new MyObject(42, "Hello");

int intArray[] = new int[100];

double [][] doubleArray = new double[10][10];
```

null

This value is used to indicate that an object does not reference anything. It is frequently used in equivalence tests, as shown in this example:

```
if(currentItem == null)
    SelectAnItem();
```

operator

This keyword is reserved for future use.

outer

This keyword is reserved for future use.

package

The package keyword is used to place a class into a Java package. A *package* is a collection of classes that are combined for ease of reference and use. A package is made accessible to a file by the use of the import keyword. If a package statement is used, it must be the first statement in a file. The following example creates a package named mystuff.ui:

```
package mystuff.ui;
```

private

The private keyword is used to make a member method or variable accessible only within the class in which it is declared.

protected

The protected keyword is used to make a member method or variable accessible only to the following classes:

- [ ] The class in which it is declared
- [ ] Any subclasses of that class
- [ ] Throughout the package in which the class is located

public

The public keyword can be applied to classes, interfaces, methods, and variables. If a class or interface is public, it is accessible throughout the program. A public method or variable is accessible anywhere the class is accessible.

rest

This keyword is reserved for future use.

return

The return keyword is used to pass flow control back to the calling method. The following examples illustrate the use of return:

```
void foo() {
    // do something
    return;
}
int doubleIt(int x) {
    return (x * 2);
}
```

short

The short keyword represents a 16-bit signed number that can hold a value between –32,768 and 32,767.

static

The static keyword can be applied to member methods or variables. A static variable exists once for all instances of a class. A static method may be invoked without using an instance of the class.

super

The keyword super, like this, refers to the object for which a method was invoked. However, super refers to the immediate superclass of the object.

switch

The switch keyword is used to begin a body of code that selects among alternatives and executes code within either a specific case or a default block. This can be seen in the following example:

```
switch(x) {
    case 0:
        System.out.println("Sunday");
        break;
    case 6:
        System.out.println("Saturday");
        break;
    default:
        System.out.println("Weekday");
        break;
}
```

synchronized

The synchronized keyword can be applied to methods or used to indicate critical sections of code whose execution cannot be interrupted. These uses are illustrated in the following example:

```
class MyClass {
    synchronized void method1() {
        // all code in this method is synchronized
    }

    void method2() {
        // this code is not synchronized
        synchronized (this) {
            // this code IS synchronized
        }
        // this code is not synchronized
    }
}
```

this

The keyword this refers to the object for which a method was invoked. This can be seen in the following example:

```
class MyClass {
    int myVariable;
    public MyClass(int myVariable) {
        this.myVariable = myVariable;
    }
}
```

throw

The throw keyword is used to generate an exception and to pass control flow to the closest catch statement. The following example throws the exception NullPointerException if a variable is equal to null:

```
if(a == null)
    throw new NullPointerException("missing argument");
```

throws

The throws keyword is used to specify any exceptions that may be thrown by a method. This can be seen in the following example:

```
public compare(Object a, Object b) throws NullPointerException {
    // method body goes here
}
```

transient

The transient keyword is used to indicate that a class member variable does not represent part of an object's persistent state. Although this keyword can be used in Java code, it is currently ignored. Presumably, support for transient will be added in a future version of Java and transient member variables will not be written to persistent storage (such as a database).

try

The try keyword is used to begin a block of code that may generate an exception you wish to handle. Exceptions can be caught by using the catch keyword. Code in a finally block is always executed, regardless of any exceptions that are thrown. The following example illustrates the interaction of these keywords:

```
public void paint(Graphics g) {
    String [] stringArray = {"A", "Four", "Element", "Array"};

    try {
        for(int i=0;i<5;i++)
            g.drawString(stringArray[i], 10, 30+10*i);
    }
    catch (ArrayIndexOutOfBoundsException e) {
        g.drawString("oops: array too small", 10, 10);
    }
    finally {
        g.drawString("Always executed", 10, 70);
    }
}
```

var

This keyword is reserved for future use.

void

The void keyword is used to indicate that a method has no return value. For example, the signature of Component.paint is as follows:

```
public void Paint(Graphics g);
```

volatile

The volatile keyword is used to inform the compiler that the variable may change asynchronously and that its value should be read from and written to memory each time it is used.

while

The while keyword is used to initiate a while loop or to evaluate a do...while loop. If the Boolean expression within the while statement evaluates to true, the loop continues. If it evaluates to false, the loop terminates. The following two loops are functionally equivalent:

```
int count = 0;
do {
    System.out.println("Hello\r\n");
} while (++count < 5);

count = 0;
while (count++ < 5)
    System.out.println("Hello\r\n");
```

APPENDIX

D

Answers

This appendix includes the answers to all the quiz questions from each day.

Quiz Answers for Day 1, "A Java Language Refresher"

1. A package is a collection of classes grouped together for ease of reference and use.

2. A public member is visible to other classes. A protected member is visible only within its class, its subclasses, and its package. A private member is visible only within its class.

3. Java's eight primitive types are `byte`, `short`, `int`, `long`, `float`, `double`, `char`, and `boolean`.

4. There are 4 bytes (32 bits) in a Java `int` and 8 bytes (64 bits) in a `long`.

5. An example of a widening conversion is from `int` to `long`, `float`, or `double`. For more examples, refer to Table 1.7.

6. `NaN` stands for "Not a Number" and is used to represent numbers that do not fit within the scale ranging from negative infinity to positive infinity.

7. Because no explicit superclass is given for `MyClass`, its immediate superclass is `Object`.

8. A class refers to itself with `this`.

9. A class can have only one immediate superclass.

10. A class can have an unlimited number of superclasses but has only one immediate superclass.

11. A class can implement as many interfaces as desired.

12. A class that is declared as `final` cannot serve as a superclass for another class.

13. The Java keywords `try`, `catch`, and `finally` support exception handling.

Quiz Answers for Day 2, "Getting Started with Visual Café"

1. You can invoke the Interaction wizard by selecting it from a context menu for a component in the Form Designer or by clicking the Interaction Wizard button on the toolbar and dragging a line between two components.

2. Invoking the Interaction wizard by dragging a line from one component to another tells the Interaction wizard which two components are involved in the interaction.

On the other hand, selecting Add Interaction from a component's context menu is sometimes more convenient because the Interaction wizard can be started without moving the mouse pointer back and forth over the desktop.

3. An easy way to write event-handling methods is to use the Objects list and the Events/Methods list in a source-code window.

4. Components can be dragged from the Component palette and dropped onto the Form Designer.

5. Setting values in the Property List will cause Visual Café to generate code that corresponds to your actions in the Property List.

6. To create the Hello World applet, you created a new applet, optionally changed the name of the applet in the Property List, dragged a `TextField` component onto the Form Designer, and set the `Text` property of the text field to `Hello World`.

7. The source code tags you saw in this chapter include `INIT_CONTROLS`, `DECLARE_CONTROLS`, `CONNECTION`, `INIT_MENUS`, and `DECLARE_MENUS`.

8. There is no reason not to edit the source code in tagged sections. However, after you do so, you might need to reparse the file by selecting Parse All from the Project menu.

Quiz Answers for Day 3, "Programming Applets and Handling Events"

1. The `init` method is called when the applet is loaded; the `start` method is called each time the user loads the host Web page.

2. The `stop` method is called each time the user leaves the host Web page; the `destroy` method is called when the browser closes the applet.

3. The `init`, `destroy`, `start`, and `stop` methods will be called in the following order: `init`, `start`, `stop`, `destroy`.

4. A low-level event corresponds to a low-level, user-interface action or to system events such as a mouse move, mouse click, or key press. A semantic event is generated as a result of a higher-level event such as a mouse click over a specific button or movement of a scrollbar.

5. Adapter classes are useful when you do not need to write a method body for each method required by a semantic event listener's interface.

6. The `code` attribute indicates the name of a class file to run. The `codebase` attribute can be used to specify the directory in which the class can be found.

7. One advantage of using inner classes is that they allow you to separate a class's event-handling code from its logic.

Quiz Answers for Day 4, "Java Strings"

1. To select three characters starting with the tenth character in a string, use `substring(9, 12)`.

2. The `String.equalTo` method returns `true` if the strings are equal or `false` if they are not. The `String.compareTo` method returns an integer value indicating any difference between the strings.

3. To compare an object of an unknown type to a string without using `toString` on the unknown object, use the `String.quals(Object)` method.

4. To search a string for the first occurrence of a given character, use `indexOf`. To search for the last occurrence, use `lastIndexOf`.

5. You should use a `StringBuffer` object instead of a `String` object when you expect to change the contents of the object.

6. The length of a string buffer is based on its current contents; the capacity of a string buffer is the amount of text that could be stored in the currently allocated space. A string buffer's capacity will always equal or exceed its length.

7. When text is appended to a `StringBuffer` object, it is added to the end of the string. Text can be placed in the middle of a string buffer with `insert`.

Quiz Answers for Day 5, "Using the Abstract Windowing Toolkit"

1. The Java idea of a *toolkit* is a way of encapsulating platform-specific aspects of a user interface. A *peer* is a platform-specific representation of an AWT user-interface component.

2. A text field is only one row tall; a text area can contain multiple rows.

3. The `TextComponent` class serves as the superclass for both `TextField` and `TextArea`.

4. To right-justify a label, specify `Label.RIGHT` in the constructor or in a subsequent call to `setAlignment`.

5. *Radio button* is another name for a grouped checkbox.

6. When creating a radio button instead of a checkbox, you must remember to assign the radio button to a checkbox group. This can be done in the Property List, in the `Checkbox` constructor, or with a call to `setCheckboxGroup`.

7. Only one item at a time can be selected in a `Choice` object.

8. Normally, only one item can be selected at a time in a List object. However, if the List is a multiple-selection list, there is no limit to the number of simultaneous selections.

9. In the Scrollbar class, the page-increment value indicates the amount by which the value of the scrollbar will change when moved forward or back one page.

Quiz Answers for Day 6, "Debugging, Customizing, and Managing Projects"

1. There are three ways you can examine the value of a variable in the debugger: by adding it to the Watch window, examining it in the Variables window, or positioning the mouse pointer over the variable.

2. You can use the Call Stack window to determine the order in which methods have been called.

3. A conditional breakpoint is a line of code that will stop the execution of the debugger if a specified condition is true.

4. If you have finished debugging a method and wish to return to the calling method, you should step out of the current method.

5. Visual Café loads the Debug workspace when the debugger is started so that you can work with the most useful set of windows at the appropriate points in the development cycle. The Debug workspace includes breakpoint and watch windows that would not be useful while writing code but are useful while debugging it.

6. Visual Café *does* allow you to configure the Component palette.

7. You can tailor Visual Café's toolbars to your working style by dragging them to any position on the desktop. Additionally, you can right-click to use a toolbar's context menu to disable the toolbar.

8. You can create a new class by selecting Class from the Insert menu or you can do so visually in the Hierarchy editor.

Quiz Answers for Day 7, "The Form Designer, Layout Managers, and Panels"

1. Component is a superclass of Container.

2. The five layout managers are FlowLayout, BorderLayout, CardLayout, GridLayout, and GridBagLayout.

3. The FlowLayout manager continues to place components on the current line until it runs out of room. It then starts placing components on the next line.

4. Components on a BorderLayout can be placed in the north, south, east, west, and center.

5. If all components on a form using GridBagLayout have Weight X and Weight Y values of 0, the components will cluster toward the center of the form.

6. The four values that can be used for the Fill property of a GridBagLayout are VERTICAL, HORIZONTAL, BOTH, and NONE. VERTICAL causes the component to expand vertically to fill the allotted space. HORIZONTAL does the same horizontally. BOTH causes the component to expand in both directions, and NONE leaves the component's size unchanged.

7. The subpanels of a splitter panel should be designed to the side of the splitter panel in the Form Designer so that you can visually design them. After they have been laid out in the Form Designer, they are moved at runtime from the form to the splitter panel.

Quiz Answers for Day 8, "Using the Object Library"

1. The alignment styles that can be used with WrappingLabel are ALIGN_LEFT, ALIGN_RIGHT, and ALIGN_CENTERED.

2. The bevel styles that can be used with Label3D are BEVEL_NONE, BEVEL_LINE, BEVEL_LOWERED, BEVEL_RAISED.

3. The items in a TreeView component are commonly referred to as *nodes*. A *visible node* is one that can be seen on the screen at the present time. A *viewable* node is one whose parent has been expanded so that the node will be visible if the user scrolls appropriately within the TreeView. A node can be viewable but not visible. A node cannot be visible but not viewable.

4. The setTreeStructure method can be used to load an initial set of nodes into a TreeView object.

5. A TreeView object can have as many root nodes as necessary.

6. The HTML link components are used within an applet to load a different HTML page.

7. A ComboBox component is the combination of the TextField and List components.

8. There are 1,000 milliseconds in a second.

9. When used as mask characters, a 9 allows any digit, a + allows the addition (+) or subtraction (–) signs, and a – allows anything allowed by 9 or +.

Quiz Answers for Day 9, "More Object Library Components"

1. The setHeading method of MultiList considers the first column to be 1. Other methods consider it to be column 0.

2. LabelButton improves upon Button by supporting multiple border styles and by optionally generating events for the duration the button is depressed.

3. The setNotifyWhilePressed allows a component to continue receiving events while the mouse button is depressed.

4. If the statement setNotifyWhilePressed(true) has been executed, a component will receive continuous events at the frequency set by a call to setNotifyDelay.

5. Both the MultiList and ImageListBox components allow multiple selection.

6. When a spinner reaches its maximum value, it can either stop or wrap to its minimum value.

7. A two-state StateCheckBox is either checked or unchecked. A three-state StateCheckBox adds a default state.

Quiz Answers for Day 10, "Windows, Frames, and Dialogs"

1. Figure D.1 shows the correct inheritance hierarchy for Frame, Container, Window, and Dialog.

2. The dispose method is used to release the resources in use by a window, frame, or dialog.

3. You are unlikely to directly use the Window class because windows do not include borders or a title bar. The Frame and Dialog classes are used much more frequently.

4. Before constructing a Dialog, you must have a frame that can be passed as a parameter to the dialog.

5. A modal dialog requires user input before allowing the user to interact with other parts of the program. A modeless dialog is simply another window on the screen that the user can ignore.

6. The FileDialog class can never be used in an applet due to Java security restrictions.

7. Visual Café provides four canned dialogs: AboutDialog, AttentionDialog, PasswordDialog, and ProgressDialog.

8. By default, nothing happens when the OK button on an `AttentionDialog` is clicked. You must code specific behavior for this button yourself.

Figure D.1.

Correct inheritance hierarchy for `Container`, `Window`, `Dialog`, *and* `Frame`.

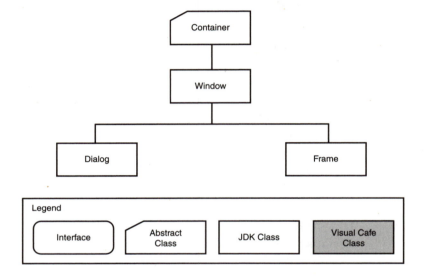

Quiz Answers for Day 11, "Menus and Toolbars"

1. See Figure D.2.

2. A menu can be attached to any class that implements the `MenuContainer` interface. `Frame` is the only provided class that implements this interface.

3. Both `getState` and `setState` are available in `CheckboxMenuItem` but not in `MenuItem`.

4. Create a submenu in the Menu editor by right-clicking a menu item and selecting Create Submenu from the context menu.

5. There is no maximum depth to which you can nest submenus.

6. `ToolBarPanel` and `ToolBarSpacer` are provided with Visual Café specifically for creating a toolbar.

7. You might want to use a toolbar instead of a menu if you need to present a very limited number of options, if you want to include nonbutton components such as choice fields, or if you are working with an applet and do not want to create a frame. Additionally, you might want to use a toolbar in addition to a menu to provide your user with multiple ways to perform an action.

Figure D.2.

The components of a Java menu system.

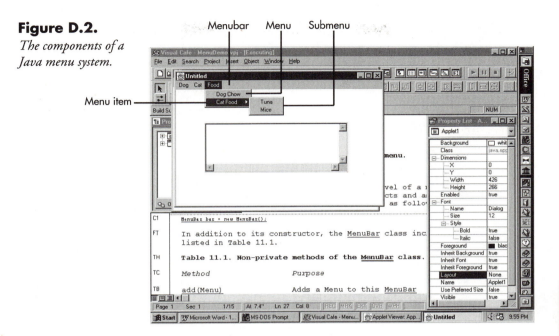

Quiz Answers for Day 12, "The Java Utility Classes"

1. The `milliseconds` parameter of `Date(long milliseconds)` represents the number of milliseconds since January 1, 1970.

2. In the `Date` class, months are numbered from 0–11, but days are numbered from 1–31.

3. The `contains` method searches a `Hashtable` object's elements; `containsKey` searches its keys.

4. The difference between `Hashtable` and `Properties` is that `Properties` can be read from and written to a stream.

5. If you use the same seed value to create two random number generators, each of the random number generators will generate the same sequence of numbers.

6. The `update` method for a class implementing the `Observer` interface is called whenever the object being observed executes the `notifyObservers` method.

7. `Stack` is a subclass of `Vector`. Within a stack you can access or remove only the most recently added element. Any element of a vector can be accessed at any time.

8. The methods `nextElement` and `nextToken` of `StringTokenizer` are identical, differing in name only.

Quiz Answers for Day 13, "Using Streams for Input and Output"

1. Because it is an abstract class, you would not create a new `InputStream` object at runtime.

2. The integer parameter passed to `InputStream.mark(int)` indicates the read ahead limit.

3. Blocking means that a method will suspend execution of its thread until some condition is met (for example, the desired bytes are read).

4. Both `InputStream` and `Reader` are abstract classes that are superclasses for the Java input stream hierarchies. Their chief difference is that `InputStream` is for byte streams and `Reader` is for character streams.

5. An example of chaining the `FileInputStream` and `BufferedInputStream` constructors is as follows:

```
BufferedInputStream bis = new BufferedInputStream(
        new FileInputStream("BufferedInputDemo.java"));
```

6. `PushbackReader` allows you to unread characters.

7. For a class to be streamable, it must implement the `Serializable` interface. It must also provide bodies for the `writeObject` and `readObject` methods.

8. When `defaultWriteObject` is used, all nonstatic, nontransient member variables are written to the stream.

Quiz Answers for Day 14, "Multithreading"

1. You can add support for threads to a class by making it a subclass of `Thread` or by implementing the `Runnable` interface.

2. Before a new thread instance will run, you must call `start`.

3. To stop a thread for a specified number of milliseconds, use `sleep`. You can use `suspend` to stop a thread until `resume` is called. Finally, `yield` temporarily stops a thread so that other threads have a chance to execute.

4. `Thread.MIN_PRIORITY` is defined as 1, `Thread.NORM_PRIORITY` is defined as 5, and `Thread.MAX_PRIORITY` is defined as 10.

5. When `synchronized` is used to synchronize a block of code, the object reference enclosed in parentheses indicates the object that will be locked while the synchronized block runs.

6. No object reference is specified when synchronizing an entire method. The method's object will be used for synchronization.

7. The only method that must be overridden for a class to implement the `Runnable` interface is `run`.

Quiz Answers for Day 15, "Client/Server Programming with Sockets"

1. There is no theoretical maximum number of clients that can be supported by a server. However, the practical limit will depend on the server and the computer on which it is run.

2. The `accept` method of `ServerSocket` is a blocking method and will wait until a client connects to the server.

3. The `accept` method blocks until a client connects. Any code after this will not be executed until a client connects.

4. The value `127.0.0.1` can be used as the hostname in Telnet to specify that the host is the same computer running Telnet.

5. The member method of `Socket` that can be used to return the input stream of the socket is `getInputStream`.

6. Line 76 in Listing 15.6 cannot be replaced with a simple test for equality, such as `if (currentValue == winners[i])`, because that test will evaluate correctly when a player wins with only three moves. Because the value of the current board is calculated based on all cells filled by a shape, the current value of the board will equal a winning value only when no extra moves have been made.

Quiz Answers for Day 16, "Working with Graphics"

1. The seven shapes that can be drawn by the `Graphics` class are line, rectangle, rounded rectangle, 3D rectangle, polygon, arc, and oval.

2. The difference between `drawRect` and `fillRect` is that `fillRect` paints a solid shape while `drawRect` paints only the outline of the shape.

3. The `Graphics` class does not include a `drawCircle` method because you can use `drawOval`, passing it the same value for the width and height of the oval.

4. The main advantage of using the `Canvas` class is that doing so allows you to paint on a screen that also uses layout managers to place its components.

5. You can use the `CropImageFilter` class to display only a portion of an image.

6. When you create your own filter by extending `RGBImageFilter`, the method `public int filterRGB(int x, int y, int rgb)` is called once for every pixel in the image. It returns the desired color to use for the pixel.

7. You do not need to do anything for a subclass of `Applet` to implement the `ImageObserver` interface. Because `Applet` is a subclass of `Component`, `ImageObserver` is already implemented.

Quiz Answers for Day 17, "Multimedia Programming"

1. To control the image displayed in a slide show, you might use `nextImage`, `previousImage`, or `setImage`.

2. If `myAnimation.setClearFrame(false)` is executed before the animation is run, the images in the animation will be drawn on top of each other.

3. `MovingAnimation` enhances `Animator` by allowing each successive image to be drawn in a different location to give the appearance of movement.

4. The `Animator`, `Firework`, `Plasma`, and `NervousText` components all extend `Canvas` and implement the `Runnable` interface.

5. When a sound player is in synchronized mode, it will play all of its sounds in sequence rather than simultaneously.

6. The `SoundPlayer` class supports only Sun's AU format.

7. The `MediaTracker.waitForAll` starts the process of loading all images registered with the `MediaTracker` object and then waits until all images have been loaded or had an error occur.

Quiz Answers for Day 18, "Java Beans"

1. A bean that is added to the Component Library by using Insert | Component from the main menu will be immediately available for use and can be removed from the Component Library. A bean whose JAR file is placed in the bin/components directory will only become available when Visual Café is restarted.

2. A JAR file is a "Java Archive" and is used to collect all of the associated files for one or more beans into a single file.

3. The `setValue` method of the `PropertyDescriptor` class is used to restrict a property to an enumerated set of values.

4. To create a custom event, you will typically create a subclass of `EventObject`. To create a custom event listener, you will typically create a new interface that is a subclass of `EventListener`.

5. If a class needs to listen for veotable property change events it must implement the `VetoableChangeListener` interface.

6. A bound property will send an event to any registered listeners whenever its value is changed. A constrained property will send an event to any registered listeners whenever an attempt is made to change the property's value. The listeners have the option of vetoing, or canceling, the proposed change.

Quiz Answers for Day 19, "Adding Native Methods"

1. To create the header file that gets included in C or C++ native method implementation source files, run the javah program.

2. The `System.loadLibrary` method loads the dynamically linked library (under Windows) or shared library (under Solaris) that contains a native method implementation.

3. When naming a native language function that implements a native method, Java uses the following naming convention:

   `Java[_PackageName][_ClassName][_MethodName]`

4. A native method is always passed `JNIENV *` and `jobject`. The first is a pointer to the JNI environment and the second is a reference to the object that is invoking the native method.

5. If a native method uses `GetStringUTFChars` to get a string, it must eventually call `ReleaseStringUTFChars` to release the memory allocated for the string.

6. The three basic steps involved in calling a Java method from within a native method are as follows:

   1. Use `GetObjectClass` to retrieve the Java class object for the object that contains the method.

   2. Use `GetMethodID` to find the desired method within the class.

   3. Invoke the method with one of the methods such as `CallVoidMethod`, `CallDoubleMethod`, or `CallBooleanMethod`.

7. Use one of the `Release<Type>ArrayElements` methods to tell the Java Virtual Machine that a native method is finished with an array that was locked in place by a call to one of the `Get<Type>ArrayElements` methods.

8. Only one object can be retrieved from an array at a time.

9. A native method *can* throw an exception that will be caught in Java code.

Quiz Answers for Day 20, "The Visual Café Database Tools"

1. A self-hosted architecture is one in which a component that could be distributed across a network is instead located on the local machine. Both dbANYWHERE and SQL Anywhere can be self-hosted.

2. dbANYWHERE supports Oracle, Sybase, Sybase SQL Anywhere, Microsoft SQL Server, Microsoft Access, and any ODBC data source.

3. The dbAware project wizard is used to create a new project based on a database table of your own design. The dbAware template wizard creates a project and adds a predesigned table to its data source.

4. To create a new database with visual tools in SQL Anywhere, use SQL Central.

5. To easily add database support to an existing project, use the Add Table wizard, which can be selected from Visual Café's Insert menu.

6. The ISQL program, which is provided with SQL Anywhere, is useful for executing or testing SQL statements in an interactive environment.

7. You can find out what columns are in a table in a database without leaving Visual Café by using the dbNAVIGATOR.

8. You can activate the dbNAVIGATOR window by selecting it from the Window menu in Visual Café.

Quiz Answers for Day 21, "Using the dbAWARE Components"

1. The three dbAWARE nonvisual components are `Session`, `ConnectionInfo`, and `RelationView`.

2. You can create a new `RelationView` object by using `Request.ExecuteRequest`.

3. A `ConnectionInfo` component connects to a data source (database).

4. *Projection* is a more technical term for a column in a database table.

5. A `RecordStateLabel` component can be used to display the state of the current record (existing, modified, deleted, and so on). A `RecordNumberLabel` displays the current record's sequence within the view.

6. There are many additional examples of master-detail relationships (for example, an invoice and the line items on it, a doctor and his patients, a mother and her children, and so on).

Quiz Answers for Day 22, "Bonus Day: Reusable Packages, Forms, and Projects"

1. When a program is run in the Visual Café development environment, Visual Café looks in the directories listed in the CLASSPATH entry of the SC.INI file.

2. To ensure that the CLASSPATH entry in SC.INI stays synchronized with your environment's CLASSPATH variable, include %CLASSPATH% in the CLASSPATH entry of SC.INI.

3. If a file is located in C:\Projects\Reusable\Utilities and the class is in the Reusable.Utilities package, then C:\Projects (or \Projects) must be included in the CLASSPATH for the class to be located.

4. To create a reusable form, take the following three steps:
    1. Create the form.
    2. Add the form to the Component Library.
    3. Reuse the form in another program.

Quiz Answers for Day 23, "Bonus Day: Using JavaDoc"

1. The @param tag is used to document the parameters used by a method.

2. To show the name of the programmer who wrote a class, use the @author tag.

3. This will generate one string of text that says This is a two-line comment for GetMaxSalary. Although it is shown as two lines in the source-code file, it will not necessarily be displayed as two lines when viewed in a browser. This will depend on the width of the browser's display area.

4. No documentation will be genereated for this method because the method is private.

Quiz Answers for Day 24, "Bonus Day: An Introduction to SQL"

1. SQL's four most common verbs are insert, update, select, and delete.

2. To select only the name column from a table named Employee, do the following:

```
select name from employee
```

3. To retrieve employee names in alphabetical order, do

   ```
   select name from employee order by name
   ```

4. To retrieve only the employees whose last name is Smith, do

   ```
   select name from employee where name = 'Smith'
   ```

5. This code joins the Book and Character tables on their `title` columns and selects all columns.

6. Existential quantification is a test to see whether any value exists that satisfies a test. Universal quantification is a test to see whether every value satisfies a test.

INDEX

MACMILLAN COMPUTER PUBLISHING USA

A VIACOM COMPANY

Technical Support:

If you need assistance with the information in this book or with a CD/Disk accompanying the book, please access the Knowledge Base on our Web site at **http://www.superlibrary.com/general/support**. Our most Frequently Asked Questions are answered there. If you do not find the answer to your questions on our Web site, you may contact Macmillan Technical Support **(317) 581-3833** or e-mail us at **support@mcp.com**.

Maximum Security: A Hacker's Guide to Protecting Your Internet Site and Network

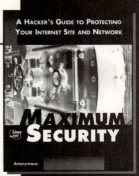

Anonymous

Now more than ever, it is imperative that users be able to prevent hackers from trashing their Web sites or stealing information. Written by a reformed hacker, this comprehensive resource identifies security holes in common computer and network systems, allowing system administrators to discover faults inherent within their network and work toward a solution to those problems. This book explores the most commonly used hacking techniques so users can safeguard their systems, and includes step-by-step lists and discussions of the vulnerabilities inherent in each operating system on the market. The CD-ROM is loaded with source code, technical documents, system logs, utilities, and other practical items for understanding and implementing Internet and computer system security. This book covers all platforms.

Price: $49.99 USA/$70.95 CDN　　　*User Level: Accomplished–Expert*
ISBN: 1-57521-268-4　　　　　　　*650 pages*

Java 1.1 Unleashed, Third Edition

Michael Morrison, et al.

Completely revised, updated, and expanded, this comprehensive reference provides users with all the information they need to master Java 1.1 programming, program advanced Java applets, and successfully integrate Java with other technologies. This book contains extensive coverage of Java 1.1, the Java extension APIs, Java Beans, JavaOS, and more. The CD-ROM contains Sun's JDK and other Java development tools, sample applets and applications, the book's entire reference selection in HTML format, as well as a selection of related titles in electronic format.

Price: $49.99 USA/$70.95 CDN　　　*User Level: Accomplished–Expert*
ISBN: 1-57521-298-6　　　　　　　*1,400 pages*

Teach Yourself Java 1.1 in 21 Days, Second Edition

Laura Lemay and Charles Perkins

This updated bestseller is the definitive guide to learning Java 1.1. *Teach Yourself Java 1.1 in 21 Days, Second Edition* carefully steps you through the fundamental concepts of the Java language, as well as the basics of applet design and integration with Web presentations. Using this book, you will learn the basics of object-oriented programming and Java development and create standalone, cross-platform applications. The CD-ROM includes Sun's Java Development Kit 1.1, Sun's Java Development Kit 1.02 for Macintosh, and Sun's Bean Development Kit for Windows 95, Windows NT, and Solaris.

Price: $39.99 USA/$56.95 CDN　　　*User Level: New–Casual*
ISBN: 1-57521-142-4　　　　　　　*816 pages*

Java 1.1 Developer's Guide, Second Edition

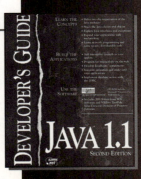

Jamie Jaworski

Written by a highly technical and experienced Web programmer, this detailed guide uses many illustrations and examples to show users how to exploit Java to develop real-world applications. It's a must-have resource for experienced Web developers. Explore the Java interface, Java in client/server environments, debugging, VRML extensions, network programming, protocol handlers, Java and the World Wide Web, and more.

Price: $49.99 USA/$70.95 CDN　　　*User Level: Accomplished–Expert*
ISBN: 1-57521-283-8　　　　　　　*800 pages*

Add to Your Sams.net Library Today
with the Best Books for Internet Technologies

ISBN	Quantity	Description of Item	Unit Cost	Total Cost
1-57521-268-4		Maximum Security: A Hacker's Guide	$49.99	
1-57521-298-6		Java 1.1 Unleashed, Third Edition	$49.99	
1-57521-142-4		Teach Yourself Java 1.1 in 21 Days, Second Edition	$39.99	
1-57521-283-8		Java 1.1 Developer's Guide, Second Edition	$49.99	
		Shipping and Handling: See information below.		
		TOTAL		

Shipping and Handling: $4.00 for the first book and $1.75 for each additional book. If you need to have it immediately, we can ship product to you in 24 hours for an additional charge of approximately $18.00, and you will receive your item overnight or in two days. For overseas shipping and handling, add $2.00. Prices subject to change. Call between 9:00 a.m. and 5:00 p.m. EST for availability and pricing information on latest editions.

201 W. 103rd Street, Indianapolis, Indiana 46290

1-800-428-5331 — Orders   1-800-835-3202 — Fax   1-800-858-7674 — Customer Service

Book ISBN 1-57521-303-6